Introductio

4th Ed

Ted M. Preston, Ph.D.
Rio Hondo College

A Local Source Textbook™ Company

Introduction to Ethics

Preface to 4th Edition

The fourth edition of this text corrects minor errors from the third, and expands existing material in several places, including expansions to the chapters on critical thinking and virtue ethics. I have also added two entirely new chapters. One explores the natural law tradition understanding of ethics, and the other is another applied ethics chapter, with a focus on helping the "less fortunate." These changes are the product of the "living laboratory" provided by my students, for whom I am grateful.

Acknowledgments

Ethics was the first philosophical topic that got me "hooked" on philosophy. Although my interests shifted over time, ethics still retains a special place in my heart.

It is with excitement, anticipation, and satisfaction that I present this text, and with which I would like to thank some of the people that made it possible.

I would first like to honor my first philosophy professor, and the one who introduced me to Kant (with whom I continue to have a love/hate relationship): Professor Clark Arthur Kucheman (2/7/1931 - 12/27/2009). Professor Kucheman's passion for both ethics and "professing" inspired me and set me on my path. I thank him and miss him.

I would (once again) like to thank my colleague Dr. Adam Wetsman for his vision of Gnutext, and his promotion of these books that I write with pleasure. I would also like to (again) thank my friend and colleague Professor Scott Dixon for his (Aristotelian) friendship, helpful comments, and stimulating conversations.

Finally, I would be remiss if I did not thank my students, for whom I write.

Table of Contents

Introduction

This is a book meant to introduce you to the study of philosophy—specifically the study of ethics. If you have not already taken an introductory philosophy class, it's safe to assume that many (if not most) of you do not yet know for certain what philosophy is. Or, perhaps you have an idea of what philosophy is, but one in need of correction (from my perspective).

There are a variety of ways in which to chop up the philosophical landscape, and these ways tend to correspond to the different approaches an instructor might take to teaching an introduction to philosophy course. Some instructors (including myself) like to organize and teach topically. That is, we divide philosophy into sub-categories, and teach a little bit from each one. There are several ways to divide up the topics covered by philosophy. Some people (like myself) prefer four broad categories, while others prefer five, six, or even more categories. To be honest, it doesn't matter all that much! The point of identifying these sub-divisions of philosophy is to provide some shared vocabulary, and a shared sense of important themes. My own preferred method of dividing up philosophical themes is as follows:

1. Metaphysics: an investigation into the ultimate nature of reality itself
2. Epistemology: an investigation into the nature of knowledge
3. Logic: an investigation into reason and argumentation
4. Value theory/axiology: an investigation into the nature of those things to which we assign value

Starting with metaphysics, I'll now provide just a little bit more detail for each. As mentioned, metaphysics concerns the ultimate nature of reality, beyond what the physical sciences can tell us. Once physics has done all it can accomplish, there remain "deep" questions about reality that are not necessarily subject to empirical verification or testing.

Metaphysics is as old as philosophy itself. One of the central concerns of the pre-Socratic philosophers (the "first philosophers") was to understand the "first principle," that which gives structure and explanation to everything we observe. Their answers were varied and sometimes amusing, from our privileged vantage point thousands of years later. Thales thought that reality was, ultimately, water. Democritus proposed "atoms." Many of these philosophers were materialists, in that they believed that the "first principle" was physical. Later philosophers, such as Plato, endorsed a dualistic understanding of metaphysics, according to which some things were physical, but other things were non-physical (e.g., "mental," or "spiritual"). This is a basic metaphysical distinction. Is reality, ultimately, purely physical? Matter and energy governed by the laws of physics? Or, is there something about reality not reducible to a purely physical description? Something "spiritual," or "mental?"

Our answer to that most basic metaphysical question leads naturally to many others. What is the ultimate nature of a person? Purely physical? A biological machine? A sophisticated animal? Or, is there something about us that is different, something "spiritual" or "mental?" Our answer to those questions immediately informs our understanding of our own behavior (a critical issue in the free will debate). It also contributes to our understanding of the nature of mind (merely *brain*? Something more?), the nature of life and death, the possibility of an afterlife, etc. Many issues in the philosophy of religion also fall into this large and fascinating category of metaphysics.

Epistemology concerns the nature of knowledge. Just as old as metaphysics, philosophers have long agonized over whether knowledge is possible, and, if possible, what it means to know something (as opposed to merely believing something). The skeptics argued that knowledge was unattainable, while other philosophers across the centuries sought to demonstrate that it is.

Another epistemological concern is the nature of truth. Is there any such thing as "the Truth? Objective truth? Absolute truth? Or, is truth always a matter of perspective? The sophist Protagoras claimed that "man is the measure of all things," and that truth is always a matter of perspective. Others, such as Plato, claimed that Truth is something objective and independent of our perspectives, and that the task of philosophy is to help us arrive at that Truth.

With regard to both metaphysical and epistemological issues, *arguments* have been employed by philosophers at least since Thales. Argument and reason is perhaps the most distinguishing feature of philosophy. Philosophy does not rely on tradition or appeals to authority to prove a point—philosophers *prove* their points. Such attempts involve arguments and the exercise of reason, and this is the domain of logic. Logical issues include methods of reasoning, in general, different kinds of argument (e.g., deductive and inductive), and how we evaluate the quality of arguments in terms of their validity, soundness, absence of fallacies, etc.

This book will focus on the last remaining category: ethics. When one begins to study ethics it might not be immediately obvious what one is "doing." Are you training yourself to be a morally better person? Is the study of ethics a form of "self-help?" Possibly, but not necessarily, or even primarily.[1]

Realistically, the vast majority of us (including you, I presume) are already morally-motivated persons. That is simply to say that you already have a sense of what is right or wrong, that you already have a "conscience," that you are already (generally) motivated to be a good person. If that is not the case, this course is unlikely to help you, sociopath that you are! Clearly, there are many different interpretations of what is morally good or bad, but that most of us are already concerned with "morality" is a given. If not, it is unlikely that a formal study of ethics will change that.

Ethics, by the way, is the formal study of moral concepts and moral decision-making. Ethics concerns the study of questions such as, but certainly not limited to, the following:

1. How do we know what is right, or wrong?
2. Is there any such thing as an "objective" moral code?
3. Is "selfishness" a virtue, or a vice?
4. Is abortion morally acceptable?
5. Am I morally obligated to donate a portion of my resources (such as time or money or effort) to those "worse off" than me?

[1] Though I do believe that the practice of philosophy, in general, is therapeutic in that sense.

These are all interesting questions, and there are many more besides. If you find this material interesting, I encourage you to continue your study, perhaps by reading other books, or taking other courses, focusing specifically on ethics. Our focus, of necessity, will be limited in scope, designed to offer you an introduction to several central issues and themes within the field of ethics.

 Before officially addressing ethics at all, we will spend some time on critical thinking skills. A central exercise of philosophy is understanding and evaluating arguments, and we need to make sure you have the tools necessary for that, before proceeding to the arguments themselves.

After covering some critical thinking basics, the next several chapters will address some "challenges" to traditional interpretations of ethics and moral values. We will consider the descriptive theory of human nature known as psychological egoism, and its prescriptive "cousin" ethical egoism. We will then consider two variations on the view that moral value judgments are matters of opinion (rather than fact): subjectivism and Ethical Relativism. Our next two chapters will focus on the role of emotion with respect to ethics, considering both emotivism and moral sentimentalism. Having done so, we will wade into the controversial waters of evolution and religion, first by considering a purely naturalistic/evolutionary interpretation of ethics, followed by an examination of divine command theory. Elements of each of those approaches will be considered when we then turn to the natural law tradition.

We will round out our examination of objective approaches to ethics by considering the "big three" ethical theories: Utilitarianism, Kantianism, and Virtue Theory.

Finally, we will consider how all these wonderful ideas might be applied to particular moral issues, such as the moral status of non-human animals, the moral status of abortion, and whether we have a moral obligation to help the "less fortunate."

Each chapter will begin with a few comprehension questions. These are questions that you should be able to answer once you have read that chapter, and digested the information you read. They are also, therefore, indicators of key ideas from each chapter—especially important things that I think you should know. The questions are there for your benefit, so I encourage you to use them. Read the questions before reading the chapter, so as to give yourself a preview of the especially important ideas on which to focus. Then, when you have finished a chapter, see if you can answer those questions, with confidence. They are meant to provide a means of self-assessment, a way for you to gauge how well you understood the material.

Finally, at the end of nearly every chapter you will find one or more reading selections pertaining to the main topic of that chapter. These are excerpts from some of the larger works of some of the finest minds from the history of Western philosophy, going all the way back to the 4th century (BCE). Although I like to think that my own summaries and introductions are illuminating, engaging primary source materials is an essential part of studying philosophy. You will discover that (with a few exceptions), I have not provided specific summaries or explanations of the text selections themselves. There is a reason for that. Engaging the readings yourself, grappling with the arguments, and coming to your own understanding—even if initially hesitant—is one of the primary tasks of philosophy. Your instructor will undoubtedly offer assistance along the way, but it's important to meet with these thinkers, your mind to their minds, and participate in the great conversation that we call philosophy. It's also important to remember that we all stand on the shoulders of those who came before us. To remain ignorant of their ideas and achievements, and to attempt to "reinvent the wheel" ourselves, is inefficient at best, and intellectually dishonest and disrespectful, at worst.

Chapter 1: Critical Thinking

Comprehension questions you should be able to answer after reading this chapter:

1. What is "epistemology?"

2. What is the definition of "knowledge?"

3. What is a "claim?" What does it mean to say that a claim has a "truth-value?"

4. What is an argument?

5. What is meant by a "relevance-relationship" between premises and a conclusion? What does it mean for a deductive argument to be "valid?"

6. What does it mean for a deductive argument to be "sound?"

7. Why is the soundness of arguments often difficult to establish?

8. What is the principle of charity?

9. What is a "worldview?" What do we usually do (in general) when a claim fits with our worldview? What about when it conflicts with it? If a claim that conflicts with our worldview is proven to be true, what should we do with our worldview?

10. What are the four conditions under which it is reasonable to accept an unsupported claim as true?

11. What are the ways in which we establish the expertise of sources?

12. What are the two justification questions we ask when presented with a new piece of information?

13. What are different meanings of "fake news?" Why is "fake news" a problem?

14. When should we suspend judgment concerning the truth or falsity of a claim?

15. How is "truth" understood by epistemic relativism and by the correspondence theory?

Argument

When one thinks of "ethics," the word "argument" probably comes to mind—though probably for the wrong reason! It's an old cliché that one doesn't talk about politics or religion at parties, and ethical issues are often regarded in the same way. For most of us, if you want to start an "argument" at a family dinner, we should bring up either politics or religion or some sort of moral issue. That is not usually, however, what an "argument" means in the context of philosophy.

Before delving into the nuances of arguments, though, we need to back up and develop a basic understanding of epistemology, so that we *know* what we're talking about.

Epistemology, the focus of this chapter, is the study of knowledge. Believe it or not, there's some pretty serious debate concerning how best to understand "knowledge." Some, for example, believe that we can never possess knowledge. Classical skeptics fit this description. Others believe that "knowledge" is never more than personal perspective.

Despite the plurality of views, there is a generally accepted definition of knowledge that seems to work for most people, in most cases. There are some complications, of course, and some disagreements here and there, but, for the most part, Plato's understanding of knowledge is pretty good. In his dialogue, the *Theaetetus*, Plato has the character Socrates (his real life mentor and friend) explore the proper definition of knowledge. The most promising candidate that emerges is that knowledge is "justified, true belief." Or, as Plato puts it, "true belief with an account."

Why should we accept Plato's definition? Plato is a giant in Western Philosophy, to say the least. A student of Socrates himself, Plato (428/427 BCE—348/347 BCE) founded the first institution of higher education (an "Academy") in the Western world. He also developed very impressive accounts of virtually every major topic of philosophical interest. Indeed, the 20th century philosopher Alfred North Whitehead said of Plato and Philosophy:

> *The safest general characterization of the European philosophical tradition is that it consists of a series of footnotes to Plato. I do not mean the systematic scheme of thought which scholars have doubtfully extracted from his writings. I allude to the wealth of general ideas scattered through them....*[2]

Still, just because a definition comes from Plato doesn't *automatically* make it correct. To assume so is a fallacy—an "appeal to authority." The *reason* why (most of us) use this definition is because it seems like a pretty good one! You'll soon see why.

Knowledge: justified, true belief

Plato's definition has three components, each of which requires a little bit of explanation.

1. Belief

It is generally accepted that in order to know something, one must also believe it. It seems odd to say that I know Donald Trump is the current U.S. President, but that I don't believe that he is. Note that the reverse is not also true. We are quite comfortable with the idea that someone can believe something without also knowing it. For example, at the moment I'm writing this sentence, I believe my mother is at her home, but I wouldn't claim to *know* that she is. It's entirely possible that I'm not

---

[2] Alfred North Whitehead, *Process and Reality*, Free Press, 1979. p. 39.

remembering her schedule accurately, and that she's volunteering somewhere. Or, perhaps she's on an errand? As we can see, to know something, one must also believe it, but one can believe without knowing.

An easy way to think of the relationship between belief and knowledge, in this sense, is with the language of a "promotion." We believe all kinds of things, but some of the things we believe have a special quality to them. These beliefs earn a "promotion," and a new title: knowledge. What is this quality that earns the belief a promotion to knowledge? As it turns out, this quality concerns the other two parts of our definition of knowledge: justification, and truth.

Before delving into justification, we'll spend a little more time on belief and complicate matters by asking what a belief *is*. A good chunk of my doctoral dissertation was devoted to just that question, but, once again, that level of analysis and expertise is not needed for our own purposes right now. At the minimum, we can simply talk about what form beliefs take in our language, so that we may easily identify them in speech and writing.

Very simply, beliefs appear in the form of "claims." *Claims* are statements, assertions, or propositions (different terms meaning *roughly* the same thing, in most cases). Claims have what is called a *"truth-value."* To say that a claim has a truth-value is simply to say that it must be either true or false (if true, then its truth-value is true; if false, then its truth-value is false). Note that we do not need to know *which* truth-value applies to a claim to know that it is a claim. Consider the examples below.

Claims	Not Claims
• You are reading this sentence right now.	• What time is it?
• Donald Trump is the current U.S. president.	• Please shut the door.
• There is intelligent life elsewhere in the universe.	• Ouch.

Remember, a claim is a statement that has to be either true or false (even if we're not sure which it is). You either are, or you are not, reading this book right now. Donald Trump either is, or is not, the current U.S. President. You're probably pretty confident about those two. What about life elsewhere in the universe? Well, you might not be certain either way. But (and this is the important part), we know that there either is, or there is not, intelligent life elsewhere in the universe. In other words, that claim has a truth-value, even though we don't know (for sure, right now) if that value is "true" or if it is "false."

Now, consider the other column of examples. What time is it? True or false? You probably had to reread those sentences just now, and my question probably still doesn't make any sense. There's a reason for that. "What time is it?" is not the sort of thing that can be either true or false. Neither is "Please shut the door." Neither is "ouch." None of those has a truth-value, because none is a claim, and therefore none is a belief. Why does this matter? Because claims are the building blocks of arguments, and arguments form the core of what we study and what we do in philosophy.

An argument is an attempt to establish the truth of a claim (the conclusion) by offering evidence (premises) in support of that claim. No name-calling, no chair-throwing, no raised voices—not even any presumption of disagreement. In a philosophical context, an argument is not a fight, but simply an attempt to make a point, using evidence, and following certain rules of reason.

Although we don't usually encounter arguments in the following format (except in philosophy courses), all arguments (at least implicitly) have the same general form:

> Premise$_1$
> Premise$_2$
> Conclusion

Please note that we have not yet specified any particular content for that argument. That is because arguments can be about *anything*. Any time you try to persuade someone to believe anything at all, on the basis of some kind of reason/evidence, you are offering an argument. Also note that although there were two premises in the generic argument above, there is nothing special about that number. You might have only a single premise (piece of evidence), or you might have a hundred premises, or any other number whatsoever. So long as you have at least one piece of evidence, at least one reason to believe that the conclusion is true, you have provided an argument.

Every philosophical essay that you read in this book (or any other) is an argument, or at least contains arguments. What all arguments have in common is that they are attempts to prove that a claim (the conclusion) is true, by offering other claims (premises) as evidence. Note that both the conclusion of an argument and all the premises in an argument, are *claims*. This is not a trivial observation! Every (proper) piece of every argument is a claim. Therefore, every (proper) piece of every argument has a truth-value—which is what makes argument evaluation possible.

However, although some professional philosophers will sometimes write out their arguments in obvious "premise$_1$, premise$_2$, therefore conclusion" format, most philosophical readings are not so blatantly reader-friendly. Philosophical arguments will be made in the context of paragraphs, essays, chapters, or even entire books. As we read, then, our job is to identify the main point the author seems to be trying to make. This is the conclusion. Then, we must try to identify all of the supporting points the author provides in defense of that conclusion. These are the premises. Once we have identified the conclusion and premises, we are prepared to evaluate the argument.

I hope it's obvious that not all arguments are created equal. Just because you have offered a reason to believe something is true doesn't mean you have provided a *good* reason, or even a relevant one. Consider the following example:

Argument (A)
1. Egg yolks are high in cholesterol.
2. High cholesterol is associated with increased risk of heart disease.
3. Therefore, abortion is morally wrong.

Argument (A) is laughably bad, and I'm sure you realize that, but it's important to recognize *why*. It doesn't take much reflection, or any fancy vocabulary, to describe what's going "wrong" with that argument: the premises don't have anything to do with the conclusion! You might rightfully be wondering what the heck eggs and cholesterol have to do with abortion. Clearly, the premises aren't *relevant* to the conclusion.

Relevance-relationships are an important initial way to evaluate the quality of an argument. In general, if the premises aren't "relevant," then we would say that little (if any) support has been provided for the conclusion—and that doesn't make for a very good argument! One specific example of this relevance relationship occurs with deductive arguments

Deductive arguments are constructed with the intent to provide for the certainty of the conclusion, on the assumption that the premises are true. Such arguments are (generally) evaluated in terms of their validity, and soundness. Both of those words (valid, sound) have specific meaning in the context of argument, and both (especially validity) have different uses in everyday speech. For example, you might hear someone say "that's a valid point." What that person means is that you have made a good point. In that usage, valid means something like "good," or "apt," or "true." That is not what "valid" means for our purposes, though.

Validity

A deductive argument is <u>valid</u> if the conclusion necessarily follows (logically) from the premises. Another way of putting that idea is that an argument is valid when, *if* the premises are true, the conclusion must also be true. Or, an argument is valid if it's impossible for the conclusion to be false, *if* all the premises are true. To repeat: validity indicates the right kind of "relevance-relationship" between the premises and the conclusion.

You might have noticed that I italicized the word "if" in a couple of places in the previous paragraph. There's a good reason for that. When we assess an argument's validity, it's a hypothetical exercise. We're not making any claim that the premises are, in fact, true—we're just asking what would happen *if* the premises are true. Consider the following:

1.   All humans are mortal.
2.   Preston is a human.
3.   Therefore, Preston is mortal.

Is this argument "valid," according to our definition? To find out if it is, ask yourself the following: *if* all the premises are true, must the conclusion also be true? *If* it's true that all humans are mortal, and *if* it's true that Preston is a human, then, must it also be true that Preston is mortal? The answer, of course, is "yes." Therefore, this is a valid argument. This indicates that there is the right kind of logical relationship between the premises and conclusion, there is a relationship of relevance between them. We haven't yet established that the premises are, in fact, true (that's a later step), but we have established that *if* they are true, the conclusion is as well. That is very important. Let's reconsider example (A) from above:

Argument (A)
1. Egg yolks are high in cholesterol.
2. High cholesterol is associated with increased risk of heart disease.
3. Therefore, abortion is morally wrong.

Just a few paragraphs ago, we articulated the "badness" of this argument using ordinary language. Presumably, you recognized that eggs, cholesterol, and heart disease risks have nothing to do with whether or not abortion is morally wrong! There isn't the right kind of relationship between those premises, and the conclusion. If we consider this in terms of validity, the problem becomes clear.

Is it possible for it to be true that egg yolks are high in cholesterol, and true that high cholesterol is associated with increased risk of heart disease, and yet for it to be false that abortion is morally wrong? Of course that's possible! So, if, for some weird reason, you try to prove the moral wrongness of abortion by appealing to the cholesterol content of eggs, you will fail in grand, embarrassing fashion. Even if all your evidence is proven to be true, you still will not have proven that your conclusion ("abortion is morally wrong") is true.

Soundness

If validity appeals to the hypothetical truth of the premises, soundness refers to their actual truth. *A deductive argument is "sound" when it is both valid and all its premises are, in fact, true.* Notice that in order for an argument to be sound, it must first already be valid. You can imagine an implicit checklist for argument evaluation:

☐   Is the argument valid?
☐   Is the argument sound?

Only if we can "check the first box" do we bother to consider whether the argument is sound. Let's go back to one of our earlier examples:

1. All humans are mortal.
2. Preston is a human.
3. Therefore, Preston is mortal.

Is the argument valid? Yes, it is (as established above).

✓   Is the argument valid?
☐   Is the argument sound?

Since it's valid, we can now move on to consider its soundness. Are all of the premises, in fact, true? To be honest, the question of "truth" opens Pandora's proverbial box.

What does "truth" mean? What does it take for something to be true, let alone known to be true? You could spend an entire career as a philosophy professor focusing solely on the concept of "truth," and still have plenty of questions remaining. We will not spend entire careers on the concept of truth, but we will spend some time later in this chapter on two different interpretations of what it means for a claim to be true. For now, however, let's set aside the murky notion of "truth" and assume (for the sake of argument) that we know what it means for a claim to be true. Even so, how can we tell if a particular claim is, in fact, true?

Obviously, not all claims will be easily verifiable as true. While we might be fairly confident that it is true that egg yolks are high in cholesterol, some truth-values (unfortunately, probably the ones we tend to care the most about—truth-values for claims about morality, religion, politics, etc.), might be especially difficult to establish.

4Do aliens exist, or not? Hard to say, since we haven't explored the entire universe just yet. Is abortion immoral? Hard to say, since there's so much disagreement, and so many compelling arguments that can be given on both sides. Does God exist? Hard to say, since there are compelling arguments on both sides of the debate, and legitimate debate as to what does or could count as evidence for God's existence in the first place. And so forth. . . .

Recognizing that some claims will be difficult to establish, let us return to a relatively easy argument just to complete our discussion of "soundness."

1. All humans are mortal.
2. Preston is a human.
3. Therefore, Preston is mortal.

In order for this argument to be sound, it has to be valid, and all of its premises must be true. We've already established that it's valid. Are its premises, in fact, true? Does the claim that "all humans are mortal" seem to be true? If we interpret "mortal" in its usual sense ("liable or subject to death"), then it does, in fact, appear to be true. That all humans are subject to death seems to be true, like it or not. What about the second premise? Is it, in fact, true that Preston (the author of this book) is a human? Again, if we're assuming the usual sense of "human" ("a member of the genus *Homo* and especially of the species *H. sapiens*"), then it would appear that Preston being human is true as well. Given that both premises are, in fact, true, we have established that the argument is not only valid, but sound.

✓ Is the argument valid?
✓ Is the argument sound?

If you have established that an argument is sound, you have proven that the conclusion is true. It doesn't get any better than that! Unfortunately, whenever we're dealing with serious, important arguments, it's usually pretty challenging to establish that the argument is sound. Consider another argument for the wrongness of abortion:

Argument (B)
1. Murder is morally wrong.
2. Abortion is murder.
3. Therefore, abortion is morally wrong.

You should know the routine by now:

☐   Is the argument valid?
☐   Is the argument sound?

If it's true that murder is morally wrong, and it's also true that abortion is murder, must it also be true that abortion is morally wrong? Yes, this is a valid argument. Is it sound? Perhaps, but this is far from obvious. Murder, by its usual definition, is the unjustified killing of an innocent person, so I suspect *most* people would agree that premise 1 is true.[3] Premise 2 is going to be much more controversial, though. Is abortion the unjustified killing of an innocent person? People who argue that abortion is (at least sometimes) morally acceptable will usually argue either that the fetus is not a "person," or that the killing is justified (or both). Such persons would not grant the truth of premise 2, and would not recognize the argument as sound, even though it is valid.

Let's take a moment to summarize the ground we've covered so far. An argument is an attempt to prove some point by appealing to reasons that support that point. In order for an argument to be a good argument, the premises need to be relevant (valid, in the case of deductive arguments), and preferably true as well.

Some of you might have wondered about that last sentence. Only "preferably" true? Ideally, of course, good arguments will exhibit both relevance between premises and the conclusion, and contain premises that are, in fact, true. But, if we insist that an argument have only premises known to be true in order to be "good," we might be setting the bar so high that few, if any, arguments are "good." This is because, as we have already seen, the actual truth of premises can be difficult and controversial to establish. Consider one more argument:

Argument (C)
1.   If God does not exist, objective moral values and duties do not exist.
2.   Objective moral values and duties do exist.
3.   Therefore, God exists.

This is actually one of the more famous arguments for God's existence known as the "moral argument." For our purposes, though, let's just consider our checklist:

☐   Is the argument valid?
☐   Is the argument sound?

If both premises are true, must the conclusion also be true? Yes—and this shouldn't be surprising. Any of the "major" arguments for God's existence, the arguments that have withstood the test of time (often centuries, if not millennia), are presumably going to be valid—otherwise they would have been abandoned long ago.

✓   Is the argument valid?
☐   Is the argument sound?

---

[3] In fairness, there might even be disagreement as to the truth of *this* premise!

Now that we know it's valid, is it sound? Is it, in fact, true that if God does not exist, objective moral values and duties do not exist? Is it, in fact, true that objective moral values and duties do exist? Those who use the moral argument for God's existence will offer reasons to accept both premises as true. If you find those reasons compelling, you will presumably conclude that both premises are, in fact, true—in which case you will conclude that the argument is sound. But, if you think the reasons are not compelling, you will instead conclude that the premises are not true—in which case you will conclude that the argument is not sound. Or, perhaps some of you, even after serious consideration, will come to the honest conclusion that you're just *not sure* if those premises are true—in which case you will conclude that you don't know whether the argument is sound.

    ✓   Is the argument valid?
    ?   Is the argument sound?

That the soundness of this (or any other of the major arguments for, *or against,* God's existence) is in question should not be surprising. Remember: if an argument is sound, its conclusion *is, in fact, true.* So, if an argument for God's existence can be shown to be sound, that would mean that it is, in fact, true that God exists—and that this has been proven! Conversely, if an argument against God's existence were shown to be sound, it would mean that God has been proven not to exist. Had either of these events occurred, you probably would have heard about it!

Similarly, if the soundness of various arguments concerning moral or political issues could be easily established, you would think that there would no longer be any debate about things like abortion, eating meat, the death penalty, the value of democracy, etc. The fact that people still passionately debate these issues should tell us something about the difficulty in establishing the soundness of those sorts of arguments.

Don't be discouraged, though. Just because it's difficult to establish the soundness of these sorts of arguments doesn't mean that there's no point in evaluating them, nor does it mean that we will be unable to say anything evaluative or interesting about them. Even if we're not *sure* if argument B is sound, it's clearly a better argument for the wrongness of abortion than the one referencing the risks of high cholesterol (argument A)!

To summarize thus far: when someone is trying to convince you of something, the first thing to ask is whether or not any support is being offered. If the answer is "no," then that person is just making a statement, and we will consider how to evaluate unsupported claims a little later in this chapter. If, however, support is being offered, then you have been presented with an *argument.*

If someone is presenting you with an argument, you need to determine whether that support is relevant to the conclusion. With deductive arguments, this is a question of *validity*—but generally speaking you can just ask whether the premises are "relevant." If they are not relevant, that doesn't mean their conclusion is false, but it does mean their evidence doesn't really count as support, and you should treat the conclusion as an unsupported claim. If the premises are relevant, then the next step is to determine if they are true.

When relevant premises are not actually true, then they don't properly support their conclusion, and you should treat the conclusion as an unsupported claim. If the premises are true, however, then the argument is in pretty good shape. After all, we already determined they were relevant, and now we've determined they're also true! With deductive arguments, that means the argument is *sound*, and the conclusion has been *proven* to be true. Even if the argument isn't deductive, though, there is still probably some very impressive support for the conclusion such that it's at least likely to be true. In that case, you should consider how well that newly-proven conclusion fits with your worldview.

We will discuss worldviews in greater detail later in this chapter, but, for now, just know that your worldview is your basic understanding of the world and how it works. When claims fit with our worldview, they don't tend to surprise us, and we usually presume they are true (even though they might not be). When they conflict with our worldviews, however, we tend to be skeptical and presume they are false (even though they might be true). When a conclusion has been proven to be true, though, that should make a difference to your worldview.

If, for example, my current worldview includes a general skepticism about the existence of aliens, but I then see live footage of an alien spacecraft on every major news network, and I am personally abducted by aliens and experimented upon, you better believe that I will revise my worldview to now include the existence of aliens!

Whatever the content of the argument, and perhaps especially when the conclusion conflicts with our own worldview, we need to be self-aware when we are evaluating it. One important element of (honest) argument evaluation is what's known as the "*principle of charity.*" Basically, we want to be "charitable" when evaluating arguments—especially if we're inclined to disagree with them.

It's all too easy to develop a "straw man" interpretation of someone else's position, and then dismiss it as foolish, fallacious, or misguided. This is perhaps especially the case when dealing with ethics.

The fact of the matter is that people don't tend to view their own arguments as foolish. This doesn't mean they aren't, but in order to perform an honest evaluation of an argument, we need to present it in its best possible light. We must put ourselves in the position of the person who presented the argument, consider the argument in the strongest possible way (given the original author's intentions), and then evaluate the argument, so charitably constructed. This is a good approach to evaluating arguments, in general, but it's especially apt in the context of considering formal philosophical arguments in a book like this one.

The sorts of arguments and theories we will consider have stood the test of time. They're considered in this book for a reason. No matter what your personal views happen to be, it's <u>un</u>charitable to casually dismiss "the other side" as fools offering lousy arguments. You might well conclude that "their" arguments fail, but to be justified in that conclusion you need to consider those arguments charitably, in their best light.

2. Justification

Having just spent a lot of time on arguments, and determining the relevance-relationship and truth of their premises, let us now turn to (perhaps) the most critical component of argument evaluation: justification.

Justification is probably the most critical aspect of this process because it is the process by which we attempt to determine whether claims (e.g., premises or conclusions) are (in fact) true, and therefore whether arguments are *good* arguments, and therefore whether or not we can "know" whether the conclusion of an argument is true. Justification is crucially involved in determining the truth of the premises in argument (once relevance has been established), and in evaluating the truth of an unsupported claim when no proper argument is present at all.

Justification is also probably the most controversial element of our definition of knowledge, primarily because we can bicker over what, exactly, counts as sufficient justification. Again, this is a very complicated subject, but this is not an extended treatment of epistemology, so we can get by with a basic understanding of the key ideas.

To say that knowledge requires justification is simply to say that you can only "know" something on the basis of good reasons. If I present you with a jar filled with marbles, and you guess there are 457 marbles in the jar (just pulling a number "out of the air," at random), and, with a startled look on my face, I tell you that there are, in fact, 457 marbles in the jar, we wouldn't want to say that you *knew* the number of marbles in the jar at the time you guessed. We call it a guess for a reason! You didn't know, but you took a shot at it, and happened to get lucky. That's not knowledge; it's a lucky guess.

Sometimes, we like to distinguish "believing" from "knowing" by making explicit appeals to how much justification we have for the belief in question. I claimed to believe that my mother was at home, because I have reason to think that she is. However, my confidence in those reasons is pretty low, so I don't think I have sufficient justification to claim to *know* that she's at home.

As I mentioned, justification can be a thorny issue. How can we tell when we have enough justification to claim that we know something, as opposed to merely believing it? As with many questions in philosophy, there's no obvious, uncontroversial answer to that question. We can, however, talk about ways in which our beliefs are justified, and the degree to which our beliefs are supported by evidence.

When we are presented with an unsupported claim (including the premises of most arguments), our three basic options are to accept it as true, reject it as false, or to suspend judgment because we're not sure either way. How do we know which one of those three options is the right one to exercise?

Generally speaking, it is reasonable to *accept* an *unsupported* claim if the claim:

1. Does not conflict with our own observations
2. Does not conflict with other credible claims
3. Comes from a credible source that offers us no compelling reason to expect bias
4. Does not conflict with our background information/worldview

1) The Claim does not Conflict with our own Observations

We are justifiably skeptical about claims that directly contradict what we have personally observed! If you're texting with a friend, and he is telling you that he's in his car and on the way to meet you at Starbuck's, but you are personally observing him (in secret), right then and there, standing outside the Apple Store talking to your girlfriend, then either your friend is saying something false or you are hallucinating (or something else equally unlikely). Not surprisingly, in such a case you would be inclined to reject his claim as false. On the other hand, if you just came in from the rain and are shaking off your umbrella, and your friend calls and tells you he's running late because it's raining out, you're probably going to accept his claim as true. After all, you personally witnessed the rain too.

2)   The Claim does not Conflict with other Credible Claims

In courtroom settings, one of the best ways for an attorney to undermine the evidence offered by a witness or expert is to provide another witness or expert who will contradict that evidence. This is often very successful in creating "reasonable doubt" in jurors. So, for example, if one blood-splatter expert testifies that the spray patterns suggest the killer was at least six feet tall (which is bad news for the 6-foot-tall defendant), that claim is undermined if another, equally respectable, blood splatter expert says the patterns are inconclusive. In the context of philosophy, this is a notorious experience for philosophy students. One philosopher offers a compelling case that we have no free will, but then another equally impressive philosopher says the opposite. In such cases, we often must suspend judgment, even if we don't outright reject the original claim. If, on the other hand, there is no such conflict, if the claim is not being contradicted by other (credible) claims—let alone if there is consensus from a variety of sources—then we are likely to accept the claim as true.

3)   The Claim comes from a Credible Source that Offers Us no Compelling Reason to Expect Bias

This criterion actually has two elements: bias, and credibility. "Bias" is an issue when the person making the claim is suspected to have an ulterior motive. For example, if someone is trying to sell you their used car, they have a personal incentive for you to buy it, and they might be inclined to be less than completely honest about the condition of the vehicle. This doesn't mean they're automatically lying, of course, but careful car buyers will inspect the vehicle, and even enlist the help of someone who knows a thing or two about cars (e.g., an automotive mechanic) to confirm the car really is in good condition. Similarly, when the Tobacco industry spent decades denying the link between smoking and cancer, a clear case can be made that they had an ulterior motive to make that claim.[4] After all, if they admitted smoking caused cancer, it might reduce the number of people who smoke, and therefore their profits. Similarly, we might be reasonably skeptical when the petroleum industry funds lobbying groups denying the link between automobile emissions and climate change.[5] The possibility of bias doesn't demonstrate the *falsity* of the claim, of course. To presume so would actually be an example of what is called the "genetic fallacy"— denying (or accepting) the truth of a claim *solely* because of its source. However, while

---

[4] http://www.who.int/tobacco/media/en/TobaccoExplained.pdf
[5] https://www.theguardian.com/environment/2015/jul/15/exxon-mobil-gave-millions-climate-denying-lawmakers

a possibly-biased source doesn't necessarily indicate their claim is false, it should inspire us to be especially vigilant when evaluating the evidence (if any) that they provide in support of their claim.

Setting aside issues of bias, we can now turn to credibility. Unless one is a radical epistemic relativist, we recognize that not all sources are equally credible. When evaluating a claim, the source matters—especially if the subject matter is significant or if the claim conflicts with our own worldview. I should hope that you trust the testimony of your medical doctor more than you trust the testimony of your neighbor when it comes to your health—unless of course your neighbor also happens to be a medical doctor!

If someone is especially knowledgeable about a particular topic, we tend to give extra "weight" to their claims made about that topic. Sometimes, we consider such persons "experts."

We establish expertise, generally, by considering the following criteria:

1) Education
2) Experience
3) Accomplishments

Education is just what you think it is. Generally speaking, the more educated someone is on a topic, the more likely we are to (reasonably) take him or her to be an expert on that topic. Someone who majored in chemistry as an undergraduate probably knows a lot more about chemistry than someone who majored in something else—let alone someone who has never studied chemistry at all. Someone who has a Master's degree (M.S.) in chemistry probably knows even more, and someone with a doctorate (Ph.D.) probably knows even more than that. To be skeptical of this would require you to be profoundly skeptical of the effectiveness of our education system, in general! Keep in mind, of course, that expertise based on education is limited to the focus of one's education. That Ph.D. in chemistry doesn't mean the chemist is also an expert on criminal law.

Experience is also just what you think it is. While education is terribly valuable, relevant experience is valuable as well. *All else being equal*, a medical doctor who has been in practice for 20 years is probably more knowledgeable than a first-year M.D. Once again, we have to be careful of relevance. The fact that I have been a philosophy professor for fifteen years doesn't mean that I "know better" than a first year lawyer when it comes to *legal* issues. Despite the fact that President Donald Trump has been an ostensibly successful business man for decades, his claim that he "knows more about ISIS than the generals" is dubious on its surface.[6] For all his business acumen, and despite his clear mastery of the media, then-candidate Trump had literally *no* experience relevant to ISIS, in contrast to "the Generals" and their combined decades of military experience, including years of recent experience specifically opposing ISIS.

Accomplishments often (though not always) come from education and experience, as well as merit. If a cancer researcher, for example, has won a Nobel Prize for her research, that scientist is probably pretty knowledgeable! Sometimes, some awards or "achievements" are questionable, and serve primarily to stoke the vanity

---

[6] https://www.youtube.com/watch?v=kul34O_yMLs

of their recipients. For example, I get solicitations every year to be an "invited speaker" at a conference called the Oxford Round Table. It is held at the very prestigious Oxford University, and being able to put "invited speaker" on your résumé is usually a respectable achievement, for a professor like myself. However, the Oxford Round Table has no affiliation with Oxford University at all (they just rent space!), "invited speakers" (or their campuses) must *pay* several thousand dollars for the privilege to attend, and whether or not one is invited seems to be much more about whether you're on their email list than actual achievements or status on the field. In other words, this conference is largely a scam designed to make money for the organizers of the event. Today, with the increasing influence of social media, we have to be careful not to confuse "notoriety" with being "accomplished." As of 2017, Katy Perry has over 95 *million* twitter followers compared to only 45 million for CNN. It would be absurd to think that somehow Katy Perry is a more credible source of information, however, based solely on her superior popularity.

Putting all these ideas together, we can consider a "real-life" example of two experts.

Richard Dawkins:
- BA, Ph.D.: Oxford University Professor (emeritus) Oxford
- Specialization: evolutionary biology
- Achievements: numerous awards and publications

William Lane Craig:
- BA (Wheaton College),
- MA Phil of Religion & History of Christian Thought (Trinity Evangelical Divinity School), Ph.D. in PHIL (University of Birmingham),
- Ph.D. in Theology (University of Munich).
- Professor: Trinity Evangelical school and Talbot School of Theology
- Specialization: Philosophy of religion & Christian doctrine
- Achievements: numerous awards and publications

A legitimate evaluation of these two scholars recognizes that they are both very well educated and accomplished in their respective fields. Both are undoubtedly intelligent persons who deserve respect. This doesn't mean they are always correct, of course—but it does mean we should take them seriously when they offer claims concerning their areas of expertise.

An interesting application that applies to these two, specifically, is that they are considered "rivals." Craig is an outspoken Christian who debates prominent atheists around the world, trying to demonstrate the rationality of Christian faith. Dawkins, on the other hand, is a notorious critic of religion, and the author of such books as "The God Delusion."

While both men are credible experts, even legitimate experts can be guilty of stepping outside their areas of genuine expertise. Dawkins, for example, while one of the finest scholars on evolution living today, is *not* an expert on Western philosophy—let alone the philosophy of religion. Not surprisingly, when he writes a book like "The God Delusion" that deals with philosophy, rather than evolution, his credibility is strained. His critiques of the most famous arguments for God's existence in the Western tradition are undeniably outdated, and rely heavily on the criticisms offered by David Hume—written some two and a half centuries ago. What's worse is that what he calls his "central argument" is demonstrably invalid (according to the very standards we have addressed earlier in this chapter). Indeed, Craig has described the argument as "the worst atheistic argument in the history of Western thought."[7] In fairness, Craig should be equally cautious about extending his own expertise into the realm of biology. . . .

4)   The Claim does not Conflict with our own Worldview

We each have, at our disposal, what we may call our "background knowledge," or "background information, or our "worldview." Whatever we want to call it, it is that vast collection of everything we have heard, seen, read, and otherwise learned, throughout our lives. This collection is everything we know (or think we know) about the world and how it works. It includes your understanding of hugely important questions such as whether or not God (somehow conceived) exists, to your understanding of human psychology, world history, economics, State capitals, and even sports statistics. If you have learned about it, it is part of your worldview.

When presented with a claim, we all immediately evaluate that claim not only in terms of evidence, source, and our own observations, but also with respect to how well it "fits" with our worldview. We can summarize and simplify this process by asking two general questions about that claim.

1.   To what extent is the belief supported by good reasons and compelling evidence from reliable sources?

Is the belief in question supported by your own first-hand observations? Or, is it in conflict with your own observations? If you're receiving your evidence from another source, how reliable is that source? How credible is the source? Does the source have any relevant expertise? Is there any reason to be biased?

2.   To what extent is the belief consistent with my worldview?

Every time we are confronted with a piece of information, we automatically and instantly evaluate it against our background knowledge. If the new information seems to "fit" with our background knowledge, we're likely to accept it as true. If it does not fit, however, if the claim is surprising to us, we're likely to hesitate and to demand more justification before accepting it as true.

For example, if I were to claim that I drove home on the Southbound 605 freeway at 5 PM on a Thursday afternoon, and the freeway was wide open, with hardly any cars on it at all, anyone living in Southern California (that is, anyone for whom the 605 freeway, on a weekday, at 5 PM, is part of their background knowledge/worldview) would immediately doubt what I'm saying. Why? Because her understanding of the world and how it works is that Southern California freeways are jammed at that time

---

[7] http://www.reasonablefaith.org/dawkins-delusion

of day.

When it comes to justification, then, we'll want to know if the belief is consistent with other things that we know about the world and how it works. If the belief is consistent, so far, so good. If it is not, then we'll naturally be skeptical, and we'll require further evidence before accepting the belief.

We always need to be aware, however, that our own background knowledge can be flawed. For example, it used to be part of most people's worldview that the Sun revolved around the Earth. Now, it's part of our worldview that it's the Earth that moves relative to the Sun. Background knowledge is subject to revision. So, the mere fact that a piece of information conflicts with your understanding of the world does not automatically mean that the claim is false. It's possible that it's true, and that it's your worldview that needs revision.

Whenever you get presented with a claim (including the conclusion of an argument) that conflicts with your worldview, but for which you're confident it's true, the reasonable thing to do is to revise your worldview accordingly. Obviously, the more you know, the better equipped you are to evaluate claims, and to be accurate in your evaluations.

It is also important to be honest about the threat of bias posed by our worldviews when evaluating information—a bias that we are *all* subject to. Thus far, I have casually commented on our tendency to accept claims that fit with our worldview, and to be skeptical of those that clash with it. This is a well-known and studied psychological tendency known as the "confirmation bias." What makes the confirmation bias dangerous, though, is that it distorts our ability to honestly and objectively evaluate claims. This is not merely some anecdotal complaint about the state of debate today. There is scientific evidence to suggest that our brains are "wired" to be resistant to change with respect to "firmly held beliefs."

A study published in 2016 showed, via neuroimaging, that when subjects were presented with arguments that contradicted their strongly held political views, they experienced "increased activity in the default mode network—a set of interconnected structures associated with self-representation and disengagement from the external world."[8] The default mode network is normally shown to active during such states as daydreaming and mind-wandering. It is labeled "default" because the network activates "by default" when the person is not engaged in a task requiring attention. This is fascinating, if true! It suggests that when our firmly-held political beliefs are challenged, our brains "check out" in ways analogous to daydreaming. How responsive to evidence and argument are we likely to be if our brains are in a "day-dreaming" state when evidence contrary to our firmly held beliefs is presented?

In the final speech President Obama gave as President, he warned against our increasing tendency to operate within our own ideological "bubbles."

For too many of us, it's become safer to retreat into our own bubbles, whether in our neighborhoods or college campuses or places of worship or our social media feeds, surrounded by people who look like us and share the same political

---

[8] Kaplan, J. T. et al. Neural correlates of maintaining one's political beliefs in the face of counterevidence. Sci. Rep. 6, 39589; doi: 10.1038/srep39589 (2016). Available at http://www.nature.com/articles/srep39589

outlook and never challenge our assumptions. The rise of naked partisanship, increasing economic and regional stratification, the splintering of our media into a channel for every taste – all this makes this great sorting seem natural, even inevitable. And increasingly, we become so secure in our bubbles that we accept only information, whether true or not, that fits our opinions, instead of basing our opinions on the evidence that's out there.[9]

This isn't merely some anecdotal cautionary tale about liberals only watching MSNBC and conservatives only watching Fox News. A study published in the Proceedings of the National Academy of Sciences of the United States of America concluded that "selective exposure to content is the primary driver of content diffusion and generates the formation of homogeneous clusters, i.e., 'echo chambers.' Indeed, homogeneity appears to be the primary driver for the diffusion of contents and each echo chamber has its own cascade dynamics."[10]

In other words, people on Facebook mostly share news that they already agree with, that is consistent with their worldview, and they don't share information that challenges it. As the researchers put it, "users show a tendency to search for, interpret, and recall information that confirm their pre-existing beliefs."

Combine this tendency with the fact that Facebook has nearly 2 billion users (out of roughly 7 billion people on the planet), and reaches 67% of U.S. adults, and that 62% of Americans get their news mainly from social media sites such as Facebook and Twitter.[11] A majority of Americans get their news primarily from social media, and research confirms the application of the confirmation bias to social media platforms. It should go without saying that these trends seriously compromise our ability to think critically, and to responsibly accept or reject claims.

A recent and ominous development of this trend has inspired me to add an entire subsection to this chapter for the first time: "Fake News."

"Fake News"

As of 2017, "Fake News" has entered into the American vocabulary, initially and specifically in the realm of politics—though the phrase is likely to "trend" and apply to other contexts as well. Initially used by liberals to describe right-wing "conspiracy theories," the phrase expanded in use just as did the frequency of fake news itself. Conservatives then adopted the phrase themselves, and the phrase now gets used to describe multiple, significantly different things. This is where philosophy has a chance to shine, considering the experience philosophers have with conceptual analysis. The primary meanings of "fake news," as it is used, seems to be the following:

- *A work of fiction, known to be so by the author, but presented as real/true for personal, political, or financial motives.* This is the original meaning of fake news,

---

[9] http://www.latimes.com/politics/la-pol-obama-farewell-speech-transcript-20170110-story.html

[10] http://www.pnas.org/content/113/3/554.full

[11] http://www.journalism.org/2016/05/26/news-use-across-social-media-platforms-2016/?utm_content=bufferae870&utm_medium=social&utm_source=twitter.com&utm_campaign=buffer

and all other meanings are a departure from this. Another word to describe this kind of fake news is a "lie." A clear illustration of this kind of fake news is the example of Cameron Harris. As reported in an interview with Harris by the New York Times, he admitted to writing multiple completely fabricated stories that he thought would be effective "click-bait" for Trump supporters.[12] He claimed to have done so for financial reasons, citing that he made $22,000 in ad-revenue from his stories, though it was later revealed that he also worked as an aide to a Maryland Republican lawmaker.[13] Eight of his fake news stories were popular enough to attract the attention of (and debunking by) Snopes.com.[14] His most "effective" story claimed "Tens of thousands of fraudulent Clinton votes found in Ohio warehouse." By his own admission, he invented an imaginary electrical worker and named him "Randall Prince." He copied and pasted a screen shot of a man standing in front of ballot boxes using a google image search. He also identified the motive for the imaginary ballot-tampering: "the Clinton campaign's likely goal was to slip the fake ballot boxes in with the real ballot boxes when they went to official election judges on November 8th." The fact that the story was a complete *lie* did nothing to stop it from being shared with 6 million people. The fake news story went sufficiently viral that the Franklin County (Ohio) board of elections was forced to investigate—after which they confirmed the story had no basis in reality.[15]

- Satire: while also a work of fiction (and known to be so by the author), the work is presented as fiction for the sake of entertainment or to make a point. Satire is a long-practiced means of both entertainment and persuasion. "The Onion" is perhaps the most famous satirical website today, and it makes no pretense that its stories are true. When The Onion runs the headline, "Trump Calms Nerves Before Inaugural Address By Reminding Himself He's The Only Person Who Actually Exists," it is presumed that the reader will know that The Onion is only trying to be funny.[16] Similarly, when Jonathan Swift famously argued that a solution to Irish poverty was for Irish parents to sell their children as food to wealthy Englishmen, he wasn't being serious! Despite eating children being presented as his "Modest Proposal," his actual proposals were much more serious (and sincere):

Therefore let no man talk to me of other expedients: Of taxing our absentees at five shillings a pound: Of using neither clothes, nor household furniture, except what is of our own growth and manufacture: Of utterly rejecting the materials

[12] https://www.nytimes.com/2017/01/18/us/fake-news-hillary-clinton-cameron-harris.html?_r=0
[13] http://www.inquisitr.com/3901102/cameron-harris-fake-news-writer-bought-christian-times-newspaper-for-5-made-22000-and-got-fired/
[14] http://www.snopes.com/tag/christian-times-newspaper/
[15] http://files.constantcontact.com/b01249ec501/58eeb35a-7d61-4807-b168-765d27ca11cf.pdf
[16] http://www.theonion.com/article/trump-calms-nerves-inaugural-address-reminding-him-55095

and instruments that promote foreign luxury: Of curing the expensiveness of pride, vanity, idleness, and gaming in our women: Of introducing a vein of parsimony, prudence and temperance: . . . Of teaching landlords to have at least one degree of mercy towards their tenants. Lastly, of putting a spirit of honesty, industry, and skill into our shop-keepers, who, if a resolution could now be taken to buy only our native goods, would immediately unite to cheat and exact upon us in the price, the measure, and the goodness, nor could ever yet be brought to make one fair proposal of just dealing, though often and earnestly invited to it.

Satire is "fake news" in the sense that it is not *real*, but nor is it intended to be— and that is a significant difference from the original meaning of "fake news."

- *A work thought to be true and intended to be true by the author, but mistaken in one or more significant details.* In another words, a mistake. An example of a mistake in reporting that was, nevertheless, denounced as "fake news" occurred on the day Donald Trump was inaugurated as President. A White House pool reporter tweeted that a bust of Martin Luther King Jr. had been removed from the Oval Office.[17] In fact, the bust had simply been moved to a different part of the office, and the reporter hadn't seen it—something the reporter later acknowledged and for which he apologized. Nevertheless, the initial report was called "fake news" by detractors all the same.[18] At the risk of editorializing: honest mistakes, while bad, are not properly "fake news." A relevant indicator of intent is whether or not the person who made the initial claim is willing to admit (and correct) the mistake, and apologize.

- *A news story deemed "irrelevant," or unimportant, or distracting from "real" news* (according to the person making the claim). An example of this might be when reporters comment on the fashion choices of a politician, rather than the substance of her policies. As another example, when Senator Jeff Sessions was nominated to be U.S. Attorney General by President Trump, some reporters (and Democratic politicians) pointed to allegations of racism from his past as a potential disqualifier for confirmation. This was labeled by some as "fake news."[19]

- *A news story disliked by the reader.* This is perhaps the most disturbing usage of "fake news" of them all, in my opinion. This usage occurs when information is dismissed as "fake" simply because it conflicts with the reader's worldview, or because it would be distressing, if accepted as true. To be blunt: not liking a piece of information doesn't mean that it's false. If your medical doctor tells you that you have cancer, dismissing it as "fake news" is of no help.

---

[17] https://twitter.com/philipindc/status/822603029950173187
[18] http://www.thegatewaypundit.com/2017/01/fakenews-media-falsely-reports-trump-removed-mlk-bust-oval-office/
[19] http://eaglerising.com/38617/cnn-fake-news-story-jeff-sessions-is-a-racist/

The problem with the varied and inconsistent usage of the phrase "fake news" isn't just an issue of conceptual fussiness from overly-picky philosophers. Words have meaning. When President Trump refused to take questions from a CNN reporter, and dismissed the network as "fake news," it's likely that what he really meant is something like "I don't like CNN, and how CNN is reporting on my presidency."[20] However, people who listen to and respect President Trump might take his words to mean that CNN intentionally prints stories they know to be false for ulterior motives, and thereby lose confidence in the network as a reliable news source.

This isn't just bad news for CNN's ratings or profit margins. If confidence in mainstream media sources is undermined, people will retreat even *further* into their ideological bubbles, and their critical thinking skills will be even further compromised. President Trump later again labeled major media sources (viz., the New York Times, NBC, ABC, CBS, and CNN) as "fake news," but went further by denouncing them as the "enemy of the American People."

Cognitive linguist George Lakoff finds this strategy to be both intentional and dangerous. The adjective "fake" modifies the function of "news." The primary purpose of "news" is to pass along factual information in service to the public good. If "news" is modified with the term "fake," it implies that the basic function of "news" has been compromised.

> It is done to serve interests at odds with the public good. It also undermines the credibility of real news sources, that is, the press. Therefore it makes it harder for the press to serve the public good by revealing truths. And it threatens democracy, which requires that the press function to reveal real truths.[21]

Perhaps we would be better and more accurately served by refraining from using the phrase "fake news" entirely? When Hillary Clinton claimed in 2008 to have run from sniper fire in Bosnia, and her claim was proven to be false, the best-case scenario

---

[20] http://www.cnn.com/videos/politics/2017/01/11/donald-trump-jim-acosta-cnn-fake-news.cnn

[21] http://www.npr.org/2017/02/17/515630467/with-fake-news-trump-moves-from-alternative-facts-to-alternative-language

is that her memory was "mistaken," and the worst-case is that she intentionally lied for some reason.[22] Why bother calling it "fake news" when a "lie" or "mistake" more accurately conveys what occurred?

When President Trump's press secretary, Sean Spicer, in his very first press briefing, not only claimed that President Trump's inauguration audience was the largest ever, but also condemned journalists for writing "fake news" downplaying the size of the crowds, several troubling things occurred. For one, his claim about viewership was demonstrably false. President Trump's Nielson television ratings were only the fifth highest since President Richard Nixon—lower than President Obama's first inauguration, for example, but higher than the inaugurations of both Presidents Clinton and George W. Bush.[23] It's likely that President Trump and his staff would have liked it if their inauguration attendance and Nielson ratings had been the highest, but that preference doesn't mean that reporters who provide the factual numbers, in contrast, are disseminating "fake news." To suggest that they are is, again, to undermine confidence in the press, in general. It also seems unlikely to be helpful when President Trump's counselor, Kellyanne Conway described Spicer's actions in the following way: "You're saying it's a falsehood, and they're giving- Sean Spicer, our press secretary, gave alternative facts to that."[24]

For the sake of conceptual clarity: facts are objective, and are, by definition, true. An "alternative fact," therefore, is a clever term for something that is false—either a mistake, or a lie.

If it is a fact that 2+2 = 4, it is silly to label 2+2 = 5 as an "alternative fact." If it is a fact that Donald Trump is the 45th President of the United States, to claim that Bernie Sanders is the 45th President is not to offer an "alternative fact," but is simply to claim something that *is not true*. That President Trump's Nielson ratings for his inauguration were *not* the highest ever is a *fact*. To assert otherwise is not to provide an "alternative fact," but is simply to be either mistaken, or lying.

If you agree that "fake news" is troubling, and if you are motivated to be a good critical thinker, what can *you* do to be more wary when it comes to the news stories you accept or reject? The good news is that you have already learned how, earlier in this chapter! All of our previous discussion of justification, and how we should evaluate claims, is directly relevant to discerning whether a claim is "fake news," a lie, a mistake, or just simply true or false.

First of all, is the claim supported by evidence? In other words, is it an argument? Press Secretary Spicer didn't offer any evidence in support of his claim about the inauguration Nielson ratings—he just made an assertion. If he had offered an argument, you could try to determine whether his premises were relevant to the conclusion, and ultimately whether they were true. Had he cited Nielson numbers, you could easily fact-check them—probably on your smart phone!

---

[22]https://www.washingtonpost.com/news/fact-checker/wp/2016/05/23/recalling-hillary-clintons-claim-of-landing-under-sniper-fire-in-bosnia/?utm_term=.e6222cd61035

[23] http://www.washingtonexaminer.com/trump-inaugurations-nielsen-ratings-fourth-highest-since-nixon/article/2612602

[24]http://time.com/4642689/kellyanne-conway-sean-spicer-donald-trump-alternative-facts/

Don't forget the general process of evaluating unsupported claims. Recall that it's generally reasonably to accept an unsupported claim if it:

1. Does not conflict with our own observations
2. Does not conflict with other credible claims
3. Comes from a credible source that offers us no compelling reason to expect bias
4. Does not conflict with our background information/worldview

While it might not always be practical for you to investigate the source, at the very least you can try to be aware of the influence of your own worldview. If you know you are firm Trump supporter, then be aware that you are especially vulnerable to believing negative stories about Hillary Clinton—just as Hillary supporters would be especially vulnerable to believing negative stories about President Trump. Before getting indignant (and retweeting or sharing) an incendiary piece of news, try taking a few moments to carefully reflect on the claims being made, and maybe even do some fact-checking before taking a stance. Snopes.com is as very helpful resource in this regard.

Another very simple tip is to be initially skeptical about any stories riddled with spelling or grammar problems, or that use lots of CAPS or exclamation marks!!! Actual, serious journalists are usually pretty good writers, and poor writing can be a sign of an amateur blogger or internet troll.

You might be wondering why we just spent so much time on "fake news" and examples that were obviously political in nature, considering that this is an ethics text book. The explanation for that is because of the common overlap between "ethics" and "politics." Abortion is both a moral and political issue, as is the death penalty, as is torturing suspected terrorists, as is providing assistance to refugees, etc. Our moral values inform our political views (and vice versa). Most of us don't read articles or books on ethics (present company excluded, of course!), but most of us do engage with books, articles, television broadcasts, radio programs (etc.,) that deal with politics. The strategy is the same in any case. The very same precautions we should take when evaluating "political" claims will apply to claims made in the context of ethics.

Having completed our treatment of "fake news," we can now resume our discussion of processing claims, in general. Thus far, we've only seriously addressed the conditions under which we accept or reject a claim, but there is a third alternative that requires some attention as well: *suspending judgment*. Basically, to *accept* a claim means you think it's true, to reject it means you think it's false, and to *suspend judgment* means you're just not sure either way.

It is OK to suspend judgment.

Let me repeat that: it is OK to suspend judgment. You certainly don't want to spend your whole life shrugging your shoulders and pleading ignorance, but nor should you pretend to know the truth value of a claim if you honestly don't. Far too often, people accept or reject claims, and take stances on issues, when they know little, if anything, about the subject in question. Pardon my coarse language, but when people do so they are engaging in "bullshit."

Believe it not, "bullshit" is officially a philosophical term, thanks to the philosopher Harry Frankfurt. Is his aptly title book, "On Bullshit," he discusses this tendency in human behavior, and distinguishes it from lying. According to Frankfurt, "bullshit" occurs when "a person's obligations or opportunities to speak about some topic exceed his or her knowledge of the facts that are relevant to the topic."[25]

In other words, if you ask me what I think about President Trump's choice for Secretary of the Interior, and I have no idea who that is (or even what he or she does), and instead of admitting "I don't know," I say that I don't approve of the choice, I have engaged in some "bullshit."[26] The claim I have made exceeds the relevant knowledge I actually have on that topic.

It's clear, I hope, that the proper thing to do in a situation like that is to suspend judgment. Yet, all kinds of people "bullshit" all the time. Why? According to Frankfurt: "Closely related instances arise from the widespread conviction that it is the responsibility of a citizen in democracy to have opinions about everything, or at least everything that pertains to the conduct of his country's affairs."[27]

In other words, there is a perceived social expectation that everyone is supposed to have (and be ready to provide) an opinion about everything. When this is combined with a crude presumption of epistemic relativism,[28] then we get an especially troubling situation: everyone feels obliged to opine about everything, and no matter how uninformed they might be, somehow their own opinion is just as good as anyone else's, and therefore worth sharing.

An intellectually honest alternative to "bullshitting," and one that, frankly, requires both self-awareness and some courage, is to be willing to suspend judgment if you honestly don't know whether a claim is true or false.

To put this "justification" process to the test, we can apply our understanding by evaluating the following two claims.

1. **"I believe that, someday, my body will die."**

- Question: To what extent is the belief supported by good reasons and compelling evidence from reliable sources?
- Answer: Ample evidence is supplied every day, every time someone dies. Obituaries, news stories about deaths, and personal experiences and memories of people (and every other animal on Earth) dying all serve as evidence.

---

[25] Harry Frankfurt, *On Bullshit*. Princeton University Press, 2005. p. 63.

[26] In case you are curious, President Trump's Secretary of the Interior is Ryan Zinke (as of the time of this writing), and the Secretary's job is to manage the Department of the Interior, which is the government department that oversees federal land, natural resources, and the administration of programs relating to Native Americans, Alaskans, and Hawaiians.

[27] Harry Frankfurt, On Bullshit. Princeton University Press, 2005. p. 63.

[28] A view according to which all opinions are equally legitimate—and one we will consider later in this chapter.

- Question: To what extent is the belief consistent with my worldview?
- Answer: The claim is consistent with the complex web of our beliefs involving the natural sciences. Biology and history both inform our worldview, and our worldview certainly includes bodily death.

2. "I believe that I will win the Powerball jackpot this week."

- Question: To what extent is the belief supported by good reasons and compelling evidence from reliable sources?
- Answer: Excluding the possibility of cheating, there is no compelling evidence to indicate I will win. Indeed, it's unclear what could possibly count as evidence of this in the first place.

- Question: To what extent is the belief consistent with other my worldview?
- Answer: The claim that I will win the Powerball jackpot conflicts with our understanding of probability in general, and with our experience of lotteries, in particular. For example, the odds of winning the Powerball grand prize are 1 in 292,201,338. To win a million dollars has odds of 1 in 11,688,053.[29] In comparison, the odds of being struck by lightning *twice* in your lifetime are 1 in 9,000,000—something much more likely than being made a millionaire by the lottery![30]

When we compare these examples, we can detect a sharp contrast. In both cases, you probably (rightfully) think you do not have to suspend judgment, but can actually take a stance. The first claim (concerning bodily death) is so strongly justified that you probably not only accept it as true, but with sufficient justification to constitute knowledge. If you disagree with this, and deny that you *know* that your body will die someday, you probably think it's impossible to know *anything*.[31]

The second example (me winning the lottery) is so poorly justified as to be little better than wishful thinking—certainly *not* knowledge. In fairness, the lottery claim is about the future, and many epistemologists would say that future-indexed claims have an indeterminate truth-value, since they haven't happened yet. For that reason, you might be inclined to suspend judgment-and that is a fair position to take. However, even if you're suspending judgment for that reason, you probably think the claim is very likely to turn out to be false.

3. Truth

As a reminder: "knowledge" is defined as "justified, true belief." We have already discussed both belies and justification, and may now turn to truth.

---

[29] http://www.powerball.com/powerball/pb_prizes.asp
[30] http://wncn.com/2016/01/12/odds-of-winning-powerball-jackpot-less-than-being-hit-by-lightning-twice/
[31] That's not necessarily a bad thing. There is a respectable and ancient school of thought called "Skepticism" that regards knowledge as impossible to obtain.

It is generally accepted that one can't know something that is false. I can't know (as of 2017) that George Washington is the current U.S. President—because he isn't!

Note that we can *think* that we know all kinds of things, and then discover that we were mistaken. In those cases, we never *really* knew what we believed we knew at all. This is complicated, but only a very basic understanding is needed for our purposes. In summary, if we really do know something, it must be something that is true.

What does it *mean* for something to be true? Once again, this is a complicated issue, but, once again, we can avoid needless complications by focusing just on some key concepts. Though there are several ways of understanding truth, we will focus on just two: epistemic relativism and correspondence theory.

Epistemic Relativism

Epistemic relativism claims that truth is "relative" to the observer. Truth is a matter of perspective. Truth depends on one's point of view. Several ancient Sophists were known to hold this perspective, including Protagoras who allegedly claimed that "man is the measure of all things."[32]

Now, at a certain level, there is something obvious and unobjectionable about this idea. Most everyone would agree that there are certain kinds of claims we can make, certain kinds of judgments, which are merely expressions of personal opinion, or personal taste. One's favorite color, or whether or not one likes a band, or whether or not one likes spicy food—all such things seem to be matters of perspective. I like spicy food. My mother doesn't. She's not "wrong" or "mistaken" about spicy food—she just has different taste preferences. I really like the band "Switchfoot." I'm sure some people couldn't bear them (as hard as that is for me to believe). Again, no one is in error over such matters.

We call these sorts of claims "subjective claims." When we're dealing with subjective claims, there is no one "correct" point of view. There is no single correct answer to questions involving subjective claims. In cases of disagreement, it's not the case that someone must be wrong. Also, in cases of disagreement, there's little that can be accomplished from debate. I can sing the praises of spicy food for hours, but my mother will never be convinced of the truth of my claims and change her mind. This isn't because she's stubborn, it's because she just doesn't like spicy food! Her opinion on this matter is no better, or worse, than my own. It's just different.

Think about this, briefly, in the context of politics. To apply epistemic relativism to politics would mean believing that claims about political matters are simply matters of opinion. Such claims that would be opinions (as opposed to facts) might include the following:

---

[32] Strictly speaking, he is reported to have said "Of all things the measure is man, of the things that are, that [or "how"] they are, and of things that are not, that [or "how"] they are not." Hermann Diels and Kranz Walther. *Die Fragmente der Vorsokratiker*. Zurich: Weidmann, 1985. DK80b1. More "recently," and perhaps more famously, the character Obi Wan Kenobi implied this view in the film Return of the Jedi. "Luke, you're going to find that many of the truths we cling to depend greatly on our own point of view."

- Abortion is morally wrong.
- It is morally acceptable to use lethal force in self-defense.
- The use of violence is always wrong.
- It is morally wrong to eat meat.

So far, there's nothing terribly interesting or controversial about epistemic relativism. Where epistemic relativism does become controversial, however, is when we realize that the theory claims that *all* truths are relative; that all claims are subjective, and that none are objective.

If you stop to reflect on that for a moment, you can start to see how extraordinary that view really is (whether true, or not). If all "truths" are matters of perspective, and if no perspective is inherently any more privileged than any other, then everyone is always "right" about everything.

You believe the Earth is a sphere. I believe it's flat (I don't, really). Assuming each claim represents our own respective opinions, why would your opinion be any more "right" than mine? In a sense, we're both right—even though we're making mutually exclusive claims.

I think George W. Bush is the current U.S. President (I don't believe that either). That's my opinion, and I'm entitled to it, and your opinion isn't any more accurate than mine. "But," you might counter, "no one else shares your opinion, while lots of people share mine." Fine. That just means your opinion is more popular—it doesn't mean it's more accurate.

If all truth is subjective, then all truth is like my taste in music. If 99% of the world population couldn't stand Country music, but I loved it, my opinion that Country music is great would be no less legitimate than the nearly seven billion who disagree—it would just be a lot less popular.

To make matters even more interesting, consider this: "all truth is relative" is a claim. That means it's either true, or it's false. If it's false, then we obviously have no good reason to entertain it any further. If, on the other hand, it's true that all truth is relative, then that very claim is itself only relatively true. That is, it's just a matter of opinion, a matter of perspective. In that case, if I disagree, then my opinion is no worse, no less correct, than that of those who embrace epistemic relativism.

To sum this up, either "all truth is relative" is a relative truth, or it's not-relative. If it's relative, then it's merely an opinion that is no "more true" than an opposing opinion. If it's not-relative, then not all truth is relative, and the claim refutes itself.

There is something seemingly self-refuting, or internally inconsistent, with epistemic relativism. Since all opinions are equally true, it is simultaneously and equally true that epistemic relativism is, itself, both true and false.

Beyond this conceptual puzzle, a figure no less prominent than Socrates himself points out that we do not, in fact, regard all opinions as equally true. Consider the following examples:

Subject	Expert
Medicine	Medical Doctor
Nutrition	Nutritionist
Carpentry	Carpenter
Botany	Botanist
Chemistry	Chemist
Physics	Physicist
Philosophy	Philosopher

I'll start with a deeply personal example. If you don't believe that my understanding of philosophy, on the basis of my several degrees (B.A., M.A., and Ph.D.), years of experience (more than 20 years at the time of this writing), and "accolades" (e.g., being a tenured professor, and having published multiple articles and textbooks, etc.), is any more informed than your own, why on Earth are you bothering to read this book, or take my class? What is the point of education, in general, if every student is equally informed as his or her teacher?

Let's make it more absurd. Why bother going to the doctor when you are sick and injured? If all opinions are equal, your own opinion about your medical condition is just as good as that doctor's!

Those astrophysicists who have spent decades studying the universe and who are debating whether or not this universe is situated within a broader multiverse? Their views are no better informed than a random person who has never studied that stuff a day in his or her life. Does that seem true to you? That they are equally true opinions?

You almost certainly don't believe that, I'll wager—and that is the critic's point. In actual practice, we don't really believe that "all opinions are equal," but instead recognize that some people know what they're talking about, and others don't. If we recognize that this sort of relativism is rife with problems in non-moral contexts,[33] why should we entertain the notion in political contexts?

Does it seem plausible that every person's perspective is equally informed and "true" as any other person's when it comes to the various systems of government? To interpreting the Constitution? To various economic policies and how different systems of taxation will impact the Gross Domestic Product? To when and whether war is morally justifiable?

The question we must now consider is whether political claims concern a matter of possible expertise ("politics"), in which case we would presumably recognize that some people are better informed than others, and that not all views are equally good. Or, if we reject that, then we are presumably treating political claims as mere indicators of personal taste.

I might recognize that some people might be experts at "baking," and are certainly better informed than I am when it comes to how best to bake a cake, but I don't recognize that anyone else is somehow more informed than I am about what sort of cake *I* like! If you've gone to culinary school, your understanding of how to bake a red velvet cake is probably better informed than my own, but it makes no sense to suggest

---

[33] For example, think about what it would mean for it to be "just a matter of opinion" that humans require oxygen to survive.

that you know better than I do regarding whether or not I *like* red velvet cake. Is politics more like baking, or more like the kind of cake you like?

Using cake as our guide, consider the following examples and inferences:

Two people taste the same chocolate cake. One thinks it's overly sweet. The other thinks it could stand to be sweeter. Therefore, the sweetness of the chocolate is merely a matter of individual perspective. There is no "Truth" regarding its sweetness.

I look at a flower and perceive it to be yellow. A bee looks at the same flower and perceives it to be blue with a red center. Therefore, the appearance of the flower is a matter of individual perspective. There is no "Truth" regarding the appearance of the flower.

Such common sense differences in perspective *seem* to suggest that epistemic relativism might be the correct way to understand truth. However, if one considers carefully these examples, it will soon be clear that these examples do *not* imply that "*all* truth is relative"—indeed they presuppose something very different.

Epistemic relativism is driven by the force of the relativity of acts of perception. That is, because it is such a common experience for people to perceive "the same thing" in very different ways, it's easy to conclude that truth is relative. Be careful, though! The relativity of perception, even if true, doesn't imply that *all* truth is relative. In fact, some truths must be held to be objective in order for the relativity of other truths to make any sense.

Reconsider the chocolate cake. Two people taste the same cake with different results. Therefore, perception is relative. What is *not* thought to be relative in this example is the existence of the cake, the tasters, and the world in which both cake and tasters exist! The same sorts of presuppositions apply to the flower example. The bee and I perceive the flower with different results, but what is *not* thought to be relative is the existence of the flower itself, the bee, myself, and the reality in which all three of us reside.

In order to even make sense of the relativity of perception, one must presuppose that it is "True" that observers exist, and that a reality exists that may be perceived differently. The commonsense observation that initially gives rise to relativism is that the "real world" exists, that perceivers (such as you, me, and the bee) exist, but that we experience the "real world" in different ways.

Much more relevant to the subject of politics, even the all-too-common claim that politicians "lie" presupposes that there is such a thing as "truth."

The 2016 U.S. Presidential election was contentious, to say the least. Both Republicans and Democrats demonized their opposition by claiming that they were liars. Trump supporters condemned Hillary Clinton for lying about emails, and "Benghazi," and countless other things. Hillary supporters condemned Donald Trump for lying about his taxes, charitable donations, his treatment of women, and various other statements made and stances taken. Politifact affirmed that they *both* lied about a variety of things, with Trump having lied more often.[34]

To use just one example, consider that on September 26th, 2016, at one of the televised President debates, Hillary Clinton said that Donald Trump had claimed

---

[34] http://www.politifact.com/truth-o-meter/lists/people/comparing-hillary-clinton-donald-trump-truth-o-met/

climate change was a hoax. He interjected, "I did not, I did not, . . . I do not say that."[35] However, there is documentation of multiple instances of him saying precisely that, including a Tweet from November 6th, 2012, in which he said "The concept of global warming was created by and for the Chinese in order to make U.S. manufacturing non-competitive."[36]

This is not about Hillary Clinton, Donald Trump, or global warming. It is, however, about whether or not there is a notion of truth that goes beyond personal opinion. If you think that lies are possible, and that either Trump or Clinton lied about something, what do you *mean* by that, if not that there is some *fact* (e.g., Trump said global warming is a hoax), but the person in question knowingly made a claim that contradicts that fact (e.g., "I did not say that.")? If Hillary Clinton lied about her use of a private email server during her tenure as Secretary of State, that implies that there is some independent truth of the matter, and that her claims don't match up to that truth. This common sense assumption about lies not "matching up" brings us to our alternative to epistemic relativism: correspondence theory.

Correspondence Theory
Consider the following statements:

- The claim that George W. Bush is the current U.S. President is true if and only if he really is the current U.S. President.
- The claim that there are exactly 457 marbles in the jar is true if and only if there really are exactly 457 marbles in the jar.
- The claim that there was life on Mars is true if and only if there really was life on Mars.

---

[35] https://www.youtube.com/watch?time_continue=1&v=PlI5l41Hpww
[36]https://twitter.com/realDonaldTrump/status/265895292191248385?ref_src=twsrc%5Etfw

Are these statements reasonable? If you think so, you're probably sympathetic to what is known as the correspondence theory of truth.

According to correspondence theory, a claim is true if it "corresponds" to the way things "really are" in the world, if the claim "matches up" with reality, if it "maps on" to how the world actually is. This theory claims that there is a way that the universe "really is," and our claims are true, or not, depending on whether they match up with the world. This is the approach implicitly employed by most people, whether they realize it or not.

Imagine that you intercept a fellow student on the way to class, and she tells you that the class has been cancelled. Has she told you the truth? What would you need to know in order to make that assessment? Simply this: you would need to know if the class really had been cancelled. If it had, her statement was true. If it had not, her statement was false. Her claim either "corresponded" to the world, or it didn't.

Obviously, not all of our claims will be so easily verifiable. Some truth claims, including, unfortunately, the ones we tend to care the most about (i.e., claims about morality, religion, politics, etc.), might be especially difficult to establish because we might not know how "the world is" concerning that particular subject.

Do aliens exist, or not? Hard to say, since we haven't explored the entire universe just yet. Is abortion immoral? Hard to say, since there's so much disagreement, and so many compelling arguments that can be given on both sides. Should governments promote a strong middle class, primarily promote the interests of the working class, or sit back and let "the Market" decide? Hard to say, since there's so much disagreement, and so many compelling arguments that can be given on both sides. . .
.

What correspondence theorists *will* claim is that even if we're not sure what the answers to some of these difficult questions are, we nevertheless can be confident that there *are* answers, and not merely equally legitimate opinions, out there for us to discover.

Conclusion

The purpose of this introductory chapter is to provide a basic overview of arguments as understood in philosophy, provide a few key vocabulary terms (e.g., validity, soundness, claim, premise, etc.), and provide a framework within which to understood how we evaluate arguments. This will serve us for the remainder of this book.

Every chapter that follows this one will be offering one or more perspectives from across the history of Western political philosophical thought. Each of these famous philosophers will be offering *arguments*—which is just to say that they will be defending their positions, offering reasons for what they believe. Your task going forward will be the following:

1. Using the Principle of Charity, identity the main points (conclusions) being made by these philosophers.
2. Using the Principle of Charity, identity the reasons/evidence (premises) being offered in support of those main points.
3. As best you can, and when possible, determine whether their premises are relevant. In some cases, this will be an indicator as to whether the argument

is "valid."

4. As best you can, and when possible, use the process of justification discussed in this chapter (i.e., considering evidence, source, and fit with your worldview) to determine whether the premises are also true—and if this entails that their conclusion is true.

5. Determine your own degree of agreement or disagreement with these various philosophers and their ideas. Presumably, if you have concluded that their arguments are "sound," you should agree! Conversely, if you still disagree, that should indicate that their arguments are somehow flawed.

With this foundation in place, we will move on, in the next chapter, to consider our first "argument:" the one made by the psychological egoist in defense of their claim that all human actions are fundamentally motivated by self-interest.

Chapter 2: Psychological Egoism

> *Comprehension questions you should be able to answer after reading this chapter:*
>
> 1. What are altruistic motivations?
>
> 2. What are egoistic motivations?
>
> 3. What is the difference between a descriptive theory and a prescriptive theory?
>
> 4. What is psychological egoism? What does it claim about human motivation?
>
> 5. Why would psychological egoism, if true, have such a significant impact on our understanding of ethics?
>
> 6. What are some possible problems for (objections to) psychological egoism?

Ethics is the formal study of moral principles, decision making, right and wrong behavior, virtue and vice, etc. It concerns what we should, or should not, do. To even speak in terms of what we should do presupposes that we have a choice. This is why the free will debate is so intimately bound to ethics. It is a curious thing to tell me that I should not lie if it is literally impossible for me to tell the truth. A taken-for-granted principle in ethics is that "ought implies can." That is, if I ought to do X, it must be possible for me to do X; and, if I ought to refrain from X, that must be possible for me to refrain from doing X.

One of the first "challenges" to ethics we will consider is what sorts of moral obligations might apply to us. To begin, it will be useful to distinguish two basic kinds of motivation: altruistic, and egoistic.

Altruism: acting for the benefit of others; acting for the sake of others; foregoing some benefit for oneself so that another may enjoy a benefit instead

Egoism: acting for self-benefit; acting from self-interest; promoting one's own good (possibly at the expense of another's)

Presumably, the most morally relevant of those two types of motivations is the altruistic variety. After all, it's easy to think of moral obligations that involve acting for the benefit of others. The most obvious examples involve anything charitable. Giving money to help the poor instead of spending on something for yourself, or donating time to work for the good of others (instead of using that time for your own benefit), are both examples of altruistically motivated actions. Whether or not a particular altruistic behavior is morally required of us would, of course, be subject to interpretation and debate, but the mere idea that we are all, at least sometimes, morally obligated to put other people's interests ahead of our own seems uncontroversial.

What if altruistically motivated behavior is impossible, though?

Psychological Egoism

Psychological egoism is a *descriptive theory* of human nature. That is, rather than making recommendations (as we find in *prescriptive theories*), it seeks merely to describe the nature of something—in this case, human motivation. As such, it claims to be empirical and scientific. According to psychological egoism (henceforth referred to as PE), every single human being, without exception, is always driven *solely* by egoistic motivations. Altruism is an illusion, a myth. Even those actions that we *believe* to be altruistic in intention actually serve self-interest—otherwise, they would not be performed.

A very early account of PE is found in Plato's *Republic*, as presented by Glaucon (Plato's half-brother, in real life). It is important to note that Plato was not himself a psychological egoist. At most, a character (Glaucon) in one of Plato's dialogues (*Republic*) promotes PE, sort of....[37]

In seeking to explain the nature and origin of justice, Glaucon appeals to the myth of Gyges' ring. According to this myth, a shepherd named Gyges is tending his flock one day, when an earthquake splits the ground. He explores the fissure and discovers a large tomb in the shape of a horse. Inside, he finds the body of a giant. The dead giant is wearing a ring. Gyges takes the ring. The shepherd-turned-grave robber discovers that this is no ordinary ring. When he manipulates the ring a certain way, he becomes invisible! When he twists it back, he becomes visible once more. After mastering the ring, he arranges to have himself sent as the representative of his village to the royal court. Once there, he uses to power of the ring to murder the king and claim power for himself.

Before we come to any harsh judgments against Gyges, Glaucon recommends a thought experiment. Imagine there are two such magic rings, each of which renders the wearer invisible. These days, we might need to get a little more sophisticated. Perhaps you suppose that even invisible persons might still leave behind fingerprints, or hair samples, or other means by which a clever forensic investigator could identify a perpetrator. They're magic rings. We can make them do whatever we want! Suppose the rings render the wearer invisible, magically cloaks any heat signatures, erases fingerprints, eliminates DNA evidence, etc. Now, give one of the two rings to someone whom you regard as tremendously virtuous and just. Give the other to someone quite the opposite: a vicious and unjust jerk. What, do you suppose, each would do with the ring? Glaucon believes that both the "just" and the "unjust" would come "at last to the same point." That is, they would each, eventually, do the same thing: whatever it is that each wanted. To make matters more interesting, give yourself one of the rings.

What would you do? Honestly....If your answer includes anything you would not already do right now, without the ring, you have confirmed Glaucon's point (and his

---

[37] A footnote for those truly interested: not even Glaucon endorses PE. He finds himself in the awkward position of wanting to believe that morality and justice are intrinsically valuable, and worthy for their own sake, but concerned that this might not be true. So, he plays the role of a devil's advocate, arguing in favor of a selfish view of human nature and justice in the hopes that Socrates will leap into the conversation and prove him wrong.

fear). If you would do something with the ring, that you would not do without it, it suggests that the reason why you refrain from that action now is not any commitment to moral principle, but fear of getting caught and punished. Remove the fear, and watch out....

The outcome of Glaucon's thought experiment provides a possible insight into human nature. If it is true that any one of us would ultimately and inevitably abuse the power of Gyges' ring, then the reason why most of us usually obey the rules and "play nice" with one another is fear. Although we would like to be able to do whatever we want, to whomever we want, whenever we want, we recognize that such behavior just isn't possible. None of us is Superman.

However powerful a given individual might be, she isn't bulletproof (to put it bluntly). No matter how wealthy, how powerful, how well-connected, each one of us is all-too-human, and all-too-vulnerable. Realizing that, and wishing to minimize the risk we face from others, we make mutual promises to "play nice." I won't rob you so long as you don't rob me. I won't kill you, so long as you don't kill me. We surrender some of our own power, and our own freedom, when we make those promises, but in exchange for that we gain security. We behave ourselves because it is in our self-interest to do so. If it were no longer necessary, no *longer* in our self-interest (e.g., if we had Gyges' ring), we would no longer be inclined to "play nice." Notice that the common theme in both cases is the same: self-interest. When we obey the law, it is because we perceive it is in our self-interest to do so. When we instead break the law, it is because we perceive it is in our self-interest to break it, instead.

These are understandable and even inevitable behaviors, according to psychological egoism. According to PE, each person *always* pursues her own self-interest, without exception. We can't help but do so. We're "wired" to always pursue our own self-interest. If this is true, it has profound implications for our understanding of moral obligation. The following argument illustrates why.

1. Everyone always acts from self-interest (PE).
2. If one can't do something, one is not obligated to do it ("ought implies can").
3. Altruism requires putting others' interests ahead of our own.
4. Altruism is therefore impossible (from lines 1 and 3).
5. Altruism is therefore never required (from lines 2 and 4).

Notice just how significant this is, if true. Every major ethical system in the world (with the notable exception of ethical egoism) claims that altruism is at least sometimes required of us. I'm confident that no matter what your own approach to ethics is, you believe that at least *sometimes* the morally right thing to do is to put another person's interests ahead of your own.

PE says that to do so is impossible.

You and I are *incapable* of putting other people first. Since it's impossible for us, we are never obligated to put others first. Therefore, we never have a moral obligation to behave altruistically. That means every major ethical system in the world (except for ethical egoism) is mistaken. Unless you happen to be an ethical egoist, you will need to revise your understanding of moral obligation.

If PE is true, it clearly has a profound impact on ethics. But, *is* it true? Should we believe it is? Why would anyone? The most often provided reason is because it appears that PE can provide an egoistic explanation for any action whatsoever, no matter how altruistic it might appear on the surface.

I'm going to pretend to be a psychological egoist, and set the bar very high, right from the beginning: I'm going to prove that Mother Teresa was selfish.[38]

"Mother Teresa was selfish?" you might ask.

"Certainly," I reply.

She was a nun, right? That suggests she took her religion pretty seriously. She believed in heaven and hell. As a Roman Catholic, she likely placed even greater emphasis on "works" (as opposed to faith alone) than would Protestants. "I heard the call to give up all and follow Christ into the slums to serve Him among the poorest of the poor. It was an order. I was to leave the convent and help the poor while living among them."

On the very reasonable assumption that she believed that her actions in this world would impact her prospects in the next, the cost-benefit analysis is embarrassingly simple: a few decades of service and sacrifice in exchange for an eternity of indescribable bliss. This is easy math! By living "altruistically," Mother Teresa was promoting her own Salvation. Maybe she even didn't even have to wait in line to get into Heaven....

What's more, she was a celebrity, and not merely well-known, but beloved and admired by millions, if not billions, of people.

Finally, by her own description, she was happy! "Poverty for us is a freedom. It is not mortification, a penance. It is joyful freedom. There is no television here, no this, no that. But we are perfectly happy." She was happy in her life. She was happy being poor. She was happy serving others.

To sum up, by serving the sick and the poor, Mother Teresa became famous and beloved (which presumably feels pretty good), she made herself happy, and she engineered an eternity of reward for herself. Was she motivated by self-interest? So it would seem! And, if someone like Mother Teresa falls prey to egoistic interpretation, how much more easily do the rest of us? It seems that everyone (even Mother Teresa) is always driven by self-interest

Summary (so far):

It appears to be a fact that people do indeed act for the sake of self-interest. That is, it's not difficult to think of examples where it is obvious that people acted for their own benefit, sometimes at the expense of others. It also appears that any action can be explained in terms of self-interest (e.g., Mother Teresa "serving" the poor). PE offers itself as an explanatory theory to account for those facts: all people necessarily

---

[38] For those who aren't familiar with Mother Teresa: she was a globally-recognized Catholic nun who spent most of her life in India. She founded the "Missionaries of Charity" that included over 4,500 nuns and is active in over 130 countries. The organization runs hospices and homes for people with HIV/AIDS, leprosy and tuberculosis. It also operates soup kitchens, dispensaries and mobile clinics, child and family counseling programs, and orphanages and schools. Nuns of the order must take (and adhere to) vows of chastity, poverty and obedience, as well as a fourth vow: to give "wholehearted free service to the poorest of the poor".

(and exclusively) act from self-interest.

We now face the following question: is this explanatory theory (PE) the only, or at least the best, way to understand human behavior? If the answer is "yes," then we would have good reason to accept PE, and consequently accept the serious implications it would have on our understanding of ethics. If the answer is "no," however, then we may reject both PE and its serious implications. We have reviewed reasons to think PE is true, so we will consider some reasons to reject it.

Possible Problems for PE

Possible Problem #1: the "post hoc ergo propter hoc" fallacy

"Post hoc ergo propter hoc" is a Latin phrase. Roughly translated: "after the fact, therefore because of the fact."

The post hoc fallacy is an abuse of what is otherwise a perfectly legitimate form of causal inference. As I write this sentence, I first tap a key, then a letter appears on the monitor. Therefore, tapping the key causes the letter to appear. Nothing weird or presumptuous about that piece of reasoning! First one thing happens (tapping the key), then another thing happens (a letter appears), therefore the first thing (tapping) causes the second thing (appearing). Try a different example, though. I had some eggs for breakfast. Later in the day, the Dow Jones Industrial Average lost several hundred points. Therefore, my eating eggs caused the Dow to lose hundreds of points. Who would have guessed that my dietary practices exerted so much terrible influence over the U.S. economy?

They don't, of course—and I'm sure you recognize that it's silly to think that just because one thing happened first (eggs for breakfast), and then something else happened later (Dow loss), the two are somehow causally connected. When such a causal connection is hastily drawn, we have an example of the post hoc fallacy.

This kind of fallacious reasoning can occur not just with respect to causes, but also with *reasons*. For example, prior to obtaining full time employment at Rio Hondo College, I taught at several campuses, usually in the same academic terms. Some semesters, I taught at CSU Long Beach, Cal Poly Pomona, *and* UC Riverside. A typical day might involve starting in Long Beach and teaching there, then driving to Riverside and teaching a class there, then driving to Pomona to teach another class, and returning home to Long Beach to collapse from exhaustion, grade exams, prep for the next day, or whatever else seemed most appropriate. As a result of all that commuting, I burned up a lot of gasoline. It would be a mistake, though, to think in the following way:

1. Ted drove to work.
2. As a result, he burned gasoline.
3. Therefore, he drove in order to burn gasoline.

I assure you that burning gas was not my goal. If I could have avoided it, I would have. My goals were many (e.g., to earn a paycheck, to advance my career, to do what I love, etc.), but burning gas was not among them. Just because an action produced a particular outcome (and a predictable one, at that) does not mean that the action was done for the sake of that outcome.

How does this apply to PE, you might wonder? Psychological egoists note that Mother Teresa helped the poor. As a consequence, she was made happy, became famous, and possibly earned herself eternal reward. Therefore, she helped the poor *for the sake* of her own happiness, fame, and eternal reward.

This is possibly true, of course, but may we simply *assume* it to be true? Just because helping others made her happy, does that mean she did it *in order* to promote her own happiness? Are we justified in assuming that to be the case, when we weren't justified in assuming that I commuted for the sake of burning gas? Isn't it possible (simply *possible*) that she helped the poor for some other reason (e.g., because it was the right thing to do, or because she thought it was God's will), and, as a result of her actions, she was made happy—but that her own happiness wasn't her goal? Consider (and compare) the following:

(A)

Action		Result	(inferred) Goal
i.	Help the poor	Feel happy	Feel happy
ii.	Commute	Burn gas	Burn gas

V.

(B)

Action		Result	(actual) Goal
i.	Help the poor	Feel happy	Do the right thing
ii.	Commute	Burn gas	Earn a paycheck

PE seems to assume that the egoistic explanation, represented in (Ai), is the correct explanation—but assuming and proving are two very different things. One might also assume that I commuted in order to burn gas (Aii)! But, the critic of PE might allege that just as the correct explanation of my commuting is something other than burning gas (e.g., earning a paycheck, Bii), so too might the correct explanation of Mother Teresa's behavior be something other than self-interest. In other words, the explanation offered in (Bi) could be the correct kind of explanation. Unless a reasonable causal connection can be traced and *demonstrated*, it appears that PE is possibly guilty of the post hoc fallacy.

Can such a causal connection be demonstrated? Seemingly not. Consult your own experience. How often do you perform an action with your goal being "to satisfy self-interest?" Isn't it, instead, usually the case that your goal is something else altogether, and that when you achieve *that* goal, your self-interest is (at least sometimes, somehow conceived) served?

For example, suppose you buy your mother a nice present for Mother's Day, and she is visibly happy when you give it to her. You then feel proud and happy, and have a wonderful Mother's Day with her. Presumably, you could not have felt "proud and happy" if you had not desired to make your mother happy with the gift. If you couldn't care less about that, why would her happiness have made you proud and happy yourself? Implicitly, then, your desire was to make your mother happy—*that* is what you were pursuing. To have experienced happiness when your desire was satisfied, you had to have a desire other than your own happiness! If so, this suggests that it is not the case that *all* our actions are motivated by our own happiness, or self-interest. Rather, our actions seem to be motivated by all kinds of other desires, and when those desires are satisfied we often experience happiness or the fulfillment of our self-interest as a *result*.

Possible Problem #2: Unfalsifiability

PE is often regarded as very convincing (at least initially) because it seems capable of providing an egoistic explanation for *any and every* action whatsoever.

<u>Example</u>	<u>Egoistic Explanation</u>
Helping the poor	Feeling self-righteous
Donating to charity	Tax deduction
Risking your life for another	Avoiding survivor's guilt
Donating a kidney to a friend	Adulation for being a hero

On the surface, at least, this might seem like an incredible strength of the theory. No matter what example you provide, a psychological egoist can show how it is motivated by self-interest, even if this requires appealing to subconscious motivations.

You think you helped the poor because it was the "right thing to do," but really you did it to feel good about yourself. Don't think so? Well, that should come as no surprise. It's in your self-interest to not think of yourself as selfish, and instead to think of yourself as truly generous and charitable. If you were honest with yourself, though, and dug deeply enough into the layers of your motivation, you would eventually uncover your own self-interest. Don't think so? You obviously haven't delved deeply, and honestly enough, yet. Keep up the soul-searching! When may you stop? When you finally realize that your motivation was self-interested, of course!

Do you sense the problem, yet? Taken to this extreme, PE's explanatory power is quickly revealed to be unfalsifiable. This is not a virtue for a theory. If there is no possible way to disprove the theory, no possible counter-example that can be provided, the theory is unfalsifiable. This is another way of saying that it is unverifiable, untestable.

This is a not a good thing for a theory of human nature, for a theory that claims to be an explanatory theory, for a theory that cloaks itself in the language of science. In science, if a hypothesis is not testable, it is not scientific. End of discussion.

If the hypothesis that all human acts are egoistic is not testable (because it is not falsifiable), it is not scientific. End of discussion. Proponents of PE may *assume* that all our motivations are egoistic, they may *assert* that all our motivations are egoistic, but assuming and asserting and not at all the same thing as *proving*.

Possible Problem #3: Defining "self-interest"

PE claims that all our motivations are egoistic, that we always act in our own self-interest. By now, you're probably wondering what, exactly, that means. After all, "acting in self-interest" may mean any number of things, some of which being more plausible than others. Let us consider some possible meanings of "self-interest."

1.   We always do what is best for us.

Perhaps "self-interest," as understood by PE, means that we always do what is best for ourselves. If so, PE appears to be mistaken in rather obvious ways. It's clear that we do not always do what is best for ourselves. Sometimes we behave foolishly, recklessly, and dangerously. Sometimes we ruin our lives by making stupid mistakes. Sometimes the damage isn't so dire, but we recognize our errors all the same. Clearly, we do not always do what is best, even for ourselves.

2.   We always do what we *think* is best for us.

This seems more plausible, as it allows for honest mistakes. Perhaps we always do what seems to be best, but it turns out, in retrospect, that we were wrong. "I thought that cheating on the exam would be best for me, but it turns out I was mistaken. I had no idea the professor was so skilled at catching cheaters...."
While this interpretation is more plausible than #1, it still seems false. If you're anything like me, you've had experiences in which you've said to yourself something along the lines of:

"I know I shouldn't do this, but...."
"I know I'm going to regret this...."
"I know this is a bad idea, however...."

It seems to be the case that we sometimes do something while fully aware of the fact that it's not smart, or wise, or healthy, or prudent, or even the least bit a good idea. But, we do it anyway. If so, it would appear that it is not the case that we always do even what we *think* to be best.

3.   We always do what we want most to do, all things considered.

This seems most plausible of all. Perhaps what PE boils down to is that we always do what we most want, and sometimes what we most want is pretty stupid, or harmful, or reckless. For example, a smoker wants to quit, and knows she should, but she continues smoking anyway. How can we understand that? Simply: although she wanted to quit, she wanted another cigarette even more. A person wants to lose weight, but still doesn't begin to exercise or control caloric intake. Explanation? Although he wants to lose weight, he wants to enjoy food and avoid strenuous exercise even more. What about when the smoker finally quits? Simple: at that point, her desire to quit was stronger than her desire to smoke. Whatever it is that we do, it's what we most wanted to do—otherwise, we'd have done something else.
So far, so good. A critic might wonder, however, just how it is that we discern what we most want to do. How can such things be identified? Easily, according to this interpretation of PE. We simply identify the action performed. We can identify what we most want, retroactively, by observing behavior. The mere fact that we perform

an action X is evidence that what we most wanted was to do X---otherwise, we'd have done Y (or Z, etc.). Closer inspection, however, reveals this understanding to be problematic—circular, in fact. Consider the following:

1.   We always do what *we most want to do*.

Now, what is it that we most want to do? What does that phrase mean?

2.   What we most want to do, is *whatever it is that we actually do* (otherwise, we would have done something else).

So, "what we most want to do" is understood to be "what we actually do." If this is correct, I should be able to substitute "what we actually do" for "what we most want to do" wherever I find it expressed (such as in statement #1 above). Behold.

3.   We always do what we actually do.

Brilliant! Obviously true. Also trivially true. Meaninglessly true. "We always do what we actually do?" How about simplifying that expression?

4.   We do what we do.

This is what is called a "tautology." A tautology involves a repetition of meaning, saying (essentially) the same thing, but using different words—especially when the additional words fail to provide additional clarity. Of course it is true that "we do what we do." The problem is that this tells us nothing interesting. It's a safe assumption that all intentional human action is motivated by some sort of desire, that we perform actions on the basis of some sort of motivation. But, does it seem accurate to identify every and any desire or motive with "self-interest?"

> *In assessing whether an action is self-interested, the issue is not whether the action is based on a desire; the issue is what kind of desire it is based on. If what you want is to help someone else, then your motive is altruistic, not self-interested.*[39]

PE claims that all actions are motivated by self-interest, that all motivations are egoistic. This seems obviously false, if we understand "self-interest" to mean something like "putting yourself first, at the expense of others." One can immediately begin to generate counter-examples: charitable giving, the life and work of Mother Theresa, sacrificing your own life to save another's, etc. Given the categorical nature of PE, all it takes is a single counter-example to refute the theory. In order to defeat these sorts of counter-examples, PE must be understood in such a way that even examples like those can be understood as egoistically motivated. This requires stretching the meaning of "self-interest" so as to incorporate every possible action

---

[39] James Rachels, The Elements of Moral Philosophy, Chapter 5.2.

whatsoever. Concepts are kind of like gum, though: the more you stretch it, the weaker and more transparent it becomes. Concepts have meaning not only by what they include, but also by what they *exclude*. Stretch a concept so that *nothing* is excluded, and *everything* is included, and the concept ceases to have meaning!

For example, in sports, the "MVP" is literally *the* "most valuable player." "The most" is a superlative term. By definition, only one member of the team can be the MVP. Imagine that a well-intentioned Little League coach is trying to increase the self-esteem of his players, and at the annual awards banquet announces that *every* player is the MVP that year. What does "MVP" now mean? When every player is the MVP, all MVP means (now) is "player." The word has literally lost its meaning, by being misapplied—no matter how well-intentioned the gesture might have been.

As another example, pretend you are an anthropologist, and you are visiting a recently discovered tribe of people called "Prestonians," where the inhabitants speak "Prestonian" due to the pervasiveness of the word "Preston" in their language. You are trying to learn this language, and a member of the Preston tribe points to what you call a tree, and says "Preston." He then points to what you call a dog and says "Preston." He points to another tribesman punching someone in the face and says "Preston," then points to a local couple kissing passionately: "Preston." He later points to a woman giving birth and says "Preston," and then to a man who just died of a heart attack: "Preston." After several days, you realize that everything he points to, he calls "Preston," and whenever you attempt to ask him a question in your own language, with the additional use of pointing and hand gestures, he always pauses, seems to reflect, and then answers "Preston."

What does the word Preston mean, in his language? You don't have the slightest clue, do you? *Everything* seemed to be "Preston"—which made it impossible for you to discern what the word *actually means*.

In the same way, psychological egoists point to "everything" and call it "egoistic," or "selfish." Saving a life? Selfish. Taking a life? Selfish. Helping the poor? Selfish. Hurting the poor? Selfish. Going to class? Selfish. Skipping class? Selfish. Given this usage, "selfish" or "self-interested" has no more meaning than does "Preston!" If "Preston" means "everything," it actually means *nothing*. So too with selfishness, or self-interest.

PE has an easy way to fix this problem: tighten up the meaning of self-interest so that "acting from self-interest" ceases to imply a tautology. If PE does this, the "definitional" problem can be resolved—but it is soon replaced by a new problem: it is no longer anything close to obvious that all actions really are motivated by self-interest!

It is possible that even seemingly heroic actions are motivated by self-interest, but is it plausible? Think about what this would mean. On September 11th, 2001, 346 firefighters were killed. They were moving into the World Trade Towers, while everyone else was trying to get out. PE does provide a possible explanation for their seemingly heroic behavior: self-interest. Perhaps they wanted to feel like heroes. Perhaps they didn't want to avoid losing their jobs, or being scorned by their peers for cowardice. In any event, PE claims their motivations must have been self-interested. On September 12th, 2001, USA Today reported that two men (Michael Benfante and John Cerqueira) spent an hour carrying an unnamed woman who used a wheelchair down 68 flights of stairs, at clear and obvious risk to their own life. PE offers an explanation for why they did so: self-interest (somehow conceived). Millions of ordinary citizens donated money, and time, and blood for the relief effort after 9-11. Why did they all do so? Self-interest, according to PE.

When I was a senior in high school, my father lost his job due to "downsizing." He ended up finding another job, but there's a story behind it. My dad had been a broadcast engineer for most of his working life. He had left a position as the Director of Engineering at a television station to take a sales job with a large company. He sold the broadcasting equipment he had used, purchased, and knew so much about in his capacity as an engineer. Much earlier in his career, he had worked for a boss he disliked very much—so much so that he took another job in another State to get away from him. Years later, that same boss became the boss of the television station my dad had left when he took the sales position. Then, he was "downsized" from his sales position, and found himself unemployed, and wondering how he was going to support his family. As I mentioned, he did find another job—an entry level engineer position at his old television station. He was the lowest seniority person in the very same department that he used to manage. He was working beneath the same guys that he used to supervise—and his boss was the *same guy* that inspired him to move across the country just to get away from him. Only as an adult now myself, can I appreciate how humbling that must have been for him: to have to take a job from a man he disliked, and did not respect; to have once been the manager, and to then be the "low man on the totem pole," with the worst shifts and the least seniority. What I found out from him decades later, but had never known before, was that he had been offered *another* job. It would have required us to move, however, and he refused to move during my senior year in high school. He knew how disruptive that would be to me socially, and emotionally, and (more importantly) academically. I was a good student, and was poised to be the first person in our immediate family to go to college, and one of only a handful in our entire extended family. He didn't want to mess things up for me. So, instead, he humbled himself and essentially started over in his career working for a man he despised. It seems to me that he acted *selflessly*, for my sake—certainly not for his own. However, the psychological egoist must interpret his actions as having been motivated by his own self-interest.

It is possible that self-interest is the explanation for all those actions, and for any other you or I might imagine. Since PE is unfalsifiable, we can't, of course, know with certainty whether those actions (or any other) really are motivated by self-interest. So, all you and I can do is try to figure out what seems to make the most sense. If, based on your experience of the world and how it works, it appears to you that PE offers the best explanation of human behavior, including the examples above, then PE is probably a compelling theory to you. On the other hand, if it appears to you that humans are at least sometimes capable of genuine altruism, that not every action is motivated by self-interest, then you will probably reject PE.

Plato (424 BCE – 328 BCE) is a very well-known ancient Greek philosopher and student of the possibly more well-known Socrates. Because Socrates wrote nothing himself, most of what we think we know about Socrates comes from the writings of others, most notably Plato. Socrates appears as the main character in numerous Platonic dialogues, including "The Republic," from which the following is an excerpt. In this section of that dialogue, Socrates is discussing the nature of justice with several other persons. Glaucon argues that justice is a necessary inconvenience that we agree to in the style of a social contract. This agreement is accepted by virtue of the fact that none of us has sufficient power to behave as we truly desire without fear of consequences. The Myth of Gyges' Ring is offered as evidence in support of this. Note that this brief section provides an incredibly early account of both the social contract approach to political philosophy, as well as the theory of human motivation known as psychological egoism.

The Republic
Plato

Book II - The Individual, The State, and Education

Socrates - Glaucon

WITH these words I was thinking that I had made an end of the discussion; but the end, in truth, proved to be only a beginning. For Glaucon, who is always the most pugnacious of men, was dissatisfied at Thrasymachus' retirement; he wanted to have the battle out. So he said to me: Socrates, do you wish really to persuade us, or only to seem to have persuaded us, that to be just is always better than to be unjust?

I should wish really to persuade you, I replied, if I could.

Then you certainly have not succeeded. Let me ask you now:--How would you arrange goods--are there not some which we welcome for their own sakes, and independently of their consequences, as, for example, harmless pleasures and enjoyments, which delight us at the time, although nothing follows from them?

I agree in thinking that there is such a class, I replied.

Is there not also a second class of goods, such as knowledge, sight, health, which are desirable not only in themselves, but also for their results?

Certainly, I said.

And would you not recognize a third class, such as gymnastic, and the care of the sick, and the physician's art; also the various ways of money-making--these do us good but we regard them as disagreeable; and no one would choose them for their own sakes, but only for the sake of some reward or result which flows from them?

There is, I said, this third class also. But why do you ask?

Because I want to know in which of the three classes you would place justice?

In the highest class, I replied,--among those goods which he who would be happy desires both for their own sake and for the sake of their results.

Then the many are of another mind; they think that justice is to be reckoned in the troublesome class, among goods which are to be pursued for the sake of rewards and of reputation, but in themselves are disagreeable and rather to be avoided.

I know, I said, that this is their manner of thinking, and that this was the thesis which Thrasymachus was maintaining just now, when he censured justice and praised injustice. But I am too stupid to be convinced by him.

I wish, he said, that you would hear me as well as him, and then I shall see whether you and I agree. For Thrasymachus seems to me, like a snake, to have been charmed by your voice sooner than he ought to have been; but to my mind the nature of justice and injustice have not yet been made clear. Setting aside their rewards and results, I want to know what they are in themselves, and how they inwardly work in the soul. If you, please, then, I will revive the argument of Thrasymachus. And first I will speak of the nature and origin of justice according to the common view of them. Secondly, I will show that all men who practise justice do so against their will, of necessity, but not as a good. And thirdly, I will argue that there is reason in this view, for the life of the unjust is after all better far than the life of the just--if what they say is true, Socrates, since I myself am not of their opinion. But still I acknowledge that I am perplexed when I hear the voices of Thrasymachus and myriads of others dinning in my ears; and, on the other hand, I have never yet heard the superiority of justice to injustice maintained by any one in a satisfactory way. I want to hear justice praised in respect of itself; then I shall be satisfied, and you are the person from whom I think that I am most likely to hear this; and therefore I will praise the unjust life to the utmost of my power, and my manner of speaking will indicate the manner in which I desire to hear you too praising justice and censuring injustice. Will you say whether you approve of my proposal?

Indeed I do; nor can I imagine any theme about which a man of sense would oftener wish to converse.

I am delighted, he replied, to hear you say so, and shall begin by speaking, as I proposed, of the nature and origin of justice.

Glaucon

They say that to do injustice is, by nature, good; to suffer injustice, evil; but that the evil is greater than the good. And so when men have both done and suffered injustice and have had experience of both, not being able to avoid the one and obtain the other, they think that they had better agree among themselves to have neither; hence there arise laws and mutual covenants; and that which is ordained by law is termed by them lawful and just. This they affirm to be the origin and nature of justice;--it is a mean or compromise, between the best of all, which is to do injustice and not be punished, and the worst of all, which is to suffer injustice without the power of retaliation; and justice, being at a middle point between the two, is tolerated not as a good, but as the lesser evil, and honoured by reason of the inability of men to do injustice. For no man who is worthy to be called a man would ever submit to such an agreement if he were able to resist; he would be mad if he did. Such is the received account, Socrates, of the nature and origin of justice.

Now that those who practise justice do so involuntarily and because they have not the power to be unjust will best appear if we imagine something of this kind: having given both to the just and the unjust power to do what they will, let us watch and see whither desire will lead them; then we shall discover in the very act the just and unjust man to be proceeding along the same road, following their interest, which all natures deem to be their good, and are only diverted into the path of justice by the force of law. The liberty which we are supposing may be most completely given to them in the form of such a power as is said to have been possessed by Gyges the ancestor of Croesus the Lydian. According to the tradition, Gyges was a shepherd in the service of the king of Lydia; there was a great storm, and an earthquake made an opening in the earth at the place where he was feeding his flock. Amazed at the sight, he descended into the opening, where, among other marvels, he beheld a hollow brazen horse, having doors, at which he stooping and looking in saw a dead body of stature, as appeared to him, more than human, and having nothing on but a gold ring; this he took from the finger of the dead and reascended. Now the shepherds met together, according to custom, that they might send their monthly report about the flocks to the king; into their assembly he came having the ring on his finger, and as he was sitting among them he chanced to turn the collet of the ring inside his hand, when instantly he became invisible to the rest of the company and they began to speak of him as if he were no longer present. He was astonished at this, and again touching the ring he turned the collet outwards and reappeared; he made several trials of the ring, and always with the same result-when he turned the collet inwards he became invisible, when outwards he reappeared. Whereupon he contrived to be chosen one of the messengers who were sent to the court; where as soon as he arrived he seduced the queen, and with her help conspired against the king and slew him, and took the kingdom. Suppose now that there were two such magic rings, and the just put on one of them and the unjust the other; no man can be imagined to be of such an iron nature that he would stand fast in justice. No man would keep his hands off what was not his own when he could safely take what he liked out of the market, or go into houses and lie with any one at his pleasure, or kill or release from prison whom he would, and in all respects be like a God among men. Then the actions of the just would be as the actions of the unjust; they would both come at last to the same point. And this we may truly affirm to be a great proof that a man is just, not willingly or because he thinks that justice is any good to him individually, but of necessity, for wherever any one thinks that he can safely be unjust, there he is unjust. For all men believe in their hearts that injustice is far more profitable to the individual than justice, and he who argues as I have been supposing, will say that they are right. If you could imagine any one obtaining this power of becoming invisible, and never doing any wrong or touching what was another's, he would be thought by the lookers-on to be a most wretched idiot, although they would praise him to one another's faces, and keep up appearances with one another from a fear that they too might suffer injustice. Enough of this....

Adeimantus

On what principle, then, shall we any longer choose justice rather than the worst injustice? when, if we only unite the latter with a deceitful regard to appearances, we shall fare to our mind both with gods and men, in life and after death, as the most numerous and the highest authorities tell us. Knowing all this, Socrates, how can a man who has any superiority of mind or person or rank or wealth, be willing to honour justice; or indeed to refrain from laughing when he hears justice praised? And even if there should be some one who is able to disprove the truth of my words, and who is satisfied that justice is best, still he is not angry with the unjust, but is very ready to forgive them, because he also knows that men are not just of their own free will; unless, peradventure, there be some one whom the divinity within him may have inspired with a hatred of injustice, or who has attained knowledge of the truth--but no other man. He only blames injustice who, owing to cowardice or age or some weakness, has not the power of being unjust. And this is proved by the fact that when he obtains the power, he immediately becomes unjust as far as he can be.

The cause of all this, Socrates, was indicated by us at the beginning of the argument, when my brother and I told you how astonished we were to find that of all the professing panegyrists of justice--beginning with the ancient heroes of whom any memorial has been preserved to us, and ending with the men of our own time--no one has ever blamed injustice or praised justice except with a view to the glories, honours, and benefits which flow from them. No one has ever adequately described either in verse or prose the true essential nature of either of them abiding in the soul, and invisible to any human or divine eye; or shown that of all the things of a man's soul which he has within him, justice is the greatest good, and injustice the greatest evil. Had this been the universal strain, had you sought to persuade us of this from our youth upwards, we should not have been on the watch to keep one another from doing wrong, but every one would have been his own watchman, because afraid, if he did wrong, of harbouring in himself the greatest of evils. I dare say that Thrasymachus and others would seriously hold the language which I have been merely repeating, and words even stronger than these about justice and injustice, grossly, as I conceive, perverting their true nature. But I speak in this vehement manner, as I must frankly confess to you, because I want to hear from you the opposite side; and I would ask you to show not only the superiority which justice has over injustice, but what effect they have on the possessor of them which makes the one to be a good and the other an evil to him. And please, as Glaucon requested of you, to exclude reputations; for unless you take away from each of them his true reputation and add on the false, we shall say that you do not praise justice, but the appearance of it; we shall think that you are only exhorting us to keep injustice dark, and that you really agree with Thrasymachus in thinking that justice is another's good and the interest of the stronger, and that injustice is a man's own profit and interest, though injurious to the weaker. Now as you have admitted that justice is one of that highest class of goods which are desired indeed for their results, but in a far greater degree for their own sakes--like sight or hearing or knowledge or health, or any other real and natural and not merely conventional good--I would ask you in your praise of justice to regard one point only: I mean the essential good and evil which justice and injustice work in the possessors of them. Let others praise justice and censure injustice, magnifying the rewards and honours of the one and abusing the other; that is a manner of arguing which, coming from them, I am ready to tolerate, but from you who have spent your whole life in the consideration of this question, unless I hear the contrary from your own lips, I expect something better. And therefore, I say, not only prove to us that justice is better than injustice, but show what they either of them do to the possessor of them, which makes the one to be a good and the other an evil, whether seen or unseen by gods and men.

Chapter 3: Ethical Egoism

Comprehension questions you should be able to answer after reading this chapter:

1. What is the difference between psychological egoism and ethical egoism? Why does ethical egoism actually presuppose the falsity of psychological egoism?

2. What (in general) is the morally right thing to do, according to ethical egoism?

3. What is the "capitalist" argument in favor of ethical egoism, and why might it be seen as problematic as an argument for ethical egoism?

4. What does Rand mean by "selfishness?

5. According to Rand, what is a "value"? What is the "ultimate value" for humans? What makes something good or evil, given this ultimate value?

6. What is the role of reason, according to Rand?

7. What does Rand mean by our "rational self-interest"?

8. What is our "highest moral purpose" according to Rand?

9. Why does Rand reject "altruism"?

10. How can one explain the "straw man/false dilemma" possible problem for Rand's argument?

In our previous chapter, we considered the descriptive theory known as psychological egoism (PE). PE is not really an ethical theory, as it takes no stance with regard to what is morally right or wrong, what we should or should not do. Instead, it claims that all of our decisions, all of our actions, "ethical" or otherwise, are driven by self-interest. Although it was not itself an ethical theory, we considered the claims of PE because of their impact on ethics, in general. After all, if it is true that all people always act from self-interest, it will make no sense to ever claim that people *should* behave altruistically, to say that the right thing to do would be to put someone else's interests before your own, as that would be an impossible obligation to fulfill.

PE and Ethical egoism do have one very important common denominator: self-interest. However, whereas PE appeals to self-interest as an explanation for how all people *do* behave, EE appeals to self-interest as the guide for how people *should* behave. Ethical egoism (hereafter, EE), in contrast to PE, is a *prescriptive* theory. That is, EE is not describing how people do, in fact, behave, but is prescribing how people *should* behave. Indeed, EE actually presupposes the *falsity* of PE. After all, there's no need to recommend that people pursue their own self-interest if we are all hardwired to do so anyway!

Nathaniel Branden, a psychotherapist and former (long-time) associate of Ayn Rand wrote an essay entitled "Isn't Everyone Selfish?" Within it, he not only demonstrates that ethical egoism is distinct from psychological egoism, but he also argues that PE is a confused, false theory. In response to PE's more extravagant claim that everyone always acts selfishly (knowingly or not), because every purposeful action is motivated by some sort of value or goal desired by the agent, Branden clarifies that the selfishness (or unselfishness) of an action is determined *objectively*, not by the particular feelings of the agent performing the act. Of course it's true that every intentional action must be motivated by some "want," but whether or not the action is selfish depends on *why* the agent wants to do it.

> To equate 'motivated behavior' with 'selfish behavior' is to blank out the distinction between an elementary fact of human psychology and the phenomenon of ethical choice. It is to evade the central problem of ethics, namely: by what is a man to be motivated?...Those who assert that 'everyone is selfish' commonly intend their statement as an expression of cynicism and contempt. But the truth is that their statement pays mankind a compliment it does not deserve.[40]

This critique of PE should sound familiar, as it was voiced by James Rachels in our previous chapter on PE (i.e., that "acting on a desire" is not sufficient for "self-interest," but rather what determines self-interest is the type of desire upon which one acts). Notice the interesting phrasing at the end of that quotation from Branden, though: to say that all people are selfish is to pay them a *compliment* that they *don't deserve*. Rather obviously, Brandon perceives "selfishness" as something good, something complimentary. This brings us to the basic elements of EE.

As stated, EE prescribes that we *should* pursue our own self-interest. It's important to realize that "should," in this case, is not merely a recommendation of prudence. EE is not claiming that it is shrewd, or clever, or useful to pursue your own self-interest—though it may well be so. EE is claiming that it is *morally right* to pursue your own self-interest, that the pursuit of self-interest is morally good. Indeed, the most well-known advocate of ethical egoism, the philosopher and novelist Ayn Rand (1905-1982) entitled a collection of essays addressing this idea, *The Virtue of Selfishness*.

On its surface, this might seem to be an outrageous and provocative claim. Selfishness, after all, has traditionally been regarded as a vice. Selfish people are greedy, petty individuals. One wants a reputation for being generous and charitable, not self-centered—and yet, Rand boldly proclaims that selfishness is a *virtue*. We will expand on Rand's position a bit later in this chapter, but for now we will consider some other arguments in favor of EE.

The "Capitalist" defense of EE

According to this argument, the appeal of EE is that the pursuit of self-interest, ultimately, benefits *everyone*. It is sometimes called the "capitalist" defense of EE because it makes the same appeal as do defenders of free market ("laissez-faire") capitalism: by leaving people free to pursue their own self-interest, the optimal

---

[40] Nathaniel Branden, "Isn't Everyone Selfish?" in *The Virtue of Selfishness*, by Ayn Rand.

results for all involved are achieved. The "patron saint" of capitalism, Adam Smith, alludes to this idea in a couple of different texts:

> *But the annual revenue of every society is always precisely equal to the exchangeable value of the whole annual produce of its industry, or rather is precisely the same thing with that exchangeable value. As every individual, therefore, endeavours as much as he can both to employ his capital in the support of domestic industry, and so to direct that industry that its produce may be of the greatest value; every individual necessarily labours to render the annual revenue of the society as great as he can. He generally, indeed, neither intends to promote the public interest, nor knows how much he is promoting it. By preferring the support of domestic to that of foreign industry, he intends only his own security; and by directing that industry in such a manner as its produce may be of the greatest value, he intends only his own gain, and he is in this, as in many other cases, led by an invisible hand to promote an end which was no part of his intention. Nor is it always the worse for the society that it was no part of it. By pursuing his own interest he frequently promotes that of the society more effectually than when he really intends to promote it. I have never known much good done by those who affected to trade for the public good. It is an affectation, indeed, not very common among merchants, and very few words need be employed in dissuading them from it."[41]*

> *The proud and unfeeling landlord views his extensive fields, and without a thought for the wants of his brethren, in imagination consumes himself the whole harvest ... [Yet] the capacity of his stomach bears no proportion to the immensity of his desires ... the rest he will be obliged to distribute among those, who prepare, in the nicest manner, that little which he himself makes use of, among those who fit up the palace in which this little is to be consumed, among those who provide and keep in order all the different baubles and trinkets which are employed in the economy of greatness; all of whom thus derive from his luxury and caprice, that share of the necessaries of life, which they would in vain have expected from his humanity or his justice...The rich...are led by an invisible hand to make nearly the same distribution of the necessaries of life, which would have been made, had the earth been divided into equal portions among all its inhabitants, and thus without intending it, without knowing it, advance the interest of the society...[42]*

Consider a very common example: selecting a check-out line at a store. Barring unusual circumstances, I'm confident that your basic strategy when it comes to line selection is the same as mine: you select the shortest line. Why? Because it serves your self-interest to do so—just as it serves mine when I do so. I have no desire to wait in line any longer than I must, so I pick the shortest line (all else being equal),

---

[41] Adam Smith, <u>An Inquiry into the Nature and Causes of the Wealth of Nations</u>, IV.2.9.
[42] Adam Smith, <u>The Theory of Moral Sentiments</u>, IV.1.

and so does everyone else. Now, it just so happens that when everyone selects the shortest line (all else being equal), the number of people in each available line becomes roughly equal, and the most efficient rate of completing transactions is achieved. Customers, as a whole, and the employees and managers, as a whole, arguably achieve maximal benefit from this outcome. But, notice that no one was deliberately trying to "maximize efficiency," or make things best for "everyone." Each one of us is pursuing what we perceive to be in our own interest, and it just so happens that when we do, the best available result for everyone is achieved.

With respect to capitalism, the basic prescription is that people should be maximally free to pursue their own self-interest, with as little (government) interference as possible. When this occurs, the optimal result for everyone involved is achieved, whether we're talking about the prices of products, or the wage of workers, etc.

As is true of our economic interactions, so too with all our interactions. If we all pursue our own self-interest, we will obtain the optimal "result" for everyone involved. We might offer a formal version of this argument as follows:

1. We ought to do whatever will best promote everyone's interests.
2. The best way to promote everyone's interests is for each of us to adopt the policy of pursuing our own interests exclusively.
3. Therefore, each of us should adopt the policy of pursuing our own interests exclusively.

Whether or not this is true is an empirical matter, more so than a philosophical one—but for our purposes we can set aside the truth or falsity of this "capitalist" claim. As it turns out, this is an odd defense of EE. Why odd? Because this argument is really an argument for a *different* ethical theory: utilitarianism.

We will consider utilitarianism in a later chapter, but for now all you need to know is that utilitarians claim that the morally right thing to do is whatever will maximize "utility" for all involved, whatever will produce the best result for all involved. Sounds pretty similar to the argument above, doesn't it? As it turns out, the "capitalist" argument for EE isn't really claiming that what is morally right is to pursue self-interest. Instead, it's claiming that what is morally right is to "maximize utility," and that the best way to achieve that goal is by the pursuit of self-interest. That is, our moral goal is to achieve the best result for all involved, and the *means* to achieve this is the pursuit of self-interest. The pursuit of self-interest, then, is, at best, merely instrumentally valuable. Whether or not the pursuit of self-interest is always the best way to "maximize utility" is certainly subject to debate, and if the reason why someone endorses the pursuit of self-interest is because of this "capitalist" argument, it seems that such persons would have to acknowledge that if it could be shown that altruism could better achieve that end, then altruistic behavior would be recommended instead. This suggests that an appeal to what is "best for all involved" is not actually a very compelling endorsement of EE, after all.

This is by no means a refutation of EE, nor is it meant to be. Instead, this merely indicates that if EE is appealing to you is because it seems to "optimize outcomes," you're probably actually a utilitarian, and not an ethical egoist.

The "Ayn Rand" defense of EE

Perhaps the most well-known and sophisticated advocate for ethical egoism was the philosopher and writer, Ayn Rand. Although Rand did not call her ethical system "ethical egoism," but instead called it "Objectivist Ethics," the basic elements (for our purposes) are (effectively) the same. Importantly, her own approach is not subject to the "isn't this just utilitarianism in disguise" critique we considered previously. Rand's emphasis on self-interest is not tied, implicitly or explicitly, to some "greater good." In fact, she repeatedly rails against utilitarianism and other "altruistic" systems that sacrifice the individual for the sake of the "greater good." Instead, she advocates unapologetic *self*-interest, the pursuit of one's *own* good. "Selfishness," according to Rand, is a *virtue*.

To proclaim selfishness a virtue is both bold and controversial, but before attempting to justify this claim, it's important to clarify what is meant by it. Neither Rand, nor ethical egoists in general, propose the reckless and wanton pursuit of (so-called) "self-interest." The caricature of a sociopath flouting social conventions and ruthlessly exploiting others is just that: a caricature. Selfishness, according to Rand, is simply "concern with one's own interests." There is nothing (yet) morally good or bad about selfishness.

"Selfishness" ("concern with one's own interests") is preferable, according to Rand, in contrast to its opposite: altruism. Rand understands "altruism" in a particular way (one that, admittedly, might not be agreed upon by altruists themselves). According to her understanding of "altruism," and altruistic ethical systems, any action taken for the benefit of others is good, and any action taken for one's own benefit is evil. In this way, the only standard of moral value is the beneficiary. If I'm the one performing the action, and the beneficiary is "me," then the action is morally "bad;" but, if the beneficiary is "you," then it's "good."

Rand claims that this standard of moral value makes morality our "enemy." Doing what is morally right is always something that benefits others, that causes others to gain, but that causes oneself to lose. Sure, we might hope that we will benefit from the actions of others from time to time, just as they benefit from our own actions, but this breeds mutual resentment rather than happiness. "Morally, their pursuit of values will be like an exchange of unwanted, unchosen Christmas presents, which neither is morally permitted to buy for himself."[43]

In contrast to this, her "Objectivist Ethics" (for us, still EE) claims that the moral agent herself should always be the beneficiary of her own actions.[44] In order to understand Rand's advocacy for the pursuit of self-interest, and to give it a fair hearing, we need to understand the premises by which she comes to her conclusion, the foundation on which she builds her ethical system.

Rand defines morality or ethics as a code of values to *guide* choices and actions, and it is our choices and actions that determine the *purpose and course* of one's life. Historically, the two major types of ethical codes in the West have been associated with "mystics" or "neo-mystics." Rand claims that "mystics" proclaim that the

---

[43] Ayn Ran, *The Virtue of Selfishness*, Introduction, p. viii.
[44] The text of her essay, "The Objectivist Ethics," is available at the following URL: http://aynrandlexicon.com/ayn-rand-ideas/the-objectivist-ethics.html

"arbitrary, unaccountable 'will of God'" is the standard of "the good," whereas "neo-mystics" hold the "good of society" as the standard of "the good" instead.[45] The obvious candidates for "mystics" are any sort of "divine command" ethical theory, and the most obvious candidate for "neo-mystics" are utilitarians—though any system that posits a "good" other than oneself could be lumped into this "neo-mystic" camp as well.

In either case, Rand claims that some persons, claiming to be spokespersons for either God or society, are ethically entitled to interpret this "good" while everyone else is obliged to spend their lives in service to that "gang's" desires. In practice, it's not difficult to see the force of this interpretation. Religious leaders, throughout history, have been the official spokespersons of their faith, have interpreted what their deity (or deities) demand, and have then attempted to encourage (or outright compel) the faithful to obey. In secular systems, particular people (e.g., politicians) decide what is "best" for society, and then enact legislation to inspire (or compel) everyone else to play along. Rand is a fan of neither camp....

Central to understanding Rand's emphasis on self-interest is her concept of "value." A value, for Rand, is simply "That which one acts to gain and/or keep." Any meaningful concept of value presupposes alternatives (choices), and an agent capable of choosing from amongst those options, and acting in pursuit of that value. For living organisms of all kinds (including humans), the most fundamental choice, the most basic alternative, is life or death. When a living organism fails to sustain itself, it dies. When it succeeds in sustaining itself, it lives. Rand claims that life is what makes "value" possible. Only living things are capable of choices, and only living things can pursue the objects of those choices. Accordingly, only to living things can other things be "good" or "evil/bad."

In that only living things can make choices, only living things can have goals, and engage in goal-directed action. All living livings have at least one implicit goal in common: the automatic (unintentional) function of all living organisms is the maintenance of its own life. The natural pursuit of all living things is the continuation of its own existence. This functions automatically and "unintentionally" for most living things, such as plants and most animals. That is just to say that my rosemary bush doesn't consciously *intend* to remain alive—it automatically functions in pursuit of its continued life until something kills it. This seems to be the case for most living things.

For any living thing, life depends on two factors: "fuel" (food), and the actions of its body in using that fuel properly. What determines a "proper" use of the fuel? Simply, that which is required for the organism's survival. This is not a matter of subjective preference, but is objectively determined by a thing's nature. A plant doesn't choose photosynthesis—not only because a plant is incapable of choice but because the plant doesn't have any other option. Although humans are capable of choice, I don't have the luxury of choosing to be "fed" by photosynthesis, as my "nature" does not allow it.[46]

For any living thing, its life is maintained only by virtue of constant self-sustaining action. The implicit goal of those actions, and their ultimate value ("that which one

---

[45] Rand, "The Objectivist Ethics," *The Virtue of Selfishness*, 14.
[46] Despite the claims and wishes of those at www.humanphotosynthesis.com.

acts to gain/keep") is the organism's life. Life itself, then, is the *ultimate* value, the final end/goal to which all lesser goals are means, and the standard by which lesser goals are evaluated.

With this standard in place, "good" is that which furthers one's life, and "evil" is that which threatens it. Plants, of course, are incapable of cognition and moral judgment, but "good" for a plant would be things like sunlight, water, and nutrient rich soil (and the actions of the plant that pursue/promote those things), while "evil" for a plant would be things like drought, locust swarms, over-zealous gardeners, etc.

Humans are more sophisticated than plants, of course, but our "good" and "evil" is built upon the same foundation: the preservation and promotion of our own lives. Unlike plants, humans have a crude (but effective) capacity to become aware of what is good and evil (in its simplest form): our capacity for pleasure and pain. Pain is a warning signal to any animal, including humans, that it is pursuing the "wrong" course of action, while pleasure is a signal that it is pursuing the "right" course of action. These judgments can get complicated, of course, but in many cases this is obviously true. Pain is *usually* an indicator that the body is being damaged. Suffer enough damage, and you will die. This basic recognition signals that we should eat when hungry, remove our hands from fires, run away or fight back if we're being eaten, stop stepping on jagged rocks, etc. Pleasure is usually an indicator that the body is being "nurtured" or benefitted. Physical comfort suggests safe living conditions, the pleasure of eating encourages us to sustain ourselves with "fuel"—even sexual pleasure promotes the continued life of the species itself. Just as pain is a signal of a "wrong course of action," and pleasure is a signal of a "right course of action," happiness is an indicator of a successful state of life, while suffering is a warning signal of "failure."

As we've seen with plants, some living things automatically pursue their "good." A plant doesn't need instruction on how to absorb and convert sunlight, nor can it make a mistake and choose to try to eat nuts and berries instead. For conscious living beings, such as humans, though, our bodies can only automatically *use* fuel—we can't automatically *obtain* it. A plant can just stay in place and absorb its fuel from its environment. In contrast, if I just "stay in place" I will grow increasingly hungry and thirsty and then die.

Unlike plants and (most?) non-human animals, humans have no "automatic" knowledge of how to survive, no automatic set of values, no automatic understanding of good and evil, and no automatic set of goals proper to our nature, nor knowledge of how to obtain those goals. We humans must *discover* these things (e.g., which plants are nutritious, and which are poison; how to hunt and prepare meat, etc.), and then *choose* to pursue them. Humans are *volitional*, which is to say that our intentional actions are voluntary, we must *intend* them. The faculty/capacity that directs this process of discovery and volition is *reason*. The process, itself, is *thinking*. Rand observes that thinking is *not* automatic, but is also a choice. We must focus our consciousness, focus our thoughts, direct our minds, or else we sink to the level of an undirected "sensory-perceptual mechanism," such as that presumably exhibited by most non-human animals.

For humans, reason is an indispensable tool. Reason is our basic means of survival. We don't benefit from roots and the capacity for photosynthesis. We don't have instincts to hunt or spin webs to catch flies. Although we automatically feel hunger, and automatically digest food once it's in our bellies, we don't automatically know how to get that food into our stomachs, or even what qualifies as food to begin with! We have to use our reason and *think* our way to a full stomach. This is not anything subjective or arbitrary either. What is required for our survival is not *determined* by us, any more than it is determined by the plant, but is instead discovered by us, and whether we rightly pursue these requirements is chosen by us. As Rand says of "Man," "He is free to make the wrong choice, but not free to succeed with it." I am free to choose to eat rocks, but not free to be nourished by them.

A *successful* life, at its most basic level, is simply one that continues, one in which life is maintained. For volitional creatures like humans, this requires recognizing and pursuing goals and values proper to our survival. *Ethics*, as a discipline, seeks to answer these questions: what are the right goals to pursue? What are the values required for survival?

Again, for Rand, there is nothing subjective about this. "Ethics is *not* a mystic fantasy—nor a social convention—nor a dispensable subjective luxury, to be switched or discarded in any emergency. Ethics is an *objective, metaphysical necessity of man's survival*—not by the grace of the supernatural nor of your neighbors nor of your whims, but by the grace of reality and the nature of life."[47]

In determining what is necessary for our survival, though, we must remember what sort of living thing we are. Humans are *rational* animals. Since reason is our means of survival, that which is proper to the life of a *rational* being is "the good;" that which opposes/destroys it is the "evil." This is a very important point. The survival proper to the human animal is not merely what is needed to prevent organ failure, and to keep the heart beating, but what is needed to maintain a human *as a rational animal.* There might be some actions that maintain life, but at the expense of reason. In such a case, we would be surviving as an animal, but not as a person.

What *is* proper to the life of a person, as a rational animal? Everything a human need to survive has to be discovered by his own mind, and produced by his own effort. Essential to *proper* survival, then, are thinking and productive work. Seeming exceptions to this (e.g., "looters," "robbers") are mere parasites on those who *do* the productive work, and these so-called exceptions could not survive without the work of the producers. Herein is to be found Rand's complaint against altruism (as she understands it).

"Altruism" commands that we act in service to others, that we sacrifice our own interests for the good of others. However, for Rand, this is simply *unnatural*. As a living creature, my ultimate value is the maintenance of my own life, and every other value is subordinate to (and in service of) that ultimate value. Your life is of ultimate value to you, but it is not of ultimate value to me—nor should it be. Altruism demands that we make someone else's life (indeed, *anyone* else's life) our ultimate value. That's like asking the flower to live for the sake of the bee....

Rand advocates that each person should act for her own *rational* self-interest, her own *actual* self-interest. This is not some license to "do as one pleases." Just as not everything one chooses to eat must necessarily be food, so too is it the case that not everything someone desires and pursues is in her self-interest. Remember, our actual (rational) self-interest is not determined by our whims, but by our nature, by the sort

---

[47] Rand, "The Objectivist Ethics," *The Virtue of Selfishness*, 23.

of living thing we are, by the values required for human survival. "Self-interest" is not identical to "what I want," or even "what I *think* is in my self-interest. "One's own independent judgment is the means by which one must choose one's actions, but one's own judgment is not itself the moral criterion of action."[48] I might think that a poisonous plant is safe to eat, and then die from my mistake. Similarly, I might think a course of life is in my self-interest, but be mistaken about that as well, and sow the seeds of my own unhappiness and failure.

That we should each pursue our own self-interest doesn't entail that we must be in conflict with each other, and certainly doesn't entail that we each live our lives trying to "use" other people for our own benefit. If we recognize that life (in general) is an end in itself (i.e., our ultimate value), then this implies that every living human life is therefore an end in itself, and not a mere means to another end.[49] Each person should live for his own sake, neither sacrificing himself to others, not sacrificing others to himself. According to Rand, "to live for his own sake means that *the achievement of his own happiness is man's highest moral purpose.*"[50]

Although happiness is our highest moral *purpose*, happiness is not the primary *standard* of evaluation or our primary value. "Man's life" is primary, and pursuing the rational values that life requires allows one to *achieve* happiness. "Happiness can properly be the purpose of ethics, but not the standard."[51] In contrast, employing some subjective emotional standard of what "makes you happy" is to let yourself be guided by emotional whims.

> *The subjectivist theory of ethics is, strictly speaking, not a theory, but a negation of ethics. And more: it is a negation of reality, a negation not merely of man's existence, but of all existence. Only the concept of a fluid, plastic, indeterminate, Heraclitean universe could permit anyone to think or to preach that man needs no objective principles of action—that reality gives him a blank check on values—that anything he cares to pick as the good or the evil, will do—that a man's whim is a valid moral standard, and that the only question is how to get away with it. The existential monument to this theory is the present state of our culture.*[52]

> *If desire (regardless of its nature, or cause, regardless of what the desire happens to be) is primary, and the gratification of desire is taken as an ethical goal (such as "the greatest happiness for the greatest number"), then desires and interests will inevitably clash. You desire to produce, but I desire to steal. If mere desire is the standard of the good, then every desire has equal moral validity. Here is where conflict is born, according to Rand. Her objectivist ethic, in contrast, entails no such conflict.*

---

[48] Ayn Ran, *The Virtue of Selfishness*, Introduction, p. x.
[49] Rand agrees with Kant on at least this much....
[50] Rand, "The Objectivist Ethics," *The Virtue of Selfishness*, 27.
[51] Ibid., 29.
[52] Ibid., 34.

The Objectivist ethics proudly advocates and upholds rational selfishness—which means: the values required for man's survival qua man—which means: the values required for human survival—not the values produced by the desires, the emotions, the "aspirations," the feelings, the whims or the needs of irrational brutes, who have never outgrown the primordial practice of human sacrifices, have never discovered an industrial society and can conceive of no self-interest but that of grabbing the loot of the moment.

The Objectivist ethics holds that human good does not require human sacrifices and cannot be achieved by the sacrifice of anyone to anyone. It holds that the rational interests of men do not clash—that there is no conflict of interests among men who do not desire the unearned, who do not make sacrifices nor accept them, who deal with one another as traders, giving value for value.

The principle of trade is the only rational ethical principle for all human relationships, personal and social, private and public, spiritual and material. It is the principle of justice.

A trader is a man who earns what he gets and does not give or take the undeserved. He does not treat men as masters or slaves, but as independent equals. He deals with men by means of a free, voluntary, unforced, uncoerced exchange—an exchange which benefits both parties by their independent judgment. A trader does not expect to be paid for his defaults, only for his achievements. He does not switch to others the burden of his failures, and he does not mortgage his life into bondage to the failure of others.

In spiritual issues—(by 'spiritual' I mean: 'pertaining to man's consciousness')—the currency or medium of exchange is different, but the principle is the same. Love, friendship, respect, admiration are the emotional response of one man to the virtues of another, the spiritual payment given in exchange for the personal, selfish pleasure which one man derives from the virtues of another man's character.[53]

Rand's ideal is that all persons greet and interact with each other as equals, offering and accepting terms of interaction that are of mutual benefit. This includes not only our obvious economic exchanges, such as offering labor to an employer in exchange for wages, but even our personal relationships are "contractual" in that sense. We are friends with someone because we find value in it, we benefit from the continued companionship of that person. If that ceases to be true, we cease to be friends.

Contrary to the caricature of ruthless "selfishness," Rand thinks her promotion of rational self-interest is the only ethical system that honors the value of the individual, is consistent with our nature, and that avoids the evils of altruistic moral codes. Indeed, Rand's condemnation of altruistic systems is both persistent and harsh. A few sections from her novel, "Atlas Shrugged," demonstrate this.

---

[53] Ibid., 31.

This much is true: the most selfish of all things is the independent mind that recognizes no authority higher than its own and no value higher than its judgment of truth. You are asked to sacrifice your intellectual integrity, your logic, your reason, your standard of truth-in favor of becoming a prostitute whose standard is the greatest good for the greatest number.

If you search your code for guidance, for an answer to the question: 'What is the good?'-the only answer you will find is 'The good of others.' The good is whatever others wish, whatever you feel they feel they wish, or whatever you feel they ought to feel. 'The good of others' is a magic formula that transforms anything into gold, a formula to be recited as a guarantee of moral glory and as a fumigator for any action, even the slaughter of a continent. Your standard of virtue is not an object, not an act, not a principle, but an intention. You need no proof, no reasons, no success, you need not achieve in fact the good of others-all you need to know is that your motive was the good of others, not your own. Your only definition of the good is a negation: the good is the 'non-good for me.'...

If you wish it, it's evil; if others wish it, it's good; if the motive of your action is your welfare, don't do it; if the motive is the welfare of others, then anything goes.

As this double-jointed, double-standard morality splits you in half, so it splits mankind into two enemy camps: one is you, the other is all the rest of humanity. You are the only outcast who has no right to wish to live. You are the only servant, the rest are the masters, you are the only giver, the rest are the takers, you are the eternal debtor, the rest are the creditors never to be paid off. You must not question their right to your sacrifice, or the nature of their wishes and their needs: their right is conferred upon them by a negative, by the fact that they are 'non-you.'...

I, who do not accept the unearned, neither in values nor in guilt, am here to ask the questions you evaded. Why is it moral to serve the happiness of others, but not your own? If enjoyment is a value, why is it moral when experienced by others, but immoral when experienced by you? If the sensation of eating a cake is a value, why is it an immoral indulgence in your stomach, but a moral goal for you to achieve in the stomach of others? Why is it immoral for you to desire, but moral for others to do so? Why is it immoral to produce a value and keep it, but moral to give it away? And if it is not moral for you to keep a value, why is it moral for others to accept it? If you are selfless and virtuous when you give it, are they not selfish and vicious when they take it? Does virtue consist of serving vice? Is the moral purpose of those who are good, self-immolation for the sake of those who are evil?...

Under a morality of sacrifice, the first value you sacrifice is morality; the next is self-esteem. When need is the standard, every man is both victim and parasite. As a victim, he must labor to fill the needs of others, leaving himself in the position of a parasite whose needs must be filled by others. He cannot approach his fellow men except in one of two disgraceful roles: he is both a beggar and a sucker.

You fear the man who has a dollar less than you, that dollar is rightfully his, he makes you feel like a moral defrauder. You hate the man who has a dollar more than you, that dollar is rightfully yours, he makes you feel that you are morally defrauded. The man below is a source of, your guilt, the man above is a source of your frustration.[54]

The writing here is rhetorically powerful, to be sure. We might formalize Rand's argument in the following (far less rhetorically powerful) way:

1. Each person has only one life to life to live.
2. If we value the individual (i.e., if the individual has moral worth), then this life is of supreme importance, as it is all one has, and all one is.
3. The ethics of altruism regards the life of the individual as something one must be ready to sacrifice for the good of others.
4. Therefore, the ethics of altruism does not take seriously the value of the individual.
5. Ethical egoism regards the individual's own life as being of ultimate value.
6. Ethical egoism is the only moral philosophy to take seriously the value of the individual.
7. Therefore, ethical egoism is the moral philosophy we ought to accept.

Considering how awful altruistic systems are, EE will be commendable even if only by contrast—and herein lies a possible criticism of Rand's version of EE.

Possible Problems
One possible problem with Rand's system involves the fact that it presupposes a particular worldview, a purely naturalistic worldview. Rand is quite clear on this. With regard to the role and value of reason, she claims that reason "means the rejection of any form of mysticism, i.e., any claim to some non-sensory, non-rational, non-definable, supernatural source of knowledge."[55] Against divine command approaches to ethics, in particular, she is even blunter.

The mystic theory of ethics is explicitly based on the premise that the standard of value of man's ethics is set beyond the grave, by the laws or requirements of another, supernatural dimension, that ethics is impossible for man to practice, that it is unsuited for and opposed to man's life on earth, and that man must take the blame for it and suffer through the whole of his earthly existence, to atone for the guilt of being unable to practice the impracticable. The Dark Ages and the Middle Ages are the existential monument to this theory of ethics.[56]

---

[54] Ayn Rand, *Atlas Shrugged*, 388-389.
[55] Rand, "The Objectivist Ethics," *The Virtue of Selfishness*, 26.
[56] Ibid., 34.

To be fair, *if* this presupposition of a purely naturalistic worldview is a "problem," it is only a problem for those who embrace a worldview that includes the supernatural (e.g., God). I mention this issue for one reason only: because of the internal tension between some enthusiasts of Rand who also happen to subscribe to a theistic worldview.

As an example, Congressman Paul Ryan (the Vice-Presidential candidate for the Republican Party in 2012) mentioned Rand in a speech he gave in 2005. "[T]he reason I got involved in public service, by and large, if I had to credit one thinker, one person, it would be Ayn Rand. And the fight we are in here, make no mistake about it, is a fight of individualism versus collectivism." Then, in 2009, he credited her again: "what's unique about what's happening today in government, in the world, in America, is that it's as if we're living in an Ayn Rand novel right now. I think Ayn Rand did the best job of anybody to build a moral case of capitalism, and that morality of capitalism is under assault."

Unless one finds Rand's approach to EE controversial in and of itself, there would be nothing "interesting" (let alone controversial) about Paul Ryan acknowledging the intellectual debt he owes to Ayn Rand. However, Paul Ryan is also a self-professed Catholic, and his Catholicism is credited for informing his position on numerous social issues. Indeed, Presidential Candidate Mitt Romney introduced Ryan as a "faithful Catholic [who] believes in the dignity and worth of every life." Given the added public scrutiny of being the Vice-Presidential candidate for a political party with a significant Christian base of support, Ryan backed away from his enthusiasm for Rand. "I reject her philosophy. It's an atheist philosophy. It reduces human interactions down to mere contracts and it is antithetical to my worldview."

This is not meant as commentary on one politician possibly "flip-flopping" for the sake of political expediency. Instead, it is meant to illustrate that ideas neither arise in a vacuum nor operate in a vacuum. Rand's ethical system is built upon a metaphysical system that denies the existence of the supernatural. It is only against this backdrop that her ethics "makes sense." If this (earthly) life is the one and only experience of existence that any of us will ever have, then the second premise of the formal argument for EE above ("If we value the individual (i.e., if the individual has moral worth), then this life is of supreme importance, as it is all one has, and all one is.") makes sense. If there is no afterlife, then the only value that exists is to be found in this world, in this life. Self-sacrifice when you're anticipating an eternity of reward in Heaven is not a bad deal at all, but self-sacrifice in the absence of any of that is a sacrifice of the only value there is—a sacrifice of "everything."

This is not to suggest that if one is a naturalist, one must embrace EE. From a purely naturalistic perspective, one might embrace utilitarianism, Kantianism, virtue ethics, Ethical Relativism, etc. What the implicit naturalism behind Rand's version of EE *does* rule out, though, is a non-naturalistic worldview! This was Ryan's problem, and what should have been a source of cognitive dissonance. As a Catholic, Ryan's metaphysical worldview is opposed to Rand's metaphysics—but he tried (tries?) to embrace her ethics anyway. What's the point? If your worldview isn't naturalism, you are starting from fundamentally different premises than Rand, and it will be difficult, if not impossible, to come to her same conclusions with regards to ethics.

Another possible problem involves Rand's rhetorical force. Rand's denunciation of altruism is powerful. The selections from "Atlas Shrugged" include some rather provocative vocabulary; the language of "masters" and "slaves," "beggars," "suckers," and "parasites." Altruism makes you a "prostitute," and turns morality into "self-immolation." Certainly if altruistic moral systems are that bad, we would want to be very cautious about following them, to say the least!

Some critics of Rand, however, think that her argument relies upon the combination of two fallacies: a "false dilemma" and a "straw man?" Generally, a false dilemma occurs when you are forced to pick from two options, despite other options being theoretically available. A famous example of this was uttered by President George W. Bush in a speech before Congress on September 20, 2001.

> *Every nation, in every region, now has a decision to make. Either you are with us, or you are with the terrorists. From this day forward, any nation that continues to harbor or support terrorism will be regarded by the United States as a hostile regime.*

In the context of the impending "war on terror," President Bush proclaimed that every nation is either "with us" or "with the terrorists." Clearly, that's a false dilemma in that it's entirely possible for a nation to not support every single action taken by the U.S. Government and yet also not be "with the terrorists." The next sentence is more reasonable in its formulation. A nation that "harbors" or "supports" terrorism is more plausibly "with the terrorists" than one that is either neutral or else not "with us" with respect to particular actions.

A "straw man" occurs when an exaggerated caricature of a position or person (or group) is presented for rhetorical effect. This is a common argumentative strategy, and exhibited perhaps nowhere so often and as readily as in politics.

- "Republicans only care about the 1%."
- "Only people on welfare vote for Democrats."
- "People who advocate for the 2nd amendment are gun nuts."
- "People who support universal health care access are communists."

Rhetorically, the appeal of a straw man is obvious: a straw man is much easier to "defeat!" An over-the-top caricature of a political position is likely to appear extreme and unreasonable. It is much easier to refute such a position than it is to refute a subtle, nuanced, and carefully argued version of the same basic position. It should come as no surprise, then, that politicians often try to "demonize" their opponents. This is the primary function of "attack ads."

The use of a straw man is often combined with a false dilemma for extra impact. Once again, both the strategy and the appeal are obvious. If "the other guy" is so *awful* (thanks to a straw man portrayal), and if the only other option is me (thanks to a false dilemma, perhaps), then I will look like a good choice in comparison. The problem with this, however rhetorically effective it might be, is that the "enemy" you defeat isn't real.

Imagine I urge someone to not support the Affordable Care Act ("Obamacare") because it requires "Death Panels." Actually, we don't have to imagine this. Some opponents of the ACA have been appealing to death panels for years now.

Former Governor and Republican Vice-Presidential candidate Sarah Palin said the following in a Facebook post:

Statement on the Current Health Care Debate

August 7, 2009 at 1:26pm

As more Americans delve into the disturbing details of the nationalized health care plan that the current administration is rushing through Congress, our collective jaw is dropping, and we're saying not just no, but hell no!

The Democrats promise that a government health care system will reduce the cost of health care, but as the economist Thomas Sowell has pointed out, government health care will not reduce the cost; it will simply refuse to pay the cost. And who will suffer the most when they ration care? The sick, the elderly, and the disabled, of course. The America I know and love is not one in which my parents or my baby with Down Syndrome will have to stand in front of Obama's "death panel" so his bureaucrats can decide, based on a subjective judgment of their "level of productivity in society," whether they are worthy of health care. Such a system is downright evil.

The Democrats promise that a government health care system will reduce the cost of health care, but as the economist Thomas Sowell has pointed out, government health care will not reduce the cost; it will simply refuse to pay the cost. And who will suffer the most when they ration care? The sick, the elderly, and the disabled, of course. The America I know and love is not one in which my parents or my baby with Down Syndrome will have to stand in front of Obama's 'death panel' so his bureaucrats can decide, based on a subjective judgment of their 'level of productivity in society,' whether they are worthy of health care. Such a system is downright evil.

That same year, former NY Lieutenant Governor, Betsy McCaughey, told listeners of Fred Thompson's radio show that "Congress would make it mandatory — absolutely require — that every five years people in Medicare have a required counseling session that will tell them how to end their life sooner."

This *does* sound pretty evil! Indeed, if we are faced with a choice between "death panels" and no health care reform at all, most of us would pick "no reform."

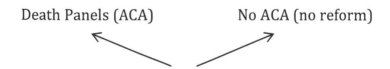

Death Panels (ACA)   No ACA (no reform)

The problem, however, is that the "death panel" argument was denounced as the "politifact 'lie of the year.'"[57] In reality, the "death panels" alleged to be in the ACA served a function far less scary, and much more benign—a provision that would compensate doctors (via Medicare) if they counseled their patients about their end-of-life options (e.g., living wills, "do not resuscitate" orders, etc.), and how to make sure they were honored. In reality, many times hospital staff members have no idea what a patient would want if in a coma, terminally ill, mortally wounded, etc., and often times families bicker over these things. "Dad wouldn't want to live like this!"

---

[57] http://www.politifact.com/truth-o-meter/article/2009/dec/18/politifact-lie-year-death-panels/

"No, Dad would want to fight!" The "infamous" provision of the ACA simply provided a way for doctors to get paid for answering questions their patients had about their options, whereas prior to that they would have to do it for free, on their own time, as it were.

The "death panel" was (and is) a straw man version of one aspect of the ACA because it exaggerates and flat out misrepresents what the ACA does (in that respect). It's probably not difficult to get someone to agree that "death panels" are a bad idea, but if that person actually understands the ACA she can simply reply that the ACA *doesn't have* death panels, so the argument is pointless.

Death Panels   [Actual ACA]   No ACA (no
("ACA")   reform)

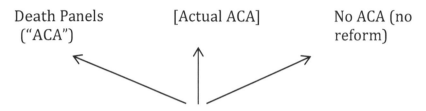

Of course it's easier to garner opposition to the "death panel" version of the ACA, and to steer people towards "no reform" in comparison—but this is misleading because another option exists: the *actual* ACA. Someone with enough information can defeat this strategy (in theory) simply by revealing the false dilemma and straw man it employs.

How does this potentially apply to Rand? Some of her critics think she's doing the same sort of thing with regard to altruistic ethical theories. Recall Rand's depiction of altruistic moral theories, using such language as "masters" and "slaves," "beggars," "suckers," "parasites," and "prostitutes." Certainly, if altruistic ethical theories make us slaves, beggars, parasites, and prostitutes, then we would be concerned about embracing any such theory! EE, in contrast, is going to look rather appealing!

"Altruism"   Ethical
                                            Egoism

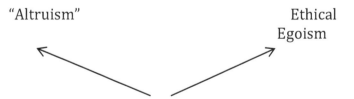

The possible problem here is not everyone thinks that her depiction of altruistic ethical theories is accurate—especially advocates of those theories! We have yet to review these sorts of theories (e.g., Divine Command, Utilitarianism, Kantianism, and Virtue Ethics), but will do so in later chapters. I leave it to you, on the basis of your study of those theories, to determine for yourself whether Rand's general description of them is accurate. If you think they are, then you will agree with Rand and not this criticism. If, on the other hand, you think Rand's portrayal of these sorts of theories is misleading, then you might think she has employed a combination of a straw man and false dilemma. If so, her arguments have not necessarily refuted these theories, because she never actually engaged what they *really* are, what they *really* demand.

"Altruism"   *Actual* Altruism   Ethical Egoism

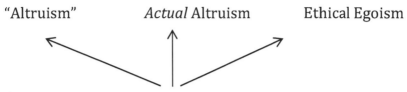

Conclusion

At first glance, EE might seem like an outrageous approach to ethics. An ethical theory that advocates selfishness? That encourages each one of us to be concerned for ourselves alone? We must be careful not to create a caricature of EE, however. Some versions, such as Rand's, are quite sophisticated, well thought-out, and based upon a comprehension philosophical worldview. Whether you agree with Rand's version of EE, or not, it deserves to be taken seriously. As we've seen, Rand's EE presupposes a particular (naturalistic) worldview. If you are a naturalist as well, you might find her views compelling—though if you are a theist this seems much less likely.

As we consider several additional theories over the next several chapters, try to consider how each measures up to Rand's very-different system, and consider which of them, if any, seems to make the most sense given your own worldview.

Chapter 4: Subjectivism

> *Comprehension questions you should be able to answer after reading this chapter:*
>
> 1. What are subjective claims? What are objective claims?
>
> 2. How do "Simple Subjectivists" understand moral claims? What makes a moral claim "true," according to subjectivism?
>
> 3. What do subjectivists mean when they say moral claims are neither analytically true nor empirically verifiable? Why would this be an argument for moral claims being subjective, rather than objective?
>
> 4. If subjectivism is true, can anyone ever be mistaken about a moral value judgment? Why or why not?
>
> 5. If subjectivism is true, how would we have to interpret claims that some people (e.g., Martin Luther King Jr.) were morally better than other people (e.g., Osama Bin Laden)?
>
> 6. If subjectivism is true, how must we understand "disagreement" on moral issues? How will moral conflict be resolved?
>
> 7. What is "justice" (moral rightness) according to Thrasymachus?

As you might recall from our earlier critical thinking chapter, "claims" are statements, assertions, propositions. An important epistemological issue concerns the status of claims. Are they subjectively true (true by virtue of personal opinion), or, are some claims objectively true (true, by themselves, regardless of personal opinion).

If a claim is objective, its truth or falsity is independent of whatever I believe or desire. It is sometimes said that "facts don't discriminate." If it is a fact that $2 + 2 = 4$, then it is true that $2 + 2 = 4$ even if I believe that $2 + 2 = 17$, even if my deepest desire is that $2 + 2 = 17$. Bluntly, it doesn't matter what I believe or desire. If it is a fact that $2 + 2 = 4$, then the truth of that claim applies equally to every person at every time and at every place. If I disagree, I am just plain mistaken. If a billion people disagree, then a billion people are mistaken.

If a claim is subjective, on the other hand, then the truth or falsity of the claim is *not* independent of the person making the claim. Indeed, whether the claim is true or false depends *entirely* on what the speaker or writer believes. If I claim that spicy food is delicious, I'm expressing my personal taste preferences. Is it true that spicy food is delicious? Well, it's true to *me*. I suspect some of you might disagree. Which one of us is correct, then? When we're dealing with a subjective claim, that question doesn't make a whole lot of sense. It's entirely consistent that "spicy food is delicious" is true for me, but not true for you. There is no "right" answer to the question of whether spicy food is delicious—it depends upon the person tasting the food.

This indicates a fairly reliable way to gauge whether a claim is objective, or subjective. Ask yourself what it would mean if two people disagreed about the truth of the claim. If disagreement indicates that at least one person is wrong, such as would be the case if we came up with two different answers to the same math problem, then that is a pretty reliable indicator that the claim is subjective. On the other hand, if it would make perfect sense for both persons to be "right," as would be the case should you and I disagree about the deliciousness of spicy food, then that is a pretty reliable indicator that the claim is subjective.

One of the kinds of claims we make—indeed, one of the most important kinds of claims we can make—are moral claims. Moral claims are simply assertions involving some moral issue. "Eating meat is wrong." "War is never justifiable." "Abortion is wrong." "Premarital sex is morally acceptable." These are all examples of moral claims. What we now have to address is whether moral claims are subjective or objective. Are moral claims more like answers to math problems, or more like food preferences? First, consider a visual representation that applies if moral claims are *objective.*

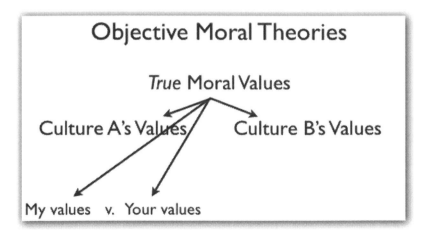

If moral claims are objective, then they appeal to facts (as opposed to opinions). I am going to begin an extended analogy that should resonate with most of you: tests and answer keys.

An answer key for a test is a version of the test that includes all of the correct answers. When a student takes a test for which there is an answer key, the student's answers are compared to the answer key for grading purposes. Consider the following mathematical example.

X + 3 = 5

Solve for X.

My answer: X = 1
Your answer: X = 2
Answer key: X = 2

The correct answer (i.e., the answer found in the answer key) is that X = 2. Your answer was 2. You got it right. My answer was 1. I got it wrong. As mentioned a few paragraphs ago, before we even looked at the answer key, we had reason to believe at least one of us was wrong. After all, we gave two different answers to the same math problem. It was possible that neither one of us got the correct answer, but what wasn't possible was that *both* of us got the correct answer.

If moral claims are objective, then there are moral facts. As facts, they apply equally to all people at all times. Facts don't discriminate. These moral facts are our moral "answer key." We can imagine that we are all continually engaged in a process of moral "test-making." Each day, by virtue of what we do, or fail to do, we are morally tested. As communities, too, we are being "tested" by virtue of the laws, policies, and actions we take (or fail to take) as communities. What determines whether an action taken by either an individual or by a community is morally correct? The "answer key."

If, for example, it is a moral fact that killing innocent people is morally wrong, then if you and I give two different "answers" to that same moral "question," one of us right, and the other wrong (here's a hint: whichever one of us is a murderer, is wrong). If a particular culture allows, let alone perpetrates, the killing of innocent people, then that culture is *wrong* on that particular issue. Obviously, there is room for plenty of spirited debate as to just which moral values are "facts" belonging in the universal moral answer key, but what any objective approach to ethics will have in common is the belief that there is such an answer key, even if we don't fully agree as to its contents.

According to a subjectivist approach to morality, moral claims are matters of personal opinion. As such, there is no "fact" that validates some opinions, but refutes others. Very simply, if I believe something is morally wrong, then, for me, it is morally wrong. If you believe differently, then it's not wrong for you. If you and I disagree, it's not the case that one of us is mistaken—we simply have different opinions on the matter.

If subjectivism is true, then moral claims share the same (or at least a similar) status as other claims indicating personal preference or perspective. A comparison of objective and subjective claims might make this clearer, as well as make clear one of the significant implications of subjectivism.

<u>Objective claims</u>
- 2+2 = 4
- Bachelors are unmarried men
- The final two Democratic presidential candidates in 2016 are Hillary Clinton and Bernie Sanders
- The director of *The Hateful Eight* is Quentin Tarantino
- Bacon is usually made from pork
- Abortion is the intentional termination of a pregnancy.

<u>Subjective claims</u>
- Math is boring
- It's better to be a bachelor than married
- Bernie Sanders is the better Presidential candidate
- *The Hateful Eight* was awesome!
- Bacon is delicious.
- Abortion is morally wrong.

One of the observations we can make about these groupings is that all of the examples of objective claims are either "analytic" claims or are empirically verifiable.

An analytic claim is a claim that is true (or false) by definition, by the very meaning of the words it contains. 2 + 2 = 4 is an analytic claim. Given the meaning of two, four, plus, and equals, we know that it is true that 2 + 2 = 4. The same is also true of our second example: bachelors are unmarried men. That is simply the definition of a bachelor. Assuming you know what the word means, you know that it is true that bachelors are unmarried men, "by definition." The final example from the objective column is also an analytic claim. Abortion just is the intentional termination of a pregnancy.

The remaining examples of objective claims are not true by definition, but can be demonstrated to be true (or false) with a little bit of research and effort. Simply by checking to see which were the final two candidates for the Democratic Party in 2016 on primary ballots and in Democratic debates allows us to verify that the claim is true. Similarly, we can check the film credits for *The Hateful Eight* using resources such as "IMDb" allows to verify who directed that film.[58] Finally, a survey of bacon production, or even a simple examination at a grocery store, would allow us to verify that most bacon is pork (as opposed to turkey, for example).

Now turn to the examples of subjective claims, and notice a stark contrast: they are neither analytic claims nor empirically verifiable. Starting with the claim that math is boring, regardless of whether *you* find math to be boring, you undoubtedly recognize that there is nothing inherent to our very concept of math that renders it boring (unlike being unmarried being inherent to our concept of a bachelor), nor is there any way to "prove" that math is boring. Even if you survey thousands of people, and discover that most people describe math as boring, all you have proven is that "*most people surveyed describe math as boring,*" not that math *is* boring.

With regard to whether it's better to be married or a bachelor, once again we would all recognize that responses will vary. Some people love being married, others love being single—and neither preference is either analytically true or empirically verifiable as "correct." So, too, with preferring Bernie Sanders to Hillary Clinton, whether or not *The Hateful Eight* was "awesome," and even whether or not bacon is delicious.

Last, but certainly not least, what about that claim that abortion is morally wrong? This is clearly a moral claim (i.e., a claim concerning a moral issue), and some subjectivists will say that, like those other claims, it is neither analytic nor capable of empirical verification. This leads us to an official argument for moral subjectivism.

- Moral claims are not objective because moral claims aren't provable

  1. Objective claims must be either analytic claims or empirically verifiable.
  2. Moral claims are not analytic claims.
  3. Moral claims are not empirically verifiable.
  4. Therefore, moral claims are not objective claims.
  5. Therefore, moral claims are subjective claims.

Let us now consider the argument, one line at a time. As with any subject in

---

[58] http://www.imdb.com/title/tt3460252/?ref_=nv_sr_1

philosophy, the first premise is subject to disagreement.[59] However, that objective claims must be either analytic or empirically verifiable is a widely-accepted understanding of objective claims, and will be our working definition, given our limited purposes.

The second and third premises are much more important and interesting. The second premise claims that moral claims are not analytic claims. That is, they are not inherently true or false in the way that "bachelors are unmarried men" is inherently true, and "Ted is a married bachelor" is inherently false.

Consider the moral claim that it is wrong to steal. You might agree with that statement. You might think it is "obviously" true. However, you probably also acknowledge that if someone disagrees, and asserts that it is *not* wrong to steal (perhaps because they have a particular understanding of "property" and "property rights?"), that person has not uttered a literal logical contradiction. You might think that person is mistaken, but the person hasn't said something literally incoherent—unlike someone who says a bachelor is married. Even in cases of passionate disagreement, such as between "Pro-Life" and "Pro-Choice" camps, there is no notion that the "other side" believes something literally incoherent and logically impossible. If you agree with this reasoning, then this indicates that moral claims are not *analytic* claims, not true (or false) *by definition*.

The third premise claims that moral claims are not empirically verifiable. To return to our example of theft, supporters of this argument would say that there is no way to *prove* that stealing is wrong (or disprove it). After all, what test could someone propose that would *prove* the wrongness of stealing?

You could certainly prove the financial impact of stealing, or you could verify what someone (e.g., the thief, or the victim) *said* about stealing, or you could try to document the ownership of the item in question to determine whether a theft actually occurred, or you could verify that the act was indeed a violation of the law simply by consulting the laws in the place where the act occurred—but what verifiable fact or feature of reality corresponds to the *wrongness* of the stealing? Some subjectivists answer that there is no such verifiable fact or feature, and therefore moral claims are not empirically verifiable.

If objective claims must be either analytic, or empirically verifiable, and if moral claims are neither, then it seems to follow from that that moral claims are not objective. If they are not objective, but are, nevertheless, claims, then what remains for them is to be *subjective* claims.

Another argument for subjectivism relies upon the judgment that moral claims are not "natural." That is, they do not come from "Nature," but are rather the product of human conventions, and are therefore arbitrary and subjective, as opposed to objective.

- Moral claims aren't objective because they are merely conventional

By way of analogy, consider the game of chess. In chess, there are certain rules

---

[59] Indeed, an amusing possible criticism of this claim is that it is, itself, neither analytic nor empirically verifiable, and therefore not an objective claim, according to its own standards.

that govern the movement of the pieces. Rooks can only move forward and backward, or from side to side. Bishops can only move diagonally. Knights can only move in "L" shapes. If I try to move a Knight one space directly forward, I have broken one of the rules of chess—but the rules themselves are completely conventional and arbitrary. There is nothing "natural" and necessary about chess. Human beings happened to invent a game, and came up with a handful of arbitrary rules that govern it. Unlike the "rules" (i.e., Laws) of Nature, though, they are optional and arbitrary. Gravity, in contrast, is neither arbitrary, conventional, nor optional.

Some subjectivists will argue that moral "laws" (rules) are far more like the rules of chess than like the Laws of Nature, and for that reason are subjective rather than objective. Or, to put it a bit differently, natural laws are descriptive (i.e., they tell us how things in nature will behave) whereas moral claims are prescriptive (i.e., they tell us how moral agents *should* behave).

1. Natural Laws are descriptive, not prescriptive
2. Moral claims, though, are prescriptive.
3. Therefore, moral claims are not natural/objective but are conventional/subjective.

In support of the first premise, note that we recognize that natural laws don't make recommendations, but instead describe, explain, and predict. For example, Newton's law of Universal Gravitation claims that "any two bodies in the universe attract each other with a force that is directly proportional to the product of their masses and inversely proportional to the square of the distance between them." There is nothing to be recommended here. Newton wasn't suggesting how bodies should behave, but describing how they do behave. There are no value judgments in that description.

Even when we describe the behavior of other living things, we don't imply any sort of value judgments, but merely offer amoral descriptions of their behavior.

> *A hawk that seizes a fish from the sea kills it, but does not murder it; and another hawk that seizes the fish from the talons of the first takes it, but does not steal it - for none of these things is forbidden.*[60]

The comparison here is interesting. The behavior of a hawk taking a fish from another hawk and a human taking a fish from another human are outwardly the same—or at least very similar. Why is one "taking" and the other "stealing?" Chimpanzees are somewhat notorious among primatologists for killing other (rival) chimps.[61] Most of us, however, would call that behavior "killing" rather than "murder"—and even if we use the word "murder" we would probably acknowledge that we are using the word differently than when we use it with human actions. If, by chance, you think chimps are sufficiently self-conscious that such killing really *is* murder, then switch my example to a black widow spider killing and eating her mate,

---

[60] Richard Taylor, Ethics, Faith, and Reason, pp.14.
[61] http://www.bbc.com/news/science-environment-29237276

and now ponder how killing became murder when it reached the chimpanzee.

What, though, justifies our different judgment? Why is it "killing" if a chimpanzee ends the life of another chimpanzee through violence, but "murder" if a human does the same thing to another human? From a purely naturalistic perspective, humans are primates just as are chimpanzees, after all. . . .

At this point, the subjectivist could say that it is clear that Nature does not prohibit killing. In fact, killing (in the form of predation) is a *necessity* for a great many species! Killing fellow humans is "wrong" not because "Nature" says so, but because humans have said so. In effect, we have set up some "rules" for a "game," and one of those more common rules is that we're not (usually) allowed to kill one another. There is, however, nothing "natural" about that rule any more than there is something "natural" about the rules of chess. We can easily imagine different rules for human behavior just as we can imagine different rules for chess. Accordingly, given the difference between moral claims and Natural Laws, we should recognize moral claims as arbitrary, conventional prescriptions rather than objective descriptions.

Consider, now, the implications of this, if true. Given the subjective nature of moral claims, some will focus on the "rules" of the "games" we create as communities, and identify morality in terms of those collective rules. We will consider this interpretation in the form of Ethical Relativism in a later section.

Others, though, will question the validity of the "game" itself, and emphasize the arbitrary nature of those rules. If the moral rules are "arbitrary," what could make one rule more legitimate than another? There are a lot of different ways to play Poker. In some versions, the Joker is in play, and is "wild"—meaning it can stand for any card you want. Or, in some versions, it can only stand for specific cards. Or, some people don't include the Joker at all.

Which of those variations is "true" Poker? Who has the authority to make such a judgment? Maybe some people like playing Poker without a Joker, and others like playing with the Joker being wild. Which of those groups is "right?" Does that question even make any sense? How could one style of play somehow be more "correct" than the other, if we acknowledge that the rules of Poker are completely arbitrary and products of human convention to begin with?

Now imagine that we consider moral "rules" (i.e., moral claims) in the same way. There are many different styles of "play," representing many different personal preferences. If you and I disagree about some particular moral issue, neither one of us is "mistaken." For one of us to be mistaken, there would need to be some sort of independent "answer key" against which we could compare our own values.

What or who could provide that "answer key?" Someone else? Why should her opinion count for more than our own? What about majority opinion? Isn't that just popularity?

Just because lots of people enjoy Country Music doesn't mean someone is mistaken for not liking it. Similarly, just because more people like to play Poker without the Joker than with it doesn't mean that those who like playing with the Joker are mistaken—they're just outnumbered.

What about appealing to the law? This sounds like an appeal to the "rules of the game." But, given the arbitrariness of those rules in the first place, no one could be "mistaken" if they prefer, instead, to substitute their own "house rules." Of course, if you're playing Poker at someone else's table, you might be bound to play by their rules, but that doesn't mean your own version of the game is "wrong." It might well be prudent of you to play by the rules of your host, but that is just a practical consideration, and in no way implies that your host's rules are somehow more correct than your own! If the only sources to which we may appeal are other humans, the question remains: why would one human's values be somehow more authoritative, more morally accurate, than another's?

If you and I disagree about spicy food, we tend to think that's not a big deal. I'll eat spicy food, and you won't. Everyone's happy. But, what if I think it's OK for me to steal your identity and charge a bunch of merchandise in your name? I keep all the stuff, and you get stuck with the bill. You find out it was me, and you come complaining:

You: "Hey, Ted! What's wrong with you? Why did you steal my credit card and buy all that stuff for yourself? I just got a huge credit card bill in the mail?"

Me: "Um, I wanted the stuff, and I also didn't want to pay for it myself. Seemed like a pretty good way to handle that particular problem...."

You: "But you can't just steal my credit card because *you* want something and don't want to have to pay for it! That's *wrong!*"

Me: "No it's not...."

You: "What are you talking about? Of course it is!"

Me: "I don't think it is—and I would appreciate it if you would drop that self-righteous tone. The way you're speaking to me, it's as if you think your opinion concerning identity theft is somehow better, or more accurate, than mine. How arrogant...."

At this point it will be helpful to distinguish two kinds of moral subjectivism: "simple subjectivism," and "emotivism." We will devote a chapter to emotivism later in this book, so for now we will focus on simple subjectivism, and only offer a preview of emotivism, in contrast.

Simple Subjectivism

Simple Subjectivism (i.e., the focus of this chapter) is the view that has been lurking in the background for this entire section, thus far. According to Simple Subjectivism, moral claims are matters of opinion, rather than fact. They are subjective, rather than objective. Moral claims are indicators of personal preference or taste, and are therefore more similar to a claim concerning whether I liked a movie than to a claim concerning who directed the movie. According to Simple Subjectivism, being opposed to abortion is more like offering your opinion about a painting than answering a math problem. Because moral claims appeal to opinions rather than facts, there are no "right" answers to our moral questions. Instead, something is morally right or wrong (to me) just to the extent that I believe it is, and if you should disagree with me, your opinion is no more (or less) correct than my own.

Emotivism

Although Emotivists agree with subjectivists that moral claims are about the individual/subject rather than the act/object (i.e., subjective, rather than objective), Emotivists go even further. Emotivists wouldn't even say that moral claims are subjective claims. Rather, they believe that moral "claims" are not *claims* at all! Instead, they are indicators of positive or negative emotional attitudes only.

Subjectivism and emotivism are similar, but not identical. According to subjectivism, an action is morally right (to me) simply if I approve of it. Moral claims are simply statements concerning a person's approval or disapproval of an action.

To claim that "eating meat is morally wrong" is just a way of that person saying "I don't approve of eating meat." This claim has a truth value. It is either true, or false. It is true if that person really does disapprove of eating meat (i.e., she is telling the truth), and it is false if she doesn't really disapprove of eating meat (i.e., she is lying).

Emotivists, in contrast, deny that there is any sort of claim being made at all, preferring instead to interpret so-called moral claims as mere expressions of a *feeling*—and feelings are neither true or false.

Whether or not someone is *experiencing* a particular feeling can be interpreted as true or false. If someone asks if you are sad, and you say "yes," your implied statement of "I am feeling sad" is true if you really are sad, or false if you're lying. But, while the statement *about* your sadness can be true or false, the *sadness itself* can't be. For emotivists, moral claims aren't statements about our feelings, but the actual "emoting" of the feeling itself.

With either of these versions of subjectivism, the impact on our understanding of ethics, moral claims, and the weight of moral obligations would be tremendous. But, is either interpretation true, or at least compelling?

We will now consider some possible criticism of moral subjectivism so you can decide, for yourself, whether it's the best interpretation of moral claims.

Possible problems for subjectivism

What most of these possible problems will have in common is that they involve "intuition tests." In a previous chapter, we addressed how we process new pieces of information. As you might recall, we each have, at our disposal, what we may call our "background knowledge," "background information," or our "worldview." Whatever we want to call it, it is that vast collection of everything we have heard, seen, read, and otherwise learned, throughout our lives. This collection is everything we know (or think we know) about the world and how it works. Every time we are confronted with a piece of information, we automatically and instantly evaluate it against our background knowledge. If the new information seems to "fit" with our background knowledge, we're likely to accept it as true. If it does not fit, however, if the claim is surprising to us, we're likely to hesitate and to demand more justification before accepting it as true.

Each of the possible problems for subjectivism we will consider involves an implication of subjectivism. In each case the strategy is the same: "if subjectivism is true, then [something else] is also true." That "something else" is being presented as a "possible problem," in the following way: each implication of subjectivism is a new piece of information. It either fits nicely with your worldview, sounding "right"—in which case you are likely to accept it as true, and this indicates that you might well be a subjectivist. On the other hand, this new piece of information might conflict with your worldview, and sound "wrong"—in which case you are likely to reject it as false, or at least be skeptical and demand some convincing evidence before revising your worldview.

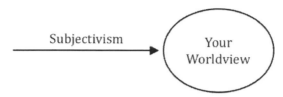

If any of these implications conflicts with your worldview, that doesn't necessarily mean that subjectivism is *false*, of course, but it would indicate that subjectivism *seems* at least unlikely to be true, given your understanding of the world and how it works.

Possible problem #1: Simple Subjectivism is counter-intuitive because no one is ever "mistaken" about moral value judgments

We can now consider a possible (and disturbing) possible problem arising from Simple Subjectivism: no one is ever "wrong"—at least not in any strong sense.

Professor Emeritus Harry Jaffa (from my own Alma Mater, Claremont McKenna College), penned a fictionalized account of a conversation between the serial killer Ted Bundy and one of his victims, "Laura." Jaffa has admitted that it was "composed on the same principle as the speeches in Thucydides' History of the Peloponnesian War, attributing to each speaker the words that fit his character and the circumstances in which he spoke." In other words, he made it up—but in a way that he thought was at least consistent with the character of Bundy. Though I can't express enough how much I disagree with Professor Jaffa on certain subjects, he has managed to make the crux of a subjectivist understanding of morality clear in this dialogue. A brief excerpt follows:

Bundy: I recognize that your life and your freedom are very valuable to you, but you must recognize that they are not so valuable to me. And if I must sacrifice your life and freedom to mine, why should I not do so? The unexamined life was not worth living to Socrates. And a life without raping and murdering is not worth living to me. What right do you—or does anyone—have, to deny this to me?

Laura: But rape and murder are wrong. The Bible says they are wrong, and the law says they are wrong.

Bundy: What do you mean by wrong? What you call wrong, I call attempts to limit my freedom. The Bible punished both sodomy and murder with death. Sodomy is no longer regarded as a crime, or even as immoral. Why then should murder—or rape? . . . I want you to know that once upon a time I too believed that God and the moral law prescribed boundaries within which my life had to be lived. That was before I took my first college courses in philosophy. Then it was that I discovered how unsophisticated—nay, primitive—my earlier beliefs had been. Then I learned that all moral judgments are "value judgments," that all value judgments are subjective, and that none can be proved to be either "right" or "wrong." . . . And I quickly discovered that the greatest obstacle to my freedom, the greatest block and limitation to it, consisted in the insupportable "value judgment" that I was bound to respect the rights of others. I asked myself, who were these "others"? Other human beings, with human rights? Why is it more wrong to kill a human animal than any other animal, a pig or a sheep or a steer? Is our life more to you than a hog's life to a hog? Why should I be willing to sacrifice my pleasures more for the one than for the other? Surely, you would not, in this age of scientific enlightenment, declare that God or nature has marked some pleasures as "moral" or "good" and others as "immoral" or "bad?"

Jaffa's point is pretty simple: if moral truth is relative to the individual, then, strictly speaking, Bundy isn't *wrong* (as in, "incorrect") to believe that raping and murdering is a fine form of entertainment.

I disagree with Bundy, of course, and so do you (I hope!). But, if moral claims are subjective, then all that means is that we have a different *opinion* about rape and murder than he does. Our opinion is neither better, nor worse, than Bundy's—in much the same way that someone who dislikes spicy food isn't "wrong" (whatever I might believe about their taste preferences). Similarly, someone who believes it's acceptable to have sex with young children isn't "wrong" according to a subjectivist approach. Such a person's opinion is no doubt quite unpopular, but "unpopular" isn't the same thing as "wrong."

I like garlic. For the most part, you can't put too much garlic in food as far as I'm concerned. Garlic ice cream is a feature at the Gilroy Garlic Festival, and can be purchased at the garlic-themed "Stinking Rose" restaurant in Los Angeles. Despite my love of garlic, I have never been excited about garlic ice cream. To be honest, garlic ice cream doesn't sound very appealing to me at all, though there are clearly some people who *do* like garlic ice cream—after all, the makers wouldn't bother making it if no one bought it!

I don't think those garlic ice cream enthusiasts are mistaken. If they like garlic ice cream, how can they be wrong about that? At the same time, those garlic ice cream fans must recognize that their ice cream preference is not very popular. They shouldn't be surprised when they can't find garlic ice cream in the freezer section of the grocery store, or at Baskin-Robbins. Instead, such venders cater to much more popular taste preferences such as mint chip, cookies and cream, etc. That doesn't mean that those of us who prefer mint chip are "correct" and those who prefer garlic ice cream are "incorrect"—but it does mean that we're in the majority, that our preference is more popular, and that our preference is much more likely to be honored in our community.

If subjectivism is true, then Ted Bundy's preference for rape and murder is like another person's preference for garlic ice cream. He was not "mistaken," but his view was unpopular, and he was outnumbered by those of us who believe rape and murder are wrong. That helps to explain why rape and murder are illegal, and why he was punished (executed!) once he was caught.

None of that indicates that he was *mistaken* about rape and murder, though. If Simple Subjectivism is true, none of us can be "mistaken" about any moral claim, no matter what example we might conjure.

People who like garlic ice cream aren't mistaken. That's just what they like. Is that true of pedophiles as well? Are we willing to think of "I like garlic ice cream" and "I like raping children" as the same kinds of claims? I'm being intentionally provocative here, because it's essential that we understand what it means if subjectivism is the proper way to understand morality. It's possible that moral truths really are simply matters of personal opinion. I don't personally think that is true, but it's *possible*. If that's the case, "morality," as most of us commonly understand it, doesn't exist—and this is why Simple Subjectivism is presented as a "challenge" to ethics.

Critics of Simple Subjectivism will point out that we do not, in fact, regard all opinions as equally true. This is evident, according to the critic, by the fact that we recognize areas of expertise, and experts whose views are regarded as more credible and authoritative as a result of that expertise.

Consider the following examples:

Subject	Expert
Medicine	Medical Doctor
Nutrition	Nutritionist
Carpentry	Carpenter
Botany	Botanist
Chemistry	Chemist
Physics	Physicist
Philosophy	Philosopher

I'll start with a deeply personal example. If you don't believe that my understanding of philosophy, on the basis of my several degrees (B.A., M.A., and Ph.D.), years of experience (more than 20 years at the time of this writing), and "accolades" (e.g., being a tenured professor, and having published multiple articles and textbooks, etc.), is any more informed than your own, why on Earth are you bothering to read this book, or take my class? What is the point of education, in general, if every student is equally informed as his or her teacher?

Let's make it more absurd. Why bother going to the doctor when you are sick and injured? If all opinions are equal, your own opinion about your medical condition is just as good as that doctor's!

Those astrophysicists who have spent studying the universe and who are debating whether or not this universe is situated within a broader multiverse? Their views are no better informed than the random person who has never studied that stuff a day in his or her life. . . .

You don't accept that as true, of course—and this is the critics point. In actual practice, we don't really believe that "all opinions are equal," but instead recognize that some people know what they're talking about, and others don't. Socrates himself criticized epistemic relativism (and moral subjectivism) thousands of years ago:

Why, that all those mercenary individuals, whom the many call Sophists and whom they deem to be their adversaries, do, in fact, teach nothing but the opinion of the many, that is to say, the opinions of their assemblies; and this is their wisdom. I might compare them to a man who should study the tempers and desires of a mighty strong beast who is fed by him—he would learn how to approach and handle him, also at what times and from what causes he is dangerous or the reverse, and what is the meaning of his several cries, and by what sounds, when another utters them, he is soothed or infuriated; and you may suppose further, that when, by continually attending upon him, he has become perfect in all this, he calls his knowledge wisdom, and makes of it a system or art, which he proceeds to teach, although he has no real notion of what he means by the principles or passions of which he is speaking, but calls this honourable and that dishonourable, or good or evil, or just or unjust, all in accordance with the tastes and tempers of the great brute. Good he pronounces to be that in which the beast delights and evil to be that which he dislikes; and he can give no other account of them except that the just and noble are the necessary, having never himself seen, and having no power of explaining to others the nature of either, or the difference between them, which is immense.[62]

In other words, these intellectual mercenaries know nothing of good or evil, justice or injustice. Instead, they merely *observe* what actually happens in the world, what people seem to like and dislike, and *proclaim* those things to be good or bad, just or unjust.

If we recognize that this sort of relativism is rife with problems in a non-moral context (e.g., think about what it would mean for it to be "just a matter of opinion" that humans require oxygen to survive), why should we entertain the notion in moral contexts?

The question we must now consider is whether moral claims concern a matter of possible expertise ("morality"), in which case we would presumably recognize that some people are better informed than others, and that not all views are equally good. Or, if we reject that, then we are presumably treating moral claims as mere indicators of personal taste. I might recognize that some people might be experts at "baking," and are certainly better informed than I am when it comes to how best to bake a cake, but I don't recognize that anyone else is somehow more informed than I am about what sort of cake I like! If you've gone to culinary school, your understanding of how to bake a red velvet cake is probably better informed than my own, but it makes no sense to suggest that you know better than I do regarding whether or not I *like* red velvet cake.

Herein lies the intuition test: based upon your worldview, is "morality" more like a skill that allows for expertise ("e.g., "baking"), or is it more like a personal taste preference ("red velvet cake is my favorite")?

---

[62] Plato, *Republic*, 493a-c

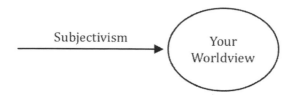

Possible problem #2: Simple Subjectivism is counter-intuitive because of how it interprets language use

This possible problem might sound mysterious and abstract, but it's really not very complicated. Language is a rich and sophisticated tool with which we may accomplish many things. We use language in a lot of different ways, and we intend different sorts of things when we use language.

Sometimes, when we make a claim (whether spoken or written), all we are intending to do is to express a personal preference or experience. For example, if I tell you that "*The Martian* was a good movie," it's very likely that all I am intending to do is to convey the fact that I liked the movie. In fact, if someone had to "translate" my claim using other words, but conveying the same meaning, that person might very well just translate it as "Ted liked *The Martian*."

As another example, suppose I go to see my doctor, and he refers me to an oncologist—a doctor who specializes in cancer diagnosis and treatment. Suppose that, after some tests, that oncologist says to me, "You have cancer." Presumably, the intention of my oncologist is not at all the same as with my first example. She's not saying anything at all like "I like cancer," or even "I don't like cancer." She's not offering an indicator of her personal preference at all. Instead, she is intending to provide a medically-accurate, *factual* diagnosis of my medical condition.

She is not intending to offer a mere *opinion*. Presumably, she regards that diagnosis as a medical *fact*. Given her presumed expertise, I am going to treat it as a fact, and certainly not as a mere personal perspective than is no more informed than anyone else's! Even if I seek a "second opinion," that doesn't mean that I think her diagnosis is "just an opinion." It means that I want a second doctor to double-check the tests, and to confirm the diagnosis, just in case any mistakes were made. In the same sort of way, if you complete a math problem, and you ask for someone to check your work, it's not because you think that answers to math problems are merely matters of opinion! Instead, you want something else to verify that your answer is correct.

Here is another example of a claim, but this time concerning a moral issue. "Abortion is the ending of pregnancy by removing a fetus or embryo before it can survive outside the uterus." If I offer a claim like that, it seems pretty clear that my intention is to define abortion. What I am hoping to accomplish is to convey the meaning of abortion, in the literal sense of what an abortion *is*.

Finally, let us consider the claim that "Abortion is morally wrong." As with all the other examples, we need to ask what is being intended by this claim, and how else might we "translate" it.

Simple Subjectivists seem to be assuming that the intention behind that claim is to convey personal taste preference, and therefore an accurate "translation" would be "I don't like abortion." Certainly, that is a possible interpretation of what's going on, but is it the only one? The best one?

Some critics of Simple Subjectivism will claim that an expression of personal preference is not the only intention someone might have, or even the most common one. Instead, someone who is claiming "abortion is morally wrong" might be intending to accurately describe an objective feature of a particular act; in this case, abortion. If so, the accurate "translation" would *not* be "I don't like abortion," but something like "abortion has the property of being morally wrong."

It's a statement of the obvious to point out that when someone tells us something, that person is offering his or her opinion—but it doesn't necessarily follow from that that the person is therefore offering something that is *only* subjectively true, nor that the intention is to offer a *mere* opinion. We can agree, without controversy, that if someone makes a claim (and the person is being sincere, as opposed to deceptive), that person is *at least* offering an opinion. What remains to be seen is whether it's possible to offer anything more: a fact.

Which seems more accurate to you? That all moral claims are intending merely as expressions of personal taste, or that at least some moral claims are intended as an accurate description of an objective property of a particular act?

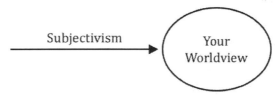

Possible problem #3: subjectivism is counter-intuitive because it doesn't allow for objective moral progress or regress in individuals

A third possible problem with subjectivism is what it does to our notions of moral progress and regress. In actual practice, we speak about people becoming morally better or worse people over time. "He's really turned his life around!" "What happened to Jane? She used to be such a good person?" What would such statements mean from a subjectivist perspective?

Stanley "Tookie" Williams was executed by the State of California in 2005. His impending execution was covered extensively in the California media not only because executions are infrequent in California, but also because Tookie had become a bit of a celebrity, and had numerous actual celebrities lobbying for a stay of execution. Although several different arguments were offered for why he should not be executed, one particular argument was, by far, employed most often: Tookie had "reformed."

Although he was convicted of several murders from 1979, and although he was a co-founder of the notorious Crips gang, his supporters claimed that he had transformed himself while in prison, and was no longer the man he used to be. He had become a morally better person, and didn't deserve to die (at least not any more).

I no longer participate in the so-called gangster lifestyle, and I deeply regret that I ever did . . . I vow to spend the rest of my life working toward solutions.

—William's 1997 open apology for his gang activities.

What would it mean to say that Tookie was a better person in 2005 than he was in 1979? Better how? By what standard? By *whose* standard? Remember, if moral truths are subjective, his beliefs and values in 1979 were not *wrong* (mistaken). Whatever he believed was right, *really was* right (for him).

In 2005, he allegedly possessed a different set of values. Those values were neither better nor worse than his values from 1979. They were simply different.

If you think he had become a better person, then, according to Simple Subjectivism, that's simply *your* opinion. One can imagine that some of his still-dedicated Crips associates might disagree.

From a subjectivist perspective, to say that Tookie became a better person is to say something like the following:

- "*I* like Tookie a lot more than I used to."
- "*I* wouldn't have wanted to hang out with Tookie in 1979, but I would have in 2005."
- "*I* didn't have much in common with Tookie back in 1979, but now I do."
- "Tookie would have made me uncomfortable back in 1979, but now I feel good about him and his values."

Only if morality is *not* simply a matter of opinion, only if there is some non-subjective notion of truth behind it, can we have any strong notion of people becoming better or worse over time. Perhaps progress and regress are merely matters of perspective, but if you disagree and think there is a more powerful sense in which people can become morally better or worse, then you presumably disagree with the claims of subjectivism.

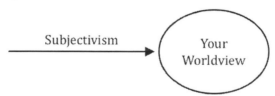

Possible problem #4: subjectivism is counter-intuitive because it doesn't allow for objective moral comparisons between individuals.

We've just seen how subjectivism can't provide strong comparisons of the *same* person over time. Now we can see how it also can't provide for strong comparisons of *different* people at the *same* time.

Consider these two men:

Now consider these two quotations. One is attributed to each man. I'll let you make an educated guess as to who is responsible for each quotation....

The pieces of the bodies of infidels were flying like dust particles. If you would have seen it with your own eyes, you would have been very pleased, and your heart would have been filled with joy.

Nonviolence is the answer to the crucial political and moral questions of our time; the need for mankind to overcome oppression and violence without resorting to oppression and violence. Man must evolve for all human conflict a method which rejects revenge, aggression and retaliation. The foundation of such a method is love.

Shameless moral imperialist that I am, I'm going to boldly proclaim that MLK was morally superior to bin Laden. I'm even going to assume that most of you agree. What would that mean, though, given a subjectivist framework? It certainly could *not* mean that King was morally better in any "objective sense"—after all, there is no such thing as moral objectivity from the point of view of the subjectivist. Instead, it must mean that my own *personal opinion* (yours too, presumably) is that King was morally superior.

That's just *my* opinion, though, and one that is no more or less correct than that of the most zealous fan of al-Qu'aida or bin Laden. If someone else thinks bin Laden to be the morally superior man, he or she is not "wrong"—we just have different moral taste preferences. To say that MLK is the better man is really just an indicator of my own values, as opposed to any claim about some moral truth—at least not any truth that is more than mere opinion.

One must grant, in all fairness and honesty, that the subjectivists *could* be right. It might be the case that all our moral judgments are simply expressions of personal opinion, and nothing stronger than that. You must ask yourself, in light of what is *possible*, if it's also *probable* that subjectivism is true. Are we incapable of any stronger moral comparison than the expression of our personal tastes? Is proclaiming King to be the morally better man the same kind of claim as pronouncing Switchfoot to be the best contemporary rock band?

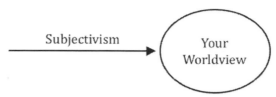

Possible problem #5: subjectivism is counter-intuitive because moral conflict must be resolved by appeals to power, rather than truth

One final (potentially disturbing) implication of subjectivism: if all moral judgments are mere expressions of personal opinion, and if no opinion can claim the mantle of truth, then moral disagreements cannot be resolved by appealing to the truth. Indeed, some subjectivists would deny that disagreement on moral claims is even possible!

Such subjectivists believe that there can be no such thing as contradictory moral claims. For example, the Pro-Life and Pro-Choice crowds aren't actually declaring contrary beliefs, according to this interpretation, but are instead expressing different emotional attitudes about abortion. Obviously, the Pro-Life people have a negative emotional attitude about abortion, while the Pro-Choice people have a positive emotional attitude about reproductive choice. It would be misguided, though, to think that one of the two groups could ever, somehow, be proven to be "right." No party to the pseudo-debate can be proved to be "right" and the other "wrong" because there is nothing objectively right or wrong, or objectively true or false about our moral "claims."

In a non-moral context, if I claim that a painting is "beautiful," I'm not declaring any objective fact about the painting, but simply indicating my own positive attitude towards the painting. I like the painting. It appeals to me. The beauty isn't something objective in the painting, but rather something subjective about me and my experience of the painting—otherwise, everyone would think the painting is beautiful.

Similarly, if subjectivism is correct, then claiming that "abortion is immoral" is not a declaration of any objective fact (about which someone else could be mistaken), but merely an indicator of the speaker's own attitude towards abortion (i.e., a negative attitude). If that is the case, there is no genuine disagreement possible when it comes to abortion, or any other moral issue.

If you and I agree disagree on an objective matter, disagreement indicates error. If I claim that Barack Obama was the 42nd President of the United States, and you claim that George W. Bush was the 42nd President of the United States, at least one of us must be mistaken, since only one person could have been the 42nd President.[63] However, if I claim that George W. Bush is handsome and you claim that he is not, it

---

[63] Actually, in that case both of us would be mistaken, since Bill Clinton was the 42nd President. Congratulations to those of you paying attention!

is entirely consistent that both of us can be correct, since we are not actually contradicting each other. Note the comparison:

Objective claim	Subjective claim
Barack Obama was the 42nd President	*I* think G. W. Bush is handsome
George W Bush was the 42nd President	*You* think G. W. Bush isn't handsome

The claims in the first column can't be both be true at the same time, but the claims in the second can certainly both be true at the same time. This indicates, to subjectivists, that moral disagreement doesn't involve anything like the simultaneous utterance of contradictory claims, but merely the simultaneously different personal attitudes about something experienced by two different people.

Earlier in this chapter, we considered a criticism of subjectivism based on language use. The complaint was that our use of moral claims doesn't seem to be merely an indicator of personal taste preference, but that sometimes we are honestly trying to argue for or against a position. Ayer recognizes this experience, and has an interpretation to account for it (underlining added for emphasis).

> *This may seem, at first sight to be a very paradoxical assertion. For we certainly do engage in disputes which are ordinarily regarded as disputes about questions of value, But, in all such cases, we find, if we consider the matter closely, that the dispute is not really about a question of value, but about a question of fact. When someone disagrees with us about the moral value of a certain action or type of action, we do admittedly resort to argument in order to win him over to our way of thinking.* <u>*But we do not attempt to show by our arguments that he has the 'wrong' ethical feeling towards a situation whose nature he has correctly apprehended. What we attempt to show is that he is mistaken about the facts of the case.*</u> *We argue that he has misconceived the agent's motive: or that he has misjudged the effects of the action, or its probable effects in view of the agent's knowledge; or that he has failed to take into account the special circumstances in which the agent was placed. Or else we employ more general arguments about the effects which actions of a certain type tend to produce, or the qualities which are usually manifested in their performance.* <u>*We do this in the hope that we have only to get our opponent to agree with us about the nature of the empirical facts for him to adopt the same moral attitude towards them as we do. And as the people with whom we argue have generally received the same moral education as ourselves, and live in the same social order, our expectation is usually justified.*</u>

For a different example, consider moral opposition to homosexuality. Some people believe that homosexual behavior is immoral, while others seemingly disagree. But, according to Ayer, they're not *really* "disagreeing." What could this mean?

Recall the following: "When someone disagrees with us about the moral value of a certain action or type of action, we do admittedly resort to argument in order to win him over to our way of thinking. But we do not attempt to show by our arguments that he has the 'wrong' ethical feeling towards a situation whose nature he has correctly apprehended. What we attempt to show is that he is mistaken about the facts of the case."

Consider how much effort has been made on both sides of the sexuality debate to determine whether or not homosexuality is a "lifestyle choice" or whether people are "born that way." 2016 Presidential candidate Ben Carson stirred some controversy when he argued that homosexuality is a choice "because a lot of people who go into prison go into prison straight -- and when they come out, they're gay. So, did something happen while they were in there? Ask yourself that question."[64] The American Psychological Association disagrees, claiming that "most people experience little or no sense of choice about their sexual orientation."

Why would it matter whether or not homosexuality is a choice? Presumably because most people (or most Americans, at least) think that it is unfair to condemn someone for something over which they have no control. If homosexuality is no more a choice than is heterosexuality, then to condemn homosexual activity between consenting adults while endorsing heterosexual activity between consenting adults might seem unfair, or even arbitrary.

One of the reasons Gay-rights activists have argued so consistently for the acceptance that homosexuality is not a lifestyle choice is so that an analogy with the American Civil Rights movement can be made. To discriminate against African-Americans on the basis of their skin color (something that was not a choice) is now regarded as unfair and unacceptable by most Americans. If sexuality is similar to skin color by virtue of being something we are born with, then discrimination on the basis of sexuality could also be argued to be unfair and unacceptable. On the other hand, if someone could prove that there is no biological basis for sexual orientation, if it could be proven that people choose their attractions, then the analogy breaks down, and other analogies are possible:

> We never, ever judge someone on who's going to heaven, hell. That's the Almighty's job. We just love 'em, give 'em the good news about Jesus—whether they're homosexuals, drunks, terrorists. We let God sort 'em out later, you see what I'm saying?[65]

In this quotation, "Duck Dynasty" patriarch Phil Robertson compares homosexuals to drunks and terrorists. Just as people choose to drink to excess (and that is wrong), and others choose to commit acts of terrorism (and that is wrong), so too do some people choose to engage in homosexual activity (and that is wrong). People are no more born to be gay than they are born to be terrorists, according to this logic.

Ayer would interpret the disagreement between these two camps as not actually being a disagreement about the rightness or wrongness of homosexuality, which is merely a subjective preference, but instead a disagreement about the objective nature

---

[64] http://www.cnn.com/2015/03/04/politics/ben-carson-prisons-gay-choice/
[65] http://entertainment.time.com/2013/12/18/duck-dynasty-star-compares-gay-people-to-drunks-terrorists-and-prostitutes/

of sexual orientation. Similarly, disagreement about abortion is really disagreement about the objective fact as to whether or not a fetus is an innocent person with rights, analogous to adult humans that are protected under the law.

For the subjectivist, there is no "truth" concerning the moral status of the abortion itself other than the truth or falsity of someone's personal attitudes about abortion. Truth, it may be said, has no role to play in this dispute.

If truth can't be used to settle moral conflict and debate, what can? If you and I disagree about some moral issue, and it's impossible (even in principle) for either one of us to establish who is correct (or at least closer to the truth), then what will resolve the conflict? The only thing left: power.

Thrasymachus, in Plato's *Republic*, argued famously that "might makes right."

I declare justice is nothing but the advantage of the stronger.[66]

Rather than viewing morality and justice as anything lofty and noble, a much simpler (and more cynical) interpretation is offered: the people in charge get to make the rules. Whatever they say is right, is, for all practical purposes, "right." One of the perks of being the most powerful person is that you get to enshrine your own personal values into law and custom—at least until someone more powerful comes along with a different set of values.

From the standpoint of subjectivism, those of us who think it abhorrent to have sex with a child don't have "better" values than a pedophile. We're not "right." What we are, is more powerful, if for no other reason than because we are more numerous. It just so happens that the no-sex-with-children crowd gained control at some point in our history, and has remained more populous and more powerful than the percentage of our population who think it acceptable to have sex with children. We have no (objective) moral advantage over them, but we can force them to follow our values rather than theirs. After all, if they refuse, we'll throw them in jail.

Returning to our abortion example, neither side is "correct" or "incorrect," but in an ostensibly democratic society like the United States of America, whichever side can generate more votes and elect candidates that agree with them will have more power, and will "win."

Once again, the subjectivist could reply that, like it or not, that's just how things are. Moral judgments are all matters of personal opinion (or expressions of feelings), and the values supported by our laws and customs are not superior (in any strong, objective sense) to those values we label deviant.

Moral disagreement *could*, in fact, always be a power struggle, and is only ever resolved by force (social, or physical). That's possible, but does it seem to be true? Is there nothing more to your value judgments than opinion, or feelings? No way to resolve disagreement than by force? Can we only ever hope to be the most powerful, as opposed to the most right? Is it ever possible for someone to have no power, but nevertheless be *right*? If subjectivism is the best way to understand morality, it truly does require a radical revision of our understanding of morality, a revision that many of you might find untenable.

---

[66] Plato, *Republic*, 338c

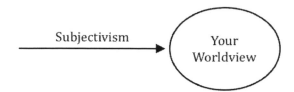

In this second excerpt (from Book 1 of The Republic), Socrates is debating Thrasymachus. Thrasymachus argues that justice is simply the will of the stronger; that "might makes right." Socrates presses Thrasymachus on this, forcing him to acknowledge seeming contradictions and counter-examples, in an attempt to establish that there is a standard of justice that transcends the interests of the stronger, and that injustice is never more "profitable" than justice.

The Republic
Plato

Book I

Socrates - Polemarchus – Thrasymachus

He roared out to the whole company: What folly. Socrates, has taken possession of you all? And why, sillybillies, do you knock under to one another? I say that if you want really to know what justice is, you should not only ask but answer, and you should not seek honour to yourself from the refutation of an opponent, but have your own answer; for there is many a one who can ask and cannot answer. And now I will not have you say that justice is duty or advantage or profit or gain or interest, for this sort of nonsense will not do for me; I must have clearness and accuracy.

I was panic-stricken at his words, and could not look at him without trembling. Indeed I believe that if I had not fixed my eye upon him, I should have been struck dumb: but when I saw his fury rising, I looked at him first, and was therefore able to reply to him.

Thrasymachus, I said, with a quiver, don't be hard upon us. Polemarchus and I may have been guilty of a little mistake in the argument, but I can assure you that the error was not intentional. If we were seeking for a piece of gold, you would not imagine that we were 'knocking under to one another,' and so losing our chance of finding it. And why, when we are seeking for justice, a thing more precious than many pieces of gold, do you say that we are weakly yielding to one another and not doing our utmost to get at the truth? Nay, my good friend, we are most willing and anxious to do so, but the fact is that we cannot. And if so, you people who know all things should pity us and not be angry with us.

How characteristic of Socrates! he replied, with a bitter laugh;--that's your ironical style! Did I not foresee--have I not already told you, that whatever he was asked he would refuse to answer, and try irony or any other shuffle, in order that he might avoid answering?

You are a philosopher, Thrasymachus, I replied, and well know that if you ask a person what numbers make up twelve, taking care to prohibit him whom you ask from answering twice six, or three times four, or six times two, or four times three, 'for this sort of nonsense will not do for me,'--then obviously, that is your way of putting the question, no one can answer you. But suppose that he were to retort, 'Thrasymachus, what do you mean? If one of these numbers which you interdict be the true answer to the question, am I falsely to say some other number which is not the right one?--is that your meaning?'--How would you answer him?

Just as if the two cases were at all alike! he said.

Why should they not be? I replied; and even if they are not, but only appear to be so to the person who is asked, ought he not to say what he thinks, whether you and I forbid him or not?

I presume then that you are going to make one of the interdicted answers?

I dare say that I may, notwithstanding the danger, if upon reflection I approve of any of them.

But what if I give you an answer about justice other and better, he said, than any of these? What do you deserve to have done to you?

Done to me!--as becomes the ignorant, I must learn from the wise--that is what I deserve to have done to me.

What, and no payment! a pleasant notion!

I will pay when I have the money, I replied.

Socrates - Thrasymachus - Glaucon

But you have, Socrates, said Glaucon: and you, Thrasymachus, need be under no anxiety about money, for we will all make a contribution for Socrates.

Yes, he replied, and then Socrates will do as he always does--refuse to answer himself, but take and pull to pieces the answer of some one else.

Why, my good friend, I said, how can any one answer who knows, and says that he knows, just nothing; and who, even if he has some faint notions of his own, is told by a man of authority not to utter them? The natural thing is, that the speaker should be some one like yourself who professes to know and can tell what he knows. Will you then kindly answer, for the edification of the company and of myself?

Glaucon and the rest of the company joined in my request and Thrasymachus, as any one might see, was in reality eager to speak; for he thought that he had an excellent answer, and would distinguish himself. But at first he to insist on my answering; at length he consented to begin. Behold, he said, the wisdom of Socrates; he refuses to teach himself, and goes about learning of others, to whom he never even says thank you.

That I learn of others, I replied, is quite true; but that I am ungrateful I wholly deny. Money I have none, and therefore I pay in praise, which is all I have: and how ready I am to praise any one who appears to me to speak well you will very soon find out when you answer; for I expect that you will answer well.

Listen, then, he said; I proclaim that justice is nothing else than the interest of the stronger. And now why do you not me? But of course you won't.

Let me first understand you, I replied. Justice, as you say, is the interest of the stronger. What, Thrasymachus, is the meaning of this? You cannot mean to say that because Polydamas, the pancratiast, is stronger than we are, and finds the eating of beef conducive to his bodily strength, that to eat beef is therefore equally for our good who are weaker than he is, and right and just for us?

That's abominable of you, Socrates; you take the words in the sense which is most damaging to the argument.

Not at all, my good sir, I said; I am trying to understand them; and I wish that you would be a little clearer.

Well, he said, have you never heard that forms of government differ; there are tyrannies, and there are democracies, and there are aristocracies?

Yes, I know.

And the government is the ruling power in each state?

Certainly.

And the different forms of government make laws democratical, aristocratical, tyrannical, with a view to their several interests; and these laws, which are made by them for their own interests, are the justice which they deliver to their subjects, and him who transgresses them they punish as a breaker of the law, and unjust. And that is what I mean when I say that in all states there is the same principle of justice, which is the interest of the government; and as the government must be supposed to have power, the only reasonable conclusion is, that everywhere there is one principle of justice, which is the interest of the stronger.

Now I understand you, I said; and whether you are right or not I will try to discover. But let me remark, that in defining justice you have yourself used the word 'interest' which you forbade me to use. It is true, however, that in your definition the words 'of the stronger' are added.

A small addition, you must allow, he said.

Great or small, never mind about that: we must first enquire whether what you are saying is the truth. Now we are both agreed that justice is interest of some sort, but you go on to say 'of the stronger'; about this addition I am not so sure, and must therefore consider further.

Proceed.

I will; and first tell me, Do you admit that it is just for subjects to obey their rulers?

I do.

But are the rulers of states absolutely infallible, or are they sometimes liable to err?

To be sure, he replied, they are liable to err.

Then in making their laws they may sometimes make them rightly, and sometimes not?

True.

When they make them rightly, they make them agreeably to their interest; when they are mistaken, contrary to their interest; you admit that?

Yes.

And the laws which they make must be obeyed by their subjects,--and that is what you call justice?

Doubtless.

Then justice, according to your argument, is not only obedience to the interest of the stronger but the reverse?

What is that you are saying? he asked.

I am only repeating what you are saying, I believe. But let us consider: Have we not admitted that the rulers may be mistaken about their own interest in what they command, and also that to obey them is justice? Has not that been admitted?

Yes.

Then you must also have acknowledged justice not to be for the interest of the stronger, when the rulers unintentionally command things to be done which are to their own injury. For if, as you say, justice is the obedience which the subject renders to their commands, in that case, O wisest of men, is there any escape from the conclusion that the weaker are commanded to do, not what is for the interest, but what is for the injury of the stronger?

Nothing can be clearer, Socrates, said Polemarchus.

Socrates - Cleitophon - Polemarchus - Thrasymachus

Yes, said Cleitophon, interposing, if you are allowed to be his witness.

But there is no need of any witness, said Polemarchus, for Thrasymachus himself acknowledges that rulers may sometimes command what is not for their own interest, and that for subjects to obey them is justice.

Yes, Polemarchus,--Thrasymachus said that for subjects to do what was commanded by their rulers is just.

Yes, Cleitophon, but he also said that justice is the interest of the stronger, and, while admitting both these propositions, he further acknowledged that the stronger may command the weaker who are his subjects to do what is not for his own interest; whence follows that justice is the injury quite as much as the interest of the stronger.

But, said Cleitophon, he meant by the interest of the stronger what the stronger thought to be his interest,--this was what the weaker had to do; and this was affirmed by him to be justice.

Those were not his words, rejoined Polemarchus.

Socrates - Thrasymachus

Never mind, I replied, if he now says that they are, let us accept his statement. Tell me, Thrasymachus, I said, did you mean by justice what the stronger thought to be his interest, whether really so or not?

Certainly not, he said. Do you suppose that I call him who is mistaken the stronger at the time when he is mistaken?

Yes, I said, my impression was that you did so, when you admitted that the ruler was not infallible but might be sometimes mistaken.

You argue like an informer, Socrates. Do you mean, for example, that he who is mistaken about the sick is a physician in that he is mistaken? or that he who errs in arithmetic or grammar is an arithmetician or grammarian at the me when he is making the mistake, in respect of the mistake? True, we say that the physician or arithmetician or grammarian has made a mistake, but this is only a way of speaking; for the fact is that neither the grammarian nor any other person of skill ever makes a mistake in so far as he is what his name implies; they none of them err unless their skill fails them, and then they cease to be skilled artists. No artist or sage or ruler errs at the time when he is what his name implies; though he is commonly said to err, and I adopted the common mode of speaking. But to be perfectly accurate, since you are such a lover of accuracy, we should say that the ruler, in so far as he is the ruler, is unerring, and, being unerring, always commands that which is for his own interest; and the subject is required to execute his commands; and therefore, as I said at first and now repeat, justice is the interest of the stronger.

Indeed, Thrasymachus, and do I really appear to you to argue like an informer?

Certainly, he replied.

And you suppose that I ask these questions with any design of injuring you in the argument?

Nay, he replied, 'suppose' is not the word--I know it; but you will be found out, and by sheer force of argument you will never prevail.

I shall not make the attempt, my dear man; but to avoid any misunderstanding occurring between us in future, let me ask, in what sense do you speak of a ruler or stronger whose interest, as you were saying, he being the superior, it is just that the inferior should execute--is he a ruler in the popular or in the strict sense of the term?

In the strictest of all senses, he said. And now cheat and play the informer if you can; I ask no quarter at your hands. But you never will be able, never.

And do you imagine, I said, that I am such a madman as to try and cheat, Thrasymachus? I might as well shave a lion.

Why, he said, you made the attempt a minute ago, and you failed.

Enough, I said, of these civilities. It will be better that I should ask you a question: Is the physician, taken in that strict sense of which you are speaking, a healer of the sick or a maker of money? And remember that I am now speaking of the true physician.

A healer of the sick, he replied.

And the pilot--that is to say, the true pilot--is he a captain of sailors or a mere sailor?

A captain of sailors.

The circumstance that he sails in the ship is not to be taken into account; neither is he to be called a sailor; the name pilot by which he is distinguished has nothing to do with sailing, but is significant of his skill and of his authority over the sailors.

Very true, he said.

Now, I said, every art has an interest?

Certainly.

For which the art has to consider and provide?

Yes, that is the aim of art.

And the interest of any art is the perfection of it--this and nothing else?

What do you mean?

I mean what I may illustrate negatively by the example of the body. Suppose you were to ask me whether the body is self-sufficing or has wants, I should reply: Certainly the body has wants; for the body may be ill and require to be cured, and has therefore interests to which the art of medicine ministers; and this is the origin and intention of medicine, as you will acknowledge. Am I not right?

Quite right, he replied.

But is the art of medicine or any other art faulty or deficient in any quality in the same way that the eye may be deficient in sight or the ear fail of hearing, and therefore requires another art to provide for the interests of seeing and hearing--has art in itself, I say, any similar liability to fault or defect, and does every art require another supplementary art to provide for its interests, and that another and another without end? Or have the arts to look only after their own interests? Or have they no need either of themselves or of another?--having no faults or defects, they have no need to correct them, either by the exercise of their own art or of any other; they have only to consider the interest of their subject-matter. For every art remains pure and faultless while remaining true--that is to say, while perfect and unimpaired. Take the words in your precise sense, and tell me whether I am not right."

Yes, clearly.

Then medicine does not consider the interest of medicine, but the interest of the body?

True, he said.

Nor does the art of horsemanship consider the interests of the art of horsemanship, but the interests of the horse; neither do any other arts care for themselves, for they have no needs; they care only for that which is the subject of their art?

True, he said.

But surely, Thrasymachus, the arts are the superiors and rulers of their own subjects?

To this he assented with a good deal of reluctance.

Then, I said, no science or art considers or enjoins the interest of the stronger or superior, but only the interest of the subject and weaker?

He made an attempt to contest this proposition also, but finally acquiesced.

Then, I continued, no physician, in so far as he is a physician, considers his own good in what he prescribes, but the good of his patient; for the true physician is also a ruler having the human body as a subject, and is not a mere money-maker; that has been admitted?

Yes.

And the pilot likewise, in the strict sense of the term, is a ruler of sailors and not a mere sailor?

That has been admitted.

And such a pilot and ruler will provide and prescribe for the interest of the sailor who is under him, and not for his own or the ruler's interest?

He gave a reluctant 'Yes.'

Then, I said, Thrasymachus, there is no one in any rule who, in so far as he is a ruler, considers or enjoins what is for his own interest, but always what is for the interest of his subject or suitable to his art; to that he looks, and that alone he considers in everything which he says and does.

When we had got to this point in the argument, and every one saw that the definition of justice had been completely upset, Thrasymachus, instead of replying to me, said: Tell me, Socrates, have you got a nurse?

Why do you ask such a question, I said, when you ought rather to be answering?

Because she leaves you to snivel, and never wipes your nose: she has not even taught you to know the shepherd from the sheep.

What makes you say that? I replied.

Because you fancy that the shepherd or neatherd fattens of tends the sheep or oxen with a view to their own good and not to the good of himself or his master; and you further imagine that the rulers of states, if they are true rulers, never think of their subjects as sheep, and that they are not studying their own advantage day and night. Oh, no; and so entirely astray are you in your ideas about the just and unjust as not even to know that justice and the just are in reality another's good; that is to say, the interest of the ruler and stronger, and the loss of the subject and servant; and injustice the opposite; for the unjust is lord over the truly simple and just: he is the stronger, and his subjects do what is for his interest, and minister to his happiness, which is very far from being their own. Consider further, most foolish Socrates, that the just is always a loser in comparison with the unjust. First of all, in private contracts: wherever the unjust is the partner of the just you will find that, when the partnership is dissolved, the unjust man has always more and the just less. Secondly, in their dealings with the State: when there is an income tax, the just man will pay more and the unjust less on the same amount of income; and when there is anything to be received the one gains nothing and the other much. Observe also what happens when they take an office; there is the just man neglecting his affairs and perhaps suffering other losses, and getting nothing out of the public, because he is just; moreover he is hated by his friends and acquaintance for refusing to serve them in unlawful ways. But all this is reversed in the case of the unjust man. I am speaking, as before, of injustice on a large scale in which the advantage of the unjust is more apparent; and my meaning will be most clearly seen if we turn to that highest form of injustice in which the criminal is the happiest of men, and the sufferers or those who refuse to do injustice are the most miserable--that is to say tyranny, which by fraud and force takes away the property of others, not little by little but wholesale; comprehending in one, things sacred as well as profane, private and public; for which acts of wrong, if he were detected perpetrating any one of them singly, he would be punished and incur great disgrace--they who do such wrong in particular cases are called robbers of temples, and man-stealers and burglars and swindlers and thieves. But when a man besides taking away the money of the citizens has made slaves of them, then, instead of these names of reproach, he is termed happy and blessed, not only by the citizens but by all who hear of his having achieved the consummation of injustice. For mankind censure injustice, fearing that they may be the victims of it and not because they shrink from committing it. And thus, as I have shown, Socrates, injustice, when on a sufficient scale, has more strength and freedom and mastery than justice; and, as I said at first, justice is the interest of the stronger, whereas injustice is a man's own profit and interest.

Thrasymachus, when he had thus spoken, having, like a bathman, deluged our ears with his words, had a mind to go away. But the company would not let him; they insisted that he should remain and defend his position; and I myself added my own humble request that he would not leave us. Thrasymachus, I said to him, excellent man, how suggestive are your remarks! And are you going to run away before you have fairly taught or learned whether they are true or not? Is the attempt to determine the way of man's life so small a matter in your eyes--to determine how life may be passed by each one of us to the greatest advantage?

And do I differ from you, he said, as to the importance of the enquiry?

You appear rather, I replied, to have no care or thought about us, Thrasymachus--whether we live better or worse from not knowing what you say you know, is to you a matter of indifference. Prithee, friend, do not keep your knowledge to yourself; we are a large party; and any benefit which you confer upon us will be amply rewarded. For my own part I openly declare that I am not convinced, and that I do not believe injustice to be more gainful than justice, even if uncontrolled and allowed to have free play. For, granting that there may be an unjust man who is able to commit injustice either by fraud or force, still this does not convince me of the superior advantage of injustice, and there may be others who are in the same predicament with myself. Perhaps we may be wrong; if so, you in your wisdom should convince us that we are mistaken in preferring justice to injustice.

And how am I to convince you, he said, if you are not already convinced by what I have just said; what more can I do for you? Would you have me put the proof bodily into your souls?

Heaven forbid! I said; I would only ask you to be consistent; or, if you change, change openly and let there be no deception. For I must remark, Thrasymachus, if you will recall what was previously said, that although you began by defining the true physician in an exact sense, you did not observe a like exactness when speaking of the shepherd; you thought that the shepherd as a shepherd tends the sheep not with a view to their own good, but like a mere diner or banqueter with a view to the pleasures of the table; or, again, as a trader for sale in the market, and not as a shepherd. Yet surely the art of the shepherd is concerned only with the good of his subjects; he has only to provide the best for them, since the perfection of the art is already ensured whenever all the requirements of it are satisfied. And that was what I was saying just now about the ruler. I conceived that the art of the ruler, considered as ruler, whether in a state or in private life, could only regard the good of his flock or subjects; whereas you seem to think that the rulers in states, that is to say, the true rulers, like being in authority.

Think! Nay, I am sure of it.

Then why in the case of lesser offices do men never take them willingly without payment, unless under the idea that they govern for the advantage not of themselves but of others? Let me ask you a question: Are not the several arts different, by reason of their each having a separate function? And, my dear illustrious friend, do say what you think, that we may make a little progress.

Yes, that is the difference, he replied.

And each art gives us a particular good and not merely a general one--medicine, for example, gives us health; navigation, safety at sea, and so on?

Yes, he said.

And the art of payment has the special function of giving pay: but we do not confuse this with other arts, any more than the art of the pilot is to be confused with the art of medicine, because the health of the pilot may be improved by a sea voyage. You would not be inclined to say, would you, that navigation is the art of medicine, at least if we are to adopt your exact use of language?

Certainly not.

Or because a man is in good health when he receives pay you would not say that the art of payment is medicine?

I should say not.

Nor would you say that medicine is the art of receiving pay because a man takes fees when he is engaged in healing?

Certainly not.

And we have admitted, I said, that the good of each art is specially confined to the art?

Yes.

Then, if there be any good which all artists have in common, that is to be attributed to something of which they all have the common use?

True, he replied.

And when the artist is benefited by receiving pay the advantage is gained by an additional use of the art of pay, which is not the art professed by him?

He gave a reluctant assent to this.

Then the pay is not derived by the several artists from their respective arts. But the truth is, that while the art of medicine gives health, and the art of the builder builds a house, another art attends them which is the art of pay. The various arts may be doing their own business and benefiting that over which they preside, but would the artist receive any benefit from his art unless he were paid as well?

I suppose not.

But does he therefore confer no benefit when he works for nothing?

Certainly, he confers a benefit.

Then now, Thrasymachus, there is no longer any doubt that neither arts nor governments provide for their own interests; but, as we were before saying, they rule and provide for the interests of their subjects who are the weaker and not the stronger--to their good they attend and not to the good of the superior.

And this is the reason, my dear Thrasymachus, why, as I was just now saying, no one is willing to govern; because no one likes to take in hand the reformation of evils which are not his concern without remuneration. For, in the execution of his work, and in giving his orders to another, the true artist does not regard his own interest, but always that of his subjects; and therefore in order that rulers may be willing to rule, they must be paid in one of three modes of payment: money, or honour, or a penalty for refusing.

Socrates - Glaucon

What do you mean, Socrates? said Glaucon. The first two modes of payment are intelligible enough, but what the penalty is I do not understand, or how a penalty can be a payment.

You mean that you do not understand the nature of this payment which to the best men is the great inducement to rule? Of course you know that ambition and avarice are held to be, as indeed they are, a disgrace?

Very true.

And for this reason, I said, money and honour have no attraction for them; good men do not wish to be openly demanding payment for governing and so to get the name of hirelings, nor by secretly helping themselves out of the public revenues to get the name of thieves. And not being ambitious they do not care about honour. Wherefore necessity must be laid upon them, and they must be induced to serve from the fear of punishment. And this, as I imagine, is the reason why the forwardness to take office, instead of waiting to be compelled, has been deemed dishonourable. Now the worst part of the punishment is that he who refuses to rule is liable to be ruled by one who is worse than himself. And the fear of this, as I conceive, induces the good to take office, not because they would, but because they cannot help--not under the idea that they are going to have any benefit or enjoyment themselves, but as a necessity, and because they are not able to commit the task of ruling to any one who is better than themselves, or indeed as good. For there is reason to think that if a city were composed entirely of good men, then to avoid office would be as much an object of contention as to obtain office is at present; then we should have plain proof that the true ruler is not meant by nature to regard his own interest, but that of his subjects; and every one who knew this would choose rather to receive a benefit from another than to have the trouble of conferring one. So far am I from agreeing with Thrasymachus that justice is the interest of the stronger. This latter question need not be further discussed at present; but when Thrasymachus says that the life of the unjust is more advantageous than that of the just, his new statement appears to me to be of a far more serious character. Which of us has spoken truly? And which sort of life, Glaucon, do you prefer?

I for my part deem the life of the just to be the more advantageous, he answered.

Did you hear all the advantages of the unjust which Thrasymachus was rehearsing?

Yes, I heard him, he replied, but he has not convinced me.

Then shall we try to find some way of convincing him, if we can, that he is saying what is not true?

Most certainly, he replied.

If, I said, he makes a set speech and we make another recounting all the advantages of being just, and he answers and we rejoin, there must be a numbering and measuring of the goods which are claimed on either side, and in the end we shall want judges to decide; but if we proceed in our enquiry as we lately did, by making admissions to one another, we shall unite the offices of judge and advocate in our own persons.

Very good, he said.

And which method do I understand you to prefer? I said.

That which you propose.

Well, then, Thrasymachus, I said, suppose you begin at the beginning and answer me. You say that perfect injustice is more gainful than perfect justice?

Socrates - Glaucon - Thrasymachus

Yes, that is what I say, and I have given you my reasons.

And what is your view about them? Would you call one of them virtue and the other vice?

Certainly.

I suppose that you would call justice virtue and injustice vice?

What a charming notion! So likely too, seeing that I affirm injustice to be profitable and justice not.

What else then would you say?

The opposite, he replied.

And would you call justice vice?

No, I would rather say sublime simplicity.

Then would you call injustice malignity?

No; I would rather say discretion.

And do the unjust appear to you to be wise and good?

Yes, he said; at any rate those of them who are able to be perfectly unjust, and who have the power of subduing states and nations; but perhaps you imagine me to be talking of cutpurses.

Even this profession if undetected has advantages, though they are not to be compared with those of which I was just now speaking.

I do not think that I misapprehend your meaning, Thrasymachus, I replied; but still I cannot hear without amazement that you class injustice with wisdom and virtue, and justice with the opposite.

Certainly I do so class them.

Now, I said, you are on more substantial and almost unanswerable ground; for if the injustice which you were maintaining to be profitable had been admitted by you as by others to be vice and deformity, an answer might have been given to you on received principles; but now I perceive that you will call injustice honourable and strong, and to the unjust you will attribute all the qualities which were attributed by us before to the just, seeing that you do not hesitate to rank injustice with wisdom and virtue.

You have guessed most infallibly, he replied.

Then I certainly ought not to shrink from going through with the argument so long as I have reason to think that you, Thrasymachus, are speaking your real mind; for I do believe that you are now in earnest and are not amusing yourself at our expense.

I may be in earnest or not, but what is that to you?--to refute the argument is your business.

Very true, I said; that is what I have to do: But will you be so good as answer yet one more question? Does the just man try to gain any advantage over the just?

Far otherwise; if he did would not be the simple, amusing creature which he is.

And would he try to go beyond just action?

He would not.

And how would he regard the attempt to gain an advantage over the unjust; would that be considered by him as just or unjust?

He would think it just, and would try to gain the advantage; but he would not be able.

Whether he would or would not be able, I said, is not to the point. My question is only whether the just man, while refusing to have more than another just man, would wish and claim to have more than the unjust?

Yes, he would.

And what of the unjust--does he claim to have more than the just man and to do more than is just.

Of course, he said, for he claims to have more than all men.

And the unjust man will strive and struggle to obtain more than the unjust man or action, in order that he may have more than all?

True.

We may put the matter thus, I said--the just does not desire more than his like but more than his unlike, whereas the unjust desires more than both his like and his unlike?

Nothing, he said, can be better than that statement.

And the unjust is good and wise, and the just is neither?

Good again, he said.

And is not the unjust like the wise and good and the just unlike them?

Of course, he said, he who is of a certain nature, is like those who are of a certain nature; he who is not, not.

Each of them, I said, is such as his like is?

Certainly, he replied.

Very good, Thrasymachus, I said; and now to take the case of the arts: you would admit that one man is a musician and another not a musician?

Yes.

And which is wise and which is foolish?

Clearly the musician is wise, and he who is not a musician is foolish.

And he is good in as far as he is wise, and bad in as far as he is foolish?

Yes.

And you would say the same sort of thing of the physician?

Yes.

And do you think, my excellent friend, that a musician when he adjusts the lyre would desire or claim to exceed or go beyond a musician in the tightening and loosening the strings?

I do not think that he would.

But he would claim to exceed the non-musician?

Of course.

And what would you say of the physician? In prescribing meats and drinks would he wish to go beyond another physician or beyond the practice of medicine?

He would not.

But he would wish to go beyond the non-physician?

Yes.

And about knowledge and ignorance in general; see whether you think that any man who has knowledge ever would wish to have the choice of saying or doing more than another man who has knowledge. Would he not rather say or do the same as his like in the same case?

That, I suppose, can hardly be denied.

And what of the ignorant? would he not desire to have more than either the knowing or the ignorant?

I dare say.

And the knowing is wise?

Yes.

And the wise is good?

True.

Then the wise and good will not desire to gain more than his like, but more than his unlike and opposite?

I suppose so.

Whereas the bad and ignorant will desire to gain more than both?

Yes.

But did we not say, Thrasymachus, that the unjust goes beyond both his like and unlike? Were not these your words? They were.

They were.

And you also said that the lust will not go beyond his like but his unlike?

Yes.

Then the just is like the wise and good, and the unjust like the evil and ignorant?

That is the inference.

And each of them is such as his like is?

That was admitted.

Then the just has turned out to be wise and good and the unjust evil and ignorant.

Thrasymachus made all these admissions, not fluently, as I repeat them, but with extreme reluctance; it was a hot summer's day, and the perspiration poured from him in torrents; and then I saw what I had never seen before, Thrasymachus blushing. As we were now agreed that justice was virtue and wisdom, and injustice vice and ignorance, I proceeded to another point:

Well, I said, Thrasymachus, that matter is now settled; but were we not also saying that injustice had strength; do you remember?

Yes, I remember, he said, but do not suppose that I approve of what you are saying or have no answer; if however I were to answer, you would be quite certain to accuse me of haranguing; therefore either permit me to have my say out, or if you would rather ask, do so, and I will answer 'Very good,' as they say to story-telling old women, and will nod 'Yes' and 'No.'

Certainly not, I said, if contrary to your real opinion.

Yes, he said, I will, to please you, since you will not let me speak. What else would you have?

Nothing in the world, I said; and if you are so disposed I will ask and you shall answer.

Proceed.

Then I will repeat the question which I asked before, in order that our examination of the relative nature of justice and injustice may be carried on regularly. A statement was made that injustice is stronger and more powerful than justice, but now justice, having been identified with wisdom and virtue, is easily shown to be stronger than injustice, if injustice is ignorance; this can no longer be questioned by any one. But I want to view the matter, Thrasymachus, in a different way: You would not deny that a state may be unjust and may be unjustly attempting to enslave other states, or may have already enslaved them, and may be holding many of them in subjection?

True, he replied; and I will add the best and perfectly unjust state will be most likely to do so.

I know, I said, that such was your position; but what I would further consider is, whether this power which is possessed by the superior state can exist or be exercised without justice.

If you are right in you view, and justice is wisdom, then only with justice; but if I am right, then without justice.

I am delighted, Thrasymachus, to see you not only nodding assent and dissent, but making answers which are quite excellent.

That is out of civility to you, he replied.

You are very kind, I said; and would you have the goodness also to inform me, whether you think that a state, or an army, or a band of robbers and thieves, or any other gang of evil-doers could act at all if they injured one another?

No indeed, he said, they could not.

But if they abstained from injuring one another, then they might act together better?

Yes.

And this is because injustice creates divisions and hatreds and fighting, and justice imparts harmony and friendship; is not that true, Thrasymachus?

I agree, he said, because I do not wish to quarrel with you.

How good of you, I said; but I should like to know also whether injustice, having this tendency to arouse hatred, wherever existing, among slaves or among freemen, will not make them hate one another and set them at variance and render them incapable of common action?

Certainly.

And even if injustice be found in two only, will they not quarrel and fight, and become enemies to one another and to the just.

They will.

And suppose injustice abiding in a single person, would your wisdom say that she loses or that she retains her natural power?

Let us assume that she retains her power.

Yet is not the power which injustice exercises of such a nature that wherever she takes up her abode, whether in a city, in an army, in a family, or in any other body, that body is, to begin with, rendered incapable of united action by reason of sedition and distraction; and does it not become its own enemy and at variance with all that opposes it, and with the just? Is not this the case?

Yes, certainly.

And is not injustice equally fatal when existing in a single person; in the first place rendering him incapable of action because he is not at unity with himself, and in the second place making him an enemy to himself and the just? Is not that true, Thrasymachus?

Yes.

And O my friend, I said, surely the gods are just?

Granted that they are.

But if so, the unjust will be the enemy of the gods, and the just will be their friend?

Feast away in triumph, and take your fill of the argument; I will not oppose you, lest I should displease the company.

Well then, proceed with your answers, and let me have the remainder of my repast. For we have already shown that the just are clearly wiser and better and abler than the unjust, and that the unjust are incapable of common action; nay ing at more, that to speak as we did of men who are evil acting at any time vigorously together, is not strictly true, for if they had been perfectly evil, they would have laid hands upon one another; but it is evident that there must have been some remnant of justice in them, which enabled them to combine; if there had not been they would have injured one another as well as their victims; they were but half--villains in their enterprises; for had they been whole villains, and utterly unjust, they would have been utterly incapable of action. That, as I believe, is the truth of the matter, and not what you said at first. But whether the just have a better and happier life than the unjust is a further question which we also proposed to consider. I think that they have, and for the reasons which to have given; but still I should like to examine further, for no light matter is at stake, nothing less than the rule of human life.

Proceed.

I will proceed by asking a question: Would you not say that a horse has some end?

I should.

And the end or use of a horse or of anything would be that which could not be accomplished, or not so well accomplished, by any other thing?

I do not understand, he said.

Let me explain: Can you see, except with the eye?

Certainly not.

Or hear, except with the ear?

No.

These then may be truly said to be the ends of these organs?

They may.

But you can cut off a vine-branch with a dagger or with a chisel, and in many other ways?

Of course.

And yet not so well as with a pruning-hook made for the purpose?

True.

May we not say that this is the end of a pruning-hook?

We may.

Then now I think you will have no difficulty in understanding my meaning when I asked the question whether the end of anything would be that which could not be accomplished, or not so well accomplished, by any other thing?

I understand your meaning, he said, and assent.

And that to which an end is appointed has also an excellence? Need I ask again whether the eye has an end?

It has.

And has not the eye an excellence?

Yes.

And the ear has an end and an excellence also?

True.

And the same is true of all other things; they have each of them an end and a special excellence?

That is so.

Well, and can the eyes fulfil their end if they are wanting in their own proper excellence and have a defect instead?

How can they, he said, if they are blind and cannot see?

You mean to say, if they have lost their proper excellence, which is sight; but I have not arrived at that point yet. I would rather ask the question more generally, and only enquire whether the things which fulfil their ends fulfil them by their own proper excellence, and fall of fulfilling them by their own defect?

Certainly, he replied.

I might say the same of the ears; when deprived of their own proper excellence they cannot fulfil their end?

True.

And the same observation will apply to all other things?

I agree.

Well; and has not the soul an end which nothing else can fulfil? for example, to superintend and command and deliberate and the like. Are not these functions proper to the soul, and can they rightly be assigned to any other?

To no other.

And is not life to be reckoned among the ends of the soul?

Assuredly, he said.

And has not the soul an excellence also?

Yes.

And can she or can she not fulfil her own ends when deprived of that excellence?

She cannot.

Then an evil soul must necessarily be an evil ruler and superintendent, and the good soul a good ruler?

Yes, necessarily.

And we have admitted that justice is the excellence of the soul, and injustice the defect of the soul?

That has been admitted.

Then the just soul and the just man will live well, and the unjust man will live ill?

That is what your argument proves.

And he who lives well is blessed and happy, and he who lives ill the reverse of happy?

Certainly.

Then the just is happy, and the unjust miserable?

So be it.

But happiness and not misery is profitable.

Of course.

Then, my blessed Thrasymachus, injustice can never be more profitable than justice.

Let this, Socrates, he said, be your entertainment at the Bendidea.

For which I am indebted to you, I said, now that you have grown gentle towards me and have left off scolding. Nevertheless, I have not been well entertained; but that was my own fault and not yours. As an epicure snatches a taste of every dish which is successively brought to table, he not having allowed himself time to enjoy the one before, so have I gone from one subject to another without having discovered what I sought at first, the nature of justice. I left that enquiry and turned away to consider whether justice is virtue and wisdom or evil and folly; and when there arose a further question about the comparative advantages of justice and injustice, I could not refrain from passing on to that. And the result of the whole discussion has been that I know nothing at all. For I know not what justice is, and therefore I am not likely to know whether it is or is not a virtue, nor can I say whether the just man is happy or unhappy?

Chapter 5: Ethical Relativism

Comprehension questions you should be able to answer after reading this chapter:

1. What makes something morally right or wrong, according to Ethical Relativism?

2. What is meant by an "observation of cultural differences?" Why is this not necessarily identical to Ethical Relativism?

3. Explain Benedict's argument concerning "normality" and "morality." What is she trying to prove? How might someone try to refute her argument?

4. What is the "argument from tolerance" and how does it show a mistaken understanding of Ethical Relativism, if actually used to support ER?

5. Why is it that ER can't require universal toleration or respect for diversity?

6. If ER is true, how would we have to understand cross-cultural comparisons on moral issues?

7. If ER is true, how would we have to understand the moral status of moral reformers, at the time of their reform efforts?

8. Why is the claim that "culture" is a "vague concept" a possible problem for ER?

9. What does James Rachels mean when he suggests that some "cultural differences" are actually just different manifestations/expressions of the same moral values?

10. Why does Rachels think that there are some universal moral values, found in every culture? How does he try to prove this?

11. What are Lewis' criticisms of ER?

Ethical Relativism

Consider the image above. It represents the kinds of judgments and comparisons possible according to Ethical Relativism. No such image was provided for subjectivism, in our previous chapter, since, if subjectivism is true, no comparisons of values are possible anyway—at least not anything other than a "taste test." Ethical Relativism (ER henceforth, for short) does allow some comparisons, some strong moral judgments, but it too is limited, and in very similar ways to subjectivism.

Ethical Relativism operates on just the same assumptions as subjectivism with one notable difference: whereas subjectivism claims that moral judgments are matters of personal opinion, and gain whatever legitimacy they have from the endorsement of the individual, ER claims that morality is a matter of *collective* judgment. What is right and wrong is determined by the prevailing values of a given community. You've probably heard the expression, "when in Rome, do as the Romans do." Assuming this is meant as more than just practical advice, this is an expression of ER.

According to ER, what is morally right and morally wrong is established by the dominant values of a given culture. This allows for moral judgments and comparisons concerning individuals—at least within the same community. The standard we would use for such judgments would be the dominant values of the culture in question. For example, in the United States, an adult male marrying a 9 year-old girl would not merely be considered morally wrong, he would be prosecuted for a sex crime! Thus, because the dominant cultural values of the U.S. frown upon such marriages, it is morally wrong to marry 9 year old girls in the U.S. Not so, elsewhere, however.

Tihun, a 9 year old Ethiopian girl, was arranged to marry a 19 year old Orthodox Church deacon by her father. This is not an aberration. According to UN and Ethiopian statistics, in some parts of Ethiopia almost 90 percent of the local girls are married before age 15 (technically, it is against Ethiopian law to marry anyone under the age of 18, but the punishment is a $12 fine, is rarely enforced, and is generally ignored by the conservative population.). "'In truth, if a girl reaches 13, she is already too old to be married,' declares Nebiyu Melese, 54, Tihun's wiry farmer father. 'I know some people say this is uncivilized. But they don't live here. So how can they judge?'" (As reported By Paul Salopek, Chicago Tribune foreign correspondent, published December 12, 2004)

"How can they judge?" According to ER, we can't—at least not with any special credibility. Because ER claims, like subjectivism, that there is no set of "true" moral values that apply to all people, everywhere, and at all times, there is no objective standard with which to judge the values of a culture. From *within* a given culture, one may (and should) employ the values of that culture, and individuals can (and should) be judged according to those standards. In the U.S., if you marry a 9 year old and I don't, I'm a morally superior person than you are (on that one issue, at least) because my values and behavior are more in harmony with those prescribed by our culture. Outside of our own culture, however, we are in no position to judge.

Why would anyone accept this view? There are several reasons, and not all of them rest on mistakes. One that *does* rest on a mistake, however, involves the *observation of cultural differences* throughout the world.

One need not be especially well-traveled, or cosmopolitan, to know that different cultures have different practices, and (seemingly) different values. Certain examples are obvious. Australian aborigines eat the "witchety grub" and consider it a welcome delicacy. Most Americans would only eat grubs if on a reality TV show. Americans eat meat with reckless abandon (171 pounds per person, in 2011, according to the U.S. Department of Agriculture), but Indian Hindus abstain from eating meat.[67]

It is not only our diets that vary, from one culture to the next. Marriage practices, sexual taboos, notions of masculinity and femininity, notions of "family," clothing practices, funerary practices, and many other activities vary. One need not be a world traveler to know this, just watch PBS or National Geographic.

Some cultural relativists, such as Ruth Benedict, observe these cultural differences, and make something morally significant out of it. Benedict claims that standards of normalcy and deviance vary from one culture to the next.

The above picture shows former President George Herbert Walker Bush ("the Elder") walking hand-in-hand with Saudi King Abdullah. In the United States, this is an interesting event, because in the U.S. it isn't "normal" for grown (heterosexual) men to hold hands. That is, when we see two adult men holding hands, we assume they are homosexual, and that their hand-holding means basically the same thing as

---

[67] "He who desires to augment his own flesh by eating the flesh of other creatures lives in misery in whatever species he may take his birth." (Mahabharat 115.47—for those unfamiliar, the Mahabharat is one of two major Sanskrit epics of ancient India. It is also an important part of Hindu mythology. Thus, quoting sections and verses from the Mahabarat is analogous to quoting from chapter and verse from the Christian Bible.)

when straight men and straight women hold each other's hands. Even for straight allies, men holding hands is seen as a sub-cultural practice for homosexuals—there's been little, if any, infiltration of this practice into the (straight) mainstream culture. The practice, and its meaning, however, is quite different in Saudi culture. Men hold hands as a display of friendship, not as a display of a romantic relationship.

"We" give a "high-five," "they" hold hands.

Americans eat with forks, the Chinese eat with chopsticks.

American men wear pants, traditional Scotsmen wear kilts. Different strokes for different folks....

Most of us are willing to acknowledge that certain practices vary from one culture to the next, and that each is a *legitimate* practice. That is, it's hard to find someone who would claim, in any serious tone, that it's "wrong" to eat with chop-sticks, Chinese or not, and that eating with a fork is the only morally legitimate means to transport food to one's mouth. Benedict goes quite a bit farther than this, though, by claiming not only that "normalcy" varies (legitimately) from one culture to the next, but also that "normalcy" and "morally good" are synonymous terms. In other words, when we say that something is morally good, what we're really saying is that the practice in question is what we consider "normal," and if we label something to be morally bad, that's just another way of saying it's "weird." A slight bit of logic allows us to see the implication of this.

1. What is considered "normal" varies (legitimately) across cultures.
2. Therefore, there is no single standard of normalcy for humankind.
3. "Normal" and "morally good" are synonymous terms.
4. Therefore, there is no single standard of moral goodness for humankind.

A few points require immediate attention.

1. It is far from obvious that "normalcy" and "morality" are, in fact, synonymous terms—at least not across the whole range of practices deemed either normal/deviant, or good/bad.

For example, it's possible that there are practices deemed normal or abnormal that we don't regard as having any moral significance whatsoever. Talking to oneself in public is seen as "weird" in the U.S. culture, and is often assumed to be a sign of mental illness, but it's not obvious that it would also be considered morally wrong. Piercing one's face is still considered "extreme," despite the increasing popularity of body piercings, but it's not easy to find someone who would claim that those who do so have committed a moral offense.

Similarly, it's not obvious that we would all agree that certain practices, deemed immoral, are of the same type as those we also deem "abnormal." Child-rape is certainly considered deviant, and perceived as "weird," but the act seems to be more than just "weird." Intentionally urinating on oneself in public is weird. Very weird, in fact. Is raping a child just very, very weird? Very, very, very weird? Or, are some acts qualitatively different, such that they no longer fit into our categories or normalcy/deviancy, but require their own (distinct) category: good/evil?

If we consider the Venn diagram below, it seems possible that certain actions (e.g., extensive facial piercings) might be considered "abnormal/deviant" within a community, but *not* considered immoral. In fact, every time I survey my students and ask them if having facial piercings is morally wrong, almost no one ever says "yes"—though nearly everyone acknowledges that it is outside the "norm." Other actions might be considered "immoral," but are not abnormal in the sense of unusual or atypical. For example, pre-marital sex is the "norm" in the United States. The overwhelming majority of Americans has sex before marriage, across most demographic groups—but many (even if grudgingly) consider pre-marital sex to be (technically) morally wrong. Here we have an example of something "normal" (as in "common") but possibly immoral. Some actions, though, are generally considered to be *both* abnormal *and* immoral. Pedophilia is certainly outside the norm, but also widely regarded as morally wrong.

On the "positive" side, certain actions are "normal" in the United States (e.g., shaking hands as a form of greeting), but without necessarily attributing any moral "goodness" to the act. Other actions are regarded as possibly morally good (e.g., abstaining from pre-marital sex), but are not the norm. Still other actions might be regarded as both the "norm" as well as being morally good (e.g., honesty). We can dispute particular examples, but the key question to ask is whether this preceding discussion, in general, seems plausible? If the relationship depicted in the Venn diagram seems plausible, then it would indicate that "normal" and "moral," while related, are *not* synonymous terms.

"Normal/abnormal" v. "Moral/immoral"(?)

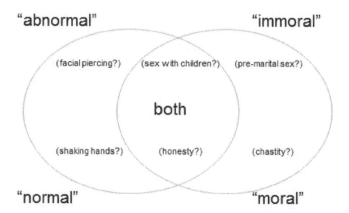

2. As James Rachels has argued, the mere fact of difference does not mean that there are no values that apply to all people everywhere. The observation of cultural differences is consistent with *both* ER *and* objective approaches to ethics, therefore the fact of cultural differences is not automatically support for ER.

In cases of difference, a relativist will conclude that there are no universal values. Someone who believes morality is objective will look at those same differences and conclude that at least one of the cultures is *mistaken*.

Consider an analogy: if two people come up with two different answers to the same math problem, we would be foolish to leap to the conclusion that both of them are correct, or (more foolish still) that there is no "correct" answer at all. Much more plausibly, we would infer that at least one of those persons (and maybe both!) is mistaken and came up with the wrong answer.

Similarly, just because two different cultures come up with two different "answers" to the same (moral) question, that doesn't necessarily mean that both cultures are equally morally correct or that no "correct" answer exists. It's possible that one culture is mistaken. It might be difficult to discern who is in the right, but there is nothing logically inconsistent with looking at two cultures, one of which prosecutes the rapist when a woman is raped, the other of which stones the woman to death for adultery, noting the different responses, and concluding that one of them is in error. My own vote is against stoning rape survivors. What's the point? Simply this: the fact of cultural differences, by itself, is not necessarily an indicator of the truth of ER.

Cultural differences alone do not require one to accept ER, but there might well be other reasons to do so. One reason is a general skepticism that a universal moral code could ever be agreed upon. After all, that there is deep division on numerous moral issues (e.g., abortion, the death penalty, homosexuality, etc.) is obvious. One might think that agreement will never be reached and take that as a sign that no such set of universal values could exist. That might be true, but it's a hasty conclusion.

Even if humanity never does come to consensus on the requirements of morality, that might say far more about our own limitations than about moral values. Humans might never fully understand the laws of Nature, or the true origin of the universe, but that doesn't mean that there is no explanation, no right answer—just none that *we* can reach. Moreover, even if it's true that we can never know, with certainty, the truth concerning our moral obligations, that doesn't mean that we can't *progress towards* the truth, that we can't come ever closer to a full and accurate ethical theory.

One additional reason someone might embrace ER is a result of rejecting its perceived alternative: objective ethical theories.[68] This approach is presumably well-intentioned, and rooted in a recognition that, for most of recorded history, "tribes" have always assumed their own moral superiority over their neighbors.

In the West, we have a long and bloody history of European (and eventually, American) powers taking notice of a group of people, taking note of how different those people are, judging that to be different is to be wrong and in need of correction, and then using that judgment to justify campaigns of invasion, colonization, exploitation, and even genocide.

If "savages" engage in morally inferior practices, then one is doing them a "favor" by "correcting" them. After all, they're being made "better." Since *our* way is the only *right* way, they should be made to dress like us, marry like us, speak like us, worship like us, govern like us, and so on.

Many of us, looking back on history, and even on contemporary policies and practices, are repulsed by the cruelties and atrocities that were perpetrated by virtue of the self-righteous assumption of one's own moral superiority. If the inspiration for such actions is the belief that there is one set of true moral values (undoubtedly, one's own!), then a rejection of such an assumption might prevent such actions. ER is seen

---

[68] The argument from tolerance was developed by the anthropologist Melville Herskovits. Cynics might call this the "liberal guilt argument" for ER.

as the tolerance-producing alternative to objective ethics, and is sometimes, for that reason, embraced. This "argument from tolerance" may be formulated as follows:

The Argument from Tolerance

1. If morality is relative to its culture, then there is no independent basis for criticizing the moral values of any other culture.
2. If there is no independent way of criticizing any other culture, then we ought to be tolerant of the moral values of other cultures.
3. Morality is relative to culture.
4. Therefore, (by 1-3) we ought to be tolerant of the moral values of other cultures.

If this argument works, from Ethical Relativism we may derive that we ought to be tolerant of other cultures.

Tolerance is a good thing, right? Not necessarily! Ask yourself this question: is there any limit as to what should be tolerated? And what does it even mean to be "tolerant?" Does it mean to let people do whatever they want? Does it allow for judgment, but not intervention? Does it just mean we have to be "polite" when judging others? Which of the following should be (or should have been) "tolerated?" What would it mean to "tolerate" such practices?

- South African apartheid.
- Nazi mass-extermination of Jews.
- The Armenian genocide perpetrated by Turkey?
- The Cherokee "Trail of Tears?"
- The thousands of African-Americans lynched in the American South?[69]
- The internment of Japanese-Americans during WWII?
- Female Genital Mutilation that currently affects approximately 2 million girls each year?
- The harvesting of organs from executed criminals in China?
- Saddam Hussein's gassing of Kurdish villages?
- Beheadings and crucifixion of "infidels" by ISIS?

(If you don't know what some of these examples refer to, look them up!)

A first problem with the argument from tolerance is that it's not at all obvious that tolerance is always a good thing. It certainly seems to be the case that some practices, and some values, should *not* be tolerated. Which values fit into that category will be subject to spirited debate, of course, but it does seem that such a category exists.

A second problem with the argument from tolerance is a problem of internal consistency. Premise 1 seems uncontroversial, but premise 2 requires a close examination.

Premise 2 claims that "we" ought to be tolerant. Two words are significant: "we,"

---

[69] At least 3,400 from 1882-1968.

and "ought." Notice that "ought" is a value-term. To say that we ought to do something is to make a prescriptive claim. We *should* be tolerant. It's *good* to be tolerant. It's *right* to be tolerant. Who, exactly, are "we" who are being told that "we" *ought* to be tolerant? There are three possibilities:

1. "We" are all of humanity—all people, in all places, at all times.
2. "We" are people from the same culture as the person making the argument.
3. "We" are people from a different culture than that of the person making the argument.

No matter which is intended (1-3), a problem emerges. Let's work backwards. If (3), then we are from a *different* culture than that of the person urging us to be tolerant. Why should we listen to her? Her values might be right for her own people, but they don't apply to us. If ER is true, we should heed the moral requirements of our own culture, and not hers.

If (2), then she is speaking to us as a peer. Now we must figure out what the values of our (shared) culture happen to be. Is tolerance, in fact, a dominant value in our culture? If so, then we *should*, in fact, be tolerant (whatever that means), but *not because of her argument*. We should be tolerant because that is what our cultural values prescribe. She's merely "preaching to the choir."

On the other hand, what if our culture is not tolerant? What if we come from an imperialist culture that believes that other cultures' values are savage and wrong? In that case, according to ER, we should be *in*tolerant! In fact, that tolerance-promoting troublemaker is actively encouraging us to be immoral by going against the values of our culture. This is something no self-aware, self-respecting cultural relativist could prescribe!

If (1), then she is claiming that there is at least one value (tolerance) that applies to all people, everywhere, at all times. That flatly contradicts a central feature of ER: namely, that there are *no* values that apply to all people, everywhere, at all times. She has contradicted herself and supplied the counter-example to her own theory. How embarrassing for her!

None of this means that a cultural relativist cannot, or will not, be tolerant. Instead, it simply demonstrates that tolerance is not a necessary consequence of ER. Indeed, anyone who alleges that ER *does* require, or even recommend, toleration reveals that he simply has not correctly understood ER!

Consider an analogy: suppose I were to tell you that my favorite thing about soccer (in America, soccer—football everywhere else in the world) is the fact that any player, at any time, can pick up the ball with his or her hands and run with it.

If you know anything about soccer, you immediately realize that I do not, given the fact that most players are *not* allowed to use their hands during the game. My comment is no commentary on soccer, but rather on my own *misunderstanding* of soccer.

Similarly, if someone tells me how ER requires (or even promotes) tolerance or respect for diversity, I immediately realize that this is no commentary on ER, but rather an indicator of that person's *misunderstanding* of ER.

According to ER, you should be tolerant only if that is what your culture demands, and if a culture is intolerant, that culture is not "wrong" for being so. This indicates a very important feature of ER: *ER does not take a stance on any moral issue whatsoever.* Instead, it provides a decision-making procedure with regard to the moral rightness or wrongness of whatever example we might entertain: "ask your culture."

This is simple to illustrate. According to ER, all moral values are relative to a particular culture. Therefore, ER (itself) does not indicate that abortion is morally acceptable (or unacceptable). Instead, it claims that the rightness or wrongness of abortion will depend upon the culture in question. In some cultures, abortion is morally wrong, but in others cultures it is acceptable. Similarly, ER takes no stance on the death penalty. The death penalty will be morally acceptable in some cultures, and unacceptable in others. Slavery is neither morally right nor wrong according to ER— but it will be morally right (or wrong) in *particular cultures*. So, too, with homosexual sex acts, human sacrifice, eating meat, pre-marital sex, etc.

Toleration and/or respect for diversity are moral values like *any other* just mentioned. ER does not endorse, or reject, toleration or respect for diversity. Instead, according to ER, the rightness or wrongness of toleration will depend upon the culture in question. ER does not—and can't—require toleration, though a particular culture *might*.

One final time, the preceding discussion is neither an indictment of ER, nor of toleration, but is simply meant to illustrate that the idea that ER somehow requires or promotes toleration is a *myth*. There might well be good reasons to endorse ER as an ethical theory, but the belief that it requires or promotes tolerance should not be one of them.

Possible Problems with ER

We now know that ER claims that all moral values are relative to particular cultures, and we have considered several reasons why someone might think this interpretation is correct (e.g., a general skepticism concerning universal moral values, a (misguided) association of ER with tolerance, or Benedict's argument concerning normalcy and morality). As we have done with both PE and subjectivism, we will now consider some reasons to reject ER, and enable you to make your own assessment.

Ultimately, ER is potentially vulnerable to the very same criticisms that were leveled against subjectivism, but adjusted to reflect ER's emphasis on collective values as opposed to personal opinion. Also, just as with subjectivism, most of these possible problems amount to "intuition tests" in which a new piece of information (an implication of ER) is evaluated against your worldview.

Possible problem #1: ER allows no objective stance from which to evaluate other cultures' values.

Much as subjectivism does not allow moral comparisons of individuals (beyond expressions of our own personal opinions), ER is incapable of strong cross-cultural comparisons.

Consider the Taliban. Prior to the U.S. led overthrow of the Taliban (2001), the laws and practices of Afghanistan drew considerable international criticism. Here are a few examples:

- Public executions, including stonings, were common.
- Kite-flying (a "frivolous" activity) was outlawed.
- TV, music, and the internet were banned (to remove "decadent" Western influences).
- Men were *required* to wear beards.
- Girls were forbidden to attend school.
- Women could not be examined by male doctors.
- Women could no longer work *as* doctors (think about what these last two mean for women's health care under the Taliban).
- Women could not leave the home without a male escort.
- "Idolatrous" art was destroyed--such as the giant statues of Buddha (constructed 2nd and 3rd centuries A.D., destroyed in 2001).

Much more recently (and similarly), the practices of ISIS (or ISIL)[70] have drawn international criticism. Public executions, including stonings and crucifixions occur "daily" in ISIS-controlled parts of Syria, women are lashed if not sufficiently "covered," international journalists are beheaded on camera, and (interestingly enough, given the context of this book) philosophy has been banned as a form of blasphemy.[71]

If ER is true, then the practices of the Taliban (or ISIS) are neither better nor worse than those of any other culture—just "different." Of course, the U.S. overthrow of the Taliban could not be condemned either, as long as it was consistent with the dominant values of U.S. culture. Moreover, neither the Taliban (or ISIS) nor the U.S.-led overthrow could be judged by other cultures—after all, they have no privileged position from which to judge the U.S. any more than the U.S. has a privileged position from which to judge the Taliban.

Perhaps this is accurate, and no community is ever in a position to judge another. If so, though, we must face a radical revision of our common practices, since we do, in fact, tend to condemn cultures such as Nazi Germany, the Taliban, and apartheid-era South Africa. Many countries condemn the actions of ISIS. Is there *any* behavior, *any* cultural practice, from *any* period in human history that you think is just plain *wrong*, period? Slavery? Human sacrifice? Child rape? Genocide? Anything at all?

If there is even one act, practice, or behavior that you think is always morally wrong, regardless of time, place, or opinion, you have an intuitive disagreement with ER. If you think condemnation that is more than a mere expression of collective taste is possible, then you would have reason to reject ER.

Possible problem #2: Moral reformers are always morally "wrong."

According to ER, the right thing to do is, by definition, whatever one's culture tells one to do. Since the dominant values of one's culture are the ultimate arbiter of morality (the "supreme court" of morality, as it were), there is nothing to which one

---

[70] "Islamic State of Iraq and al-Sham," or the "Islamic State of Iraq and the Levant," respectively.
[71]http://www.cnn.com/2014/09/04/world/meast/isis-inside-look/index.html?hpt=hp_t1

can appeal that is "higher" than one's culture. You can never go "over the head" of your culture in the event that you disagree with its values. So where does that leave reformers?

A reformer, by definition, is trying to change her culture. All reformers detect something about their culture that they think is morally wrong, or unjust, and they try to change it. According to ER, though, *it is not the individual's judgment* that establishes what is right and wrong; *it is the collective judgment of the entire culture as expressed in its dominant values.*

By definition, then, someone who is trying to change the values of the culture is trying to change what is "right." That makes them *wrong*, doesn't it?

Both Martin Luther King Jr. and Rosa Parks were icons of the American Civil Rights era. Both fought against racism and segregation laws. Both were also criminals, by definition, since they deliberately disobeyed segregation laws, and both were arrested for their "offenses." Both believed that the values of their culture, at the time, were wrong, and in need of correction. But who were they to challenge the values of their culture? By offering a set of values different from that of their culture, at the time, weren't they morally in the wrong, by definition? And yet, don't we tend to have precisely the *opposite* view of reformers, at least in retrospect?

When Rosa Parks died in 2005, her body was displayed in the Capitol Rotunda. The tribute, which requires an act of Congress, has taken place only 31 times in this country's history. Those receiving this rare honor include President Abraham Lincoln and several other Presidents, eight members of Congress, and two Capitol police officers slain at their posts, among a handful of others.[72] President Bill Clinton delivered a eulogy for her. In it, he said that she made us a "better people, and a better country."

If ER is true, what could it mean that she made us "better?" The segregationist values prior to the Civil Rights Movement were not "wrong," after all—just "wrong" given our *current* dominant values.

Much as individuals cannot get morally better or worse, in any strong sense, from a subjectivist perspective, neither can cultures get morally better or worse over time from the perspective of ER. Cultures become "different," but their former values were not "wrong;" they were "right," at the time. This aspect is especially fascinating considering how often proponents of ER condemn the "imperialist" practices of their own culture! If ER is true, on what grounds can they complain about their own culture's values?

In fairness, the advocate of ER could reply in the following way: "when we complain about our own culture, our complaint is that the practices of our culture are not consistent with its values. So, too, with reformers in general. What reformers do is appeal to the already existing values of their culture that are not being honored, to some extent."

Using the example of the Civil Rights Movement, a relativist could say that King and others appealed to the values of equality, brotherhood, freedom, and dignity that were already found in Christianity and in the political philosophy that shaped our government and society. When King advocated equality, he was not introducing some

---

[72] If you are interested in a full and up-to-date listing, check the following URL: http://www.aoc.gov/nations-stage/lying-state

new, alien value into the culture, but was simply pointing out that U.S. society was not living up to its very own ideals, by virtue of the rampant discrimination at the time. Indeed, the advocate of ER could argue that had those basic values of equality, freedom, opportunity, and the like not already been present in the culture, the Movement could have never taken hold and been successful. *If* that's true, then Civil Rights activists were not "in the wrong," but were, instead, champions of the actual cultural values of the United States. Historians will be better prepared to address this issue, but it seems (to me) overly generous to think that racism and segregationism were not expressions of the dominant values at the time, considering how pervasive and enduring racism, and its legacy, has proven to be. Anti-"race-mixing" laws were not overturned by the Supreme Court until 1967. Lest one think such laws were regional only, found in the deep South alone, bear in mind that California's anti-miscegenation law was not overturned by a California Supreme Court until 1948, a mere seven years prior to the beginning of the Civil Rights Movement.

Let us suppose, however, for the sake of argument, that interpreting successful reform movements (such as the Civil Rights Movement, for example) as cases where reformers were actually appealing to pre-existing cultural values is plausible. This approach nevertheless seems limited, however, in that it would appear that a culture could never undergo a radical transformation from within. Social change would always need to be somehow consistent with already existing and honored values. Any radical change would have to be understood in terms of an "invasion" of a foreign value, and in terms of that initially-"wrong" value "vanquishing" and ultimately replacing the native values, much as a foreign usurper may claim a throne. Small changes might be understood as a somewhat different application of an already dominant value, while major change must come from the outside. Major changes, at the least, and the advocates of major change, would have to be considered "wrong," at the time.

This produces a potentially counter-intuitive evaluation of moral reformers—at least those advocating "major" change. In trying to change the "right" values of their culture, moral reformers are always "wrong." If they succeed, and their own values become dominant later on, they will be hailed as moral visionaries, in retrospect. But, in their own time, they are moral villains.

Perhaps that's just "how it is." We must acknowledge the possibility that our own perception that a culture (including our own) has gotten morally better or worse over time is just an expression of the bias of our own time and place. *We* think segregation laws are wrong because, in our own time, they are considered wrong. Had we been born (Caucasian, presumably) a half-century ago, though, we would have likely thought differently. Perhaps, at the time, we would have been "right."

On the other hand, if you have any strong intuition that cultures really *do* get morally better or worse over time (e.g., that a culture that abandons slavery has become objectively morally better than it had been), and that such judgments are not mere expressions of current collective opinion, then you presumably have a hard time accepting the implications of ER. What is certain is that ER requires a radical revision of our everyday notions of cultural moral progress and regress.

Possible problem #3: "Culture" is a vague concept.

You've perhaps noticed that I've tossed around words like "we" and "our" quite a bit in these past few pages. I've been speaking of U.S. culture, on the reasonably safe assumption that the overwhelming majority of you are Americans, or at least reside in the U.S., but to speak of the U.S. culture as if it were some obvious and monolithic thing is problematic. Just what is a "culture," anyway?

Merriam-Webster defines "culture" as "the customary beliefs, social forms, and material traits of a racial, religious, or social group." This is extraordinarily vague, and maybe even hopelessly so. To see why this is a problem, think of yourself, and your own social context. How do you self-identify, according to the following criteria?

- Race/ethnicity
- National origin
- Gender
- Sexual orientation
- Ability/disability
- Socio-economic status
- Religious affiliation (atheist, agnostic, or secular humanist are each acceptable responses to this)
- Generation (e.g., "baby-boomer," "Gen-X," "Gen-Next.")
- Citizenship status
- State, county, and city of residence
- Group memberships (e.g., fraternal orders, Freemasons, etc.)

This is a partial list, to be sure, but serves to illustrate the possible problem. If you live on a small, remote island in which everyone comes from the same ethnic stock, belongs to the same religious tradition, and shares the same values, the identification of your culture is probably pretty simple. I, however, live in Southern California, and it's hard to imagine a more diverse, pluralistic region than L.A. County. According to the U.S. Census Bureau, in 2010, the following was true of the people of L.A. County:[73]

RACE	People	% American
Indian and Alaska Native	72,828	0.7
Asian	1,346,865	13.7
Filipino	322,110	3.3
Japanese	102,287	1.0
Korean	216,501	2.2
Vietnamese	87,468	0.9
Other Asian [1]	145,842	1.5
Asian Indian	79,169	0.8
Black or African American	856,874	8.7

[73] More detail information is available here:
http://factfinder2.census.gov/faces/tableservices/jsf/pages/productview.xhtml?sr c=bkmk

RACE	People	% American
Chinese	393,488	4.0
Cuban	41,350	0.4
Mexican	3,510,677	35.8
Native Hawaiian and Other Pacific Islander	26,094	0.3
Native Hawaiian	4,013	0.0
Guamanian or Chamorro	3,447	0.0
Samoan	12,115	0.1
Other Pacific Islander	6,519	0.1
Puerto Rican	44,609	0.5
White	4,936,599	50.3
Two or More Races	438,713	4.5

With respect to religion, the Association of Religion Data Archives tracked over 100 different denominations/faith traditions in 2010 within L.A. County, from the American Baptist Association to Zoroastrians.[74] That's over a hundred different faith traditions in only one county, of one region, of one state, in the United States.

I (and probably you, as well) live in a diverse, pluralistic society. Why does this matter so much? ER tells us that what determines moral rightness and wrongness is the dominant values of one's culture—but what is my culture? What is yours? Which values are the dominant ones?

If you're considering the moral permissibility of an abortion, for example, isn't it possible that you might get one answer if you live in Salt Lake City, Utah, and another if you live in San Francisco, California? One answer if you are Catholic, and another if you are Episcopalian? One answer if you live in L.A. County, another if you live in Orange County (both within the State of California)? One answer if your family has just immigrated to the U.S., and another if your ancestors arrived on the Mayflower? One answer if you were born between 1940 and 1960 ("Baby-Boomer"), another if you were born between 1961 and 1981 ("Generation X"), and still another if you were born after 1982 ("Generation Y"/"Generation Next")?

Just how big and influential does a group have to be to count as a culture? As of 1995, the North American Man/Boy Love Association (N.A.M.B.L.A.) boasted a membership of 1,100. Is that enough to constitute a culture (one that advocates what the rest of us call pedophilia and pederasty, but a "culture" nonetheless)? If it is not a culture, why not? How large must a "social group" be to count as a culture? If it is a culture, then, according to ER, are its values just as legitimate as any others'? How do we handle the fact that the N.A.M.B.L.A. "culture" (or perhaps sub-culture) is found within other, broader cultures in which "man-boy love" is condemned as child rape?

From which group does one get one's values? Do we just pick for ourselves which group's values we'll adopt and value? If so, isn't that just subjectivism?

Whatever other challenges ER faces, a key feature of any ethical theory is its ability to provide a decision-making procedure, a method for resolving what to do when faced with a difficult ethical decision. If ER fails to provide this decision-making

---

[74] More detail information is available here:
http://www.thearda.com/rcms2010/r/c/06/rcms2010_06037_county_name_2010.asp

procedure, due to the vagueness of the very concept of "culture," then it fails as an ethical theory.

"Just consult the laws of the land," one might reply. "If it's against the law, then it's morally wrong according to your culture." This is probably too simplistic, though, given the fact that we recognize a distinction between what is legal/illegal and what is right/wrong. Lying, in most contexts, is not illegal, but is nevertheless generally regarded as wrong. African-Americans sitting at certain lunch counters was illegal at one time in the U.S., but most of us would deny that doing so was also morally wrong. Indeed, the very fact that we have a concept of "just" *and* "unjust" laws tells us that legality and morality, while usually overlapping, are not always the same thing. This is just one more challenge for this already besieged approach to ethics, but I'm not done yet!

All other challenges to ER aside, if one can establish that there are, in fact, at least some values that are found in all societies, at all times, and in all places, then such a finding would lend much credence to the claim that at least *some* moral values are universal, and that ER is false. James Rachels has attempted to provide a compelling argument that this is so.

James Rachels: Universal Moral Values

Rachels proposes that there is more moral "universality" across cultures than we might initially recognize. One reason for this is because cultures might manifest the same underlying value in different ways, given contingent historical, geographical, climatic, and other circumstances.

For example, throughout most of the U.S., the dead are buried below ground, but in New Orleans, they are buried above ground. Why? New Orleans is below sea-level, and has a high water table. Graves fill with water, and caskets float, creating an unhealthy, as well as deeply disturbing, result.[75] This is an example of how geography can influence the *manifestation* (burial below v. above ground) of the *same underlying value* (honor the dead). Other cultures cremate. Ancient Egyptians mummified their dead. All believed it to be morally right to honor the dead, but due to different circumstances, they demonstrated that belief in different ways.

As another example, consider child-rearing. Some cultures adopt the so-called "nuclear family" (mom, dad, and 2.5 kids under the same roof). Others prefer extended families (multiple generations in the same home), and still others embrace communal child-rearing in which responsibility for caring for the young is shared by the larger community, including non-blood relatives.

There is any number of explanations for why one culture might manifest its child-care in one fashion, while a different culture does so in another, but the allegation is that the underlying value is the same, even though the manifestation is different.

The moral value that the young should be cared for is, in fact, one of a handful of values that Rachels claims that all cultures must have, if they are to survive as a culture. It is thus a *universal* (non-relative) value. Consider the alternative.

Try to imagine a culture in which no moral value was placed on caring for the young. There is no stigma, no shame, no pressure, no laws associated with child-rearing. How could such a culture persist? In order to survive, a culture must produce

---

[75] http://www.experienceneworleans.com/deadcity.html

new members who will survive long enough to continue its traditions, and then create the next generation themselves. Although people care for children in a variety of formats, we struggle to even *imagine* a culture that does not care for them at all.

As another example, Rachels claims that no culture could survive if it did not have some prohibition against murder. Try to imagine what it would be like to live in a society in which no positive value was placed on innocent life, and in which there was nothing wrong with killing innocent people. What an anxiety-filled existence! How could such a culture avoid self-destruction?

As a final example, consider honesty. Rachels claims that all cultures, in order to survive as cultures, must endorse honesty and condemn deception. Why? Consider the alternative. If there was no stigma attached to deception, and no expectation of honesty, under normal circumstances, why would you ever believe what other people tell you? What you read? What you hear? Why would you assume the words you're reading right now are sincere and accurate? Why go to school, if it's just as likely that your instructors are lying as they are not? Why read the newspaper (or, more likely, internet news sources), if it's no worse for it to be filled with lies than the truth? Clearly, without an expectation of honesty, there's no basis for trust. Without trust, there's no basis for cooperation, and without cooperation, there is no society—not even family units can survive without trust-enabled cooperation. Obviously, people can and do lie, but this is the exception, rather than the rule. Imagine trying to get through your day if it was just as likely that everyone you met was lying to you as that they were telling the truth!

If Rachels is correct, then this is a major accomplishment. Though we might bicker as to just *which* moral principles and values are necessary for any society to survive (and are, therefore, "universal"), it would appear that there are some that fit that description. If so, then ER is wrong with respect to its claim that all values are relative, and that none is universal. That, at the very least, is a very important start for the rest of our process, in that it would allow us to operate on the assumption that (at least some) moral claims are objective.

If at least some moral claims are objective, then it's possible to make strong, meaningful comparisons of individuals, and of entire cultures. What will be the standard by which such comparisons are possible? The set of true moral values that apply to all people, everywhere, at all times.

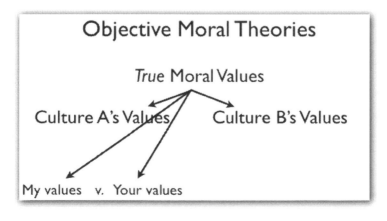

C.S. Lewis

Although his reasons are very different from those of James Rachels, C.S. Lewis agrees that there are universal (objective) moral values.

Lewis starts from what he takes to be the universal recognition of objective moral "rights" and "wrongs." This is evident, he thinks, from the fact that we all tend to *judge* the behavior of others (and ourselves). We really do think that some actions are good, and others bad—and morally so, not merely so in terms of what's prudent. We really do think that some actions are virtuous, and others vile, and that some people are heroes, and others villains. Although our particular examples might vary, we all engage in this general behavior. In addition, we have behavioral expectations of others, and we are upset when people violate them. We all think there are certain things that people just shouldn't do, and we get upset with them if they do it anyway. Spouses shouldn't be unfaithful. Friends shouldn't lie to you. Politicians shouldn't accept (or expect) bribes. Your neighbor shouldn't steal from you. No one should molest your child. And so forth. We don't merely blithely announce our expectations, and then shrug when they're violated, as though it didn't matter. We are offended, indignant, outraged, betrayed, hurt. . . With respect to our own behavior, when someone else accuses *us* of violating moral norms, we usually try to make excuses for the behavior, if we don't outright confess—thereby implying the need for an explanation in the first place. Compare the following hypothetical exchanges:

You: "Hey! Don't cut in line in front of me."
Me: "My friend has been saving my spot."

You: "Hey! Don't cut in line in front of me."
Me: "I'll do whatever I want!"

While there certainly are some people who flout convention, and are unashamed to do, we tend to judge those people very harshly—sometimes going so far as to label them sociopaths. Most of us play by the rules, try to justify our actions if we're caught "bending" them, get upset with others when they break them, and all the while at least implicitly acknowledge the existence of "the rules" in the first place. The implicit premise here seems to be that we all know that there exist certain (objective) moral principles.

Lewis is aware that not everyone would so readily agree to that claim, and he anticipates (and addresses) several possible objections. A first, obvious, objection is the theory of Ethical Relativism itself. But, just as Rachels argued that there are fewer differences in values across cultures as there might appear, Lewis makes a similar point.

Think of a country where people were admired for running away in battle, or where a man felt proud of double-crossing all the people who had been kindest to him. You might just as well try to imagine a country where two and two made five. Men have differed as regards what people you ought to be unselfish to—whether it was only your own family, or your fellow countrymen, or everyone. But they have always agreed that you ought not to put yourself first. Selfishness has never been admired. Men have differed as to whether you should have one wife or four. But they have always agreed that you must not simply have any woman you liked.[76]

Indeed, Lewis echoes most of the objections we have thus far considered. With regard to the fact that, if ER is true, there is no objective stance from which to evaluate or criticize any culture's values or practices, Lewis draws on his own experience of facing the threat of the Nazis in his lifetime. The Nazis were, for him, an example of a people and a cultural program gone *wrong*, and the mere fact that some Nazis might have thought differently doesn't change that fact. "People may be sometimes mistaken about [morals], just as people sometimes get their sums wrong; but they are not a matter of mere taste and opinion any more than the multiplication table."

A related objection was that, if ER is true, moral reformers are, paradoxically, always morally wrong. And yet, as Lewis points out, people *do* argue that reform is possible, and desirable.

If no set of moral ideas were truer or better than any other, there would be no sense in preferring civilised morality to savage morality, or Christian morality to Nazi morality. In fact, of course, we all do believe that some moralities are better than others. We do believe that some of the people who tried to change the moral ideas of their own age were what we would call Reformers or Pioneers-people who understood morality better than their neighbours did.

Another objection to the existence of objective moral values, very much in the spirit of ER, is that "morality" is merely social conditioning produced by our education and upbringing. Lewis, however, replies that *how* something is learned doesn't necessarily indicate its ultimate source or status (e.g., we learn the multiplication tables at school without this implying that math is merely a human convention). "But," the skeptic might wonder, "Why think that morality is objective in a way analogous to math?" Because, says Lewis, the "Moral Law" is (generally, at its core) the same across cultures, whereas mere convention (e.g., which side of the road one drives on) is not.

Returning to his arguments against ER, Lewis reiterates that we do, in actual practice, hold some cultural norms to be "better" or "worse" than others (e.g., Nazis are worse!), and alleged differences in values are often just differences in matters of fact. We have already rehearsed this point about alleged differences in values being just differences in local expressions of those values previously in this chapter, but Lewis uses an interesting example that's worth quoting: witch burning.

I have met people who exaggerate the differences, because they have not distinguished between differences of morality and differences of belief about facts. For example, one man said to me, 'Three hundred years ago people in England were putting witches to death. Was that what you call the Rule of Human Nature or Right Conduct?' But surely the reason we do not execute witches is that we do not believe there are such things. If we did-if we really thought that there were people going about who had sold themselves to the devil and received supernatural powers from him in return and were using these powers to kill their neighbours or drive them mad or bring bad weather, surely we would all agree that if anyone deserved the death penalty, then these filthy quislings did. There is no difference of moral principle here: the difference is simply about matter of fact. It may be a great advance in knowledge not to believe in witches: there is no moral advance in not executing them when you do not think they are there. You would not call a man humane for ceasing to set mousetraps if he did so because he believed there were no mice in the house.

A different sort of objection to the claim that morality is objective brings us back to the evolutionary understanding of morality previously considered by our appeals to Dawkins and Rachels. Perhaps "morality" is just our evolution-produced "herd instinct," just one instinctive drive amongst other instinctive drives? Lewis replies that desires are not identical to our sense of obligation with respect to those desires. For example, my awareness that I *ought* to be forgiving is not at all the same as a *desire* to be forgiving. Indeed, often our desires are in sharp contrast to our sense of obligation. Moreover, Lewis thinks that it makes little sense to understand moral prescriptions as impulses or desires amongst others, as he can identify no particular impulses or desires that the "Moral Law" tells us always to restrain or to pursue. Indeed, our sense of moral obligation seems to be a different sort of thing *by which we judge between* desires and impulses.

Supposing you hear a cry for help from a man in danger. You will probably feel two desires-one a desire to give help (due to your herd instinct), the other a desire to keep out of danger (due to the instinct for self-preservation). But you will find inside you, in addition to these two impulses, a third thing which tells you that you ought to follow the impulse to help, and suppress the impulse to run away. Now this thing that judges between two instincts, that decides which should be encouraged, cannot itself be either of them. You might as well say that the sheet of music which tells you, at a given moment, to play one note on the piano and not another, is itself one of the notes on the keyboard. The Moral Law tells us the tune we have to play: our instincts are merely the keys.

Nor does it seem plausible, according to Lewis, that morally good behavior is merely socially useful behavior (e.g., what's needed for community flourishing, as Rachels might argue). According to Lewis, morally good behavior *is* socially useful, but that doesn't explain its purpose (in a non-circular way), since being "socially useful" *is* of those behaviors we label "good."

If a man asked what was the point of playing football, it would not be much good saying 'in order to score goals,' for trying to score goals is the game itself, not the reason for the game, and you would really only be saying that football was football-which is true, but not worth saying. In the same way, if a man asks what is the point of behaving decently, it is no good replying, 'in order to benefit society,' for trying to benefit society, in other words being unselfish (for 'society' after all only means 'other people'), is one of the things decent behaviour consists in; all you are really saying is that decent behaviour is decent behaviour.

While Lewis and Rachels agree, then, on the existence of universal moral values, they very much disagree as the nature of the source and grounding of those values. For Rachels, our objective moral values arise as dispositions to behave that promoted our survival, and are, indeed, necessary for human survival and flourishing in communities. For Lewis, the ultimate source of those moral values is a transcendent, morally perfect God—though his defense of that claim is beyond the scope of this chapter, or even this book.

Although we have seen two critiques of ER from Rachels and Lewis, it's important to make three concessions:

1. Some differences are probably so significant that they're not best understood as merely different manifestations of the same underlying values. For example, someone might claim that marriage is one way of expressing the value that human sexuality should be constrained, and Female Genital Mutilation (FGM) is simply another. I, for one, find the practices different enough that I doubt they express the same value at all. This is certainly subject to debate. The point, at this stage, though, is simply to acknowledge that it would be too easy, and too sloppy, to gloss over the genuine and controversial differences between various cultural practices by suggesting that they are just different manifestations of the same value. While there might be more universality than there appears, there's probably also less universality than we might wish were the case.

2. Both subjectivism and ER have something worthwhile to offer. There is certainly a category of value judgments that we make that is best understood using the subjectivist model. Our judgments concerning aesthetic preferences, for example, music, art, food, and so on, all very reasonably seem to be nothing more (or less) than expressions of personal opinion. They can, and should, be understood through the subjectivist lens.

There is another category of values and behaviors that seem to be based on cultural standards, and is both more than mere personal opinion, and less than a universal moral value. Once again, the exact content of this category is probably difficult to articulate, but things like expectations of behavior in particular settings (e.g., how to behave with respect to greetings, when visiting holy sites, when a guest in someone's home, etc.) are probably examples.

3. A lesson to be learned from both subjectivism and ER is to be cautious of hasty assumptions and self-righteousness. It's all too easy to presume one's own view of the world, and one's own values, are the absolute truth and worthy of promulgation. History is filled with the tragic consequences of such assumptions. Both subjectivism and ER give us reason to slow down, restrain our arrogant tendencies, and pay careful attention to what other individuals, and other communities, have to say.

Where both go too far, however, is in thinking that no truth is possible, that there are no right answers at all, that no meaningful comparisons and judgments are possible, and that no individual (or group) ever does wrong (in any strong sense beyond our own personal or collective opinion).

Indeed, there's a dangerous irony lurking behind both theories: the subjectivist judgment that all values are mere opinions is *itself* a mere opinion (according to its own standards), yet is offered as a rule for all; and the ER view that all values are relative to one's culture is also usually (implicitly, and mistakenly) offered as a reason for all people to be accepting, respectful, and tolerant, of other culture's values, even when some cultures clearly value doing just the opposite.

Herodotus (484 BCE – 425 BCE) was an ancient Greek historian and is often credited with being the first true historian in that he was the first (known) to systematically gather information, test the accuracy of accounts, and present historical narratives in a systematic and compelling fashion. In this incredibly brief excerpt we get a report showcasing the differences between ancient Greek and Callatian cultural practices with regard to how to dispose of their dead. Noting the fierce disagreement between cultures, "custom" is proclaimed "king o'er all"—that is, cultural standards dictate what is right and wrong for communities.

The History of Herodotus
Herodotus

Book III, Chapter 38

...Many other wild outrages of this sort did Cambyses commit, both upon the Persians and the allies, while he still stayed at Memphis; among the rest he opened the ancient sepulchres, and examined the bodies that were buried in them. He likewise went into the temple of Vulcan, and made great sport of the image. For the image of Vulcan is very like the Pataeci of the Phoenicians, wherewith they ornament the prows of their ships of war. If persons have not seen these, I will explain in a different way- it is a figure resembling that of a pigmy. He went also into the temple of the Cabiri, which it is unlawful for any one to enter except the priests, and not only made sport of the images, but even burnt them. They are made like the statue of Vulcan, who is said to have been their father.

Thus it appears certain to me, by a great variety of proofs, that Cambyses was raving mad; he would not else have set himself to make a mock of holy rites and long-established usages. For if one were to offer men to choose out of all the customs in the world such as seemed to them the best, they would examine the whole number, and end by preferring their own; so convinced are they that their own usages far surpass those of all others. Unless, therefore, a man was mad, it is not likely that he would make sport of such matters. That people have this feeling about their laws may be seen by very many proofs: among others, by the following. Darius, after he had got the kingdom, called into his presence certain Greeks who were at hand, and asked- "What he should pay them to eat the bodies of their fathers when they died?" To which they answered, that there was no sum that would tempt them to do such a thing. He then sent for certain Indians, of the race called Callatians, men who eat their fathers, and asked them, while the Greeks stood by, and knew by the help of an interpreter all that was said - "What he should give them to burn the bodies of their fathers at their decease?" The Indians exclaimed aloud, and bade him forbear such language. Such is men's wont herein; and Pindar was right, in my judgment, when he said, "Law [custom] is the king o'er all."...

Marcus Tullius Cicero (106 BCE – 43 BCE) was not merely a "fan" of Greek philosophy who shared his interests with others. He was a careful thinker and a skilled writer who translated Greek thought into the Roman (Latin) language not only in the literal sense of translation, but also to the extent that he coined new Latin vocabulary to help elucidate difficult philosophical concepts. He helped bring ancient Greek thought to the Romans, and then helped to bring both Greek and Roman philosophy to the rest of Europe, somewhat in the Middle Ages—but especially in the Renaissance. His oratory skill and political talents caught the eye of Julius Caesar, who (in 60 BCE) invited Cicero to be the 4th member of his "partnership" with Pompey and Marcus Licinius Crassus. Cicero declined the offer to join what would become the First Triumvirate due to his concern that it would undermine the Republic.). In February, 44 BCE, Caesar was appointed "dictator for life." Roughly a month later, he was assassinated on the Ides of March (March 15th). Cicero had not, himself, participated in the conspiracy or assassination. However, Marcus Junius Brutus allegedly called out Cicero's name, bloodstained dagger in hand, and asked him to restore the Republic, and Cicero's own endorsement of the assassination was unmistakable. In the political instability that followed the assassination, a power struggle broke out between the assassins (led by Brutus and Cassius) and "loyalists" to Caesar (led by Mark Antony and Octavian). Cicero was a political leader—and found himself in direct opposition to Mark Antony. Cicero was the spokesman for the Senate, and Antony was a consul and the unofficial executor of Caesar's will. Cicero tried to manipulate Octavian into opposing Antony, but ultimately failed. Cicero wrote and spoke publicly against Antony in a series of speeches called the "Phillipics"—actions and writing that ultimately cost him his life. In 43 BCE, Antony, Octavian, and Lepidus formed the Second Triumvirate. They issued proscriptions against Roman citizens, including Cicero (and his brother and nephew). Cicero was assassinated on December 7th, 43 BCE. Antony then displayed Cicero's severed head and hands (the ones that wrote the Phillipics) in the Roman Forum in a final act of humiliation. In this very brief selection from "The Republic" that follows, Cicero has the character Philus advocate against any sort of universal notion of justice/goodness, and argue, instead, for what we would today call Ethical Relativism.

The Republic
Cicero

Book 3: 8-18

. . .

Scipio and his friends having again assembled, Scipio spoke as follows: — In our last conversation I promised to prove that honesty is the best policy in all states and commonwealths whatsoever. But if I am to plead in favour of strict honesty and justice in all public affairs, no less than in private, I must request Philus, or some one else, to take up the advocacy of the other side; the truth will then become more manifest, from the collision of opposite arguments, as we see every day exemplified at the Bar.

Philus.

—In good truth you have allotted me a marvellous creditable cause. So you wish me to plead for vice, do you?

Lælius.

—Perhaps you are afraid, lest in reproducing the ordinary objections made to justice in politics, you should seem to express your own sentiments. But this caution is ridiculous in you, my Philus; you, who are so universally respected as an almost unique example of the ancient probity and good faith; you, who are so familiar with the legal habit of disputing on both sides of a question, because you think this is the best way of getting at the truth.

Philus.

—Very well; I obey you, and wilfully with my eyes open, I will undertake this dirty business. Since those who seek for gold do not flinch at the sight of the mud, we, who search for justice, which is far more precious than gold, must overcome all dainty scruples. I will therefore, make use of the antagonist arguments of a foreigner, and assume his character in using them. The pleas, therefore, now to be delivered by Philus are those once employed by the Greek Carneades, accustomed to express whatever served his turn. Let it be understood, therefore, that I by no means express my own sentiments, but those of Carneades, in order that you may refute this philosopher, who was wont to turn the best causes into joke, through the mere wantonness of wit.

When Philus had thus spoken, he took a general review of the leading arguments that Carneades had brought forward to prove that justice was neither eternal, immutable, nor universal. Having put these sophistical arguments into their most specious and plausible form, he thus continued his ingenious pleadings.

Aristotle has treated this question concerning justice, and filled four large volumes with it. As to Chrysippus, I expected nothing grand or magnificent in him, for, after his usual fashion, he examines everything rather by the signification of words, than the reality of things. But it was surely worthy of those heroes of philosophy to ennoble by their genius a virtue so eminently beneficent and liberal, which every where exalts the social interests above the selfish, and teaches to love others rather than ourselves. It was worthy of their genius, we say, to elevate this virtue to a divine throne, close to that of Wisdom. Certainly they wanted not the intention to accomplish this. What else could be the cause of their writing on the subject, or what could have been their design? Nor could they have wanted genius, in which they excelled all men. But the weakness of their cause was too great for their intention and their eloquence to make it popular. In fact, this justice on which we reason may be a civil right, but no natural one; for if it were natural and universal, then justice and injustice would be recognized similarly by all men, just as the elements of heat and cold, sweet and bitter.

Now if any one, carried in the chariot of winged serpents, of which the poet Pacuvius makes mention, could take his flight over all nations and cities, and accurately observe their proceedings, he would see that the sense of justice and right varies in different regions. In the first place he would behold among the unchangeable people of Egypt, which preserves in its archives the memory of so many ages and events, a bull adored as a deity, under the name of Apis, and a multitude of other monsters, and all kinds of animals admitted by the natives into the number of the gods.

The Persians, on the other hand, regard all these forms of idolatry as impious, and it is affirmed that the sole motive of Xerxes for commanding the conflagration of the Athenian temples, was the belief that it was a superstitious sacrilege to keep confined within narrow walls the gods, whose proper home was the entire universe. Afterwards Philip, in his hostile projects against the Persians, and Alexander, in his expedition, alleged this plea for war, that it was necessary to avenge the temples of Greece. And the Greeks thought proper never to rebuild these fanes, that this monument of the impiety of the Persians might always remain before the eyes of their posterity.

How many, such as the inhabitants of Taurica along the Euxine Sea—as the King of Egypt Busiris—as the Gauls and the Carthaginians—have thought it exceedingly pious and agreeable to the gods to sacrifice men. Besides these religious discrepancies, the rules of life are so contradictory that the Cretans and Ætolians regard robbery as honourable. And the Lacedæmonians say that their territory extends to all places which they can touch with a lance. The Athenians had a custom of swearing by a public proclamation, that all the lands which produced olives and corn were their own. The Gauls consider it a base employment to raise corn by agricultural labour, and go with arms in their hands, and mow down the harvests of neighbouring peoples. And our Romans, the most equitable of all nations, in order to raise the value of our vines and olives, do not permit the races beyond the Alps to cultivate either vineyards or oliveyards. In this respect, it is said, we act with prudence, but not with justice. You see then that wisdom and policy are not always the same as equity. Lycurgus, the inventor of a most admirable jurisprudence, and most wholesome laws, gave the lands of the rich to be cultivated by the common people, who were reduced to slavery.

If I were to describe the diverse kinds of laws, institutions, manners, and customs, not only as they vary in the numerous nations, but as they vary likewise in single cities, as Rome for example, I should prove that they have had a thousand revolutions. For instance, that eminent expositor of our laws who sits in the present company, I mean Malilius, if you were to consult him relative to the legacies and inheritances of women, he would tell you that the present law is quite different from that he was accustomed to plead in his youth, before the Voconian enactment came into force— an edict which was passed in favour of the interests of the men, but which is evidently full of injustice with regard to women. For why should a woman be disabled from inheriting property? Why can a vestal virgin become an heir, while her mother cannot? And why, admitting that it is necessary to set some limit to the wealth of women, should Crassus' daughter, if she be his only child, inherit thousands without offending the law, while my daughter can only receive a small share in a bequest?

If this justice were natural, innate, and universal, all men would admit the same law and right, and the same men would not enact different laws at different times. If a just man and a virtuous man is bound to obey the laws, I ask what laws do you mean? Do you intend all the laws indifferently? Virtue does not permit this inconstancy in moral obligation—such a variation is not compatible with natural conscience. The laws are, therefore, based not on our sense of justice, but on our fear of punishment. There is, therefore, no natural justice, and hence it follows that men cannot be just by nature. . . .

Chapter 6: Emotivism

Comprehension questions you should be able to answer after reading this chapter:

1. What is a claim? What is a truth-value?

2. What is an analytic claim? What is a synthetic claim?

3. What is the "principle of verification?"

4. Why do emotivists think that moral claims are not "cognitively meaningful" (i.e., not actually claims at all) according to the principle of verification?

5. What do emotivists think we are doing when we offer moral "claims?"

6. Why are the standards of the principle of verification a possible problem for the principle of verification itself?

7. Is our only use of moral language the expression of emotional approval or disapproval? If not, what other functions might moral claims serve?

All of the remaining theories in the book will assume that moral value judgments are claims (with truth values), and then debate whether moral claims are factual (objective) or non-factual (subjective), and what will determine the truth value of the claim (in either case). But, what if moral value judgments aren't *claims* at all? Not value *judgments* at all?

"Emotivism" is an ethical theory that proposes those very ideas. As mentioned briefly in an earlier chapter, according to emotivism, there are no moral facts—but then there are no actual moral opinions either! Our moral terminology such as "good" and "bad," "right" and "wrong," "just" and "unjust" doesn't indicate moral properties of people or acts. Grammatically, we might say that "good" and "bad" don't serve as predicates.

A predicate is a fancy grammatical term that (roughly) means the same thing as "property" or "quality." A thing (e.g., an apple) will have various properties (e.g., being edible, being red, being a certain size, having a certain mass, etc.). Those properties are also its "predicates." According to emotivism, our moral concepts don't point out any actual properties of people or actions. They don't make "claims" at all. Instead, moral "claims" are expressions of the speaker's own emotions, and indicate attitudes of either approval or disapproval.

For example, according to emotivists, if I say that "murder is morally wrong," I haven't reported any fact about murder (i.e., its wrongness). Instead, I have expressed my own negative attitude about murder. Famously, this is sometimes referred to as the "boo/hurrah!" interpretation of moral claims. Today, we might replace "boo" with ☹ and "hurrah" with ☺.

Before delving further into this interpretation of ethics, it's important to explain why certain emotivists (at least) thought that moral claims are not actually *claims*. One of the most famous emotivists, A.J. Ayer, was identified with the philosophical movement known as "logical positivism."

According to logical positivists like Ayer, in order for a claim to be "meaningful," in order for it to have a truth value, the claim must either be an analytic claim, or, if a synthetic claim, that synthetic claim must be empirically verifiable (testable).

An analytic claim is one that can be known to be true, by definition. It doesn't tell us anything interesting about the "real world," as it actually is. It just provides information about concepts. Examples of analytic claims are as follows:

- 2 +2 = 4 (true, by definition)
- Bachelors are unmarried men (true, by definition)
- My biological uncle is not the brother of either my biological father, or biological mother (false, by definition)

Simply put, if you know what the word "bachelor" means, then you already know that it is true that bachelors are unmarried men. You don't have to go out and survey the world to verify this. In fact, no amount of research could impact the fact that it is true that bachelors are unmarried men. You might discover which men (in particular) are bachelors, and which are married, or you might discover the number of bachelors alive at any given place and time, but what a bachelor *is* does not require such research.

Synthetic claims, on the other hand, involve the application of our concepts to the world around us. Such claims *do* require "research," and their truth or falsity *does* depend upon features of the world. For example, "Professor Preston is a bachelor" is a synthetic claim. Nothing about "Professor Preston" entails "bachelor" in the same way that "bachelor" entails "unmarried man." My ex-*wife* used to be a "Professor Preston"—and she was not (and is not) a bachelor. I (Professor Preston) am a man, but whether or not it is true that I am bachelor depends on when the claim is made. At times that has been true, at other times it has been false. The point, of course, is that synthetic claims such as "Professor Preston is a bachelor" are not merely definitional statements, but are statements made about particular features of the world, and are therefore neither necessarily true nor necessarily false, but must be discovered to be true, or false.

The Principle of Verification

As mentioned, a key principle of logical positivism is the "principle of verification." According to the Principle of Verification (or verificationist principle), "a statement is held to be literally meaningful if and only if it is either analytic or empirically verifiable."[77] Let us consider moral claims with this standard in mind.

1. Moral claims do not appear to be analytic statements.

For example, "it is not wrong to steal" does not seem to be *logically contradictory*, even if you believe it to be *false*. In other words, even if you believe that stealing *is*

---

[77] From the introduction of A.J. Ayer's, *Language, Truth, and Logic*.

wrong, if someone disagrees with you and claims that stealing is not wrong, you might think the person is mistaken, but you don't believe the person is uttering a contradictory claim—not as if he had claimed that some bachelors are married. This indicates that moral claims are not analytic claims, not true (or false) *by definition*. If not analytic, then in order to be "meaningful" moral claims must be synthetic—but this leads to another problem, according to emotivists.

2.   Moral claims do not appear to be empirically verifiable.

According to emotivists like Ayer, at least, there is no way to *prove* that stealing is wrong (or disprove it). If the claim is that "Professor Preston is a bachelor," there are certainly ways to prove (or disprove) that claim. One could search marriage records, for example. But, what test could someone propose that would prove the wrongness of stealing? You could certainly prove the financial impact of stealing, or you could verify what someone (e.g., the thief, or the victim) *said* about stealing, or you could try to document the ownership of the item in question to determine whether a theft actually occurred, or you could verify that the act was indeed a violation of the law simply by consulting the laws in the place where the act occurred—but what verifiable fact of reality corresponds to the *wrongness* of the stealing?

According to the verificationist principle, then, since moral claims are neither analytic nor empirically verifiable, they are not cognitively meaningful, they are not claims at all, and are therefore not the sorts of things which can be either true *or* false.

If moral "claims" aren't actually *claims*, and if we're not actually describing any properties of people or actions when me make moral statements, then what *are* we doing when we say that one person is evil, and another person a moral role-model? When we say that abortion is wrong, or that eating meat is wrong, or that it's good to help the less fortunate?

According to emotivists like Ayer, what we're *really* doing when we make moral "claims" is expressing our own positive or negative attitudes about the person or act in question, we're expressing our emotional approval or disapproval.

To say that "murder is wrong," for example, doesn't report any fact about murder, and doesn't declare anything that is either true or false. Instead, to say that "murder is wrong" is to express a negative attitude towards murder. This is sometimes (at times, dismissively) referred to as the "boo! /hurrah!" interpretation of moral statements.

We begin by admitting that the fundamental ethical concepts are unanalysable, inasmuch as there is no criterion by which one can test the validity of the judgments in which they occur. So far we are in agreement with the absolutists. But, unlike the absolutists, we are able to give an explanation of that fact about ethical concepts. We say that the reason why they are unanalysable is that they are mere pseudo-concepts. The presence of an ethical symbol in a proposition adds nothing to its factual content. Thus if I say to someone, 'You acted wrongly in stealing that money,' I am not stating anything more than if I had simply said, 'You stole that money.' In adding that this action is wrong I am not making any further statement about it. I am simply evincing my moral disapproval of it. It is as if I had said, 'You stole that money,' in a peculiar tone of horror, or written it with the addition of some special exclamation marks. The tone, or the exclamation marks, adds nothing to the literal meaning of the sentence. It merely serves to show that the expression of it is attended by certain feelings in the speaker.

If now I generalize my previous statement and say, 'Stealing money is wrong.' I produce a sentence which has no factual meaning - that is, expresses no proposition which can be either true or false, it is as if I had written 'Stealing money!!' - where the shape and thickness of the exclamation marks show, by a suitable convention, that a special sort of moral disapproval is the feeling which is being expressed. It is clear that there is nothing said here which can be true or false.

Given modern linguistic developments, I'm going to rebrand this approach in terms of emoticons, with approval being expressed by the "smiling" emoticon (or emoji) [☺] and disapproval being expressed by the "frowning" emoticon [☹].

- "Murder is wrong" = "Murder.☹"
- Charity is good." = "Charity.☺"
- Martin Luther King Jr. was a righteous person." = "Martin Luther King Jr. ☺."
- Osama bin Laden was evil" = "Osama bin Laden.☹"

I'm sure you get the idea, by now.

Don't confuse emotivism with subjectivism, by the way. As you might recall, subjectivism is an ethical theory that holds that moral claims are matters of personal opinion. When we say that something is morally right or wrong, good or bad, we're simply describing our own beliefs and preferences. On this view, moral claims are still *claims*, still have a truth-value—they just get their truth-value solely from the speaker. So, according to subjectivism, if I claim that "murder is wrong," what I'm implicitly saying is "[I think] murder is wrong." I'm not describing some objective, independent fact about the world, but I am describing a fact about my own beliefs—and that description can be either true or false. For example, I might *lie* about my moral beliefs. It's not difficult to imagine a person who actually believes that same-sex marriage is morally wrong publicly proclaiming it to be morally acceptable (or vice versa). In that case, the opponent of same-sex marriage is making a false moral claim: "[I think] same-sex marriage is morally acceptable."

The emotivist, in contrast, doesn't even think that we're offering descriptions of our own beliefs, when we make moral "claims." Instead, we're indicating positive or negative emotional attitudes towards the person or behavior in question. For the emotivist:

- "Same-sex marriage is wrong" = "Same sex marriage.☹"
- "Same-sex marriage is good" = Same-sex marriage. ☺"

Because emotivists deny that moral "claims" are even *claims* at all (in the traditional sense), moral disagreement is not about facts or changing beliefs. If this is true, then a surprising implication of emotivism is that there can be no such thing as contradictory moral claims. If you and I seemingly disagree about some moral claim, we are simply expressing different moral sentiments. Pro-life and Pro-choice crowds aren't declaring contrary beliefs, but are instead expressing different emotional attitudes about abortion. No party to the pseudo-debate can be proved to be "right" and the other "wrong" because there is nothing right or wrong, true or false about our moral "claims."

> *Another man may disagree with me about the wrongness of stealing, in the sense that he may not have the same feelings about stealing as I have, and he may quarrel with me on account of my moral sentiments. But he cannot, strictly speaking, contradict me. For in saying that a certain type of action is right or wrong, I am not making any factual statement, not even a statement about my own state of mind. I am merely expressing certain moral sentiments. And the man who is ostensibly contradicting me is merely expressing his moral sentiments. So that there is plainly no sense in asking which of us is in the right. For neither of us is asserting a genuine proposition.*

So why do we bother to "argue" with one another concerning moral issues, then? Clearly, we *do* "argue" with each other about all kinds of moral issues. We seemingly argue about the morality of abortion, torturing suspected terrorists, the death penalty, eating meat, environmental regulations, tax policies, sexual activities, narcotics use, etc.

According to the emotivist, in those cases what we are actually doing is trying to arouse similar feelings (positive, or negative, as the case might be) in other people, and thereby cause them to change their behavior in ways that harmonize with our own moral attitudes. As Ayer says, "It is worth mentioning that ethical terms do not serve only to express feeling. They are calculated also to arouse feeling, and so to stimulate action."

Animal rights activists have negative emotions concerning things like eating meat, wearing furs and experimenting on animals. When they engage others, seemingly trying to convince them that such actions are morally wrong, they are trying to cause similar negative feelings to arise in their audience so that those people will stop engaging in those behaviors.

Anti-abortion activists have negative emotions concerning abortion. When they engage others, seemingly trying to convince them that abortion is morally wrong, they are trying to cause similar negative feelings to arise in their audience so that those people will be opposed to abortion as well.

People who support universal health care access have positive emotions concerning things like everyone having access to basic health care. When they engage others, seemingly trying to convince them of the moral rightness of universal health care access, they are trying to cause their audience to develop similarly positive emotions about universal health care, and thereby act in ways that support it.

And so forth...

Let's be honest: there is certainly something plausible about this interpretation of moral "discourse." Think of the tactics that the groups of people mentioned above tend to employ. PETA ("People for the Ethical Treatment of Animals") is notorious for "pulling on the heart strings" of people in television commercials and print ads.[78] It's no secret why they display adorable baby seals, and then show footage of such adorable baby seals being clubbed to death for their fur; why they show sad, scared dogs and cats being experimented upon, and why they show graphic footage of slaughter houses. They are trying to upset you—upset you so much that you will develop negative emotions towards those practices (if you don't already have them), in the hopes that your feelings will cause you to change your behavior.

Think of how most Pro-Life activists operate. They don't organize dispassionate debates in lecture halls. They stand in front of abortion clinics with giant signs depicting bloody, dismembered fetuses, contrasted with pictures of adorable babies with captions like "Take my hand, not my life." They are trying to make abortion disgusting to you (if it's not already), and to inspire sufficient negative feeling that it will cause you to behave in certain ways (e.g., not have an abortion, vote for Pro-Life candidates, etc.).

Additional examples of these tactics are abundant, and lend support to Ayers' claim that so-called "debate" is actually an attempt to influence emotion. Ayer acknowledges that this be a counter-intuitive interpretation to accept, initially.

> This may seem, at first sight to be a very paradoxical assertion. For we certainly do engage in disputes which are ordinarily regarded as disputes about questions of value, But, in all such cases, we find, if we consider the matter closely, that the dispute is not really about a question of value, but about a question of fact. When someone disagrees with us about the moral value of a certain action or type of action, we do admittedly resort to argument in order to win him over to our way of thinking. But we do not attempt to show by our arguments that he has the 'wrong' ethical feeling towards a situation whose nature he has correctly apprehended. What we attempt to show is that he is mistaken about the facts of the case. We argue that he has misconceived the agent's motive: or that he has misjudged the effects of the action, or its probable effects in view of the agent's knowledge; or that he has failed to take into account the special circumstances in which the agent was placed. Or else we employ more general arguments about the effects which actions of a certain type tend to produce, or the qualities which are usually manifested in their performance. We do this in the hope that we have only to get our opponent to agree with us about the nature of the empirical facts for him to adopt the same moral attitude towards them as we do. And as the people with whom we argue have generally received the same moral education as ourselves, and live in the same social order, our expectation is usually justified.

According to Ayer, even in cases of actual debate, we are not trying to prove someone wrong (i.e., prove that someone's moral claim is false), but are actually trying to prove that the person's interpretation of the non-moral facts is wrong. For example, within the context of the abortion debate, it's safe to assume that both sides agree that murder is wrong—where they disagree is whether or not abortion is

---

[78] You can view many of them at their website: www.peta.org.

murder.

If we accept the definition of "murder" to be "the unjustified killing of an innocent person," whether or not abortion is murder is going to depend on whether a fetus is an "innocent person," and whether it is "unjustified." Not surprisingly, then, when Pro-Choice activists argue for the availability of abortion services, they don't argue in favor of "murder," but try to demonstrate that a fetus is not a "person" (i.e., that the fetus lacks the relevant qualities necessary for personhood, such as self-awareness, rationality, the ability to enter into reciprocal relationships with others, etc.), or else try to demonstrate that there are mitigating factors (e.g., health and well-being of the mother, the value of reproductive autonomy, etc.) that *justifies* the termination of the fetus, thereby causing it not to be an *un*justified killing (person, or not). On the other side of the protest line, the Pro-Life crowd agrees (of course) that murder is wrong, and because they think that abortion *is* (in fact) the "unjustified killing of an innocent person," they think abortion is wrong as well.

Whether or not emotivism is the best way to understand ethics, there is certainly something intuitively "right" about this observation of what actually transpires in moral "debates," and it helps to explain why participants in the abortion debate are often so dumbfounded and frustrated when the other side doesn't agree with them. It's just "obvious" that "abortion is murder", or "obvious" that a "fetus is not a person." The reason why we think it should be "obvious" to the "other side" is because we assume that they have a similar moral outlook as we do, based on similar basic values, upbringing, and conditioning—and most of the time, this is a fairly safe assumption. Where the assumption becomes hasty, however, is when there are, in fact, considerable differences in upbringing, cultural conditioning, etc. Without such shared sentiments, we discover that reasoning with such a person is "impossible," and we give up—writing the other person or group off as "brainwashed," or "savage," or "perverse," or "sick."

> But if our opponent happens to have undergone a different process of moral 'conditioning' from ourselves, so that, even when he acknowledges all the facts, he still disagrees with us about the moral value of the actions under discussion, then we abandon the attempt to convince him by argument. We say that it is impossible to argue with him because he has a distorted or undeveloped moral sense; which signifies merely that he employs a different set of values from our own. We feel that our own system of values is superior, and therefore speak in such derogatory terms of his. But we cannot bring forward any arguments to show that our system is superior. For our judgment that it is so is itself a judgment of value, and accordingly outside the scope of argument. It is because argument fails us when we come to deal with pure questions of value, as distinct from questions of fact, that we finally resort to mere abuse.

Possible problems

One immediate (and infamous) possible problem for emotivists concerns the verificationist principle itself. Recall that the principle of verification asserts that a claim is meaningful (i.e., has a truth-value) if and only if it is either an analytic claim, or else empirically verifiable. Critics of logical positivism (and the emotivism that proceeds from logical positivism) point out, however, that the verificationist principle *itself* is neither analytic, nor empirically verifiable. That is to say the principle of verification is not necessarily true (i.e., it is unlike a claim such as "bachelors are unmarried men"), and it is not subject to empirical verification. What test could possibly "verify" that the principle of verification is, itself, true? According to its own standards, then, the principle of verification is, itself, neither true nor false, and is therefore not "cognitively meaningful!"

Defenders of the verificationist principle could retort that it serves as an axiom, and is therefore not something that can be (or should) be "proven" to be true, in much the same way that mathematical axioms are not themselves "proven" true within their own mathematical systems. For example, one does not have to "prove" the Euclidean axiom that "the whole is greater than the part," or that things which are equal to the same thing are equal to each other (e.g., If X = 3, and Y = 3, then X = Y).

On the other hand, axioms, traditionally conceived, were claims perceived to be "self-evident," accepted as true without controversy. It is "self-evident" that a whole is greater than its part simply by virtue of knowing what a "part" means in relation to the "whole" *of which it is a part*. But it's far from obvious that it is "self-evident" that the verificationist principle is true. Indeed, all of the controversy long surrounding the verificationist principle is evidence that it is *not* self-evident.

Another possible problem with emotivism is that some think that while moral claims do indeed *sometimes* serve to express emotional approval or disapproval, or to arouse those emotions in others, this is not the *only* function moral claims serve in our language. Other uses imply that they function as descriptive sentences, with truth-values

According to this line of criticism, it's not obvious that all moral discourse aims (merely) to arouse emotion. If we reconsider the abortion debate, for example, we can certainly see that many elements of the "debate" are attempts to arouse emotion—and that this occurs on both sides. A "Pro-Lifer" might show large pictures of dismembered fetuses in hopes of arousing disgust, while a "Pro-Choicer" might share the tale of a botched "back-alley abortion" and ask, rhetorically, "what if it were your daughter, bleeding to death from an unlicensed, unsafe abortion?"

Not all debate tactics are necessarily so emotionally driven, though. While that hypothetical "Pro-Choicer" might attempt to inspire sympathy or empathetic fear with that horror story about "back-alley abortions," she might also (or instead) offer a systematic and formal argument for reproductive autonomy in an intentionally dispassionate manner. Indeed, in philosophy it's often regarded as bad form (a fallacy!) to appeal to emotion rather than reasons. Appeals to emotion seem an *alternative* to argument, "rhetoric" rather than reasoning. But, if appeals to emotion are at least sometimes an alternative to argument, this would suggest that arguments and appeals to emotion are not always the same thing.

Moreover, some uses of moral "claims" don't seem so easily reducible to mere expressions of moral approval or disapproval. Consider the following example:

1. If cheating is wrong, then you ought not to cheat on your philosophy exam.
2. Cheating is wrong.
3. Therefore, you ought not to cheat on your philosophy exam.

Logically, this looks like a perfectly standard example of *"modus ponens,"* and therefore a logically valid argument.[79] In everyday use, we might not be likely to actually construct a formalized argument in this fashion, when trying to convince someone that she ought not to cheat on a test, but this is at least implicitly the logical form of our argument. However, according to emotivists, we can't actually employ his kind of reasoning, since "cheating is wrong" isn't really a claim at all, and has no truth-value to transfer across the argument. Remember, "cheating is wrong" just means something like: "cheating!☹"

It's possible that when we are seemingly engaged in what appears to be an ethical argument (such as in the example above) all we are *really* doing is wringing our hands and saying "cheating!" with a look of disapproval and a fist shaking at our audience. Critics of emotivism think this is implausible, though, because we really do seem to be using *logic* and *argument* to make our point. Is it plausible that we're all just self-deceived about what we're actually doing, in those cases?

Consider all the various (and common) uses of moral claims:

- Assertions: Murder is wrong.
- Conditional statements: If murder is wrong, then Maria shouldn't get an abortion.
- Questions: Is murder wrong?
- Belief attribution: Scott thinks that murder is wrong.

If emotivism is correct, and moral claims are just expressions of emotional approval or disapproval, then the following substitutions should work:

- Assertions: Murder! ☹
- Conditional statements: If murder! ☹ , then Maria shouldn't get an abortion.
- Questions: Murder! ☹?
- Belief attribution: Scott thinks that murder! ☹.

Does each of those substitutions "work?" Critics of emotivism think they do not, and that our moral language and use of moral claims, while *sometimes* indicating emotional approval or disapproval, also sometimes intend something else, such as actually offering a proposition and assuming it has a truth-value.

Conclusion

Emotivism offers an intriguing interpretation of moral discourse, and shines a spotlight on the undoubtedly real practice of attempting to stir emotion when advocating for moral position or policies. It also is potentially refreshing in that it highlights the role of emotion, in contrast to reason—which so dominates virtually every other ethical theory. Nevertheless, there are few ethicists who espouse emotivism anymore, largely due to the decline of the principle of verification, and the recognition that our use of moral claims is more varied and rich than mere expressions of emotional approval or disapproval.

In the remaining chapters, we will operate off the assumption that moral claims

---

[79] Modus ponens is usually the first inference rule one learns in any logic class.

are, indeed, *claims*, and focus on how best to understand and interpret those claims, and how best to establish their truth or falsity.

Sir Alfred Jules Ayer (29 October 1910 – 27 June 1989) was a British philosopher best known for contribution to the school of thought known as Logical Positivism. In this selection, Ayer applies the principle of verification to moral claims in an effort to show that moral claims are not actually "claims" at all, but are rather expressions of feelings of approval or disapproval. Accordingly, for ethics to be meaningful, it must restrict itself to clarifying moral concepts and definitions, leaving other aspects to psychology and sociology.

Language, Truth and Logic
A.J. Ayer

CHAPTER 6
CRITIQUE OF ETHICS AND THEOLOGY

There is still one objection to be met before we can claim to have justified our view that all synthetic propositions are empirical hypotheses. This objection is based on the common supposition that our speculative knowledge is of two distinct kinds - that which relates to questions of empirical fact, and that which relates to questions of value. It will be said that 'statements of value' are genuine synthetic propositions, but that they cannot with any show of justice be represented as hypotheses, which are used to predict the course of our sensations; and, accordingly, that the existence of ethics and aesthetics as branches of speculative knowledge presents an insuperable objection to our radical empiricist thesis.

In face of this objection, it is our business to give an account of 'judgments of value' which is both satisfactory in itself and consistent with our general empiricist principles. We shall set ourselves to show that in so far as statements of value are significant, they are ordinary 'scientific' statements; and that in so far as they are not scientific, they are not in the literal sense significant, but are simply expressions of emotion which can be neither true nor false. In maintaining this view, we may confine ourselves for the present to the case of ethical statements. What is said about them will be found to apply, mutatis mutandis, to the case of aesthetic statements also.

The ordinary system of ethics, as elaborated in the works of ethical philosophers, is very far from being a homogeneous whole. Not only is it apt to contain pieces of metaphysics, and analyses of non-ethical concepts: its actual ethical contents are themselves of very different kinds. We may divide them, indeed, into four main classes. There are, first of all, propositions which express definitions of ethical terms, or judgments about the legitimacy or possibility of certain definition, Secondly, there are propositions describing the phenomena of moral experience, and their causes. Thirdly, there are exhortations to moral virtue. And, lastly, there are actual ethical judgments. It is unfortunately the case that the distinction between these four classes, plain as it is, is commonly ignored by ethical philosophers; with the result that it is often very difficult to tell from their works what it is that they are seeking to discover or prove.

In fact, it is easy to see that only the first of our four classes, namely that which comprises the propositions relating to the definitions of ethical terms, can be said to constitute ethical philosophy. The propositions which describe the phenomena of moral experience, and their causes, must be assigned to the science of psychology, or sociology. The exhortations to moral virtue are not propositions at all, but ejaculations or commands which are designed to provoke the reader to action of a certain sort. Accordingly, they do not belong to any branch of philosophy or science. As for the expressions of ethical judgments, we have not yet determined how they should be classified. But inasmuch as they are certainly neither definitions nor comments upon, definitions, nor quotations, we may say decisively that they do not belong to ethical philosophy. A strictly philosophical treatise on ethics should therefore make no ethical pronouncements. But it should, by giving an analysis of ethical terms, show what is the category to which all such pronouncements belong. And this is what we are now about to do.

A question which is often discussed by ethical philosophers is whether it is possible to find definitions which would reduce all ethical terms to one or two fundamental terms. But this question, though it undeniably belongs to ethical philosophy, is not relevant to our present inquiry. We are not now concerned to discover which term, within the sphere of ethical terms, is to be taken as fundamental; whether, for example, 'good' can be defined in terms of 'right' or 'right' in terms of 'good', or both in terms of 'value'. What we are interested in is the possibility of reducing the whole sphere of ethical terms to non-ethical terms. We are inquiring whether statements of ethical value can be translated into statements of empirical fact.

That they can be so translated is the contention of those ethical philosophers who are commonly called subjectivists, and of those who are known as utilitarians. For the utilitarian defines the rightness of actions, and the goodness of ends, in terms of the pleasure, or happiness, or satisfaction, to which they give rise; the subjectivist, in terms of the feelings of approval which a certain person, or group of people, has towards them. Each of these types of definition makes moral judgments into a sub-class of psychological or sociological judgments; and for this reason they are very attractive to us. For, if either was correct, it would follow that ethical assertions were not generally different from the factual assertions which are ordinarily contrasted with them; and the account which we have already given of empirical hypotheses would apply to them also.

Nevertheless we shall not adopt either a subjectivist or a utilitarian analysis of ethical terms. We reject the subjectivist view that to call an action right, or a thing good, is to say that it is generally approved of, because it is not self-contradictory to assert that some actions which are generally approved of are not right, or that some things which are generally approved of are not good. And we reject the alternative subjectivist view that a man who asserts that a certain action is right, or that a certain thing is good, is saying that he himself approves of it, on the ground that a man who confessed that he sometimes approved of what was bad or wrong would not be contradicting himself. And a similar argument is fatal to utilitarianism. We cannot agree that to call an action right is to say that of all the actions possible in the circumstances it would cause, or be likely to cause, the greatest happiness, or the greatest balance of pleasure over pain, or the greatest balance of satisfied over unsatisfied desire, because we find that it is not self-contradictory to say that it is sometimes wrong to perform the action which would actually or probably cause the greatest happiness, or the greatest balance of pleasure over pain, or of satisfied over unsatisfied desire, And since it is not self-contradictory to say that some pleasant things are not good, or that some bad things are desired, it cannot be the case that the sentence 'x is good' is equivalent to 'x is pleasant', or to 'x is desired'. And to every other variant of utilitarianism with which I am acquainted the same objection can be made. And therefore we should, I think, conclude that the validity of ethical judgments is not determined by the felicific tendencies of actions, any more than, by the nature of people's feelings; but that it must be regarded as 'absolute' or 'intrinsic', and not empirically calculable.

If we say this, we are not, of course, denying that it is possible to invent a language in which all ethical symbols are definable in non-ethical terms, or even that it is desirable to invent such a language and adopt it in place of our own; what we are denying is that the suggested reduction of ethical to non-ethical statements is consistent with the conventions of our actual language. That is, we reject utilitarianism and subjectivism, not as proposals to replace our existing ethical notions by new ones, but as analyses of our existing ethical notions. Our contention is simply that in our language, sentences which contain normative ethical symbol are not equivalent to sentences which express psychological propositions, or indeed empirical propositions of any kind.

It is advisable here to make it plain that it is only normative ethical symbols, and not descriptive ethical symbols, that are held by us to be indefinable in factual terms. There is a danger of confusing these two types of symbols, because they are commonly constituted by signs of the same sensible form. Thus a complex sign of the form 'x is wrong' may constitute a sentence which expresses a moral judgment concerning a certain type of Conduct, or it may constitute a sentence which states that a certain type of conduct is repugnant to the moral sense of a particular society. In the latter case, the symbol 'wrong' is a descriptive ethical symbol, and the sentence in which it occurs expresses an ordinary sociological proposition; in the former case, the symbol 'wrong' is a normative ethical symbol, and the sentence in which it occurs does not, we maintain, express an empirical proposition at all. It is only with normative ethics that we are at present concerned; so that whenever ethical symbols are used in the course of this argument without qualification, they are always to be interpreted as symbols of the normative type.

In admitting that normative ethical concepts are irreducible to empirical concepts, we seem to be leaving the way clear for the "absolutist" view of ethics - that is, the view that statements of value are not controlled by observation, as ordinary empirical propositions are, but only by a mysterious 'intellectual intuition'. A feature of this theory, which is seldom recognized by its advocates, is that it makes statements of value unverifiable. For it is notorious that what seems intuitively certain to one person may seem doubtful, or even false, to another. So that unless it is possible to provide some criterion by which one may decide between conflicting intuitions, a mere appeal to intuition is worthless as a test of a proposition's validity. But in the case of moral judgments no such criterion can be given. Some moralists claim to settle the matter by saying that they 'know' that their own moral judgments are correct. But such an assertion is of purely psychological interest, and has not the slightest tendency to prove the validity of any moral judgment. For dissentient moralists may equally well 'know' that their ethical views are correct. And, as far as subjective certainty goes, there will be nothing to choose between them. When such differences of opinion arise in connexion with an ordinary empirical proposition, one may attempt to resolve them by referring to, or actually carrying out, some relevant empirical test. But with regard to ethical statements, there is, on the 'absolutist' or "intuitionist' theory, no relevant empirical test. We are therefore justified in saying that on this theory ethical statements are held to be unverifiable. They are, of course, also held to be genuine synthetic propositions.

Considering the use which we have made of the principle that a synthetic proposition is significant only if it is empirically verifiable, it is clear that the acceptance of an 'absolutist' theory of ethics would undermine the whole of our main argument. And as we have already rejected the 'naturalistic' theories which are commonly supposed to provide the only alternative to 'absolutism' in ethics, we seem to have reached a difficult position. We shall meet the difficulty by showing that the correct treatment of ethical statements is afforded by a third theory, which is wholly compatible with our radical empiricism.

We begin by admitting that the fundamental ethical concepts are unanalysable, inasmuch as there is no criterion by which one can test the validity of the judgments in which they occur. So far we are in agreement with the absolutists. But, unlike the absolutists, we are able to give an explanation of that fact about ethical concepts. We say that the reason why they are unanalysable is that they are mere pseudo-concepts. The presence of an ethical symbol in a proposition adds nothing to its factual content. Thus if I say to someone, 'You acted wrongly in stealing that money,' I am not stating anything more than if I had simply said, 'You stole that money.' In adding that this action is wrong I am not making any further statement about it. I am simply evincing my moral disapproval of it. It is as if I had said, 'You stole that money,' in a peculiar tone of horror, or written it with the addition of some special exclamation marks. The tone, or the exclamation marks, adds nothing to the literal meaning of the sentence. It merely serves to show that the expression of it is attended by certain feelings in the speaker.

If now I generalize my previous statement and say. 'Stealing money is wrong.' I produce a sentence which has no factual meaning - that is, expresses no proposition which can be either true or false, it is as if I had written 'Stealing money! ! ' - where the shape and thickness of the exclamation marks show, by a suitable convention, that a special sort of moral disapproval is the feeling which is being expressed. It is clear that there is nothing said here which can be true or false, Another man may disagree with me about the wrongness of stealing, in the sense that he may not have the same feelings about stealing as I have, and he may quarrel with me on account of my moral sentiments. But he cannot, strictly speaking, contradict me. For in saying that a certain type of action is right or wrong, I am not making any factual statement, not even a statement about my own state of mind. I am merely expressing certain moral sentiments. And the man who is ostensibly contradicting me is merely expressing his moral sentiments. So that there is plainly no sense in asking which of us is in the right. For neither of us is asserting a genuine proposition.

What we have just been saying about the symbol 'wrong' applies to all normative ethical symbols. Sometimes they occur in sentences which record ordinary empirical facts besides expressing ethical feeling about those facts: sometimes they occur in sentences which simply express ethical feeling about a certain type of action, or situation, without making any statement of fact. But in every case in which one would commonly be said to be making an ethical judgment, the function of the relevant ethical word is purely 'emotive'. It is used to express feeling about certain objects, but not to make any assertion about them. It is worth mentioning that ethical terms do not serve only to express feeling. They are calculated also to arouse feeling, and so to stimulate action. Indeed some of them are used in such a way as to give the sentences in which they occur the effect of commands. Thus the sentence 'It is your duty to tell the truth' may be regarded both as the expression of a certain sort of ethical feeling about truthfulness and as the expression of the command 'Tell the truth.' The sentence 'You ought to tell the truth' also involves the command 'Tell the truth', but here the tone of the command is less emphatic. In the sentence 'It is good to tell the truth' the command has become little more than a suggestion. And thus the 'meaning' of the word 'good', in its ethical usage, is differentiated from that of the word 'duty' or the word 'ought'. In fact we may define the meaning of the various ethical words in terms both of the different feelings they are ordinarily taken to express, and also the different responses which they are calculated to provoke.

We can now see why it is impossible to find a criterion for determining the validity of ethical judgments. It is not because they have an 'absolute' validity which is mysteriously independent of ordinary sense-experience, but because they have no objective validity whatsoever. If a sentence makes no statement at all, there is obviously no sense in asking whether what it says is true or false. And we have seen, that sentences which simply express moral judgments do not say anything. They are pure expressions of feeling and as such do not come under the category of truth and falsehood. They are unverifiable for the same reason as a cry of pain or a word of command is unverifiable - because they do not express genuine propositions.

Thus, although our theory of ethics might fairly be said to be radically subjectivist, it differs in a very important respect from the orthodox subjectivist theory. For the orthodox subjectivist does not deny, as we do, that the sentences of a moralizer express genuine propositions, All he denies is that they express propositions of a unique non-empirical character- His own view is that they express propositions about the speaker's feelings. If this were so, ethical judgments clearly would be capable of being true or false. They would be true if the speaker had the relevant feelings, and false if he had not. And this is a matter which is in principle, empirically verifiable. Furthermore they could be significantly contradicted. For if I say, 'Tolerance is a virtue.' and someone answers, 'You don't approve of it,' he would, on the ordinary subjectivist theory, be contradicting me. On our theory, he would not be contradicting me, because, in saying that tolerance was a virtue, I should not be making any statement about my own feelings or about anything else. I should simply be evincing my feelings, which is not at all the same thing as saying that I have them.

The distinction between the expression of feeling and the assertion of feeling is complicated by the fact that the assertion that one has a certain feeling often accompanies the expression of that feeling, and is then, indeed, a factor in the expression of that feeling. Thus I may simultaneously express boredom and say that I am bored, and in that case my utterance of the words 'I am bored' is one of the circumstances which make it true to say that I am expressing or evincing boredom. But I can express boredom without actually saying that I am bored. I can express it by my tone and gestures, while making a statement about something wholly unconnected with it, or by an ejaculation, or without uttering any words at all. So that even if the assertion that one has a certain feeling always involves the expression of that feeling, the expression of a feeling assuredly does not always involve the assertion that one has it. And this is the important point to grasp in considering the distinction between our theory and the ordinary subjectivist theory. For whereas the subjectivist holds that ethical statements actually assert the existence of certain feelings, we hold that ethical statements: are expressions and excitants of feeling which do not necessarily involve any assertions.

We have already remarked that the main objection to the ordinary subjectivist theory is that the validity of ethical judgments is not determined by the nature of their author's feelings. And this is an objection which our theory escapes. For it does not imply that the existence of any feelings is a necessary and sufficient condition of the validity of an ethical judgment. It implies, on the contrary, that ethical judgments have no validity. There is, however, a celebrated argument against subjectivist theories which our theory does not escape. It has been pointed out by Moore that if ethical statements were simply statements about the speaker's feelings, it would be impossible to argue about questions of value.' To take a typical example: if a man said that thrift was a virtue, and another replied that it was a vice, they would not, on this theory, be disputing with one another. One would be saying that he approved of thrift, and the other that he didn't; and there is no reason why both these statements should not be true. Now Moore held it to be obvious that we do dispute about questions of value, and accordingly concluded that the particular form of subjectivism which he was discussing was false.

It is plain that the conclusion that it is impossible to dispute about questions of value follows from our theory also. For as we hold that such sentences as 'Thrift is a virtue' and 'Thrift is a vice' do not express propositions at all, we clearly cannot hold that they express incompatible propositions. We must therefore admit that if Moore's argument really refutes the ordinary subjectivist theory, it also refutes ours. But, in fact, we deny that it does refute even the ordinary subjectivist theory. For we hold that one really never does dispute about questions of value.

This may seem, at first sight to be a very paradoxical assertion. For we certainly do engage in disputes which are ordinarily regarded as disputes about questions of value, But, in all such cases, we find, if we consider the matter closely, that the dispute is not really about a question of value, but about a question of fact. When someone disagrees with us about the moral value of a certain action or type of action, we do admittedly resort to argument in order to win him over to our way of thinking. But we do not attempt to show by our arguments that he has the 'wrong' ethical feeling towards a situation whose nature he has correctly apprehended. What we attempt to show is that he is mistaken about the facts of the case. We argue that he has misconceived the agent's motive: or that he has misjudged the effects of the action, or its probable effects in view of the agent's knowledge; or that he has failed to take into account the special circumstances in which the agent was placed. Or else we employ more general arguments about the effects which actions of a certain type tend to produce, or the qualities which are usually manifested in their performance. We do this in the hope that we have only to get our opponent to agree with us about the nature of the empirical facts for him to adopt the same moral attitude towards them as we do. And as the people with whom we argue have generally received the same moral education as ourselves, and live in the same social order, our expectation is usually justified. But if our opponent happens to have undergone a different process of moral 'conditioning' from ourselves, so that, even when he acknowledges all the facts, he still disagrees with us about the moral value of the actions under discussion, then we abandon the attempt to convince him by argument. We say that it is impossible to argue with him because he has a distorted or undeveloped moral sense; which signifies merely that he employs a different set of values from our own. We feel that our own system of values is superior, and therefore speak in such derogatory terms of his. But we cannot bring forward any arguments to show that our system is superior. For our judgment that it is so is itself a judgment of value, and accordingly outside the scope of argument. It is because argument fails us when we come to deal with pure questions of value, as distinct from questions of fact, that we finally resort to mere abuse.

In short, we find that argument is possible on moral questions only if some system of values is presupposed. If our opponent concurs with us in expressing moral disapproval of all actions of a given type t, then we may get him to condemn a particular action A, by bringing forward arguments to show that A is of type t. For the question whether A does or does not belong to that type is a plain question of fact. Given that a man has certain moral principles, we argue that he must, in order to be consistent, react morally to certain things in a certain way. What we do not and cannot argue about is the validity of these moral principles. We merely praise or condemn them in the light of our own feelings.

If anyone doubts the accuracy of this account of moral disputes, let him try to construct even an imaginary argument on a question of value which does not reduce itself to an argument about a question of logic or about an empirical matter of fact, I am confident that he will not succeed in producing a single example. And if that is the case, he must allow that its involving the impossibility of purely ethical arguments is not, as Moore thought, a ground of objection to our theory, but rather a point in favour of it.

Having upheld our theory against the only criticism which appeared to threaten it, we may now use it to define the nature of all ethical inquiries. We find that ethical philosophy consists simply in saying that ethical concepts are pseudo-concepts and therefore unanalysable. The further task of describing the different feelings that the different ethical terms are used to express, and the different reactions that they customarily provoke, is a task for the psychologist. There cannot be such a thing as ethical science, if by ethical science one means the elaboration of a 'true' system of morals. For we have seen that, as ethical judgments are mere expressions of feeling, there can be no way of determining the validity of any ethical system, and, indeed, no sense in asking whether any such system is true. All that one may legitimately inquire in this connection is, What are the moral habits of a given person or group of people, and what causes them to have precisely those habits and feelings? And this inquiry falls wholly within the scope of the existing social sciences.

It appears, then, that ethics, as a branch of knowledge, is nothing more than a department of psychology and sociology. And in case anyone thinks that we are overlooking the existence of casuistry, we may remark that casuistry is not a science, but is a purely analytical investigation of the structure of a given moral system. In other words, it is an exercise in formal logic.

When one comes to pursue the psychological inquiries which constitute ethical science, one is immediately enabled to account for the Kantian and hedonistic theories of morals. For one finds that one of the chief causes of moral behaviour is fear, both conscious and unconscious, of a god's displeasure, and fear of the enmity of society. And this, indeed, is the reason, why moral precepts present themselves to some people as 'categorical' commands. And one finds, also, that the moral code of a society is partly determined by the beliefs of that society concerning the conditions of its own happiness - or, in other words, that a society tends to encourage or discourage a given type of conduct by the use of moral sanctions according as it appears to promote or detract from the contentment of the society as a whole. And this is the reason why altruism is recommended in most moral codes and egotism condemned. It is from the observation of this connexion between morality and happiness that hedonistic or eudaemonistic theories of morals ultimately spring, just as the moral theory of Kant is based on the fact, previously explained, that moral precepts have for some people the force of inexorable commands. As each of these theories ignores the fact which lies at the root of the other, both may be criticized as being one-sided; but this is not the main objection to either of them. Their essential defect is that they treat propositions which refer to the causes and attributes of our ethical feelings as if they were definitions of ethical concepts. And thus they fail to recognize that ethical concepts are pseudo-concepts and consequently indefinable.

Chapter 7: Moral Sentimentalism

Comprehension questions you should be able to answer after reading this chapter:

1. Describe the role of "sympathy" in moral judgment, according to Smith.

2. What is the "impartial spectator?" What function does it serve?

3. How are general moral rules formed, according to Smith?

4. What is the "invisible hand?" What purpose does it serve? What is its source/origin?

5. What is the value of the pursuit of self-interest, for Smith?

6. How does the division of labor (and specialization) create wealth?

7. How can the division of labor dull the intellect, according to Smith? How can this be prevented?

8. How is it a mistake to admire the wealthy, according to Smith? Why is this envy threatening to the accuracy of our moral judgments?

9. Why does Smith think it is right for the government to provide for the poor, including, at least, universal education?

Background

Adam Smith was the "Founding Father" of capitalism. He was a tireless crusader for "laissez-faire" economics, a ceaseless foe of taxation, and a firm believer in the value of wealth, and the virtues of the wealthy. He was opposed to government intervention, in general, and believed that government efforts to help the poor, especially at the expense of the wealthy, were woefully misguided and illegitimate.

Most of that preceding paragraph was much more mythology than reality! Indeed, some of it is patently and demonstrably false.

In truth, although Smith is very often quoted, he is very rarely read (even by those who quote him), and even more rarely understood. This is not to say that the myth of Adam Smith bears no resemblance to the real man at all. Smith did offer offers accounts of the division of labor, free trade, self-interest in economic transactions, limited government intervention, pricing, and general market structures. He was not, however, primarily an economist, and the free market is just *one* component of his broader theory of human interaction.

Smith was born in June of 1723, in Kirkcaldy (Eastern Scotland). In 1737 he went to Glasgow College at the age of 13, and then on to Oxford University, where he was taught by Francis Hutcheson, an early leader of the "Scottish Enlightenment." More so than an economist, Smith was a philosopher. Smith held the Chair of Logic from 1751-1752, and then was appointed to Hutcheson's old chair: the Chair of Moral Philosophy.

His *Theory of Moral Sentiments* (first published in 1759) is an account of morality:

how we ought to behave, and how we are to know such things. The book was well-received, including by his equally-if-not-more-famous friend David Hume.

> ... *Supposing, therefore, that you have duly prepared yourself for the worst by all these reflections, I proceed to tell you the melancholy news that your book has been very unfortunate, for the public seem disposed to applaud it extremely. It was looked for by the foolish people with some impatience; and the mob of literati are beginning already to be very loud in its praises. Three bishops called yesterday at Millar's shop in order to buy copies, and to ask questions about the author. The Bishop of Peter-borough said he had passed the evening in a company where he heard it extolled above all books in the world. You may conclude what Opinion true Philosophers will entertain of it, when these Retainers of Superstition praise it so highly.*[80]

After the success of the *Theory of Moral Sentiments*, Smith was offered a lucrative tutoring position by Charles Townshend (the Chancellor of Exchequer responsible for the taxes that triggered the American Revolution!). He moved with the family to France in 1763, where he became bored. The abundance of free time gave him time to write the *Wealth of Nations*, however.

> *The Duke is acquainted with no Frenchman whatever. I cannot cultivate the acquaintance of the few with whom I am acquainted, as I cannot bring them to our house, and am not always at liberty to go to theirs. The life which I led at Glasgow was a pleasurable dissipated life in comparison of that which I lead here at Present. I have begun to write a book in order to pass away the time.*[81]

He eventually returned to London and continued working for Townshend until 1767. He was elected to the Royal Society at this time, and published the *Wealth of Nations* in 1776—four months before the signing of the United States Declaration of Independence. This book, too, was immediately well-received. He published nothing else of significance in his life, and died on July 17th, 1790.

Although it is tempting to leap into a discussion of Smith's economic views, this neglects the fact that his views on economics were derived, in part, from his earlier philosophical work. Moreover, this is an ethics textbook, not a text on economics nor even political philosophy! As such, we will focus, instead, on his account of "sympathy" as developed in the *Theory of Moral Sentiments*.

Sympathy

Smith rejected any purely "self-interested" interpretation of human nature. The very first sentence of the *Theory of Moral Sentiments* makes this clear. "How selfish soever man may be supposed, there are evidently some principles in his nature, which interest him in the fortune of others, and render their happiness necessary to him, though he derives nothing from it except the pleasure of seeing it."

In contrast to selfish individualists, Smith considers people to be social beings.

---

[80] Letter from Hume to Smith, April 12th, 1759.
[81] Letter from Smith to Hume, July 5th, 1764.

We care about others, with their happiness or unhappiness bringing us our own pleasure or pain. Smith was undoubtedly influenced by his close friend, David Hume, with regard to "sympathy." What follows is a section not from Smith, but from Hume's *Treatise on Human Nature.*

When experience has once given us a competent knowledge of human affairs, and has taught us the proportion they bear to human passion, we perceive, that the generosity of men is very limited, and that it seldom extends beyond their friends and family, or, at most, beyond their native country. Being thus acquainted with the nature of man, we expect not any impossibilities from him; but confine our view to that narrow circle, in which any person moves, in order to form a judgment of his moral character. When the natural tendency of his passions leads him to be serviceable and useful within his sphere, we approve of his character, and love his person, by a sympathy with the sentiments of those, who have a more particular connexion with him. We are quickly oblig'd to forget our own interest in our judgments of this kind, by reason of the perpetual contradictions, we meet with in society and conversation, from persons that are not plac'd in the same situation, and have not the same interest with ourselves. The only point of view, in which our sentiments concur with those of others, is, when we consider the tendency of any passion to the advantage or harm of those, who have any immediate connexion or intercourse with the person possess'd of it. And tho' this advantage or harm be often very remote from ourselves, yet sometimes 'tis very near us, and interests us strongly by sympathy. This concern we readily extend to other cases, that are resembling; and when these are very remote, our sympathy is proportionably weaker, and our praise or blame fainter and more doubtful. The case is here the same as in our judgments concerning external bodies. All objects seem to diminish by their distance: But tho' the appearance of objects to our senses be the original standard, by which we judge of them, yet we do not say, that they actually diminish by the distance; but correcting the appearance by reflection, arrive at a more constant and establish'd judgment concerning them. In like manner, tho' sympathy be much fainter than our concern for ourselves, and a sympathy with persons remote from us much fainter than that with persons near and contiguous; yet we neglect all these differences in our calm judgments concerning the characters of men. Besides, that we ourselves often change our situation in this particular, we every day meet with persons, who are in a different situation from ourselves, and who cou'd never converse with us on any reasonable terms, were we to remain constantly in that situation and point of view, which is peculiar to us. The intercourse of sentiments, therefore, in society and conversation, makes us form some general inalterable standard, by which we may approve or disapprove of characters and manners. And tho' the heart does not always take part with those general notions, or regulate its love and hatred by them, yet are they sufficient for discourse, and serve all our purposes in company, in the pulpit, on the theatre, and in the schools.

From these principles we may easily account for that merit, which is commonly ascrib'd to generosity, humanity, compassion, gratitude, friendship, fidelity,

zeal, disinterestedness, liberality, and all those other qualities, which form the
character of good and benevolent. A propensity to the tender passions makes a
man agreeable and useful in all the parts of life; and gives a just direction to all
his other qualities, which otherwise may become prejudicial to society. Courage
and ambition, when not regulated by benevolence, are fit only to make a tyrant
and public robber. 'Tis the same case with judgment and capacity, and all the
qualities of that kind. They are indifferent in themselves to the interests of
society, and have a tendency to the good or ill of mankind, according as they are
directed by these other passions.[82]

Sympathy is, arguably, the basis for Smith's entire moral philosophy.[83] Sympathy
(for Smith) arises when we imagine how we would feel in the circumstances of others.
The "process" of sympathy is roughly as follows:

1.   The observer witnesses the actions/reactions of the actor.
2.   The observer imagines what it's like to be the actor in those circumstances,
     and imagines what he (the observer) would do in their place.
3.   If the imagined reaction is similar to the observed reaction, the observer
     sympathizes with the actor.
4.   If the imagined reaction is significantly different from the observed
     reaction, the observer does not sympathize.

This process, one must note, requires imagination. Sympathy is a reaction not just
to someone's experience, but their experience in a context. "Fury" might inspire
compassion for the furious, if they have been horribly wronged, but unwarranted
anger (given the circumstances) can actually produce the opposite effect. Similarly,
we might feel sadness in a situation, even when the actor, himself, does not. Our
ability to discern what an "impartial spectator" would feel in contexts drives this
ability, and also helps us to be sympathetic even when our own actual feelings are
lacking. For example, if we just lost a loved one, our grief might prevent us from
feeling joy at a friend's good fortune—but our recognition of the appropriateness of
that joy allows us to still "be happy" for that person, even if we're not feeling it
ourselves.

Although sympathy (empathy) is about what we imagine we would feel as the
other in those same circumstances, sympathy is not about *me* (or you, respectively).
That is, it is not a self-interested, let alone "selfish," orientation.

Sympathy, however, cannot, in any sense, be regarded as a selfish principle.
When I sympathize with your sorrow or your indignation, it may be pretended,
indeed, that my emotion is founded in self-love, because it arises from bringing
your case home to myself, from putting myself in your situation, and thence
conceiving what I should feel in the like circumstances. But though sympathy is
very properly said to arise from an imaginary change of situations with the

---

[82] Hume, *A Treatise of Human Nature*, 3.3.3.2-3.3.3.4.
[83] What Smith calls sympathy is what, today, we more often call *empathy*.

person principally concerned, yet this imaginary change is not supposed to happen to me in my own person and character, but in that of the person with whom I sympathize. When I condole with you for the loss of your only son, in order to enter into your grief I do not consider what I, a person of such a character and profession, should suffer, if I had a son, and if that son was unfortunately to die: but I consider what I should suffer if I was really you, and I not only change circumstances with you, but I change persons and characters. My grief, therefore, is entirely upon your account, and not in the least upon my own. It is not, therefore, in the least selfish. How can that be regarded as a selfish passion, which does not arise even from the imagination of any thing that has befallen, or that relates to myself, in my own proper person and character, but which is entirely occupied about what relates to you? A man may sympathize with a woman in child-bed; though it is impossible that he should conceive himself as suffering her pains in his own proper person and character. That whole account of human nature, however, which deduces all sentiments and affections from self-love, which has made so much noise in the world, but which, so far as I know, has never yet been fully and distinctly explained, seems to me to have arisen from some confused misapprehension of the system of sympathy.[84]

This quotation should make it clear that Smith did not regard sympathy as egoistic. It is not a matter of imagining myself in similar circumstances, but of imagining myself as *you*.

In order to produce this concord, as nature teaches the spectators to assume the circumstances of the person principally concerned, so she teaches this last in some measure to assume those of the spectators. As they are continually placing themselves in his situation, and thence conceiving emotions similar to what he feels; so he is as constantly placing himself in theirs, and thence conceiving some degree of that coolness about his own fortune, with which he is sensible that they will view it. As they are constantly considering what they themselves would feel, if they actually were the sufferers, so he is as constantly led to imagine in what manner he would be affected if he was only one of the spectators of his own situation. As their sympathy makes them look at it, in some measure, with his eyes, so his sympathy makes him look at it, in some measure, with theirs, especially when in their presence and acting under their observation: and as the reflected passion, which he thus conceives, is much weaker than the original one, it necessarily abates the violence of what he felt before he came into their presence, before he began to recollect in what manner they would be affected by it, and to view his situation in this candid and impartial light.[85]

It is not always easy to truly imagine yourself in another person's situation. *Effective* sympathy requires information about events and people. Without it, it's difficult for us to sympathize. There are limits to our actual capacity for sympathy,

---

[84] *The Moral Sentiments*, Part VI, Section iii, chapter 1.
[85] Ibid., Part I, Section i, chapter 4.

and sympathy can be impeded by ignorance of particular circumstances, or personal biases.

If I don't really understand "you," or your life circumstances—if you and your life is something "foreign" to me—then it will likely be difficult for me to imagine myself "in your shoes." The problem with this is that, among other things, it can interfere with sympathy.

> Let us suppose that the great empire of China, with all its myriads of inhabitants, was suddenly swallowed up by an earthquake, and let us consider how a man of humanity in Europe, who had no sort of connexion with that part of the world, would be affected upon receiving intelligence of this dreadful calamity. He would, I imagine, first of all, express very strongly his sorrow for the misfortune of that unhappy people, he would make many melancholy reflections upon the precariousness of human life, and the vanity of all the labours of man, which could thus be annihilated in a moment. He would too, perhaps, if he was a man of speculation, enter into many reasonings concerning the effects which this disaster might produce upon the commerce of Europe, and the trade and business of the world in general. And when all this fine philosophy was over, when all these humane sentiments had been once fairly expressed, he would pursue his business or his pleasure, take his repose or his diversion, with the same ease and tranquillity, as if no such accident had happened. The most frivolous disaster which could befal himself would occasion a more real disturbance. If he was to lose his little finger to-morrow, he would not sleep to-night; but, provided he never saw them, he will snore with the most profound security over the ruin of a hundred millions of his brethren, and the destruction of that immense multitude seems plainly an object less interesting to him, than this paltry misfortune of his own. To prevent, therefore, this paltry misfortune to himself, would a man of humanity be willing to sacrifice the lives of a hundred millions of his brethren, provided he had never seen them? Human nature startles with horror at the thought, and the world, in its greatest depravity and corruption, never produced such a villain as could be capable of entertaining it. But what makes this difference? When our passive feelings are almost always so sordid and so selfish, how comes it that our active principles should often be so generous and so noble? When we are always so much more deeply affected by whatever concerns ourselves, than by whatever concerns other men; what is it which prompts the generous, upon all occasions, and the mean upon many, to sacrifice their own interests to the greater interests of others? It is not the soft power of humanity, it is not that feeble spark of benevolence which Nature has lighted up in the human heart, that is thus capable of counteracting the strongest impulses of self-love. It is a stronger power, a more forcible motive, which exerts itself upon such occasions. It is reason, principle, conscience, the inhabitant of the breast, the man within, the great judge and arbiter of our conduct. It is he who, whenever we are about to act so as to affect the happiness of others, calls to us, with a voice capable of astonishing the most presumptuous of our passions, that we are but one of the multitude, in no respect better than any other in it; and that when we prefer ourselves so shamefully and so blindly to others, we become the proper objects of resentment, abhorrence, and

execration. It is from him only that we learn the real littleness of ourselves, and of whatever relates to ourselves, and the natural misrepresentations of self-love can be corrected only by the eye of this impartial spectator.[86]

Thinking only from our own perspective, my might feel more sorrow for the loss of our own little finger than we would at the deaths of numerous strangers from "strange" lands. To correct for this limitation, our goal should be to judge and act based on how an "impartial spectator" would. This idea of the "impartial spectator" is crucial for understanding Smith's theory of moral judgment, and it is repeated throughout the *Theory of Moral Sentiments*.

When I endeavour to examine my own conduct, when I endeavour to pass sentence upon it, and either to approve or condemn it, it is evident that, in all such cases, I divide myself, as it were, into two persons; and that I, the examiner and judge, represent a different character from that other I, the person whose conduct is examined into and judged of. The first is the spectator, whose sentiments with regard to my own conduct I endeavour to enter into, by placing myself in his situation, and by considering how it would appear to me, when seen from that particular point of view. The second is the agent, the person whom I properly call myself, and of whose conduct, under the character of a spectator, I was endeavouring to form some opinion. The first is the judge; the second the person judged of. But that the judge should, in every respect, be the same with the person judged of, is as impossible, as that the cause should, in every respect, be the same with the effect.[87]

And again:

But we admire that noble and generous resentment which governs its pursuit of the greatest injuries, not by the rage which they are apt to excite in the breast of the sufferer, but by the indignation which they naturally call forth in that of the impartial spectator; which allows no word, no gesture, to escape it beyond what this more equitable sentiment would dictate; which never, even in thought, attempts any greater vengeance, nor desires to inflict any greater punishment, than what every indifferent person would rejoice to see executed.[88]

Smith thinks that the feelings the impartial spectator would have are the ones that correctly fit the situation. They are the feelings that we *should* feel, in that situation, as well.

To sympathize with another's feelings is to implicitly approve of them, and to sympathize as we imagine an impartial spectator would, is to bestow moral approval on those feelings.

Of course, not every "feeling" we have is equally legitimate! I might feel revulsion, when none is called for. Or, I might feel "nothing," when I should feel sorrow. The

---

[86] Ibid., Part III, Chapter 3.
[87] Ibid., Part III, Chapter 1.
[88] Ibid., Part I, Section i, Chapter 5.

feelings of the impartial spectator are thus the measure by which our own sentiments can be judged, indicating that some emotional responses are "correct," and others are "incorrect."

The impartial spectator provides a guide for our feelings, and, ultimately, a guide for our actions as well. We desire the sympathy of others, and so will regulate our actions to procure it. We will limit our displays of anger, and be humble in our moments of triumph—all to garner the sympathy of spectators, based on what we anticipate would seem appropriate to them. We can imagine what someone *should* feel (e.g., that the death of millions of people is far more tragic than the loss of a single finger!), and then act accordingly. Moral norms, then, can be understood in terms of the feelings expressed by the impartial spectator.

From the imagined feelings of the impartial spectator, we derive moral norms, and from moral norms we can develop moral rules. Moral rules are formed on the basis of our reactions to specific instances of especially disturbing actions (e.g., rape, murder). Our experience of such events is so repulsive that we, in effect, vow that we would never do such a thing—and surely the "impartial spectator" has the same revulsion, and would limit his or her actions in the same way.

> *It is thus that the general rules of morality are formed. They are ultimately founded upon experience of what, in particular instances, our moral faculties, our natural sense of merit and propriety, approve, or disapprove of. We do not originally approve or condemn particular actions; because, upon examination, they appear to be agreeable or inconsistent with a certain general rule. The general rule, on the contrary, is formed, by finding from experience, that all actions of a certain kind, or circumstanced in a certain manner, are approved or disapproved of. To the man who first saw an inhuman murder, committed from avarice, envy, or unjust resentment, and upon one too that loved and trusted the murderer, who beheld the last agonies of the dying person, who heard him, with his expiring breath, complain more of the perfidy and ingratitude of his false friend, than of the violence which had been done to him, there could be no occasion, in order to conceive how horrible such an action was, that he should reflect, that one of the most sacred rules of conduct was what prohibited the taking away the life of an innocent person, that this was a plain violation of that rule, and consequently a very blamable action. His detestation of this crime, it is evident, would arise instantaneously and antecedent to his having formed to himself any such general rule. The general rule, on the contrary, which he might afterwards form, would be founded upon the detestation which he felt necessarily arise in his own breast, at the thought of this, and every other particular action of the same kind.*[89]

These general rules give us minimal guidelines to follow, even if our own actual feelings haven't caught up with those of the impartial spectator. I might not personally feel revulsion at the thought of killing someone I hate, but I recognize that the impartial spectator would feel that revulsion, and so I can guide my behavior accordingly, despite my lack of appropriate sentiment.

---

[89] Ibid., Part 3, Chapter 4.

Although Smith's teacher, Frances Hutcheson, as well as his friend Hume, were arguably "proto-utilitarians," Smith resisted the temptation to reduce all of morality to just an emphasis on consequences." If anything, he said his own approach aligned more with the (virtue) approach of Aristotle.

> *Virtue, according to Aristotle, consists in the habit of mediocrity according to right reason. Every particular virtue, according to him, lies in a kind of middle between two opposite vices, of which the one offends from being too much, the other from being too little affected by a particular species of objects. Thus the virtue of fortitude or courage lies in the middle between the opposite vices of cowardice and of presumptuous rashness, of which the one offends from being too much, and the other from being too little affected by the objects of fear. Thus too the virtue of frugality lies in a middle between avarice and profusion, of which the one consists in an excess, the other in a defect of the proper attention to the objects of self-interest. Magnanimity, in the same manner, lies in a middle between the excess of arrogance and the defect of pusillanimity, of which the one consists in too extravagant, the other in too weak a sentiment of our own worth and dignity. It is unnecessary to observe that this account of virtue corresponds too pretty exactly with what has been said above concerning the propriety and impropriety of conduct.[90]*

For Smith, the foundation, of all virtue is "self-command," which allows us to control and restrain our passions, and feel compassion for (and empathize with) others. We develop and internalize this capacity only after experiencing the disapproval of others. This first occurs as children at play. As adults, the major sphere in which this trait is developed and displayed is the "market" (i.e., in economic transactions). As an example, try getting (and keeping) a job if you are exclusively focused only on your own desires and gratification! "I know I'm supposed to be to work by 9 AM, but I'd prefer to sleep in later." To be blunt, my employer is unlikely to care that I "prefer" to sleep later than 9, if I'm supposed to be teaching a class at that time!

Market interactions require a careful consideration of "self-love."

> *But man has almost constant occasion for the help of his brethren, and it is in vain for him to expect it from their benevolence only. He will be more likely to prevail if he can interest their self-love in his favour, and shew them that it is for their own advantage to do for him what he requires of them. Whoever offers to another a bargain of any kind, proposes to do this. Give me that which I want, and you shall have this which you want, is the meaning of every such offer; and it is in this manner that we obtain from one another the far greater part of those good offices which we stand in need of. It is not from the benevolence of the butcher, the brewer, or the baker that we expect our dinner, but from their regard to their own interest. We address ourselves, not to their humanity, but to their self-love, and never talk to them of our own necessities, but of their advantages. Nobody but a beggar chooses to depend chiefly upon the*

---

[90] Ibid., Part VII, Section i, Chapter 2.

benevolence of his fellow-citizens. Even a beggar does not depend upon it entirely. The charity of well-disposed people, indeed, supplies him with the whole fund of his subsistence. But though this principle ultimately provides him with all the necessaries of life which he has occasion for, it neither does nor can provide him with them as he has occasion for them. The greater part of his occasional wants are supplied in the same manner as those of other people, by treaty, by barter, and by purchase. With the money which one man gives him he purchases food. The old clothes which another bestows upon him he exchanges for other clothes which suit him better, or for lodging, or for food, or for money, with which he can buy either food, clothes, or lodging, as he has occasion.[91]

Market interactions, despite the common ("mythological") interpretation of Smith, are *not* about channeling the raw self-interest of others to one's own advantage, but are interactions in which we must subordinate our exclusive focus on *our own* self-interest, and consider the *other*, in order to come to an agreement. As an example, if I am applying for a job, and the only thing I consider is what I want, and what will be good for me—as opposed to also considering how my services might be of value to my prospective employer—then it is unlikely that I will successfully "sell myself" to that employer. If it's "all about me," I probably won't get the job, and (perhaps ironically), my own self-interest will not be served after all. In contrast, if I approach the negotiation with a mind to what will be of interest to the employer, and if the employer is doing the same with regard to me, then it seems more likely that we will come to a mutually satisfactory agreement.

It is no accident that we have this capacity for sympathy, an ability to imagine how an impartial spectator would feel (using that to guide our own reactions and behavior), and a tendency to produce mutually beneficial outcomes when the interest of others are considered. For Smith, these things are all the product of the "Deity," an "invisible hand" guiding our conduct.

The "invisible hand," while usually understood only in the context of the free market, is actually a reference to the covert work of a (deistic) God intervening in human affairs for the betterment of all. The "invisible hand" thus refers to the several ways in which our "natural" pursuits (e.g., the pursuit of our self-interest, our pursuit of the sympathy of others, our pursuit of wealth, etc.) helps us, collectively. Certainly one of the arenas in which the invisible hand leads us is economics, but it is not the only, nor even the primary. First, it guides our sentiments and moral judgments.

This Deity gave humanity a surer guide to our collective well-being than reason alone: our "passions." Sympathy *moves* us, and then reason can be employed through the thought experiment of the impartial spectator, to expand the scope of our sympathy so that it reaches people and situations that our feelings, all by themselves, wouldn't reach. Sympathy (a feeling) is the foundation for our moral judgments, but it is reason that allows us to render moral judgments in fair and less partial (even if not *im*partial) ways.

---

[91] *Wealth of Nations*, Book I, Chapter 2.

Economics

Having established Smith's basic moral foundations, we will now turn to that for which he was most famous: his views on capitalism, and (more importantly for our purposes) the *ethical* dimensions of those views.

Smith, technically, did not actually endorse "capitalism," as that term didn't acquire widespread use until the next century. However, vocabulary notwithstanding, there is no doubt as to type of economic system he had in mind.

In Smith's view, a free market harnesses personal desire not just for the individual's benefit, but that of the community, as a whole. What makes the pursuit of self-interest in a free market *good*, and morally permissible, is the presumed fact that it benefits the *community*, and *not just the individual*. As a basic (and important) psychological premise, Smith argues that we all naturally seek our own betterment.

> *But the principle which prompts to save, is the desire of bettering our condition; a desire which, though generally calm and dispassionate, comes with us from the womb, and never leaves us till we go into the grave. In the whole interval which separates those two moments, there is scarce, perhaps, a single instance, in which any man is so perfectly and completely satisfied with his situation, as to be without any wish of alteration or improvement of any kind.[92]*

It is not by accident that we all seek to "better" our economic condition. Smith believed that the "invisible hand" implants in us a *confusion* of wealth with "betterment." That is, we think that having more money (or more resources, in general), will make our lives "better."

If we take the example of the iconic "small business owner," she will be driven by invisible hand to increase her wealth, and as a result, will *work* to do so. The fruits of her labor won't just be stored up in a bank, though, but will be reinvested in her business so as to acquire *more* wealth. She will invest in new and better technology, which will require not only more workers, but more specialized workers. This division of labor will increase production, and therefore increase profit—leading to economic growth and the betterment of all—once again emphasizing what is good for all, and not merely the individual.

> *Observe the accommodation of the most common artificer or day-labourer in a civilized and thriving country, and you will perceive that the number of people, of whose industry a part, though but a small part, has been employed in procuring him this accommodation, exceeds all computation. The woollen coat, for example, which covers the day-labourer, as coarse and rough as it may appear, is the produce of the joint labour of a great multitude of workmen. The shepherd, the sorter of the wool, the wool-comber or carder, the dyer, the scribbler, the spinner, the weaver, the fuller, the dresser, with many others, must all join their different arts in order to complete even this homely production. How many merchants and carriers, besides, must have been employed in transporting the materials from some of those workmen to others who often live*

---

[92] Ibid., Book II, Chapter 3.

in a very distant part of the country? How much commerce and navigation in particular, how many ship-builders, sailors, sail-makers, rope-makers, must have been employed in order to bring together the different drugs made use of by the dyer, which often come from the remotest corners of the world? What a variety of labour, too, is necessary in order to produce the tools of the meanest of those workmen! To say nothing of such complicated machines as the ship of the sailor, the mill of the fuller, or even the loom of the weaver, let us consider only what a variety of labour is requisite in order to form that very simple machine, the shears with which the shepherd clips the wool. The miner, the builder of the furnace for smelting the ore, the feller of the timber, the burner of the charcoal to be made use of in the smelting-house, the brickmaker, the bricklayer, the workmen who attend the furnace, the millwright, the forger, the smith, must all of them join their different arts in order to produce them. Were we to examine, in the same manner, all the different parts of his dress and household furniture, the coarse linen shirt which he wears next his skin, the shoes which cover his feet, the bed which he lies on, and all the different parts which compose it, the kitchen-grate at which he prepares his victuals, the coals which he makes use of for that purpose, dug from the bowels of the earth, and brought to him, perhaps, by a long sea and a long land-carriage, all the other utensils of his kitchen, all the furniture of his table, the knives and forks, the earthen or pewter plates upon which he serves up and divides his victuals, the different hands employed in preparing his bread and his beer, the glass window which lets in the heat and the light, and keeps out the wind and the rain, with all the knowledge and art requisite for preparing that beautiful and happy invention, without which these northern parts of the world could scarce have afforded a very comfortable habitation, together with the tools of all the different workmen employed in producing those different conveniencies; if we examine, I say, all these things, and consider what a variety of labour is employed about each of them, we shall be sensible that, without the assistance and co-operation of many thousands, the very meanest person in a civilized country could not be provided, even according to, what we very falsely imagine, the easy and simple manner in which he is commonly accommodated. Compared, indeed, with the more extravagant luxury of the great, his accommodation must no doubt appear extremely simple and easy; and yet it may be true, perhaps, that the accommodation of an European prince does not always so much exceed that of an industrious and frugal peasant, as the accommodation of the latter exceeds that of many an African king, the absolute masters of the lives and liberties of ten thousand naked savages.[93]

Setting aside the needless and breathtaking racism (no doubt the product of his time and culture, as it certainly is not warranted by his philosophical system), the basic point of his fantastic anecdote is that the production (and sale) of something even as simple as a wool coat involves, and enriches, far more people than we might initially realize—and that, within a market economy, even the "common day-labourer" who is but an "industrious and frugal peasant" has a lifestyle that exceeds

---

[93] Ibid., Book I, Chapter 1.

that of "many an African king."

A more culturally sensitive way to express his idea is that even "poor" people achieve levels of comparative wealth within capitalist systems—at least as compared to their counterparts within mercantilist, feudal, or other economic systems.

Key to this enrichment and aggrandizement, of course, is competition. The value of competition within a capitalist society is that individuals are driven by their desire for wealth, and competition dismantles rigid class structures by allowing for social mobility. In theory, the "best" will prevail, whether it be the best applicant for a job, or the best product in the marketplace. The "best" isn't determined by your last name, or gender, or race, or noble title, or anything else other than what is (in theory) truly most marketable. Competition attracts labor and capital when the market price is above the "natural price" (what it costs to produce the product or service), and labor and capital will move elsewhere if the market price is below the natural price.

This is another demonstration of the "invisible hand" at work. Competition turns self-interest towards socially useful goals—so long, that is, as people are free to market their labor, and competition (rather than monopolies) reign.

Interestingly, the "invisible hand" of the Deity implants in us a desire for self-enrichment, and an envy of the wealthy. This causes us to believe that the lives of the wealthy are better and happier, and we therefore work improve our circumstances. Although we might well eventually discover that the rich are not necessarily happier than anyone else, our original perception has fulfilled its function. Our hard work and ambition has made us productive, and has increased the wealth and usable resources around us. Land that otherwise might have been left fallow has been cultivated. Time that otherwise might have been spent at leisure has used "productively," supplying humanity with inventions, goods, and services it otherwise would not have enjoyed.

The poor man's son, whom heaven in its anger has visited with ambition, when he begins to look around him, admires the condition of the rich. He finds the cottage of his father too small for his accommodation, and fancies he should be lodged more at his ease in a palace. He is displeased with being obliged to walk a-foot, or to endure the fatigue of riding on horseback. He sees his superiors carried about in machines, and imagines that in one of these he could travel with less inconveniency. He feels himself naturally indolent, and willing to serve himself with his own hands as little as possible; and judges, that a numerous retinue of servants would save him from a great deal of trouble. He thinks if he had attained all these, he would sit still contentedly, and be quiet, enjoying himself in the thought of the happiness and tranquillity of his situation. He is enchanted with the distant idea of this felicity. It appears in his fancy like the life of some superior rank of beings, and, in order to arrive at it, he devotes himself for ever to the pursuit of wealth and greatness. To obtain the conveniencies which these afford, he submits in the first year, nay in the first month of his application, to more fatigue of body and more uneasiness of mind than he could have suffered through the whole of his life from the want of them. He studies to distinguish himself in some laborious profession. With the most unrelenting industry he labours night and day to acquire talents superior to all his competitors. He endeavours next to bring those talents into public view, and with equal assiduity solicits every opportunity of employment. For this purpose he makes his court to all mankind; he serves those whom he hates, and is obsequious to those whom he despises.

Through the whole of his life he pursues the idea of a certain artificial and elegant repose which he may never arrive at, for which he sacrifices a real tranquillity that is at all times in his power, and which, if in the extremity of old age he should at last attain to it, he will find to be in no respect preferable to that humble security and contentment which he had abandoned for it. It is then, in the last dregs of life, his body wasted with toil and diseases, his mind galled and ruffled by the memory of a thousand injuries and disappointments which he imagines he has met with from the injustice of his enemies, or from the perfidy and ingratitude of his friends, that he begins at last to find that wealth and greatness are mere trinkets of frivolous utility, no more adapted for procuring ease of body or tranquillity of mind than the tweezer-cases of the lover of toys; and like them too, more troublesome to the person who carries them about with him than all the advantages they can afford him are commodious. . . . If we consider the real satisfaction which all these things are capable of affording, by itself and separated from the beauty of that arrangement which is fitted to promote it, it will always appear in the highest degree contemptible and trifling. But we rarely view it in this abstract and philosophical light. We naturally confound it in our imagination with the order, the regular and harmonious movement of the system, the machine or oeconomy by means of which it is produced. The pleasures of wealth and greatness, when considered in this complex view, strike the imagination as something grand and beautiful and noble, of which the attainment is well worth all the toil and anxiety which we are so apt to bestow upon it.

And it is well that nature imposes upon us in this manner. It is this deception which rouses and keeps in continual motion the industry of mankind. It is this which first prompted them to cultivate the ground, to build houses, to found cities and commonwealths, and to invent and improve all the sciences and arts, which ennoble and embellish human life; which have entirely changed the whole face of the globe, have turned the rude forests of nature into agreeable and fertile plains, and made the trackless and barren ocean a new fund of subsistence, and the great high road of communication to the different nations of the earth. The earth by these labours of mankind has been obliged to redouble her natural fertility, and to maintain a greater multitude of inhabitants.[94]

If one believes Smith to be the "patron saint" of Capitalism, and unapologetic advocate for the unrestricted accumulation of wealth, then one might form some very *false* conclusions about his actual system. Smith did indeed favor the accumulation of societal wealth—but for the betterment of all, not merely for the sake of the wealthy.

Smith neither despised the poor, nor adored the rich. Indeed, the poor are not essentially different from the rich, according to Smith.

[94] *TMS*, Part IV, Chapter 1.

The difference of natural talents in different men, is, in reality, much less than we are aware of; and the very different genius which appears to distinguish men of different professions, when grown up to maturity, is not upon many occasions so much the cause, as the effect of the division of labour. The difference between the most dissimilar characters, between a philosopher and a common street porter, for example, seems to arise not so much from nature, as from habit, custom, and education. When they came in to the world, and for the first six or eight years of their existence, they were, perhaps, very much alike, and neither their parents nor play-fellows could perceive any remarkable difference. About that age, or soon after, they come to be employed in very different occupations.[95]

In sharp contrast to the crudely "social Darwinist" ideas that some hold today, according to which the wealthy are so because of their inherent talent and merit, whereas the poor are so from their character flaws and incompetence, Smith is claiming that the rich and poor alike start out very similar to each other, but as they grow up, different experiences, resources, and educational opportunities cause them to be "employed in very different occupations."

Not only does Smith not advocate any sort of presumption of moral superiority in the wealthy, he explicitly argues *against* such a presumption, claiming that many *mistakenly* envy the rich, and pursue wealth at the expense of virtue.

It is from our disposition to admire, and consequently to imitate, the rich and the great, that they are enabled to set, or to lead what is called the fashion. Their dress is the fashionable dress; the language of their conversation, the fashionable style; their air and deportment, the fashionable behaviour. Even their vices and follies are fashionable; and the greater part of men are proud to imitate and resemble them in the very qualities which dishonour and degrade them. Vain men often give themselves airs of a fashionable profligacy, which, in their hearts, they do not approve of, and of which, perhaps, they are really not guilty. They desire to be praised for what they themselves do not think praise-worthy, and are ashamed of unfashionable virtues which they sometimes practise in secret, and for which they have secretly some degree of real veneration. There are hypocrites of wealth and greatness, as well as of religion and virtue; and a vain man is as apt to pretend to be what he is not, in the one way, as a cunning man is in the other. He assumes the equipage and splendid way of living of his superiors, without considering that whatever may be praise-worthy in any of these, derives its whole merit and propriety from its suitableness to that situation and fortune which both require and can easily support the expence. Many a poor man places his glory in being thought rich, without considering that the duties (if one may call such follies by so very venerable a name) which that reputation imposes upon him, must soon reduce him to beggary, and render his situation still more unlike that of those whom he admires and imitates, than it had been originally.

---

[95] Ibid., Book I, Chapter 2.

To attain to this envied situation, the candidates for fortune too frequently abandon the paths of virtue; for unhappily, the road which leads to the one, and that which leads to the other, lie sometimes in very opposite directions. But the ambitious man flatters himself that, in the splendid situation to which he advances, he will have so many means of commanding the respect and admiration of mankind, and will be enabled to act with such superior propriety and grace, that the lustre of his future conduct will entirely cover, or efface, the foulness of the steps by which he arrived at that elevation. In many governments the candidates for the highest stations are above the law; and, if they can attain the object of their ambition, they have no fear of being called to account for the means by which they acquired it. They often endeavour, therefore, not only by fraud and falsehood, the ordinary and vulgar arts of intrigue and cabal; but sometimes by the perpetration of the most enormous crimes, by murder and assassination, by rebellion and civil war, to supplant and destroy those who oppose or stand in the way of their greatness. They more frequently miscarry than succeed; and commonly gain nothing but the disgraceful punishment which is due to their crimes. But, though they should be so lucky as to attain that wished-for greatness, they are always most miserably disappointed in the happiness which they expect to enjoy in it. It is not ease or pleasure, but always honour, of one kind or another, though frequently an honour very ill understood, that the ambitious man really pursues. But the honour of his exalted station appears, both in his own eyes and in those of other people, polluted and defiled by the baseness of the means through which he rose to it."[96]

Though written over 150 years ago, this could just have easily been written today. Imitation of the wealthy achieved new heights of absurdity with the "Kylie Jenner Lip Challenge" that swept Instagram in 2015, only to be supplanted by the "Kylie Jenner 'Thighbrow' Challenge" in that same year. A young woman known only for her wealth and status on a reality TV show ("Keeping up with the Kardashians") became an object of imitation for countless young girls who sought to acquire the same puffy lips, and particular thigh creases. This is only an extreme example from social media, but countless more examples abound of the ways in which the wealthy set fashion trends, and how their behavior—no matter how scandalous—inspires imitation from persons who want to be "just like" their "role-models."

This envy of the wealthy, and the confusing of wealth with virtue, is problematic because it can distort our sympathies, and even the objectivity of the "impartial spectator." It skews our moral judgments by causing us to be insufficiently sympathetic to the poor, and overly sympathetic to the wealthy. The following excerpt is lengthy, but worth quoting at length.

This disposition to admire, and almost to worship, the rich and the powerful, and to despise, or, at least, to neglect persons of poor and mean condition, though necessary both to establish and to maintain the distinction of ranks and the order of society, is, at the same time, the great and most universal cause of the corruption of our moral sentiments. That wealth and greatness are often

---

[96] *TMS*, Part I, Section iii, Chapter 8.

regarded with the respect and admiration which are due only to wisdom and virtue; and that the contempt, of which vice and folly are the only proper objects, is often most unjustly bestowed upon poverty and weakness, has been the complaint of moralists in all ages.

We desire both to be respectable and to be respected. We dread both to be contemptible and to be contemned. But, upon coming into the world, we soon find that wisdom and virtue are by no means the sole objects of respect; nor vice and folly, of contempt. We frequently see the respectful attentions of the world more strongly directed towards the rich and the great, than towards the wise and the virtuous. We see frequently the vices and follies of the powerful much less despised than the poverty and weakness of the innocent. To deserve, to acquire, and to enjoy the respect and admiration of mankind, are the great objects of ambition and emulation. Two different roads are presented to us, equally leading to the attainment of this so much desired object; the one, by the study of wisdom and the practice of virtue; the other, by the acquisition of wealth and greatness. Two different characters are presented to our emulation; the one, of proud ambition and ostentatious avidity. the other, of humble modesty and equitable justice. Two different models, two different pictures, are held out to us, according to which we may fashion our own character and behaviour; the one more gaudy and glittering in its colouring; the other more correct and more exquisitely beautiful in its outline: the one forcing itself upon the notice of every wandering eye; the other, attracting the attention of scarce any body but the most studious and careful observer. They are the wise and the virtuous chiefly, a select, though, I am afraid, but a small party, who are the real and steady admirers of wisdom and virtue. The great mob of mankind are the admirers and worshippers, and, what may seem more extraordinary, most frequently the disinterested admirers and worshippers, of wealth and greatness.

The respect which we feel for wisdom and virtue is, no doubt, different from that which we conceive for wealth and greatness; and it requires no very nice discernment to distinguish the difference. But, notwithstanding this difference, those sentiments bear a very considerable resemblance to one another. In some particular features they are, no doubt, different, but, in the general air of the countenance, they seem to be so very nearly the same, that inattentive observers are very apt to mistake the one for the other.

In equal degrees of merit there is scarce any man who does not respect more the rich and the great, than the poor and the humble. With most men the presumption and vanity of the former are much more admired, than the real and solid merit of the latter. It is scarce agreeable to good morals, or even to good language, perhaps, to say, that mere wealth and greatness, abstracted from merit and virtue, deserve our respect. We must acknowledge, however, that they almost constantly obtain it; and that they may, therefore, be considered as, in some respects, the natural objects of it. Those exalted stations may, no doubt, be completely degraded by vice and folly. But the vice and folly must be very great, before they can operate this complete degradation. The profligacy of a man of fashion is looked upon with much less contempt and aversion, than that of a man of meaner condition. In the latter, a single transgression of the rules of temperance and propriety, is commonly more resented, than the constant and avowed contempt of them ever is in the former.

In the middling and inferior stations of life, the road to virtue and that to fortune, to such fortune, at least, as men in such stations can reasonably expect to acquire, are, happily in most cases, very nearly the same. In all the middling and inferior professions, real and solid professional abilities, joined to prudent, just, firm, and temperate conduct, can very seldom fail of success. Abilities will even sometimes prevail where the conduct is by no means correct. Either habitual imprudence, however, or injustice, or weakness, or profligacy, will always cloud, and sometimes depress altogether, the most splendid professional abilities. Men in the inferior and middling stations of life, besides, can never be great enough to be above the law, which must generally overawe them into some sort of respect for, at least, the more important rules of justice. The success of such people, too, almost always depends upon the favour and good opinion of their neighbours and equals; and without a tolerably regular conduct these can very seldom be obtained. The good old proverb, therefore, That honesty is the best policy, holds, in such situations, almost always perfectly true. In such situations, therefore, we may generally expect a considerable degree of virtue; and, fortunately for the good morals of society, these are the situations of by far the greater part of mankind.

In the superior stations of life the case is unhappily not always the same. In the courts of princes, in the drawing-rooms of the great, where success and preferment depend, not upon the esteem of intelligent and well-informed equals, but upon the fanciful and foolish favour of ignorant, presumptuous, and proud superiors; flattery and falsehood too often prevail over merit and abilities. In such societies the abilities to please, are more regarded than the abilities to serve. In quiet and peaceable times, when the storm is at a distance, the prince, or great man, wishes only to be amused, and is even apt to fancy that he has scarce any occasion for the service of any body, or that those who amuse him are sufficiently able to serve him. The external graces, the frivolous accomplishments of that impertinent and foolish thing called a man of fashion, are commonly more admired than the solid and masculine virtues of a warrior, a statesman, a philosopher, or a legislator. All the great and awful virtues, all the virtues which can fit, either for the council, the senate, or the field, are, by the insolent and insignificant flatterers, who commonly figure the most in such corrupted societies, held in the utmost contempt and derision. When the duke of Sully was called upon by Lewis the Thirteenth, to give his advice in some great emergency, he observed the favourites and courtiers whispering to one another, and smiling at his unfashionable appearance. 'Whenever your majesty's father,' said the old warrior and statesman, 'did me the honour to consult me, he ordered the buffons of the court to retire into the antechamber.'[97]

---

[97] Ibid., Part 1, Section 3, Chapter 3.

This breathtaking commentary on the unfair treatment, and even the unfair judgment, of the poor (and in favor of the wealthy) is shocking, given the myth of Adam Smith as the champion of the wealthy. The myth is precisely that, though: a myth.

Smith joins his voice to the "complaint of moralists in all ages" that the admiration rightfully bestowed upon wisdom and virtue is misguidedly being extended to "wealth and greatness," whereas the contempt rightfully reserved for "vice and folly" is being bestowed instead upon "poverty."

We all desire to be respected, but we soon discover that wisdom and good character are not the only means by which one can become requested, nor even the surest ones! Instead, we discover that esteem is bestowed due to wealth and celebrity, and even the vice of the wealthy seems to be overlooked and more easily forgiven than the "poverty and weakness of the innocent."

As a political example, consider the fact that the Republican nominee for the Presidency in 2016 is Donald Trump. Setting aside any actual policy issues, it's impossible to set aside the perception that much of Trump's popularity is the result of his wealth and social status. During the 2016 primary season, he "flip-flopped" on various issues again and again, made controversial statements about women, the nation of Mexico, Muslims (in general), illegal immigrants, and "Mexican" judges (i.e., Judge Gonzalo Curiel, who, while of Latino heritage, was born in Indiana[98]); he mocked a journalist with a disability, insulted (on a personal level) all of his political rivals, boasted of his penis size in a nationally-televised debate,[99] and all while being sued for having founded an allegedly fraudulent "University" (among other things). And yet, Donald Trump won the Republican nomination, in State after State, winning millions of votes in the process—and could ultimately be elected President of the United States.

There might be any number of reasons for Trump's political success, and this is not the book to delve into them. One possible explanation, though, is that many people simply overlook what might be considered his moral shortcomings because they are awed by his material success. Donald Trump is undeniable a very wealthy man, and he has so successfully branded his image that his very name is associated with "success." As a result, he is admired and esteemed by others—and we all notice that fact!

Smith thinks that, in general, we conclude that there are two roads to the esteem we desire: virtue, or wealth.

Virtue is difficult to acquire and display, and often not even noticed by any "but the most studious and careful observer." Someone has to get to know you pretty well to perceive that you are wise and good—but wealth is noticed right away! When someone pulls up in their expensive sports car at the most exclusive restaurant in town, with an entourage of well-dressed tag-alongs, and surrounded by the paparazzi, there is no mistaking their wealth and "greatness."

---

[98]http://www.cnn.com/2016/06/07/politics/donald-trump-mexican-judge-trump-university-racist/index.html
[99]http://www.cnn.com/2016/03/03/politics/donald-trump-small-hands-marco-rubio/index.html

Even though we recognize that the respect we feel for wisdom and virtue is different from that we feel for wealth and celebrity, the feelings "bear a considerable resemblance to one another," and so are easily confused, or substituted, in our minds. While we might be willing to proclaim that the wealthy who are without virtue don't deserve our respect, we also have to acknowledge "that they almost certainly obtain it" anyway! Celebrities of all kinds (most of whom are wealthy) are admired, and copied, their opinions on *anything* seems worthy of publication; they acquire millions of followers of twitter or other social media vehicles. We try to dress like them, live like them, speak like them. Indeed, many wish they could be just like them. There is no question that Western cultures (at least) virtually *worship* the rich and famous. Small wonder that so many seek esteem from wealth than from the much more difficult, and less noteworthy path of virtue!

And so much the worse for us, if we do, according to Smith. Interestingly, he suggests that there is something advantageous, with respect to building and maintaining moral character, and even with respect to being poor.

Poor people can't get away with acting as if they were above the law (unlike the rich), but must instead regulate their behavior if they want to avoid trouble. Similarly, the success of a poor person depends much more heavily on their reputation among their peers, who tend to not be very forgiving of foolish behavior. Poorer people must therefore maintain "tolerably regular conduct." In wealthier circles, however, "flattery and falsehood too often prevail over merit and abilities," and "frivolous accomplishments . . . are commonly more admired than the solid and masculine virtues of a warrior, a statesman, a philosopher, or a legislator."

Bemoaning this false equivalence of "wealth" with "virtue" and "poverty" with "vice," Smith recommends that education is needed to correct any gaps of understanding with regard to the merits of the rich and the poor (just as education is needed to correct any misunderstanding of Smith himself!).

While it is mythological thinking to imagine Smith as hostile to the poor, it would be equally mythological to imagine Smith as some sort of socialist champion of the "Proletariat," in contrast. He was far from either. He did, however, explicitly argue that a legitimate and important role for the government was to intervene on behalf of the poor. Book five of the *Wealth of Nations* addresses the importance of universal education, social unity, religious toleration, and the need to regulate against the dangers of religious extremism. Our focus will be limited to what he has to say about universal education.

Although the division of labor (and the subsequent specialization) is what makes possible the economic growth and general prosperity for which capitalism is known, Smith argues that, without education, the very division of labor that makes possible the economic growth that promotes the "universal opulence which extends itself to the lowest ranks of all people" can be mentally stultifying. In "primitive economies," on the other hand, the variety of tasks keeps the mind active and engaged.

> *In the progress of the division of labour, the employment of the far greater part of those who live by labour, that is, of the great body of the people, comes to be confined to a few very simple operations; frequently to one or two. But the understandings of the greater part of men are necessarily formed by their ordinary employments. The man whose whole life is spent in performing a few*

simple operations, of which the effects, too, are perhaps always the same, or very nearly the same, has no occasion to exert his understanding, or to exercise his invention, in finding out expedients for removing difficulties which never occur. He naturally loses, therefore, the habit of such exertion, and generally becomes as stupid and ignorant as it is possible for a human creature to become. The torpor of his mind renders him not only incapable of relishing or bearing a part in any rational conversation, but of conceiving any generous, noble, or tender sentiment, and consequently of forming any just judgment concerning many even of the ordinary duties of private life. Of the great and extensive interests of his country he is altogether incapable of judging; and unless very particular pains have been taken to render him otherwise, he is equally incapable of defending his country in war. The uniformity of his stationary life naturally corrupts the courage of his mind, and makes him regard, with abhorrence, the irregular, uncertain, and adventurous life of a soldier. It corrupts even the activity of his body, and renders him incapable of exerting his strength with vigour and perseverance in any other employment, than that to which he has been bred. His dexterity at his own particular trade seems, in this manner, to be acquired at the expense of his intellectual, social, and martial virtues. But in every improved and civilized society, this is the state into which the labouring poor, that is, the great body of the people, must necessarily fall, unless government takes some pains to prevent it.

It is otherwise in the barbarous societies, as they are commonly called, of hunters, of shepherds, and even of husbandmen in that rude state of husbandry which precedes the improvement of manufactures, and the extension of foreign commerce. In such societies, the varied occupations of every man oblige every man to exert his capacity, and to invent expedients for removing difficulties which are continually occurring. Invention is kept alive, and the mind is not suffered to fall into that drowsy stupidity, which, in a civilized society, seems to benumb the understanding of almost all the inferior ranks of people. In those barbarous societies, as they are called, every man, it has already been observed, is a warrior. Every man, too, is in some measure a statesman, and can form a tolerable judgment concerning the interest of the society, and the conduct of those who govern it. How far their chiefs are good judges in peace, or good leaders in war, is obvious to the observation of almost every single man among them. In such a society, indeed, no man can well acquire that improved and refined understanding which a few men sometimes possess in a more civilized state. Though in a rude society there is a good deal of variety in the occupations of every individual, there is not a great deal in those of the whole society.

Every man does, or is capable of doing, almost everything which any other man does, or is capable of being. Every man has a considerable degree of knowledge, ingenuity, and invention but scarce any man has a great degree. The degree, however, which is commonly possessed, is generally sufficient for conducting the whole simple business of the society. In a civilized state, on the contrary, though there is little variety in the occupations of the greater part of individuals, there is an almost infinite variety in those of the whole society. These varied occupations present an almost infinite variety of objects to the contemplation of those few, who, being attached to no particular occupation themselves, have leisure and inclination to examine the occupations of other people. The contemplation of so great a variety of objects necessarily exercises their minds in endless comparisons and combinations, and renders their understandings, in an extraordinary degree, both acute anti comprehensive. Unless those few, however, happen to be placed in some very particular situations, their great abilities, though honourable to themselves, may contribute very little to the good government or happiness of their society. Notwithstanding the great abilities of those few, all the nobler parts of the human character may be, in a great measure, obliterated and extinguished in the great body of the people.[100]

The concern here is not difficult to imagine. Suppose a lower-skilled "blue collar" worker is trained and specializes in fulfilling a very specific function at a factory, such as taping boxes shut for shipment at the end of an assembly line. He performs the same motion (swiping a tape dispenser) again and again, hour after hour, five days (at minimum!) each week, every week of the year, for 30-40 years. Now imagine that this worker is employed in Smith's era, when workers worked longer hours, and poor workers had even fewer resources than today for recreation and mental stimulation. "The man whose whole life is spent in performing a few simple operations, of which the effects, too, are perhaps always the same, or very nearly the same, has no occasion to exert his understanding, or to exercise his invention, in finding out expedients for removing difficulties which never occur. He naturally loses, therefore, the habit of such exertion, and generally becomes as stupid and ignorant as it is possible for a human creature to become."

Such a repetitive task requires no creativity, no problem-solving. There is nothing new or stimulating. It's as though the mind is a muscle, and it atrophies from lack of stimulation. The concern isn't just that the worker might grow "bored." "The torpor of his mind renders him not only incapable of relishing or bearing a part in any rational conversation, but of conceiving any generous, noble, or tender sentiment, and consequently of forming any just judgment concerning many even of the ordinary duties of private life. Of the great and extensive interests of his country he is altogether incapable of judging . . ."

Such a person loses his ability to problem-solve, in general, from lack of use; loses the ability to participate in rational conversation, and given the crucial role of the imagination in anticipating what the "impartial spectator" would do in a situation, such persons are even stunted in their capacity for correct moral judgment.

It's implausible that employers will take it upon themselves to remodel the workplace for the sake of mental stimulation. After all, it would reduce their efficiency and profits if they did so. That means that it is by education that we must combat this mental atrophy to which most of the work force is subject. Since the poor, by virtue of being poor, are unlikely to be able to pay for private schools or tutors, it will fall to the State to provide that education at public expense. This means, of course, that taxes will have to be levied to pay for that education.

---

[100] *WN*, Book V, Chapter 1, Part 3, Article 1.

Smith did not regard taxation as theft,[101] nor even as something bad. "Every tax, however, is to the person who pays it a badge, not of slavery, but of liberty. It denotes that he is subject to government, indeed, but that, as he has some property, he cannot himself be the property of a master."[102] The very fact that someone has property subject to taxation means that the person has private property, personal wealth (to whatever extent). This is the mark of a citizen, not a subject or slave. Smith, while critical of government meddling, was not critical of taxation, or even "redistribution of wealth."

> When the carriages which pass over a highway or a bridge, and the lighters which sail upon a navigable canal, pay toll in proportion to their weight or their tonnage, they pay for the maintenance of those public works exactly in proportion to the wear and tear which they occasion of them. It seems scarce possible to invent a more equitable way of maintaining such works. This tax or toll, too, though it is advanced by the carrier, is finally paid by the consumer, to whom it must always be charged in the price of the goods. As the expense of carriage, however, is very much reduced by means of such public works, the goods, notwithstanding the toll, come cheaper to the consumer than they could otherwise have done, their price not being so much raised by the toll, as it is lowered by the cheapness of the carriage. The person who finally pays this tax, therefore, gains by the application more than he loses by the payment of it. His payment is exactly in proportion to his gain. It is, in reality, no more than a part of that gain which he is obliged to give up, in order to get the rest. It seems impossible to imagine a more equitable method of raising a tax. When the toll upon carriages of luxury, upon coaches, post-chaises, etc. is made somewhat higher in proportion to their weight, than upon carriages of necessary use, such as carts, waggons, etc. the indolence and vanity of the rich is made to contribute, in a very easy manner, to the relief of the poor, by rendering cheaper the transportation of heavy goods to all the different parts of the country.[103]

In fact, Smith even argues for what today would be called "progressive taxation" (i.e., taxing the wealthy at higher rates).

> The necessaries of life occasion the great expense of the poor. They find it difficult to get food, and the greater part of their little revenue is spent in getting it. The luxuries and vanities of life occasion the principal expense of the rich; and a magnificent house embellishes and sets off to the best advantage all the other luxuries and vanities which they possess. A tax upon house-rents, therefore, would in general fall heaviest upon the rich; and in this sort of inequality there would not, perhaps, be any thing very unreasonable. It is not very unreasonable that the rich should contribute to the public expense, not only in proportion to

---

[101] In contrast to the view espoused by Judge Andrew Napolitano: https://reason.com/archives/2013/04/18/taxation-is-theft
[102] *WN*, Book V, Chapter 2.
[103] Ibid., Book V, Chapter 1.

their revenue, but something more than in that proportion.[104]

Even Smith's genuine libertarian strain is not so completely "hands off" as one might think.

> *A superior may, indeed, sometimes, with universal approbation, oblige those under his jurisdiction to behave, in this respect, with a certain degree of propriety to one another. The laws of all civilized nations oblige parents to maintain their children, and children to maintain their parents, and impose upon men many other duties of beneficence. The civil magistrate is entrusted with the power not only of preserving the public peace by restraining injustice, but of promoting the prosperity of the commonwealth, by establishing good discipline, and by discouraging every sort of vice and impropriety; he may prescribe rules, therefore, which not only prohibit mutual injuries among fellow-citizens, but command mutual good offices to a certain degree.*[105]

Don't gloss over that last sentence! Smith is claiming that the legitimate application of law and coercion by the State is not merely "negative," to protect us from injuries from each other, but can, "to a certain degree," be "positive" as well—commanding "mutual good offices." In other words, to an extent, at least, it is legitimate to use the State, and taxation, to provide for the needs of the poor.

Conclusion

Very often misunderstood and wrongly applied, Adam Smith, though famous for his economic ideas, must be understood as a moral philosopher first. His understanding of ethics as being based on sympathy situate him among the few Western moral philosophers who focus on feelings, rather than Reason. This places him in sharp contrast to someone like Immanuel Kant (who allegedly regarded Smith as his favorite "sentimentalist"), but also to outcome-oriented utilitarians—both of whom will be considered in future chapters.

---

[104] Ibid., Book V, Chapter 2. Emphasis added.
[105] *TMS*, Part II, Section ii, Chapter 1. Emphasis added.

In what follows, you will find selections from the Theory of Moral Sentiments. It is a lengthy work, and much material has been cut for the sake of space and reasonable reading requirements. In this selection, we have Smith's account of sympathy, the impartial spectator, and the "corruption" of our moral sentiments due to unwarranted envy of the rich. We also find mentions of the infamous "invisible hand."

The Theory of Moral Sentiments[106]
Adam Smith
**Professor of Moral Philosophy in the University of Glasgow.
London Printed for A. Millar, in the Strand; And A. Kincaid and J. Bell in Edinburgh.
MDCCLIX**

Part I: Of the Propriety of Action Consisting of Three Sections
Section I: Of the Sense of Propriety
Chap. I: Of Sympathy

How selfish soever man may be supposed, there are evidently some principles in his nature, which interest him in the fortune of others, and render their happiness necessary to him, though he derives nothing from it except the pleasure of seeing it. Of this kind is pity or compassion, the emotion which we feel for the misery of others, when we either see it, or are made to conceive it in a very lively manner. That we often derive sorrow from the sorrow of others, is a matter of fact too obvious to require any instances to prove it; for this sentiment, like all the other original passions of human nature, is by no means confined to the virtuous and humane, though they perhaps may feel it with the most exquisite sensibility. The greatest ruffian, the most hardened violator of the laws of society, is not altogether without it.

As we have no immediate experience of what other men feel, we can form no idea of the manner in which they are affected, but by conceiving what we ourselves should feel in the like situation. Though our brother is upon the rack, as long as we ourselves are at our ease, our senses will never inform us of what he suffers. They never did, and never can, carry us beyond our own person, and it is by the imagination only that we can form any conception of what are his sensations. Neither can that faculty help us to this any other way, than by representing to us what would be our own, if we were in his case. It is the impressions of our own senses only, not those of his, which our imaginations copy. By the imagination we place ourselves in his situation, we conceive ourselves enduring all the same torments, we enter as it were into his body, and become in some measure the same person with him, and thence

---

[106]http://web.archive.org/web/20030324040029/http://etext.lib.virginia.edu/etc bin/toccer-new2?id=SmiMora.xml&images=images/modeng&data=/texts/ english/modeng/parsed&tag=public&part=all

form some idea of his sensations, and even feel something which, though weaker in degree, is not altogether unlike them. His agonies, when they are thus brought home to ourselves, when we have thus adopted and made them our own, begin at last to affect us, and we then tremble and shudder at the thought of what he feels. For as to be in pain or distress of any kind excites the most excessive sorrow, so to conceive or to imagine that we are in it, excites some degree of the same emotion, in proportion to the vivacity or dulness of the conception.

That this is the source of our fellow-feeling for the misery of others, that it is by changing places in fancy with the sufferer, that we come either to conceive or to be affected by what he feels, may be demonstrated by many obvious observations, if it should not be thought sufficiently evident of itself. When we see a stroke aimed and just ready to fall upon the leg or arm of another person, we naturally shrink and draw back our own leg or our own arm; and when it does fall, we feel it in some measure, and are hurt by it as well as the sufferer. The mob, when they are gazing at a dancer on the slack rope, naturally writhe and twist and balance their own bodies, as they see him do, and as they feel that they themselves must do if in his situation. Persons of delicate fibres and a weak constitution of body complain, that in looking on the sores and ulcers which are exposed by beggars in the streets, they are apt to feel an itching or uneasy sensation in the correspondent part of their own bodies. The horror which they conceive at the misery of those wretches affects that particular part in themselves more than any other; because that horror arises from conceiving what they themselves would suffer, if they really were the wretches whom they are looking upon, and if that particular part in themselves was actually affected in the same miserable manner. The very force of this conception is sufficient, in their feeble frames, to produce that itching or uneasy sensation complained of. Men of the most robust make, observe that in looking upon sore eyes they often feel a very sensible soreness in their own, which proceeds from the same reason; that organ being in the strongest man more delicate, than any other part of the body is in the weakest.

Neither is it those circumstances only, which create pain or sorrow, that call forth our fellow-feeling. Whatever is the passion which arises from any object in the person principally concerned, an analogous emotion springs up, at the thought of his situation, in the breast of every attentive spectator. Our joy for the deliverance of those heroes of tragedy or romance who interest us, is as sincere as our grief for their distress, and our fellow-feeling with their misery is not more real than that with their happiness. We enter into their gratitude towards those faithful friends who did not desert them in their difficulties; and we heartily go along with their resentment against those perfidious traitors who injured, abandoned, or deceived them. In every passion of which the mind of man is susceptible, the emotions of the by-stander always correspond to hat, by bringing the case home to himself, he imagines should be the sentiments of the sufferer.

Pity and compassion are words appropriated to signify our fellow-feeling with the sorrow of others. Sympathy, though its meaning was, perhaps, originally the same, may now, however, without much impropriety, be made use of to denote our fellow-feeling with any passion whatever.

Upon some occasions sympathy may seen to arise merely from the view of a certain emotion in another person. The passions, upon some occasions, may seem to be transfused from one man to another, instantaneously and antecedent to any knowledge of what excited them in the person principally concerned. Grief and joy, for example, strongly expressed in the look and gestures of any one, at once affect the spectator with some degree of a like painful or agreeable emotion. A smiling face is, to every body that sees it, a cheerful object; as a sorrowful countenance, on the other hand, is a melancholy one.

This, however, does not hold universally, or with regard to every passion. There are some passions of which the expressions excite no sort of sympathy, but before we are acquainted with what gave occasion to them, serve rather to disgust and provoke us against them. The furious behaviour of an angry man is more likely to exasperate us against himself than against his enemies. As we are unacquainted with his provocation, we cannot bring his case home to ourselves, nor conceive any thing like the passions which it excites. But we plainly see what is the situation of those with whom he is angry, and to what violence they may be exposed from so enraged an adversary. We readily, therefore, sympathize with their fear or resentment, and are immediately disposed to take part against the man from whom they appear to be in so much danger.

If the very appearances of grief and joy inspire us with some degree of the like emotions, it is because they suggest to us the general idea of some good or bad fortune that has befallen the person in whom we observe them: and in these passions this is sufficient to have some little influence upon us. The effects of grief and joy terminate in the person who feels those emotions, of which the expressions do not, like those of resentment, suggest to us the idea of any other person for whom we are concerned, and whose interests are opposite to his. The general idea of good or bad fortune, therefore, creates some concern for the person who has met with it, but the general idea of provocation excites no sympathy with the anger of the man who has received it. Nature, it seems, teaches us to be more averse to enter into this passion, and, till informed of its cause, to be disposed rather to take part against it.

Even our sympathy with the grief or joy of another, before we are informed of the cause of either, is always extremely imperfect. General lamentations, which express nothing but the anguish of the sufferer, create rather a curiosity to inquire into his situation, along with some disposition to sympathize with him, than any actual sympathy that is very sensible. The first question which we ask is, What has befallen you? Till this be answered, though we are uneasy both from the vague idea of his misfortune, and still more from torturing ourselves with conjectures about what it may be, yet our fellow-feeling is not very considerable.

Sympathy, therefore, does not arise so much from the view of the passion, as from that of the situation which excites it. We sometimes feel for another, a passion of which he himself seems to be altogether incapable; because, when we put ourselves in his case, that passion arises in our breast from the imagination, though it does not in his from the reality. We blush for the impudence and rudeness of another, though he himself appears to have no sense of the impropriety of his own behaviour; because we cannot help feeling with what confusion we ourselves should be covered, had we behaved in so absurd a manner.

Of all the calamities to which the condition of mortality exposes mankind, the loss of reason appears, to those who have the least spark of humanity, by far the most dreadful, and they behold that last stage of human wretchedness with deeper commiseration than any other. But the poor wretch, who is in it, laughs and sings perhaps, and is altogether insensible of his own misery. The anguish which humanity feels, therefore, at the sight of such an object, cannot be the reflection of any sentiment of the sufferer. The compassion of the spectator must arise altogether from the consideration of what he himself would feel if he was reduced to the same unhappy situation, and, what perhaps is impossible, was at the same time able to regard it with his present reason and judgment.

What are the pangs of a mother, when she hears the moanings of her infant that during the agony of disease cannot express what it feels? In her idea of what it suffers, she joins, to its real helplessness, her own consciousness of that helplessness, and her own terrors for the unknown consequences of its disorder; and out of all these, forms, for her own sorrow, the most complete image of misery and distress. The infant, however, feels only the uneasiness of the present instant, which can never be great. With regard to the future, it is perfectly secure, and in its thoughtlessness and want of foresight, possesses an antidote against fear and anxiety, the great tormentors of the human breast, from which reason and philosophy will, in vain, attempt to defend it, when it grows up to a man.

We sympathize even with the dead, and overlooking what is of real importance in their situation, that awful futurity which awaits them, we are chiefly affected by those circumstances which strike our senses, but can have no influence upon their happiness. It is miserable, we think, to be deprived of the light of the sun; to be shut out from life and conversation; to be laid in the cold grave, a prey to corruption and the reptiles of the earth; to be no more thought of in this world, but to be obliterated, in a little time, from the affections, and almost from the memory, of their dearest friends and relations. Surely, we imagine, we can never feel too much for those who have suffered so dreadful a calamity. The tribute of our fellow-feeling seems doubly due to them now, when they are in danger of being forgot by every body; and, by the vain honours which we pay to their memory, we endeavour, for our own misery, artificially to keep alive our melancholy remembrance of their misfortune. That our sympathy can afford them no consolation seems to be an addition to their calamity; and to think that all we can do is unavailing, and that, what alleviates all other distress, the regret, the love, and the lamentations of their friends, can yield no comfort to them, serves only to exasperate our sense of their misery. The happiness of the dead, however, most assuredly, is affected by none of these circumstances; nor is it the thought of these things which can ever disturb the profound security of their repose. The idea of that dreary and endless melancholy, which the fancy naturally ascribes to their condition, arises altogether from our joining to the change which has been produced upon them, our own consciousness of that change, from our putting ourselves in their situation, and from our lodging, if I may be allowed to say so, our own living souls in their inanimated bodies, and thence conceiving what would be our emotions in this case. It is from this very illusion of the imagination, that the foresight of our own dissolution is so terrible to us, and that the idea of those circumstances, which undoubtedly can give us no pain when we are dead, makes us miserable while we are alive. And from thence arises one of the most important principles in human nature, the dread of death, the great poison to the happiness, but the great restraint upon the injustice of mankind, which, while it afflicts and mortifies the individual, guards and protects the society.

. . .

Chap. III: Of the manner in which we judge of the propriety or impropriety of the affections of other men, by their concord or dissonance with our own.

When the original passions of the person principally concerned are in perfect concord with the sympathetic emotions of the spectator, they necessarily appear to this last just and proper, and suitable to their objects; and, on the contrary, when, upon bringing the case home to himself, he finds that they do not coincide with what he feels, they necessarily appear to him unjust and improper, and unsuitable to the causes which excite them. To approve of the passions of another, therefore, as suitable to their objects, is the same thing as to observe that we entirely sympathize with them; and not to approve of them as such, is the same thing as to observe that we do not entirely sympathize with them. The man who resents the injuries that have been done to me, and observes that I resent them precisely as he does, necessarily approves of my resentment. The man whose sympathy keeps time to my grief, cannot but admit the reasonableness of my sorrow. He who admires the same poem, or the same picture, and admires them exactly as I do, must surely allow the justness of my admiration. He who laughs at the same joke, and laughs along with me, cannot well deny the propriety of my laughter. On the contrary, the person who, upon these different occasions, either feels no such emotion as that which I feel, or feels none that bears any proportion to mine, cannot avoid disapproving my sentiments on account of their dissonance with his own. If my animosity goes beyond what the indignation of my friend can correspond to; if my grief exceeds what his most tender compassion can go along with; if my admiration is either too high or too low to tally with his own; if I laugh loud and heartily when he only smiles, or, on the contrary, only smile when he laughs loud and heartily; in all these cases, as soon as he comes from considering the object, to observe how I am affected by it, according as there is more or less disproportion between his sentiments and mine, I must incur a greater or less degree of his disapprobation: and upon all occasions his own sentiments are the standards and measures by which he judges of mine.

To approve of another man's opinions is to adopt those opinions, and to adopt them is to approve of them. If the same arguments which convince you convince me likewise, I necessarily approve of your conviction; and if they do not, I necessarily disapprove of it: neither can I possibly conceive that I should do the one without the other. To approve or disapprove, therefore, of the opinions of others is acknowledged, by every body, to mean no more than to observe their agreement or disagreement with our own. But this is equally the case with regard to our approbation or disapprobation of the sentiments or passions of others.

There are, indeed, some cases in which we seem to approve without any sympathy or correspondence of sentiments, and in which, consequently, the sentiment of approbation would seem to be different from the perception of this coincidence. A little attention, however, will convince us that even in these cases our approbation is ultimately founded upon a sympathy or correspondence of this kind. I shall give an instance in things of a very frivolous nature, because in them the judgments of mankind are less apt to be perverted by wrong systems. We may often approve of a jest, and think the laughter of the company quite just and proper, though we ourselves do not laugh, because, perhaps, we are in a grave humour, or happen to have our attention engaged with other objects. We have learned, however, from experience, what sort of pleasantry is upon most occasions capable of making us laugh, and we observe that this is one of that kind. We approve, therefore, of the laughter of the company, and feel that it is natural and suitable to its object; because, though in our present mood we cannot easily enter into it, we are sensible that upon most occasions we should very heartily join in it.

The same thing often happens with regard to all the other passions. A stranger passes by us in the street with all the marks of the deepest affliction; and we are immediately told that he has just received the news of the death of his father. It is impossible that, in this case, we should not approve of his grief. Yet it may often happen, without any defect of humanity on our part, that, so far from entering into the violence of his sorrow, we should scarce conceive the first movements of concern upon his account. Both he and his father, perhaps, are entirely unknown to us, or we happen to be employed about other things, and do not take time to picture out in our imagination the different circumstances of distress which must occur to him. We have learned, however, from experience, that such a misfortune naturally excites such a degree of sorrow, and we know that if we took time to consider his situation, fully and in all its parts, we should, without doubt, most sincerely sympathize with him. It is upon the consciousness of this conditional sympathy, that our approbation of his sorrow is founded, even in those cases in which that sympathy does not actually take place; and the general rules derived from our preceding experience of what our sentiments would commonly correspond with, correct upon this, as upon many other occasions, the impropriety of our present emotions.

The sentiment or affection of the heart from which any action proceeds, and upon which its whole virtue or vice must ultimately depend, may be considered under two different aspects, or in two different relations; first, in relation to the cause which excites it, or the motive which gives occasion to it; and secondly, in relation to the end which it proposes, or the effect which it tends to produce.

In the suitableness or unsuitableness, in the proportion or disproportion which the affection seems to bear to the cause or object which excites it, consists the propriety or impropriety, the decency or ungracefulness of the consequent action.

In the beneficial or hurtful nature of the effects which the affection aims at, or tends to produce, consists the merit or demerit of the action, the qualities by which it is entitled to reward, or is deserving of punishment.

Philosophers have, of late years, considered chiefly the tendency of affections, and have given little attention to the relation which they stand in to the cause which excites them. In common life, however, when we judge of any person's conduct, and of the sentiments which directed it, we constantly consider them under both these aspects. When we blame in another man the excesses of love, of grief, of resentment, we not only consider the ruinous effects which they tend to produce, but the little occasion which was given for them. The merit of his favourite, we say, is not so great, his misfortune is not so dreadful, his provocation is not so extraordinary, as to justify so violent a passion. We should have indulged, we say; perhaps, have approved of the violence of his emotion, had the cause been in any respect proportioned to it.

When we judge in this manner of any affection, as proportioned or disproportioned to the cause which excites it, it is scarce possible that we should make use of any other rule or canon but the correspondent affection in ourselves. If, upon bringing the case home to our own breast, we find that the sentiments which it gives occasion to, coincide and tally with our own, we necessarily approve of them as proportioned and suitable to their objects; if otherwise, we necessarily disapprove of them, as extravagant and out of proportion.

Every faculty in one man is the measure by which he judges of the like faculty in another. I judge of your sight by my sight, of your ear by my ear, of your reason by my reason, of your resentment by my resentment, of your love by my love. I neither have, nor can have, any other way of judging about them.

Chap. IV: The same subject continued

We may judge of the propriety or impropriety of the sentiments of another person by their correspondence or disagreement with our own, upon two different occasions; either, first, when the objects which excite them are considered without any peculiar relation, either to ourselves or to the person whose sentiments we judge of; or, secondly, when they are considered as peculiarly affecting one or other of us.

1. With regard to those objects which are considered without any peculiar relation either to ourselves or to the person whose sentiments we judge of; wherever his sentiments entirely correspond with our own, we ascribe to him the qualities of taste and good judgment. The beauty of a plain, the greatness of a mountain, the ornaments of a building, the expression of a picture, the composition of a discourse, the conduct of a third person, the proportions of different quantities and numbers, the various appearances which the great machine of the universe is perpetually exhibiting, with the secret wheels and springs which product them; all the general subjects of science and taste, are what we and our companion regard as having no peculiar relation to either of us. We both look at them from the same point of view, and we have no occasion for sympathy, or for that imaginary change of situations

from which it arises, in order to produce, with regard to these, the most perfect harmony of sentiments and affections. If, notwithstanding, we are often differently affected, it arises either from the different degrees of attention, which our different habits of life allow us to give easily to the several parts of those complex objects, or from the different degrees of natural acuteness in the faculty of the mind to which they are addressed.

When the sentiments of our companion coincide with our own in things of this kind, which are obvious and easy, and in which, perhaps, we never found a single person who differed from us, though we, no doubt, must approve of them, yet he seems to deserve no praise or admiration on account of them. But when they not only coincide with our own, but lead and direct our own; when in forming them he appears to have attended to many things which we had overlooked, and to have adjusted them to all the various circumstances of their objects; we not only approve of them, but wonder and are surprised at their uncommon and unexpected acuteness and comprehensiveness, and he appears to deserve a very high degree of admiration and applause. For approbation heightened by wonder and surprise, constitutes the sentiment which is properly called admiration, and of which applause is the natural expression. The decision of the man who judges that exquisite beauty is preferable to the grossest deformity, or that twice two are equal to four, must certainly be approved of by all the world, but will not, surely, be much admired. It is the acute and delicate discernment of the man of taste, who distinguishes the minute, and scarce perceptible differences of beauty and deformity; it is the comprehensive accuracy of the experienced mathematician, who unravels, with ease, the most intricate and perplexed proportions; it is the great leader in science and taste, the man who directs and conducts our own sentiments, the extent and superior justness of whose talents astonish us with wonder and surprise, who excites our admiration, and seems to deserve our applause: and upon this foundation is grounded the greater part of the praise which is bestowed upon what are called the intellectual virtues.

The utility of those qualities, it may be thought, is what first recommends them to us; and, no doubt, the consideration of this, when we come to attend to it, gives them a new value. Originally, however, we approve of another man's judgment, not as something useful, but as right, as accurate, as agreeable to truth and reality: and it is evident we attribute those qualities to it for no other reason but because we find that it agrees with our own. Taste, in the same manner, is originally approved of, not as useful, but as just, as delicate, and as precisely suited to its object. The idea of the utility of all qualities of this kind, is plainly an after-thought, and not what first recommends them to our approbation.

2. With regard to those objects, which affect in a particular manner either ourselves or the person whose sentiments we judge of, it is at once more difficult to preserve this harmony and correspondence, and at the same time, vastly more important. My companion does not naturally look upon the misfortune that has befallen me, or the injury that has been done me, from the same point of view in which I consider them. They affect me much more nearly. We do not view them from the same station, as we do a picture, or a poem, or a system of philosophy, and are,

therefore, apt to be very differently affected by them. But I can much more easily overlook the want of this correspondence of sentiments with regard to such indifferent objects as concern neither me nor my companion, than with regard to what interests me so much as the misfortune that has befallen me, or the injury that has been done me. Though you despise that picture, or that poem, or even that system of philosophy, which I admire, there is little danger of our quarrelling upon that account. Neither of us can reasonably be much interested about them. They ought all of them to be matters of great indifference to us both; so that, though our opinions may be opposite, our affections may still be very nearly the same. But it is quite otherwise with regard to those objects by which either you or I are particularly affected. Though your judgments in matters of speculation, though your sentiments in matters of taste, are quite opposite to mine, I can easily overlook this opposition; and if I have any degree of temper, I may still find some entertainment in your conversation, even upon those very subjects. But if you have either no fellow-feeling for the misfortunes I have met with, or none that bears any proportion to the grief which distracts me; or if you have either no indignation at the injuries I have suffered, or none that bears any proportion to the resentment which transports me, we can no longer converse upon these subjects. We become intolerable to one another. I can neither support your company, nor you mine. You are confounded at my violence and passion, and I am enraged at your cold insensibility and want of feeling.

In all such cases, that there may be some correspondence of sentiments between the spectator and the person principally concerned, the spectator must, first of all, endeavour, as much as he can, to put himself in the situation of the other, and to bring home to himself every little circumstance of distress which can possibly occur to the sufferer. He must adopt the whole case of his companion with all its minutest incidents; and strive to render as perfect as possible, that imaginary change of situation upon which his sympathy is founded.

After all this, however, the emotions of the spectator will still be very apt to fall short of the violence of what is felt by the sufferer. Mankind, though naturally sympathetic, never conceive, for what has befallen another, that degree of passion which naturally animates the person principally concerned. That imaginary change of situation, upon which their sympathy is founded, is but momentary. The thought of their own safety, the thought that they themselves are not really the sufferers, continually intrudes itself upon them; and though it does not hinder them from conceiving a passion somewhat analogous to what is felt by the sufferer, hinders them from conceiving any thing that approaches to the same degree of violence. The person principally concerned is sensible of this, and at the same time passionately desires a more complete sympathy. He longs for that relief which nothing can afford him but the entire concord of the affections of the spectators with his own. To see the emotions of their hearts, in every respect, beat time to his own, in the violent and disagreeable passions, constitutes his sole consolation. But he can only hope to obtain this by lowering his passion to that pitch, in which the spectators are capable of going along with him. He must flatten, if I may be allowed to say so, the sharpness of its natural tone, in order to reduce it to harmony and concord with the emotions of those who are about him. What they feel, will, indeed, always be, in some respects, different from what he feels, and compassion can never be exactly the same with original sorrow; because the secret consciousness that the change of situations, from which the sympathetic sentiment arises, is but imaginary, not only lowers it in degree, but, in some measure, varies it in kind, and gives it a quite different modification. These two sentiments, however, may, it is evident, have such a correspondence with one another, as is sufficient for the harmony of society. Though they will never be unisons, they may be concords, and this is all that is wanted or required.

In order to produce this concord, as nature teaches the spectators to assume the circumstances of the person principally concerned, so she teaches this last in some measure to assume those of the spectators. As they are continually placing themselves in his situation, and thence conceiving emotions similar to what he feels; so he is as constantly placing himself in theirs, and thence conceiving some degree of that coolness about his own fortune, with which he is sensible that they will view it. As they are constantly considering what they themselves would feel, if they actually were the sufferers, so he is as constantly led to imagine in what manner he would be affected if he was only one of the spectators of his own situation. As their sympathy makes them look at it, in some measure, with his eyes, so his sympathy makes him look at it, in some measure, with theirs, especially when in their presence and acting under their observation: and as the reflected passion, which he thus conceives, is much weaker than the original one, it necessarily abates the violence of what he felt before he came into their presence, before he began to recollect in what manner they would be affected by it, and to view his situation in this candid and impartial light.

The mind, therefore, is rarely so disturbed, but that the company of a friend will restore it to some degree of tranquillity and sedateness. The breast is, in some measure, calmed and composed the moment we come into his presence. We are immediately put in mind of the light in which he will view our situation, and we begin to view it ourselves in the same light; for the effect of sympathy is instantaneous. We expect less sympathy from a common acquaintance than from a friend: we cannot open to the former all those little circumstances which we can unfold to the latter: we assume, therefore, more tranquillity before him, and endeavour to fix our thoughts upon those general outlines of our situation which he is willing to consider. We expect still less sympathy from an assembly of strangers, and we assume, therefore, still more tranquillity before them, and always endeavour to bring down our passion to that pitch, which the particular company we are in may be expected to go along with. Nor is this only an assumed appearance: for if we are at all masters of ourselves, the presence of a mere acquaintance will really compose us, still more than that of a friend; and that of an assembly of strangers still more than that of an acquaintance.

Society and conversation, therefore, are the most powerful remedies for restoring the mind to its tranquillity, if, at any time, it has unfortunately lost it; as well as the best preservatives of that equal and happy temper, which is so necessary to self-satisfaction and enjoyment. Men of retirement and speculation, who are apt to sit brooding at home over either grief or resentment, though they may often have more humanity, more generosity, and a nicer sense of honour, yet seldom possess that equality of temper which is so common among men of the world.

...

Section III: Of the Effects of Prosperity and Adversity upon the Judgment of Mankind with regard to the Propriety of Action; and why it is more easy to obtain their Aprobation in the one state than in the other

...

Chap. II: Of the origin of Ambition, and of the distinction of Ranks

It is because mankind are disposed to sympathize more entirely with our joy than with our sorrow, that we make parade of our riches, and conceal our poverty. Nothing is so mortifying as to be obliged to expose our distress to the view of the public, and to feel, that though our situation is open to the eyes of all mankind, no mortal conceives for us the half of what we suffer. Nay, it is chiefly from this regard to the sentiments of mankind, that we pursue riches and avoid poverty. For to what purpose is all the toil and bustle of this world? what is the end of avarice and ambition, of the pursuit of wealth, of power, and preheminence? Is it to supply the necessities of nature? The wages of the meanest labourer can supply them. We see that they afford him food and clothing, the comfort of a house, and of a family. If we examined his oeconomy with rigour, we should find that he spends a great part of them upon conveniencies, which may be regarded as superfluities, and that, upon extraordinary occasions, he can give something even to vanity and distinction. What then is the cause of our aversion to his situation, and why should those who have been educated in the higher ranks of life, regard it as worse than death, to be reduced to live, even without labour, upon the same simple fare with him, to dwell under the same lowly roof, and to be clothed in the same humble. attire? Do they imagine that their stomach is better, or their sleep sounder in a palace than in a cottage? The contrary has been so often observed, and, indeed, is so very obvious, though it had never been observed, that there is nobody ignorant of it. From whence, then, arises that emulation which runs through all the different ranks of men, and what are the advantages which we propose by that great purpose of human life which we call bettering our condition? To be observed, to be attended to, to be taken notice of with sympathy, complacency, and approbation, are all the advantages which we can propose to derive from it. It is the vanity, not the ease, or the pleasure, which interests us. But vanity is always founded upon the belief of our being the object of attention and approbation. The rich man glories in his riches, because he feels that they naturally draw upon him the attention of the world, and that mankind are disposed to go along with him in all those agreeable emotions with which the advantages of his situation so readily inspire him. At the thought of this, his heart seems to swell and dilate itself within him, and he is fonder of his wealth, upon this account, than for all the other advantages it procures him. The poor man, on the contrary, is ashamed of his poverty. He feels that it either places him out of the sight of mankind, or, that if they take any notice of him, they have, however, scarce any fellow-feeling with the misery and distress which he suffers. He is mortified upon both accounts. for though to be overlooked, and to be disapproved of, are things entirely different, yet as obscurity covers us from the daylight of honour and approbation, to feel that we are taken no notice of, necessarily damps the most agreeable hope, and disappoints the most ardent desire, of human nature. The poor man goes out and comes in unheeded, and when in the midst of a crowd is in the same obscurity as if shut up in his own hovel. Those humble cares and painful attentions which occupy those in his situation, afford no amusement to the dissipated and the gay. They turn away their eyes from him, or if the extremity of his distress forces them to look at him, it is only to spurn so disagreeable an object from among them. The fortunate and the proud wonder at the insolence of human wretchedness, that it should dare to present itself before them, and with the loathsome aspect of its misery presume to disturb the serenity of their happiness. The man of rank and distinction, on the contrary, is observed by all the world. Every body is eager to look at him, and to conceive, at least by sympathy, that joy and exultation with which his circumstances naturally inspire him. His actions are the objects of the public care. Scarce a word, scarce a gesture, can fall from him that is altogether neglected. In a great assembly he is the person upon whom all direct their eyes; it is upon him that their passions seem all to wait with expectation, in order to receive that movement and direction which he shall impress upon them; and if his behaviour is not altogether absurd, he has, every moment, an opportunity of interesting mankind, and of rendering himself the object of the observation and fellow-feeling of every body about him. It is this, which, notwithstanding the restraint it imposes, notwithstanding the loss of liberty with which it is attended, renders greatness the object of envy, and compensates, in the opinion of all those mortifications which must mankind, all that toil, all that anxiety, be undergone in the pursuit of it; and what is of yet more consequence, all that leisure, all that ease, all that careless security, which are forfeited for ever by the acquisition.

When we consider the condition of the great, in those delusive colours in which the imagination is apt to paint it. it seems to be almost the abstract idea of a perfect and happy state. It is the very state which, in all our waking dreams and idle reveries, we had sketched out to ourselves as the final object of all our desires. We feel, therefore, a peculiar sympathy with the satisfaction of those who are in it. We favour all their inclinations, and forward all their wishes. What pity, we think, that any thing should spoil and corrupt so agreeable a situation! We could even wish them immortal; and it seems hard to us, that death should at last put an end to such perfect enjoyment. It is cruel, we think, in Nature to compel them from their exalted stations to that humble, but hospitable home, which she has provided for all her children. Great King, live for ever! is the compliment, which, after the manner of eastern adulation, we should readily make them, if experience did not teach us its absurdity. Every calamity that befals them, every injury that is done them, excites in the breast of the spectator ten times more compassion and resentment than he would have felt, had the same things happened to other men. It is the misfortunes of Kings only which afford the proper subjects for tragedy. They resemble, in this respect, the misfortunes of lovers. Those two situations are the chief which interest us upon the theatre; because, in spite of all that reason and experience can tell us to the contrary, the prejudices of the imagination attach to these two states a happiness superior to any other. To disturb, or to put an end to such perfect enjoyment, seems to be the most atrocious of all injuries. The traitor who conspires against the life of his monarch, is thought a greater monster than any other murderer. All the innocent blood that was shed in the civil wars, provoked less indignation than the death of Charles I. A stranger to human nature, who saw the indifference of men about the misery of their inferiors, and the regret and indignation which they feel for the misfortunes and sufferings of those above them, would be apt to imagine, that pain must be more agonizing, and the convulsions of death more terrible to persons of higher rank, than to those of meaner stations.

Upon this disposition of mankind, to go along with all the passions of the rich and the powerful, is founded the distinction of ranks, and the order of society. Our obsequiousness to our superiors more frequently arises from our admiration for the advantages of their situation, than from any private expectations of benefit from their good-will. Their benefits can extend but to a few. but their fortunes interest almost every body. We are eager to assist them in completing a system of happiness that approaches so near to perfection; and we desire to serve them for their own sake, without any other recompense but the vanity or the honour of obliging them. Neither is our deference to their inclinations founded chiefly, or altogether, upon a regard to the utility of such submission, and to the order of society, which is best supported by it. Even when the order of society seems to require that we should oppose them, we can hardly bring ourselves to do it. That kings are the servants of the people, to be obeyed, resisted, deposed, or punished, as the public conveniency may require, is the doctrine of reason and philosophy; but it is not the doctrine of Nature. Nature would teach us to submit to them for their own sake, to tremble and bow down before their exalted station, to regard their smile as a reward sufficient to compensate any services, and to dread their displeasure, though no other evil were to follow from it, as the severest of all mortifications. To treat them in any respect as men, to reason and dispute with them upon ordinary occasions, requires such resolution, that there are few men whose magnanimity can support them in it, unless they are likewise assisted by familiarity and acquaintance. The strongest motives, the most furious passions, fear, hatred, and resentment, are scarce sufficient to balance this natural disposition to respect them: and their conduct must, either justly or unjustly, have excited the highest degree of all those passions, before the bulk of the people can be brought to oppose them with violence, or to desire to see them either punished or deposed. Even when the people have been brought this length, they are apt to relent every moment, and easily relapse into their habitual state of deference to those whom they have been accustomed to look upon as their natural superiors. They cannot stand the mortification of their monarch. Compassion soon takes the place of resentment, they forget all past provocations, their old principles of loyalty revive, and they run to re-establish the ruined authority of their old masters, with the same violence with which they had opposed it. The death of Charles I brought about the Restoration of the royal family. Compassion for James II when he was seized by the populace in making his escape on ship-board, had almost prevented the Revolution, and made it go on more heavily than before.

Do the great seem insensible of the easy price at which they may acquire the public admiration; or do they seem to imagine that to them, as to other men, it must be the purchase either of sweat or of blood? By what important accomplishments is the young nobleman instructed to support the dignity of his rank, and to render himself worthy of that superiority over his fellow-citizens, to which the virtue of his ancestors had raised them? Is it by knowledge, by industry, by patience, by self-denial, or by virtue of any kind? As all his words, as all his motions are attended to, he learns an habitual regard to every circumstance of ordinary behaviour, and studies to perform all those small duties with the most exact propriety. As he is conscious how much he is observed, and how much mankind are disposed to favour all his inclinations, he acts, upon the most indifferent occasions, with that freedom and elevation which the thought of this naturally inspires. His air, his manner, his deportment, all mark that elegant and graceful sense of his own superiority, which those who are born to inferior stations can hardly ever arrive at. These are the arts by which he proposes to make mankind more easily submit to his authority, and to govern their inclinations according to his own pleasure: and in this he is seldom disappointed. These arts, supported by rank and preheminence, are, upon ordinary occasions, sufficient to govern the world. Lewis XIV during the greater part of his reign, was regarded, not only in France, but over all Europe, as the most perfect model of a great prince. But what were the talents and virtues by which he acquired this great reputation? Was it by the scrupulous and inflexible justice of all his undertakings, by the immense dangers and difficulties with which they were attended, or by the unwearied and unrelenting application with which he pursued them? Was it by his extensive knowledge, by his exquisite judgment, or by his heroic valour? It was by none of these qualities. But he was, first of all, the most powerful prince in Europe, and consequently held the highest rank among kings; and then, says his historian, 'he surpassed all his courtiers in the gracefulness of his shape, and the majestic beauty of his features. The sound of his voice, noble and affecting, gained those hearts which his presence intimidated. He had a step and a deportment which could suit only him and his rank, and which would have been ridiculous in any other person. The embarrassment which he occasioned to those who spoke to him, flattered that secret satisfaction with which he felt his own superiority. The old officer, who was confounded and faultered in asking him a favour, and not being able to conclude his discourse, said to him: Sir, your majesty, I hope, will believe that I do not tremble thus before your enemies: had no difficulty to obtain what he demanded.' These frivolous accomplishments, supported by his rank, and, no doubt too, by a degree of other talents and virtues, which seems, however, not to have been much above mediocrity, established this prince in the esteem of his own age, and have drawn, even from posterity, a good deal of respect for his memory. Compared with these, in his own times, and in his own presence, no other virtue, it seems, appeared to have any merit. Knowledge, industry, valour, and beneficence, trembled, were abashed, and lost all dignity before them.

But it is not by accomplishments of this kind, that the man of inferior rank must hope to distinguish himself. Politeness is so much the virtue of the great, that it will do little honour to any body but themselves. The coxcomb, who imitates their manner, and affects to be eminent by the superior propriety of his ordinary behaviour, is rewarded with a double share of contempt for his folly and presumption. Why should the man, whom nobody thinks it worth while to look at, be very anxious about the manner in which he holds up his head, or disposes of his arms while he walks through a room? He is occupied surely with a very superfluous attention, and with an attention too that marks a sense of his own importance, which no other mortal can go along with. The most perfect modesty and plainness, joined to as much negligence as is consistent with the respect due to the company, ought to be the chief characteristics of the behaviour of a private man. If ever he hopes to distinguish himself, it must be by more important virtues. He must acquire dependants to balance the dependants of the great, and he has no other fund to pay them from, but the labour of his body, and the activity of his mind. He must cultivate these therefore: he must acquire superior knowledge in his profession, and superior industry in the exercise of it. He must be patient in labour, resolute in danger, and firm in distress. These talents he must bring into public view, by the difficulty, importance, and, at the same time, good judgment of his undertakings, and by the severe and unrelenting application with which he pursues them. Probity and prudence, generosity and frankness, must characterize his behaviour upon all ordinary occasions; and he must, at the same time, be forward to engage in all those situations, in which it requires the greatest talents and virtues to act with propriety, but in which the greatest applause is to be acquired by those who can acquit themselves with honour. With what impatience does the man of spirit and ambition, who is depressed by his situation, look round for some great opportunity to distinguish himself? No circumstances, which can afford this, appear to him undesirable. He even looks forward with satisfaction to the prospect of foreign war, or civil dissension; and, with secret transport and delight, sees through all the confusion and bloodshed which attend them, the probability of those wished-for occasions presenting themselves, in which he may draw upon himself the attention and admiration of mankind. The man of rank and distinction, on the contrary, whose whole glory consists in the propriety of his ordinary behaviour, who is contented with the humble renown which this can afford him, and has no talents to acquire any other, is unwilling to embarrass himself with what can be attended either with difficulty or distress. To figure at a ball is his great triumph, and to succeed in an intrigue of gallantry, his highest exploit. He has an aversion to all public confusions, not from the love of mankind, for the great never look upon their inferiors as their fellow-creatures; nor yet from want of courage, for in that he is seldom defective; but from a consciousness that he possesses none of the virtues which are required in such situations, and that the public attention will certainly be drawn away from him by others. He may be willing to expose himself to some little danger, and to make a campaign when it happens to be the fashion. But he shudders with horror at the thought of any situation which demands the continual and long exertion of patience, industry, fortitude, and application of thought. These virtues are hardly ever to be met with in men who are born to those high stations. In all governments accordingly, even in monarchies, the highest offices are generally possessed, and the whole detail of the administration conducted, by men who were educated in the middle and inferior ranks of life, who have been carried forward by their own industry and abilities, though loaded with the jealousy, and opposed by the resentment, of all those who were born their superiors, and to whom the great, after having regarded them first with contempt, and afterwards with envy, are at last contented to truckle with the same abject meanness with which they desire that the rest of mankind should behave to themselves.

It is the loss of this easy empire over the affections of mankind which renders the fall from greatness so insupportable. When the family of the king of Macedon was led in triumph by Paulus Aemilius, their misfortunes, it is said, made them divide with their conqueror the attention of the Roman people. The sight of the royal children, whose tender age rendered them insensible of their situation, struck the spectators, amidst the public rejoicings and prosperity, with the tenderest sorrow and compassion. The king appeared next in the procession; and seemed like one confounded and astonished, and bereft of all sentiment, by the greatness of his calamities. His friends and ministers followed after him. As they moved along, they often cast their eyes upon their fallen sovereign, and always burst into tears at the sight; their whole behaviour demonstrating that they thought not of their own misfortunes, but were occupied entirely by the superior greatness of his. The generous Romans, on the contrary, beheld him with disdain and indignation, and regarded as unworthy of all compassion the man who could be so mean-spirited as to bear to live under such calamities. Yet what did those calamities amount to? According to the greater part of historians, he was to spend the remainder of his days, under the protection of a powerful and humane people, in a state which in itself should seem worthy of envy, a state of plenty, ease, leisure, and security, from which it was impossible for him even by his own folly to fall. But he was no longer to be surrounded by that admiring mob of fools, flatterers, and dependants, who had formerly been accustomed to attend upon all his motions. He was no longer to be gazed upon by multitudes, nor to have it in his power to render himself the object of their respect, their gratitude, their love, their admiration. The passions of nations were no longer to mould themselves upon his inclinations. This was that insupportable calamity which bereaved the king of all sentiment; which made his friends forget their own misfortunes; and which the Roman magnanimity could scarce conceive how any man could be so mean-spirited as to bear to survive.

'Love,' says my Lord Rochfaucault, 'is commonly succeeded by ambition; but ambition is hardly ever succeeded by love.' That passion, when once it has got entire possession of the breast, will admit neither a rival nor a successor. To those who have been accustomed to the possession, or even to the hope of public admiration, all other pleasures sicken and decay. Of all the discarded statesmen who for their own ease have studied to get the better of ambition, and to despise those honours which they could no longer arrive at, how few have been able to succeed? The greater part have spent their time in the most listless and insipid indolence, chagrined at the thoughts of their own insignificancy, incapable of being interested i n the occupations of private life, without enjoyment, except when they talked of their former greatness, and without satisfaction, except when they were employed in some vain project to recover it. Are you in earnest resolved never to barter your liberty for the lordly servitude of a court, but to live free, fearless, and independent? There seems to be one way to continue in that virtuous resolution; and perhaps but one. Never enter the place from whence so few have been able to return; never come within the circle of ambition; nor ever bring yourself into comparison with those masters of the earth who have already engrossed the attention of half mankind before you.

Of such mighty importance does it appear to be, in the imaginations of men, to stand in that situation which sets them most in the view of general sympathy and attention. And thus, place, that great object which divides the wives of aldermen, is the end of half the labours of human life; and is the cause of all the tumult and bustle, all the rapine and injustice, which avarice and ambition have introduced into this world. People of sense, it is said, indeed despise place; that is, they despise sitting at the head of the table, and are indifferent who it is that is pointed out to the company by that frivolous circumstance, which the smallest advantage is capable of overbalancing. But rank, distinction pre-eminence, no man despises, unless he is either raised very much above, or sunk very much below, the ordinary standard of human nature; unless he is either so confirmed in wisdom and real philosophy, as to be satisfied that, while the propriety of his conduct renders him the just object of approbation, it is of little consequence though he be neither attended to, nor approved of; or so habituated to the idea of his own meanness, so sunk in slothful and sottish indifference, as entirely to have forgot the desire, and almost the very wish, for superiority.

As to become the natural object of the joyous congratulations and sympathetic attentions of mankind is, in this manner, the circumstance which gives to prosperity all its dazzling splendour; so nothing darkens so much the gloom of adversity as to feel that our misfortunes are the objects, not of the fellow-feeling, but of the contempt and aversion of our brethren. It is upon this account that the most dreadful calamities are not always those which it is most difficult to support. It is often more mortifying to appear in public under small disasters, than under great misfortunes. The first excite no sympathy; but the second, though they may excite none that approaches to the anguish of the sufferer, call forth, however, a very lively compassion. The sentiments of the spectators are, in this last case, less wide of those of the sufferer, and their imperfect fellow-feeling lends him some assistance in supporting his misery. Before a gay assembly, a gentleman would be more mortified to appear covered with filth and rags than with blood and wounds. This last situation would interest their pity; the other would provoke their laughter. The judge who orders a criminal to be set in the pillory, dishonours him more than if he had condemned him to the scaffold. The great prince, who, some years ago, caned a general officer at the head of his army, disgraced him irrecoverably. The punishment would have been much less had he shot him through the body. By the laws of honour, to strike with a cane dishonours, to strike with a sword does not, for an obvious reason. Those slighter punishments, when inflicted on a gentleman, to whom dishonour is the greatest of all evils, come to be regarded among a humane and generous people, as the most dreadful of any. With regard to persons of that rank, therefore, they are universally laid aside, and the law, while it takes their life upon many occasions, respects their honour upon almost all. To scourge a person of quality, or to set him in the pillory, upon account of any crime whatever, is a brutality of which no European government, except that of Russia, is capable.

A brave man is not rendered contemptible by being brought to the scaffold; he is, by being set in the pillory. His behaviour in the one situation may gain him universal esteem and admiration. No behaviour in the other can render him agreeable. The sympathy of the spectators supports him in the one case, and saves him from that shame, that consciousness that his misery is felt by himself only, which is of all sentiments the most unsupportable. There is no sympathy in the other; or, if there is any, it is not with his pain, which is a trifle, but with his consciousness of the want of sympathy with which this pain is attended. It is with his shame, not with his sorrow. Those who pity him, blush and hang down their heads for him. He droops in the same manner, and feels himself irrecoverably degraded by the punishment, though not by the crime. The man, on the contrary, who dies with resolution, as he is naturally regarded with the erect aspect of esteem and approbation, so he wears himself the same undaunted countenance; and, if the crime does not deprive him of the respect of others, the punishment never will. He has no suspicion that his situation is the object of contempt or derision to any body, and he can, with propriety, assume the air, not only of perfect serenity, but of triumph and exultation.

'Great dangers,' says the Cardinal de Retz, 'have their charms, because there is some glory to be got, even when we miscarry. But moderate dangers have nothing but what is horrible, because the loss of reputation always attends the want of success.' His maxim has the same foundation with what we have been just now observing with regard to punishments.

Human virtue is superior to pain, to poverty, to danger, and to death; nor does it even require its utmost efforts do despise them. But to have its misery exposed to insult and derision, to be led in triumph, to be set up for the hand of scorn to point at, is a situation in which its constancy is much more apt to fail. Compared with the contempt of mankind, all other external evils are easily supported.

Chap. III: Of the corruption of our moral sentiments, which is occasioned by this disposition to admire the rich and the great, and to despise or neglect persons of poor and mean condition

This disposition to admire, and almost to worship, the rich and the powerful, and to despise, or, at least, to neglect persons of poor and mean condition, though necessary both to establish and to maintain the distinction of ranks and the order of society, is, at the same time, the great and most universal cause of the corruption of our moral sentiments. That wealth and greatness are often regarded with the respect and admiration which are due only to wisdom and virtue; and that the contempt, of which vice and folly are the only proper objects, is often most unjustly bestowed upon poverty and weakness, has been the complaint of moralists in all ages.

We desire both to be respectable and to be respected. We dread both to be contemptible and to be contemned. But, upon coming into the world, we soon find that wisdom and virtue are by no means the sole objects of respect; nor vice and folly, of contempt. We frequently see the respectful attentions of the world more strongly directed towards the rich and the great, than towards the wise and the virtuous. We see frequently the vices and follies of the powerful much less despised than the poverty and weakness of the innocent. To deserve, to acquire, and to enjoy the respect and admiration of mankind, are the great objects of ambition and emulation. Two different roads are presented to us, equally leading to the attainment of this so much desired object; the one, by the study of wisdom and the practice of virtue; the other, by the acquisition of wealth and greatness. Two different characters are presented to our emulation; the one, of proud ambition and ostentatious avidity. the other, of humble modesty and equitable justice. Two different models, two different pictures, are held out to us, according to which we may fashion our own character and behaviour; the one more gaudy and glittering in its colouring; the other more correct and more exquisitely beautiful in its outline: the one forcing itself upon the notice of every wandering eye; the other, attracting the attention of scarce any body but the most studious and careful observer. They are the wise and the virtuous chiefly, a select, though, I am afraid, but a small party, who are the real and steady admirers of wisdom and virtue. The great mob of mankind are the admirers and worshippers, and, what may seem more extraordinary, most frequently the disinterested admirers and worshippers, of wealth and greatness.

The respect which we feel for wisdom and virtue is, no doubt, different from that which we conceive for wealth and greatness; and it requires no very nice discernment to distinguish the difference. But, notwithstanding this difference, those sentiments bear a very considerable resemblance to one another. In some particular features they are, no doubt, different, but, in the general air of the countenance, they seem to be so very nearly the same, that inattentive observers are very apt to mistake the one for the other.

In equal degrees of merit there is scarce any man who does not respect more the rich and the great, than the poor and the humble. With most men the presumption and vanity of the former are much more admired, than the real and solid merit of the latter. It is scarce agreeable to good morals, or even to good language, perhaps, to say, that mere wealth and greatness, abstracted from merit and virtue, deserve our respect. We must acknowledge, however, that they almost constantly obtain it; and that they may, therefore, be considered as, in some respects, the natural objects of it. Those exalted stations may, no doubt, be completely degraded by vice and folly. But the vice and folly must be very great, before they can operate this complete degradation. The profligacy of a man of fashion is looked upon with much less contempt and aversion, than that of a man of meaner condition. In the latter, a single transgression of the rules of temperance and propriety, is commonly more resented, than the constant and avowed contempt of them ever is in the former.

In the middling and inferior stations of life, the road to virtue and that to fortune, to such fortune, at least, as men in such stations can reasonably expect to acquire, are, happily in most cases, very nearly the same. In all the middling and inferior professions, real and solid professional abilities, joined to prudent, just, firm, and temperate conduct, can very seldom fail of success. Abilities will even sometimes prevail where the conduct is by no means correct. Either habitual imprudence, however, or injustice, or weakness, or profligacy, will always clouD, and sometimes Depress altogether, the most splendid professional abilities. Men in the inferior and middling stations of life, besides, can never be great enough to be above the law, which must generally overawe them into some sort of respect for, at least, the more important rules of justice. The success of such people, too, almost always depends upon the favour and good opinion of their neighbours and equals; and without a tolerably regular conduct these can very seldom be obtained. The good old proverb, therefore, That honesty is the best policy, holds, in such situations, almost always perfectly true. In such situations, therefore, we may generally expect a considerable degree of virtue; and, fortunately for the good morals of society, these are the situations of by far the greater part of mankind.

In the superior stations of life the case is unhappily not always the same. In the courts of princes, in the drawing-rooms of the great, where success and preferment depend, not upon the esteem of intelligent and well-informed equals, but upon the fanciful and foolish favour of ignorant, presumptuous, and proud superiors; flattery and falsehood too often prevail over merit and abilities. In such societies the abilities to please, are more regarded than the abilities to serve. In quiet and peaceable times, when the storm is at a distance, the prince, or great man, wishes only to be amused, and is even apt to fancy that he has scarce any occasion for the service of any body, or that those who amuse him are sufficiently able to serve him. The external graces, the frivolous accomplishments of that impertinent and foolish thing called a man of fashion, are commonly more admired than the solid and masculine virtues of a warrior, a statesman, a philosopher, or a legislator. All the great and awful virtues, all the virtues which can fit, either for the council, the senate, or the field, are, by the insolent and insignificant flatterers, who commonly figure the most in such corrupted societies, held in the utmost contempt and derision. When the duke of Sully was called upon by Lewis the Thirteenth, to give his advice in some great emergency, he observed the favourites and courtiers whispering to one another, and smiling at his unfashionable appearance. 'Whenever your majesty's father,' said the old warrior and statesman, 'did me the honour to consult me, he ordered the buffoons of the court to retire into the antechamber.'

It is from our disposition to admire, and consequently to imitate, the rich and the great, that they are enabled to set, or to lead what is called the fashion. Their dress is the fashionable dress; the language of their conversation, the fashionable style; their air and deportment, the fashionable behaviour. Even their vices and follies are fashionable; and the greater part of men are proud to imitate and resemble them in the very qualities which dishonour and degrade them. Vain men often give themselves airs of a fashionable profligacy, which, in their hearts, they do not approve of, and of which, perhaps, they are really not guilty. They desire to be praised for what they themselves do not think praise-worthy, and are ashamed of unfashionable virtues which they sometimes practise in secret, and for which they have secretly some degree of real veneration. There are hypocrites of wealth and greatness, as well as of religion and virtue; and a vain man is as apt to pretend to be what he is not, in the one way, as a cunning man is in the other. He assumes the equipage and splendid way of living of his superiors, without considering that whatever may be praise-worthy in any of these, derives its whole merit and propriety from its suitableness to that situation and fortune which both require and can easily support the expence. Many a poor man places his glory in being thought rich, without considering that the duties (if one may call such follies by so very venerable a name) which that reputation imposes upon him, must soon reduce him to beggary, and render his situation still more unlike that of those whom he admires and imitates, than it had been originally.

To attain to this envied situation, the candidates for fortune too frequently abandon the paths of virtue; for unhappily, the road which leads to the one, and that which leads to the other, lie sometimes in very opposite directions. But the ambitious man flatters himself that, in the splendid situation to which he advances, he will have so many means of commanding the respect and admiration of mankind, and will be enabled to act with such superior propriety and grace, that the lustre of his future conduct will entirely cover, or efface, the foulness of the steps by which he arrived at that elevation. In many governments the candidates for the highest stations are above the law; and, if they can attain the object of their ambition, they have no fear of being called to account for the means by which they acquired it. They often endeavour, therefore, not only by fraud and falsehood, the ordinary and vulgar arts of intrigue and cabal; but sometimes by the perpetration of the most enormous crimes, by murder and assassination, by rebellion and civil war, to supplant and destroy those who oppose or stand in the way of their greatness. They more frequently miscarry than succeed; and commonly gain nothing but the disgraceful punishment which is due to their crimes. But, though they should be so lucky as to attain that wished-for greatness, they are always most miserably disappointed in the happiness which they expect to enjoy in it. It is not ease or pleasure, but always honour, of one kind or another, though frequently an honour very ill understood, that the ambitious man really pursues. But the honour of his exalted station appears, both in his own eyes and in those of other people, polluted and defiled by the baseness of the means through which he rose to it. Though by the profusion of every liberal expence; though by excessive indulgence in every profligate pleasure, the wretched, but usual, resource of ruined characters; though by the hurry of public business, or by the prouder and more dazzling tumult of war, he may endeavour to efface, both from his own memory and from that of other people, the remembrance of what he has done; that remembrance never fails to pursue him. He invokes in vain the dark and dismal powers of forgetfulness and oblivion. He remembers himself what he has done, and that remembrance tells him that other people must likewise remember it. Amidst all the gaudy pomp of the most ostentatious greatness; amidst the venal and vile adulation of the great and of the learned; amidst the more innocent, though more foolish, acclamations of the common people; amidst all the pride of conquest and the triumph of successful war, he is still secretly pursued by the avenging furies of shame and remorse; and, while glory seems to surround him on all sides, he himself, in his own imagination, sees black and foul infamy fast pursuing him, and every moment ready to overtake him from behind. Even the great Caesar, though he had the magnanimity to dismiss his guards, could not dismiss his suspicions. The remembrance of Pharsalia still haunted and pursued him. When, at the request of the senate, he had the generosity to pardon Marcellus, he told that assembly, that he was not unaware of the designs which were carrying on against his life; but that, as he had lived long enough both for nature and for glory, he was contented to die, and therefore despised all conspiracies. He had, perhaps, lived long enough for nature. But the man who felt himself the object of such deadly resentment, from those whose favour he wished to gain, and whom he still wished to consider as his friends, had certainly lived too long for real glory; or for all the happiness which he could ever hope to enjoy in the love and esteem of his equals.

. . .

Part IV: Of the Effect of Utility upon the Sentiment of Approbation Consisting of One Section

Chap. I: Of the Beauty which the Appearance of Utility bestows upon all the Productions of Art, and of the extensive Influence of this Species of Beauty

That utility is one of the principal sources of beauty has been observed by every body, who has considered with any attention what constitutes the nature of beauty. The conveniency of a house gives pleasure to the spectator as well as its regularity, and he is as much hurt when he observes the contrary defect, as when he sees the correspondent windows of different forms, or the door not placed exactly in the middle of the building. That the fitness of any system or machine to produce the end for which it was intended, bestows a certain propriety and beauty upon the whole, and renders the very thought and contemplation of it agreeable, is so very obvious that nobody has overlooked it.

The cause too, why utility pleases, has of late been assigned by an ingenious and agreeable philosopher, who joins the greatest depth of thought to the greatest elegance of expression, and possesses the singular and happy talent of treating the abstrusest subjects not only with the most perfect perspicuity, but with the most lively eloquence. The utility of any object, according to him, pleases the master by perpetually suggesting to him the pleasure or conveniency which it is fitted to promote. Every time he looks at it, he is put in mind of this pleasure; and the object in this manner becomes a source of perpetual satisfaction and enjoyment. The spectator enters by sympathy into the sentiments of the master, and necessarily views the object under the same agreeable aspect. When we visit the palaces of the great, we cannot help conceiving the satisfaction we should enjoy if we ourselves were the masters, and were possessed of so much artful and ingeniously contrived accommodation. A similar account is given why the appearance of inconveniency should render any object disagreeable both to the owner and to the spectator.

But that this fitness, this happy contrivance of any production of art, should often be more valued, than the very end for which it was intended; and that the exact adjustment of the means for attaining any conveniency or pleasure, should frequently be more regarded, than that very conveniency or pleasure, in the attainment of which their whole merit would seem to consist, has not, so far as I know, been yet taken notice of by any body. That this however is very frequently the case, may be observed in a thousand instances, both in the most frivolous and in the most important concerns of human life.

When a person comes into his chamber, and finds the chairs all standing in the middle of the room, he is angry with his servant, and rather than see them continue in that disorder, perhaps takes the trouble himself to set them all in their places with their backs to the wall. The whole propriety of this new situation arises from its superior conveniency in leaving the floor free and disengaged. To attain this conveniency he voluntarily puts himself to more trouble than all he could have suffered from the want of it; since nothing was more easy, than to have set himself down upon one of them, which is probably what he does when his labour is over. What he w.anted therefore, it seems, was not so much this conveniency, as that arrangement of things which promotes it. Yet it is this conveniency which ultimately recommends that arrangement, and bestows upon it the whole of its propriety and beauty.

A watch, in the same manner, that falls behind above two minutes in a day, is despised by one curious in watches. He sells it perhaps for a couple of guineas, and purchases another at fifty, which will not lose above a minute in a fortnight. The sole use of watches however, is to tell us what o'clock it is, and to hinder us from breaking any engagement, or suffering any other inconveniency by our ignorance in that particular point. But the person so nice with regard to this machine, will not always be found either more scrupulously punctual than other men, or more anxiously concerned upon any other account, to know precisely what time of day it is. What interests him is not so much the attainment of this piece of knowledge, as the perfection of the machine which serves to attain it.

How many people ruin themselves by laying out money on trinkets of frivolous utility? What pleases these lovers of toys is not so much the utility, as the aptness of the machines which are fitted to promote it. All their pockets are stuffed with little conveniencies. They contrive new pockets, unknown in the clothes of other people, in order to carry a greater number. They walk about loaded with a multitude of baubles, in weight and sometimes in value not inferior to an ordinary Jew's-box, some of which may sometimes be of some little use, but all of which might at all times be very well spared, and of which the whole utility is certainly not worth the fatigue of bearing the burden.

Nor is it only with regard to such frivolous objects that our conduct is influenced by this principle; it is often the secret motive of the most serious and important pursuits of both private and public life.

The poor man's son, whom heaven in its anger has visited with ambition, when he begins to look around him, admires the condition of the rich. He finds the cottage of his father too small for his accommodation, and fancies he should be lodged more at his ease in a palace. He is displeased with being obliged to walk a-foot, or to endure the fatigue of riding on horseback. He sees his superiors carried about in machines, and imagines that in one of these he could travel with less inconveniency. He feels himself naturally indolent, and willing to serve himself with his own hands as little as possible; and judges, that a numerous retinue of servants would save him from a great deal of trouble. He thinks if he had attained all these, he would sit still contentedly, and be quiet, enjoying himself in the thought of the happiness and tranquillity of his situation. He is enchanted with the distant idea of this felicity. It appears in his fancy like the life of some superior rank of beings, and, in order to arrive at it, he devotes himself for ever to the pursuit of wealth and greatness. To obtain the conveniencies which these afford, he submits in the first year, nay in the first month of his application, to more fatigue of body and more uneasiness of mind than he could have suffered through the whole of his life from the want of them. He studies to distinguish himself in some laborious profession. With the most unrelenting industry he labours night and day to acquire talents superior to all his competitors. He endeavours next to bring those talents into public view, and with equal assiduity solicits every opportunity of employment. For this purpose he makes his court to all mankind; he serves those whom he hates, and is obsequious to those whom he despises. Through the whole of his life he pursues the idea of a certain artificial and elegant repose which he may never arrive at, for which he sacrifices a real tranquillity that is at all times in his power, and which, if in the extremity of old age he should at last attain to it, he will find to be in no respect preferable to that humble security and contentment which he had abandoned for it. It is then, in the last dregs of life, his body wasted with toil and diseases, his mind galled and ruffled by the memory of a thousand injuries and disappointments which he imagines he has met with from the injustice of his enemies, or from the perfidy and ingratitude of his friends, that he begins at last to find that wealth and greatness are mere trinkets of frivolous utility, no more adapted for procuring ease of body or tranquillity of mind than the tweezer-cases of the lover of toys; and like them too, more troublesome to the person who carries them about with him than all the advantages they can afford him are commodious. There is no other real difference between them, except that the conveniencies of the one are somewhat more observable than those of the other. The palaces, the gardens, the equipage, the retinue of the great, are objects of which the obvious conveniency strikes every body. They do not require that their masters should point out to us wherein consists their utility. Of our own accord we readily enter into it, and by sympathy enjoy and thereby applaud the satisfaction which they are fitted to afford him. But the curiosity of a tooth-pick, of an ear-picker, of a machine for cutting the nails, or of any other trinket of the same kind, is not so obvious. Their conveniency may perhaps be equally great, but it is not so striking, and we do not so readily enter into the satisfaction of the man who possesses them. They are therefore less reasonable subjects of vanity than the magnificence of wealth and greatness; and in this consists the sole advantage of these last. They more effectually gratify that love of distinction so natural to man. To one who was to live alone in a desolate island it might be a matter of doubt, perhaps, whether a palace, or a collection of such small conveniencies as are commonly contained in a tweezer-case, would contribute most to his happiness and enjoyment. If he is to live in society, indeed, there can be no comparison, because in this, as in all other cases, we constantly pay more regard to the sentiments of the spectator, than to those of the person principally concerned, and consider rather how his situation will appear to other people, than how it will appear to himself. If we examine, however, why the spectator distinguishes with such admiration the condition of the rich and the great, we shall find that it is not so much upon account of the superior ease or pleasure which they are supposed to enjoy, as of the numberless artificial and elegant contrivances for promoting this ease or pleasure. He does not even imagine that they are really happier than other people: but he imagines that they possess more means of happiness. And it is the ingenious and artful adjustment of those means to the end for which they were intended, that is the principal source of his admiration. But in the languor of disease and the weariness of old age, the pleasures of the vain and empty distinctions of greatness disappear. To one, in this situation, they are no longer capable of recommending those toilsome pursuits in which they had formerly engaged him. In his heart he curses ambition, and vainly regrets the ease and the indolence of youth, pleasures which are fled for ever, and which he has foolishly sacrificed for what, when he has got it, can afford him no real satisfaction. In this miserable aspect does greatness appear to every man when reduced either by spleen or disease to observe with attention his own situation, and to consider what it is that is really wanting to his happiness. Power and riches appear then to be, what they are, enormous and operose machines contrived to produce a few trifling conveniencies to the body, consisting of springs the most nice and delicate, which must be kept in order with the most anxious attention, and which in spite of all our care are ready every moment to burst into pieces, and to crush in their ruins their unfortunate possessor. They are immense fabrics, which it requires the labour of a life to raise, which threaten every moment to overwhelm the person that dwells in them, and which while they stand, though they may save him from some smaller inconveniencies, can protect him from none of the severer inclemencies of the season. They keep off the summer shower, not the winter storm, but leave him always as much, and sometimes more exposed than before, to anxiety, to fear, and to sorrow; to diseases, to danger, and to death.

But though this splenetic philosophy, which in time of sickness or low spirits is familiar to every man, thus entirely depreciates those great objects of human desire, when in better health and in better humour, we never fail to regard them under a more agreeable aspect. Our imagination, which in pain and sorrow seems to be confined and cooped up within our own persons, in times of ease and prosperity expands itself to everything around us. We are then charmed with the beauty of that accommodation which reigns in the palaces and oeconomy of the great; and admire how everything is adapted to promote their ease, to prevent their wants, to gratify their wishes, and to amuse and entertain their most frivolous desires. If we consider the real satisfaction which all these things are capable of affording, by itself and separated from the beauty of that arrangement which is fitted to promote it, it will always appear in the highest degree contemptible and trifling. But we rarely view it in this abstract and philosophical light. We naturally confound it in our imagination with the order, the regular and harmonious movement of the system, the machine or oeconomy by means of which it is produced. The pleasures of wealth and greatness, when considered in this complex view, strike the imagination as something grand and beautiful and noble, of which the attainment is well worth all the toil and anxiety which we are so apt to bestow upon it.

And it is well that nature imposes upon us in this manner. It is this deception which rouses and keeps in continual motion the industry of mankind. It is this which first prompted them to cultivate the ground, to build houses, to found cities and commonwealths, and to invent and improve all the sciences and arts, which ennoble and embellish human life; which have entirely changed the whole face of the globe, have turned the rude forests of nature into agreeable and fertile plains, and made the trackless and barren ocean a new fund of subsistence, and the great high road of communication to the different nations of the earth. The earth by these labours of mankind has been obliged to redouble her natural fertility, and to maintain a greater multitude of inhabitants. It is to no purpose, that the proud and unfeeling landlord views his extensive fields, and without a thought for the wants of his brethren, in imagination consumes himself the whole harvest that grows upon them. The homely and vulgar proverb, that the eye is larger than the belly, never was more fully verified than with regard to him. The capacity of his stomach bears no proportion to the immensity of his desires, and will receive no more than that of the meanest peasant. The rest he is obliged to distribute among those, who prepare, in the nicest manner, that little which he himself makes use of, among those who fit up the palace in which this little is to be consumed, among those who provide and keep in order all the different baubles and trinkets, which are employed in the oeconomy of greatness; all of whom thus derive from his luxury and caprice, that share of the necessaries of life, which they would in vain have expected from his humanity or his justice. The produce of the soil maintains at all times nearly that number of inhabitants which it is capable of maintaining. The rich only select from the heap what is most precious and agreeable. They consume little more than the poor, and in spite of their natural selfishness and rapacity, though they mean only their own conveniency, though the sole end which they propose from the labours of all the thousands whom they employ, be the gratification of their own vain and insatiable desires, they divide with the poor the produce of all their improvements. They are led by an invisible hand to make nearly the same distribution of the necessaries of life, which would have been made, had the earth been divided into equal portions among all its inhabitants, and thus without intending it, without knowing it, advance the interest of the society, and afford means to the multiplication of the species. When Providence divided the earth among a few lordly masters, it neither forgot nor abandoned those who seemed to have been left out in the partition. These last too enjoy their share of all that it produces. In what constitutes the real happiness of human life, they are in no respect inferior to those who would seem so much above them. In ease of body and peace of mind, all the different ranks of life are nearly upon a level, and the beggar, who suns himself by the side of the highway, possesses that security which kings are fighting for.

The same principle, the same love of system, the same regard to the beauty of order, of art and contrivance, frequently serves to recommend those institutions which tend to promote the public welfare. When a patriot exerts himself for the improvement of any part of the public police, his conduct does not always arise from pure sympathy with the happiness of those who are to reap the benefit of it. It is not commonly from a fellow-feeling with carriers and waggoners that a public-spirited man encourages the mending of high roads. When the legislature establishes premiums and other encouragements to advance the linen or woollen manufactures, its conduct seldom proceeds from pure sympathy with the wearer of cheap or fine cloth, and much less from that with the manufacturer or merchant. The perfection of police, the extension of trade and manufactures, are noble and magnificent objects. The contemplation of them pleases us, and we are interested in whatever can tend to advance them. They make part of the great system of government, and the wheels of the political machine seem to move with more harmony and ease by means of them. We take pleasure in beholding the perfection of so beautiful and grand a system, and we are uneasy till we remove any obstruction that can in the least disturb or encumber the regularity of its motions. All constitutions of government, however, are valued only in proportion as they tend to promote the happiness of those who live under them. This is their sole use and end. From a certain spirit of system, however, from a certain love of art and contrivance, we sometimes seem to value the means more than the end, and to be eager to promote the happiness of our fellow-creatures, rather from a view to perfect and improve a certain beautiful and orderly system, than from any immediate sense or feeling of what they either suffer or enjoy. There have been men of the greatest public spirit, who have shown themselves in other respects not very sensible to the feelings of humanity. And on the contrary, there have been men of the greatest humanity, who seem to have been entirely devoid of public spirit. Every man may find in the circle of his acquaintance instances both of the one kind and the other. Who had ever less humanity, or more public spirit, than the celebrated legislator of Muscovy? The social and well-natured James the First of Great Britain seems, on the contrary, to have had scarce any passion, either for the glory or the interest of his country. Would you awaken the industry of the man who seems almost dead to ambition, it will often be to no purpose to describe to him the happiness of the rich and the great; to tell him that they are generally sheltered from the sun and the rain, that they are seldom hungry, that they are seldom cold, and that they are rarely exposed to weariness, or to want of any kind. The most eloquent exhortation of this kind will have little effect upon him. If you would hope to succeed, you must describe to him the conveniency and arrangement of the different apartments in their palaces; you must explain to him the propriety of their equipages, and point out to him the number, the order, and the different offices of all their attendants. If any thing is capable of making impression upon him, this will. Yet all these things tend only to keep off the sun and the rain, to save them from hunger and cold, from want and weariness. In the same manner, if you would implant public virtue in the breast of him who seems heedless of the interest of his country, it will often be to no purpose to tell him, what superior advantages the subjects of a well-governed state enjoy; that they are better lodged, that they are better clothed, that they are better fed. These considerations will commonly make no great impression. You will be more likely to persuade, if you describe the great system of public police which procures these advantages, if you explain the connexions and dependencies of its several parts, their mutual subordination to one another, and their general subserviency to the happiness of the society; if you show how this system might be introduced into his own country, what it is that hinders it from taking place there at present, how those obstructions might be removed, and all the several wheels of the machine of government be made to move with more harmony and smoothness, without grating upon one another, or mutually retarding one another's motions. It is scarce possible that a man should listen to a discourse of this kind, and not feel himself animated to some degree of public spirit. He will, at least for the moment, feel some desire to remove those obstructions, and to put into motion so beautiful and so orderly a machine. Nothing tends so much to promote public spirit as the study of politics, of the several systems of civil government, their advantages and disadvantages, of the constitution of our own country, its situation, and interest with regard to foreign nations, its commerce, its defence, the disadvantages it labours under, the dangers to which it may be exposed, how to remove the one, and how to guard against the other. Upon this account political disquisitions, if just, and reasonable, and practicable, are of all the works of speculation the most useful. Even the weakest and the worst of them are not altogether without their utility. They serve at least to animate the public passions of men, and rouse them to seek out the means of promoting the happiness of the society.

Chapter 8: Evolutionary Ethics

Comprehension questions you should be able to answer after reading this chapter:

1. What is evolution? What is natural selection?

2. According to the evolutionary account of ethics, why would "morality" be "selected" via natural selection?

3. What does Dawkins mean by the "selfish gene"?

4. What are the four "strategies" (offered by Dawkins) for promoting the survival of the selfish gene, and how do they work?

5. For each of the four strategies explained in (4) above, explain why behavior resulting from those strategies would be seen as "moral"?

6. What does Dawkins mean when he calls morality a "blessed, precious mistake"?

One of the first, core differences of opinion arising in the study of morality is the ultimate origin of and explanation for our concepts of good and evil, rightness and wrongness, duty, obligation, justice, fairness, etc. Some philosophers will claim that these things could not exist given a purely naturalistic worldview, and that some "higher" source is needed—at least if our moral values and duties are to be *objective*.

Other thinkers believe that not only *could* such things arise within a purely naturalistic worldview, but that they *did*. According to this view, humans have evolved to be "moral" animals, to have a sense of moral requirements, and to be motivated (variously) to behave according to moral standards.

Research has been conducted for decades in the "Baby Lab" (formally known as the "Infant Cognition Center") at Yale University, with the test subjects being babies under 24 months of age. The purpose of the research has been to gauge how much (if at all) babies understand "good" and "bad" behavior. The details are somewhat complicated, but the basic elements of one of the experiments are not: show a baby a puppet show in which a puppet displays "helping" behavior, and a different puppet engages in "unhelpful" behavior, and then see which puppet the babies prefer. More than 80% of the babies preferred the "nice" puppet (controlling for various other factors that might contribute to the choice)—and the percentage rises to 87% by the age of three.

Paul Bloom (a psychology professor connected to the lab) concludes that the research shows that babies are born with a rudimentary (though admittedly limited) sense of justice. Babies are born with a natural preference for "nice" behavior over "mean" behavior, but it takes development and instruction before they extend these moral notions outside their immediate circle of family.[107]

What could account for this astonishing indicator that even *babies* have at least a

---

[107] According to Bloom, "We are by nature indifferent, even hostile to strangers; we are prone towards parochialism and bigotry."

crude sense of morality? Evolutionary approaches to ethics claim that humans have evolved to possess and display a moral sense in much the same way that we have evolved to have and display sexual desire, or any other "selected for" adaptations. Before delving into the details of this evolutionary approach to ethics, it's important to make sure we all have at least a rudimentary understanding of evolution. Please bear in mind that I am a philosophy professor, not a professor of evolutionary biology, and that my Ph.D. is in philosophy, not evolutionary biology. If you're hoping for a nuanced and advanced exposition of evolutionary theory, you need to read someone else's book! But, for our purposes, we need only the basics.

"Evolution 101"

- Evolution: a change in the gene pool of a population over time.
- Gene pool: the set of all genes in a species or population.
- Species: all the individuals of a group that can exchange genes with one another
- Gene: hereditary unit that can be passed on (usually unaltered) for many generations.

Now that we have some core vocabulary in place, we can summarize the (general, basic) process of evolution:

1. Genes mutate.
2. Individuals are "selected," as a result of competition.
3. Populations evolve.

Mutation is a random process that increases genetic variation within a population. Mutations can be beneficial, harmful, or neither with respect to the organism in question—but most mutations are either neutral or harmful. Only a very small percentage of mutations are somehow beneficial.

A simple way to think of mutation is as a copying error in which gene sequences are altered. When cells divide, they make copies of their DNA. Sometimes, the process is not executed perfectly, and the copy is not exactly the same. This deviance is a mutation. In movies and comic books, mutation occurs as the result of exposure to chemicals or radiation. Exposure to certain chemicals or radiation causes DNA to break down. Cells repair themselves, but sometimes the repairs are imperfect— resulting in a mutation. Although this is a "real thing," don't expect super-powered mutants to rampage through neighborhoods any time soon. Also, although environmental factors (such as radiation) might influence the rate of mutation, most evolutionary biologists believe that those factors don't influence the "direction" or mutation. In other words, living in an environment with high radiation levels might cause mutations to occur more often, but they won't cause mutations specifically pertaining to radiation, such as resistance to it. Mutation is capricious, and this is why it's called *random* genetic mutation. Whether or not a mutation occurs is independent of whether the mutation will actually be useful to the organism, let alone with respect to how, specifically, it might be useful.

The only sorts of mutations that matter on an evolutionary scale are those that will get passed on to offspring ("germ line mutations"). Such mutations can produce no perceivable effect on the phenotype (observable characteristics). In such cases, a mutation might occur in a portion of DNA that has no function, for example. Or, such mutations can produce a small change in the phenotype, such as a change in coloration, or ear shape, for example. Or, such mutations could produce a significant change in the phenotype, such as resistance to antibiotics in bacteria strains.

Random genetic mutation increases genetic variation within a gene pool, but natural selection *decreases* genetic variation by culling "unfit" variants from the pool.

Some types of organisms within a population produce more offspring than others. Given time, this greater frequency will increase the numbers of this more prolific type within a population, and the population will change (evolve) to resemble that type. Living things are in competition with each other for food and reproductive access. Some members of each species are better (even if only slightly) at surviving and reproducing. This could be for any number of reasons. Perhaps they are stronger, or faster, or cleverer, or blend in with their surroundings, or store fat more easily, or are resistant to a certain disease, etc. Survival is "sexy." To put it bluntly: dead creatures aren't very good at reproducing.

Arguably the most cited example of this process at work involves the "peppered moths" of England. Two major variants of this moth species occur in that area, and they are genetically identical except that one variant (of a single gene) produces more melanin, causing it to be much darker in color. As a result, some moths within the population are white with black speckles, and others are just black. Historical records (such as records of moth specimen collections) reveal that the population has changed over time. Prior to the Industrial Revolution, and in rural areas far from industrial centers, the white speckled variants were more common, and the black variation quite rare. During and after the Industrial Revolution, when lots of coal was being burned, the population of moths shifted such that the black variant was much more prominent—up to 90%, in fact, although in rural areas the white speckled variation was still more numerous. What could account for these facts?

This species of moth spends much of its time perched on tree trunks. Before the Industrial Revolution, or in rural areas, such trees would grow lichen and the "speckled" moths would blend in very nicely against the trunks. This made them difficult to see, whereas the black variants were much more visible. As a result, the black ones got eaten more often, and therefore were less likely to reproduce. The population of moths favored the speckled variant. During the Industrial Revolution, however, urban areas were polluted by the soot of burning coal. This soot settled on tree trunks, killing the lichen and causing the trunks to appear black. In that context, the speckled moth is more visible, while the black variant blends in. The speckled moth gets eaten more often, the black variant reproduces more successfully, and the population of moths changed over time to favor the black variant. As a footnote to this story, with the imposition of environmental regulations since the 1950's, the air has gotten cleaner, soot has been reduced, and the tree trunks grow lichen again. The result? Once again, the speckled variant is favored, and the black variant has diminished within the population of moths.[108]

---

[108] For any interested readers, the precise mechanism of this process has been discovered: http://blogs.discovermagazine.com/d-brief/2016/06/01/jumping-gene-painted-the-peppered-moth-

To summarize this example: as a result of random genetic mutation, some moths are darker in color than their white/speckled peers. Given a particular environmental context ("sooty trees"), this mutation was advantageous and was therefore "selected" via natural selection. Over time, the population of moths changed (evolved) to reflect this.

Please note that the claim is that it is *populations* that evolve, not individual organisms (though *natural selection* occurs at the level of the individual). Continuing with that example, it's not as though a particular moth grows darker over the span of its life, with its chance for survival increasing incrementally all the while. Rather, some moths exhibit the mutation, and others don't. It just so happens that the mutation, in that case, is beneficial, and therefore gets passed down to new generations of moths. The population of moths, over a long span of time and many generations, changes to reflect this advantageous trait. As another example, *humans* have evolved, and continue to evolve, but individual human beings do not. In other words "Ted Preston" (me, the author) does not "evolve," but rather the species to which I belong evolves. To illustrate this, consider the uncomfortable example of obesity.

I have weighed various amounts over the span of my life thus far, sometimes "thinner," sometimes "heavier." The general explanation for why I weigh more or less at various times of my life (excluding obvious factors like being a tiny child as opposed to being a grown adult!) probably doesn't require much more insight than daily calorie intake and physical activity variations. My behavior contributes to my personal weight increases and losses, but it's not as if "humanity" is somehow being genetically altered to be fatter or thinner along with me.

That being said, a case can be made that humans, in general (at least in populations where food is abundant) *are* growing "heavier." Much talk is generated about the "obesity epidemic" in America, for example. Some medical doctors and nutritionists think there is an evolutionary explanation for this general trend of obesity. The idea is (roughly) this: *long* ago our human ancestors had far less reliable access to food. Hunting and gathering was not always successful, and sometimes humans starved. In that kind of environment, the disposition to store and retain fat would be advantageous. Those fat reserves could be used in "lean" times to allow the human to survive a bit longer, when food is scarce. Some humans were born, as a result of random genetic mutations, with a gene (or sequence of genes) that caused them to store fat more readily than other humans. That was advantageous to them. They were more likely to survive than their skinny, high-metabolism neighbors. Because they were more likely to survive, they were more likely to reproduce, and they passed this "store fat" gene down to their children. Over time, this advantageous trait continued to be "selected for" and the population of humans changed, over a *long* span of time, such that the tendency to store fat became a common feature.

In those days, long ago, the tendency to store fat didn't entail that those early humans were all pleasantly plump, of course. There wasn't a surplus of food to make that possible, and there was plenty of physical activity with which to burn calories.

Instead, it just meant that they didn't become "famine skinny" so easily, and were more likely to survive. Needless to say, times and circumstances have changed. In America, for example, you find very few "hunter/gatherers." We have an abundance of high calorie (processed) foods at our disposal, and many of us lead sedentary lives. Exercise is no longer a necessity for most of us, but a hobby, or a luxury pursued (often) for the sake of vanity. We still have our ancestors' disposition to retain fat, but we don't have our ancestors' food or lifestyle. The result? Many of us "retain" fat far more readily, and in excess, of what we would prefer, or is healthy.

On the assumption that this evolutionary account of our expanding waistlines is accurate, it reveals an important feature of natural selection: what is advantageous (selected for) is contingent upon the environmental circumstances at the time. The ability to retain fat might have promoted survival thousands of years ago, but might prove to impede survival now that our diets and lifestyles have changed.[109] Similarly, being a black moth rather than a speckled moth might be advantageous when the tree trunks are black with soot and free from lichen, but should the soot go away and the lichen return, being black (and not speckled) is no longer advantageous.

Let us now return to our original focus: morality. According to the evolutionary account of the development of the human animal, our sense of morality (like everything else about us) is the result of evolutionary forces, such as natural selection. Compassion, charity, justice, fairness, and any and every other moral notion exists because they met the test of natural selection, or are byproducts of something *else* that met that test.

Before delving deeper, it's important to note that to offer an evolutionary origin as the explanation for moral values is not to somehow deny the existence of those values, or denounce them as fake. To say, for example, that a mother's love for her child evolved because those creatures who cared for their young were more successful at passing along their genes than those who didn't doesn't somehow mean that mothers don't actually love their children! That would be like claiming that because sexual desire evolved for the sake of procreation, whenever anyone feels amorous that person is really, secretly, only trying to reproduce. That inference is hard to reconcile with the use of birth control, homosexual sex, masturbation, or any sexual activity other than unprotected vaginal intercourse. Just because sex evolved because it promoted the propagation of our genes doesn't mean that its only use is that propagation, nor that propagation is what we intend by it. Compassion might exist because the disposition to feel compassion, and respond accordingly, promoted the survival of those human communities in which it was found. That doesn't mean compassion is an illusion, or that when we feel compassion and act on it we are "really" only intending to promote our species' survival.

Another common assumption that must be addressed concerns the association of evolution with the doctrine of the "survival of the fittest." If evolutionary forces favor "survivors," then wouldn't we expect to find nature promoting selfish creatures, and selfish behaviors? If that were so, how could we explain the seeming existence of altruism? Cooperative behavior? Charity? Even self-sacrifice? This is the so-called

---

[109] Of course, strictly speaking, we need only to survive long enough to reproduce. So long as we delay our strokes and heart attacks long enough to have children, we've done the job our genes need us to do.

"problem of altruism," for evolutionary approaches to ethics. How could a purely naturalistic (evolutionary) understanding of morality explain moral values and behaviors that seem to defy the "eat or be eaten" code of nature?

One attempt to answer such questions comes from the famed evolutionary biologist Richard Dawkins. In his book, *The Selfish Gene*, he argues that natural selection does not work at the level of the individual organism, but rather at the level of the individual *gene*. When he refers to "the selfish gene," he makes explicitly clear that he's not imagining that a gene is *actually* selfish, or capable of any sort of motives or intentions at all. It is a metaphorical way of describing the behaviors that promote the gene's survival *as though the gene were "selfish."* He has since admitted that it was perhaps a poor and misleading choice of words—but there's nothing to be done about that now!

Natural selection operates at the level of the gene, according to Dawkins, because living creatures (such as humans) don't last long enough (historically) to be a proper unit of natural selection. If I have a child, that child will possess ½ of my genes. If that child has a child, my grandchild will possess ¼ of my genes, and so on. Within just a few generations, so much gene mixing has taken place that "I" (as a temporary aggregation of genes) am no longer present in any genetically meaningful capacity. "I" am not found in my descendants in any meaningful sense, but some of the particular genes that, at one point, comprised me, *are* found in my descendants. So, "I" don't survive long enough to participate much in evolution, but some of my genes might.

Consider an analogy with poker. Imagine that genes are the cards found in a deck. The deck is the gene pool. Some of those cards form a small collection (a "hand"). That hand represents an individual organism. Shuffling and reshuffling the deck represents the gene-mixing that takes place when we reproduce, resulting in new hands being dealt—new collections of genes. Notice that the cards survive the shuffling process, but specific hands do not. So, if I am symbolically represented by all four kings and the ace of spades, "I" am gone and used up as soon as the cards are shuffled again—but those specific cards (i.e., the kings and the ace of spades) might well find themselves in a new hand that has been dealt. It might not be glorious, but we could imagine ourselves as giant, complicated machines that exist, ultimately, to replicate the genes that comprise us. Once we serve that function, and have promoted those genes, we are cast aside, but the genes endure.

Still *metaphorically speaking*, genes "want" to survive. Genes are "selfish" (metaphorically speaking!) in that way. But, we must understand that the so-called "selfish gene" isn't just one particular occurrence of the gene, but *every* occurrence of that gene, every replica of it found in any organism anywhere in the world. If we go back to our card analogy, it's as though the ace of spades isn't just seeking its own promotion into future hands of cards, but that of every ace of spades in any deck anywhere in the world. So, imagine that there is a gene that is part of my DNA. We'll call it gene X. Gene X is "selfish" (metaphorically speaking) in that it "wants" (metaphorically speaking) to survive and continue through history. There are a variety of behaviors and traits that would help gene X to survive, and would therefore potentially pass the test of natural selection.

1. Individual selfishness

The first and most obvious way of promoting gene X's survival (which, like any other gene, is "the selfish gene") would be programming individual organisms, such as myself, to be selfish. After all, in a statement of the obvious, I share 100% of my genes with myself. The longer I live, the longer those genes (including gene X) lives. So, behaviors and dispositions to behave that cause me to put myself first, to look after my own needs (even at the expense of others'), and other such tendencies, would promote gene X, make it more likely that I survive long enough to pass gene X on to my children, and therefore promote the survival of the "selfish gene." Perhaps this can explain the fact that we humans are, admittedly, pretty self-centered a lot of the time? However, individual selfishness is not the only way to promote the survival of gene X.

2. Kin selection/Kin altruism

Recall that part of the logic of individual selfishness was that it kept the organism (me) alive longer, ultimately increasing my odds of passing along my genes. Passing along the gene is a terribly important part of the process. After all, if the only creature carrying around gene X is me, it doesn't help gene X all that much to keep just me alive for a 100 years. Gene X would die with me. But, if I have children, gene X gets to keep surviving.

Any biological child of mine will have 50% of my genes, including, possibly, gene X. So, a good strategy for keeping gene X alive would be to program me to take care of creatures that probably carry gene X as well—like my own children, for example. A possible evolutionary explanation for why living creatures, in general (certainly mammals, at least) instinctively care for their own offspring is that those offspring carry copies of "the selfish gene" (such as gene X) within them as well. If the ultimate unit of evolutionary interest is the gene, rather than the organism, this could explain self-sacrifice—a mother dying to protect her child, for example. The mother dies, but the genes live on.

Consider the math of a biological family. I share 100% of my genes, so of course promoting my own well-being serves the selfish gene. But, any children of mine would carry 50% of my genes, so helping them makes sense too. My parents also have 50% of my genes each (they're the source of them, after all), so it makes sense that I would be concerned about their survival. Any siblings of mine also share 50% of my genes. Uncles and aunts and cousins have fewer genes in common, but there's still a decent chance that gene X is in them too. Same with grandkids, etc. Heck, given the genetic similarity between humans, complete strangers have a chance of sharing some genes with me—but this is less obvious, and less likely, so it might make sense if humans had been programmed to look after themselves and their kin first and foremost.

3. Reciprocal altruism

Obviously, when we observe human behavior (and that of other animals as well), we don't observe that humans only help their own biological family. We also engage in behaviors that help non-relatives. The notion of reciprocal altruism could be used to help explain some of those behaviors. Reciprocal altruism can be summed up by the slogan, "you scratch my back, and I'll scratch yours." In other species, these sorts of arrangements are common. In fact, sometimes the arrangement literally involves scratching each other's backs! Reciprocal grooming promotes the health and well-being of each participant (e.g., two monkeys, two birds, etc.). Each one is helping another organism, who is not necessarily a blood relative, but is helped in return, thereby promoting the survival of its own genes. Such arrangements can even cross species lines. If you've ever seen video footage of little birds riding around on wildebeests, eating the insects crawling around on the wildebeests' hide, you have observed "reciprocal altruism." The wildebeest gets pesky and possibly-health-threatening insects removed, and the bird gets a meal. Bees get food, and the flower gets pollinated.

The flower and bee example should make it obvious that reciprocal altruism doesn't require an explicit "deal" to made, or even the capacity to form intentions. It would be silly to suggest that a flower and a bee drew up a mutually beneficial contract, or that the flower even "wants" anything at all. Nevertheless, in a metaphorical sort of way, both the flower and the bee are getting what they "want," and each organism's survival (and therefore the selfish gene's survival) is promoted.

4.   Altruism as a show of dominance

Finally, one more possible explanation of altruistic behavior involves cases of benevolence in which (seemingly) *nothing* is received in return. Allow me to use an admittedly cynical example. Suppose I walk into a bar, dressed in obviously expensive clothes, wearing a gold watch and some gold rings, and I buy myself a glass of top-shelf whiskey. Then, to the presumed delight of some of my fellow patrons, I announce that I'm buying a round of drinks for everyone. Everyone gets a free drink at my expense. Let's assume that I have no good reason to think that any of those patrons is one of my blood relatives. Let's also assume that I have no good reason to think that any of them is going to buy me a drink (or the equivalent) in return. What could explain this seemingly gratuitous display of generosity? I'll give you a moment to become equally cynical and ponder the possibilities....

Women.

Maybe that's my angle? After all, I've just walked into this bar, sharply dressed, and now I'm throwing money around like I've got it to burn. I'm flaunting it. A reasonable inference is that I must be a pretty good provider, and therefore a good candidate for a mate. I'm so good at "survival" that I can "waste" my resources on others, expecting nothing in return, and still get along just fine. I just (theoretically) made myself look more "attractive" than all those other males in the bar—those "losers" who rely on my free drinks! Ladies, you better snatch me up while you can....

I'm being facetious, of course—but, joking or not, this kind of explanation gets to the heart of the idea of altruism as a show of dominance. By "dominance" we don't have to mean something cruel, or oppressive. Treating someone to dinner, or giving money to charity, is hardly an oppressive act, after all. But, the effect is, nevertheless, that the giver ends up looking like a good, resourceful mate. This is by no means to suggest that people (in general—let alone women, in particular) care only about how much money their prospective partners have, or what their earning potential is, but evolution provides an explanation for the common sense (anecdotal) observation that, all else being equal, most of us (male and female alike) would probably prefer that our partners be "rich" rather than "poor."

Consider, too, how, for most of human history, women did not have the opportunity to be financially independent. Historically, women were first dependent upon their parents, and then upon a husband. There's a perfectly decent evolutionary explanation for why a woman (in that case) would prefer a capable provider over a deadbeat! A capable provider makes her own survival more likely (thereby satisfying individual selfishness) as well as that of her children (thereby satisfying kin selection/kin altruism). Accordingly, it is advantageous for the would-be provider (historically, men—though not necessarily so today) to display his potential to be a good provider. Altruistic displays of "giving" (without receiving something in return) could be just such a display.

In summary, through a variety of mechanisms (e.g., individual selfishness, kin selection, reciprocal altruism, and altruism as a show of dominance), behaviors that manifest as altruistic at the level of the organism, and within communities, are "selfish" at the level of the gene (e.g., the hypothetical gene X).

Does this "selfish gene" explanation (and the four strategies we just discussed) account for all of our moral behaviors and tendencies? Probably not, even under the best of interpretations. However, Dawkins thinks that our generalized notions of morality can be understood as a "blessed, precious mistake" of evolution.

A mistake? Yes. But, do keep in mind that he called the mistake a "blessed, precious" one. In calling morality a mistake, he means the same sort of thing when an evolutionary biologist calls any number of other generalized tendencies a "mistake."

Natural selection does not operate with laser precision. Rather, behavioral "rules of thumb" that prove advantageous get selected and passed on. A simple example of this is the fact that birds, as a "rule of thumb," feed chicks that are in their nests. Some gene or sequence of gene that produced that "rule of thumb" made survival of those chicks much more likely (obviously!), and was therefore passed along to future generations of chicks, and "nested" quite comfortably within the gene pools of birds. The rule of thumb that programs birds to feed chicks isn't precise and discriminating, though. We can imagine it (metaphorically) to be something like "feed noisy creatures in the nest." In the overwhelming majority of cases, that noisy creature in the nest is the bird's own chick. However, the Cuckoo is a species of bird that knocks the eggs of other birds from their own nests, and then places its own eggs in their place. When the eggs hatch, it's a cuckoo. The oblivious other bird (a robin, let's say) isn't savvy enough to recognize that the noisy creature isn't its own, and feeds it anyway. Technically, it is making a "mistake," since its behavior is not promoting its own genes—but you shouldn't expect especially nuanced behaviors from genes!

To return to our previous example of human sexuality, a good case can be made that sexual desire evolved because it caused us to seek out sex, and that tends to result in reproduction. The selfish gene survives into a new generation of humans. "Reproduction" might have been what made sexual desire and sexual satisfaction adaptive, but once Pandora's Box had been opened, we were hardly limited to reproduction only. Humans simply desire, and seek out, sex—and most of the time we're *not* trying to reproduce. From a certain perspective, any of our sexual activities that don't lead to reproduction are "mistakes" in that they don't promote the purpose for which they were "selected" in the first place. But, the disposition that got bred into us wasn't so precise as to specify "have intercourse, but only when reproduction can occur."

Dawkins suggests that morality operates in similar fashion.

Perhaps tendencies such as compassion, charity, self-sacrifice, mercy, fairness, and the like, were originally "selected" in the context of very small human communities in which most of the members were probably blood relatives. Altruistic behaviors towards members of that community could probably be explained in terms of kin selection, or reciprocal altruism, or altruism as a show of dominance—but the genes responsible for those tendencies couldn't specify precise behaviors like "feel compassion for distressed little creatures—but only if it's your own child." Instead, "compassion" got bred into the human gene pool. Maybe compassion originally served to motivate us to feed our babies, and care for those in need within our tiny (family) communities, but, once again, Pandora's Box has been opened. Disposed to feel compassion, we can now feel compassion not just towards our own babies, but towards "creatures in distress" in general. We can watch a commercial showing footage of a starving child on the other side of the world and feel compassion and be moved to help. We can even see a non-human suffer (e.g., a cat or dog) and feel compassion at that as well. As Dawkins puts it:

> *Sexual lust is the driving force behind a large proportion of human ambition and struggle, and much of it constitutes a misfiring. There is no reason why the same should not be true of the lust to be generous and compassionate, if this is the misfired consequence of ancestral village life. The best way for natural selection to build in both kinds of lust in ancestral times was to install rules of thumb in the brain. Those rules still influence us today, even where circumstances make them inappropriate to their original functions.[110]*

As a final note, Dawkins suggests that if this approach is correct, if our moral sense is "Darwinian" in origin, then we should expect species-level (i.e., "universal") trends in morality. We should observe some similarities in moral codes and intuitions, and researchers have indeed found the presence of cross-cultural, trans-religious, and trans-lingual moral "intuitions" that often defy our ability to articulate. Indeed, as indicated at the beginning of this chapter, some researchers claim that even babies possess this moral sense.

---

[110] The God Delusion, p.254

Chapter 9: Divine Command Theory

Comprehension questions you should be able to answer after reading this chapter:

1. What is the difference between objective and subjective claims?

2. Why does Craig think that objective moral values/duties could not exist, unless God exists?

3. How do divine command theories (in general) determine what is morally right and morally wrong?

4. How does a divine command approach to ethics (if successful) establish objective, "transcendent" moral values, and would this be seen as a selling point for the theory?

5. What is the purpose of Craig's "perceptual analogy" with regard to our "perception" of objective moral values?

6. Explain how Craig rejects "evolutionary" approaches to establishing objective moral values and duties, as well as those based on human "flourishing."

7. How does a divine command approach to ethics (if successful) answer the question, "why be moral?"

8. What is the "Euthyphro Problem," and why might it be regarded as a problem for divine command approaches to ethics? How does William Lane Craig try to "solve" the Euthyphro Problem?

As I hope you recall from our earlier critical thinking chapter, a "claim" (in this context) is simply a statement, an assertion, a proposition. One of the features of claims is that they have a "truth value." This is just a fancy way of saying that a claim must be either true or false, even if we're not sure which one it is. For example, "Ted Preston is a philosophy professor" is a claim. That claim is either true, or it isn't. If you have no idea who Ted Preston is (or to which Ted Preston I refer), you might not be sure whether it is a true statement, but you can be confident that it's either true or it's false. If you have enough information, you might be confident as to which one of those two truth values is accurate. But, what is it that would make the claim true (or false)? How would we know? The answer depends upon the kinds of claims we're talking about.

We may divide claims into two basic categories: objective claims, and subjective claims. Objective claims concern facts, while subjective claims concern opinion. The typical view is that the truth or falsity of objective claims is *independent* of whatever I (or you) happen to think, or desire, or prefer. Facts don't discriminate. They apply equally to all people at all times. If it is a fact that 2 +2 = 4, then that fact applies just as much to me as it does to you—and if I happen to believe that 2 +2 = 17, I'm *wrong*. Error is possible when we're dealing with objective claims. In fact, one of the ways to figure out if a claim is objective is to ask yourself what it would mean if two or more people disagreed about the claim. If their disagreement indicates at least one of the people is mistaken, that's a pretty good sign that the claim is objective. If I think that 2 + 2 = 17, and you think that it equals 4, that's an indicator that one of us mistaken (or maybe both of us are mistaken, and the correct answer is some third option that neither one of us came up with).

Subjective claims, in contrast, concern opinions and personal taste preferences. Disagreement does not indicate error. If I think a meal is delicious, and you think it's too spicy, it's not the case that one of us is "wrong" about the meal. If I love the band "Switchfoot," and you can't bear to listen to them, it's not the case that one of us is in error. Opinions are indexed to particular people, at particular times and places. The truth or falsity of a subjective claim is "up to me" in a meaningful sort of way—unlike the truth or falsity of objective (factual) claims.

One of the kinds of claims we make—indeed, one of the most important kinds of claims we can make—is a moral claim. Moral claims are simply assertions involving some moral issue. "Eating meat is wrong." "War is never justifiable." "Abortion is wrong." "Premarital sex is morally acceptable." These are all examples of moral claims.

According to a subjectivist approach to morality, moral claims are matters of personal opinion. As such, there is no "fact" that validates some opinions, but refutes others. Very simply, if I believe something is morally wrong, then, for me, it is morally wrong. If you believe differently, then it's not wrong for you. If you and I disagree, it's not the case that one of us is mistaken—we simply have different perspectives on the matter. A variant of this subjectivist approach claims that moral claims are not matters of individual opinion, but collective opinion. Each culture develops its own "taste" with regard to various traits and behaviors, and things are morally good or bad depending upon whether they conform to the "taste preferences" of that community. This is known as Ethical Relativism (or sometimes ethical relativism). In either case, however, moral claims are matters of opinion, rather than fact. We will now consider a few of the most prominent "objective" approaches to ethics.

As objective, each of these theories will presuppose that the project of ethics is meaningful, and although it might be difficult to discern the right thing to do in a particular situation, and although there will undoubtedly be disagreement amongst persons regarding that right thing to do, there is, nevertheless such a thing as *the* (one, exclusively) right thing to do in a given situation. All the theories we'll investigate over the next several chapters will have at least that belief in common. Where they will differ is with regard to what determines the right thing to do, and how we ought to go about discerning it.

Divine Command

Divine Command theories are just what they sound like: they identify moral goodness with the divine will, often specifically in terms of commandments thought to come from a divine source. A somewhat generic formulation is offered by William Lane Craig.

- An action (A) is *required* of a moral agent (S) if and only if a just and loving God commands S to do A.

- An action (A) is *permitted* for S if and only if a just and loving God does not command S not to do A.
- An action (A) is *forbidden* to S if and only if a just and loving God commands S not to do A.

This formulation might be somewhat controversial in that Craig builds the assumption of "just and loving" into the concept of the Divinity doing the commanding—but Craig is operating within the Christian tradition, so this should come as no surprise (more on this later). Also note that "commands" may be implied or derived from other commands, such that it need not be the case that every single thing we ought or ought not to do appears in clear black and white text in some Holy book. An easy, culturally accessible example of this kind of theory is the Ten Commandments from the Book of *Exodus* (shared by Christianity, Judaism, and Islam).

Exodus 20:2-17

2 I am the Lord your God, who brought you out of the land of Egypt, out of the house of slavery;
3 Do not have any other gods before me.
4 You shall not make for yourself an idol, whether in the form of anything that is in heaven above, or that is on the earth beneath, or that is in the water under the earth.
5 You shall not bow down to them or worship them; for I the Lord your God am a jealous God, punishing children for the iniquity of parents, to the third and the fourth generation of those who reject me,
6 but showing steadfast love to the thousandth generation of those who love me and keep my commandments.
7 You shall not make wrongful use of the name of the Lord your God, for the Lord will not acquit anyone who misuses his name.
8 Remember the Sabbath day and keep it holy.
9 For six days you shall labour and do all your work.
10 But the seventh day is a Sabbath to the Lord your God; you shall not do any work—you, your son or your daughter, your male or female slave, your livestock, or the alien resident in your towns.
11 For in six days the Lord made heaven and earth, the sea, and all that is in them, but rested the seventh day; therefore the Lord blessed the Sabbath day and consecrated it.
12 Honor your father and your mother, so that your days may be long in the land that the Lord your God is giving you.
13 You shall not murder.
14 You shall not commit adultery.
15 You shall not steal.
16 You shall not bear false witness against your neighbor.
17 You shall not covet your neighbor's house; you shall not covet your neighbor's wife, or male or female slave, or ox, or donkey, or anything that belongs to your

neighbor.

In this example, various things are required (e.g., honoring one's father and mother), other things are forbidden (e.g., murder), and anything else would be permitted (unless forbidden by God elsewhere!). Roughly, the first four Commandments address humanity's moral obligations to God, the next five address our moral obligations to other people, and the final Commandment addresses our own thoughts and desires.

The force of the Divine Command approach should be fairly obvious, and ought not to be disregarded lightly. The Divine Command approach offers a way to resolve some of the most difficult problems of ethics.

1. Divine Command theories offer an objective, "transcendent" foundation for morals.

Are there any reasons to believe objective moral values and duties really do exist? Craig thinks so, and employs an analogy with sensory perception to demonstrate his point.

To begin with, we would presumably all acknowledge that perceptual experience exists. Although our senses are fallible, in the absence of specific reasons to distrust our senses, we have a general reason to trust their adequacy. That is, although we are perfectly aware that our senses are limited, and imperfect, and can sometimes be misleading or just plain mistaken, we don't therefore embrace a comprehensive and crippling skepticism and dismiss our sense testimony as useless. Instead, we proceed by living our lives, reliant on sense testimony, and trusting in the general accuracy of our senses despite their imperfections. On a related note, we are also confident that the perceptible world exists, though we technically can't *prove* it. Each of us tends to accept that a material world exists rather independently of our awareness of it, and perceiving of it, and it is that very world within which we operate, and with which our senses are engaged. Of course, you can't prove that the material world exists and isn't just a construction of your mind (for example), since any "proof" would also be dismissed as a mental construct. That being said, with the notable exception of discussions in philosophy classes, no one takes seriously the idea that all reality is merely their own mental construct. We believe the material world exists (though we can't prove it), and we believe that our senses perceive that world in a generally reliable sort of way.

Here comes the analogy.

Just as we all have perceptual experiences (e.g., seeing, hearing, tasting, etc.), we all also have moral experiences. We "perceive" that certain actions are wrong, and others are right, that some people are "good" and others "bad," that some traits are "virtues" and others "vices." We acknowledge that this moral sense is fallible. Each of us makes moral mistakes from time to time, and some people are morally "blind" to the point where we label them sociopaths. However, just as the existence of people who are vision or hearing impaired doesn't inspire the rest of us to doubt the existence of visible or audible things (or even to seriously question the general accuracy of our own vision and hearing), the existence of those who are morally impaired need not inspire us to doubt the existence and (general) accuracy of moral experience and moral perception. As Craig puts it, "in moral experience we apprehend a realm of moral values and duties that impose themselves upon us. There's no more reason to deny the objective reality of moral values than the objective reality of the physical world."

Just as it would require a compelling argument to get you to deny the general reliability of sense testimony, so too should it require a compelling argument to get you to override your default recognition of moral perception and experience.

Perhaps there are such moral perceptions, but they are merely subjective perceptions, rather than objective? After all, you might acknowledge that there really is an independently existing glass of wine that we're both tasting, but point out that our taste experience of that wine is going to be *subjective*. I might love the wine for being so "fruit-forward," while you might hate it for being a "fruit bomb." Similarly, one person's moral perception of the same act might result in a judgment of "evil" while another's judgment of that same act is "good."

Suppose that morality is merely a matter of personal opinion, as claimed by the subjectivists. If you and I disagree about some particular moral issue, neither one of us is mistaken. For one of us to be mistaken, there would need to be some sort of independent "answer key" against which we could compare our own values. What or who could provide that "answer key?" Someone else? Why should her opinion count for more than our own? Popularity? Just because lots of people enjoy Country Music doesn't mean someone is mistaken for not liking. The law? Does it seem correct to conclude that everything that is against the law is wrong, and nothing that is not against the law is wrong? What about slavery? Slavery was once legal in the United States, and it was illegal to help slaves escape. Does it seem correct to say that slavery was therefore morally right, and abolition efforts wrong?

Lying is usually not illegal, but many of us would have concerns about the morality of lying in many cases. Though it might turn out to be the case that moral values just are reflections of popular opinion (as in Ethical Relativism), it seems hasty and simplistic to equate morality with popular opinion, or opinion that has been enshrined as law. We need only to review the "possible problems" for ER in our previous chapter to see why.

If the only sources to which we may appeal are other humans, the question remains: why would one human's values be somehow more authoritative, more morally accurate, than another's? What would be the basis for moral value (worth) within a purely naturalistic worldview? Most of us believe that persons, by default, share a baseline measure of moral worth, and upon this foundation we develop our notions of basic human rights, moral obligations to do (or refrain from doing) various things, etc. If there is no God, and humans have developed solely via unguided natural (evolutionary) processes, in the same fashion as every other animal on Earth, from where would we get the idea that persons have moral worth?

Certainly *I* regard my own life as having value, and I think others should (at the least) refrain from harming me, and I would like to think that my friends and family find my life to be of value as well, but of course the mere fact that I value my own life doesn't make my life *objectively* valuable. I also value certain photographs I've taken (or that have been taken of me) over the years, but it's rather obvious that those photos have their value solely because I have invested them with that value. In other words, their value is subjective, based solely upon my own whims. Should my feelings change, I can easily imagine discarding those photos as casually as I would discard an old newspaper. There is no independent basis for those photos having value. Is there an independent basis for my *life* having value? Clearly, my own feelings and preferences can't provide it, as nothing could be more subjective than my own feelings! What about the feelings and preferences of the friends and family who value my life? Aren't those just someone *else's* subjective preferences? Couldn't their affection for, and interest in, me dissipate just as it could for some old photographs? Does the worth of a person hinge on something as tenuous as subjective preferences? If my human rights are rooted in my moral worth, and my moral worth is subject to how I (and others) *feel* about me, then are my rights as contingent as the value of my old photos?

In the absence of the supra-natural, all that remains is the natural. In Nature, where do we find any notion of objective moral value, or rights, or duties? "A hawk that seizes a fish from the sea *kills* it, but does not *murder* it; and another hawk that seizes the fish from the talons of the first *takes* it, but does not *steal* it - for none of these things is forbidden. And exactly the same considerations apply to the people we are imagining.... the concept of moral obligation is unintelligible apart from the idea of God. The words remain but their meaning is gone."[111] Indeed, the utilitarian Jeremy Bentham went so far as to dismiss the notion of "natural rights" as "simple nonsense: natural and imprescriptible rights, rhetorical nonsense,—nonsense upon stilts."

Rights imply duties, of course. If you have a right to your life, I have a duty to refrain from killing you (at the least), and possibly even a duty to preserve your life (e.g., by providing you food if you're starving, etc.). But, within a purely naturalistic worldview, who or what has the legitimate authority to impose duties on us, or enforce them?

Certainly, in practice, parents have power to impose duties on their children, and rulers have power to impose duties on those they rule, but from where do they derive the authority to make those impositions? In the end, does it come down to nothing more (or less) than power? Rulers can compel the ruled to do (or refrain from doing) any number of things, but most of us believes that not all commands are just or legitimate. Is our complaint against unjust commands based on nothing more than our own personal preferences? A difference of tastes?

In response, some might propose that what makes values good or bad, and what makes duties morally legitimate (or not) isn't merely the taste preferences of those in power, but is based rather on something independent from those tastes: human flourishing.

Human flourishing as a foundation for objective moral values and duties requires us to take a side trip into an evolutionary interpretation of ethics. As we've already seen, one of the first, core differences of opinion arising in the study of morality is the ultimate origin and explanation for our concepts of good and evil, rightness and wrongness, duty, obligation, justice, fairness, etc. Some philosophers (such as Craig) will claim that these things could not exist given a purely naturalistic worldview, and that some "higher" source is needed—at least if our moral values and duties are to be objective.

---

[111] Richard Taylor, *Ethics, Faith, and Reason,* pp.14, 83-84

Other thinkers believe that not only could such things arise within a purely naturalistic worldview, but that they did. According to this view, humans have evolved to be "moral" animals, to have a sense of moral requirements, and to be motivated (variously) to behave according to moral standards. As we saw in a previous chapter, evolutionary approaches to ethics claim that humans have evolved to possess and display a moral sense in much the same way that we have evolved to have and display sexual desire, or any other "selected for" adaptations. According to the evolutionary account of the development of the human animal, our sense of morality (like everything else about us) is the result of evolutionary forces, such as natural selection. Compassion, charity, justice, fairness, and any and every other moral notion exists because they met the test of natural selection, or are byproducts of something *else* that met that test.

Richard Dawkins (the evolutionary biologist) has attempted to provide an evolutionary basis for our moral impulses, but James Rachels (the ethicist) will take this evolutionary foundation and attempt to develop a universal moral code. Rachels argues that there are some universal moral requirements in the sense that they are necessary for human community to exist and survive. These moral principles are "universal" in that they occur in every culture, and they exist in every culture because in order for a culture to persist over time these values must be honored. As examples, Rachels offers honesty, caring for children, and forbidding murder. This, too, should sound familiar, as we addressed this argument from Rachels in the context of Ethical Relativism in another previous chapter.

If Rachels is correct, then though we might bicker as to just which moral principles and values are necessary for any society to survive (and are, therefore, universal), it would appear that there are some that fit that description. That, at the very least, is a very important start for the rest of our process, in that it will allow us to operate on the assumption that morality is objective (to some degree, at least)— and this objectivity has been obtained without any appeal to (or need for) God. Therefore, objective values and duties can exist without God.

Craig, however, finds fault with this approach. In the first place, he regards Rachel's efforts as amounting to, at best, a socio-anthropological *description* of what is needed for group survival and cohesion. This doesn't entail that those requirements are (morally) "good," nor demonstrate that those who defy them are (objectively) "bad"—it just entails that those behaviors are needed for group survival and cohesion. That is a descriptive exercise, not prescriptive. He cites others who acknowledge the merely descriptive aspect of these evolutionary accounts: "Morality is just an aid to survival and reproduction,... and any deeper meaning is illusory."[112] Moreover, he suggests that this approach is arbitrary, and possibly "speciesist." Why would the conditions needed for human survival (or the cohesion of human communities) amount to *objective* moral values? If "survival value" is the standard for objective moral values, why not the conditions needed for mouse survival and flourishing? Or those conditions that promote bacterial survival? If humans are wrought from the same evolutionary forces as every other living thing, why would humans be "special," and why would our survival and group cohesion needs be the

---

[112] Michael Ruse, "Evolutionary Theory and Darwinian Ethics," *The Darwinian Paradigm*, p.289.

standard for (objective) morality in general?

In addition, Craig points out that these particular survival-based behaviors are utterly contingent on the particular path evolution took with regard to the human species. As a simple illustration, one of Rachels' "universal moral values" involves caring for children. He argued that you will find some sort of moral value placed on caring for children in any and every human community, because children must survive (or, at least the "replacement value" of children must survive) in order for the community to persist over time. Therefore, caring for children (e.g., a variety of nurturing behaviors), having been selected for via natural selection, is a universal moral value. But, imagine if humans hadn't evolved as primates, or even as mammals? If the dinosaurs had never faced an extinction event, and had never created a space for mammals to thrive, perhaps "humans" would be sophisticated reptiles instead? Rather than giving birth to live, vulnerable young, perhaps "humans" would just lay eggs and our offspring, once hatched, would "fend for themselves," as is the case with many reptile species? There would be no need to care for our young, or engage in nurturing behavior, in that case, so "caring for children" is merely contingent upon the fact that our offspring happen to helpless when born. Charles Darwin seemed to have grasped something similar to this idea. "If...men were reared under precisely the same conditions as hive-bees, there can hardly be a doubt that our unmarried females would, like the worker bees, think it a sacred duty to kill their brothers, and mothers would strive to kill their fertile daughters, and no one would think of interfering."[113]

There seems to be at least two lines of critique here:

1. The "values" described by Dawkins and Rachels aren't really (moral) values because they are descriptive, rather than prescriptive. Rather than telling us what is good, what we ought to be, they simply tell us what we must do in order for our genes to be promoted over time and for communities to be cohesive.
2. These "values" are contingent upon a particular evolutionary path, and therefore not *objective* values, even if they are values.

In fairness to Dawkins and Rachels, I imagine they would reply that morality *just is* a description of those behaviors and dispositions that promote human flourishing. To expect something more from morality, something that isn't somehow tied to the natural forces that produced and govern us, is to beg the question against naturalism in the first place. "In a universe of electrons and selfish genes, blind physical forces and genetic replication, some people are going to get hurt, other people are going to get lucky, and you won't find any rhyme or reason in it, nor any justice. The universe that we observe has precisely the properties we should expect if there is, at bottom, no design, no purpose, no evil, no good, nothing but pitiless indifference."[114] There is, on this account, something that we call "morality," but, like everything else, it results

[113] Charles Darwin, *The Descent of Man*, Amherst, NY: Prometheus Books, 1998, p.102.
[114] Richard Dawkins, "God's Utility Function," published in *Scientific American* (November, 1995), p. 85.

from evolutionary forces because of its survival value.

With regard to the contingency concern, I have my own critique of Craig. It seems to me that Craig is equivocating on "objective." Here are Craig's own words:

> Objective" means "independent of people's (including one's own) opinion." "Subjective" means "just a matter of personal opinion." If we do have objective moral duties, then in the various circumstances in which we find ourselves we are obligated or forbidden to do various actions, regardless of what we think.[115]

"Objective," then (according to Craig), means "independent of people's opinion"—as opposed to being "just a matter of personal opinion." If that's all it means for a moral value or duty to be objective (i.e., not just a matter of personal opinion), then it's not clear how the "contingency" objection is really an objection. After all, if the (basic) evolutionary story is true, then the behaviors and disposition that promote gene survival and the cohesion of community are *not* merely matters of personal opinion. It is not an opinion that children (generally) must be cared for in order for human communities to survive, but is, instead, a *fact*. Craig acknowledged that these are "merely" socio-anthropological descriptive *facts* (rather than values) in one of his other criticisms. Certainly it is true, on this account, that if humans had evolved in very different ways (e.g., as reptiles), then the behaviors that promote our flourishing would be different, and therefore those behaviors are contingent upon a particular evolutionary path—but this doesn't mean they are contingent in the sense of being merely personal opinion. My opinion is utterly irrelevant with regard to what conditions promote the survival of my genes. My opinion might be that being exposed to the vacuum of space will promote my genes' survival—but in that case my opinion is *false*.

If all "objective" means is "independent of personal opinion," then it seems that values arrived at via evolutionary forces would be "objective" in *that* sense. Granted, Craig can continue to claim that they aren't really "values" at all, in that they are merely descriptive of what's needed for survival, rather than prescriptive of what is morally good.

"Equivocation" occurs when you mean one thing by a word at one point in an argument, and then you shift to a different meaning of that same word in another part of the argument. I suspect Craig might be equivocating on "objective" in that he defines objective as "independent of personal opinion" in one part of his argument, but seems to shift the meaning of objective to mean something like "not dependent upon human needs," or "transcending the human condition," or (frankly) "supernatural" when criticizing the naturalists' attempt to provide objective moral values and duties. It seems to me, then, that Craig's criticism of a purely naturalistic approach to ethics isn't (or shouldn't be) that it fails to produce values and duties that are independent of human opinion, but rather that the products of such a naturalistic approach fail to provide *values* at all, or any duties that have binding force behind them beyond the contingent, power-based threats that other humans might make in the event of failing to follow the "rules." You can decide for yourself whether the account offered by Dawkins and Rachels actually provides "values."

---

[115] Question #347, answered 12-08-13, www.reasonablefaith.org

On the other hand, naturalists will often try to turn the tables on someone like Craig and counter that it is religiously-based systems of ethics that fail to provide objective moral values and duties. The most famous such objection is known as the "Euthyphro problem."

The Euthyphro Problem

Named for Plato's dialogue in which the argument is found, the Euthyphro problem explores the relationship between morality and the divine.

Socrates: And what do you say of piety, Euthyphro: is not piety, according to your definition, loved by all the gods?

Euthyphro: Yes.

Socrates: Because it is pious or holy, or for some other reason?

Euthyphro: No, that is the reason.

Socrates: It is loved because it is holy, not holy because it is loved?

Euthyphro: Yes.

Socrates: And that which is dear to the gods is loved by them, and is in a state to be loved of them because it is loved of them?

Euthyphro: Certainly.

Socrates: Then that which is dear to the gods, Euthyphro, is not holy, nor is that which is holy loved of God, as you affirm; but they are two different things.

Euthyphro: How do you mean, Socrates?

Socrates: I mean to say that the holy has been acknowledge by us to be loved of God because it is holy, not to be holy because it is loved.

Euthyphro: Yes.

Socrates: But that which is dear to the gods is dear to them because it is loved by them, not loved by them because it is dear to them.

Euthyphro: True.

Socrates: But, friend Euthyphro, if that which is holy is the same with that which is dear to God, and is loved because it is holy, then that which is dear to God would have been loved as being dear to God; but if that which dear to God is dear to him because loved by him, then that which is holy would have been holy because loved by him. But now you see that the reverse is the case, and that they are quite different from one another. For one (theophiles) is of a kind to be loved cause it is loved, and the other (osion) is loved because it is of a kind to be loved. Thus you appear to me, Euthyphro, when I ask you what is the essence of holiness, to offer an attribute only, and not the essence-the attribute of being loved by all the gods. But you still refuse to explain to me the nature of holiness. And therefore, if you please, I will ask you not to hide your treasure, but to tell me once more what holiness or piety really is, whether dear to the gods or not (for that is a matter about which we will not quarrel) and what is impiety?

Euthyphro: I really do not know, Socrates, how to express what I mean. For somehow or other our arguments, on whatever ground we rest them, seem to turn round and walk away from us.

In his usual clever and combative way, Socrates has teased out the tension in the "Divine Command" approach to ethics. Is something morally good because it is willed by God? Or, is something willed by God because it is morally good? It might take a minute for the difference to become clear. Go ahead and take that minute.

If God commands something <u>because it is morally good</u>, then the command results from God's <u>recognition of the act's goodness</u>. In that case, the standard of goodness *preceded* God's command. The possible problem (for theistic approaches to ethics) with this interpretation is that this might be seen as placing a limit on God's power and authority. After all, if morality is *independent* of God and *precedes* God's commands, is it possible to know what is right, and do what is right, without God entering the picture at all? This would seem to undermine Craig's claim that if God does not exist, objective moral values and duties do not exist. After all, it seems that these values could exist even if God does not.

On the other hand, if something is morally good <u>because God commands it</u>, then it is the act of God that <u>makes it good</u> in the first place. *Whatever* God commands is good, *whatever* God forbids is bad. The possible problem with this interpretation is that it appears to make morality a matter of God's whims—something too *arbitrary* for many to be comfortable with. If *anything* God commands, by definition, is the right thing to do, what if God were to command the slaughter of babies? Wouldn't that be, by definition, the morally right thing to do? If God's commands are arbitrary, then they don't appear to be "objective" anymore—but based on *God's* opinion instead of any of ours. In this case, God's existence fails to establish the existence of *objective* moral values/duties.

Some of you might be thinking, right now, "That's ridiculous. God would never order such a thing because God is perfectly good." Perhaps so, but Robert Solomon (a famous contemporary American philosopher) believes that such a reaction illustrates our powerful intuition that our conception of morality is that it does *not* depends wholly on God's will, and that a simple hypothetical example can demonstrate this. He invites us to imagine that what appears to be an authentic original manuscript from the Bible is discovered, one that appears to be older and more authentic than any other extant manuscripts. To the world's surprise, though, this manuscript provides a very different set of commandments, including the following:

Thou shalt kill.
Thou shalt steal.
Thou shalt commit adultery as much as thou wouldst.

Solomon is convinced that most believers, rather than undergoing a radical transformation in their values and practices, would instead reject the authenticity of the manuscript, in spite of all the evidence in its favor. Why? Because we are confident that God is a moral being, and such commandments would just not be the sorts of commandments issued by a moral being—let alone a perfect one. But, if we say that God would never do such a thing because God is good, what standard of goodness are we assuming here? If God *defines* goodness, then to say that God is good is simply to say that God does what God wants. It is only by presupposing an independent standard of goodness that someone could employ the defense that God wouldn't order anything "bad" because God is "good." If God defines goodness, then we beg the question when we say that God commands only good things.

This "Euthyphro problem" for divine command approaches is incredibly well known, and thought by many to be the death blow for divine command ethics—so much so that much of the time the divine command theory is offered in ethics courses only for the sake of thoroughness, or as an intellectual curiosity. However, we must keep in mind that the gods targeted by the "Euthyphro problem" (in its original historical context) were finite, anthropomorphic, and downright scandalous. For example, Zeus practiced incest (he had a daughter, Persephone, with his own sister, Demeter)—and his most famous wife, Hera, was another of his own sisters! He was also notorious for raping human women.

That the Euthyphro problem is used out of its original context should be obvious in that it would be pretty difficult to find anyone today who worships either the "gods" popular in ancient Greece (e.g., Zeus, Athena, Poseidon) or the non-personal "form of the good" that might be labeled "god" by Plato himself. Instead, the "problem" is always presented to particular religious traditions: usually Christianity, Judaism, or Islam. Each one of these traditions has its own concept of God, and its own understanding of the relationship between God and morality, but in none of these Western theistic traditions is God conceived as being very similar to Zeus, Ares, etc. To use the "Euthyphro problem" to attack the generic abstraction "god" is to attack a straw man (or, a straw deity, perhaps). That the *abstraction* fares poorly in the Euthyphro problem does not necessarily mean that any *actual* religious tradition, or any actual concept of God, is similarly imperiled.

To help illustrate this, William Lane Craig points out that for the Christian religious tradition; moral goodness is an aspect of God's very nature. If God's nature is to be (essentially) good, then goodness is neither something "separate" from God that God recognizes and endorses, nor is it something "arbitrary." Part of the Christian concept of God is that God's nature is eternal and unchanging. One aspect of God's nature is goodness. Being unchanging, that cannot and will not change.

Since our moral duties are grounded in the divine commands, they are not independent of God...God may act naturally in ways which for us would be rule-following and so constitutive of goodness in the sense of fulfilling our moral duties, so that God can be said similarly to be good in an analogical way. This fact also supplies the key to the arbitrariness objection. For our duties are determined by the commands, not merely of a supreme potentate, but of a just and loving God. God is essentially compassionate, fair, kind, impartial, and so forth, and His commandments are reflections of His own character. Thus, they are not arbitrary, and we need not trouble ourselves about counterfactuals with impossible antecedents like 'If God were to command child abuse . . . .' God may be said to be good in the sense that He possesses all these moral virtues--and He does so essentially and to the maximal degree![116]

In response, some critics have said this merely "pushes the problem back" one step. Now they can pose a differently formulated dilemma: is God's nature good because it is declared so or created so by God, or because it recognizes some other, external standard of goodness? Same dilemma, right? Not so, according to Craig. A "nature" is not the sort of thing that recognizes or declares or creates anything, including goodness. Persons recognize, or declare, or create, but properties (essential or otherwise) such as "goodness" aren't the sorts of things that can do any of that, any more than my own property of "male" can recognize, or create, or declare anything.

Craig reminds us that any notion of "goodness" must have a "stopping point." For the Christian, that stopping point is God, and the Euthyphro dilemma allegedly challenges that stopping point by asking whether God creates or merely recognizes what's good. The same alleged dilemma arises with any other possible source. Does "nature" create the good, and is therefore an arbitrary source, or does it merely recognize what's good and is therefore not necessary? Does the majority within a community create the good, and is therefore an arbitrary source, or does it merely recognize what's good and is therefore not necessary? For any "stopping point," for that which defines the good, for that which simply *is* "the good," it makes no sense to ask for the source of its own goodness. We either recognize the legitimacy of a "stopping point," a proper "ground" for goodness, or else we're stuck with an infinite regress. If we reject the infinite regress, we must then ask, of any proposed "stopping point," whether it is a plausible stopping point.

For Craig and other theists, God makes a very compelling "stopping point," as God is regarded as the metaphysical "ground" of all things, of all Creation. There is nothing "higher" or "greater" than God, as understood in the Western theistic traditions. Christians understand God to be the paradigm of goodness. "Eventually such questions must find a stopping point in the character of God. Kindness is good because that's the way God is; cruelty is evil because it is inconsistent with God's nature. Therefore He issues commands that forbid behavior which is cruel and prescribe behavior which is kind. Rape is cruel, not kind, and therefore it is forbidden by God and therefore wrong."

If this God exists, then God makes for a plausible and compelling "stopping point," to be sure. Any other "stopping point," however, based in something finite, such as "humanity," will seem arbitrary in comparison. Why stop there, rather than elsewhere? Why "humanity" rather than "my community," or "me?" If there is instead an appeal to some external, independent standard of "the good," then what could that

---

[116] Craig: http://www.bethinking.org/resources/the-coherence-of-theism---part-2.htm

be, or mean? The Platonist notion of "The Good" as an independently existing abstract object (like the number four, or the concept of a chair) hasn't been taken seriously for centuries. Goodness does not appear to be a thing existing unto itself, but rather a property borne by something else. In that case, paradoxically, "the good" could not itself be good. People can be good, but "the good" couldn't itself be morally good any more than the color blue could be morally good. Craig asserts that moral values are embodied in persons, not abstractions. God, therefore, is a proper candidate for goodness and is, indeed, the ultimate person, defining goodness by God's very nature.

Thus, when God wills something, it is not an arbitrary whim but a necessary expression of God's eternal and essential nature. The disturbing hypothetical scenario, then, of God suddenly deciding, on a whim, that raping children is now "good" works far better against an abstraction than the particular concept of God found in Christianity. The idea of the gods being whimsical was readily available at the time Plato was writing the Euthyphro. No wonder that Plato sought a source for goodness beyond these fickle deities, and questioned their legitimacy as a source for goodness!

The Christian concept of God is just plain different from those beings. In fact, early Jewish and Christian thinkers were quite sympathetic to Plato, recognizing their God as "the Good" referred to by Plato. What theism provides, according to Craig, "is a source of moral prohibition and moral obligation in the commands of a holy and loving God. God is not only the standard of moral goodness, but that standard issues in commandments, for us, that express God's nature, that are constitutive of our moral duties or obligations. And so, what theism gives you is not only a sound foundation for moral value, but it gives you a foundation for moral obligation and duty as well."

Even if Craig's response to the Euthyphro problem is effective, that doesn't mean that the Euthyphro no longer has any teeth—though it bites in a different spot now.

Having a concept of God whose eternal nature includes moral goodness solves the original dilemma, (or else shows that any moral framework suffers from the same "stopping point" issue) but the critic might now wonder whether it's plausible that such a concept of God actually matches up to the God actually described in Western religious traditions. Consider the following from Deuteronomy 20:16-18: "However, in the cities of the nations the LORD your God is giving you as an inheritance, do not leave alive anything that breathes. Completely destroy them—the Hittites, Amorites, Canaanites, Perizzites, Hivites and Jebusites—as the LORD your God has commanded you. Otherwise, they will teach you to follow all the detestable things they do in worshiping their gods, and you will sin against the LORD your God."

Such "Old Testament challenges" have inspired some atheists to decry the God of Christianity as a "monster." "What makes my jaw drop is that people today should base their lives on such an appalling role model as Yahweh-and even worse, that they should bossily try to force the same evil monster (whether fact or fiction) on the rest of us."[117]

Craig seems to acknowledge this revised threat from the Euthyphro problem. He points out that in order to condemn God (as recorded in the Bible), one must presuppose that objective moral value *do* exist, and, Biblical atrocities, even if truly atrocities, at best, this point would prove that certain Biblical accounts are mistaken

---

[117] Richard Dawkins, *The God Delusion* (Boston: Houghton Mifflin, 2006), 248.

in attributing to God certain actions, or that the Christian "God" isn't really God. At most, this would require an abandonment of belief in Biblical inerrancy, but not belief in God, nor even the Christian God (if one can address the "atrocities" in a reasonable way).[118]

For the Divine Command theorist, the proper source and grounding for moral truths is God. If, as is believed in the Western religious traditions, God is all-knowing, then God is the perfect knower of moral truths. Additionally, if God is sovereign over all God's Creation, then God's authority extends to each one of us as well. God's will is the final authority with regard to morality not only because God is never mistaken, but also because there is literally no possible higher authority. The Divine Command approach is thought to "ground" ethics in the most stable foundation possible: the will of God.

2. Divine Command theories provide an answer to the question, "why be moral?"

Supposing we can discern right from wrong in the first place, what would motivate me to *do* the right thing, especially in those cases when I'm confident I can "get away" with acting wrongly? Plato grappled with this problem in the *Republic*. As you might have studied in another chapter, several characters in that dialogue question the value of justice (morality), and the reasons people ought to be just. Thrasymachus thought that so-called "justice" was nothing more than the will of the stronger. Those in power get to enshrine their own values into law and custom, and everyone else must obey, but there is nothing grand or noble about justice in that case: it's nothing more than power and prudence. Those in power decide what is "right," and those below obey out of self-interest, so they're not punished by the powerful.

Glaucon was concerned that humans only act rightly because it's necessary for the sake of safety and security. What we'd all really prefer to do is whatever we want, without regard to consequences, or to anyone else. We recognize, though, that none of us is powerful enough to get away with that, so we agree amongst ourselves to play nicely with each other, so long as everyone else does the same. However, his thought experiment involving the Myth of Gyges' ring reveals his concern about human nature: give someone the power to defy the rules without fear of punishment, and he will—and so will you.

Do you disagree? Ask yourself if you would always obey the posted speed limit if

---

[118] An example of such a (possibly reasonable) way is offered by Craig: because all moral duties are ultimately grounded in divine commands which themselves issue from God's own nature, God is not bound by moral duties, since God does not issue commands to himself. Therefore, God may have prerogatives forbidden to us, and may issue morally righteous commands involving actions that would otherwise be morally forbidden in the absence of such a command" (in effect, "thou shalt not kill, unless God commands you to"). I (personally) think this approach is still problematic, and honest theists must grapple with the meaning of certain Biblical passages in an effort to harmonize God's perfectly good nature with actions or commandments attributed to God as recorded in the Bible.

you knew you wouldn't get caught and ticketed for speeding. . . .

Glaucon's (and Plato's) brother, Adeimantus, thought that what was best was to be *perceived* as good. Really, perception is all that matters. So long as others *believe* us to be good, we get all the benefits of that reputation, whether we're actually morally good or not. In that case, why not act "badly" whenever one has a chance? For the Divine Command theorist, the answer is obvious: there is no such thing as "getting away with it."

Once again using the Western religious traditions as examples, if there is an all-knowing God, no one ever escapes notice. And, if judgment and eternal reward (or punishment) awaits us when we die, there is no such thing as "getting away with it."

Why be moral? Perhaps because an all-knowing Judge will punish us in the afterlife if we don't! In fairness, Divine Command approaches need not be so obviously fear-driven or calculating. Some proponents of these theories claim that we can be motivated not only by fear, but by love. That is, an awareness of God's love and perfect justice can inspire us to *want* to act rightly from a sense of gratitude, and love for God.

Conclusion

The strength and appeal of Divine Command theories (beyond possible "fit" with theistic worldviews) is that they offer a compelling answer to the motivation question of ethics ("why be moral?"), as well as offering a clear strategy with regard to how to provide an objective foundation for moral values and duties. Despite their merits, Divine Command approaches are not without their own challenges. For one, claiming that "God" is our source of guidance and motivation invites a host of questions:

- Do we have good reason (other than its benefit for ethics) to believe that there *is* a God in the first place? Obviously, the Divine Command approach will not be persuasive for atheists and agnostics.
- Which God is the "true" God? After all, numerous religious traditions exist, with some significant differences between them. If objective moral values and duties are supplied by God, and if there are numerous (competing) interpretations of God, which of those (if any) is the correct interpretation? Which values are the correct (objective) values?
- Assuming we can settle on a particular religion, which interpretation of it? Within Christianity, for example, some churches are vehemently opposed to homosexuality, and others welcome gay and lesbian persons as their brothers and sisters in Christ. The same Christian Bible seems to be *for* capital punishment in some places (Genesis 9:6: "Yes, you must execute anyone who murders another person, for to kill a person is to kill a living being made in God's image."), but *opposed* to it in others (Matthew 5: 38-39: "You have heard that it was said, 'Eye for eye, and tooth for tooth,' but I tell you, do not resist an evil person."). There are passages that can be read in support (or at least not in condemnation) of polygamy (e.g., Deuteronomy 25: 5-6) as well as those that appear to promote monogamy (Mark 10:8).

In fairness, interpretive questions will plague any and all objective theories. You will find disagreement and difficulty with utilitarianism, for example, as well. It is wise to recognize, however, that the Divine Command approach is not as simple as some would like to believe—though it could provide a compelling foundation for objective moral values and duties.

Chapter 10: Natural Law

Comprehension questions you should be able to answer after reading this chapter:

1. What is the difference between a naturalistic worldview and a theistic worldview?

2. What does Cicero think about human laws that fail to conform to the "Natural Law?"

3. How does Cicero explain the existence of so many diverse opinions about moral values?

4. What does Aquinas mean by each of the following? Eternal Law, Natural Law, Human Law, Synderesis, Conscience.

5. What is a "conclusion" from the natural law? What is a "determination" from the natural law?

6. How does "Divine Law" (understood as "Divine Command theory") supplement the Natural Law?

7. Explain Phillipa Foot's comparison of moral "goodness" to the "goodness" of living things, such as plants.

8. What role do "virtues" play in the "goodness" of human beings, according to Foot?

9. With regard to human beings, explain the four "aspects" and the four "ends" (according to Hursthouse) that determine human "goodness."

In previous chapters, we considered interpretations of moral claims that assumed such claims were subjective, rather than objective. Simple Subjectivism claimed that moral values are matters of personal opinion, whereas Ethical Relativism claimed that moral values were matters of the dominant opinions of the community—but both were united in their denial of the objectivity of moral claims. In each case, we considered some possible objections to those views, but a criticism of subjective theories is not, by itself, a compelling argument *for* an objective alternative.

In this chapter, we will consider several arguments in favor of an objective approach to ethics. This will not be just a review of the criticisms from previous chapters. Instead, positive arguments will be advanced, along with explanations for how objective moral principles and values could exist and be discovered.

As a reminder of what you probably learned in the previous chapter, if there are objective moral values, then the moral claims that describe them are matters of fact, rather than opinion. As factual, they apply equally to persons regardless of personal opinion or contingent cultural circumstances. Using these values as a "universal answer key," we may "grade" both individuals and communities according to these objective standards. But where would this answer key come from? Who, or what, would be able to provide the "correct answers" for this answer key?

We will consider two broad approaches to objective moral values: one from a purely naturalistic worldview, and the other from a generically theistic worldview. Both of these approaches follow nicely our previous two chapters, since one is purely naturalistic and has a connection to the evolutionary ethics approach we have already considered, and the other is theistic and will incorporate and review some of the ideas from the divine command theory chapter. In this way, whether one is a theist or an atheist, the possibility of objective moral values will be explored. Admittedly, if the theistic worldview is correct, then "Nature" is part of God's Creation, as is our human nature, specifically. In that case, rather than being separate sources for objective moral values, the naturalistic source would be absorbed into the theistic worldview, and would be ultimately explainable by it. However, providing separate explanations will result in two independent arguments for objective moral values and principles, and should be of much greater appeal than one that depends exclusively on a particular type of worldview.

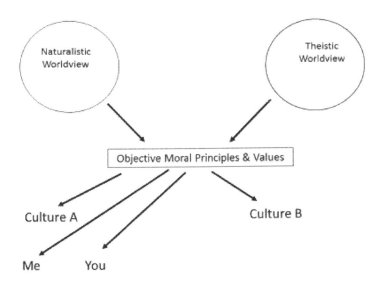

This chapter's exploration of an objective basis for moral values and duties will be based in the "Natural Law" tradition. Going back at least to Aristotle, this approach is versatile in that it will allow us to develop objective values/duties from within either a theistic ("religious") worldview or naturalistic ("atheistic") worldview. We will begin with a version of natural law developed by St. Thomas Aquinas. Not surprisingly, that is the theistic version! We will then consider naturalistic versions based on the views of two contemporary philosophers: Phillipa Foot and Rosalind Hursthouse.

Theistic Worldview: St. Thomas Aquinas

Saint Thomas Aquinas was born in either 1224 or 1225 CE. His education began at an early age, when, at age 5, he was placed in a Benedictine monastery to receive his elementary and religious education. In 1239, he enrolled at the University of Naples to study Liberal Arts. While there, he was exposed to Aristotle's writings, and came into contact with members of the Dominican Order—an order to which he declared his intention to join at the age of 19.

Aquinas' brilliance was such that he was alleged to be capable of dictating multiple treatises to multiple scribes simultaneously! One of those treatises was begun in 1266, his *Summa Theologica*. His talent and wisdom attracted notice, and he became an advisor to Popes Alexander IV and Urban IV.

It is somewhat accurate (though admittedly oversimplified) to state that Aquinas offered an adaptation of the philosophy of Aristotle, modified and supplemented to fit a Christian worldview. His debt to Aristotle is undeniable, going so far as to refer to Aristotle simply as "*The* Philosopher!"

Thanks to Aquinas' heavy, systematic, and sympathetic use of Aristotle, the Catholic Church moved away from Platonism (which had been adopted, in part, due to St. Augustine's influence) and towards a harmonizing of Aristotle and Christian doctrine. In fairness, it would be both uncharitable and inaccurate to suggest that he *merely* "Christianized" Aristotle. Aquinas draws on other sources of inspiration as well, including Plato, and Cicero—particularly Cicero's Stoic notion of natural law. In fact, before considering Aquinas, we will first briefly explore Cicero's (Stoic) foundations of natural law.

Cicero

Marcus Tullius Cicero (106 BCE – 43 BCE) was a careful thinker and a skilled writer who translated Greek thought into the Roman (Latin) language not only in the literal sense of translation, but also to the extent that he coined new Latin vocabulary to help elucidate difficult philosophical concepts. He helped bring ancient Greek thought to the Romans, and then helped to bring both Greek and Roman philosophy to the rest of Europe, somewhat in the Middle Ages—but especially in the Renaissance.

Not many philosophers can rival Cicero's world-historic status. Beyond his wisdom and talents, he was an associate, at times, friend, and at other times, rival, of some of the most famous and powerful (and notorious) politicians to ever grace the world's stage.[119]

---

[119] For those interested in history: Cicero was a gifted writer, speaker, and transmitter of ideas, in general, but he was no mere theorist. Cicero was an actual politician in his time, rising to the role of Consul (and helping to put down a coup d'etat during his tenure!). His oratory skill and political talents caught the eye of Julius Caesar, who (in 60 BCE) invited Cicero to be the 4th member of his "partnership" with Pompey and Marcus Licinius Crassus. Cicero declined the offer to join what would become the First Triumvirate due to his concern that it would undermine the Republic. Cicero did not, himself, participate in the conspiracy or assassination of Julius Caesar. However, Marcus Junius Brutus allegedly called out

Cicero was no mere theoretician, imaging how certain political principles might apply in various hypothetical scenarios. Instead, he spoke of the decay of republicanism and the rise of tyranny as a first hand witness, and wrote of resisting tyranny and affirming the rights of all persons as someone who was literally doing so—even at the eventual cost of his own life.

Cicero was able to affirm the rights of "all" because of his Stoic view that because all persons share in Reason, all people have some measure of moral value. In addition, he thought a "natural law" governs all people, regardless of political lines drawn on a map. "There is only one justice which constitutes the bond among humans, and which is established by one law, which is the right reason in commands and prohibitions."[120]

This natural law can't be overruled by any human decree, nor any considerations of convenience or self-interest. The natural law is the foundation and judge of all human laws, whether domestic or international.

We can distinguish good from bad laws by the standard of nature.[121]

There is one, single, justice. It binds together human society and has been established by one, single, law.[122]

Law in the proper sense is right reason in harmony with nature. It is spread through the whole human community, unchanging and eternal, calling people to their duty by its commands and deterring them from wrong-doing by its prohibitions. . . . This law cannot be countermanded, nor can it be in any way amended, nor can it be totally rescinded. We cannot be exempted from this law by any decree of the Senate or the people; nor do we need anyone to else to

---

Cicero's name, bloodstained dagger in hand, and asked him to restore the Republic, and Cicero's own endorsement of the assassination was unmistakable. "For Heaven will bear witness that Rome—that any nation throughout the whole world—has never seen a greater act than theirs. There has never been an achievement more glorious—more greatly deserving of renown for all eternity." In the political instability that followed the assassination, a power struggle broke out between the assassins (led by Brutus and Cassius) and "loyalists" to Caesar (led by Mark Antony and Octavian). Cicero was a political leader—and found himself in direct opposition to Mark Antony. Cicero was the spokesman for the Senate, and Antony was a consul and the unofficial executor of Caesar's will. Cicero tried to manipulate Octavian into opposing Antony, but ultimately failed. Cicero wrote and spoke publicly against Antony in a series of speeches called the "Phillipics"—actions and writing that ultimately cost him his life. In 43 BCE, Antony, Octavian, and Lepidus formed the Second Triumvirate. They issued proscriptions against Roman citizens, including Cicero (and his brother and nephew). Cicero was assassinated on December 7th, 43 BCE. Antony then displayed Cicero's severed head and hands (the ones that wrote the Phillipics) in the Roman Forum in a final act of humiliation.

[120] Cicero, *Laws*, 1.42
[121] Ibid., 1.44
[122] Ibid., 1.42

expound or explain it. There will not be one such law in Rome and another in Athens, one now and another in the future, but all people at all times will be embraced by a single and eternal and unchangeable law; and there will be, as it were, one lord and master of us all—the god who is the author, proposer, and interpreter of that law.[123]

Human laws that fail to conform to the standard provided by natural law are not, properly speaking, "laws" at all!

If ignorant unqualified people prescribe a lethal, instead of a healing, treatment, that treatment cannot properly be called 'medical.' In a community a law of just any kind will not be a law, even if the people (in spite of its harmful character) have accepted it. Therefore law means drawing a distinction between just and unjust, formulated in accordance with that most ancient and important of all things—nature; by her, human laws are guided in punishing the wicked and defending and protecting the good.[124]

And yet, one might wonder why, if there is allegedly "one single law for all humanity," there are there so many *different* opinions, customs, and human laws? How do we explain all the cultural differences, variations in laws across geographic location and time, and all the differences in opinion even within the same community? How do we explain how same-sex marriage can be celebrated by a majority of the population in some countries, today, while homosexuals are being executed in brutal fashion in other parts of the world? Prescient thinker that he was, Cicero had an answer for that conundrum, as well.

Yet we are confused by the variety and variability of men's opinions; and because the same disagreement does not occur in regard to the senses. We think the senses are reliable by nature whereas we brand as illusory those ideas that vary from one person to another and do not always remain consistent within the same person. This distinction is far from the truth. In the case of our senses, no parent or nurse or teacher or poet or stage-show distorts them, nor does popular opinion lead them astray. For our minds, however, all kinds of traps are laid, either by the people just mentioned, who on receiving young untrained minds stain them and twist them as they please, or else by that power which lurks within, entwined with every one of our senses, namely pleasure, which masquerades as goodness but is in fact the mother of all ills. Seduced by her charms, our minds fail to see clearly enough the things that are naturally good, because those things lack the sweetness and the exciting itch of pleasure.[125]

Think of it this way: most of us are not skeptics or relativists with respect to *basic* claims about perceptible things. As an example, most people are pretty confident that elephants are larger than house flies—and anyone who claims otherwise is either

---

[123] Cicero, *Republic*, 3.33
[124] *Laws*, 2.13
[125] *Laws*, 1.47

doing something odd with language, or else likely adopting an insincere philosophical pose for the sake of being contrary. Because sense-testimony is generally conducive to agreement, we imagine that empirical matters are factual, objective. However, when it comes to moral judgments, there are a variety of views.

Some people think that abortion is acceptable, and others think it is murder. Some people believe it's wrong to eat meat, and others worship at the altar of bacon. Same-sex marriage is now a Constitutional right in the United States, but homosexuals are executed by being thrown off of buildings in ISIS-controlled parts of Syria.[126]

We are taught one thing by our parents, perhaps another by teachers, perhaps another by friends, still another by our church, and yet another by the media and pop culture. This dizzying influx of contrary moral messages can cause us to conclude that there is no moral "truth" at all—only opinion.

What's more, Cicero points out that we can be "charmed" by pleasure into thinking that certain actions, because they are pleasurable, are also therefore "good"—while our senses generally provide no such ulterior motive.

For all these reasons, Cicero explains how people can come to the *false* conclusion that there is no objective moral law. However, Cicero is confident that there is. He is confident that, because we are social beings, unjust acts are contrary to our natural fellowship, and true laws, therefore, are intended to maintain social order and harmony. These beliefs will be adopted by Aquinas, and adapted to his Christian worldview, centuries later.

Aquinas' Natural Law

As mentioned in the introduction to this chapter, Aquinas was influenced not only by his Christian worldview, but by ancient philosophy—especially Aristotle and Cicero. We have already discussed Cicero, and his recognition of a universal "law" that applies to all people because of our kinship in Reason.

From Aristotle, Aquinas draws (among other things) the idea that humans have a nature/essence, as well as a *telos* (goal or "end") specific to our nature.[127] Human nature is to be a rational, social, and political animal. Our "end" is *eudaimonia* (flourishing/happiness), and our *areté* (excellence/virtue) that serves that end will be those qualities that fulfill our nature and facilitate our flourishing.

Although Aquinas will incorporate all of these ideas (or at least adaptations of them), where Aquinas *differs* from Aristotle is obvious: Christianity! Aristotle did not assume that there exists a universal human community with one supreme Lawgiver as its creator and Lord (i.e., God). For Aquinas, this amounts to a substantial difference.

For Aquinas, when it comes to human laws, the idea the ruler has in his mind as to what his subjects should be or do is "law." This same notion will be applied to God, except for the fact that God is the supreme Law-Giver of all of Nature. The rational pattern within God's mind supplies the "Eternal Law," which "is nothing but the rational pattern of the Divine wisdom considered as directing all actions and

---

[126]http://www.nydailynews.com/news/world/isis-militants-throw-gay-man-building-death-article-1.2041416

[127] For a fuller discussion of this, see the "virtue ethics" chapter in this book.

motions."[128] In other words, the Eternal Law is all the laws of Nature.

Most things are governed by the Eternal Law without the possibility of disobedience. For example, most things in the universe simply "obey" the laws of nature, and couldn't do otherwise. Imagine the absurdity of a rock "rebelling" against the pull of gravity, or an acorn defiantly growing into a zebra, rather than an oak tree! Humans, however, complicate the Eternal Law by virtue of our free will.

> *Wherefore, since all things subject to Divine providence are ruled and measured by the eternal law, as was stated above (Article [1]); it is evident that all things partake somewhat of the eternal law, in so far as, namely, from its being imprinted on them, they derive their respective inclinations to their proper acts and ends. Now among all others, the rational creature is subject to Divine providence in the most excellent way, in so far as it partakes of a share of providence, by being provident both for itself and for others. Wherefore it has a share of the Eternal Reason, whereby it has a natural inclination to its proper act and end: and this participation of the eternal law in the rational creature is called the natural law.[129]*

Because human subjection to the Eternal Law is different, Aquinas calls it being under the "Natural Law"—but "The Natural Law is nothing else than the rational creature's participation of the Eternal Law." That is, the natural law is simply the eternal law as it is applied to humans. We have to be careful here, and be painstakingly precise with our language.

Although they sound very similar, "laws of Nature" and "natural law" aren't the same thing. "Laws of nature," which would include things like the law of gravitation, are included in what Aquinas calls the Eternal Law. Clearly, I am no more immune to the pull of gravity than is a rock. The natural law, in contrast, refers specifically to intentional human *behavior*. The natural law guides humans via natural inclinations toward the natural perfection to which God intends us. This includes, among other things, moral instruction.

Aquinas calls the natural knowledge humans have concerning fundamental moral requirements of our human nature "synderesis."

> *Now it is clear that, as the speculative reason argues about speculative things, so that practical reason argues about practical things. Therefore we must have, bestowed on us by nature, not only speculative principles, but also practical principles. Now the first speculative principles bestowed on us by nature do not belong to a special power, but to a special habit, which is called "the understanding of principles," as the Philosopher explains (Ethic. vi, 6). Wherefore the first practical principles, bestowed on us by nature, do not belong to a special power, but to a special natural habit, which we call "synderesis." Whence "synderesis" is said to incite to good, and to murmur at evil, inasmuch as through first principles we proceed to discover, and judge of what we have*

---

[128] Aquinas, *Summa Theologica*, I-II, 93.1.
[129] Ibid., I-II, 91.2

discovered.[130]

A more familiar term for most of us is "conscience." He defines conscience as an act of applying synderesis to concrete situations.

> *For conscience, according to the very nature of the word, implies the relation of knowledge to something: for conscience may be resolved into "cum alio scientia," i.e. knowledge applied to an individual case. . . . Wherefore, properly speaking, conscience denominates an act. But since habit is a principle of act, sometimes the name conscience is given to the first natural habit---namely, 'synderesis': thus Jerome calls 'synderesis' conscience (Gloss. Ezech. 1:6); Basil [*Hom. in princ. Proverb.], the "natural power of judgment," and Damascene [*De Fide Orth. iv. 22] says that it is the "law of our intellect." For it is customary for causes and effects to be called after one another.*[131]

To illustrate: according to Aquinas, by synderesis we understand that adultery is morally wrong, but by conscience we understand that having sex with a particular woman who is not my wife is a case of adultery. Synderesis recognizes general principles, while conscience applies them. Synderesis reveals that stealing is wrong, and conscience tells me that taking office supplies is a case of stealing.

The natural knowledge of our moral requirements as supplied by synderesis is universal, unchangeable, and can't be "abolished from the hearts of men."[132] With this notion of a universal moral code applying to all humans, regardless of race or nationality, Aquinas is clearly drawing more from Cicero than Aristotle.

Assuming that synderesis supplies basic moral instruction, we may now turn to the specifics of that instruction. According to Aquinas, the first moral precept of the natural law is that "good is to be done and pursued and evils is to be avoided."[133]

Aquinas does not bother to prove this. Instead, he claims that this precept of practical reason is analogous to the law of non-contradiction for speculative reason: neither can be demonstrated (proven), but both are principles without which reasoning to conclusions (logical, or moral, respectively) is impossible.

Think of it this way: how would you even talk about *any* notion, *any* interpretation, of "good" or "evil" at all without presupposing that "good" is *good*, and "evil" is *bad*? And yet, how could you possibly "prove" that "good" is *good*? These notions appear intuitive and unavoidable in the abstract, even if we might disagree as to their specific applications.

If we accept that good is to be pursued, and evil avoided, how do we know what *qualifies as* good or evil? Aquinas thinks that our natural inclinations provide a rudimentary guide to "natural goods." For example, our natural inclination to self-preservation, avoidance of pain, pursuit of pleasure, reproduction and care of our offspring, living within a community, etc., are indicators of natural goods.

These inclinations are not infallible, of course. They can (and often are) corrupted

---

130 Ibid., I, 79.12
131 Ibid., I, 79.13
132 Ibid., I-II, 94.4-94.6
133 Ibid., I-II, 94.2

by sin (according to Aquinas' Christian worldview). Accordingly, we are not merely to act on just *any* inclination we happen to have! Instead, we need to recognize the "natural purpose" of the inclination, and then act on it only insofar as that purpose is being respected.

For example, according to Aquinas (and the official Natural Law doctrine of the Catholic Church), our sexual inclination has a "natural purpose" of reproduction. Therefore, the only "proper" way to act on that inclination is one which "respects" its purpose: reproduction. Not surprisingly, then, Aquinas (and the Catholic Church) are opposed to homosexual activities, masturbation, oral sex, the use of contraception— and any sexual activity that can't (feasibly) result in conception.[134]

In general, Aquinas specifies that all inclinations belong to the natural law only insofar as they are "ruled by reason."[135] We experience inclinations, but must test them with Reason to determine whether it is right to indulge and pursue them.

Although the natural law provides basic moral guidelines for human life, it does not provide specific guidance. For example, it is "natural" that those who commit crimes should be punished, but what nature does not reveal to us is what exact punishment is appropriate based on the crime. "Human law" is needed to flesh out the details.

The first function of human law is to provide the details left out by natural law. The second function of human law is to *enforce* the specific interpretation of natural law that is expressed in human law.

In some cases, human laws are so close to what is offered by natural law that we find them existing "universally" in all human communities. To use Aquinas' vocabulary, some human laws constitute *"conclusions"* from natural law. These pertain to matters about which natural law offers clear guidance (e.g., murder is wrong). Aquinas refers to these "conclusions" as the "law of nations," as they are (or ought to be) found in all nations, given that all humans have the same nature, and are subject to the same natural law. Indeed, a human law that opposes natural law is no longer properly "law" at all.

> As Augustine says (De Lib. Arb. i, 5) "that which is not just seems to be no law at all": wherefore the force of a law depends on the extent of its justice. Now in human affairs a thing is said to be just, from being right, according to the rule of reason. But the first rule of reason is the law of nature, as is clear from what has been stated above (Q[91], A[2], ad 2). Consequently every human law has just so much of the nature of law, as it is derived from the law of nature. But if in any point it deflects from the law of nature, it is no longer a law but a perversion of law.[136]

Other human laws involve much longer chains of reasoning to link them back to natural law, and so might be specific to certain communities only. These laws

---

[134] It's worth pointing out that if you think sexual activity has ends *other* than reproduction (e.g., expressing love, mere pleasure, etc.), then it ceases to be obvious that any of those activities are "unnatural."

[135] Ibid., I-II, 94.2

[136] Ibid., I-II, 95.2

constitute *"determinations"* from natural law, and these pertain to the particular details/applications that are based in the conclusions from natural law.

> *Some things are therefore derived from the general principles of the natural law, by way of conclusions; e.g. that "one must not kill" may be derived as a conclusion from the principle that "one should do harm to no man": while some are derived therefrom by way of determination; e.g. the law of nature has it that the evil-doer should be punished; but that he be punished in this or that way, is a determination of the law of nature.[137]*

Aquinas offers his own analogy to try to clarify the relationship between conclusions and determinations of natural law. All houses have certain essential elements (e.g., having a foundation, a roof, etc.), but may have particular details added to them that may vary from house to house (e.g., whether the house is built from brick or wood, whether the roof is tile or shingle, how many windows it has, etc.).

Analogously, human laws are to be based on general natural law principles (e.g., murder is a criminal offense), but may vary with regard to details (e.g., punishing murder with execution as opposed to life imprisonment).

"Conclusions" of natural law give us the basic moral "foundation" for any person or community. The inclusion of "determinations" of natural law allows for diversity of expression, so long as the particular values don't contradict the natural law itself. To reuse an example, we might think that a conclusion from natural law is that murderers should be punished, but some chains of reasoning ("determinations") might lead some communities to punish with the death penalty, and others with life imprisonment. Either could be consistent with the natural law. A community that did not prohibit murder at all, however, would be contradicting the natural law.

In addition to the guidance offered by both human laws and the natural law, *Divine Law* is needed for several reasons. One reason is because human laws can be made in error. That is, it is possible that a human law is an unjust law (by virtue of contradicting the natural law).

Another reason is because human laws can't direct the soul (the intentions) of the citizen, but only his outward acts. That is, a human law might cause someone to abstain from adultery from the threat of punishment, but that person can still commit adultery "in his heart."

Finally, human law is imperfect in its ability to punish or forbid *all* evil deeds. The Divine Law regulates and punishes us as sinners, not criminals. There might be actions which are not illegal, but are nevertheless "sinful."

> *Wherefore laws imposed on men should also be in keeping with their condition, for, as Isidore says (Etym. v, 21), law should be "possible both according to nature, and according to the customs of the country." Now possibility or faculty of action is due to an interior habit or disposition: since the same thing is not possible to one who has not a virtuous habit, as is possible to one who has. Thus the same is not possible to a child as to a full-grown man: for which reason the law for children is not the same as for adults, since many things are permitted*

---

[137] Ibid., I-II, 95.2

to children, which in an adult are punished by law or at any rate are open to blame. In like manner many things are permissible to men not perfect in virtue, which would be intolerable in a virtuous man.

Now human law is framed for a number of human beings, the majority of whom are not perfect in virtue. Wherefore human laws do not forbid all vices, from which the virtuous abstain, but only the more grievous vices, from which it is possible for the majority to abstain; and chiefly those that are to the hurt of others, without the prohibition of which human society could not be maintained: thus human law prohibits murder, theft and such like.[138]

The need for "supplement" and specific guidance (via the Divine Law) can be provided by what is generally called "divine command" approaches to ethics. Divine Command theories are just what they sound like: they identify moral goodness with the divine will, often specifically in terms of commandments thought to come from a divine source.[139] A somewhat generic formulation is offered by contemporary Christian philosopher William Lane Craig.

- An action (A) is *required* of a moral agent (S) if and only if a just and loving God commands S to do A.
- An action (A) is *permitted* for S if and only if a just and loving God does not command S not to do A.
- An action (A) is *forbidden* to S if and only if a just and loving God commands S not to do A.[140]

Note that "commands" may be implied or derived from other commands, such that it need not be the case that every single thing we ought or ought not to do appears in clear black and white text in some Holy book. An easy, culturally accessible example of this kind of theory is the Ten Commandments from the Book of *Exodus* (shared by Christianity, Judaism, and Islam).

Exodus 20:2-17

2 I am the Lord your God, who brought you out of the land of Egypt, out of the house of slavery;
3 Do not have any other gods before me.
4 You shall not make for yourself an idol, whether in the form of anything that is in heaven above, or that is on the earth beneath, or that is in the water under the earth.
5 You shall not bow down to them or worship them; for I the Lord your God am

---

[138] Ibid., I-II, 96.2
[139] Note: some of this material will also be found in the chapter of this book specifically focused on Divine Command theory.
[140] William Lane Craig, *Reasonable Faith: Christian Truth and Apologetics.* Crossway, 2008. p. 182.

a jealous God, punishing children for the iniquity of parents, to the third and the fourth generation of those who reject me,
6 but showing steadfast love to the thousandth generation of those who love me and keep my commandments.
7 You shall not make wrongful use of the name of the Lord your God, for the Lord will not acquit anyone who misuses his name.
8 Remember the Sabbath day and keep it holy.
9 For six days you shall labour and do all your work.
10 But the seventh day is a Sabbath to the Lord your God; you shall not do any work—you, your son or your daughter, your male or female slave, your livestock, or the alien resident in your towns.
11 For in six days the Lord made heaven and earth, the sea, and all that is in them, but rested the seventh day; therefore the Lord blessed the Sabbath day and consecrated it.
12 Honor your father and your mother, so that your days may be long in the land that the Lord your God is giving you.
13 You shall not murder.
14 You shall not commit adultery.
15 You shall not steal.
16 You shall not bear false witness against your neighbor.
17 You shall not covet your neighbor's house; you shall not covet your neighbor's wife, or male or female slave, or ox, or donkey, or anything that belongs to your neighbor.

In this example, various things are required (e.g., honoring one's father and mother), other things are forbidden (e.g., murder), and anything else would be permitted, unless forbidden by God elsewhere—or, to use Aquinas' vocabulary: unless in violation of what is revealed to us by the natural law.

In the case of the Ten Commandments, the first four Commandments address humanity's moral obligations to God, the next five address our moral obligations to other people, and the final Commandment addresses our own thoughts and desires.

In Christianity, specifically, this approach is distilled and simplified in Matthew 22:35-40, when Jesus is asked "which is the great commandment in the law?" In answer, Jesus said "Thou shalt love the Lord thy God with all thy heart, and with all thy soul, and with all thy mind. This is the first and great commandment. And the second is like unto it, Thou shalt love thy neighbour as thyself. On these two commandments hang all the law and the prophets."

In essence, love God (and act accordingly), and love others as you love yourself (and act accordingly).

Note the possible collaboration with Aquinas' approach. While we might know as a "conclusion" from natural law that murder is wrong ("thou shalt not kill"), we could certainly not detect something as specific as "remember the Sabbath and keep it holy." And, while the first moral precept of the natural law is that "good is to be done and pursued and evil is to be avoided," this precept is given more clarity by the command that we "shalt love thy neighbor as thyself."

What's essential to remember, however, is that this theistically informed natural law tradition does not require that one be "religious" in order to detect and be bound by objective moral values and duties. Indeed, even atheists, according to this view, have the capacities of synderesis and conscience, and are aware of the natural law. This same tradition can cite the Apostle Paul: "When Gentiles who have not the law do by nature what the law requires, they are a law to themselves, even though they do not have the law. They show that what the law requires is written on their hearts."[141] Given free will, humans are able to resist the natural law, but we are just as "bound" to it as we are to all the other laws of Nature.

Although influenced by the "pagan" philosophies of both Aristotle and the Stoics (through Cicero), the natural law tradition we just explored took on an unmistakable Christian "flavor" thanks to Aquinas. While this might make it a perfect fit for some people, there are others who subscribe to a purely naturalistic worldview. For those persons, alternative versions of natural law are necessary, and, fortunately, available. The naturalistic versions of natural law we will consider from Phillipa Foot and Rosalind Hursthouse both rely on biological foundations and/or analogies, and do not require a "religious" worldview at all.

Natural Law: Naturalistic Worldview

Phillipa Foot

Phillipa Foot (1920-2010) was a British ethicist, and a founder of contemporary virtue ethics. She relies largely on Aristotle and Aquinas as her philosophical foundation, though her system does not presuppose Aquinas' Christian worldview. She describes moral evil not in terms of "sin," but as a kind of "natural defect." In a 2001 interview with the magazine "Philosophy Now," Foot explains that moral "goodness" is analogous to the way in which we describe living things and parts of living things as "good."[142]

When we say that someone's eyes are "good," we mean that they are functioning as they should, given the normal functioning of human eyes. For example, my own eyes are "bad" in the sense that I have astigmatism, and need glasses in order to see certain things without them being blurry, or giving me a headache.

This "goodness" is species-relative. The normal functioning of human eyes is not the same as the normal functioning of owl eyes. "So there's this notion of defect which is species-relevant. Things aren't just good or bad, they're good in a certain individual, in relation to the manner of life of his or hers or its species. That's the basic idea. And I argue that moral defects are just one more example of this kind of defect."[143]

Foot adopts Elizabeth Anscombe's notion of an "Aristotelian necessity," understood as "that which is necessary because and insofar as good hangs on it."[144] For example, it is necessary that plants have water, that wolves hunt in packs, and that lionesses teach their cubs how to hunt. These necessities are dependent upon the particular species of plant or animal in question, what they need, their natural habitat, etc. All of these things together establish what it is for members of that species to be

---

[141] Rom. 2:14-15
[142] https://philosophynow.org/issues/41/Philippa_Foot
[143] "Philosophy Now," Issue 41.
[144] Phillipa Foot, *Natural Goodness*. Oxford University Press, 2001. p. 15.

as they ought to be, and to do that which they ought to do – as members of that species.

Not all activities of an organism are "necessities," or good. For example, leaves rustling in the wind is not a necessary part in the life of a tree—unlike pollination. Those things that *are* necessary (according to Foot) "all have to do, directly or indirectly, with self maintenance, as by defence and the obtaining of nourishment, or with the reproduction of the individual, as by the building of nests... what 'plays a part' in this life is that which is causally and teleologically related to it, as putting out roots is related to obtaining nourishment, and attracting insects is related to reproduction in plants.[145]"

In general, "the way an individual *should be* is determined by what is needed for development, self-maintenance, and reproduction: in most species involving defense and in some way the rearing of the young.[146]"

While humans don't need to build nests like a bird, we do have our own necessities and our own defects. In the case of plants and animals, "flourishing" is understood simply in terms of survival and reproduction. But in humans, that is not enough. A life that is long-lived and filled with children, but also deeply unhappy would not be a "life well lived." Therefore, for humans, flourishing (as a human) necessarily involves happiness.

To be "successful" as a human, we need more than just food and water and shelter. We also need to be industrious and social. "They need the ability to form family ties, friendships, and special relations with neighbors. They also need codes of conduct. And how could they have all these things without virtues such as loyalty, fairness, kindness, and in certain circumstances obedience?"[147]

We can see now the connection between "morality" and a "good" life. Given the sorts of creatures we are, humans need "goodness" to flourish much as plants need water.

Virtues are beneficial, and humans do not generally get on that well without them. Virtues such as courage, temperance, and wisdom benefit both the possessor and others. Vices such as pride, vanity and greed *harm* both the possessor as well as others.

While some virtues such as justice and charity seem mostly about others, it seems that anyone and everyone is generally better off for being charitable and just. In addition to being seen as beneficial traits, virtues may also be regarded as "correctives," given some deficiencies in our nature.

Aquinas says of our passions: "they may incite us to something against reason, and so we need a curb, which we call temperance. Or they may make us shirk a course of action dictated by reason, through fear of dangers or hardships. Then a person needs to be steadfast and not run away from what is right; and for this courage is named."[148]

It is because we experience fear in the face of danger that courage is necessary. It is because we are tempted by desires, that temperance is necessary. We need the

---

[145] Ibid., 31.
[146] Ibid., 33.
[147] Ibid,. 45.
[148] Aquinas, *Summa Theologica*, 1a2ae Q.61 a.3.

virtue of industriousness because we are tempted by idleness, and humility because of our pride. We need charity and justice because we often neglect the good of others. This is another way of saying that we need virtue (and morality) to live well, given the sorts of species we are.

When a behavior or person is "defective" given their nature, that is bad. In the previous example of the human eye, defect was understood in terms of visual impairment. According to Foot, to speak of a good person is not to speak of his sight or memory, or most any other physical ability or disability, but rather his "rational will."[149]

> *Vice is a defect of the human will, but what counts as virtue or vice can legitimately vary at different times and in different communities. Courage, for example, will take different forms based on what is needed in the community at that time. Sometimes courage will be "soldier" courage, but at other times it might require peaceful protest against an oppressive law. The needs of a nomadic culture vary from those of city-dwellers, as do those of a people threatened by war and enemies, versus those who enjoy peace and prosperity. When religion gets involved, things vary even more. "In that sense, a lot of what's right and wrong will be relative to different cultures, of course. But that doesn't mean there isn't the same underlying basis for right and wrong.[150]*

This indicates room for diversity with respect to the expression of virtues. Courage is universally necessary, but the *kind* of courage needed might vary based on context. All plants need nourishment, but the needs of a Venus Fly Trap are met quite differently than that of a Rose.

Rosalind Hursthouse

Virtue ethicist Rosalind Hursthouse (born 1943, and still alive at the time of this writing) likewise bases her ethical system on "biology," and likewise starts with plants.

With regard to plants, an individual plant is a good specimen of its species based on its _parts_ (e.g., leaves, roots, petals) and _operations_ (e.g., growing, taking in water, developing buds), and _reactions_ (e.g., turning towards the sun). These parts and operations are evaluated as "good" based on two "ends" (purposes/goals):

1. Whether they are contributing in a way characteristic of the species to individual survival through the characteristic lifespan of such a member of that species.
2. Whether they are contributing in a way characteristic of the species to continuance of the species itself.

With regard to animals, we still evaluate "parts and operations," but add additional aspects and ends. Animals do not merely react, but also act. "_Acting_" is

---

[149] Foot, *Natural Goodness*, 66.
[150] Foot, "Philosophy Now," Issue 41, Autumn 2001

another aspect with regard to which an animal is good (or not) based on their species. Animals do not merely "produce seed," as do plants, but must do many additional things to promote not only their own survival but the continuance of the species. For example, a lioness that doesn't suckle her cubs and teach them to hunt is "defective."

The more complicated the animal, the more complicated its nervous system, and this introduces the capacity for pleasure and pain. This capacity introduces a third end. In addition to individual survival and continuance of the species, we add:

3. Whether their lives exhibit "characteristic freedom from pain and characteristic pleasure or enjoyment."[151]

This is not to say that the ideal for an animal is to experience no pain ever. An animal incapable of pain would also be incapable of detecting that it was being damaged – and this would be a *defect*. So, while the capacity for pain is not itself a defect, a life of abundant and unrelenting pain would be a defective life.

Creatures capable of pleasure and pain are also possibly capable of experiencing emotion and desire, and this suggests a notion of proper functioning with regard to those capacities as well. For example, a creature that never experiences fear even when it is warranted probably has low survival value, but a creature that is always frightened no matter how secure it might be, is likewise defective.

To summarize thus far: for sophisticated animals we now have four aspects under consideration:

(1) Parts
(2) Operations/reactions
(3) Actions
(4) Emotions/desires.

We also have three ends with respect to which individual creatures are evaluated:

1. Individual survival
2. The continuance of the species
3. Characteristic pleasure or enjoyment/characteristic freedom from pain.

Once we arrive at animals that are also *social*, an additional (4th) end is added:

4. The good functioning of the social group.

Wolves, for example, hunt in packs. A so-called "lone wolf," that doesn't participate in hunting with the pack, is "defective" in its capacity as a wolf and a member of that pack. An ape that doesn't participate in mutual grooming with other apes in his group isn't "doing it right," from a certain perspective. One might immediately wonder how we establish what constitutes the good functioning of the social group.

---

[151] Rosalind Hursthouse, *On Virtue Ethics*. Oxford University Press, 1999. p.199.

The function of such a group is to enable its members to live well (in the way characteristic of their species); that is, to foster their characteristic individual survival, their characteristic contribution to the continuance of the species, and their characteristic freedom from pain and enjoyment of such things as it is characteristic of their species to enjoy. And all this involves its fostering the development of its members' characteristic capacities. That is what a social group should do. So if it is doing it well, it is functioning well.[152]

So, a good *social* animal is one that is well fitted with respect to its parts, operations, actions, and desires/emotions. Whether it is deemed well fitted is determined by whether those things well serve its <u>individual survival</u>, the <u>continuance of its species</u>, its <u>characteristic freedom from pain and characteristic enjoyment</u>, and the <u>good functioning of its social group</u> – all in ways characteristic of the species.[153]

It is worth pointing out that the truth of these evaluations is not subjective – not based on individual desires, interests, or values. We do not get to simply decide what is, in fact, characteristic of a species and conducive to its flourishing. I couldn't claim, for example, with any credibility, that rapid flight and a keen sense of smell are characteristic features of spiders, or that skillful cello playing is a characteristic end for spiders. Analogously, given that humans are social beings, the traits of a sociopath could hardly be considered to satisfy the aspects and ends characteristic of human beings.

Conclusion

If you find the theistic/teleological worldview plausible, then there would be reason to believe that there are objective moral principles and values available for humans to discover, and follow (or not!). This might be understood in terms of explicit commandments (e.g., "thou shalt not kill"), or in terms of our having been created with a particular nature and purpose to fulfill (e.g., political and social animal who needs and benefits from group cohesion and harmonious conflict resolution).

If there is a God, then presumably our "nature" would be explained by that God. But, even in the absence of an overtly "theistic" worldview, we might still find a basis for objective moral principles and values from a purely naturalistic perspective instead, by appealing to the traits we evolved to value and display, given the sorts of creatures that we are. Given that these are species-level traits, they are not merely matters of personal (or even cultural) preference, but exist independently of those, and are therefore "objective."

---

[152] Ibid., 201-202.
[153] Ibid., 202.

St. Thomas Aquinas was a hugely influential philosopher and theologian. His brilliant adaptation of Aristotle to Christian theology provided a philosophical complement to revealed religion, and set the foundation for Christian natural law theory. His massive magnum opus, the Summa Theologica, is far too lengthy, and contains arguments far too irrelevant to be included, in entirety. Instead, just a very few excerpts have been provided. These excerpts primarily concern the natural law.

Summa Theologica[154]
St. Thomas Aquinas
Translated by The Fathers of the English Dominican Province
[1947]

OF THE NATURAL LAW (SIX ARTICLES)

We must now consider the natural law; concerning which there are six points of inquiry:

(1) What is the natural law?
(2) What are the precepts of the natural law?
(3) Whether all acts of virtue are prescribed by the natural law?
(4) Whether the natural law is the same in all?
(5) Whether it is changeable?
(6) Whether it can be abolished from the heart of man?

Whether the natural law is a habit?

Objection 1: It would seem that the natural law is a habit. Because, as the Philosopher says (Ethic. ii, 5), "there are three things in the soul: power, habit, and passion." But the natural law is not one of the soul's powers: nor is it one of the passions; as we may see by going through them one by one. Therefore the natural law is a habit.

Objection 2: Further, Basil [*Damascene, De Fide Orth. iv, 22] says that the conscience or "synderesis is the law of our mind"; which can only apply to the natural law. But the "synderesis" is a habit, as was shown in the FP, Q[79], A[12]. Therefore the natural law is a habit.

Objection 3: Further, the natural law abides in man always, as will be shown further on (A[6]). But man's reason, which the law regards, does not always think about the natural law. Therefore the natural law is not an act, but a habit.

On the contrary, Augustine says (De Bono Conjug. xxi) that "a habit is that whereby something is done when necessary." But such is not the natural law: since it is in infants and in the damned who cannot act by it. Therefore the natural law is not a habit.

I answer that, A thing may be called a habit in two ways. First, properly and essentially: and thus the natural law is not a habit. For it has been stated above (Q[90],

---

A[1], ad 2) that the natural law is something appointed by reason, just as a proposition is a work of reason. Now that which a man does is not the same as that whereby he does it: for he makes a becoming speech by the habit of grammar. Since then a habit is that by which we act, a law cannot be a habit properly and essentially.

Secondly, the term habit may be applied to that which we hold by a habit: thus faith may mean that which we hold by faith. And accordingly, since the precepts of the natural law are sometimes considered by reason actually, while sometimes they are in the reason only habitually, in this way the natural law may be called a habit. Thus, in speculative matters, the indemonstrable principles are not the habit itself whereby we hold those principles, but are the principles the habit of which we possess.

Reply to Objection 1: The Philosopher proposes there to discover the genus of virtue; and since it is evident that virtue is a principle of action, he mentions only those things which are principles of human acts, viz. powers, habits and passions. But there are other things in the soul besides these three: there are acts; thus "to will" is in the one that wills; again, things known are in the knower; moreover its own natural properties are in the soul, such as immortality and the like.

Reply to Objection 2: "Synderesis" is said to be the law of our mind, because it is a habit containing the precepts of the natural law, which are the first principles of human actions.

Reply to Objection 3: This argument proves that the natural law is held habitually; and this is granted.

To the argument advanced in the contrary sense we reply that sometimes a man is unable to make use of that which is in him habitually, on account of some impediment: thus, on account of sleep, a man is unable to use the habit of science. In like manner, through the deficiency of his age, a child cannot use the habit of understanding of principles, or the natural law, which is in him habitually.

Whether the natural law contains several precepts, or only one?

Objection 1: It would seem that the natural law contains, not several precepts, but one only. For law is a kind of precept, as stated above (Q[92], A[2]). If therefore there were many precepts of the natural law, it would follow that there are also many natural laws.

Objection 2: Further, the natural law is consequent to human nature. But human nature, as a whole, is one; though, as to its parts, it is manifold. Therefore, either there is but one precept of the law of nature, on account of the unity of nature as a whole; or there are many, by reason of the number of parts of human nature. The result would be that even things relating to the inclination of the concupiscible faculty belong to the natural law.

Objection 3: Further, law is something pertaining to reason, as stated above (Q[90], A[1]). Now reason is but one in man. Therefore there is only one precept of the natural law.

On the contrary, The precepts of the natural law in man stand in relation to practical matters, as the first principles to matters of demonstration. But there are several first indemonstrable principles. Therefore there are also several precepts of the natural law.

I answer that, As stated above (Q[91], A[3]), the precepts of the natural law are to the practical reason, what the first principles of demonstrations are to the speculative reason; because both are self-evident principles. Now a thing is said to be self-evident in two ways: first, in itself; secondly, in relation to us. Any proposition is said to be self-evident in itself, if its predicate is contained in the notion of the subject: although, to one who knows not the definition of the subject, it happens that such a proposition is not self-evident. For instance, this proposition, "Man is a rational being," is, in its very nature, self-evident, since who says "man," says "a rational being": and yet to one who knows not what a man is, this proposition is not self-evident. Hence it is that, as Boethius says (De Hebdom.), certain axioms or propositions are universally self-evident to all; and such are those propositions whose terms are known to all, as, "Every whole is greater than its part," and, "Things equal to one and the same are equal to one another." But some propositions are self-evident only to the wise, who understand the meaning of the terms of such propositions: thus to one who understands that an angel is not a body, it is self-evident that an angel is not circumscriptively in a place: but this is not evident to the unlearned, for they cannot grasp it.

Now a certain order is to be found in those things that are apprehended universally. For that which, before aught else, falls under apprehension, is "being," the notion of which is included in all things whatsoever a man apprehends. Wherefore the first indemonstrable principle is that "the same thing cannot be affirmed and denied at the same time," which is based on the notion of "being" and "not-being": and on this principle all others are based, as is stated in Metaph. iv, text. 9. Now as "being" is the first thing that falls under the apprehension simply, so "good" is the first thing that falls under the apprehension of the practical reason, which is directed to action: since every agent acts for an end under the aspect of good. Consequently the first principle of practical reason is one founded on the notion of good, viz. that "good is that which all things seek after." Hence this is the first precept of law, that "good is to be done and pursued, and evil is to be avoided." All other precepts of the natural law are based upon this: so that whatever the practical reason naturally apprehends as man's good (or evil) belongs to the precepts of the natural law as something to be done or avoided.

Since, however, good has the nature of an end, and evil, the nature of a contrary, hence it is that all those things to which man has a natural inclination, are naturally apprehended by reason as being good, and consequently as objects of pursuit, and their contraries as evil, and objects of avoidance. Wherefore according to the order of natural inclinations, is the order of the precepts of the natural law. Because in man there is first of all an inclination to good in accordance with the nature which he has in common with all substances: inasmuch as every substance seeks the preservation of its own being, according to its nature: and by reason of this inclination, whatever is a means of preserving human life, and of warding off its obstacles, belongs to the natural law. Secondly, there is in man an inclination to things that pertain to him more specially, according to that nature which he has in common with other animals: and in virtue of this inclination, those things are said to belong to the natural law, "which nature has taught to all animals" [*Pandect. Just. I, tit. i], such as sexual intercourse, education of offspring and so forth. Thirdly, there is in man an inclination to good, according to the nature of his reason, which nature is proper to him: thus man has a natural inclination to know the truth about God, and to live in society: and in this respect, whatever pertains to this inclination belongs to the natural law; for instance, to shun ignorance, to avoid offending those among whom one has to live, and other such things regarding the above inclination.

Reply to Objection 1: All these precepts of the law of nature have the character of one natural law, inasmuch as they flow from one first precept.

Reply to Objection 2: All the inclinations of any parts whatsoever of human nature, e.g. of the concupiscible and irascible parts, in so far as they are ruled by reason, belong to the natural law, and are reduced to one first precept, as stated above: so that the precepts of the natural law are many in themselves, but are based on one common foundation.

Reply to Objection 3: Although reason is one in itself, yet it directs all things regarding man; so that whatever can be ruled by reason, is contained under the law of reason.

Whether all acts of virtue are prescribed by the natural law?

Objection 1: It would seem that not all acts of virtue are prescribed by the natural law. Because, as stated above (Q[90], A[2]) it is essential to a law that it be ordained to the common good. But some acts of virtue are ordained to the private good of the individual, as is evident especially in regards to acts of temperance. Therefore not all acts of virtue are the subject of natural law.

Objection 2: Further, every sin is opposed to some virtuous act. If therefore all acts of virtue are prescribed by the natural law, it seems to follow that all sins are against nature: whereas this applies to certain special sins.

Objection 3: Further, those things which are according to nature are common to all. But acts of virtue are not common to all: since a thing is virtuous in one, and vicious in another. Therefore not all acts of virtue are prescribed by the natural law.

On the contrary, Damascene says (De Fide Orth. iii, 4) that "virtues are natural." Therefore virtuous acts also are a subject of the natural law.

I answer that, We may speak of virtuous acts in two ways: first, under the aspect of virtuous; secondly, as such and such acts considered in their proper species. If then we speak of acts of virtue, considered as virtuous, thus all virtuous acts belong to the natural law. For it has been stated (A[2]) that to the natural law belongs everything to which a man is inclined according to his nature. Now each thing is inclined naturally to an operation that is suitable to it according to its form: thus fire is inclined to give heat. Wherefore, since the rational soul is the proper form of man, there is in every man a natural inclination to act according to reason: and this is to act according to virtue. Consequently, considered thus, all acts of virtue are prescribed by the natural law: since each one's reason naturally dictates to him to act virtuously. But if we speak of virtuous acts, considered in themselves, i.e. in their proper species, thus not all virtuous acts are prescribed by the natural law: for many things are done virtuously, to which nature does not incline at first; but which, through the inquiry of reason, have been found by men to be conducive to well-living.

Reply to Objection 1: Temperance is about the natural concupiscences of food, drink and sexual matters, which are indeed ordained to the natural common good, just as other matters of law are ordained to the moral common good.

Reply to Objection 2: By human nature we may mean either that which is proper to man---and in this sense all sins, as being against reason, are also against nature, as

Damascene states (De Fide Orth. ii, 30): or we may mean that nature which is common to man and other animals; and in this sense, certain special sins are said to be against nature; thus contrary to sexual intercourse, which is natural to all animals, is unisexual lust, which has received the special name of the unnatural crime.

Reply to Objection 3: This argument considers acts in themselves. For it is owing to the various conditions of men, that certain acts are virtuous for some, as being proportionate and becoming to them, while they are vicious for others, as being out of proportion to them.

Whether the natural law is the same in all men?

Objection 1: It would seem that the natural law is not the same in all. For it is stated in the Decretals (Dist. i) that "the natural law is that which is contained in the Law and the Gospel." But this is not common to all men; because, as it is written (Rom. 10:16), "all do not obey the gospel." Therefore the natural law is not the same in all men.

Objection 2: Further, "Things which are according to the law are said to be just," as stated in Ethic. v. But it is stated in the same book that nothing is so universally just as not to be subject to change in regard to some men. Therefore even the natural law is not the same in all men.

Objection 3: Further, as stated above (AA[2],3), to the natural law belongs everything to which a man is inclined according to his nature. Now different men are naturally inclined to different things; some to the desire of pleasures, others to the desire of honors, and other men to other things. Therefore there is not one natural law for all.

On the contrary, Isidore says (Etym. v, 4): "The natural law is common to all nations."

I answer that, As stated above (AA[2],3), to the natural law belongs those things to which a man is inclined naturally: and among these it is proper to man to be inclined to act according to reason. Now the process of reason is from the common to the proper, as stated in Phys. i. The speculative reason, however, is differently situated in this matter, from the practical reason. For, since the speculative reason is busied chiefly with the necessary things, which cannot be otherwise than they are, its proper conclusions, like the universal principles, contain the truth without fail. The practical reason, on the other hand, is busied with contingent matters, about which human actions are concerned: and consequently, although there is necessity in the general principles, the more we descend to matters of detail, the more frequently we encounter defects. Accordingly then in speculative matters truth is the same in all men, both as to principles and as to conclusions: although the truth is not known to all as regards the conclusions, but only as regards the principles which are called common notions. But in matters of action, truth or practical rectitude is not the same for all, as to matters of detail, but only as to the general principles: and where there is the same rectitude in matters of detail, it is not equally known to all.

It is therefore evident that, as regards the general principles whether of speculative or of practical reason, truth or rectitude is the same for all, and is equally known by all. As to the proper conclusions of the speculative reason, the truth is the same for all, but is not equally known to all: thus it is true for all that the three angles of a triangle are together equal to two right angles, although it is not known to all. But as to the proper conclusions of the practical reason, neither is the truth or rectitude the same for all, nor, where it is the same, is it equally known by all. Thus it is right and true for all to act according to reason: and from this principle it follows as a proper conclusion, that goods entrusted to another should be restored to their owner. Now this is true for the majority of cases: but it may happen in a particular case that it would be injurious, and therefore unreasonable, to restore goods held in trust; for instance, if they are claimed for the purpose of fighting against one's country. And this principle will be found to fail the more, according as we descend further into detail, e.g. if one were to say that goods held in trust should be restored with such and such a guarantee, or in such and such a way; because the greater the number of conditions added, the greater the number of ways in which the principle may fail, so that it be not right to restore or not to restore.

Consequently we must say that the natural law, as to general principles, is the same for all, both as to rectitude and as to knowledge. But as to certain matters of detail, which are conclusions, as it were, of those general principles, it is the same for all in the majority of cases, both as to rectitude and as to knowledge; and yet in some few cases it may fail, both as to rectitude, by reason of certain obstacles (just as natures subject to generation and corruption fail in some few cases on account of some obstacle), and as to knowledge, since in some the reason is perverted by passion, or evil habit, or an evil disposition of nature; thus formerly, theft, although it is expressly contrary to the natural law, was not considered wrong among the Germans, as Julius Caesar relates (De Bello Gall. vi).

Reply to Objection 1: The meaning of the sentence quoted is not that whatever is contained in the Law and the Gospel belongs to the natural law, since they contain many things that are above nature; but that whatever belongs to the natural law is fully contained in them. Wherefore Gratian, after saying that "the natural law is what is contained in the Law and the Gospel," adds at once, by way of example, "by which everyone is commanded to do to others as he would be done by."

Reply to Objection 2: The saying of the Philosopher is to be understood of things that are naturally just, not as general principles, but as conclusions drawn from them, having rectitude in the majority of cases, but failing in a few.

Reply to Objection 3: As, in man, reason rules and commands the other powers, so all the natural inclinations belonging to the other powers must needs be directed according to reason. Wherefore it is universally right for all men, that all their inclinations should be directed according to reason.

Whether the natural law can be changed?

Objection 1: It would seem that the natural law can be changed. Because on Ecclus. 17:9, "He gave them instructions, and the law of life," the gloss says: "He wished the law of the letter to be written, in order to correct the law of nature." But that which is corrected is changed. Therefore the natural law can be changed.

Objection 2: Further, the slaying of the innocent, adultery, and theft are against the natural law. But we find these things changed by God: as when God commanded Abraham to slay his innocent son (Gn. 22:2); and when he ordered the Jews to borrow and purloin the vessels of the Egyptians (Ex. 12:35); and when He commanded Osee to take to himself "a wife of fornications" (Osee 1:2). Therefore the natural law can be changed.

Objection 3: Further, Isidore says (Etym. 5:4) that "the possession of all things in common, and universal freedom, are matters of natural law." But these things are seen to be changed by human laws. Therefore it seems that the natural law is subject to change.

On the contrary, It is said in the Decretals (Dist. v): "The natural law dates from the creation of the rational creature. It does not vary according to time, but remains unchangeable."

I answer that, A change in the natural law may be understood in two ways. First, by way of addition. In this sense nothing hinders the natural law from being changed: since many things for the benefit of human life have been added over and above the natural law, both by the Divine law and by human laws.

Secondly, a change in the natural law may be understood by way of subtraction, so that what previously was according to the natural law, ceases to be so. In this sense, the natural law is altogether unchangeable in its first principles: but in its secondary principles, which, as we have said (A[4]), are certain detailed proximate conclusions drawn from the first principles, the natural law is not changed so that what it prescribes be not right in most cases. But it may be changed in some particular cases of rare occurrence, through some special causes hindering the observance of such precepts, as stated above (A[4]).

Reply to Objection 1: The written law is said to be given for the correction of the natural law, either because it supplies what was wanting to the natural law; or because the natural law was perverted in the hearts of some men, as to certain matters, so that they esteemed those things good which are naturally evil; which perversion stood in need of correction.

Reply to Objection 2: All men alike, both guilty and innocent, die the death of nature: which death of nature is inflicted by the power of God on account of original sin, according to 1 Kings 2:6: "The Lord killeth and maketh alive." Consequently, by the command of God, death can be inflicted on any man, guilty or innocent, without any injustice whatever. In like manner adultery is intercourse with another's wife; who is allotted to him by the law emanating from God. Consequently intercourse with any woman, by the command of God, is neither adultery nor fornication. The same applies to theft, which is the taking of another's property. For whatever is taken by the command of God, to Whom all things belong, is not taken against the will of its owner, whereas it is in this that theft consists. Nor is it only in human things, that whatever is commanded by God is right; but also in natural things, whatever is done by God, is, in some way, natural, as stated in the FP, Q[105], A[6], ad 1.

Reply to Objection 3: A thing is said to belong to the natural law in two ways. First, because nature inclines thereto: e.g. that one should not do harm to another. Secondly, because nature did not bring in the contrary: thus we might say that for man to be naked is of the natural law, because nature did not give him clothes, but art invented them. In this sense, "the possession of all things in common and universal freedom" are said to be of the natural law, because, to wit, the distinction of possessions and slavery were not brought in by nature, but devised by human reason for the benefit of human life. Accordingly the law of nature was not changed in this respect, except by addition.

Whether the law of nature can be abolished from the heart of man?

Objection 1: It would seem that the natural law can be abolished from the heart of man. Because on Rom. 2:14, "When the Gentiles who have not the law," etc. a gloss says that "the law of righteousness, which sin had blotted out, is graven on the heart of man when he is restored by grace." But the law of righteousness is the law of nature. Therefore the law of nature can be blotted out.

Objection 2: Further, the law of grace is more efficacious than the law of nature. But the law of grace is blotted out by sin. Much more therefore can the law of nature be blotted out.

Objection 3: Further, that which is established by law is made just. But many things are enacted by men, which are contrary to the law of nature. Therefore the law of nature can be abolished from the heart of man.

On the contrary, Augustine says (Confess. ii): "Thy law is written in the hearts of men, which iniquity itself effaces not." But the law which is written in men's hearts is the natural law. Therefore the natural law cannot be blotted out.

I answer that, As stated above (AA[4],5), there belong to the natural law, first, certain most general precepts, that are known to all; and secondly, certain secondary and more detailed precepts, which are, as it were, conclusions following closely from first principles. As to those general principles, the natural law, in the abstract, can nowise be blotted out from men's hearts. But it is blotted out in the case of a particular action, in so far as reason is hindered from applying the general principle to a particular point of practice, on account of concupiscence or some other passion, as stated above (Q[77], A[2]). But as to the other, i.e. the secondary precepts, the natural law can be blotted out from the human heart, either by evil persuasions, just as in speculative matters errors occur in respect of necessary conclusions; or by vicious customs and corrupt habits, as among some men, theft, and even unnatural vices, as the Apostle states (Rom. i), were not esteemed sinful.

Reply to Objection 1: Sin blots out the law of nature in particular cases, not universally, except perchance in regard to the secondary precepts of the natural law, in the way stated above.

Reply to Objection 2: Although grace is more efficacious than nature, yet nature is more essential to man, and therefore more enduring.

Reply to Objection 3: This argument is true of the secondary precepts of the natural law, against which some legislators have framed certain enactments which are unjust.

...

OF HUMAN LAW (FOUR ARTICLES)

We must now consider human law; and (1) this law considered in itself; (2) its power; (3) its mutability. Under the first head there are four points of inquiry:

(1) Its utility.
(2) Its origin.
(3) Its quality.
(4) Its division.

Whether it was useful for laws to be framed by men?

Objection 1: It would seem that it was not useful for laws to be framed by men. Because the purpose of every law is that man be made good thereby, as stated above (Q[92], A[1]). But men are more to be induced to be good willingly by means of admonitions, than against their will, by means of laws. Therefore there was no need to frame laws.

Objection 2: Further, As the Philosopher says (Ethic. v, 4), "men have recourse to a judge as to animate justice." But animate justice is better than inanimate justice, which contained in laws. Therefore it would have been better for the execution of justice to be entrusted to the decision of judges, than to frame laws in addition.

Objection 3: Further, every law is framed for the direction of human actions, as is evident from what has been stated above (Q[90], AA[1],2). But since human actions are about singulars, which are infinite in number, matter pertaining to the direction of human actions cannot be taken into sufficient consideration except by a wise man, who looks into each one of them. Therefore it would have been better for human acts to be directed by the judgment of wise men, than by the framing of laws. Therefore there was no need of human laws.

On the contrary, Isidore says (Etym. v, 20): "Laws were made that in fear thereof human audacity might be held in check, that innocence might be safeguarded in the midst of wickedness, and that the dread of punishment might prevent the wicked from doing harm." But these things are most necessary to mankind. Therefore it was necessary that human laws should be made.

I answer that, As stated above (Q[63], A[1]; Q[94], A[3]), man has a natural aptitude for virtue; but the perfection of virtue must be acquired by man by means of some kind of training. Thus we observe that man is helped by industry in his necessities, for instance, in food and clothing. Certain beginnings of these he has from nature, viz. his reason and his hands; but he has not the full complement, as other animals have, to whom nature has given sufficiency of clothing and food. Now it is difficult to see how man could suffice for himself in the matter of this training: since the perfection of virtue consists chiefly in withdrawing man from undue pleasures, to which above all man is inclined, and especially the young, who are more capable of being trained. Consequently a man needs to receive this training from another, whereby to arrive at the perfection of virtue. And as to those young people who are inclined to acts of virtue, by their good natural disposition, or by custom, or rather by the gift of God, paternal training suffices, which is by admonitions. But since some are found to be depraved, and prone to vice, and not easily amenable to words, it was necessary for such to be restrained from evil by force and fear, in order that, at least, they might desist from evil-doing, and leave others in peace, and that they themselves, by being habituated in this way, might be brought to do willingly what hitherto they did from fear, and thus become virtuous. Now this kind of training, which compels through fear of punishment, is the discipline of laws. Therefore in order that man might have peace and virtue, it was necessary for laws to be framed: for, as the Philosopher says (Polit. i, 2), "as man is the most noble of animals if he be perfect in virtue, so is he the lowest of all, if he be severed from law and righteousness"; because man can use his reason to devise means of satisfying his lusts and evil passions, which other animals are unable to do.

Reply to Objection 1: Men who are well disposed are led willingly to virtue by being admonished better than by coercion: but men who are evilly disposed are not led to virtue unless they are compelled.

Reply to Objection 2: As the Philosopher says (Rhet. i, 1), "it is better that all things be regulated by law, than left to be decided by judges": and this for three reasons. First, because it is easier to find a few wise men competent to frame right laws, than to find the many who would be necessary to judge aright of each single case. Secondly, because those who make laws consider long beforehand what laws to make; whereas judgment on each single case has to be pronounced as soon as it arises: and it is easier for man to see what is right, by taking many instances into consideration, than by considering one solitary fact. Thirdly, because lawgivers judge in the abstract and of future events; whereas those who sit in judgment of things present, towards which they are affected by love, hatred, or some kind of cupidity; wherefore their judgment is perverted.

Since then the animated justice of the judge is not found in every man, and since it can be deflected, therefore it was necessary, whenever possible, for the law to determine how to judge, and for very few matters to be left to the decision of men.

Reply to Objection 3: Certain individual facts which cannot be covered by the law "have necessarily to be committed to judges," as the Philosopher says in the same passage: for instance, "concerning something that has happened or not happened," and the like.

Whether every human law is derived from the natural law?

Objection 1: It would seem that not every human law is derived from the natural law. For the Philosopher says (Ethic. v, 7) that "the legal just is that which originally was a matter of indifference." But those things which arise from the natural law are not matters of indifference. Therefore the enactments of human laws are not derived from the natural law.

Objection 2: Further, positive law is contrasted with natural law, as stated by Isidore (Etym. v, 4) and the Philosopher (Ethic. v, 7). But those things which flow as conclusions from the general principles of the natural law belong to the natural law, as stated above (Q[94], A[4]). Therefore that which is established by human law does not belong to the natural law.

Objection 3: Further, the law of nature is the same for all; since the Philosopher says (Ethic. v, 7) that "the natural just is that which is equally valid everywhere." If therefore human laws were derived from the natural law, it would follow that they too are the same for all: which is clearly false.

Objection 4: Further, it is possible to give a reason for things which are derived from the natural law. But "it is not possible to give the reason for all the legal enactments of the lawgivers," as the jurist says [*Pandect. Justin. lib. i, ff, tit. iii, v; De Leg. et Senat.]. Therefore not all human laws are derived from the natural law.

On the contrary, Tully says (Rhet. ii): "Things which emanated from nature and were approved by custom, were sanctioned by fear and reverence for the laws."

I answer that, As Augustine says (De Lib. Arb. i, 5) "that which is not just seems to be no law at all": wherefore the force of a law depends on the extent of its justice. Now in human affairs a thing is said to be just, from being right, according to the rule of reason. But the first rule of reason is the law of nature, as is clear from what has been stated above (Q[91], A[2], ad 2). Consequently every human law has just so much of the nature of law, as it is derived from the law of nature. But if in any point it deflects from the law of nature, it is no longer a law but a perversion of law.

But it must be noted that something may be derived from the natural law in two ways: first, as a conclusion from premises, secondly, by way of determination of certain generalities. The first way is like to that by which, in sciences, demonstrated conclusions are drawn from the principles: while the second mode is likened to that whereby, in the arts, general forms are particularized as to details: thus the craftsman needs to determine the general form of a house to some particular shape. Some things are therefore derived from the general principles of the natural law, by way of conclusions; e.g. that "one must not kill" may be derived as a conclusion from the principle that "one should do harm to no man": while some are derived therefrom by way of determination; e.g. the law of nature has it that the evil-doer should be punished; but that he be punished in this or that way, is a determination of the law of nature.

Accordingly both modes of derivation are found in the human law. But those things which are derived in the first way, are contained in human law not as emanating therefrom exclusively, but have some force from the natural law also. But those things which are derived in the second way, have no other force than that of human law.

Reply to Objection 1: The Philosopher is speaking of those enactments which are by way of determination or specification of the precepts of the natural law.

Reply to Objection 2: This argument avails for those things that are derived from the natural law, by way of conclusions.

Reply to Objection 3: The general principles of the natural law cannot be applied to all men in the same way on account of the great variety of human affairs: and hence arises the diversity of positive laws among various people.

Reply to Objection 4: These words of the Jurist are to be understood as referring to decisions of rulers in determining particular points of the natural law: on which determinations the judgment of expert and prudent men is based as on its principles; in so far, to wit, as they see at once what is the best thing to decide.

Hence the Philosopher says (Ethic. vi, 11) that in such matters, "we ought to pay as much attention to the undemonstrated sayings and opinions of persons who surpass us in experience, age and prudence, as to their demonstrations."

Whether Isidore's description of the quality of positive law is appropriate?

Objection 1: It would seem that Isidore's description of the quality of positive law is not appropriate, when he says (Etym. v, 21): "Law shall be virtuous, just, possible to nature, according to the custom of the country, suitable to place and time, necessary, useful; clearly expressed, lest by its obscurity it lead to misunderstanding; framed for no private benefit, but for the common good." Because he had previously expressed the quality of law in three conditions, saying that "law is anything founded on reason, provided that it foster religion, be helpful to discipline, and further the common weal." Therefore it was needless to add any further conditions to these.

Objection 2: Further, Justice is included in honesty, as Tully says (De Offic. vii).

Therefore after saying "honest" it was superfluous to add "just."

Objection 3: Further, written law is condivided with custom, according to Isidore (Etym. ii, 10). Therefore it should not be stated in the definition of law that it is "according to the custom of the country."

Objection 4: Further, a thing may be necessary in two ways. It may be necessary simply, because it cannot be otherwise: and that which is necessary in this way, is not subject to human judgment, wherefore human law is not concerned with necessity of this kind. Again a thing may be necessary for an end: and this necessity is the same as usefulness. Therefore it is superfluous to say both "necessary" and "useful."

On the contrary, stands the authority of Isidore.

I answer that, Whenever a thing is for an end, its form must be determined proportionately to that end; as the form of a saw is such as to be suitable for cutting (Phys. ii, text. 88). Again, everything that is ruled and measured must have a form proportionate to its rule and measure. Now both these conditions are verified of human law: since it is both something ordained to an end; and is a rule or measure ruled or measured by a higher measure. And this higher measure is twofold, viz. the Divine law and the natural law, as explained above (A[2]; Q[93], A[3]). Now the end of human law is to be useful to man, as the jurist states [*Pandect. Justin. lib. xxv, ff., tit. iii; De Leg. et Senat.]. Wherefore Isidore in determining the nature of law, lays down, at first, three conditions; viz. that it "foster religion," inasmuch as it is proportionate to the Divine law; that it be "helpful to discipline," inasmuch as it is proportionate to the nature law; and that it "further the common weal," inasmuch as it is proportionate to the utility of mankind.

All the other conditions mentioned by him are reduced to these three. For it is called virtuous because it fosters religion. And when he goes on to say that it should be "just, possible to nature, according to the customs of the country, adapted to place and time," he implies that it should be helpful to discipline. For human discipline depends on first on the order of reason, to which he refers by saying "just": secondly, it depends on the ability of the agent; because discipline should be adapted to each one according to his ability, taking also into account the ability of nature (for the same burdens should be not laid on children as adults); and should be according to human customs; since man cannot live alone in society, paying no heed to others: thirdly, it depends on certain circumstances, in respect of which he says, "adapted to place and time." The remaining words, "necessary, useful," etc. mean that law should further the common weal: so that "necessity" refers to the removal of evils; "usefulness" to the attainment of good; "clearness of expression," to the need of preventing any harm ensuing from the law itself. And since, as stated above (Q[90], A[2]), law is ordained to the common good, this is expressed in the last part of the description.

This suffices for the Replies to the Objections.

Whether Isidore's division of human laws is appropriate?

Objection 1: It would seem that Isidore wrongly divided human statutes or human law (Etym. v, 4, seqq.). For under this law he includes the "law of nations," so called, because, as he says, "nearly all nations use it." But as he says, "natural law is that which is common to all nations." Therefore the law of nations is not contained under positive human law, but rather under natural law.

Objection 2: Further, those laws which have the same force, seem to differ not formally but only materially. But "statutes, decrees of the commonalty, senatorial decrees," and the like which he mentions (Etym. v, 9), all have the same force. Therefore they do not differ, except materially. But art takes no notice of such a distinction: since it may go on to infinity. Therefore this division of human laws is not appropriate.

Objection 3: Further, just as, in the state, there are princes, priests and soldiers, so are there other human offices. Therefore it seems that, as this division includes "military law," and "public law," referring to priests and magistrates; so also it should include other laws pertaining to other offices of the state.

Objection 4: Further, those things that are accidental should be passed over. But it is accidental to law that it be framed by this or that man. Therefore it is unreasonable to divide laws according to the names of lawgivers, so that one be called the "Cornelian" law, another the "Falcidian" law, etc.

On the contrary, The authority of Isidore (OBJ[1]) suffices.

I answer that, A thing can of itself be divided in respect of something contained in the notion of that thing. Thus a soul either rational or irrational is contained in the notion of animal: and therefore animal is divided properly and of itself in respect of its being rational or irrational; but not in the point of its being white or black, which are entirely beside the notion of animal. Now, in the notion of human law, many things are contained, in respect of any of which human law can be divided properly and of itself. For in the first place it belongs to the notion of human law, to be derived from the law of nature, as explained above (A[2]). In this respect positive law is divided into the "law of nations" and "civil law," according to the two ways in which something may be derived from the law of nature, as stated above (A[2]). Because, to the law of nations belong those things which are derived from the law of nature, as conclusions from premises, e.g. just buyings and sellings, and the like, without which men cannot live together, which is a point of the law of nature, since man is by nature a social animal, as is proved in Polit. i, 2. But those things which are derived from the law of nature by way of particular determination, belong to the civil law, according as each state decides on what is best for itself.

Secondly, it belongs to the notion of human law, to be ordained to the common good of the state. In this respect human law may be divided according to the different kinds of men who work in a special way for the common good: e.g. priests, by praying to God for the people; princes, by governing the people; soldiers, by fighting for the safety of the people. Wherefore certain special kinds of law are adapted to these men.

Thirdly, it belongs to the notion of human law, to be framed by that one who governs the community of the state, as shown above (Q[90], A[3]). In this respect, there are various human laws according to the various forms of government. Of these, according to the Philosopher (Polit. iii, 10) one is "monarchy," i.e. when the state is governed by one; and then we have "Royal Ordinances." Another form is "aristocracy," i.e. government by the best men or men of highest rank; and then we have the "Authoritative legal opinions" [Responsa Prudentum] and "Decrees of the Senate" [Senatus consulta]. Another form is "oligarchy," i.e. government by a few rich and powerful men; and then we have "Praetorian," also called "Honorary," law. Another form of government is that of the people, which is called "democracy," and there we have "Decrees of the commonalty" [Plebiscita]. There is also tyrannical government, which is altogether corrupt, which, therefore, has no corresponding law.

Finally, there is a form of government made up of all these, and which is the best: and in this respect we have law sanctioned by the "Lords and Commons," as stated by Isidore (Etym. v, 4, seqq.).

Fourthly, it belongs to the notion of human law to direct human actions. In this respect, according to the various matters of which the law treats, there are various kinds of laws, which are sometimes named after their authors: thus we have the "Lex Julia" about adultery, the "Lex Cornelia" concerning assassins, and so on, differentiated in this way, not on account of the authors, but on account of the matters to which they refer.

Reply to Objection 1: The law of nations is indeed, in some way, natural to man, in so far as he is a reasonable being, because it is derived from the natural law by way of a conclusion that is not very remote from its premises. Wherefore men easily agreed thereto. Nevertheless it is distinct from the natural law, especially it is distinct from the natural law which is common to all animals.

The Replies to the other Objections are evident from what has been said.

Chapter 11: Utilitarianism

Comprehension questions you should be able to answer after reading this chapter:

1. How do utilitarians (in general) determine what is morally right and morally wrong?

2. Who "counts" in the utilitarian cost-benefit analysis?

3. What is the "principle of utility?" What is the "greatest happiness principle?"

4. What is the difference between "act" utilitarianism and "rule" utilitarianism?

5. What is meant by the criticism of utilitarianism that it is too "artificial" and "unrealistic?" How might a utilitarian respond to this criticism?

6. What is meant by the criticism of utilitarianism that it allows, and even requires, "unjust" actions? How might a utilitarian respond?

7. What is meant by the criticism of utilitarianism that it is a "Swinish doctrine?" How does John Stuart Mill respond?

8. What is meant by the criticism of utilitarianism that it is too difficult to anticipate the consequences of our actions? How might a utilitarian respond?

At 8:46 a.m., on September 11th, 2001, American Airlines Flight 11 was intentionally crashed into the World Trade Center's North Tower. At 9:03 a.m., it was followed by United Airlines Flight 175. At 9:37 a.m., American Airlines Flight 77 was crashed into the Pentagon. United Airlines Flight 93 is believed to have been headed to either the Capitol Building or the White House, but it never reached its intended target. Passengers on Flight 93 resisted, and the plane crashed instead in a field near Shanksville, Pennsylvania at 10:03 a.m. Had the passengers not acted, and brought the plane down themselves, it is likely that the United States Air Force would have done it for them. Consider the following excerpt from an interview with (then) U.S. Vice-President Dick Cheney.

VICE PRES. CHENEY: Well, the--I suppose the toughest decision was this question of whether or not we would intercept incoming commercial aircraft.
"TIM RUSSERT: And you decided?
"VICE PRES. CHENEY: We decided to do it. We'd, in effect, put a flying combat air patrol up over the city; F-16s with an AWACS, which is an airborne radar system, and tanker support so they could stay up a long time...
"It doesn't do any good to put up a combat air patrol if you don't give them instructions to act, if, in fact, they feel it's appropriate.
"MR. RUSSERT: So if the United States government became aware that a

hijacked commercial airline[r] was destined for the White House or the Capitol,
we would take the plane down?
"VICE PRES. CHENEY: Yes. The president made the decision...that if the plane
would not divert...as a last resort, our pilots were authorized to take them out.
Now, people say, you know, that's a horrendous decision to make. Well, it is.
You've got an airplane full of American citizens, civilians, captured
by...terrorists, headed and are you going to, in fact, shoot it down, obviously, and
kill all those Americans on board?...
          -NBC, 'Meet the Press' 16 September 2001

The United States government was prepared to shoot down a commercial passenger jet, with 40 innocent civilians onboard. Why would the government be willing to make this decision? Why, for that matter, did the passengers on Flight 93 resist their hijackers, ultimately resulting in the premature crashing of their plane? The answer, in both cases, is quite possibly the same: "It's for the greater good."

That slogan captures the central idea of utilitarianism. Utilitarianism is usually associated with Jeremy Bentham (1748-1832), James Mill (1773-1836), and his son John Stuart Mill (1806-1873)—though early traces of utilitarian thought can be found in the writings of Epicurus (341 BCE-270 BCE).

Utilitarianism is an <u>objective</u> theory, which is to say that utilitarians believe that the morally right thing to do in a given situation is not merely a matter of opinion, but is a *fact*. What, specifically, will be *the* morally right thing to do brings us back to the appeal to "the greater good."

Although utilitarians will often differ with respect to the particulars of their theories, what they will all have in common is an emphasis on the consequences of our actions. For that reason, utilitarianism is one of several theories called "<u>consequentialist</u>." Utilitarianism is not the only consequentialist theory, but it is the most famous. Consequentialist theories are just what they sound like: they are theories emphasizing the consequences, the outcomes of our decisions and actions. In our everyday evaluation of actions, we will sometimes forgive someone when their actions produce undesirable consequences so long as their "heart is in the right place." Not so with utilitarians. *Intentions do not matter* (morally speaking). The only thing that matters when evaluating the moral goodness or badness of an action are the *consequences* of that action.

Although some utilitarians are interested in the satisfaction of preferences when considering "consequences," most utilitarians (including both Bentham and Mill) focus instead on "happiness." For such a simple word, happiness is notoriously difficult to define, and utilitarians have bickered over how best to understand "happiness" for centuries. For Bentham, the founder of modern utilitarian thought, happiness was to be understood in terms of pleasure, or at least the absence of pain. Unhappiness, then, would be understood in terms of pain.

With pleasure as our focus, the first formulation of utilitarianism is that the morally right thing to do will be whichever action produces, as a *consequence*, the most happiness (pleasure), or the least unhappiness (pain) for all involved. Bentham labeled this the "principle of utility."

The Principle of Utility

By the principle of utility is meant that principle which approves or disapproves of every action whatsoever, according to the tendency which it appears to have to augment or diminish the happiness of the party whose interest is in question: or, what is the same thing in other words, to promote or to oppose that happiness....

Mill provides a very similar principle, one that he calls the "greatest happiness principle."

The Greatest Happiness Principle

The creed which accepts as the foundation of morals utility, or the greatest happiness principle, holds that actions are right in proportion as they tend to promote happiness, wrong as they tend to produce the reverse of happiness. By 'happiness' is intended pleasure, and the absence of pain; by 'unhappiness,' pain, and the privation of pleasure.

One of the appeals of this approach is how intuitively powerful—even how obvious—is its basic emphasis on pleasure and pain. We don't need any argument to justify our aversion to pain and our inclinations towards pleasure. They just "are." I like pleasure. So do you. Why? I don't know. Maybe God made me that way. Maybe there's an evolutionary advantage in creatures acquiring sentience. Maybe pleasure and pain are "Nature's" way of guiding us with respect to actions to pursue or avoid.[155] Whatever the ultimate explanation happens to be, we all naturally pursue pleasure, and we all naturally avoid pain. What could be more basic, more fundamental, than the value judgments that pleasure is good and pain is bad? What could be more obvious? And, if so obvious and so universal, doesn't it make sense to think that our notion of "good" and "bad," morally speaking, would have something to do with pleasure and pain? Don't we recognize that it's "good" to promote pleasure/happiness, and "bad" to promote pain/unhappiness? Isn't there an element of pleasure or pain to be found in every act we label morally good or bad?

---

[155] Recall that Ayn Rand makes a point similar to this in our chapter on ethical egoism.

Exercise Break

Consider the following actions usually deemed morally wrong, or at least morally suspect. Identify how each is responsible for increasing the amount of pain/unhappiness in the world. Be creative, and don't restrict yourself to short-term thinking.

- Rape
- Child abuse
- Home invasion robbery
- Smoking crack cocaine
- Politicians "selling" their support to lobbyists
- Murder
- Fraud

If you actually performed the recommended exercise, you might have been surprised to see how easy it was to identify the "pain" associated with those examples. This is certainly one of the more powerful appeals of the utilitarian approach. It just seems *obvious* that we do, in fact, care about the amount of pleasure and pain not just in our own lives, but in the lives of others—indeed, in the world in general. Very often, when we condemn the actions of another (or our own actions), one of the first explanations we can offer for our condemnation involves pain.

"Stop! That *hurts*."

Most of the time, we treat that explanation as a morally sufficient explanation. If what you are doing is hurting someone, you should stop. If you don't, you're doing something morally bad.

There is room for some sophistication with this approach. For example, we recognize that actual physical pain is not the only sort of "pain" that matters.

"When you did that, it really hurt my feelings."

Usually, this sort of appeal doesn't suggest that actual physical pain resulted (though, sometimes powerful emotions do seem to produce a physical reaction in the body, including feelings of pain in the stomach, head, throat, or chest). Nevertheless, we have a concept of emotional pain that is similarly motivating. Embarrassment, a feeling of betrayal, shame, fear ... all of these, while not necessarily physically painful, are nevertheless feelings we prefer to avoid, and we describe them in terms of "hurt." Most utilitarians therefore include "emotional" pain in their considerations as well.

Another layer of sophistication that utilitarianism offers, and needs, is the recognition that we do not always categorically avoid painful experiences, nor do we invariably pursue pleasurable experiences. For example, I don't enjoy going to the dentist. It's usually an uncomfortable experience, and sometimes actually painful. But, I go anyway (at least twice each year). I have been told that shooting heroin is an intensely pleasurable experience, but I have no intention of pursuing that pleasure—

nor do most other people. So, we have two easy examples of avoiding pleasure and pursuing pain. Doesn't that contradict the basic values-assumptions behind utilitarianism? Not at all. Although going to the dentist can be painful, avoiding the dentist can be more so. I endure a little pain to avoid the greater pain of tooth decay and gum disease. We have our children inoculated against diseases even though the needles hurt them. Are we bad utilitarians? Sadists? No. We recognize that the tiny and fleeting prick of a needle is far less painful than polio. Why do we avoid the pleasure of heroin? Because we wish to avoid the greater pain that follows! Not only is heroin deadly and debilitating, but it is powerfully addictive. No one who has ever known an addict would ever claim that the use of heroin is, on balance and all things considered, a "pleasurable" activity.

What these examples and their analyses indicate is that utilitarian thought can be complicated. When calculating the consequences of our actions, we often have to look beyond the immediate experience and anticipate what the consequences will be in the future. Getting a polio vaccination might be slightly painful the moment one receives it, but it spares you from the threat of a far more painful disease later on. In receiving the shot, you are still pursuing the greater happiness.

The final layer of sophistication we'll consider, before getting into the actual application of this kind of theory, involves sentience. As you know by now, utilitarians focus on pleasure and pain. Pain is to be avoided, pleasure is to be pursued, generally speaking. It is good to promote pleasure, bad to promote pain. What's probably obvious to you is that human beings are not the only creatures capable of pleasure and pain. My cat feels pain. So do dogs, and monkeys, and buffalo, and sparrows, and cows, and lots of other creatures. Much evidence has been gathered demonstrating that mammals, birds, reptiles and amphibians, fish, and cephalopods (such as the octopus) all have central nervous systems, all have nociceptors ("pain receptors") connected to their central nervous system, and all exhibit response to damaging stimuli similar to that of human responses. Although there is less consensus among researchers, it's at least clear that even invertebrates such as lobsters have rudimentary motor responses in response to "noxious" stimulants (e.g., being dropped in boiling water!), though whether they possess a sophisticated enough nervous system for that response to be an indicator of "pain" remains subject to debate.

Debate aside, because a great many non-human creatures can clearly experience pleasure and pain, they "count" as far as utilitarianism is concerned. If pleasure is to be pursued, and pain is to be avoided, this is so for cats and cows as well as for you and me. To ignore this and to consider only human pain is arbitrary, irrational, and "speciesist" (a phrase popularized by the utilitarian Peter Singer, who intentionally wished to conjure associations with racism and sexism). Therefore, when a utilitarian considers consequences, and seeks to maximize happiness and minimize pain (sometimes referred to simply as maximizing "utility"), she will have to consider the pleasure and pain of *every creature* capable of pleasure and pain, human and non-human alike. What's more, no one counts "more" than anyone else in this calculation. My happiness is not more valuable simply because it's mine, nor is mine more valuable simply because I'm human. Everyone's happiness counts equally, all else being equal.[156]

This has been a lengthy introduction to utilitarianism! Let's see how it actually works, in application. There are two major types of utilitarian theories: act, and rule.

Act Utilitarianism

An "act utilitarian" is a utilitarian who believes that utility is/ought to be maximized by performing a "cost-benefit analysis" for each intended action on a case-by-case basis. That is, when trying to determine the right course of action, one ought to consider all the available options, weigh their "costs" (pains) and "benefits" (pleasures) for each sentient being involved, and select the option that produces the greatest overall "utility" (i.e., most overall pleasure or least overall pain). The goal is to bring about the "best" possible consequences, given the available options.

Bentham thought that our cost-benefit analysis should be informed by the following variables. When only one sentient being is to be effected, the utility calculation will consider each of the following with regard to pleasure and pain:

1. Intensity (how pleasurable or painful the experience will be)
2. Duration (how long the pleasure or pain will last)
3. Certainty/uncertainty (how confident we can be as to the actual experiencing of the pleasure or pain)
4. Propinquity/remoteness (how soon in time the pleasure or pain will be experienced)
5. Fecundity (the tendency of the experience to produce more of its kind— more pleasure or more pain)
6. Purity (the absence of its opposite—e.g., some pleasures are mixed with pain, while others produce only pleasure)

In the likely event that more than one creature will be affected, we add one more consideration (7): the extent (number affected). This just means that if five people are involved, we will have to consider how each of the five will be affected, pleasurably or painfully, when weighing our alternatives.

If we were to adopt Bentham's method, then whenever we find ourselves presented with a number of options, and interested in doing the morally right thing, we ought to consider each option, and calculate the pleasure and pain generated with respect to each of the variables above. After we have done so, we identify the option with the greatest overall utility (i.e., the greatest quantity of pleasure or least quantity of pain), compared to the alternatives, and this will show us the morally right thing to do. Lest we think ourselves finished, please note that Mill would add one more level of complexity to this process: "quality" of the pleasures involved.

For Mill, not all pleasures are equal, and "quantity" is not the only relevant measure of pleasure. There are the so-called "lower" pleasures, the pleasures we have in common with many other animals. Such pleasures include the pleasures of eating, drinking, sex, sleep, etc. There are also "higher" pleasures, such as creating and appreciating art, pursuing knowledge, games of skill, etc. "Higher" pleasures are

---

[156] Note that having a lesser capacity for pleasure by virtue of being a fish, for example, would mean that all else is *not* equal.

qualitatively superior to lower pleasures, and Mill believes that the mere intensity of a lower pleasure is not necessarily sufficient to make it more desirable than a less intense, but superior higher pleasure. Much has been written on the controversial nature of Mill's hierarchy, and whether or not he can actually justify that qualitative distinction. For our purposes, though, let's just assume that there is *something* legitimate about his appeal to quality, and make it our eighth variable. To recap what must be calculated in order to establish the morally right thing to do:

1. Intensity
2. Duration
3. Certainty
4. Propinquity
5. Fecundity
6. Purity
7. Extent
8. Quality

Honestly, I (personally) find this to be a hopeless and fruitless method—though you are certainly not required to agree with me on this point. Bentham was brilliant, and he was certainly articulating an authentic moral insight with what he offers, but a literal assignment of positive or negative values representing pain and pleasure (often referred to as "utils"—positive when pleasure, negative when pain), somehow modified with respect to duration, certainty, "propinquity," "fecundity," and "purity" is an abominable exercise—and a needless one. Several of the variables are painfully abstract ("purity?"), speculative at best ("certainty"), and potentially arbitrary ("intensity"—not to mention Mill's notoriously subjective "quality").

Rather than create an Excel spreadsheet with a formula in an effort to discern whether the morally right thing to do, for example, is to shoot down a hijacked passenger jet with 40 innocent passengers onboard, let's try some intuition and common sense.

Hijackers had set the precedent for what they were probably going to do with United Airlines Flight 93. Three other jets had already been flown into buildings that very morning, killing everyone onboard, and many at the target sites. There was good reason to believe that the 40 passengers were going to die anyway, as terrible as that would be to admit. Prior to September 11th, that would *not* have been the reasonable assumption to make. Organizations have been hijacking passenger jets for political purposes for over 40 years. In the vast majority of those cases, the planes are forced to land somewhere, and negotiations begin. The passengers are either freed after the demands are met (usually the release of some "political prisoners") or the jet is raided by police or military forces. On many occasions, the hijackers were slain, and a few passengers, crew, or police/military personnel often die as well, but most of the passengers end up free and relatively unharmed. Whether or not it was the right thing to do, it at least made sense to *consider* waiting and negotiating with the hijackers. After the first intentional crashes on 9-11, it was no longer safe to assume that the plane would land, and that it would be possible to free the passengers. What became safe for us to assume is that the jet was going to be used as a weapon, and flown into a high-profile target, killing even more people.

Assuming that to be so, it's not hard to see how the cost-benefit analysis would recommend shooting down the plane. The 40 passengers are presumed to be doomed, so their pain, as well as the pain of their friends and family members appears unavoidable. What does appear to be avoidable is additional death and misery. If the jet is shot down, at least no additional people will die—and perhaps future hijackers will have to consider that they will be unable to strike their intended targets since they will be shot down instead. Maybe this will deter similar hijackings in the future? Is anyone being made "happy?" Probably not. This is one of those examples where the utilitarian is looking merely to minimize unhappiness. It's a terrible dilemma, with no "good" outcome available. The best the utilitarian can hope for is the "least bad" consequence.

Notice how important it was to have a sense of history. Prior to 9-11, hijackers did not have a reputation for flying planes into buildings. Now, they do. As act utilitarians, our calculations have to adjust to reflect this. Twenty years ago, the best course of action might well have been to let the plane land, and then either negotiate or use a special forces team to raid the plane. Circumstances change. Perhaps the "shoot it down" approach only makes sense when the plane has been hijacked by members of al-Qu'aida. The simple point is this: an act utilitarian will make a determination of what will maximize happiness for all involved on a case-by-case basis. Sometimes, the right thing to do is to shoot the plane down. Other times, the right thing to do might be to negotiate. Sometimes, the right thing to do is to tell the truth. Other times, the right thing to do will be to tell a lie. Sometimes, it's wrong to steal. Other times, it might be the right thing to do. Although reliable patterns might emerge, what makes an act utilitarian an *act* utilitarian is that she performs the cost-benefit analysis for each individual situation, and recognizes that as the "input" changes, so too will the "output."

That act utilitarianism is sensitive to circumstances is seen by some to be an asset. However, the time it takes to perform such calculations on a case-by-case basis can be seen as a liability. Some are additionally concerned that subjectivity can easily creep into our calculations. Sometimes lying is wrong, other times, it's acceptable. How interesting that most of the time I conclude that it's acceptable is when *I* am the one doing the lying! Isn't it possible that we might "tip the scales" in our own favor when performing our calculations, inflating the value of our own happiness while underestimating that of others?

Rule Utilitarianism

To address these concerns, and others, some turn to "rule utilitarianism." Like act utilitarianism, rule utilitarianism emphasizes happiness, and maximizing utility. Where it differs is with regard to when and how these calculations are performed. Rule utilitarians believe that we best maximize utility by following rules which themselves maximize utility. That might sound complicated, but it's really quite simple. Far more often than not, killing innocent people causes more pain than pleasure. Therefore, human beings decided, a very long time ago, that there ought to be a rule against killing innocent people. You would find it very challenging to find a community anywhere in the world that does not forbid murder. Rather than have to figure things out on a case-by-case basis, rule utilitarians propose that we just follow rules such as "don't kill innocent people." It's possible that in rare, exceptional cases, it might actually maximize utility to kill an innocent person, but it's a very safe assumption that killing innocent people *usually* brings more pain than pleasure, and when it appears otherwise, there's a very good chance we're skewing our calculation to our own benefit anyway. The safe thing to do (morally speaking) is to refrain from murdering people. Theft, more often than not, inflicts more pain than pleasure. Therefore, we should follow the rule that says we shouldn't steal. So, too, with rape. So, too, with lying. And so on.

The "shortcut" provided by rule utilitarianism serves to address at least some of several well-known criticisms of utilitarianism in general. We'll now consider these criticisms, as well as how utilitarians have been known to respond.

Possible problem #1: Utilitarianism is too "artificial" and unrealistic

The basic concern behind this criticism is the claim that no one "calculates" like Bentham proposes. Morality is not a math problem, and often times we must make judgment calls with very little time in which to perform a complex calculation. Therefore, utilitarianism is an unrealistic approach to moral decision-making.

<u>Utilitarian possible response:</u>

Sometimes we *do* perform overt cost-benefit analyses. How many of you have ever listed (either mentally, or actually on paper, or on a spread sheet) the "pros" and "cons" of the options before you, and used that list to make your decision? Even if you rarely, if ever, do so according to eight specific variables Bentham offers, it's entirely possible that the notion of a cost-benefit analysis is not alien to you. Moreover, there's no reason why many of these calculations couldn't be "unconscious," or performed at an intuitive level "instantly." It does not, for example, require very much time to conclude that choking to death the guy who cuts in front of me in line does not maximize utility! That's "easy math," to say the least.... Besides, utilitarians need not be bound by Bentham's specific calculation method, and could instead adopt a much simpler, more intuitive, less quantitative approach to the cost-benefit analysis which, if adopted, side-steps much of this criticism.

Finally, with regard to the charge that we haven't enough time to calculate utility, the rule utilitarian (specifically) has a simple response. Mill says "there is ample time, namely, the whole past duration of the human species." What Mill means by this is that it's not as though humans have to figure out fresh each day what sorts of actions promote utility and which do not. Murder is reliably bad as far as utility is concerned. Humans figured out that whole "murder is bad" thing thousands of years ago. They already "did the math" for us. We no more have to rediscover the badness of murder than we have to rediscover the hotness of fire. Much of the time, the calculations have been done, and our answers are obvious, morally speaking. It is, for most of us, a rare thing when we encounter a true moral quandary, a situation in which it is truly unclear which course of action will promote the most happiness. In those situations, we might have to work out the problem ourselves, but most of the time, no time is needed.

Possible problem #2: Utilitarianism allows, and even demands (on occasion), what we would consider to be immoral actions.

Utilitarianism promotes the greatest good for the greatest number. It is undeniable that the individual's happiness might be outweighed, and even sacrificed, for the happiness of a greater number, or even the greater happiness of another individual. There is no shortage of "nightmare" scenarios and perverse hypothetical examples meant to illustrate that such reasoning can generate powerfully (seemingly) *immoral* outcomes. Consider the following (intentionally disturbing) examples:

- The tremendous suffering of a rape survivor is morally justifiable so long as it's a gang-rape, and a sufficient number of rapists participate such that their combined pleasure outweighs her pain.
- Executing members of that "new Christian cult" in the Roman Coliseum is morally justifiable so long as the pleasure stemming from the crowd's entertainment outweighs the suffering experienced by the martyrs.
- Framing an innocent homeless person for a crime is morally justifiable so long as the pleasure generated by the public's peace of mind outweighs his suffering.
- Killing a hospital patient (who happens to be listed as an organ donor) and fabricating the cause of death is morally justifiable given the number of lives saved and benefited by the organs now available for transplant.

This counter-intuitiveness triggers an "integrity objection," according to Bernard Williams.

> *It is absurd to demand of such a man, when the sums come in from the utility network which the projects of others have in part determined, that he should just step aside from his own project and decision and acknowledge the decision which utilitarian calculation requires. It is to alienate him in a real sense from his actions and the source of his action in his own convictions....It is thus, in the most literal sense an attack on his integrity.*

If utilitarianism really does allow—let alone recommend—such counter-intuitive outcomes, then to the extent such outcomes violate our moral sensibilities, utilitarianism seems suspect, as a moral theory.

<u>Utilitarian possible response:</u>

One quick and easy reply available to utilitarians is to point out that the critic begs the question in claiming that such outcomes would be immoral. How so? According to utilitarianism, the morally correct thing to do is whatever action will maximize happiness. If (outrageous as this might sound) a gang-rape really does maximize happiness (unlikely though this would be!), then, *by definition* it is the morally right thing to do. If a critic wants to claim that the action is nevertheless immoral, then the critic is clearly appealing to a standard other than maximizing utility. That's fine. It just means the critic is not a utilitarian, and is defining moral rightness and wrongness in some other way. In that case, the conflict is deep, involving fundamental premises concerning what establishes moral rightness and wrongness.

A more compelling response, however, is to once again appeal to rule utilitarianism. A rule utilitarian would likely claim that all four of the examples above are, in fact, examples of morally wrong actions. Why? Because it's likely that each of the four examples would violate a moral rule which tends to maximize utility. Rape does not maximize happiness, in general. That should go without saying. Not surprisingly, a rule forbidding rape would be adopted by rule utilitarians. Killing "outsiders" for entertainment purposes, in general, probably does much more harm than good to any society that does so. Framing innocent people? Imagine the harm done to the justice system, specifically the public's confidence in it, should such actions ever be revealed. Killing organ donors? I don't know about you, but I would cease to be an organ donor if I ever learned that such things were happening, and the damage done to the trust *necessary* for the medical community would be profound. In summary, rule utilitarians can claim that fantastic hypothetical scenarios are likely to be irrelevant, to the extent that they don't apply to rule utilitarianism.

Possible problem #3: Utilitarianism is a "swinish doctrine"

Some think there is something low and hedonistic about such an emphasis on pleasure and pain. Perhaps animals can and should be guided by such drives, but human beings are different. We're special. We're better. To the extent that utilitarianism urges us to follow our baser inclinations, it lowers us to the level of swine. Surely human beings can be, and ought to be, guided by nobler aspirations!

<u>Utilitarian possible response:</u>

This sort of criticism was well known to John Stuart Mill. He defends utilitarianism against these charges by first agreeing with the critic that human beings *are* different from non-human animals, and for that reason the sorts of activities that please us will *not* be identical to those that please swine.

> *Now it is an unquestionable fact that those who are equally acquainted with, and equally capable of appreciating and enjoying, both, do give a most marked preference to the manner of existence which employs their higher faculties. Few human creatures would consent to be changed into any of the lower animals, for a promise of the fullest allowance of a beast's pleasures; no intelligent human being would consent to be a fool, no instructed person would be an ignoramus, no person of feeling and conscience would be selfish and base, even though they should be persuaded that the fool, the dunce, or the rascal is better satisfied with his lot than they are with theirs. They would not resign what they possess more than he for the most complete satisfaction of all the desires which they have in common with him. If they ever fancy they would, it is only in cases of unhappiness so extreme, that to escape from it they would exchange their lot*

for almost any other, however undesirable in their own eyes. A being of higher faculties requires more to make him happy, is capable probably of more acute suffering, and certainly accessible to it at more points, than one of an inferior type; but in spite of these liabilities, he can never really wish to sink into what he feels to be a lower grade of existence. We may give what explanation we please of this unwillingness; ... but its most appropriate appellation is a sense of dignity, which all human beings possess in one form or other, and in some, though by no means in exact, proportion to their higher faculties, and which is so essential a part of the happiness of those in whom it is strong, that nothing which conflicts with it could be, otherwise than momentarily, an object of desire to them.... It is better to be a human being dissatisfied than a pig satisfied; better to be Socrates dissatisfied than a fool satisfied. And if the fool, or the pig, are of a different opinion, it is because they only know their own side of the question. The other party to the comparison knows both sides.

Recall Mill's distinguishing of higher and lower pleasures from earlier in this chapter. Granted, we share the capacity for lower pleasures with other animals, but, unlike them (presumably), we have a capacity for the higher pleasures as well—and the higher pleasures are qualitatively superior. Mill is confident that the vast majority of us recognize this as a fact, and would never pursue a life consisting solely in experiencing lower pleasures, or even a life consisting primarily in experiencing lower pleasures.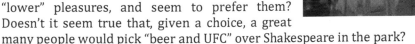

But what about *this* guy, and the many like him? Isn't it obvious that lots of people *do* pursue "lower" pleasures, and seem to prefer them? Doesn't it seem true that, given a choice, a great many people would pick "beer and UFC" over Shakespeare in the park?

Mill has an answer to that criticism as well.

It may be objected, that many who are capable of the higher pleasures, occasionally, under the influence of temptation, postpone them to the lower. But this is quite compatible with a full appreciation of the intrinsic superiority of the higher. Men often, from infirmity of character, make their election for the nearer good, though they know it to be the less valuable; and this no less when the choice is between two bodily pleasures, than when it is between bodily and mental. They pursue sensual indulgences to the injury of health, though perfectly aware that health is the greater good. It may be further objected, that many who begin with youthful enthusiasm for everything noble, as they advance in years sink into indolence and selfishness. But I do not believe that those who undergo this very common change, voluntarily choose the lower description of pleasures in preference to the higher. I believe that before they devote themselves exclusively to the one, they have already become incapable of the other. Capacity for the nobler feelings is in most natures a very tender plant, easily killed, not only by hostile influences, but by mere want of sustenance; and in the majority of young persons it speedily dies away if the occupations to which their position in life has devoted them, and the society into which it has thrown them, are not favourable to keeping that higher capacity in exercise. Men lose their high aspirations as they lose their intellectual tastes, because they have not time or opportunity for indulging them; and they addict themselves to inferior pleasures, not because they deliberately prefer them, but because they are either the only ones to which they have access, or the only ones which they are any longer capable of enjoying.

In other words, when people seem to prefer lower pleasures to higher (and not just sometimes, but in general) there is probably an explanation rooted in the life circumstances of those persons—and this is not hard to understand. Perhaps you work hard all day and come home tired and "brain-dead." You just don't feel like reading philosophy, so you opt for a cold beer and some relatively mindless diversion from the TV. Maybe you live in a neighborhood without a public theatre, or a library. Maybe the "higher" pleasures have never been modeled for you. Elitist though he might have been, Mill seems to be right about our general preference for activities that are mentally stimulating. In fact, psychological studies have suggested that extended passive pleasures actually become mildly *depressive* over time.[157]

Possible problem #4: It's too difficult to anticipate the consequences of our actions.

This criticism emerges from the fact that utilitarianism (like other consequentialist theories) focuses solely on the actual consequences of our actions. The problem is that it is often difficult to predict, with great accuracy, just what those consequences will be, and our actions often produce unintended consequences. This can produce bizarre and counter-intuitive judgments from utilitarians.

Suppose, for example that someone is a guest attending a party celebrating the 2nd birthday for the son of a wealthy business associate. The birthday boy begins to choke on a piece of food. The guest is the only one present who knows how to perform the Heimlich maneuver. Suppose also that the guest is a utilitarian. It seems like "easy math" to conclude that saving the boy's life will maximize happiness, so the guest does so, and the boy's life is saved. The year is 1959. The wealthy business associate is Muhammed Awad Bin Laden. The birthday boy is little Osama Bin Laden. By saving the boy's life, the guest has facilitated the unintended consequence of the formation of al-Qu'aida and the deadliest terrorist attack (as of the time of this writing) on U.S. soil. With all those things in mind, it seems clear that it was morally *wrong* to save the little boy from choking.

Some of you are probably thinking to yourself, "but that's not fair! How could the guest have possibly known that the two year old boy would grow up to be an international terrorist? It's unfair to expect the guest to work with information he couldn't possibly have."

---

[157]Interested readers should investigate the works of Mihaly Csikszentmihalyi, a psychologist famous for his research on happiness.

<u>Utilitarian possible response:</u>

You're correct. That *would* be unfair, and there are a couple ways we can process that. One way is to reject consequentialist theories entirely. Consequences lie in the future, and the future is not perfectly known to us. Perhaps it makes more sense to focus on something better known, such as intent. The guest "meant well," and maybe that's all that really matters. We'll explore a sophisticated approach similar to this in our later chapter on Kantianism.

However, while it's certainly possible to just reject utilitarianism as a result of this criticism, that's not the only response available—nor is it the most reasonable, I think. Why throw out the baby with the bath water? Rule utilitarianism is useful once more, in the face of this criticism. The plain fact is that most babies *don't* grow up to become the heads of terrorist organizations, nor do they become serial killers, or Hitler! For that matter, most don't grow up to cure cancer either. Most babies grow up to be *ordinary* people, sometimes doing good things, and sometimes doing bad things. It would be unreasonable (even irrational) to perceive a two year old choking to death, infer that he will become a terrorist one day, and for that reason decline to help. It makes much more sense to adhere to a "rule" that says something like "try to save the lives of other people, including children, when you're able to do so." In the vast majority of cases, this will maximize utility. Sometimes, it won't—but how could you possibly know which cases those will be? The best anyone can do, utilitarian or otherwise, is to choose the course of action which she has good reason to believe is the right thing to do. Mistakes are possible no matter which theory we adopt. Neither the fact of nor the fear of mistakes should get in the way of our trying to do the right thing, nor be used to call into question the very project of moral understanding in the first place.

Conclusion: What Utilitarians seem to be Getting Right

1. Morality *does* seem to be about reducing or preventing pain, and the promotion of happiness. Perhaps this is not the exclusive or even primary focus of morality, but the utilitarians certainly seem right to recognize the importance of pleasure and pain in our evaluation of moral claims.
2. Non-humans *do* seem to have some measure of moral value. Perhaps non-human animals are not equal to humans in many respects, and perhaps they are not even morally equal (subject to debate, of course), but any theory that simply ignores or denies the moral status of non-human animals seems insufficient, at best, and misguided, at worst.
3. Consequences *do* matter to us, morally speaking. Perhaps consequences are not the only things that matter, or are even the most important things, morally speaking, but results count. Someone can have all the best intentions, but if that person continually inflicts harm through ignorance, neglect, or just plain bad luck, we're unlikely to long uphold that person as a moral exemplar; nor are we likely to praise the person who "wants" to help others but just never gets around to actually doing so.

John Stuart Mill (20 May 1806 – 8 May 1873) was an important proponent of utilitarian philosophy and (classical) liberal political philosophy. Mill was a child genius, studying under both his father (James Mill) and Jeremy Bentham (the founder of modern utilitarianism). At the age of three, he was taught Greek, and, by eight, had read all of "Herodotus" (see the brief excerpt from Herodotus at the end of our chapter on Ethical Relativism for a sample of Herodotus—then imagine an eight year old child having read him in the original Greek). In the excerpt that follows, Mill begins with a basic statement of the "Greatest Happiness Principle," upon which he claims all moral calculations are based. Although happiness is the central motivator (and determiner) of moral action, Mill resists the criticism that utilitarianism is a "swinish" doctrine by emphasizing the qualitative distinction between "higher" and "lower" pleasures. After offering additional evidence in support of the actual use and acceptance of utilitarian cost-benefit analyses, Mill considers and attempts to respond to some of the more traditional criticisms of utilitarianism.

Utilitarianism
John Stuart Mill

Chapter 2 – What Utilitarianism Is

A passing remark is all that needs be given to the ignorant blunder of supposing that those who stand up for utility as the test of right and wrong, use the term in that restricted and merely colloquial sense in which utility is opposed to pleasure. An apology is due to the philosophical opponents of utilitarianism, for even the momentary appearance of confounding them with any one capable of so absurd a misconception; which is the more extraordinary, inasmuch as the contrary accusation, of referring everything to pleasure, and that too in its grossest form, is another of the common charges against utilitarianism: and, as has been pointedly remarked by an able writer, the same sort of persons, and often the very same persons, denounce the theory "as impracticably dry when the word utility precedes the word pleasure, and as too practically voluptuous when the word pleasure precedes the word utility." Those who know anything about the matter are aware that every writer, from Epicurus to Bentham, who maintained the theory of utility, meant by it, not something to be contradistinguished from pleasure, but pleasure itself, together with exemption from pain; and instead of opposing the useful to the agreeable or the ornamental, have always declared that the useful means these, among other things. Yet the common herd, including the herd of writers, not only in newspapers and periodicals, but in books of weight and pretension, are perpetually falling into this shallow mistake. Having caught up the word utilitarian, while knowing nothing whatever about it but its sound, they habitually express by it the rejection, or the neglect, of pleasure in some of its forms; of beauty, of ornament, or of amusement. Nor is the term thus ignorantly misapplied solely in disparagement, but occasionally in compliment; as though it implied superiority to frivolity and the mere pleasures of the moment. And this perverted use is the only one in which the word is popularly known, and the one from which the new generation are acquiring their sole notion of its meaning. Those who introduced the word, but who had for many years discontinued it as a distinctive appellation, may well feel themselves called upon to resume it, if by doing so they can hope to contribute anything towards rescuing it from this utter degradation.

The creed which accepts as the foundation of morals, Utility, or the Greatest Happiness Principle, holds that actions are right in proportion as they tend to promote happiness, wrong as they tend to produce the reverse of happiness. By happiness is intended pleasure, and the absence of pain; by unhappiness, pain, and the privation of pleasure. To give a clear view of the moral standard set up by the theory, much more requires to be said; in particular, what things it includes in the ideas of pain and pleasure; and to what extent this is left an open question. But these supplementary explanations do not affect the theory of life on which this theory of morality is grounded — namely, that pleasure, and freedom from pain, are the only things desirable as ends; and that all desirable things (which are as numerous in the utilitarian as in any other scheme) are desirable either for the pleasure inherent in themselves, or as means to the promotion of pleasure and the prevention of pain.

Now, such a theory of life excites in many minds, and among them in some of the most estimable in feeling and purpose, inveterate dislike. To suppose that life has (as they express it) no higher end than pleasure — no better and nobler object of desire and pursuit — they designate as utterly mean and grovelling; as a doctrine worthy only of swine, to whom the followers of Epicurus were, at a very early period, contemptuously likened; and modern holders of the doctrine are occasionally made the subject of equally polite comparisons by its German, French, and English assailants.

When thus attacked, the Epicureans have always answered, that it is not they, but their accusers, who represent human nature in a degrading light; since the accusation supposes human beings to be capable of no pleasures except those of which swine are capable. If this supposition were true, the charge could not be gainsaid, but would then be no longer an imputation; for if the sources of pleasure were precisely the same to human beings and to swine, the rule of life which is good enough for the one would be good enough for the other. The comparison of the Epicurean life to that of beasts is felt as degrading, precisely because a beast's pleasures do not satisfy a human being's conceptions of happiness. Human beings have faculties more elevated than the animal appetites, and when once made conscious of them, do not regard anything as happiness which does not include their gratification. I do not, indeed, consider the Epicureans to have been by any means faultless in drawing out their scheme of consequences from the utilitarian principle. To do this in any sufficient manner, many Stoic, as well as Christian elements require to be included. But there is no known Epicurean theory of life which does not assign to the pleasures of the intellect, of the feelings and imagination, and of the moral sentiments, a much higher value as pleasures than to those of mere sensation. It must be admitted, however, that utilitarian writers in general have placed the superiority of mental over bodily pleasures chiefly in the greater permanency, safety, uncostliness, etc., of the former — that is, in their circumstantial advantages rather than in their intrinsic nature. And on all these points utilitarians have fully proved their case; but they might have taken the other, and, as it may be called, higher ground, with entire consistency. It is quite compatible with the principle of utility to recognise the fact, that some kinds of pleasure are more desirable and more valuable than others. It would be absurd that while, in estimating all other things, quality is considered as well as quantity, the estimation of pleasures should be supposed to depend on quantity alone.

If I am asked, what I mean by difference of quality in pleasures, or what makes one pleasure more valuable than another, merely as a pleasure, except its being greater in amount, there is but one possible answer. Of two pleasures, if there be one to which all or almost all who have experience of both give a decided preference, irrespective of any feeling of moral obligation to prefer it, that is the more desirable pleasure. If one of the two is, by those who are competently acquainted with both, placed so far above the other that they prefer it, even though knowing it to be attended with a greater amount of discontent, and would not resign it for any quantity of the other pleasure which their nature is capable of, we are justified in ascribing to the preferred enjoyment a superiority in quality, so far outweighing quantity as to render it, in comparison, of small account.

Now it is an unquestionable fact that those who are equally acquainted with, and equally capable of appreciating and enjoying, both, do give a most marked preference to the manner of existence which employs their higher faculties. Few human creatures would consent to be changed into any of the lower animals, for a promise of the fullest allowance of a beast's pleasures; no intelligent human being would consent to be a fool, no instructed person would be an ignoramus, no person of feeling and conscience would be selfish and base, even though they should be persuaded that the fool, the dunce, or the rascal is better satisfied with his lot than they are with theirs. They would not resign what they possess more than he for the most complete satisfaction of all the desires which they have in common with him. If they ever fancy they would, it is only in cases of unhappiness so extreme, that to escape from it they would exchange their lot for almost any other, however undesirable in their own eyes. A being of higher faculties requires more to make him happy, is capable probably of more acute suffering, and certainly accessible to it at more points, than one of an inferior type; but in spite of these liabilities, he can never really wish to sink into what he feels to be a lower grade of existence. We may give what explanation we please of this unwillingness; we may attribute it to pride, a name which is given indiscriminately to some of the most and to some of the least estimable feelings of which mankind are capable: we may refer it to the love of liberty and personal independence, an appeal to which was with the Stoics one of the most effective means for the inculcation of it; to the love of power, or to the love of excitement, both of which do really enter into and contribute to it: but its most appropriate appellation is a sense of dignity, which all human beings possess in one form or other, and in some, though by no means in exact, proportion to their higher faculties, and which is so essential a part of the happiness of those in whom it is strong, that nothing which conflicts with it could be, otherwise than momentarily, an object of desire to them. Whoever supposes that this preference takes place at a sacrifice of happiness — that the superior being, in anything like equal circumstances, is not happier than the inferior — confounds the two very different ideas, of happiness, and content. It is indisputable that the being whose capacities of enjoyment are low, has the greatest chance of having them fully satisfied; and a highly endowed being will always feel that any happiness which he can look for, as the world is constituted, is imperfect. But he can learn to bear its imperfections, if they are at all bearable; and they will not make him envy the being who is indeed unconscious of the imperfections, but only because he feels not at all the good which those imperfections qualify. It is better to be a human being dissatisfied than a pig satisfied; better to be Socrates dissatisfied than a fool satisfied. And if the fool, or the pig, are of a different opinion, it is because they only know their own side of the question. The other party to the comparison knows both sides.

It may be objected, that many who are capable of the higher pleasures, occasionally, under the influence of temptation, postpone them to the lower. But this is quite compatible with a full appreciation of the intrinsic superiority of the higher. Men often, from infirmity of character, make their election for the nearer good, though they know it to be the less valuable; and this no less when the choice is between two bodily pleasures, than when it is between bodily and mental. They pursue sensual indulgences to the injury of health, though perfectly aware that health is the greater good. It may be further objected, that many who begin with youthful enthusiasm for everything noble, as they advance in years sink into indolence and selfishness. But I do not believe that those who undergo this very common change, voluntarily choose the lower description of pleasures in preference to the higher. I believe that before they devote themselves exclusively to the one, they have already become incapable of the other. Capacity for the nobler feelings is in most natures a very tender plant, easily killed, not only by hostile influences, but by mere want of sustenance; and in the majority of young persons it speedily dies away if the occupations to which their position in life has devoted them, and the society into which it has thrown them, are not favourable to keeping that higher capacity in exercise. Men lose their high aspirations as they lose their intellectual tastes, because they have not time or opportunity for indulging them; and they addict themselves to inferior pleasures, not because they deliberately prefer them, but because they are either the only ones to which they have access, or the only ones which they are any longer capable of enjoying. It may be questioned whether any one who has remained equally susceptible to both classes of pleasures, ever knowingly and calmly preferred the lower; though many, in all ages, have broken down in an ineffectual attempt to combine both.

From this verdict of the only competent judges, I apprehend there can be no appeal. On a question which is the best worth having of two pleasures, or which of two modes of existence is the most grateful to the feelings, apart from its moral attributes and from its consequences, the judgment of those who are qualified by knowledge of both, or, if they differ, that of the majority among them, must be admitted as final. And there needs be the less hesitation to accept this judgment respecting the quality of pleasures, since there is no other tribunal to be referred to even on the question of quantity. What means are there of determining which is the acutest of two pains, or the intensest of two pleasurable sensations, except the general suffrage of those who are familiar with both? Neither pains nor pleasures are homogeneous, and pain is always heterogeneous with pleasure. What is there to decide whether a particular pleasure is worth purchasing at the cost of a particular pain, except the feelings and judgment of the experienced? When, therefore, those feelings and judgment declare the pleasures derived from the higher faculties to be preferable in kind, apart from the question of intensity, to those of which the animal nature, disjoined from the higher faculties, is susceptible, they are entitled on this subject to the same regard.

I have dwelt on this point, as being a necessary part of a perfectly just conception of Utility or Happiness, considered as the directive rule of human conduct. But it is by no means an indispensable condition to the acceptance of the utilitarian standard; for that standard is not the agent's own greatest happiness, but the greatest amount of happiness altogether; and if it may possibly be doubted whether a noble character is always the happier for its nobleness, there can be no doubt that it makes other people happier, and that the world in general is immensely a gainer by it. Utilitarianism, therefore, could only attain its end by the general cultivation of nobleness of character, even if each individual were only benefited by the nobleness of others, and his own, so far as happiness is concerned, were a sheer deduction from the benefit. But the bare enunciation of such an absurdity as this last, renders refutation superfluous.

According to the Greatest Happiness Principle, as above explained, the ultimate end, with reference to and for the sake of which all other things are desirable (whether we are considering our own good or that of other people), is an existence exempt as far as possible from pain, and as rich as possible in enjoyments, both in point of quantity and quality; the test of quality, and the rule for measuring it against quantity, being the preference felt by those who in their opportunities of experience, to which must be added their habits of self-consciousness and self-observation, are best furnished with the means of comparison. This, being, according to the utilitarian opinion, the end of human action, is necessarily also the standard of morality; which may accordingly be defined, the rules and precepts for human conduct, by the observance of which an existence such as has been described might be, to the greatest extent possible, secured to all mankind; and not to them only, but, so far as the nature of things admits, to the whole sentient creation.

Against this doctrine, however, arises another class of objectors, who say that happiness, in any form, cannot be the rational purpose of human life and action; because, in the first place, it is unattainable: and they contemptuously ask, what right hast thou to be happy? a question which Mr Carlyle clenches by the addition, What right, a short time ago, hadst thou even to be? Next, they say, that men can do without happiness; that all noble human beings have felt this, and could not have become noble but by learning the lesson of Entsagen, or renunciation; which lesson, thoroughly learnt and submitted to, they affirm to be the beginning and necessary condition of all virtue.

The first of these objections would go to the root of the matter were it well founded; for if no happiness is to be had at all by human beings, the attainment of it cannot be the end of morality, or of any rational conduct. Though, even in that case, something might still be said for the utilitarian theory; since utility includes not solely the pursuit of happiness, but the prevention or mitigation of unhappiness; and if the former aim be chimerical, there will be all the greater scope and more imperative need for the latter, so long at least as mankind think fit to live, and do not take refuge in the simultaneous act of suicide recommended under certain conditions by Novalis. When, however, it is thus positively asserted to be impossible that human life should be happy, the assertion, if not something like a verbal quibble, is at least an exaggeration. If by happiness be meant a continuity of highly pleasurable excitement, it is evident enough that this is impossible. A state of exalted pleasure lasts only moments, or in some cases, and with some intermissions, hours or days, and is the occasional brilliant flash of enjoyment, not its permanent and steady flame. Of this the philosophers who have taught that happiness is the end of life were as fully aware as those who taunt them. The happiness which they meant was not a life of rapture; but moments of such, in an existence made up of few and transitory pains, many and various pleasures, with a decided predominance of the active over the passive, and having as the foundation of the whole, not to expect more from life than it is capable of bestowing. A life thus composed, to those who have been fortunate enough to obtain it, has always appeared worthy of the name of happiness. And such an existence is even now the lot of many, during some considerable portion of their lives. The present wretched education, and wretched social arrangements, are the only real hindrance to its being attainable by almost all.

The objectors perhaps may doubt whether human beings, if taught to consider happiness as the end of life, would be satisfied with such a moderate share of it. But great numbers of mankind have been satisfied with much less. The main constituents of a satisfied life appear to be two, either of which by itself is often found sufficient for the purpose: tranquillity, and excitement. With much tranquillity, many find that they can be content with very little pleasure: with much excitement, many can reconcile themselves to a considerable quantity of pain. There is assuredly no inherent impossibility in enabling even the mass of mankind to unite both; since the two are so far from being incompatible that they are in natural alliance, the prolongation of either being a preparation for, and exciting a wish for, the other. It is only those in whom indolence amounts to a vice, that do not desire excitement after an interval of repose: it is only those in whom the need of excitement is a disease, that feel the tranquillity which follows excitement dull and insipid, instead of pleasurable in direct proportion to the excitement which preceded it. When people who are tolerably fortunate in their outward lot do not find in life sufficient enjoyment to make it valuable to them, the cause generally is, caring for nobody but themselves. To those who have neither public nor private affections, the excitements of life are much curtailed, and in any case dwindle in value as the time approaches when all selfish interests must be terminated by death: while those who leave after them objects of personal affection, and especially those who have also cultivated a fellow-feeling with the collective interests of mankind, retain as lively an interest in life on the eve of death as in the vigour of youth and health. Next to selfishness, the principal cause which makes life unsatisfactory is want of mental cultivation. A cultivated mind — I do not mean that of a philosopher, but any mind to which the fountains of knowledge have been opened, and which has been taught, in any tolerable degree, to exercise its faculties — finds sources of inexhaustible interest in all that surrounds it; in the objects of nature, the achievements of art, the imaginations of poetry, the incidents of history, the ways of mankind, past and present, and their prospects in the future. It is possible, indeed, to become indifferent to all this, and that too without having exhausted a thousandth part of it; but only when one has had from the beginning no moral or human interest in these things, and has sought in them only the gratification of curiosity.

Now there is absolutely no reason in the nature of things why an amount of mental culture sufficient to give an intelligent interest in these objects of contemplation, should not be the inheritance of every one born in a civilised country. As little is there an inherent necessity that any human being should be a selfish egotist, devoid of every feeling or care but those which centre in his own miserable individuality. Something far superior to this is sufficiently common even now, to give ample earnest of what the human species may be made. Genuine private affections, and a sincere interest in the public good, are possible, though in unequal degrees, to every rightly brought up human being. In a world in which there is so much to interest, so much to enjoy, and so much also to correct and improve, every one who has this moderate amount of moral and intellectual requisites is capable of an existence which may be called enviable; and unless such a person, through bad laws, or subjection to the will of others, is denied the liberty to use the sources of happiness within his reach, he will not fail to find this enviable existence, if he escape the positive evils of life, the great sources of physical and mental suffering — such as indigence, disease, and the unkindness, worthlessness, or premature loss of objects of affection. The main stress of the problem lies, therefore, in the contest with these calamities, from which it is a rare good fortune entirely to escape; which, as things now are, cannot be obviated, and often cannot be in any material degree mitigated. Yet no one whose opinion deserves a moment's consideration can doubt that most of the great positive evils of the world are in themselves removable, and will, if human affairs continue to improve, be in the end reduced within narrow limits. Poverty, in any sense implying suffering, may be completely extinguished by the wisdom of society, combined with the good sense and providence of individuals. Even that most intractable of enemies, disease, may be indefinitely reduced in dimensions by good physical and moral education, and proper control of noxious influences; while the progress of science holds out a promise for the future of still more direct conquests over this detestable foe. And every advance in that direction relieves us from some, not only of the chances which cut short our own lives, but, what concerns us still more, which deprive us of those in whom our happiness is wrapt up. As for vicissitudes of fortune, and other disappointments connected with worldly circumstances, these are principally the effect either of gross imprudence, of ill-regulated desires, or of bad or imperfect social institutions. All the grand sources, in short, of human suffering are in a great degree, many of them almost entirely, conquerable by human care and effort; and though their removal is grievously slow — though a long succession of generations will perish in the breach before the conquest is completed, and this world becomes all that, if will and knowledge were not wanting, it might easily be made — yet every mind sufficiently intelligent and generous to bear a part, however small and unconspicuous, in the endeavour, will draw a noble enjoyment from the contest itself, which he would not for any bribe in the form of selfish indulgence consent to be without.

And this leads to the true estimation of what is said by the objectors concerning the possibility, and the obligation, of learning to do without happiness. Unquestionably it is possible to do without happiness; it is done involuntarily by nineteen-twentieths of mankind, even in those parts of our present world which are least deep in barbarism; and it often has to be done voluntarily by the hero or the martyr, for the sake of something which he prizes more than his individual happiness. But this something, what is it, unless the happiness of others, or some of the requisites of happiness? It is noble to be capable of resigning entirely one's own portion of happiness, or chances of it: but, after all, this self-sacrifice must be for some end; it is not its own end; and if we are told that its end is not happiness, but virtue, which is better than happiness, I ask, would the sacrifice be made if the hero or martyr did not believe that it would earn for others immunity from similar sacrifices? Would it be made if he thought that his renunciation of happiness for himself would produce no fruit for any of his fellow creatures, but to make their lot like his, and place them also in the condition of persons who have renounced happiness? All honour to those who can abnegate for themselves the personal enjoyment of life, when by such renunciation they contribute worthily to increase the amount of happiness in the world; but he who does it, or professes to do it, for any other purpose, is no more deserving of admiration than the ascetic mounted on his pillar. He may be an inspiriting proof of what men can do, but assuredly not an example of what they should.

Though it is only in a very imperfect state of the world's arrangements that any one can best serve the happiness of others by the absolute sacrifice of his own, yet so long as the world is in that imperfect state, I fully acknowledge that the readiness to make such a sacrifice is the highest virtue which can be found in man. I will add, that in this condition of the world, paradoxical as the assertion may be, the conscious ability to do without happiness gives the best prospect of realising such happiness as is attainable. For nothing except that consciousness can raise a person above the chances of life, by making him feel that, let fate and fortune do their worst, they have not power to subdue him: which, once felt, frees him from excess of anxiety concerning the evils of life, and enables him, like many a Stoic in the worst times of the Roman Empire, to cultivate in tranquillity the sources of satisfaction accessible to him, without concerning himself about the uncertainty of their duration, any more than about their inevitable end.

Meanwhile, let utilitarians never cease to claim the morality of self devotion as a possession which belongs by as good a right to them, as either to the Stoic or to the Transcendentalist. The utilitarian morality does recognise in human beings the power of sacrificing their own greatest good for the good of others. It only refuses to admit that the sacrifice is itself a good. A sacrifice which does not increase, or tend to increase, the sum total of happiness, it considers as wasted. The only self-renunciation which it applauds, is devotion to the happiness, or to some of the means of happiness, of others; either of mankind collectively, or of individuals within the limits imposed by the collective interests of mankind.

I must again repeat, what the assailants of utilitarianism seldom have the justice to acknowledge, that the happiness which forms the utilitarian standard of what is right in conduct, is not the agent's own happiness, but that of all concerned. As between his own happiness and that of others, utilitarianism requires him to be as strictly impartial as a disinterested and benevolent spectator. In the golden rule of Jesus of Nazareth, we read the complete spirit of the ethics of utility. To do as you would be done by, and to love your neighbour as yourself, constitute the ideal perfection of utilitarian morality. As the means of making the nearest approach to this ideal, utility would enjoin, first, that laws and social arrangements should place the happiness, or (as speaking practically it may be called) the interest, of every individual, as nearly as possible in harmony with the interest of the whole; and secondly, that education and opinion, which have so vast a power over human character, should so use that power as to establish in the mind of every individual an indissoluble association between his own happiness and the good of the whole;

especially between his own happiness and the practice of such modes of conduct, negative and positive, as regard for the universal happiness prescribes; so that not only he may be unable to conceive the possibility of happiness to himself, consistently with conduct opposed to the general good, but also that a direct impulse to promote the general good may be in every individual one of the habitual motives of action, and the sentiments connected therewith may fill a large and prominent place in every human being's sentient existence. If the impugners of the utilitarian morality represented it to their own minds in this its true character, I know not what recommendation possessed by any other morality they could possibly affirm to be wanting to it; what more beautiful or more exalted developments of human nature any other ethical system can be supposed to foster, or what springs of action, not accessible to the utilitarian, such systems rely on for giving effect to their mandates.

The objectors to utilitarianism cannot always be charged with representing it in a discreditable light. On the contrary, those among them who entertain anything like a just idea of its disinterested character, sometimes find fault with its standard as being too high for humanity. They say it is exacting too much to require that people shall always act from the inducement of promoting the general interests of society. But this is to mistake the very meaning of a standard of morals, and confound the rule of action with the motive of it. It is the business of ethics to tell us what are our duties, or by what test we may know them; but no system of ethics requires that the sole motive of all we do shall be a feeling of duty; on the contrary, ninety-nine hundredths of all our actions are done from other motives, and rightly so done, if the rule of duty does not condemn them. It is the more unjust to utilitarianism that this particular misapprehension should be made a ground of objection to it, inasmuch as utilitarian moralists have gone beyond almost all others in affirming that the motive has nothing to do with the morality of the action, though much with the worth of the agent. He who saves a fellow creature from drowning does what is morally right, whether his motive be duty, or the hope of being paid for his trouble; he who betrays the friend that trusts him, is guilty of a crime, even if his object be to serve another friend to whom he is under greater obligations.[2] But to speak only of actions done from the motive of duty, and in direct obedience to principle: it is a misapprehension of the utilitarian mode of thought, to conceive it as implying that people should fix their minds upon so wide a generality as the world, or society at large. The great majority of good actions are intended not for the benefit of the world, but for that of individuals, of which the good of the world is made up; and the thoughts of the most virtuous man need not on these occasions travel beyond the particular persons concerned, except so far as is necessary to assure himself that in benefiting them he is not violating the rights, that is, the legitimate and authorised expectations, of any one else. The multiplication of happiness is, according to the utilitarian ethics, the object of virtue: the occasions on which any person (except one in a thousand) has it in his power to do this on an extended scale, in other words to be a public benefactor, are but exceptional; and on these occasions alone is he called on to consider public utility; in every other case, private utility, the interest or happiness of some few persons, is all he has to attend to. Those alone the influence of whose actions extends to society in general, need concern themselves habitually about so large an object. In the case of abstinences indeed — of things which people forbear to do from moral considerations, though the consequences in the particular case might be beneficial — it would be unworthy of an intelligent agent not to be consciously aware that the action is of a class which, if practised generally, would be generally injurious, and that this is the ground of the obligation to abstain from it. The amount of regard for the public interest implied in this recognition, is no greater than is demanded by every system of morals, for they all enjoin to abstain from whatever is manifestly pernicious to society.

The same considerations dispose of another reproach against the doctrine of utility, founded on a still grosser misconception of the purpose of a standard of morality, and of the very meaning of the words right and wrong. It is often affirmed that utilitarianism renders men cold and unsympathising; that it chills their moral feelings towards individuals; that it makes them regard only the dry and hard consideration of the consequences of actions, not taking into their moral estimate the qualities from which those actions emanate. If the assertion means that they do not allow their judgment respecting the rightness or wrongness of an action to be influenced by their opinion of the qualities of the person who does it, this is a complaint not against utilitarianism, but against having any standard of morality at all; for certainly no known ethical standard decides an action to be good or bad because it is done by a good or a bad man, still less because done by an amiable, a brave, or a benevolent man, or the contrary. These considerations are relevant, not to the estimation of actions, but of persons; and there is nothing in the utilitarian theory inconsistent with the fact that there are other things which interest us in persons besides the rightness and wrongness of their actions. The Stoics, indeed, with the paradoxical misuse of language which was part of their system, and by which they strove to raise themselves above all concern about anything but virtue, were fond of saying that he who has that has everything; that he, and only he, is rich, is beautiful, is a king. But no claim of this description is made for the virtuous man by the utilitarian doctrine. Utilitarians are quite aware that there are other desirable possessions and qualities besides virtue, and are perfectly willing to allow to all of them their full worth. They are also aware that a right action does not necessarily indicate a virtuous character, and that actions which are blamable, often proceed from qualities entitled to praise. When this is apparent in any particular case, it modifies their estimation, not certainly of the act, but of the agent. I grant that they are, notwithstanding, of opinion, that in the long run the best proof of a good character is good actions; and resolutely refuse to consider any mental disposition as good, of which the predominant tendency is to produce bad conduct. This makes them unpopular with many people; but it is an unpopularity which they must share with every one who regards the distinction between right and wrong in a serious light; and the reproach is not one which a conscientious utilitarian need be anxious to repel.

If no more be meant by the objection than that many utilitarians look on the morality of actions, as measured by the utilitarian standard, with too exclusive a regard, and do not lay sufficient stress upon the other beauties of character which go towards making a human being lovable or admirable, this may be admitted. Utilitarians who have cultivated their moral feelings, but not their sympathies nor their artistic perceptions, do fall into this mistake; and so do all other moralists under the same conditions. What can be said in excuse for other moralists is equally available for them, namely, that, if there is to be any error, it is better that it should be on that side. As a matter of fact, we may affirm that among utilitarians as among adherents of other systems, there is every imaginable degree of rigidity and of laxity in the application of their standard: some are even puritanically rigorous, while others are as indulgent as can possibly be desired by sinner or by sentimentalist. But on the whole, a doctrine which brings prominently forward the interest that mankind have in the repression and prevention of conduct which violates the moral law, is likely to be inferior to no other in turning the sanctions of opinion against such violations. It is true, the question, What does violate the moral law? is one on which those who recognise different standards of morality are likely now and then to differ. But difference of opinion on moral questions was not first introduced into the world by utilitarianism, while that doctrine does supply, if not always an easy, at all events a tangible and intelligible mode of deciding such differences.

It may not be superfluous to notice a few more of the common misapprehensions of utilitarian ethics, even those which are so obvious and gross that it might appear impossible for any person of candour and intelligence to fall into them; since persons, even of considerable mental endowments, often give themselves so little trouble to understand the bearings of any opinion against which they entertain a prejudice, and men are in general so little conscious of this voluntary ignorance as a defect, that the vulgarest misunderstandings of ethical doctrines are continually met with in the deliberate writings of persons of the greatest pretensions both to high principle and to philosophy. We not uncommonly hear the doctrine of utility inveighed against as a godless doctrine. If it be necessary to say anything at all against so mere an assumption, we may say that the question depends upon what idea we have formed of the moral character of the Deity. If it be a true belief that God desires, above all things, the happiness of his creatures, and that this was his purpose in their creation, utility is not only not a godless doctrine, but more profoundly religious than any other. If it be meant that utilitarianism does not recognise the revealed will of God as the supreme law of morals, I answer, that a utilitarian who believes in the perfect goodness and wisdom of God, necessarily believes that whatever God has thought fit to reveal on the subject of morals, must fulfil the requirements of utility in a supreme degree. But others besides utilitarians have been of opinion that the Christian revelation was intended, and is fitted, to inform the hearts and minds of mankind with a spirit which should enable them to find for themselves what is right, and incline them to do it when found, rather than to tell them, except in a very general way, what it is; and that we need a doctrine of ethics, carefully followed out, to interpret to us the will of God. Whether this opinion is correct or not, it is superfluous here to discuss; since whatever aid religion, either natural or revealed, can afford to ethical investigation, is as open to the utilitarian moralist as to any other. He can use it as the testimony of God to the usefulness or hurtfulness of any given course of action, by as good a right as others can use it for the indication of a transcendental law, having no connection with usefulness or with happiness.

Again, Utility is often summarily stigmatised as an immoral doctrine by giving it the name of Expediency, and taking advantage of the popular use of that term to contrast it with Principle. But the Expedient, in the sense in which it is opposed to the Right, generally means that which is expedient for the particular interest of the agent himself; as when a minister sacrifices the interests of his country to keep himself in place. When it means anything better than this, it means that which is expedient for some immediate object, some temporary purpose, but which violates a rule whose observance is expedient in a much higher degree. The Expedient, in this sense, instead of being the same thing with the useful, is a branch of the hurtful. Thus, it would often be expedient, for the purpose of getting over some momentary embarrassment, or attaining some object immediately useful to ourselves or others, to tell a lie. But inasmuch as the cultivation in ourselves of a sensitive feeling on the subject of veracity, is one of the most useful, and the enfeeblement of that feeling one of the most hurtful, things to which our conduct can be instrumental; and inasmuch as any, even unintentional, deviation from truth, does that much towards weakening the trustworthiness of human assertion, which is not only the principal support of all present social well-being, but the insufficiency of which does more than any one thing that can be named to keep back civilisation, virtue, everything on which human happiness on the largest scale depends; we feel that the violation, for a present advantage, of a rule of such transcendent expediency, is not expedient, and that he who, for the sake of a convenience to himself or to some other individual, does what depends on him to deprive mankind of the good, and inflict upon them the evil, involved in the greater or less reliance which they can place in each other's word, acts the part of one of their worst enemies. Yet that even this rule, sacred as it is, admits of possible exceptions, is acknowledged by all moralists; the chief of which is when the withholding of some fact (as of information from a malefactor, or of bad news from a person dangerously ill) would save an individual (especially an individual other than oneself) from great and unmerited evil, and when the withholding can only be effected by denial. But in order that the exception may not extend itself beyond the need, and may have the least possible effect in weakening reliance on veracity, it ought to be recognised, and, if possible, its limits defined; and if the principle of utility is good for anything, it must be good for weighing these conflicting utilities against one another, and marking out the region within which one or the other preponderates.

Again, defenders of utility often find themselves called upon to reply to such objections as this — that there is not time, previous to action, for calculating and weighing the effects of any line of conduct on the general happiness. This is exactly as if any one were to say that it is impossible to guide our conduct by Christianity, because there is not time, on every occasion on which anything has to be done, to read through the Old and New Testaments. The answer to the objection is, that there has been ample time, namely, the whole past duration of the human species. During all that time, mankind have been learning by experience the tendencies of actions; on which experience all the prudence, as well as all the morality of life, are dependent. People talk as if the commencement of this course of experience had hitherto been put off, and as if, at the moment when some man feels tempted to meddle with the property or life of another, he had to begin considering for the first time whether murder and theft are injurious to human happiness. Even then I do not think that he would find the question very puzzling; but, at all events, the matter is now done to his hand. It is truly a whimsical supposition that, if mankind were agreed in considering utility to be the test of morality, they would remain without any agreement as to what is useful, and would take no measures for having their notions on the subject taught to the young, and enforced by law and opinion. There is no difficulty in proving any ethical standard whatever to work ill, if we suppose universal idiocy to be conjoined with it; but on any hypothesis short of that, mankind must by this time have acquired positive beliefs as to the effects of some actions on their happiness; and the beliefs which have thus come down are the rules of morality for the multitude, and for the philosopher until he has succeeded in finding better. That philosophers might easily do this, even now, on many subjects; that the received code of ethics is by no means of divine right; and that mankind have still much to learn as to the effects of actions on the general happiness, I admit, or rather, earnestly maintain. The corollaries from the principle of utility, like the precepts of every practical art, admit of indefinite improvement, and, in a progressive state of the human mind, their improvement is perpetually going on. But to consider the rules of morality as improvable, is one thing; to pass over the intermediate generalisations entirely, and endeavour to test each individual action directly by the first principle, is another. It is a strange notion that the acknowledgment of a first principle is inconsistent with the admission of secondary ones. To inform a traveller respecting the place of his ultimate destination, is not to forbid the use of landmarks and direction-posts on the way. The proposition that happiness is the end and aim of morality, does not mean that no road ought to be laid down to that goal, or that persons going thither should not be advised to take one direction rather than another. Men really ought to leave off talking a kind of nonsense on this subject, which they would neither talk nor listen to on other matters of practical concernment. Nobody argues that the art of navigation is not founded on astronomy, because sailors cannot wait to calculate the Nautical Almanack. Being rational creatures, they go to sea with it ready calculated; and all rational creatures go out upon the sea of life with their minds made up on the common questions of right and wrong, as well as on many of the far more difficult questions of wise and foolish. And this, as long as foresight is a human quality, it is to be presumed they will continue to do. Whatever we adopt as the fundamental principle of morality, we require subordinate principles to apply it by; the impossibility of doing without them, being common to all systems, can afford no argument against any one in particular; but gravely to argue as if no such secondary principles could be had, and as if mankind had remained till now, and always must remain, without drawing any general conclusions from the experience of human life, is as high a pitch, I think, as absurdity has ever reached in philosophical controversy.

The remainder of the stock arguments against utilitarianism mostly consist in laying to its charge the common infirmities of human nature, and the general difficulties which embarrass conscientious persons in shaping their course through life. We are told that a utilitarian will be apt to make his own particular case an exception to moral rules, and, when under temptation, will see a utility in the breach of a rule, greater than he will see in its observance. But is utility the only creed which is able to furnish us with excuses for evil doing, and means of cheating our own conscience? They are afforded in abundance by all doctrines which recognise as a fact in morals the existence of conflicting considerations; which all doctrines do, that have been believed by sane persons. It is not the fault of any creed, but of the complicated nature of human affairs, that rules of conduct cannot be so framed as to require no exceptions, and that hardly any kind of action can safely be laid down as either always obligatory or always condemnable. There is no ethical creed which does not temper the rigidity of its laws, by giving a certain latitude, under the moral responsibility of the agent, for accommodation to peculiarities of circumstances; and under every creed, at the opening thus made, self-deception and dishonest casuistry get in. There exists no moral system under which there do not arise unequivocal cases of conflicting obligation. These are the real difficulties, the knotty points both in the theory of ethics, and in the conscientious guidance of personal conduct. They are overcome practically, with greater or with less success, according to the intellect and virtue of the individual; but it can hardly be pretended that any one will be the less qualified for dealing with them, from possessing an ultimate standard to which conflicting rights and duties can be referred. If utility is the ultimate source of moral obligations, utility may be invoked to decide between them when their demands are incompatible. Though the application of the standard may be difficult, it is better than none at all: while in other systems, the moral laws all claiming independent authority, there is no common umpire entitled to interfere between them; their claims to precedence one over another rest on little better than sophistry, and unless determined, as they generally are, by the unacknowledged influence of considerations of utility, afford a free scope for the action of personal desires and partialities. We must remember that only in these cases of conflict between secondary principles is it requisite that first principles should be appealed to. There is no case of moral obligation in which some secondary principle is not involved; and if only one, there can seldom be any real doubt which one it is, in the mind of any person by whom the principle itself is recognized.

Chapter 12: Deontology (Kantianism)

> *Comprehension questions you should be able to answer after reading this chapter:*
>
> 1. What (in general) is the difference between "teleological" ethical theories and "deontological" ethical theories?
>
> 2. Why does Kant think we should be held accountable for our "will," but not for the consequences of our actions?
>
> 3. What is the difference between "acting from duty" and "acting in accordance with duty?"
>
> 4. What is a "maxim?" What are its parts?
>
> 5. What is the "categorical imperative?"
>
> 6. How do we "universalize" a maxim, and how do we assess whether an action is permitted, according to the categorical imperative?
>
> 7. What are "contradictions in conception," and "contradictions in will," and what is their connection to the categorical imperative?
>
> 8. What is the "practical imperative?" How do we assess whether an action is permitted, according to the practical imperative?
>
> 9. What is required for our actions to have "moral worth?"
>
> 10. Who "counts" (morally speaking), for Kant? What property/capacity must a being have in order to have moral status?

Utilitarianism, as you now know, is an example of a "consequentialist" theory. Another term for consequentialist theories is "teleological," from the Greek word "telos," translated as "end," or sometimes "goal." Consequentialist theories, such as utilitarianism, derive their basic orientation with respect to a particular "end" or "goal" (telos). In the case of utilitarianism, that "telos" is happiness. For a utilitarian, the "ends justify the means." That is, the good generated (happiness) morally justifies the particular acts that brought about that end.

Some people do not agree that the ends justify the means. Sometimes, for example, you might think that certain actions are just plain *wrong* no matter what good might be obtained from them. Perhaps you think a lie is always a lie, and therefore morally wrong, even if the lie would be told to spare someone's feelings. Perhaps you think it is always wrong to intentionally kill an innocent person, even if in so doing you can save the lives of even more innocent people.

Those who reject the notion that the "ends justify the means" often belong to another category of ethical theory known as "deontological," from the Greek word "deon"—which translates as "duty." Deontological theories claim that moral rightness and wrongness is not a function of any "end" sought or obtained. For that reason, such theories are fundamentally opposed to consequentialist theories.

There are several kinds of deontological theories, but the most well-known of them is the one developed by Immanuel Kant (1724–1804).

Kant is among the most famous, most influential, and most important philosophers of the Western tradition. He is also, I'm sad to say, among the most difficult to understand—and understanding is not facilitated by his notoriously difficult writing style. If it's any consolation, it's even worse in the original German....

I mention his difficulty not to discourage the reader, or to "poison the well," but to prepare you and to console you. Kant is worth studying, and he needs to be studied, but anyone who does so should be prepared to struggle with the text and not feel badly about the fact of that struggle.

Now that the intimidating prologue is behind us, what does Kant's theory actually claim?

To begin with, Kant's theory, like that of most deontological theories, centers on "agency." Briefly, this notion of agency involves the claims that we are free agents, responsive to reasons, capable of genuine free choice in response to those reasons, and therefore responsible for our actions. Genuine free will and personal responsibility is a necessary presupposition for Kant. That is, while he acknowledges that (strictly speaking) we can't *prove* that we have free will, we must act (indeed, we can't help but to act) on the *presupposition* that we are free. Also key to his approach is the appeal to reasons. Persons ("agents") seem to have the ability to make decisions based on Reason. Kant refers to this capacity as "practical reason."

Because we are responsible for our own actions (i.e., because we have free will), we are subject to moral evaluation. We are responsible only for that which is truly under our control. Strictly speaking, the consequences of our actions are *not* under our control. I can choose to perform CPR on someone whose heart has stopped, but it's not under my control whether or not I *succeed* in my efforts. The person might die anyway, despite my efforts. I can choose to tell the truth, but how that truth is received is not under my control. I can save a two year old child from choking to death, but it's not under my control whether he grows up to lead a terrorist organization. We ought to be subject to moral evaluation only with respect to those things for which we are genuinely responsible. Since "consequences" are things for which I am not responsible (or at least not *fully* responsible), I ought not to be morally evaluated on the basis of the consequences I produce. Instead, I ought to be evaluated with respect to my "will," with respect to what I "willed" by my actions. In common language we might state this in terms of whether my "heart was in the right place."

The following is a bizarre, but true story. When I was a graduate student, I was attending a logic class when one of my classmates had what appeared to be a seizure and fell from his chair, unresponsive. I'll call him Adam. There was a moment of confusion and uncertainty in which most of us did nothing but stare. One student, however, didn't hesitate at all before leaping into action. I'll call him Marc. Marc moved desks and people out of the way, placed his wallet in Adam's mouth (ostensibly to prevent him from biting or swallowing his own tongue), listened to his chest, announced that Adam wasn't breathing, and then immediately began to administer chest compressions in an effort to save his life. Others of us called for the campus police, and called "911." After the paramedics arrived, Marc went to the bathroom to splash some water on his face. I followed him and commended him for his quick thinking and heroic actions.

To shorten the story, Adam survived. To complicate the story, Marc did a lot of things "wrong." For one, you're not supposed to cram anything into the mouths of people having seizures. That's an outdated technique that no doctor recommends anymore, and it hasn't been recommended for a long time. Secondly, Adam hadn't actually stopped breathing. He had an epileptic seizure; nothing more. In the excitement and chaos of the moment, Marc had done a sloppy job checking for vital signs. Adam didn't need chest compressions. All he needed was a little bit of room and a few minutes to recover. By administering chest compressions, Marc bruised some of Adam's ribs, and could have done even more serious damage than that. From a strict consequentialist perspective, Marc screwed up. He actually did more harm than good, and therefore acted wrongly (though a rule utilitarian interpretation might be more generous and forgiving). Nevertheless, I maintain my praise for Marc, incompetence and all. I don't give him credit for being a skilled paramedic, but I did (and do) think his "heart was in the right place." His "will" was to save the life of someone he thought was dying, and I think that is praiseworthy. If you tend to agree, and think that what *really* matters with respect to moral evaluation is the intention of one's "will," then you just might be a Kantian.

When employing Kant's approach, we can engage in two levels of analysis: actions and intentions. The first level of analysis (action) establishes whether or not a particular action is *morally permissible*. The second level (intent) establishes whether or not the agent performed the action in a *morally praiseworthy manner*. What this suggests, of course, is that it's possible to do the right thing, but fail to do it in a morally praiseworthy manner. A couple of examples can help to illustrate this.

Kant believed that suicide is not morally permissible. Let's assume, for the sake of argument, that Kant was right about that. Killing myself would be wrong; not killing myself is right. At this very moment, I am acting rightly by virtue of the fact that I am not killing myself. That fact, by itself, is not sufficient to earn me any moral praise. Why? Because I *don't want* to kill myself! I have a natural inclination to maintain my life, as do nearly all persons. I like my life. I'm happy. I have no desire to die. I don't think I deserve any praise for not killing myself. Honestly, it's effortless. It's likely that the reason I maintain my life is what Kant calls "self-love." That is, I'm not maintaining my life because I recognize that it is my moral duty, but because it pleases me to do so. Contrast this with someone who actually wants to die, someone who has come to the tragic conclusion that life is no longer worth living. Now imagine that person contemplating suicide, but choosing to maintain her life simple because she recognizes that it is what morality requires of her, because it is her moral duty. *That* person has not only done the right thing, but for the right reason: moral duty.

As another example, consider honest business practices. Kant believed that shopkeepers were morally obligated to treat their customers honestly and fairly. We'll see why later. So, let's imagine two shopkeepers, Anna and Marie—both of whom manage auto shops that specialize in oil changes. Anna and Marie both treat their customers with honesty. They charge the same prices to everyone. They don't lie about the conditions of their customers' cars in order to sell extra repairs and services. Both have concluded that "honesty is the best policy." According to Kant, both are doing the right thing. Anna, however, has chosen the path of honesty for the sake of prudence. She realizes that if she gets caught cheating her customers (say, by an undercover reporter), then her reputation will be ruined, she'll lose customers, and her business will suffer greatly. The risks are too great, so she decides to play it safe. She's honest with her customers, but not out of any respect for the requirements of morality. In fact, it's reasonable to assume that if she thought she *could* get away with it, she would try, since fear of getting caught is what's determining her decision thus far.

Anna is doing the right thing, but for the wrong reason. She is *imitating* the behavior of a morally praiseworthy person, but is not herself praiseworthy—at least not with respect to her business practices. Marie, on the other hand, treats her customers with honesty because she recognizes that it's simply the right thing to do. Even if she thought she could get away with a little fraud, she wouldn't even try. It would be wrong. Period. Marie is doing the right thing, for the right reason. Good for her.

Kant provides some specific vocabulary to help us distinguish Anna's behavior from Marie's. Marie is "<u>acting from duty</u>." We act from duty when we do the right thing (what is required of us, or what is permissible) *because* it's the right thing to do. We "<u>act in accordance with duty</u>" when we do the right thing, but for any *other* reason. Anna has acted "in accordance with duty" because she was motivated by prudence, rather than duty. She has obeyed the moral law (as Kant would say), but not out of respect for the moral law. It's easy to see why merely acting in accordance with duty is not, by itself, sufficient to qualify the agent for any moral praise. Consider the following examples, all of which involve someone having done "the right thing." What do *you* think about their reasons for doing the right thing?

- "Of course I've never raped anyone. It would be just my luck that I'd be the one who actually gets reported and ends up in jail. No thanks."
- "Yes, I did make a sizable donation to that charity. I got a sweet tax write-off because of it!"
- "Why did I tell the truth? I'm a terrible liar. I always get caught when I try to lie, so why bother trying?"

For each of the examples above, imagine what would happen if their reasons for doing the right thing no longer applied. If they thought they would *not* get reported for the rape and go to jail, or if there were no tax benefit from charitable giving, or that the lie would never be exposed? Presumably, there would be rape, lying, and no charitable giving. Someone who refrains from rape simply out of fear of going to jail is technically "doing the right thing," but is hardly a candidate for our moral admiration!

Please note that acting "in accordance with duty," while not morally good, is not morally *bad* either. Instead, think of it as morally neutral. It would be silly to say that I have acted morally badly if I give to a charitable donation for the sake of a tax benefit, but it might make sense for you to refrain from showering me with praise, considering my reason.

So far, Kant has given us some vocabulary for understanding motivation, and has claimed that with regard to intent, only some people (sometimes) are worthy of moral praise. That's one level of analysis. What about the other level? It's all well and good to evaluate someone's reasons for doing the right thing, but it might seem even more important to identify "the right thing" in the first place. Kant gives us a tool to determine that as well, to determine just what our moral duties are.

Kant believes we can identify our moral duties, as dictated by Reason itself, by means of what he calls "the categorical imperative."

The categorical imperative: "act only on those maxims which you could at the same time will to be a universal law."

You should memorize that. Seriously. It's easy enough to memorize, as it's only one short statement. It's more challenging to actually understand it, and how to use it. Let's break it down into its several key elements.

First, "act." Obviously, this refers to our actions. No problem so far, I hope. Next, "maxims." "Maxim" is a word rarely used anymore except when discussing Kant. A "maxim" is a principle of conduct, an action-guiding principle, a subjective rule of action. In loose, everyday usage "honesty is the best policy" could be an example of someone's maxim if it serves to guide that person's behavior. For Kantian purposes, a maxim will be a little more demanding and complicated. A maxim is composed of several parts (each of which will get more explanation later):

- The proposed action
- The context
- The reason why.

Finally, "universal law." That's just what it sounds like: a law applying equally to all people. The categorical imperative makes a *lot* more sense once one has worked through an example, so consider the following.

Kant's most famous example involves the "lying promise." Imagine that I'm out with my friend Omar, and I spot a fancy new "smart phone" that I'd like to have. Unfortunately for me, I have no cash, and my credit cards are already at their limit. I turn to Omar and say, "Omar, would you do me a favor? I'm short on money right now, but I really want that phone. Would you buy it for me? I'll pay you back as soon as I have the money."

What Omar doesn't know is that I'm lying to him. I have no intention of paying him back. I intend to enjoy the new phone, and continue to make excuses, ignore his calls, and change the subject, etc. — all in an effort to never pay him back. Is that morally acceptable? Presumably not! But why? A utilitarian would have to offer an explanation in terms of maximizing happiness, but that sort of thing is not Kant's focus. Instead, he would have us apply the "categorical imperative" to my maxim in that example, and see what happens.

Recall the parts of any maxim: the proposed action, the context, and the reason. What's my proposed action? Lying. Specifically, I'm proposing to make a false promise to repay a loan. What's the context? When I need money, or perhaps when I would rather not pay for the item myself—whether or not I can afford it. What's the reason? Self-benefit, of course. I get the phone without paying for it!

Now, let's take those elements and construct our maxim. Remember, a maxim is a principle of conduct, so we need to make it sound like the sort of thing that could inform and guide my behavior, in general. The maxim will look something like this:

for self-benefit (reason), when I need money (context), I will make a false promise to repay a loan (action). We can take out those parenthetical reminders and we end up with the following maxim:

"For self-benefit, when I need money I will make a false promise to repay a loan."

The categorical imperative is a way for us to test our maxims. According to the categorical imperative (hereafter referred to as the CI), you (we, I, everyone) should "act only on those maxims which you could at the same time will to be a universal law." That means that I should only act on my maxim if I could will it as a universal law. What happens if I transform that maxim to make it universal? It's easy enough to do. Just substitute every particular term in the maxim for a suitable "universal" one. The universal version of my maxim would be the following: "For self-benefit, when *anyone* needs money, that person will make a false promise to repay a loan."

My maxim has now become a universal law. The behavior-guiding principle I have proposed will now guide *everyone's* behavior. Once we have universalized our maxim, we are to check for "contradictions." If a contradiction occurs, the maxim fails the test of the CI, the "universalization test." There are two kinds of contradictions that might arise.

1. Contradiction in will
2. Contradiction in conception

We'll start with the contradiction in will, since it's the easiest to understand. A contradiction in will occurs when we wouldn't *will* for the maxim to become a universal law, or, to put it differently, if we wouldn't want everyone else to be guided by the same principle that we're employing. In the case of the lying promise, it's easy to see how this generates a contradiction in will. I sure wouldn't want Omar to do the same thing to me! Nor would I want anyone else to do that to me, for that matter. I wouldn't want someone to cheat my mother or father like that, nor any of my friends.

This notion of a "contradiction in will" highlights the implicit inconsistency and downright hypocrisy that occurs with immoral behavior. Thieves don't want everyone else to steal, and they certainly don't want their own stuff stolen. Rapists don't want to be raped. Liars don't like it when other people lie to them, and cheaters don't appreciate it when they get cheated. In each case, the proposed thief, rapist, liar, or cheat is wanting to make an exception for himself. "*Everyone else* should play by the rules, but I get to break them. I'm special...." From Kant's perspective, no one is "special" in the sense that the rules of morality don't apply to them. All persons possess Reason. All persons possess free will (presumably). We're all subject to the same universal moral law.

At this point, some of you might be thinking that the CI sounds a little bit like the Golden Rule. Granted, the CI is wordier and less elegant than "do unto others as you would have them do unto you," but they seem to be thematically similar. A maxim involving a lying promise generates a contradiction in will. I wouldn't want everyone else to be guided by that same maxim. According to the Golden Rule, I shouldn't lie to Omar if I wouldn't want someone else to lie to me. Somewhat similar. Although one of my good friends and colleagues (Scott, if you're reading this, that means you) doesn't like it when I compare the CI to the Golden Rule, I think the analogy can be helpful so long as we don't take it too far. If it somehow helps you to think that the CI is *sort of* like the Golden Rule, then so be it.[158]

Contradictions in will are usually pretty easy to identify. I wouldn't want *everyone* to kill in anger. I wouldn't want *everyone* to refuse to pay their taxes. I wouldn't want *everyone* to cheat their way through school. I wouldn't want *everyone* to steal, or lie, or rape, etc. What about that other kind of contradiction, the "contradiction in conception?"

A contradiction in conception is a bit more abstract, and a bit harder to understand, but it occurs when we literally can't even *conceive* how the maxim could be universalized. Somehow, if *everyone* were to adopt that maxim, something just wouldn't make sense anymore. If a contradiction in conception occurs, you should be saying to yourself, "Wait. That maxim can't be universalized. It just wouldn't work anymore."

Let's reconsider our lying promise. The universalized version of that maxim is that *everyone* will make lying promises to repay loans. This is what *everyone* does. I do it. You do it. Omar does it. Why would Omar provide me the loan when he knows very well I'm not going to repay it? After all, *no one* repays their loans! Neither does he, or would he. If everyone were guided by that maxim, the institution of lending would cease to exist. No one would provide loans because everyone would know they wouldn't get paid back. Only if defaulting on a loan is the exception, rather than the rule, can lending take place. What this means is that my proposed action would no longer be effective, if my maxim were universalized. I wouldn't be able to get the loan from Omar. My plan just wouldn't "work."

Contradictions in conception are less common than contradictions in will, but additional examples are abundant. Not only does slavery generate a contradiction in will (*I* wouldn't want to be a slave!), it also generates a contradiction in conception. Imagine a world in which everyone has slaves. *Everyone.* That would mean that slaves have slaves. How would that even work? Rather obviously, slavery only works when some people are slaves, and other people are not. Slavery is not something that *can* be universalized (i.e., it generates a contradiction in conception), nor is it something that we would *want* to be universalized (i.e., it generates a contradiction in will). It shouldn't surprise us to discover that Kant's system concludes that slavery is not morally permissible.

You should be aware that contradictions in conception indicate what are called "perfect" duties, whereas contradictions in will indicate "imperfect duties." The vocabulary is odd, as "imperfect" suggests something "lesser"—and that is only true in a very limited sense. In brief, "perfect duties" are those that we are obliged always to fulfill, without exception or sensitivity to context. We are always to refrain from enslaving others, always to refrain from lying, from murder, etc. "Imperfect duties"

---

[158] In fairness, there *are* differences between the CI and the Golden Rule. The Golden Rule is more vulnerable to idiosyncratic desires. If we take literally the principle that we should only do to others what we would have them do to us, what would that mean in the case of a masochist? If I'm a masochist, and would be fine with you abusing me, does that mean it's OK for me to now abuse you? Since the CI requires context (e.g., "when I desire to be abused"), it seems the CI would forbid the masochist from abusing unwilling persons while certain interpretations of the GR might allow it. That being said, there remains a similar *theme* in both the CI and GR.

are also morally binding on us, but impose duties which are not as "strong" as perfect duties. As such, fulfilling imperfect duties warrants praise, but failing to fulfill them makes us less liable for blame. Another difference is that imperfect duties could not possibly be fulfilled at all times, unlike, for example, our "perfect duty" not to lie. It's entirely possible for me to always refrain from lying. All I have to do is tell only the truth, or even merely never say anything at all! One of Kant's examples of an *imperfect* duty is cultivating our own talents (as opposed to rotting away as a couch potato). I can imagine a world in which everyone is a lazy slob. The world would be very different of course, but it is conceivable. It is not desirable, however. No one would truly wish to live in a world in which everyone wasted their potential, and never developed their physical or mental talents. Since I can conceive it, but not will it, it generates only a contradiction in will, and that indicates an "imperfect duty." Accordingly, I *should* cultivate my own talents, and do things that are mentally and physically stimulating and nurturing. I can't do that every minute of the day, though. I have to sleep a few hours every day, and even the most dedicated pursuit of one's talents will be interrupted by the performance of *other* duties, from time to time. Moreover, the fulfillment of an imperfect duty is always a process, and is never completed. What would qualify me as being "finished" with the project of cultivating my talents? In this way as well, imperfect duties are less subject to blame. Just because I'm not cultivating my talents at this very moment doesn't mean I should be criticized for a moral failing. After all, I'm not required to do so every moment of every day. On the other hand, criticism with regard to perfect duties is usually pretty obvious and immediate. If I tell you a lie, I violated a perfect duty right then and there. Period. Shame on me.

Keep in mind that a maxim doesn't have to generate both kinds of contradictions in order to "fail" the test of the CI. If either contradiction is generated, it fails—but oftentimes (though not always) a maxim that generates one type contradiction will also generate the other. I couldn't will a world in which everyone kept slaves, but this doesn't merely indicate an imperfect duty. In addition, I can't even *conceive* of a world in which slavery was universalized, and that indicates a perfect duty to refrain from enslaving people. I am subject to that obligation at all times, without exception.

Exercise Break

To practice your understanding of the CI, and your ability to apply it, try to figure out how a Kantian would evaluate something like identity theft. For this example, assume that we're talking about someone stealing another person's identity for financial gain (e.g., credit card theft, forging checks, etc.).

The first thing you'll want to do is to provide the maxim. A sample answer is provided at the end of this chapter. Your answer doesn't need to be identical, but it should be pretty close, and it should express roughly the same ideas. To help you out, remember the three parts of the maxim:

1. Proposed action
2. Context
3. Reason

Now, write out the maxim (using all three parts).

Once you've come up with the maxim, "universalize" it so you can apply the CI. Just change any words like "I" or "he" to words like "everyone" or "all persons." Once you have a "universalized" version of the maxim, think about it and check for contradictions. Does it generate a contradiction in will? Would you not want that maxim to be a universal law? Does it generate a contradiction in conception? Does it even make sense that it could be a universal law?

Assuming you actually took that exercise break, you've now had some practice generating and testing maxims, and you know that if a maxim fails the test of the CI, it reveals a morally impermissible action. If it passes, if no contradictions are generated, the action is morally permissible. If you thought your work was done, you're only about half right.

Kant gives us another way to test for moral permissibility. Technically, it's just another formulation of the CI, but it's different enough that it deserves its own name: the "practical imperative" (hereafter, the PI).

The Practical Imperative: always treat self and others as an end, and never as a mere means to an end.

The good news is that the PI is simpler. No maxims to generate and universalize. No contradictions to identify. The downside is that it's a bit vaguer, but I prefer it over the CI nevertheless.

In my opinion, if there is one word that captures the essence of the PI that word is "respect." We all know what it feels like to be disrespected. Sometimes, disrespect comes in the form of open, cruel insult, but other times disrespect is something much more passive. We feel disrespected when we are ignored. We feel disrespected when people don't "see" us. We feel disrespected when we are treated as if we don't count, as if we're not persons, as though we had no minds, or lives, or dreams of our own. We feel disrespected when others treat us as if we were an object rather than a subject, a thing rather than a person of moral worth.

Another expression that illuminates the PI is "using" someone. We don't like it when we feel that we have been "used." It makes us feel like an object, like we've been disrespected. The PI commands us not to "use" people. I fail to treat you as an "end" when I instead treat you as a mere obstacle to be dealt with, or a tool to be used. I respect your personhood, on the other hand, when I recognize you for what you are: a person, capable of Reason, and a bearer of moral worth.

Notice a few key words in the PI. For one, we are required to treat *self and* others as an end. This recognizes the fact that we can disrespect ourselves as well as others. We have an obligation to treat others with respect, but also to regard ourselves as persons of dignity and worth as well.

The second key term is "mere." It is impossible to avoid treating others as a means to an end. We do so every day, so long as we have interacted with other people. The people who work in stores I visit are a means to my acquiring certain products or services. The guy at the auto repair shop is a means to my car being repaired. My students are a means to my getting paid my salary. I am a means to your getting credit for a philosophy course, or for acquiring information about philosophy in general. Interacting with other people is useful. There's a reason why humans form communities! If benefiting from another person is all it takes for an action to be immoral, than all of us would be acting immorally all of the time with almost everything we did. That's clearly not what the PI is talking about. The problem isn't when someone is a means to our ends, but when they are a *mere* means to our ends.

My first job was bussing tables at a restaurant. The worst thing about that job was the customers. Some people were fine, most were indifferent, but some were awful. Customers would literally snap their fingers at me as I hurried by, or would bark commands at me without even making eye contact. For some of those customers, I might as well have been a robot. I certainly wouldn't expect them to pause, ask me about my day, inquire about my goals for the future, and then politely request some more water—but I did expect a tiny bit of respect, the merest acknowledgment that I was a human being just like they were. It's not always easy to recognize when we are treating others (or ourselves) as mere means to an end, but I think we all have at least a rough sense of what it means to respect others, and what it means to discount them.

Although there is no formula or process analogous to that employed with the CI, there are a few things we can think about when trying to determine if we are abiding by the PI. As guidelines, we treat others as an "end" when we:

1. Make sure our interactions with them are voluntary.
2. Make sure our interactions with them are mutually beneficial, or at least just and fair.
3. Make sure to take account of their needs, desires, and interests.

If someone is not a willing participant in our interaction, there's a pretty good chance I'm using him as a mere means to an end. Victimization of all kinds fits this description.

If I'm the only person benefiting from the interaction, that should give me reason to pause and consider the morality of what I'm doing. It doesn't necessarily mean I'm doing something morally wrong, but it should raise some suspicion. Again, victimization provides easy examples of interactions where only one person benefits. Of course, it's possible that something can be morally permissible even if not every party to the interaction benefits—so long as what transpires is just and fair. Criminal punishment is an example of such an interaction. It's hard to argue that the criminal being punished is "benefiting" from his interaction with the judge, or the prison guard. However, so long as the person is actually guilty, received a fair criminal process, and is being subject to a just punishment, we consider the interaction morally permissible anyway.

Finally (and this is admittedly vague), we are advised to take into account the needs, desires, and interests of the other party. If it's "all about me," I should be concerned that I might be violating the PI.

Let's reconsider our earlier example of the lying promise using the PI instead of the CI. We don't have to identify any maxim, but we do no need to recall what's going on: I'm planning to lie to my friend in order to secure a loan that I'll never repay. Am I treating myself and Omar as ends, or as mere means to an end? Let's consider our three guidelines.

1. Make sure our interactions with them are voluntary.

Is the interaction voluntary? Not really, no. You might think that Omar is voluntarily giving me the money, but remember that *he* thinks it's a loan, whereas *I* know it's a "gift." He's not fully informed of what's going on—and that's on purpose! It's quite a different thing to ask for a gift than for a loan.

2. Make sure our interactions with them are mutually beneficial, or at least just and fair.

Is the interaction mutually beneficial? No way. I gain all the benefit, and leave my friend Omar with the bill. Literally. Is it at least just and fair? Hardly! The interaction is based on a lie and a planned betrayal of trust.

3. Make sure to take account of their needs, desires, and interests.

Am I taking into account Omar's needs, desires, and interests? Not unless he's a rare person who loves to be taken advantage of. It's pretty obvious that the only person whose interests I'm considering is my own.

The "lying promise" fails the test of the PI, as well as the CI—and that is exactly what *should* happen. Kant gives us two different "tests," but *both* should provide the same answer. If you apply the CI and conclude that something is morally permissible, but conclude that it's "OK" when using the PI, you've done something wrong. If an action "passes" one test, it should pass the other, and if it fails one, it should fail both. Must you use both tests? Only if required to do so on an ethics exam, perhaps. In "real life," if you are motivated to use Kantian methods to evaluate the morality of an action you should use whichever of the two (CI or PI) you understand best and/or prefer. If you're really motivated, you should apply both just to be extra confident in your evaluation.

Let's review what we've learned so far.

We began with an examination of "praiseworthiness." Kant claims that someone is morally praiseworthy when they act from duty, as opposed to acting merely in accordance with duty. We then saw how both the CI and the PI can be used to determine just what our "duty" is—or at least we saw how we can determine whether an action is morally permissible. We can now finally combine these efforts.

The CI and the PI concern actions. When considering a course of action, we can use either to determine whether what we are proposing to do is morally permissible, or if it violates the moral law. At that point, we can still choose to do the impermissible, of course. That's one of the "benefits" (and burdens) of free will—but if we do, we do so with full knowledge that we are acting immorally. If we choose to act rightly, however, we shift our attention to the question of intent. Even supposing that someone has done the right thing, that doesn't necessarily mean that she has acted from duty. Put simply, being a good person involves more than just doing the right thing—you also have to do it for the right reason.

Possible Problems

As with any ethical theory, Kant's is subject to some criticism. We'll consider just a few of the more prominent, or immediately obvious, concerns.

Possible problem #1: Counter-intuitive results

Kant's theory deals in moral absolutes. Remember, when we're using the test of the CI, we're offering *universal laws*. Kant is notoriously resistant to exceptions, or sensitivity to context. Perhaps the most famous example of this is his claim that lying is *always* wrong, no matter the context, no matter the reason. "To be truthful (honest) in all declarations is therefore a sacred unconditional command of reason, and not to be limited by any expediency."

In his own time, Kant was challenged on this. What if, for example, an innocent person had fled to your home, seeking sanctuary from a murderer in pursuit? You hide the person inside, and then the murderer knocks on your door, demanding to know if his intended victim is hiding within. Is it morally permissible to lie, even in such an extreme case? *No.* "A lie is a lie, and is in itself intrinsically base whether it be told with good or bad intent."

Many people, then and now, think that it's absurd to claim that honesty is demanded of us even when the lie would be for the sake of saving an innocent person from murder. Someone adhering to honesty in such a situation might seem to be treating honesty as a fetish rather than a proper moral principle. Or, couldn't one argue that the murderer is not entitled to honesty, in such a case? For many of us, it seems just plain counter-intuitive that we are morally required to tell the truth, when lying would be for the sake of saving an innocent person's life, and honesty would likely put that same innocent life in great danger.

There are several ways to address this tension. One way is by appealing to cleverness. It would be wrong to lie, but that doesn't mean you have to utter the truth. Simply remain silent. Clever, but probably not effective, in that scenario. Silence would likely be taken as an admission that the person is inside your home. If your purpose is merely to refrain from uttering a lie, you've succeeded—but you might as well have just told the truth! If the goal is to somehow protect the life of the person hiding in your home, cleverness will probably not be sufficient.

Another way to respond is to conclude that Kant is mistaken. The mistake might be at the level of his entire theory (i.e., Kantianism is fundamentally misguided), or at the level of application (i.e., Kant misapplied his own theory!). I've heard several "Kantians" offer a maxim involving a lie, but a maxim that they believe will survive the test of the CI all the same: "out of respect for innocent life (reason), I will lie (action), if doing so is necessary to save that innocent life (context)." That maxim seems fairly innocent, even when universalized. Imagine that everyone lies when doing so is necessary to save an innocent person's life. What's so bad about that? I don't think I would have a problem with everyone doing that, so it doesn't appear that any contradiction in will is generated. What about a contradiction in conception? This is where even that "innocent" maxim finds difficulty. Suppose everyone lies when necessary to save an innocent life. Everyone. You. Me. The murderer. In that case, the murderer would know that you would lie about whether the person is inside. Whether the victim actually is inside your home, or not, your answer will be "he's not here." Therefore, your claim that "he's not here" will be unconvincing. The lie won't work. A contradiction in conception results, and the maxim fails the test of the CI.

Assuming Kant is right about his own theory, we are left with two options: either lying *is* always morally impermissible, or else there is something about his theory in need of repair, replacement, or omission. You decide.

Possible problem #2: His theory is too limited in scope.

Too limited in scope? He's offering universal moral laws? What's limited about that?

Because his theory is grounded on Reason, it applies only to creatures that are bearers of Reason. Although the dividing line between creatures that possess Reason and those that do not is fuzzier now than it was in Kant's own time, for Kant, at least, it was clear that his theory did not apply to non-human animals. "The fact that the human being can have the representation 'I' raises him infinitely above all the other beings on earth. By this he is a person....that is, a being altogether different in rank and dignity from things, such as irrational animals, with which one may deal and dispose at one's discretion."

"May deal and dispose at one's discretion" is just what it sounds like. As far as non-human animals go, they have no rights, no moral standing whatsoever. Not cats, not dogs, not dolphins, not horses. Not ugly animals or cute ones. Only "persons" have rights, and non-human animals are not persons (by virtue of their lacking Reason). This does not mean that "anything goes" as far as non-human animals are concerned. That would be an unfair caricature of Kant. He does recognize limits regarding our treatment of animals, but not out of any obligation to the animals themselves. "...so far as animals are concerned, we have no direct duties....Our duties towards animals are merely indirect duties towards humanity."

In other words, indirect duties towards animals emerge from our direct duties to other persons. An obvious example involves property. To the extent that some animals are "owned" by humans, I have the same obligation to respect that person's property whether in the form of his dog or his couch. Just as it would be wrong for me to destroy his couch without permission, so too is it wrong for me to "destroy" his dog without permission. If I do, I'm not morally offending against the dog, but against the owner. Notice the important caveat: *without his permission*. What if I do have his permission? If some cruel bastard says, "Hey Ted, want to kill my dog? I'll let you...." what then?

In such a case, it is technically permissible for me to dispose of his "property" according to his desires, but Kant offers reservations even then. We ought to refrain from being cruel to animals, for example, even though animals have no moral standing. Why? Because of how our treatment of animals impacts our treatment of other humans. As Kant said: "If a man shoots his dog because the animal is no longer capable of service, he does not fail in his duty to the dog, for the dog cannot judge, but his act is inhuman and damages in himself that humanity which it is his duty to show towards mankind. If he is not to stifle his human feelings, he must practice kindness toward animals, for he who is cruel to animals becomes hard also in his treatment of men. We can judge the heart of a man by his treatment of animals." The philosopher and Nobel Peace Prize recipient Albert Schweitzer echoed this idea when he said that anyone "who has accustomed himself to regard the life of any living creature as worthless is in danger of arriving also at the idea of worthless human lives".

Some fascinating connections between animal abuse and crimes against humans have been researched and discovered. A 1997 study done by the Massachusetts Society for the Prevention of Cruelty to Animals (SPCA) and Northeastern University concludes that those who abuse animals are five times more likely to commit violent crimes against people and four times more likely to commit property crimes than those without any such history. A survey of serial killers found that 36 percent of them admitted to committing acts of animal cruelty as children, 46 percent did so as adolescents, and 36 percent as adults. A 2008 study by the Chicago police department revealed that, of 332 people arrested for animal cruelty, 70 percent of suspects had arrests on felony charges (including two homicides), 86 percent of suspects had multiple arrests, and 13 percent of suspects had been arrested on sex crime charges. This apparent connection between the abuse of animals and crimes against humans was known in Kant's time as well. Indeed, Kant references the series of engraving by William Hogarth entitled "The Four Stages of Cruelty" to illustrate the progression of the infliction of cruelty from animals to humans.[159]

To be fair to Kant, he is very far from recommending a callous disregard for animal welfare. What might make him problematic for some readers is that all of his regard, ultimately, is rooted in regard for human beings only. Even the kindness that we ought to show animals is to be understood as training for kindness to humans— or at least a means to avoid becoming cruel towards humans. For anyone who believes non-human animals have some moral standing in their own right, Kant's theory might seem insufficient, or even viciously "speciesist."

To make matters more controversial, non-human animals are excluded from

---

[159] The graphic (and centuries old) engravings may be viewed online at numerous sites, including this one (at least at the time of this writing): http://www.graphicwitness.org/coe/cruel.htm

moral standing because they lack Reason, because they (allegedly) lack self-consciousness. As Kant puts it, "Animals are not self conscious and are there merely as a means to an end. That end is man."

To be consistent, though, if lacking self-consciousness relegates one to the status of a mere "means to an end," then it would seem that that same standard should apply to *any* creature. Therefore, if a human lacks self-consciousness, it should *also* have the status of being merely a means to an end. Many so-called "marginal" cases present themselves: fetuses, infants, severely mentally disabled humans of all ages, humans in persistent vegetative states, etc. It would be challenging to argue that such humans possess self-consciousness. Are they therefore equally lacking in moral standing? Morally equivalent to non-human animals, and benefiting only from indirect duties derived from self-conscious humans? If the answer is "yes," then even more readers might find themselves uncomfortable with Kant's theory, as it excludes from the moral community not only all non-human animals, but also several categories of humans—including very young children! If the answer is "no," then a consistent Kantian will need to offer an explanation for why the lack of self-consciousness disqualifies non-human animals, but not similarly equipped humans.

Conclusion: What Kant seems to be Getting Right

- It *does* seem to matter what reasons someone has for their actions. Someone who tells the truth from fear, or who saves a life for the sake of a reward just doesn't seem to merit the kind of moral praise that would be forthcoming for a person who did the same actions from more "pure" motives.
- Respect *does* seem to be a central theme for our moral understanding. However we care to articulate it, the notion that all people deserve at least a baseline level of respect and dignity, that all people possess at least a baseline level of moral worth, seems consistent with our moral intuitions.
- "Universalizability" *does* seem to be a handy tool for evaluating our actions. Whether we understand this in terms of the CI, or the Golden Rule, or any of the variations of the Golden Rule found in virtually every major religious tradition in the world, this idea that something is acceptable for one only if it would be acceptable for all is a powerful and potentially universal moral insight.
- Reason and self-consciousness *do* seem to be important qualities with regard to moral standing. We don't have to commit ourselves to the position that anything lacking in these qualities is completely lacking in moral standing, but the possession of these qualities does seem to qualify a creature for some sort of "special" moral standing—even if in no other respect than being a bearer of greater moral responsibility! Some have expressed this distinction in terms of moral "agents" (those possessing reason and self-consciousness) and moral "patients" (those lacking the qualities of agency, but still entitled to some degree of moral consideration).

Answer to exercise break:

- Identity theft maxim: For self-benefit (reason), whenever I have the opportunity and desire (context), I will steal others' financial identity and purchase items using their credit (action).

- Universalized form of the maxim: For self-benefit, whenever anyone has the opportunity and desire, they will steal others' financial identity and purchase items using their credit.
- Contradiction in will? Of course! Who would want everyone to engage in identify theft? That would mean that you're likely to be a victim of it, since everyone does it.
- Contradiction in conception? Yes. If everyone did this, credit would either disappear, or rigorous security measures would be applied to prevent identity theft. In a world where everyone commits identity theft, purchases using credit cards, checks, online purchases, etc., would not be permitted.

Immanuel Kant (22 April 1724 – 12 February 1804) is one of the most important, and certainly one of the most challenging, philosophers of the last several centuries. Often regarded as a bridge between the "modern" period of philosophy and the "contemporary" period, Kant's philosophy is a vast and sophisticated system of thought addressing metaphysics, epistemology, logic, ethics, philosophy of religion, and political philosophy. In this excerpt, we get a glimpse at some of the key elements of Kant's moral philosophy. Kant is considered a "must study" figure in most ethics courses because of the importance of his approach. He begins by asserting that only the "good will" is unqualifiedly good, and that all other things are only instrumentally good, at best. This recognition of the importance of the will with regard to moral evaluation is then revealed with several examples, including that of the "honest shopkeeper." In that example we also see the important distinction between acting from duty and acting in accordance with duty. Perhaps most importantly, Kant offers us the means by which we can determine whether what we will is morally permissible: the categorical imperative. The categorical imperative reveals contradictions (in will or conception) that underlie immoral "maxims" (principles of conduct). Finally (for our purposes), Kant discusses the "practical imperative" as an alternate formulation of the categorical imperative. Note the sharp contrast between the Kantian approach (emphasizing the will, what we intend, and the rationality that governs our will) and the utilitarian approach (emphasizing outcomes and happiness).

Fundamental Principles of the Metaphysics of Morals
Immanuel Kant

First Section, Transition from the Common Rational Knowledge of Morality to the Philosophical

Nothing can possibly be conceived in the world, or even out of it, which can be called good, without qualification, except a good will. Intelligence, wit, judgement, and the other talents of the mind, however they may be named, or courage, resolution, perseverance, as qualities of temperament, are undoubtedly good and desirable in many respects; but these gifts of nature may also become extremely bad and mischievous if the will which is to make use of them, and which, therefore, constitutes what is called character, is not good. It is the same with the gifts of fortune. Power, riches, honour, even health, and the general well-being and contentment with one's condition which is called happiness, inspire pride, and often presumption, if there is not a good will to correct the influence of these on the mind, and with this also to rectify the whole principle of acting and adapt it to its end. The sight of a being who is not adorned with a single feature of a pure and good will, enjoying unbroken prosperity, can never give pleasure to an impartial rational spectator. Thus a good will appears to constitute the indispensable condition even of being worthy of happiness.

There are even some qualities which are of service to this good will itself and may facilitate its action, yet which have no intrinsic unconditional value, but always presuppose a good will, and this qualifies the esteem that we justly have for them and does not permit us to regard them as absolutely good. Moderation in the affections and passions, self-control, and calm deliberation are not only good in many respects, but even seem to constitute part of the intrinsic worth of the person; but they are far from deserving to be called good without qualification, although they have been so unconditionally praised by the ancients. For without the principles of a good will, they may become extremely bad, and the coolness of a villain not only makes him far more dangerous, but also directly makes him more abominable in our eyes than he would have been without it.

A good will is good not because of what it performs or effects, not by its aptness for the attainment of some proposed end, but simply by virtue of the volition; that is, it is good in itself, and considered by itself is to be esteemed much higher than all that can be brought about by it in favour of any inclination, nay even of the sum total of all inclinations. Even if it should happen that, owing to special disfavour of fortune, or the niggardly provision of a step-motherly nature, this will should wholly lack power to accomplish its purpose, if with its greatest efforts it should yet achieve nothing, and there should remain only the good will (not, to be sure, a mere wish, but the summoning of all means in our power), then, like a jewel, it would still shine by its own light, as a thing which has its whole value in itself. Its usefulness or fruitfulness can neither add nor take away anything from this value. It would be, as it were, only the setting to enable us to handle it the more conveniently in common commerce, or to attract to it the attention of those who are not yet connoisseurs, but not to recommend it to true connoisseurs, or to determine its value.

There is, however, something so strange in this idea of the absolute value of the mere will, in which no account is taken of its utility, that notwithstanding the thorough assent of even common reason to the idea, yet a suspicion must arise that it may perhaps really be the product of mere high-flown fancy, and that we may have misunderstood the purpose of nature in assigning reason as the governor of our will. Therefore we will examine this idea from this point of view.

In the physical constitution of an organized being, that is, a being adapted suitably to the purposes of life, we assume it as a fundamental principle that no organ for any purpose will be found but what is also the fittest and best adapted for that purpose. Now in a being which has reason and a will, if the proper object of nature were its conservation, its welfare, in a word, its happiness, then nature would have hit upon a very bad arrangement in selecting the reason of the creature to carry out this purpose. For all the actions which the creature has to perform with a view to this purpose, and the whole rule of its conduct, would be far more surely prescribed to it by instinct, and that end would have been attained thereby much more certainly than it ever can be by reason. Should reason have been communicated to this favoured creature over and above, it must only have served it to contemplate the happy constitution of its nature, to admire it, to congratulate itself thereon, and to feel thankful for it to the beneficent cause, but not that it should subject its desires to that weak and delusive guidance and meddle bunglingly with the purpose of nature. In a word, nature would have taken care that reason should not break forth into practical exercise, nor have the presumption, with its weak insight, to think out for itself the plan of happiness, and of the means of attaining it. Nature would not only have taken on herself the choice of the ends, but also of the means, and with wise foresight would have entrusted both to instinct.

And, in fact, we find that the more a cultivated reason applies itself with deliberate purpose to the enjoyment of life and happiness, so much the more does the man fail of true satisfaction. And from this circumstance there arises in many, if they are candid enough to confess it, a certain degree of misology, that is, hatred of reason, especially in the case of those who are most experienced in the use of it, because after calculating all the advantages they derive, I do not say from the invention of all the arts of common luxury, but even from the sciences (which seem to them to be after all only a luxury of the understanding), they find that they have, in fact, only brought more trouble on their shoulders. rather than gained in happiness; and they end by envying, rather than despising, the more common stamp of men who keep closer to the guidance of mere instinct and do not allow their reason much influence on their conduct. And this we must admit, that the judgement of those who would very much lower the lofty eulogies of the advantages which reason gives us in regard to the happiness and satisfaction of life, or who would even reduce them below zero, is by no means morose or ungrateful to the goodness with which the world is governed, but that there lies at the root of these judgements the idea that our existence has a different and far nobler end, for which, and not for happiness, reason is properly intended, and which must, therefore, be regarded as the supreme condition to which the private ends of man must, for the most part, be postponed.

For as reason is not competent to guide the will with certainty in regard to its objects and the satisfaction of all our wants (which it to some extent even multiplies), this being an end to which an implanted instinct would have led with much greater certainty; and since, nevertheless, reason is imparted to us as a practical faculty, i.e., as one which is to have influence on the will, therefore, admitting that nature generally in the distribution of her capacities has adapted the means to the end, its true destination must be to produce a will, not merely good as a means to something else, but good in itself, for which reason was absolutely necessary. This will then, though not indeed the sole and complete good, must be the supreme good and the condition of every other, even of the desire of happiness. Under these circumstances, there is nothing inconsistent with the wisdom of nature in the fact that the cultivation of the reason, which is requisite for the first and unconditional purpose, does in many ways interfere, at least in this life, with the attainment of the second, which is always conditional, namely, happiness. Nay, it may even reduce it to nothing, without nature thereby failing of her purpose. For reason recognizes the establishment of a good will as its highest practical destination, and in attaining this purpose is capable only of a satisfaction of its own proper kind, namely that from the attainment of an end, which end again is determined by reason only, notwithstanding that this may involve many a disappointment to the ends of inclination.

We have then to develop the notion of a will which deserves to be highly esteemed for itself and is good without a view to anything further, a notion which exists already in the sound natural understanding, requiring rather to be cleared up than to be taught, and which in estimating the value of our actions always takes the first place and constitutes the condition of all the rest. In order to do this, we will take the notion of duty, which includes that of a good will, although implying certain subjective restrictions and hindrances. These, however, far from concealing it, or rendering it unrecognizable, rather bring it out by contrast and make it shine forth so much the brighter.

I omit here all actions which are already recognized as inconsistent with duty, although they may be useful for this or that purpose, for with these the question whether they are done from duty cannot arise at all, since they even conflict with it. I also set aside those actions which really conform to duty, but to which men have no direct inclination, performing them because they are impelled thereto by some other inclination. For in this case we can readily distinguish whether the action which agrees with duty is done from duty, or from a selfish view. It is much harder to make this distinction when the action accords with duty and the subject has besides a direct inclination to it. For example, it is always a matter of duty that a dealer should not over charge an inexperienced purchaser; and wherever there is much commerce the prudent tradesman does not overcharge, but keeps a fixed price for everyone, so that a child buys of him as well as any other. Men are thus honestly served; but this is not enough to make us believe that the tradesman has so acted from duty and from principles of honesty: his own advantage required it; it is out of the question in this case to suppose that he might besides have a direct inclination in favour of the buyers, so that, as it were, from love he should give no advantage to one over another. Accordingly the action was done neither from duty nor from direct inclination, but merely with a selfish view.

On the other hand, it is a duty to maintain one's life; and, in addition, everyone has also a direct inclination to do so. But on this account the of anxious care which most men take for it has no intrinsic worth, and their maxim has no moral import. They preserve their life as duty requires, no doubt, but not because duty requires. On the other hand, if adversity and hopeless sorrow have completely taken away the relish for life; if the unfortunate one, strong in mind, indignant at his fate rather than desponding or dejected, wishes for death, and yet preserves his life without loving it- not from inclination or fear, but from duty- then his maxim has a moral worth.

To be beneficent when we can is a duty; and besides this, there are many minds so sympathetically constituted that, without any other motive of vanity or self-interest, they find a pleasure in spreading joy around them and can take delight in the satisfaction of others so far as it is their own work. But I maintain that in such a case an action of this kind, however proper, however amiable it may be, bas nevertheless no true moral worth, but is on a level with other inclinations, e.g., the inclination to honour, which, if it is happily directed to that which is in fact of public utility and accordant with duty and consequently honourable, deserves praise and encouragement, but not esteem. For the maxim lacks the moral import, namely, that such actions be done from duty, not from inclination. Put the case that the mind of that philanthropist were clouded by sorrow of his own, extinguishing all sympathy with the lot of others, and that, while he still has the power to benefit others in distress, he is not touched by their trouble because he is absorbed with his own; and now suppose that he tears himself out of this dead insensibility, and performs the action without any inclination to it, but simply from duty, then first has his action its genuine moral worth. Further still; if nature bas put little sympathy in the heart of this or that man; if he, supposed to be an upright man, is by temperament cold and indifferent to the sufferings of others, perhaps because in respect of his own he is provided with the special gift of patience and fortitude and supposes, or even requires, that others should have the same- and such a man would certainly not be the meanest product of nature- but if nature had not specially framed him for a philanthropist, would he not still find in himself a source from whence to give himself a far higher worth than that of a good-natured temperament could be? Unquestionably. It is just in this that the moral worth of the character is brought out which is incomparably the highest of all, namely, that he is beneficent, not from inclination, but from duty.

To secure one's own happiness is a duty, at least indirectly; for discontent with one's condition, under a pressure of many anxieties and amidst unsatisfied wants, might easily become a great temptation to transgression of duty. But here again, without looking to duty, all men have already the strongest and most intimate inclination to happiness, because it is just in this idea that all inclinations are combined in one total. But the precept of happiness is often of such a sort that it greatly interferes with some inclinations, and yet a man cannot form any definite and certain conception of the sum of satisfaction of all of them which is called happiness. It is not then to be wondered at that a single inclination, definite both as to what it promises and as to the time within which it can be gratified, is often able to overcome such a fluctuating idea, and that a gouty patient, for instance, can choose to enjoy what he likes, and to suffer what he may, since, according to his calculation, on this occasion at least, be has not sacrificed the enjoyment of the present moment to a possibly mistaken expectation of a happiness which is supposed to be found in health. But even in this case, if the general desire for happiness did not influence his will, and supposing that in his particular case health was not a necessary element in this calculation, there yet remains in this, as in all other cases, this law, namely, that he should promote his happiness not from inclination but from duty, and by this would his conduct first acquire true moral worth.

It is in this manner, undoubtedly, that we are to understand those passages of Scripture also in which we are commanded to love our neighbour, even our enemy. For love, as an affection, cannot be commanded, but beneficence for duty's sake may; even though we are not impelled to it by any inclination- nay, are even repelled by a natural and unconquerable aversion. This is practical love and not pathological- a love which is seated in the will, and not in the propensions of sense- in principles of action and not of tender sympathy; and it is this love alone which can be commanded.

The second proposition is: That an action done from duty derives its moral worth, not from the purpose which is to be attained by it, but from the maxim by which it is determined, and therefore does not depend on the realization of the object of the action, but merely on the principle of volition by which the action has taken place, without regard to any object of desire. It is clear from what precedes that the purposes which we may have in view in our actions, or their effects regarded as ends and springs of the will, cannot give to actions any unconditional or moral worth. In what, then, can their worth lie, if it is not to consist in the will and in reference to its expected effect? It cannot lie anywhere but in the principle of the will without regard to the ends which can be attained by the action. For the will stands between its a priori principle, which is formal, and its a posteriori spring, which is material, as between two roads, and as it must be determined by something, it that it must be determined by the formal principle of volition when an action is done from duty, in which case every material principle has been withdrawn from it.

The third proposition, which is a consequence of the two preceding, I would express thus Duty is the necessity of acting from respect for the law. I may have inclination for an object as the effect of my proposed action, but I cannot have respect for it, just for this reason, that it is an effect and not an energy of will. Similarly I cannot have respect for inclination, whether my own or another's; I can at most, if my own, approve it; if another's, sometimes even love it; i.e., look on it as favourable to my own interest. It is only what is connected with my will as a principle, by no means as an effect- what does not subserve my inclination, but overpowers it, or at least in case of choice excludes it from its calculation- in other words, simply the law of itself, which can be an object of respect, and hence a command. Now an action done from duty must wholly exclude the influence of inclination and with it every object of the will, so that nothing remains which can determine the will except objectively the law, and subjectively pure respect for this practical law, and consequently the maxim* that I should follow this law even to the thwarting of all my inclinations.

*A maxim is the subjective principle of volition. The objective principle (i.e., that which would also serve subjectively as a practical principle to all rational beings if reason had full power over the faculty of desire) is the practical law.

Thus the moral worth of an action does not lie in the effect expected from it, nor in any principle of action which requires to borrow its motive from this expected effect. For all these effects- agreeableness of one's condition and even the promotion of the happiness of others- could have been also brought about by other causes, so that for this there would have been no need of the will of a rational being; whereas it is in this alone that the supreme and unconditional good can be found. The pre-eminent good which we call moral can therefore consist in nothing else than the conception of law in itself, which certainly is only possible in a rational being, in so far as this conception, and not the expected effect, determines the will. This is a good which is already present in the person who acts accordingly, and we have not to wait for it to appear first in the result.*

*It might be here objected to me that I take refuge behind the word respect in an obscure feeling, instead of giving a distinct solution of the question by a concept of the reason. But although respect is a feeling, it is not a feeling received through influence, but is self-wrought by a rational concept, and, therefore, is specifically distinct from all feelings of the former kind, which may be referred either to inclination or fear, What I recognise immediately as a law for me, I recognise with respect. This merely signifies the consciousness that my will is subordinate to a law, without the intervention of other influences on my sense. The immediate determination of the will by the law, and the consciousness of this, is called respect, so that this is regarded as an effect of the law on the subject, and not as the cause of it. Respect is properly the conception of a worth which thwarts my self-love. Accordingly it is something which is considered neither as an object of inclination nor of fear, although it has something analogous to both. The object of respect is the law only, and that the law which we impose on ourselves and yet recognise as necessary in itself. As a law, we are subjected too it without consulting self-love; as imposed by us on ourselves, it is a result of our will. In the former aspect it has an analogy to fear, in the latter to inclination. Respect for a person is properly only respect for the law (of honesty, etc.) of which he gives us an example. Since we also look on the improvement of our talents as a duty, we consider that we see in a person of talents, as it were, the example of a law (viz., to become like him in this by exercise), and this constitutes our respect. All so-called moral interest consists simply in respect for the law.

But what sort of law can that be, the conception of which must determine the will, even without paying any regard to the effect expected from it, in order that this will may be called good absolutely and without qualification? As I have deprived the will of every impulse which could arise to it from obedience to any law, there remains nothing but the universal conformity of its actions to law in general, which alone is to serve the will as a principle, i.e., I am never to act otherwise than so that I could also will that my maxim should become a universal law. Here, now, it is the simple conformity to law in general, without assuming any particular law applicable to certain actions, that serves the will as its principle and must so serve it, if duty is not to be a vain delusion and a chimerical notion. The common reason of men in its practical judgements perfectly coincides with this and always has in view the principle here suggested. Let the question be, for example: May I when in distress make a promise with the intention not to keep it? I readily distinguish here between the two significations which the question may have: Whether it is prudent, or whether it is right, to make a false promise? The former may undoubtedly of be the case. I see clearly indeed that it is not enough to extricate myself from a present difficulty by means of this subterfuge, but it must be well considered whether there may not hereafter spring from this lie much greater inconvenience than that from which I now free myself, and as, with all my supposed cunning, the consequences cannot be so easily foreseen but that credit once lost may be much more injurious to me than any mischief which I seek to avoid at present, it should be considered whether it would not be more prudent to act herein according to a universal maxim and to make it a habit to promise nothing except with the intention of keeping it. But it is soon clear to me that such a maxim will still only be based on the fear of consequences. Now it is a wholly different thing to be truthful from duty and to be so from apprehension of injurious consequences. In the first case, the very notion of the action already implies a law for me; in the second case, I must first look about elsewhere to see what results may be combined with it which would affect myself. For to deviate from the principle of duty is beyond all doubt wicked; but to be unfaithful to my maxim of prudence may often be very advantageous to me, although to abide by it is certainly safer. The shortest way, however, and an unerring one, to discover the answer to this question whether a lying promise is consistent with duty, is to ask myself, "Should I be content that my maxim (to extricate myself from difficulty by a false promise) should hold good as a universal law, for myself as well as for others? and should I be able to say to myself, "Every one may make a deceitful promise when he finds himself in a difficulty from which he cannot otherwise extricate himself?" Then I presently become aware that while I can will the lie, I can by no means will that lying should be a universal law. For with such a law there would be no promises at all, since it would be in vain to allege my intention in regard to my future actions to those who would not believe this allegation, or if they over hastily did so would pay me back in my own coin. Hence my maxim, as soon as it should be made a universal law, would necessarily destroy itself.

I do not, therefore, need any far-reaching penetration to discern what I have to do in order that my will may be morally good. Inexperienced in the course of the world, incapable of being prepared for all its contingencies, I only ask myself: Canst thou also will that thy maxim should be a universal law? If not, then it must be rejected, and that not because of a disadvantage accruing from it to myself or even to others, but because it cannot enter as a principle into a possible universal legislation, and reason extorts from me immediate respect for such legislation. I do not indeed as yet discern on what this respect is based (this the philosopher may inquire), but at least I understand this, that it is an estimation of the worth which far outweighs all worth of what is recommended by inclination, and that the necessity of acting from pure respect for the practical law is what constitutes duty, to which every other motive must give place, because it is the condition of a will being good in itself, and the worth of such a will is above everything.

...

The conception of an objective principle, in so far as it is obligatory for a will, is called a command (of reason), and the formula of the command is called an imperative.

All imperatives are expressed by the word ought [or shall], and thereby indicate the relation of an objective law of reason to a will, which from its subjective constitution is not necessarily determined by it (an obligation). They say that something would be good to do or to forbear, but they say it to a will which does not always do a thing because it is conceived to be good to do it. That is practically good, however, which determines the will by means of the conceptions of reason, and consequently not from subjective causes, but objectively, that is on principles which are valid for every rational being as such. It is distinguished from the pleasant, as that which influences the will only by means of sensation from merely subjective causes, valid only for the sense of this or that one, and not as a principle of reason, which holds for every one.*

*The dependence of the desires on sensations is called inclination, and this accordingly always indicates a want. The dependence of a contingently determinable will on principles of reason is called an interest. This therefore, is found only in the case of a dependent will which does not always of itself conform to reason; in the Divine will we cannot conceive any interest. But the human will can also take an interest in a thing without therefore acting from interest. The former signifies the practical interest in the action, the latter the pathological in the object of the action. The former indicates only dependence of the will on principles of reason in themselves; the second, dependence on principles of reason for the sake of inclination, reason supplying only the practical rules how the requirement of the inclination may be satisfied. In the first case the action interests me; in the second the object of the action (because it is pleasant to me). We have seen in the first section that in an action done from duty we must look not to the interest in the object, but only to that in the action itself, and in its rational principle (viz., the law).

A perfectly good will would therefore be equally subject to objective laws (viz., laws of good), but could not be conceived as obliged thereby to act lawfully, because of itself from its subjective constitution it can only be determined by the conception of good. Therefore no imperatives hold for the Divine will, or in general for a holy will; ought is here out of place, because the volition is already of itself necessarily in unison with the law. Therefore imperatives are only formulae to express the relation of objective laws of all volition to the subjective imperfection of the will of this or that rational being, e.g., the human will.

Now all imperatives command either hypothetically or categorically. The former represent the practical necessity of a possible action as means to something else that is willed (or at least which one might possibly will). The categorical imperative would be that which represented an action as necessary of itself without reference to another end, i.e., as objectively necessary.

Since every practical law represents a possible action as good and, on this account, for a subject who is practically determinable by reason, necessary, all imperatives are formulae determining an action which is necessary according to the principle of a will good in some respects. If now the action is good only as a means to something else, then the imperative is hypothetical; if it is conceived as good in itself and consequently as being necessarily the principle of a will which of itself conforms to reason, then it is categorical.

Thus the imperative declares what action possible by me would be good and presents the practical rule in relation to a will which does not forthwith perform an action simply because it is good, whether because the subject does not always know that it is good, or because, even if it know this, yet its maxims might be opposed to the objective principles of practical reason.

Accordingly the hypothetical imperative only says that the action is good for some purpose, possible or actual. In the first case it is a problematical, in the second an assertorial practical principle. The categorical imperative which declares an action to be objectively necessary in itself without reference to any purpose, i.e., without any other end, is valid as an apodeictic (practical) principle.

Whatever is possible only by the power of some rational being may also be conceived as a possible purpose of some will; and therefore the principles of action as regards the means necessary to attain some possible purpose are in fact infinitely numerous. All sciences have a practical part, consisting of problems expressing that some end is possible for us and of imperatives directing how it may be attained. These may, therefore, be called in general imperatives of skill. Here there is no question whether the end is rational and good, but only what one must do in order to attain it. The precepts for the physician to make his patient thoroughly healthy, and for a poisoner to ensure certain death, are of equal value in this respect, that each serves to effect its purpose perfectly. Since in early youth it cannot be known what ends are likely to occur to us in the course of life, parents seek to have their children taught a great many things, and provide for their skill in the use of means for all sorts of arbitrary ends, of none of which can they determine whether it may not perhaps hereafter be an object to their pupil, but which it is at all events possible that he might aim at; and this anxiety is so great that they commonly neglect to form and correct their judgement on the value of the things which may be chosen as ends.

There is one end, however, which may be assumed to be actually such to all rational beings (so far as imperatives apply to them, viz., as dependent beings), and, therefore, one purpose which they not merely may have, but which we may with certainty assume that they all actually have by a natural necessity, and this is happiness. The hypothetical imperative which expresses the practical necessity of an action as means to the advancement of happiness is assertorial. We are not to present it as necessary for an uncertain and merely possible purpose, but for a purpose which we may presuppose with certainty and a priori in every man, because it belongs to his being. Now skill in the choice of means to his own greatest well-being may be called prudence,* in the narrowest sense. And thus the imperative which refers to the choice of means to one's own happiness, i.e., the precept of prudence, is still always hypothetical; the action is not commanded absolutely, but only as means to another purpose.

*The word prudence is taken in two senses: in the one it may bear the name of knowledge of the world, in the other that of private prudence. The former is a man's ability to influence others so as to use them for his own purposes. The latter is the sagacity to combine all these purposes for his own lasting benefit. This latter is properly that to which the value even of the former is reduced, and when a man is prudent in the former sense, but not in the latter, we might better say of him that he is clever and cunning, but, on the whole, imprudent.

Finally, there is an imperative which commands a certain conduct immediately, without having as its condition any other purpose to be attained by it. This imperative is categorical. It concerns not the matter of the action, or its intended result, but its form and the principle of which it is itself a result; and what is essentially good in it consists in the mental disposition, let the consequence be what it may. This imperative may be called that of morality....

When I conceive a hypothetical imperative, in general I do not know beforehand what it will contain until I am given the condition. But when I conceive a categorical imperative, I know at once what it contains. For as the imperative contains besides the law only the necessity that the maxims* shall conform to this law, while the law contains no conditions restricting it, there remains nothing but the general statement that the maxim of the action should conform to a universal law, and it is this conformity alone that the imperative properly represents as necessary.

*A maxim is a subjective principle of action, and must be distinguished from the objective principle, namely, practical law. The former contains the practical rule set by reason according to the conditions of the subject (often its ignorance or its inclinations), so that it is the principle on which the subject acts; but the law is the objective principle valid for every rational being, and is the principle on which it ought to act that is an imperative.

There is therefore but one categorical imperative, namely, this: Act only on that maxim whereby thou canst at the same time will that it should become a universal law.

Now if all imperatives of duty can be deduced from this one imperative as from their principle, then, although it should remain undecided what is called duty is not merely a vain notion, yet at least we shall be able to show what we understand by it and what this notion means.

Since the universality of the law according to which effects are produced constitutes what is properly called nature in the most general sense (as to form), that is the existence of things so far as it is determined by general laws, the imperative of duty may be expressed thus: Act as if the maxim of thy action were to become by thy will a universal law of nature.

We will now enumerate a few duties, adopting the usual division of them into duties to ourselves and ourselves and to others, and into perfect and imperfect duties.*

*It must be noted here that I reserve the division of duties for a future metaphysic of morals; so that I give it here only as an arbitrary one (in order to arrange my examples). For the rest, I understand by a perfect duty one that admits no exception in favour of inclination and then I have not merely external but also internal perfect duties. This is contrary to the use of the word adopted in the schools; but I do not intend to justify there, as it is all one for my purpose whether it is admitted or not.

1. A man reduced to despair by a series of misfortunes feels wearied of life, but is still so far in possession of his reason that he can ask himself whether it would not be contrary to his duty to himself to take his own life. Now he inquires whether the maxim of his action could become a universal law of nature. His maxim is: "From self-love I adopt it as a principle to shorten my life when its longer duration is likely to bring more evil than satisfaction." It is asked then simply whether this principle founded on self-love can become a universal law of nature. Now we see at once that a system of nature of which it should be a law to destroy life by means of the very feeling whose special nature it is to impel to the improvement of life would contradict itself and, therefore, could not exist as a system of nature; hence that maxim cannot possibly exist as a universal law of nature and, consequently, would be wholly inconsistent with the supreme principle of all duty.

2. Another finds himself forced by necessity to borrow money. He knows that he will not be able to repay it, but sees also that nothing will be lent to him unless he promises stoutly to repay it in a definite time. He desires to make this promise, but he has still so much conscience as to ask himself: "Is it not unlawful and inconsistent with duty to get out of a difficulty in this way?" Suppose however that he resolves to do so: then the maxim of his action would be expressed thus: "When I think myself in want of money, I will borrow money and promise to repay it, although I know that I never can do so." Now this principle of self-love or of one's own advantage may perhaps be consistent with my whole future welfare; but the question now is, "Is it right?" I change then the suggestion of self-love into a universal law, and state the question thus: "How would it be if my maxim were a universal law?" Then I see at once that it could never hold as a universal law of nature, but would necessarily contradict itself. For supposing it to be a universal law that everyone when he thinks himself in a difficulty should be able to promise whatever he pleases, with the purpose of not keeping his promise, the promise itself would become impossible, as well as the end that one might have in view in it, since no one would consider that anything was promised to him, but would ridicule all such statements as vain pretences.

3. A third finds in himself a talent which with the help of some culture might make him a useful man in many respects. But he finds himself in comfortable circumstances and prefers to indulge in pleasure rather than to take pains in enlarging and improving his happy natural capacities. He asks, however, whether his maxim of neglect of his natural gifts, besides agreeing with his inclination to indulgence, agrees also with what is called duty. He sees then that a system of nature could indeed subsist with such a universal law although men (like the South Sea islanders) should let their talents rest and resolve to devote their lives merely to idleness, amusement, and propagation of their species- in a word, to enjoyment; but he cannot possibly will that this should be a universal law of nature, or be implanted in us as such by a natural instinct. For, as a rational being, he necessarily wills that his faculties be developed, since they serve him and have been given him, for all sorts of possible purposes.

4. A fourth, who is in prosperity, while he sees that others have to contend with great wretchedness and that he could help them, thinks: "What concern is it of mine?

Let everyone be as happy as Heaven pleases, or as be can make himself; I will take nothing from him nor even envy him, only I do not wish to contribute anything to his welfare or to his assistance in distress!" Now no doubt if such a mode of thinking were a universal law, the human race might very well subsist and doubtless even better than in a state in which everyone talks of sympathy and good-will, or even takes care occasionally to put it into practice, but, on the other side, also cheats when he can, betrays the rights of men, or otherwise violates them. But although it is possible that a universal law of nature might exist in accordance with that maxim, it is impossible to will that such a principle should have the universal validity of a law of nature. For a will which resolved this would contradict itself, inasmuch as many cases might occur in which one would have need of the love and sympathy of others, and in which, by such a law of nature, sprung from his own will, he would deprive himself of all hope of the aid he desires.

These are a few of the many actual duties, or at least what we regard as such, which obviously fall into two classes on the one principle that we have laid down. We must be able to will that a maxim of our action should be a universal law. This is the canon of the moral appreciation of the action generally. Some actions are of such a character that their maxim cannot without contradiction be even conceived as a universal law of nature, far from it being possible that we should will that it should be so. In others this intrinsic impossibility is not found, but still it is impossible to will that their maxim should be raised to the universality of a law of nature, since such a will would contradict itself It is easily seen that the former violate strict or rigorous (inflexible) duty; the latter only laxer (meritorious) duty. Thus it has been completely shown how all duties depend as regards the nature of the obligation (not the object of the action) on the same principle.

If now we attend to ourselves on occasion of any transgression of duty, we shall find that we in fact do not will that our maxim should be a universal law, for that is impossible for us; on the contrary, we will that the opposite should remain a universal law, only we assume the liberty of making an exception in our own favour or (just for this time only) in favour of our inclination. Consequently if we considered all cases from one and the same point of view, namely, that of reason, we should find a contradiction in our own will, namely, that a certain principle should be objectively necessary as a universal law, and yet subjectively should not be universal, but admit of exceptions. As however we at one moment regard our action from the point of view of a will wholly conformed to reason, and then again look at the same action from the point of view of a will affected by inclination, there is not really any contradiction, but an antagonism of inclination to the precept of reason, whereby the universality of the principle is changed into a mere generality, so that the practical principle of reason shall meet the maxim half way. Now, although this cannot be justified in our own impartial judgement, yet it proves that we do really recognise the validity of the categorical imperative and (with all respect for it) only allow ourselves a few exceptions, which we think unimportant and forced from us.

We have thus established at least this much, that if duty is a conception which is to have any import and real legislative authority for our actions, it can only be expressed in categorical and not at all in hypothetical imperatives. We have also, which is of great importance, exhibited clearly and definitely for every practical application the content of the categorical imperative, which must contain the principle of all duty if there is such a thing at all. We have not yet, however, advanced so far as to prove a priori that there actually is such an imperative, that there is a practical law which commands absolutely of itself and without any other impulse, and that the following of this law is duty....

The question then is this: "Is it a necessary law for all rational beings that they should always judge of their actions by maxims of which they can themselves will that they should serve as universal laws?" If it is so, then it must be connected (altogether a priori) with the very conception of the will of a rational being generally. But in order to discover this connexion we must, however reluctantly, take a step into metaphysic, although into a domain of it which is distinct from speculative philosophy, namely, the metaphysic of morals. In a practical philosophy, where it is not the reasons of what happens that we have to ascertain, but the laws of what ought to happen, even although it never does, i.e., objective practical laws, there it is not necessary to inquire into the reasons why anything pleases or displeases, how the pleasure of mere sensation differs from taste, and whether the latter is distinct from a general satisfaction of reason; on what the feeling of pleasure or pain rests, and how from it desires and inclinations arise, and from these again maxims by the co-operation of reason: for all this belongs to an empirical psychology, which would constitute the second part of physics, if we regard physics as the philosophy of nature, so far as it is based on empirical laws. But here we are concerned with objective practical laws and, consequently, with the relation of the will to itself so far as it is determined by reason alone, in which case whatever has reference to anything empirical is necessarily excluded; since if reason of itself alone determines the conduct (and it is the possibility of this that we are now investigating), it must necessarily do so a priori.

The will is conceived as a faculty of determining oneself to action in accordance with the conception of certain laws. And such a faculty can be found only in rational beings. Now that which serves the will as the objective ground of its self-determination is the end, and, if this is assigned by reason alone, it must hold for all rational beings. On the other hand, that which merely contains the ground of possibility of the action of which the effect is the end, this is called the means. The subjective ground of the desire is the spring, the objective ground of the volition is the motive; hence the distinction between subjective ends which rest on springs, and objective ends which depend on motives valid for every rational being. Practical principles are formal when they abstract from all subjective ends; they are material when they assume these, and therefore particular springs of action. The ends which a rational being proposes to himself at pleasure as effects of his actions (material ends) are all only relative, for it is only their relation to the particular desires of the subject that gives them their worth, which therefore cannot furnish principles universal and necessary for all rational beings and for every volition, that is to say practical laws. Hence all these relative ends can give rise only to hypothetical imperatives.

Supposing, however, that there were something whose existence has in itself an absolute worth, something which, being an end in itself, could be a source of definite laws; then in this and this alone would lie the source of a possible categorical imperative, i.e., a practical law.

Now I say: man and generally any rational being exists as an end in himself, not merely as a means to be arbitrarily used by this or that will, but in all his actions, whether they concern himself or other rational beings, must be always regarded at the same time as an end. All objects of the inclinations have only a conditional worth, for if the inclinations and the wants founded on them did not exist, then their object would be without value. But the inclinations, themselves being sources of want, are so far from having an absolute worth for which they should be desired that on the contrary it must be the universal wish of every rational being to be wholly free from them. Thus the worth of any object which is to be acquired by our action is always conditional. Beings whose existence depends not on our will but on nature's, have nevertheless, if they are irrational beings, only a relative value as means, and are therefore called things; rational beings, on the contrary, are called persons, because their very nature points them out as ends in themselves, that is as something which must not be used merely as means, and so far therefore restricts freedom of action (and is an object of respect). These, therefore, are not merely subjective ends whose existence has a worth for us as an effect of our action, but objective ends, that is, things whose existence is an end in itself; an end moreover for which no other can be substituted, which they should subserve merely as means, for otherwise nothing whatever would possess absolute worth; but if all worth were conditioned and therefore contingent, then there would be no supreme practical principle of reason whatever.

If then there is a supreme practical principle or, in respect of the human will, a categorical imperative, it must be one which, being drawn from the conception of that which is necessarily an end for everyone because it is an end in itself, constitutes an objective principle of will, and can therefore serve as a universal practical law. The foundation of this principle is: rational nature exists as an end in itself. Man necessarily conceives his own existence as being so; so far then this is a subjective principle of human actions. But every other rational being regards its existence similarly, just on the same rational principle that holds for me:* so that it is at the same time an objective principle, from which as a supreme practical law all laws of the will must be capable of being deduced. Accordingly the practical imperative will be as follows: So act as to treat humanity, whether in thine own person or in that of any other, in every case as an end withal, never as means only. We will now inquire whether this can be practically carried out....

To abide by the previous examples:

Firstly, under the head of necessary duty to oneself: He who contemplates suicide should ask himself whether his action can be consistent with the idea of humanity as an end in itself. If he destroys himself in order to escape from painful circumstances, he uses a person merely as a mean to maintain a tolerable condition up to the end of life. But a man is not a thing, that is to say, something which can be used merely as means, but must in all his actions be always considered as an end in himself. I cannot, therefore, dispose in any way of a man in my own person so as to mutilate him, to damage or kill him. (It belongs to ethics proper to define this principle more precisely, so as to avoid all misunderstanding, e. g., as to the amputation of the limbs in order to preserve myself, as to exposing my life to danger with a view to preserve it, etc. This question is therefore omitted here.)

Secondly, as regards necessary duties, or those of strict obligation, towards others: He who is thinking of making a lying promise to others will see at once that he would be using another man merely as a mean, without the latter containing at the same time the end in himself. For he whom I propose by such a promise to use for my own purposes cannot possibly assent to my mode of acting towards him and, therefore, cannot himself contain the end of this action. This violation of the principle of humanity in other men is more obvious if we take in examples of attacks on the freedom and property of others. For then it is clear that he who transgresses the rights of men intends to use the person of others merely as a means, without considering that as rational beings they ought always to be esteemed also as ends, that is, as beings who must be capable of containing in themselves the end of the very same action.*

*Let it not be thought that the common "quod tibi non vis fieri, etc." could serve here as the rule or principle. For it is only a deduction from the former, though with several limitations; it cannot be a universal law, for it does not contain the principle of duties to oneself, nor of the duties of benevolence to others (for many a one would gladly consent that others should not benefit him, provided only that he might be excused from showing benevolence to them), nor finally that of duties of strict obligation to one another, for on this principle the criminal might argue against the judge who punishes him, and so on.

Thirdly, as regards contingent (meritorious) duties to oneself: It is not enough that the action does not violate humanity in our own person as an end in itself, it must also harmonize with it. Now there are in humanity capacities of greater perfection, which belong to the end that nature has in view in regard to humanity in ourselves as the subject: to neglect these might perhaps be consistent with the maintenance of humanity as an end in itself, but not with the advancement of this end.

Fourthly, as regards meritorious duties towards others: The natural end which all men have is their own happiness. Now humanity might indeed subsist, although no one should contribute anything to the happiness of others, provided he did not intentionally withdraw anything from it; but after all this would only harmonize negatively not positively with humanity as an end in itself, if every one does not also endeavour, as far as in him lies, to forward the ends of others. For the ends of any subject which is an end in himself ought as far as possible to be my ends also, if that conception is to have its full effect with me.

This principle, that humanity and generally every rational nature is an end in itself (which is the supreme limiting condition of every man's freedom of action), is not borrowed from experience, firstly, because it is universal, applying as it does to all rational beings whatever, and experience is not capable of determining anything about them; secondly, because it does not present humanity as an end to men (subjectively), that is as an object which men do of themselves actually adopt as an end; but as an objective end, which must as a law constitute the supreme limiting condition of all our subjective ends, let them be what we will; it must therefore spring from pure reason. In fact the objective principle of all practical legislation lies (according to the first principle) in the rule and its form of universality which makes it capable of being a law (say, e. g., a law of nature); but the subjective principle is in the end; now by the second principle the subject of all ends is each rational being, inasmuch as it is an end in itself. Hence follows the third practical principle of the will, which is the ultimate condition of its harmony with universal practical reason, viz.: the idea of the will of every rational being as a universally legislative will.

On this principle all maxims are rejected which are inconsistent with the will being itself universal legislator. Thus the will is not subject simply to the law, but so subject that it must be regarded as itself giving the law and, on this ground only, subject to the law (of which it can regard itself as the author).

In the previous imperatives, namely, that based on the conception of the conformity of actions to general laws, as in a physical system of nature, and that based on the universal prerogative of rational beings as ends in themselves- these imperatives, just because they were conceived as categorical, excluded from any share in their authority all admixture of any interest as a spring of action; they were, however, only assumed to be categorical, because such an assumption was necessary to explain the conception of duty. But we could not prove independently that there are practical propositions which command categorically, nor can it be proved in this section; one thing, however, could be done, namely, to indicate in the imperative itself, by some determinate expression, that in the case of volition from duty all interest is renounced, which is the specific criterion of categorical as distinguished from hypothetical imperatives. This is done in the present (third) formula of the principle, namely, in the idea of the will of every rational being as a universally legislating will.

For although a will which is subject to laws may be attached to this law by means of an interest, yet a will which is itself a supreme lawgiver so far as it is such cannot possibly depend on any interest, since a will so dependent would itself still need another law restricting the interest of its self-love by the condition that it should be valid as universal law.

Thus the principle that every human will is a will which in all its maxims gives universal laws,* provided it be otherwise justified, would be very well adapted to be the categorical imperative, in this respect, namely, that just because of the idea of universal legislation it is not based on interest, and therefore it alone among all possible imperatives can be unconditional. Or still better, converting the proposition, if there is a categorical imperative (i.e., a law for the will of every rational being), it can only command that everything be done from maxims of one's will regarded as a will which could at the same time will that it should itself give universal laws, for in that case only the practical principle and the imperative which it obeys are unconditional, since they cannot be based on any interest.

*I may be excused from adducing examples to elucidate this principle, as those which have already been used to elucidate the categorical imperative and its formula would all serve for the like purpose here.

Looking back now on all previous attempts to discover the principle of morality, we need not wonder why they all failed. It was seen that man was bound to laws by duty, but it was not observed that the laws to which he is subject are only those of his own giving, though at the same time they are universal, and that he is only bound to act in conformity with his own will; a will, however, which is designed by nature to give universal laws. For when one has conceived man only as subject to a law (no matter what), then this law required some interest, either by way of attraction or constraint, since it did not originate as a law from his own will, but this will was according to a law obliged by something else to act in a certain manner. Now by this necessary consequence all the labour spent in finding a supreme principle of duty was irrevocably lost. For men never elicited duty, but only a necessity of acting from a certain interest. Whether this interest was private or otherwise, in any case the imperative must be conditional and could not by any means be capable of being a moral command. I will therefore call this the principle of autonomy of the will, in contrast with every other which I accordingly reckon as heteronomy.

The conception of the will of every rational being as one which must consider itself as giving in all the maxims of its will universal laws, so as to judge itself and its actions from this point of view- this conception leads to another which depends on it and is very fruitful, namely that of a kingdom of ends.

By a kingdom I understand the union of different rational beings in a system by common laws. Now since it is by laws that ends are determined as regards their universal validity, hence, if we abstract from the personal differences of rational beings and likewise from all the content of their private ends, we shall be able to conceive all ends combined in a systematic whole (including both rational beings as ends in themselves, and also the special ends which each may propose to himself), that is to say, we can conceive a kingdom of ends, which on the preceding principles is possible.

For all rational beings come under the law that each of them must treat itself and all others never merely as means, but in every case at the same time as ends in themselves. Hence results a systematic union of rational being by common objective laws, i.e., a kingdom which may be called a kingdom of ends, since what these laws have in view is just the relation of these beings to one another as ends and means. It is certainly only an ideal.

A rational being belongs as a member to the kingdom of ends when, although giving universal laws in it, he is also himself subject to these laws. He belongs to it as sovereign when, while giving laws, he is not subject to the will of any other.

A rational being must always regard himself as giving laws either as member or as sovereign in a kingdom of ends which is rendered possible by the freedom of will. He cannot, however, maintain the latter position merely by the maxims of his will, but only in case he is a completely independent being without wants and with unrestricted power adequate to his will.

Morality consists then in the reference of all action to the legislation which alone can render a kingdom of ends possible. This legislation must be capable of existing in every rational being and of emanating from his will, so that the principle of this will is never to act on any maxim which could not without contradiction be also a universal law and, accordingly, always so to act that the will could at the same time regard itself as giving in its maxims universal laws. If now the maxims of rational beings are not by their own nature coincident with this objective principle, then the necessity of acting on it is called practical necessitation, i.e., duty. Duty does not apply to the sovereign in the kingdom of ends, but it does to every member of it and to all in the same degree.

The practical necessity of acting on this principle, i.e., duty, does not rest at all on feelings, impulses, or inclinations, but solely on the relation of rational beings to one another, a relation in which the will of a rational being must always be regarded as legislative, since otherwise it could not be conceived as an end in itself. Reason then refers every maxim of the will, regarding it as legislating universally, to every other will and also to every action towards oneself; and this not on account of any other practical motive or any future advantage, but from the idea of the dignity of a rational being, obeying no law but that which he himself also gives.

In the kingdom of ends everything has either value or dignity. Whatever has a value can be replaced by something else which is equivalent; whatever, on the other hand, is above all value, and therefore admits of no equivalent, has a dignity.

Whatever has reference to the general inclinations and wants of mankind has a market value; whatever, without presupposing a want, corresponds to a certain taste, that is to a satisfaction in the mere purposeless play of our faculties, has a fancy value; but that which constitutes the condition under which alone anything can be an end in itself, this has not merely a relative worth, i.e., value, but an intrinsic worth, that is, dignity.

Now morality is the condition under which alone a rational being can be an end in himself, since by this alone is it possible that he should be a legislating member in the kingdom of ends. Thus morality, and humanity as capable of it, is that which alone has dignity. Skill and diligence in labour have a market value; wit, lively imagination, and humour, have fancy value; on the other hand, fidelity to promises, benevolence from principle (not from instinct), have an intrinsic worth. Neither nature nor art contains anything which in default of these it could put in their place, for their worth consists not in the effects which spring from them, not in the use and advantage which they secure, but in the disposition of mind, that is, the maxims of the will which are ready to manifest themselves in such actions, even though they should not have the desired effect. These actions also need no recommendation from any subjective taste or sentiment, that they may be looked on with immediate favour and satisfaction: they need no immediate propension or feeling for them; they exhibit the will that performs them as an object of an immediate respect, and nothing but reason is required to impose them on the will; not to flatter it into them, which, in the case of duties, would be a contradiction. This estimation therefore shows that the worth of such a disposition is dignity, and places it infinitely above all value, with which it cannot for a moment be brought into comparison or competition without as it were violating its sanctity.

What then is it which justifies virtue or the morally good disposition, in making such lofty claims? It is nothing less than the privilege it secures to the rational being of participating in the giving of universal laws, by which it qualifies him to be a member of a possible kingdom of ends, a privilege to which he was already destined by his own nature as being an end in himself and, on that account, legislating in the kingdom of ends; free as regards all laws of physical nature, and obeying those only which he himself gives, and by which his maxims can belong to a system of universal law, to which at the same time he submits himself. For nothing has any worth except what the law assigns it. Now the legislation itself which assigns the worth of everything must for that very reason possess dignity, that is an unconditional incomparable worth; and the word respect alone supplies a becoming expression for the esteem which a rational being must have for it. Autonomy then is the basis of the dignity of human and of every rational nature.

The three modes of presenting the principle of morality that have been adduced are at bottom only so many formulae of the very same law, and each of itself involves the other two. There is, however, a difference in them, but it is rather subjectively than objectively practical, intended namely to bring an idea of the reason nearer to intuition (by means of a certain analogy) and thereby nearer to feeling. All maxims, in fact, have:

1. A form, consisting in universality; and in this view the formula of the moral

imperative is expressed thus, that the maxims must be so chosen as if they were to serve as universal laws of nature.

2. A matter, namely, an end, and here the formula says that the rational being, as it is an end by its own nature and therefore an end in itself, must in every maxim serve as the condition limiting all merely relative and arbitrary ends.

3. A complete characterization of all maxims by means of that formula, namely, that all maxims ought by their own legislation to harmonize with a possible kingdom of ends as with a kingdom of nature.* There is a progress here in the order of the categories of unity of the form of the will (its universality), plurality of the matter (the objects, i.e., the ends), and totality of the system of these. In forming our moral judgement of actions, it is better to proceed always on the strict method and start from the general formula of the categorical imperative: Act according to a maxim which can at the same time make itself a universal law. If, however, we wish to gain an entrance for the moral law, it is very useful to bring one and the same action under the three specified conceptions, and thereby as far as possible to bring it nearer to intuition.

*Teleology considers nature as a kingdom of ends; ethics regards a possible kingdom of ends as a kingdom nature. In the first case, the kingdom of ends is a theoretical idea, adopted to explain what actually is. In the latter it is a practical idea, adopted to bring about that which is not yet, but which can be realized by our conduct, namely, if it conforms to this idea.

We can now end where we started at the beginning, namely, with the conception of a will unconditionally good. That will is absolutely good which cannot be evil- in other words, whose maxim, if made a universal law, could never contradict itself. This principle, then, is its supreme law: "Act always on such a maxim as thou canst at the same time will to be a universal law"; this is the sole condition under which a will can never contradict itself; and such an imperative is categorical. Since the validity of the will as a universal law for possible actions is analogous to the universal connexion of the existence of things by general laws, which is the formal notion of nature in general, the categorical imperative can also be expressed thus: Act on maxims which can at the same time have for their object themselves as universal laws of nature. Such then is the formula of an absolutely good will.

Rational nature is distinguished from the rest of nature by this, that it sets before itself an end. This end would be the matter of every good will. But since in the idea of a will that is absolutely good without being limited by any condition (of attaining this or that end) we must abstract wholly from every end to be effected (since this would make every will only relatively good), it follows that in this case the end must be conceived, not as an end to be effected, but as an independently existing end. Consequently it is conceived only negatively, i.e., as that which we must never act against and which, therefore, must never be regarded merely as means, but must in every volition be esteemed as an end likewise. Now this end can be nothing but the subject of all possible ends, since this is also the subject of a possible absolutely good will; for such a will cannot without contradiction be postponed to any other object. The principle: "So act in regard to every rational being (thyself and others), that he may always have place in thy maxim as an end in himself," is accordingly essentially identical with this other: "Act upon a maxim which, at the same time, involves its own universal validity for every rational being." For that in using means for every end I should limit my maxim by the condition of its holding good as a law for every subject, this comes to the same thing as that the fundamental principle of all maxims of action must be that the subject of all ends, i.e., the rational being himself, be never employed merely as means, but as the supreme condition restricting the use of all means, that is in every case as an end likewise.

It follows incontestably that, to whatever laws any rational being may be subject, he being an end in himself must be able to regard himself as also legislating universally in respect of these same laws, since it is just this fitness of his maxims for universal legislation that distinguishes him as an end in himself; also it follows that this implies his dignity (prerogative) above all mere physical beings, that he must always take his maxims from the point of view which regards himself and, likewise, every other rational being as law-giving beings (on which account they are called persons). In this way a world of rational beings (mundus intelligibilis) is possible as a kingdom of ends, and this by virtue of the legislation proper to all persons as members. Therefore every rational being must so act as if he were by his maxims in every case a legislating member in the universal kingdom of ends. The formal principle of these maxims is: "So act as if thy maxim were to serve likewise as the universal law (of all rational beings)." A kingdom of ends is thus only possible on the analogy of a kingdom of nature, the former however only by maxims, that is self-imposed rules, the latter only by the laws of efficient causes acting under necessitation from without. Nevertheless, although the system of nature is looked upon as a machine, yet so far as it has reference to rational beings as its ends, it is given on this account the name of a kingdom of nature. Now such a kingdom of ends would be actually realized by means of maxims conforming to the canon which the categorical imperative prescribes to all rational beings, if they were universally followed. But although a rational being, even if he punctually follows this maxim himself, cannot reckon upon all others being therefore true to the same, nor expect that the kingdom of nature and its orderly arrangements shall be in harmony with him as a fitting member, so as to form a kingdom of ends to which he himself contributes, that is to say, that it shall favour his expectation of happiness, still that law: "Act according to the maxims of a member of a merely possible kingdom of ends legislating in it universally," remains in its full force, inasmuch as it commands categorically. And it is just in this that the paradox lies; that the mere dignity of man as a rational creature, without any other end or advantage to be attained thereby, in other words, respect for a mere idea, should yet serve as an inflexible precept of the will, and that it is precisely in this independence of the maxim on all such springs of action that its sublimity consists; and it is this that makes every rational subject worthy to be a legislative member in the kingdom of ends: for otherwise he would have to be conceived only as subject to the physical law of his wants. And although we should suppose the kingdom of nature and the kingdom of ends to be united under one sovereign, so that the latter kingdom thereby ceased to be a mere idea and acquired true reality, then it would no doubt gain the accession of a strong spring, but by no means any increase of its intrinsic worth. For this sole absolute lawgiver must, notwithstanding this, be always conceived as estimating the worth of rational beings only by their disinterested behaviour, as prescribed to themselves from that idea [the dignity of man] alone. The essence of things is not altered by their external relations, and that which, abstracting from these, alone constitutes the absolute worth of man, is also that by which he must be judged, whoever the judge may be, and even by the Supreme Being. Morality, then, is the relation of actions to the relation of actions will, that is, to the autonomy of potential universal legislation by its maxims. An action that is consistent with the autonomy of the will is permitted; one that does not agree therewith is forbidden. A will whose maxims necessarily coincide with the laws of autonomy is a holy will, good absolutely. The dependence of a will not absolutely good on the principle of autonomy (moral necessitation) is obligation. This, then, cannot be applied to a holy being. The objective necessity of actions from obligation is called duty.

From what has just been said, it is easy to see how it happens that, although the conception of duty implies subjection to the law, we yet ascribe a certain dignity and sublimity to the person who fulfils all his duties. There is not, indeed, any sublimity in him, so far as he is subject to the moral law; but inasmuch as in regard to that very law he is likewise a legislator, and on that account alone subject to it, he has sublimity. We have also shown above that neither fear nor inclination, but simply respect for the law, is the spring which can give actions a moral worth. Our own will, so far as we suppose it to act only under the condition that its maxims are potentially universal laws, this ideal will which is possible to us is the proper object of respect; and the dignity of humanity consists just in this capacity of being universally legislative, though with the condition that it is itself subject to this same legislation.

Chapter 13: Virtue Ethics

Comprehension questions you should be able to answer after reading this chapter:

1. What is a "moral saint," and why does Susan Wolf think that the life of a moral saint is not one that we would want to live?

2. What are "reasons of love?"

3. What is the "fulfillment view?" What is the "larger-than-oneself view?"

4. What two conditions of meaning have to be satisfied according to the "fitting fulfillment view?"

5. What are "virtues?"

6. What does Aristotle mean by each of the following: form/essence, telos, areté, eudaimonia? How does each apply to persons?

7. What is the most important "ingredient" for eudaimonia, according to Aristotle?

8. What are the various methods by which we become virtuous?

9. What is the Golden Mean?

10. What is meant by the complaint that virtue ethics does not offer specific moral guidance?

In previous chapters, I tried to identity several features of both utilitarianism and Kantianism that seem to be powerful, legitimate insights into the demands of morality, and the project of ethics. I did so because I believe that both offer something valuable, but each, on its own, is also lacking. I am far from the first philosopher to come to this conclusion. I think Robert Solomon makes the point quite well:

Deontological theories such as Kant's succeed precisely where utilitarian theories fail, in showing how moral principles are unconditional and not dependent on utility, especially in those cases where the greatest good for the greatest number can be realized through injustice or cruelty. Where the deontologist runs into trouble, however, is just where the utilitarian succeeds. One of the great attractions of utilitarianism is its emphasis on human happiness and well-being. The deontologist is not indifferent to such concerns, but they clearly play a secondary role in the theory of morality.... But is it possible or tolerable that happiness should be opposed to morality? To be sure, there are occasions in which we are obliged to do what we do not want to do. But could this opposition be general and imply an antagonism between doing right and living well?

Utilitarians, at their worst, devolve into bickering number-crunchers—treating morality as if it were a math problem. Kantians, at their worst, devolve into cold and obedient robots. And, just to bring divine command theory back into the mix, divine command theorists, at their worst, devolve into fearful and/or self-righteous worshippers of authority. Where is the *joy* in any of this? Where is the satisfaction of a life well-lived? To echo Solomon, is it possible that the moral life is opposed to the sort of life that we would actually *want to live*? Do our lives serve morality, or does morality serve our lives?

Imagine a morally perfect utilitarian. This person is a genius with respect to cost-benefit analyses, and does only that which will maximize utility for all involved. She lives very modestly, as there is almost always something "better" she could do with her money than to spend it on herself. Her home is modest, as is her clothing, and, of course, her lifestyle. How could she justify hosting a dinner party when that money and time could be better spent helping the poor? How could she justify going to a movie with some friends, when she could be mentoring troubled teens instead? One tragic day, she took her young daughter and her daughter's two friends out to a nearby lake to do a beach clean-up. Her daughter began to choke on the meager food they brought, just as the two friends fell into the lake and began to drown. She performed the cost-benefit analysis, and with grim determination left her daughter to choke to death so that she could save the two drowning acquaintances. Saving two lives will produce more utility than saving just one—and it's not as if her daughter counts for more in the cost-benefit analysis....

Imagine a morally perfect Kantian. She always abides by the Categorical Imperative, and when she does, she always acts *from duty*.[160] Whatever she does, she does solely because it is her duty to do so. Desires are fickle. Affection can be biased. To act from love, or from a desire for happiness is to act in accordance with duty, at best, and is neither worthy of praise, nor is a reliable indicator of one who will consistently act as duty requires. She is unerringly honest. "Do I look fat?" "Yes." "Why did you help me, just now?" "Because I could not universalize the maxim according to which I did not help you, Mother." She is dutiful, respectful, and vigilant, at all times....

Would you want to live the lives of either? Are they our only options? Our only justifiable options? If we don't wish to live the lives of a moral perfectionist, are we just selfish?

As Susan Wolf describes the state of things, most major approaches to ethics offer two basic "reasons" to explain or justify our choices, including those choices that have an ethical aspect to them: self-interest, and morality.

The first kind of explanation (viz., an appeal to self-interest) is egoistic, and is characterized as the pursuit of one's own happiness at best, or selfishness at worst. The second kind of explanation (viz., an appeal to moral reasons) instead appeals to moral concepts such as "justice," or "virtue" or what will produce the most "good."

Wolf, however, thinks that some of our choices are not best explained by either, but are better explained by what she calls "reasons of love." As examples, she offers writing philosophy (such as what I am doing at this very moment!), practicing the

---

[160] If you don't remember what the categorical imperative is, or the difference between acting from duty and acting in accordance with duty, review the Kant chapter!

cello, and weeding your garden. In each case, it is entirely possible that these activities demand more time, energy, and resources than is warranted by an appeal to "self-interest," but it is also not the case that these actions are somehow morally required of us. Instead, we do these things simply because we *love* them.

Wolf thinks that to try to understand some of the things we do in terms of either self-interest or morality is misleading. Making a fancy dinner for friends might involve more work and expense than is warranted, based on self-interest alone—but to justify it as "morally valuable" seems "both pompous and hard to sustain." This interpretation "puffs up" such activities. On the other hand, justifying them by saying that we sometimes do things "just because we want to" seems to "sell them short," as though they were mere arbitrary preferences. "I act in these cases not for my sake or the world's; I act neither out of duty nor self-interest. Rather, I am drawn by the particular values of my friend, of philosophy, of a great chocolate cake."[161]

Appealing to "reasons of love," rather than self-interest or moral requirement, expands the categories of justifiable reasons for actions, and allows us to justify intuitive distinctions we already make. "We give a wider moral berth to people's engagement with the projects or realms from which they get meaning than we do to people's pursuit of happiness, pure and simple."[162]

For example, we might tend to think that lying is morally suspect, but acknowledge that lying to protect a loved one seems somehow less blameworthy than lying to protect yourself. Or, we might think that a devoted and passionate musician spending most of her savings on a new instrument seems less "decadent" than her spending it on an expensive bottle of wine—though a devoted and informed wine collector spending that same money on that same bottle might make sense to us! Finally, we might acknowledge that an aspiring actor missing a close friend's birthday party for the sake of an audition for a "dream role" seems more justifiable than missing it from mere apathy.

This recognition and inclusion of "reasons of love" serves an important role in Wolf's understanding of meaning in life, and why "morality" is not the sole relevant consideration we should employ when fashioning our lives. Those for whom morality *is* the sole, relevant consideration, are "moral saints," and Wolf will argue that a moral saint is not someone we would, or should, want to be!

A moral saint is a person whose every action is as morally good as possible, a person who is as morally worthy as one can be. At first glance, this sounds wonderful, and enviable! Shouldn't we all aspire to be a moral saint? "No," says Wolf. This is not because Wolf is some sort of moral villain who delights in evil. Far from it. Her point, though, is that (surprising as it might sound), moral saintliness is not a desirable model of personal well-being. Ultimately, none of us would really want to be a moral saint. What's more, there's good reason for that, according to Wolf.

A moral saint's life is dominated by a commitment to improving the welfare of others, or that of society, in general. A noble ambition, to be sure! Such a person will have many character traits that render her so saintly. She will be patient, considerate,

---

[161] Susan Wolf, *Meaning in Life and Why it Matters*, Princeton University Press, 2012, p. 51.
[162] Ibid., 54.

even-tempered, hospitable, charitable in both thought and deed, quite reluctant to make negative judgments (let alone comments!), and she will be careful not to favor some people over others based on contingent properties (such as race, gender, being one's own child, etc.). What's not to like about such a person? Why wouldn't we (or shouldn't we) all want to be such a person?

Wolf claims that to have the moral virtues to such a degree requires that one neglect other, valuable, non-moral virtues, as well as interests and traits that contribute to a healthy, interesting, well-rounded character. To be maximally good, a real moral saint, think of all the sorts of things one must subordinate and neglect: hobbies, the arts, socializing, wit and humor, delicacies, etc. Wolf wonders, if one completely commits to morality alone, how little love must one have for everything else?

It's important to understand that Wolf's rejection of the life of a moral saint is not a rejection of morality for the sake of relentless self-interest. This is where the importance of those previously mentioned "reasons of love" is clear.

The characters we tend to admire, and often aspire to be, aren't admirable because they're indifferent to justice and goodness, or morality in general, but because they seem to be living meaningful, fulfilling lives—and the pursuit of what they love seems to play an important role in that. Wolf claims that a person's life can be meaningful only if she cares deeply about some things, only if she's moved by "reasons of love"—as opposed to being bored and alienated from most (or all) of what she does. Importantly, acting in ways that positively engage with a worthy object of love can be justified even if it doesn't maximally promote "self-interest" or the impartial "good" of the world. In other words, we can be justified in rejecting the life of a moral saint, without thereby being branded an egoist!

Wolf's own view on what makes for a meaningful life is a combination of two common views on life and meaning: the "fulfillment view," and the "larger-than-oneself view."

According to the "fulfillment view," you should "find your passion." It doesn't matter what you do in life, so long as it's something you love. This is a subjective condition for meaning, of course—and the usual perspective we adopt when considering one's own life, and whether it is meaningful.

"Fulfillment" occurs when we are doing what we love, when we are engaged with something that matters to us. The experience of fulfillment is the opposite of boredom and alienation, but should not to be confused with mere pleasant feelings. For example, riding a roller coaster might be exciting, and eating pizza might be satisfying, but neither would likely be described in terms of "fulfillment." Nor should fulfillment be confused with happiness. Fulfilling lives might be filled with stress, anxiety, and even pain and suffering! Think of the stereotypical "starving artist" who struggles for the sake of her art, but wouldn't give it up for anything. The fact that most of us would be willing to endure stress, anxiety, pain, etc. in pursuit of our passions indicates that fulfillment is regarded as a distinctive and important good in our lives.

This distinction between fulfillment and happiness (or other good feelings) also helps to explain why someone could have a "good" job, health, a comfortable lifestyle, a family, etc., and still feel something "missing."

As useful as it is, Wolf thinks that the fulfillment view is inadequate, by itself, because the only thing that matters according to this view are experiences of a certain subjective quality—regardless of what specific activities provide the feeling of fulfillment. To use some extreme examples, what if someone finds "fulfillment" in being a serial killer? Or what if someone finds "fulfillment" in acts of extreme hoarding? Or, to use the mythological (and philosophically popular) example of Sisyphus, what if Sisyphus is able to reframe his punishment so that he finds fulfillment in endlessly rolling a stone up a hill?

In contrast to the fulfillment view, we have the "larger-than-oneself view." According to this model, you should aspire to be "part of something larger than yourself." It is important to contribute to something whose value is independent of you, such as making the world a "better place," "making a difference," etc.

This is an objective condition for meaning. It doesn't matter if I *feel* that my life has made an impact if, in fact, my life has made no difference to anyone at all! This is also the usual perspective we adopt when considering the lives of others, and whether they are meaningful. When we think that someone is "wasting his life," or "squandering her potential," or "hasn't amounted to much," we aren't considering how that person feels about her own life, but are making a judgment based on what we take to be that person's impact on the world.

The larger-than-oneself view demands that we get involved with something whose source of value is outside of oneself. For that reason, a life of pot-smoking, serial killing, or stone-rolling probably lacks "external" value, and wouldn't be deemed as lives worth living by *others*—and the judgment of others will be relevant, as we will soon see.

To address the limitations of each view, Wolf offers a combination of the two, and calls it the "Fitting Fulfillment View." According to this (combined) view, in order for a life to be meaningful, it must satisfy two conditions:

1. A meaningful life is one the subject finds fulfilling (fulfillment view; subjective)

2. A meaningful life contributes/connects positively to something of value which has its source outside the subject (larger-than-oneself view; objective)

As was indicated, the fitting fulfillment view contains both objective and subjective elements. To be meaningful, the life has to be fulfilling to the one who is living it, but not just any life is *fitting*. Appropriately fulfilling activities are those that have independent value, and can be characterized as objectively good.

The appeal to "objectively good" activities invokes the perspective of an impartial observer. This is somewhat similar to Smith's "impartial spectator" discussed in a previous chapter. This appeal to an impartial point of view corresponds to the desire most of us have that our lives be considered good, valuable, and a rightful source of pride from others' perspectives. Whatever we might *say* in prideful moments, only psychopaths are *truly* unconcerned with what others' think of us, our lives, and whether or not our lives are meaningful. It might be proper to be unconcerned with what a random internet "troll" says about you on twitter, but shouldn't we care what our family thinks of us? Our closest friends? People whom we respect and admire?

We are social animals, and when engaged in projects of independent value, a social value is produced. Others will be able to appreciate and value what we are doing, allowing for overlapping values, and possibly an affirming experience of acceptance and appreciation.

For Wolf, *meaning* arises from loving objects *worthy* of love, and engaging with them in positive ways. This is both objective and subjective: subjective because it involves attitudes and feelings; objective because it must be "worthy" of love." As she puts it, meaning results when "subjective attraction meets objective attractiveness."[163]

One might immediately wonder how the "objective attractiveness" of certain projects and activities gets established. Why would something like playing a musical instrument have independent value, while spending every day smoking marijuana wouldn't? "Who is to say which activities have objective value?" Wolf's answer might be surprising: "No one in particular." Ultimately, *everyone*. Her own inclination is to be "generous" about what is valuable, and that "almost anything that a significant number of people have *taken* to be valuable over a long span of time is valuable."[164]

In one sense, this might be seen as dodging the question, as avoiding the difficult task of explaining how objective value is determined, if it is to be invoked. In another sense, though, this might instead be seen as an appropriately modest acknowledgment that a definitive answer to "what is valuable in life?" is understandably subject to disagreement.

At the very least, even if we can't specify with precision which activities are valuable, and which are not, we might agree that some activities seem to be better candidates for objective value than others. For example, devoting yourself to being a musician requires not only talent, but various admirable character traits such as discipline, dedication, and possibly creativity. Being a musician allows for a display of mastery of a skill, and (arguably) contributes to the world by providing music. In contrast, imagine someone dedicated to growing really-long fingernails. This might require patience, but it might instead just require laziness. What other virtues does it require, or display? What skill is involved, and what mastery is demonstrated? What is provided to the world, other than images of long fingernails?

Can we definitely identify a clear and unambiguous line that separates musicians from fingernail-growers, such that we can unquestionably declare the former independently valuable and the latter a merely subjectively satisfying pursuit? Probably not—but this doesn't rule out a reasonably confident consensus that becoming a skilled musician seems more likely to have independent value, between the two.

Assuming we can agree that, in principle, some activities have independent value, and exhibit "objective attractiveness," how does this contribute to her rejection of the life of a moral saint?

Recall that, as Wolf describes them, moral saints are people whose lives are dominated by a commitment to improving the welfare of others, or that of society, in general, and whose "every action is as morally good as possible." In addition, Wolf claimed that the kind of character capable of that kind of commitment would have to

---

[163] Ibid., 9.
[164] Ibid., 47.

neglect other traits and interests that, while not necessarily morally required, are nevertheless *valuable*.

We know what it means to "love" music, or to "love" travel, or to "love" dancing, and for Wolf these are all potentially "fitting" and "fulfilling" activities, but what would it mean to "love" *morality itself*?

We might have a sense of what it means to love "being of service," or to love "making people happy," or to love "helping those in need"—but those are all expressed in specific activities which might, themselves, be "fitting" and "fulfilling." Being a mentor to at-risk youth is probably morally praise-worthy, but also the sort of activity that, like musicianship, has independent value, allows for the development and display of skill and virtues, and that might be quite fulfilling for the mentor.

Wolf's critique of the moral saint is not that morally-motivated activities are not fitting, nor fulfilling, but that such activities shouldn't be regarded as the *only* fitting and fulfilling activities. What's more, a life that doesn't recognize that we can love more than just "goodness" is one that is *lacking* something important and valuable.

Morality itself does not seem to be a suitable object of passion. Thus, when one reflects, for example, on the Loving Saint easily and gladly giving up his fishing trip or his stereo or his hot fudge sundae at the drop of the moral hat, one is apt to wonder not at how much he loves morality, but at how little he loves these other things. One thinks that, if he can give these up so easily, he does not know what it is to truly love them.[165]

Most of us want to be morally good people, and we also want to be happy (in ways consistent with our self-interest)—but we also most to live a meaningful life. Meaning is not identical to either self-interested happiness or morality. Recognizing that meaning is something desirable in life, something we want for ourselves and others, suggests that there is "more to life" than self-interest and moral duty. There are things "worth doing" that have their value for reasons other than self-interest or moral requirement. In fact, Wolf thinks that, from the moral point of view, we have at least as much reason to promote fulfillment as we do to promote happiness. Fulfillment need not be opposed to morality, but can actually be promoted by it.

Finally, there is an existential significance to a life of meaning. What gives meaning to our lives also tends to give us reasons to live, even in bleak circumstances. Acting in ways that are fulfilling is not mere "selfishness" or immoral self-interest. If the activities satisfy the "fitting fulfillment view," they have independent value. In addition, "it is hard to see how reasons for staying within the moral order could override one's reasons for doing something without which one would lose interest in the world, and so presumably in the moral order of the world, altogether."[166] Imagine, for example, a person for whom making music gives life meaning, being told she must sell her instrument because the money could be used to feed starving people—and that such would be the better, and therefore morally obligatory, use of

---

[165] Wolf, "Moral Saints," *The Journal of Philosophy*, 1982.
[166] Susan Wolf, *Meaning in Life and Why it Matters*, Princeton University Press, 2012, p.57.

the money. Or, imagine a parent devoted to his child being told that he should let his own child drown to save the lives of three strangers (because three lives have more value than one), in the horrible scenario where four children are drowning, and he can't save them all.

Morality is, indeed, one terribly important consideration when it comes to the ordering of our lives, but, for Wolf, it's not the *only* consideration, nor the one that always and obviously "trumps" other considerations of value.

> *Morality, at least as I understand it, is chiefly concerned with integrating into our practical outlook the fact that we are each one person (or perhaps one subject) in a community of others equal in status to ourselves. It requires us to act and to restrain our actions in ways that express respect and concern for others in exchange for our right to claim the same respect and concern from them. But there is another perspective, possibly even more external, in which the demands and interests of morality are not absolute. From a perspective that considers our place in the universe (as opposed to our place in the human or sentient community) a person's obedience or disobedience to moral constraints may itself seem to be one consideration among others.[167]*

In actual practice, we admire all kinds of lives and people. We admire morally good people—and well we should! But, we also admire people who are funny (even when their humor is a little "edgy"). We admire people who have a great sense of style, or who are skilled artists, or extraordinary athletes, or amazing cooks. We admire people for the way they can tell a story, or because they can speak several languages, or because they've traveled the world, or because they have a fantastic palate for wine tasting. This is not to say that the ability to bowl a perfect game, or tell a Syrah from a Zinfandel, is somehow more important or more impressive than being the sort of person who reliably does the morally right thing. What it does indicate is that we have a sense of "the good life" that is broader than that captured by moral sainthood.

The sorts of people we really admire tend to be imperfect blends. They are people who are mostly good, reliably good, but who also possess a fascinating mix of non-moral traits and interests that "rounds them out." An honest and loyal friend who knows how to throw a great dinner party. A kind and compassionate person who plays the piano and really knows a thing or two about film. A lovable rogue with a quick wit (sometimes crossing over into sarcasm), but who always has your best interest at heart. These are not perfect people, by any stretch of the imagination, nor moral saints—but they just might be the kind of people we aspire to become ourselves.

For Wolf, morality has to be about us and for us. It has to offer a life we would actually want to live! For that reason, a perfect rule-follower or utility calculator does not suffice. What is needed is an ethic that is concerned with life, and what it means to live well. Virtue ethics is offered as just such an approach.

---

[167] Ibid., 58-59.

Virtue Ethics

As you can probably infer, virtue ethics is an approach to ethics that focuses on the virtues. Virtues are character traits, dispositions to behave, that we think are good to have, praiseworthy, and instrumental in living a good life.

One of the first questions that can arise with respect to virtues concerns whether they are "universal" or culturally relative. It's not hard to argue, for example, that one culture's virtues might be a different culture's vices. For Aristotle and his fellow Greek aristocrats, pride is a virtue. For Christian cultures, it's foremost among the seven deadly sins. The "manly" heroic virtues favored during the Trojan War (1194–1184 BCE) are seemingly different from those that would be espoused by Tibetan Buddhists today.

For some philosophers, such as Robert Solomon, the cultural relativity of the virtues is a given, by no means a "problem," and is something to be understood and embraced. If David Hume was right, and virtues are (basically) character features that are pleasing to others, then Solomon would remind us that what is pleasing to others will vary, understandably, across communities. What is pleasing to Greek aristocrats might not please a community of Christian monks, and what pleases the monks might not please feudal samurai, and what pleases the samurai might not please capitalist Americans.

Solomon points out that the virtues are understood as parts of a way of life. These "ways" vary. Everyone eats, but what and how one eats might vary considerably. Generally speaking, one should "clean one's plate" in Germany, but leave a little bit of food on your plate in the Middle East. Dinner conversation is (generally) subdued in Japan, but animate and even loud in Turkey. What is "gluttonous" in one culture might be "appreciative" in another, and what comes across as "dignified" in one place might be "aloof" in still another. "Temperance" might mean abstinence in one community, but simply "moderation" in another. The virtues of an aristocrat probably won't include those associated with labor (e.g., hard work, perseverance), whereas those labor-related traits might be highly esteemed during the "westward expansion" phase of U.S. history.

Because Solomon believes that virtues always represent the ideals of a particular "ethos" (i.e., the overall character of an entire society), we should expect that what counts as a virtue will vary to the extent that ethos vary. In a highly pluralistic society such as our own, it is difficult to establish a singular and overarching ethos—and therefore it is implausible to expect a single and shared set of recognized virtues. Instead, there will be the virtues of various defined communities. Religious communities. Academic communities. Workplace communities. Athletic communities. The qualities that make you an excellent lawyer might make you a lousy Christian! And vice versa.

On the other hand, although different communities might emphasize different virtues, this does not necessarily mean that the concept of virtue is a mere cultural creation. In fact, the similarities in virtues across cultures are perhaps even more striking than their differences. Consider the following examples of virtues celebrated by different people, at different times in their histories:

- The four "cardinal" virtues (ancient Greek/Roman): wisdom, courage, temperance, justice
- The seven "heavenly" virtues (Christianity): wisdom, courage, temperance, justice, faith, hope, charity
- Navajo virtues: generosity, loyalty, self-control, peacefulness, amity, courteousness, honesty
- Sioux virtues: bravery, fortitude, generosity, and wisdom
- From an ancient Egyptian text (*Instruction of Ptahhotep*, which is 4000 years old!): self-control, moderation, kindness, generosity, justice, truthfulness, discretion.
- Swahili proverbs: kindness, prudence, patience, courage, self-control, humbleness, honesty, fairness, responsibility, respectfulness, cooperation.
- Traditional Japanese virtues: loyalty, justice, humanity, compassion, honor, respect
- Confucian virtues: gravity, generosity of soul, sincerity, earnestness, and kindness.
- Sikh virtues: Truth, Contentment, Patience, Faith, and Daya (compassion)
- Hindu virtues: Non-violence, Truth, Purity, Self-control
- Buddhist virtues: Charity, Uprightness, Forbearance, Dispassion, Dauntlessness, Contemplation

There are differences to be found, of course, but note the many similarities. Perhaps there are certain character traits that are just plain useful for *any* human to develop and display? Perhaps, also, some of the apparent differences between different cultures values are merely differences in application rather than in the virtues themselves. In cultures accustomed to regular warfare, "courage" is likely to be interpreted as "battlefield" courage—the ability to overcome fear of death and injury and persist in combat. In the contemporary United States, few of us are called upon to be actual warriors—for better or for worse. We have a professional military and a police force for such things. Not surprisingly, our culture is not very focused on cultivating "battlefield" courage in all its citizens. Instead, we tend to talk about having the "courage of one's convictions." Standing up for what you believe in is much more likely to manifest as something like speaking up for oneself when challenged, or having the guts to disagree with powerful people, than as epic sword fights and glorious self-sacrifice. Achilles was deemed brave for risking his life. You or I might be deemed brave for risking our jobs. However courage might manifest, many regard courage as a universal virtue. Indeed, some argue that, without courage, none of the other virtues are possible for us either. More a poet than a philosopher, Maya Angelou nevertheless captured this idea when she claimed that, "without courage, we cannot practice any other virtue with consistency. We can't be kind, true, merciful, generous, or honest."

Whether or not there truly are some universal virtues, and what those virtues are, is (thankfully) beyond the scope of this chapter. For our purposes, it's enough to recognize the mere possibility of universal virtues, and to recognize the important role culture has to play in our interpretation and celebration of certain virtues.

Beyond the "relativity" debate, there is also considerable debate as to the nature of the relationship between the virtues and morality. Some believe that only a virtue-centered understanding of morality "works," and therefore reject other approaches such as utilitarianism or Kantianism. Others believe that virtues supplement or reinforce our ability to fulfill our obligations as defined by one of the other theories. For example, someone who is courageous is better able to abide by the CI, so courage is a valuable character trait to cultivate—but only for its ability to enable us to adhere to the CI. Or, perhaps temperate people are better able to calculate utility with accuracy and objectivity, so temperance is worth cultivating—but, again, for the sake of utilitarian cost-benefit analyses as opposed to for its own sake.

Still other people believe that theories that focus on rules or procedures (e.g., either Kantianism or utilitarianism) capture one important aspect of morality, while virtue ethics captures another. The different approaches, then, complement each other, and neither is dispensable.

This is my own view: that each approach offers something valuable, but that none, by themselves, fully capture what concerns us when we're engaged in the project of understanding what it means to be moral.

Virtue ethics, our final approach to ethics for this book, is older than both utilitarianism and Kantianism, and older than the specifically Christian version of divine command theory. Although virtue ethics has gained in popularity since the latter half of the 20th century, and is now widely recognized as one of the "big three" (secular) theories (alongside Kantianism and Utilitarianism), it was most popular—indeed, dominant—in ancient Greece, with Aristotle's version being the most celebrated.

Aristotle

Aristotle lived from 384 BCE to 323 BCE. At around the age of 18, he began studying under Plato. He studied and taught at Plato's Academy until the time of Plato's death, when curriculum disagreements between Aristotle and Plato's successor to head the Academy (Plato's own nephew, Speussipus) inspired Aristotle to split from the Academy. There might also have been a bit of resentment involved, as Aristotle had been a strong candidate for the position as well. Aristotle took on the job of tutor to no less a youth than Alexander the Great. He eventually opened his own school (the *Lyceum*) and his followers became known as "Peripatetics," due to their habit of walking the gardens (*peripatoi* = covered walk) while having their deep philosophical conversations.

Aristotle favored an empirical approach to knowledge (in contrast to his mentor, Plato). That is, the source of knowledge will be data collected from sense experience. Correctly interpreted, this will provide theoretical as well as scientific knowledge. As an example of his dedication to this method, he spent several years studying marine organisms, in effect inventing what we now know as the discipline of marine biology.

He was confident that from observations of particular things, we could gain insight into universal concepts. For example, to gain insight into politics, in general, he studied the particular constitutions of 158 existing states. As another example, we thought that we could learn about morality, in general, by studying actual people and how they behave.

Aristotle did not limit himself to ethics, politics, and marine biology. If it existed as a subject of inquiry, he pursued it. A "renaissance man" a millennia and a half before the Renaissance, Aristotle studied and wrote about physics, "metaphysics," poetry, theater and music, logic and rhetoric and linguistics, politics and government, ethics, biology, and zoology.

Given the specific focus of this book, we will spend little time on Aristotle's metaphysics, except with respect to some ideas that will be directly relevant to our understanding of his political/ethical theory, beginning with his concept of "causation." Aristotle provides us with *four* different notions of "cause."

Causation

1. Material cause
2. Efficient cause
3. Formal cause
4. Final cause

A thing's Material cause is its matter, the raw materials of which it is made. Using the example of a statue, its Material cause is marble (or whatever kind of stone the sculptor used).

An Efficient cause is a thing's origin—the process responsible for it being what it is. In the case of the statue, its Efficient cause is the sculptor and her tools.

The Formal cause is a thing's essence, the governing idea giving it its structure and form. For the statue, its Formal cause is the vision of the completed sculpture entertained by the sculptor. Finally, we have the Final cause. *The Final cause is the end or purpose ("telos") that the thing is to fulfill*. With the statue, perhaps its Final cause is to depict the likeness of Aristotle. For our purposes, focus on that idea of a Final cause.

When we combine Aristotle's notion of a final cause, and his notion of essence/form, we get his teleology: the goal-oriented structure of the universe.

Telos

The essence of each kind of substance includes its "inner drive" to develop in a certain kind of way, to actualize its potential. For example, part of the essence of an acorn is its *telos* (Final cause)—namely, to become an oak tree. All things have a "*telos*" relating to their essence. The *telos* of an acorn is to become an oak tree, the *telos* of a knife is to cut. Human beings also have an essence, and a potential to actualize.

To understand the essence of humans, and our *telos*, we have to understand Aristotle's different categories of soul (I know, we're diverting into quite a lot of ancient philosophy, but trust me—his ethics will make much more sense thanks to these details). Don't think that Aristotle is getting religious when he discusses souls. As a biologist, his understanding of "souls" was naturalistic. A soul was not some sort of spirit that flies away when the body dies and goes to heaven. Instead, for living things, the soul just was the "essence" (form) of that kind of living thing. Because there is no such thing as form apart from matter, clearly, Aristotle's notion of the soul is not anything that could somehow survive the death of the body. That would literally make no sense to him.

There are three basic kinds of souls: vegetative, animal, and rational. Vegetative souls (sometimes called nutritive souls) are the essences of different kinds of plants. Vegetative souls make possible growth and nourishment. Anything capable of growth, therefore, can be understood in terms of a vegetative soul. Some living things are capable of more than growth, though. Animals, unlike plants, are also capable of perception, motion, and expression. An animal soul, then, is the kind of essence that makes such things possible. Animals, therefore, are to be understood in terms of both animal and vegetative souls, whereas plants are understood only in terms of vegetative souls. Finally, some living things (e.g., humans) are capable of more than growth, motion, perception, and expression. We are also capable of thinking, judging, and belief-formation—in short, Reason. Rational souls make this possible. Humans, then, (exclusively, according to Aristotle) have aspects of all three types.

Since a thing's potential is determined by its essence, and a thing's *telos* is determined by its potential, our own *telos* (our Final cause) is likewise determined by our essence, by the kind of thing that we are. Since that which makes humans distinctly human, and different from every other living thing, is our capacity for Reason, it should come as no surprise that Reason will play a significant role in our *telos*. Once again, the practical benefit of philosophy is clear: philosophical contemplation is not only the means by which we can understand our *telos*, but, as the highest use of Reason, is the clearest expression of a fully actualized human being.

In addition to each thing having a *telos* (an end, a purpose), *each thing has an "excellence" (in Greek, "areté")* that serves that *telos*. Just like the *telos,* a thing's *areté* is likewise based on its essence, and is that by which we evaluate the quality of the thing with regard to its *telos*. That sounds complicated, but it's really fairly simple. A knife's *telos* is to cut. Its *areté* will be that which makes it excellent with regard to cutting. "Sharpness" seems like a pretty good candidate for its *areté*! The *telos* of an eyeball is to see. An eyeball's *areté*, then, will be that which makes it excellent with regard to seeing. An ophthalmologist could surely discuss this better than I, but I would assume that the overall shape of the eye, the transparency of its lens (e.g., not having any cataracts), and other such things would constitute the *areté* of an eyeball. The example that will matter to us, of course, is that of a human being. Earlier in this chapter, just after a discussion of "moral saints," I mentioned the need for an ethical system concerned with living well. Such was Aristotle's emphasis, and such was his understanding of our *telos*. What is our *telos*? What is our *areté*?

Eudaimonia

Aristotle, like many ancient philosophers, believed that the ultimate "end" in life, life's ultimate goal and purpose, was "*eudaimonia.*" This is sometimes translated as happiness, but that's misleading. To render it "happiness" suggests that *eudaimonia* is a feeling, or, worse yet, that's it's just a fancy Greek word for pleasure. Not so. *Eudaimonia is better translated as "flourishing."* It refers to an overall quality of one's life. Thus, one is not "*eudaimon*" on Monday, but not so much on Tuesday. It is one's whole life that is either "*eudaimon*," or not.

There are several ways to try to capture the meaning of a life that is "*eudaimon*." Some of them have become cliché's, but they'll suffice. Realizing your potential. Being fully alive. Thriving. Being all you can be. Exemplifying what it is to be human.

Why is *eudaimonia* our *telos*? Because all other "ends" have only instrumental value. That is, we pursue them for the sake of something else. Success, for its own sake? Wealth, for its own sake? A good reputation, for its own sake? Education, for its own sake? All these things are valuable, to be sure, and certainly worthy of attainment, but for each of them there is an implicit "because." Wealth is desirable because it enables one to live comfortably, and to pursue the things important to her. Education is valuable because it better allows us to understand ourselves, and the world. But what about *eudaimonia*? This rich notion of "happiness" involving one's entire being, culminating in a truly excellent life? Because? Just because, it seems. *Aristotle thought that eudaimonia was intrinsically valuable, pursued for its own sake— the ultimate "end" to which all other worthy ends point.*

Assuming Aristotle is right about that, what it means for a human to flourish will be defined by a human's essence. Reason is uniquely human, so our flourishing must involve Reason, a life in which our behavior and our character is determined and governed by Reason rather than our appetites. For Aristotle, this is what it means to be virtuous.

Virtue

Virtue will be the most important ingredient in a life that is *eudaimon*. Without it, *eudaimonia* will be impossible. With it, *eudaimonia* is not guaranteed, but virtue is the most reliable means to a life that is *eudaimon*. Note that even virtue does not guarantee *eudaimonia*. Aristotle recognized that other factors, admittedly often beyond our control, influence our ability to flourish as well. For Aristotle, these other factors included political stability, wealth, beauty, reputation, having a good family, having good friends, etc. For many of us, some of the elements of this list seem unfair, or even outrageous. Wealth? Why not? Being wealthy certainly doesn't guarantee an excellent character (in fact, it can be an obstacle to it), but being desperately poor probably doesn't help either! Health? Sick people can certainly have excellent character, and illness can often be a means to developing courage, patience, and other virtues. However, a life wracked with pain and suffering can hardly be called an excellent life. Beauty? Let's face it: attractive people have an easier time in life. That might be unfair, but it seems to be true. If you are considered attractive, you reap numerous benefits that others do not. Studies indicate that those perceived as being attractive have an easier time getting jobs (and better jobs), are promoted more often, receive better treatment from the police and the legal system, have more choices in romantic partners, and are even perceived as being more intelligent and morally better! All Aristotle is recognizing here is that the recipe for an excellent life includes several ingredients. Virtue is the most important, by far—but it's not the only ingredient.

Given that the most important ingredient is also the one over which we have the most control, it makes sense for us to focus on having a good character. Those with good character possess the virtues among their character traits. *Virtues are simply dispositions (habits) to behave in certain ways*. The virtues are positive dispositions, such as honesty, respectfulness, generosity, courage, etc. There are also negative dispositions (vices) such as disloyalty, cowardice, greediness, etc. Generally speaking, we want to display the virtues, and not the vices.

Aristotle had a particular understanding of the virtues. First, he thought there were two kinds: intellectual, and moral.

Intellectual virtues are based on excellence in reasoning, and can be taught. Prudence is an example of an intellectual virtue. *The moral virtues, on the other hand, can't be taught (not directly, at least), but must be lived and practiced in order for one to acquire them.* You could read a very well-written book on courage, for example, without it making you one bit more courageous. The way we acquire those sorts of virtues is by practicing them. We become courageous by putting ourselves in fearsome situations, and then overcoming that fear. We become honest by telling the truth. Aristotle says, "It is right, then, to say that by doing what is just a man becomes just, and temperate by doing what is temperate, while without doing thus he has no chance of ever becoming good. But most men, instead of doing thus, fly to theories, and fancy that they are philosophizing and that this will make them good, like a sick man who listens attentively to what the doctor says and then disobeys all his orders. This sort of philosophizing will no more produce a healthy habit of mind than this sort of treatment will produce a healthy habit of body (Nicomachean Ethics, Book 2, chapter 4)."

When I lie, I am training myself to be a liar. When I steal, I am training myself to be a thief. When I act without compassion, I am training myself to be cold and cruel. If those are all traits I would like to avoid, I had better practice their opposites! Practice, then, is essential in acquiring the virtues—and they are not our virtues until they become habitual. To say that it is habitual means that in order to qualify as generous, for example, you have to be generous most of the time. Being generous one time in your life doesn't earn you the right to be labeled generous!

Habit covers one half of Aristotle's particular understanding of virtue. The other half refers to the "mean." For Aristotle, a virtue is a character trait that hits the "mean" and is manifested in habitual action, or what he called "habituation."

This doctrine of the "mean" is often referred to as *"the Golden Mean." According to this doctrine, we should choose the "mean" over the extremes of excess and deficit.* The extremes of excess and deficiency occur when we're ruled by desires/emotions and not reason. This reminds us of the central role of reason in human excellence. Virtue serves to correct these disorders by helping us to resist our impulses and desires that interfere with us living the good life. For example, the virtue of courage corrects for inappropriate fear. The virtue of temperance corrects our impulses to overindulge or to seek immediate and harmful pleasures. The mean shows us a rational course of action by choosing between the two competing desire extremes (e.g., fear and wrath), letting neither desire have complete control.

That virtue is seen as a "mean" is interesting, and unusual. Most people see virtue as the opposite of a vice. Aristotle sees virtue as the mean between two vices, one of excess, and one of deficiency. The following is a list of virtues entertained by Aristotle. Note that the virtue is depicted as a mean between two vices.

Issue	Vice (Deficiency)	Virtue (Mean)	Vice (Excess)
Fear	Cowardice	Courage	Foolhardiness
Pleasure/Pain	Inhibition	Temperance	Overindulgence
Spending	Miserliness	Liberality	Extravagance
Spending (major)	Shabbiness	Magnificence	Vulgarity
Ambition	Lack of ambition	Proper ambition	Over-Ambition
Self-esteem	Meekness	Magnanimity	Vanity
Anger	Timidity	Righteous indignation	Hot-temperedness
Conversation	Boorishness	Wittiness	Buffoonery
Social Conduct	Crankiness	Friendliness	Obsequiousness

Notice, for example, that courage is not the opposite of cowardice, but rather the mean between cowardice (excessive fear) and foolhardiness (bravado). Being temperate doesn't mean that you never indulge any desires, but enjoy sensual delights appropriately (at the right times, and in the right amounts).

The mean is the "perfect" thing for a particular person to do in a specific situation. Note the relativity of this. Courage is different for different people. Someone with agoraphobia shows courage simply by stepping outside. A very sociable person, on the other hand, must take a very different sort of risk in order to display courage. What might count as a generous donation from you or me is probably quite different from what would qualify as a generous donation from Bill Gates.

A morally admirable person is one who has learned (over time, and with experience) what it means to be virtuous, and how to apply that understanding in ever-changing circumstances, reliably finding "just the right way" to behave, so much so that it is habitual, a reliable feature of her very character. Her reason commands her passions and appetites, and she avoids extreme emotional responses in either direction, hitting the "mean" instead. It tends to be the "extremes" in life that get us into trouble. As a result, she is not led off her path or distracted from her pursuit of the good life. With the addition of some favorable circumstances, her life could be *eudaimon*.

Although the Golden Mean sounds mathematical, it falls short of providing us a formula, or even any concrete list of "thou shalt nots." In fairness to Aristotle, he thought ethics could not be understood in that way. Ethics is not like math. If any analogy is to be made, the ancients (including Aristotle) preferred the analogy to medicine. Indeed, philosophy was often referred to as "medicine for the soul."

There is a science to medicine, to be sure, but a good doctor isn't one who has memorized all the I.C.D. codes, nor is the good psychiatrist the one who has memorized the DSM-IVTR. What makes medicine so interesting (and challenging) is those darn patients! Each one is subtly different, though their symptoms might be quite similar. Excellent doctors are the ones that can synthesize their theoretical understanding with the practical information and context before them. Martha Nussbaum, a contemporary philosopher and expert on Aristotle put it this way: "Excellent ethical choice cannot be captured completely in general rules because-like medicine-it is a matter of fitting one's choice to the complex requirements of a concrete situation, taking all of its contextual features into account."

Wisdom (understood as "practical wisdom," *phronesis*) was regarded by Aristotle as the "master" virtue. Without it, none of the other virtues enjoy guidance, and we won't know how to implement them. For example, the "Golden Mean" is the virtuous avoidance of two extremes (vices). Too much "courage" becomes recklessness, and too little becomes cowardice. How much is enough, though? We need *phronesis* to discern the answer to that question.

Similarly, virtues often come into conflict with each other. Kindness is a virtue, but so is honesty. Imagine you have a friend who is going out for the evening, and she asks you how she looks. You think her outfit is unflattering. The honest answer might not be kind, but the kind answer might not be honest. Which virtue should prevail, in such a situation of conflict? Once again, *phronesis* is needed to resolve that dilemma— and no simple, formulaic answer is possible. To know the right thing to do will require that you know your friend very well. Is she very sensitive? Will an honest answer crush her self-esteem? Will it ruin the friendship? Will she be grateful for the honest feedback? Also, you would need to know the situation. How important are her plans? Is it just an average night out, with nothing at stake? Is she on a first date? Is she interviewing for a job? Does she have other options? If you tell her the outfit is unflattering, is there anything else she could wear instead, that would be appropriate and more flattering? An understanding of all these things (and probably more) is needed, in order to discern the right course of action, for that person, in that situation. Someone who can reliably discern that right thing to do, is wise.

Returning to the example of courage, Aristotle can urge us to be courageous, but that's going to sound pretty hollow until we have a context in which to understand courage. What it means to be courageous will vary from one person to the next, from one circumstance to the next—and that's why we can't get specific "rules" from virtue approaches, like "always rush into battle." Sometimes it might be courageous to rush into battle, but other times that will be stupidity. Towards the end of the 2003 film, The Last Samurai, all of the samurai from the last holdout clan resisting "reform" enter battle knowing it will be their last, knowing they will die. This might well be courage, as they are overcoming fear of death for the sake of their principles. However, after much success in the battle, they end their fight with a cavalry charge into a line of Gatling guns. They are cut down with only one character (the main one) managing to survive. It's questionable whether that final charge was "courageous," as a case could certainly be made that it was more foolhardy. After all, courage doesn't require one to abandon sound tactics. Was their charge courageous, or reckless? No obvious and indisputable answer is available, as virtue is a subtle thing.

This is not to say that Aristotle (and virtue ethicists, in general) provides no moral guidance. For Aristotle, guidance was everywhere. Look around Athens and take note of those who are esteemed, and those who are held in disgrace. There are already people deemed virtuous. Be like those people. Robert Solomon (a contemporary American philosopher) thinks the alleged threat of virtue vagueness is overstated.

> *When we discuss the virtues in general, they can become vague and we can begin to think that almost anything can be a virtue somewhere, under some conditions, but when we look at particular communities and their practices, this vagueness is dispelled and the virtues emerge with remarkable clarity and strictness.*

We all have moral role-models in our lives, whether they are friends, family members, teachers or priests or mentors, historical figures, or even fictional characters. Each one of us is capable of thinking of a person (perhaps several) of whom we would say, "That person is an excellent human being. I wish I were more like him (or her)." Even the "What Would Jesus Do" (WWJD) movement expresses this theme. By modeling our behavior on those who have already achieved a level of personal excellence, we can practice and pursue that excellence ourselves. This is not unlike a golfer trying to model her swing after Tiger Wood's, or a pianist studying the technique of Little Richard. Perhaps looking for "human virtues" is to overreach, but to seek after what it means to be an admirable person within your own community is not so difficult.

Speaking of community, it would be a mistake to think that Aristotle's understanding of ethics is somehow focused exclusively on the self in isolation. Aristotle was especially and overtly sensitive to the demands of community.

> *The complete good is thought to be self-sufficient. Now by self-sufficient we do not mean that which is sufficient for a man all by himself, for one who lives a solitary life, but also for parents, children, wife, and in general for friends and fellow citizens, since, a human being by nature is a political animal.*

Aristotle even ties the flourishing of the individual to the flourishing of his greater society. As such, one cannot be happy unless a similar happiness is realized in the greater society. Since our *eudaimonia* is affected by life circumstances (e.g., health, political stability, wealth, etc.), a "bad" society will interfere with personal flourishing. One can be virtuous in spite of bad circumstances, but one would be impaired in the practice of one's virtue.

Still others argue that, far from being in conflict with community, the pursuit of private perfection is necessary for an excellent community. Stanley Cavell (another contemporary philosopher) argues (at least with respect to democratic societies) that our democratic institutions and principles will only be as strong and just as are the individuals who run, apply, and criticize them. Perfectionism is needed to create the sort of character needed for a healthy democracy. Second, relying solely upon institutional principles of justice inspires complacency in the face of the many sorts of injustices and brutality we witness that are not excluded by institutional principles of justice alone. "The perfectionist will never be satisfied with himself and the system as long as any injustice or misery exists. Reproaching himself and the system for not doing better, he will constantly struggle to better himself and others. Democracy, if it is to realize the best justice possible, needs this vigilance and supererogation."

The virtue approach encourages individual greatness—but not solely for our own sake, as if there is some forced choice between self and society. Instead, this approach recognizes that we are social creatures, and must understand ourselves as part of a community. Our flourishing is tied to others. Excellent individuals make for excellent communities, and excellent communities facilitate excellent individuals.

Conclusion: What Virtue Ethics Seems to be Getting Right

- One's "attitude" and general disposition with regard to morally right actions *does* seem to matter. Truly honest people don't struggle with honesty. Indeed, they probably rarely, if ever, even contemplate lying. This seems more morally impressive than the person who grits his teeth, digs in his heels, and barely manages to tell the truth despite his worst intentions.
- The "virtue" approach *does* seem to help with that pesky "altruism v. egoism" debate within the field of ethics. It overcomes the self-interest concern by acknowledging that there need be no divide between one's own happiness and the demands of morality—indeed, it claims that our own happiness depends on our being morally good. In this way, virtue ethics renders the *good* life the good *life*—a life worth having, and therefore worth pursuing.
- Who one *is* (as opposed to what one does) *does* seem significant. Moral goodness seems to be about who one is, one's basic character, and in ways that can't be captured by a checklist concerning whether one has been naughty or nice.
- The vocabulary of admiration or disgust *does* seem important for our daily moral evaluations. We are more likely to speak of how someone is a "great man," or how "you disgust me," than to speak in terms of rules violated, or utility squandered.

Just as Plato was Socrates' student, Aristotle (384 BCE – 322 BCE) was Plato's student. Aristotle is also tremendously important in the history of Western philosophy, and is often understood as a practical, empirical contrast to his idealist teacher. Aristotle seemed to study and be an expert on virtually everything, ranging from physics to poetry, to marine biology, to logic, and to ethics (to name just a few). Aristotle's thought shaped much of medieval philosophy and was so respected that Aquinas refers to him simply as "the philosopher." In this excerpt from his "Nicomachean Ethics", Aristotle argues that happiness (eudaimonia) is the ultimate aim of all our actions. Given that we are rational and social animals, this fulfillment of our "end" (telos) will require a life of reason and relationships. Virtue (areté) is the most important ingredient in living an excellent life (i.e., one that achieves eudaimonia). Intellectual virtues might be taught, but moral virtues must be practiced and trained. One means of training is to pursue the "golden mean" in our actions.

Nicomachean Ethics
Aristotle

Book I

Let us again return to the good we are seeking, and ask what it can be. It seems different in different actions and arts; it is different in medicine, in strategy, and in the other arts likewise. What then is the good of each? Surely that for whose sake everything else is done. In medicine this is health, in strategy victory, in architecture a house, in any other sphere something else, and in every action and pursuit the end; for it is for the sake of this that all men do whatever else they do. Therefore, if there is an end for all that we do, this will be the good achievable by action, and if there are more than one, these will be the goods achievable by action.

So the argument has by a different course reached the same point; but we must try to state this even more clearly. Since there are evidently more than one end, and we choose some of these (e.g. wealth, flutes, and in general instruments) for the sake of something else, clearly not all ends are final ends; but the chief good is evidently something final. Therefore, if there is only one final end, this will be what we are seeking, and if there are more than one, the most final of these will be what we are seeking. Now we call that which is in itself worthy of pursuit more final than that which is worthy of pursuit for the sake of something else, and that which is never desirable for the sake of something else more final than the things that are desirable both in themselves and for the sake of that other thing, and therefore we call final without qualification that which is always desirable in itself and never for the sake of something else.

Now such a thing happiness, above all else, is held to be; for this we choose always for self and never for the sake of something else, but honour, pleasure, reason, and every virtue we choose indeed for themselves (for if nothing resulted from them we should still choose each of them), but we choose them also for the sake of happiness, judging that by means of them we shall be happy. Happiness, on the other hand, no one chooses for the sake of these, nor, in general, for anything other than itself.

From the point of view of self-sufficiency the same result seems to follow; for the final good is thought to be self-sufficient. Now by self-sufficient we do not mean that which is sufficient for a man by himself, for one who lives a solitary life, but also for parents, children, wife, and in general for his friends and fellow citizens, since man is born for citizenship. But some limit must be set to this; for if we extend our requirement to ancestors and descendants and friends' friends we are in for an infinite series. Let us examine this question, however, on another occasion; the self-sufficient we now define as that which when isolated makes life desirable and lacking in nothing; and such we think happiness to be; and further we think it most desirable of all things, without being counted as one good thing among others- if it were so counted it would clearly be made more desirable by the addition of even the least of goods; for that which is added becomes an excess of goods, and of goods the greater is always more desirable. Happiness, then, is something final and self-sufficient, and is the end of action.

Presumably, however, to say that happiness is the chief good seems a platitude, and a clearer account of what it is still desired. This might perhaps be given, if we could first ascertain the function of man. For just as for a flute-player, a sculptor, or an artist, and, in general, for all things that have a function or activity, the good and the 'well' is thought to reside in the function, so would it seem to be for man, if he has a function. Have the carpenter, then, and the tanner certain functions or activities, and has man none? Is he born without a function? Or as eye, hand, foot, and in general each of the parts evidently has a function, may one lay it down that man similarly has a function apart from all these? What then can this be? Life seems to be common even to plants, but we are seeking what is peculiar to man. Let us exclude, therefore, the life of nutrition and growth. Next there would be a life of perception, but it also seems to be common even to the horse, the ox, and every animal. There remains, then, an active life of the element that has a rational principle; of this, one part has such a principle in the sense of being obedient to one, the other in the sense of possessing one and exercising thought. And, as 'life of the rational element' also has two meanings, we must state that life in the sense of activity is what we mean; for this seems to be the more proper sense of the term. Now if the function of man is an activity of soul which follows or implies a rational principle, and if we say 'so-and-so- and 'a good so-and-so' have a function which is the same in kind, e.g. a lyre, and a good lyre-player, and so without qualification in all cases, eminence in respect of goodness being idded to the name of the function (for the function of a lyre-player is to play the lyre, and that of a good lyre-player is to do so well): if this is the case, and we state the function of man to be a certain kind of life, and this to be an activity or actions of the soul implying a rational principle, and the function of a good man to be the good and noble performance of these, and if any action is well performed when it is performed in accordance with the appropriate excellence: if this is the case, human good turns out to be activity of soul in accordance with virtue, and if there are more than one virtue, in accordance with the best and most complete.

But we must add 'in a complete life.' For one swallow does not make a summer, nor does one day; and so too one day, or a short time, does not make a man blessed and happy.

Let this serve as an outline of the good; for we must presumably first sketch it roughly, and then later fill in the details. But it would seem that any one is capable of carrying on and articulating what has once been well outlined, and that time is a good discoverer or partner in such a work; to which facts the advances of the arts are due; for any one can add what is lacking. And we must also remember what has been said before, and not look for precision in all things alike, but in each class of things such precision as accords with the subject-matter, and so much as is appropriate to the inquiry. For a carpenter and a geometer investigate the right angle in different ways; the former does so in so far as the right angle is useful for his work, while the latter inquires what it is or what sort of thing it is; for he is a spectator of the truth. We must act in the same way, then, in all other matters as well, that our main task may not be subordinated to minor questions. Nor must we demand the cause in all matters alike; it is enough in some cases that the fact be well established, as in the case of the first principles; the fact is the primary thing or first principle. Now of first principles we see some by induction, some by perception, some by a certain habituation, and others too in other ways. But each set of principles we must try to investigate in the natural way, and we must take pains to state them definitely, since they have a great influence on what follows. For the beginning is thought to be more than half of the whole, and many of the questions we ask are cleared up by it....

Yet evidently, as we said, it needs the external goods as well; for it is impossible, or not easy, to do noble acts without the proper equipment. In many actions we use friends and riches and political power as instruments; and there are some things the lack of which takes the lustre from happiness, as good birth, goodly children, beauty; for the man who is very ugly in appearance or ill-born or solitary and childless is not very likely to be happy, and perhaps a man would be still less likely if he had thoroughly bad children or friends or had lost good children or friends by death. As we said, then, happiness seems to need this sort of prosperity in addition; for which reason some identify happiness with good fortune, though others identify it with virtue....

Must no one at all, then, be called happy while he lives; must we, as Solon says, see the end? Even if we are to lay down this doctrine, is it also the case that a man is happy when he is dead? Or is not this quite absurd, especially for us who say that happiness is an activity? But if we do not call the dead man happy, and if Solon does not mean this, but that one can then safely call a man blessed as being at last beyond evils and misfortunes, this also affords matter for discussion; for both evil and good are thought to exist for a dead man, as much as for one who is alive but not aware of them; e.g. honours and dishonours and the good or bad fortunes of children and in general of descendants. And this also presents a problem; for though a man has lived happily up to old age and has had a death worthy of his life, many reverses may befall his descendants- some of them may be good and attain the life they deserve, while with others the opposite may be the case; and clearly too the degrees of relationship between them and their ancestors may vary indefinitely. It would be odd, then, if the dead man were to share in these changes and become at one time happy, at another wretched; while it would also be odd if the fortunes of the descendants did not for some time have some effect on the happiness of their ancestors

But we must return to our first difficulty; for perhaps by a consideration of it our present problem might be solved. Now if we must see the end and only then call a man happy, not as being happy but as having been so before, surely this is a paradox, that when he is happy the attribute that belongs to him is not to be truly predicated of him because we do not wish to call living men happy, on account of the changes that may befall them, and because we have assumed happiness to be something permanent and by no means easily changed, while a single man may suffer many turns of fortune's wheel. For clearly if we were to keep pace with his fortunes, we should often call the same man happy and again wretched, making the happy man out to be chameleon and insecurely based. Or is this keeping pace with his fortunes quite wrong? Success or failure in life does not depend on these, but human life, as we said, needs these as mere additions, while virtuous activities or their opposites are what constitute happiness or the reverse.

The question we have now discussed confirms our definition. For no function of man has so much permanence as virtuous activities (these are thought to be more durable even than knowledge of the sciences), and of these themselves the most valuable are more durable because those who are happy spend their life most readily and most continuously in these; for this seems to be the reason why we do not forget them. The attribute in question, then, will belong to the happy man, and he will be happy throughout his life; for always, or by preference to everything else, he will be engaged in virtuous action and contemplation, and he will bear the chances of life most nobly and altogether decorously, if he is 'truly good' and 'foursquare beyond reproach'.

Now many events happen by chance, and events differing in importance; small pieces of good fortune or of its opposite clearly do not weigh down the scales of life one way or the other, but a multitude of great events if they turn out well will make life happier (for not only are they themselves such as to add beauty to life, but the way a man deals with them may be noble and good), while if they turn out ill they crush and maim happiness; for they both bring pain with them and hinder many activities. Yet even in these nobility shines through, when a man bears with resignation many great misfortunes, not through insensibility to pain but through nobility and greatness of soul.

If activities are, as we said, what gives life its character, no happy man can become miserable; for he will never do the acts that are hateful and mean. For the man who is truly good and wise, we think, bears all the chances life becomingly and always makes the best of circumstances, as a good general makes the best military use of the army at his command and a good shoemaker makes the best shoes out of the hides that are given him; and so with all other craftsmen. And if this is the case, the happy man can never become miserable; though he will not reach blessedness, if he meet with fortunes like those of Priam.

Nor, again, is he many-coloured and changeable; for neither will he be moved from his happy state easily or by any ordinary misadventures, but only by many great ones, nor, if he has had many great misadventures, will he recover his happiness in a short time, but if at all, only in a long and complete one in which he has attained many splendid successes.

When then should we not say that he is happy who is active in accordance with complete virtue and is sufficiently equipped with external goods, not for some chance period but throughout a complete life? Or must we add 'and who is destined to live thus and die as befits his life'? Certainly the future is obscure to us, while happiness, we claim, is an end and something in every way final. If so, we shall call happy those among living men in whom these conditions are, and are to be, fulfilled- but happy men. So much for these questions....

Since happiness is an activity of soul in accordance with perfect virtue, we must consider the nature of virtue; for perhaps we shall thus see better the nature of happiness. The true student of politics, too, is thought to have studied virtue above all things; for he wishes to make his fellow citizens good and obedient to the laws. As an example of this we have the lawgivers of the Cretans and the Spartans, and any others of the kind that there may have been. And if this inquiry belongs to political science, clearly the pursuit of it will be in accordance with our original plan. But clearly the virtue we must study is human virtue; for the good we were seeking was human good and the happiness human happiness. By human virtue we mean not that of the body but that of the soul; and happiness also we call an activity of soul. But if this is so, clearly the student of politics must know somehow the facts about soul, as the man who is to heal the eyes or the body as a whole must know about the eyes or the body; and all the more since politics is more prized and better than medicine; but even among doctors the best educated spend much labour on acquiring knowledge of the body. The student of politics, then, must study the soul, and must study it with these objects in view, and do so just to the extent which is sufficient for the questions we are discussing; for further precision is perhaps something more laborious than our purposes require.

Some things are said about it, adequately enough, even in the discussions outside our school, and we must use these; e.g. that one element in the soul is irrational and one has a rational principle. Whether these are separated as the parts of the body or of anything divisible are, or are distinct by definition but by nature inseparable, like convex and concave in the circumference of a circle, does not affect the present question.

Of the irrational element one division seems to be widely distributed, and vegetative in its nature, I mean that which causes nutrition and growth; for it is this kind of power of the soul that one must assign to all nurslings and to embryos, and this same power to fullgrown creatures; this is more reasonable than to assign some different power to them. Now the excellence of this seems to be common to all species and not specifically human; for this part or faculty seems to function most in sleep, while goodness and badness are least manifest in sleep (whence comes the saying that the happy are not better off than the wretched for half their lives; and this happens naturally enough, since sleep is an inactivity of the soul in that respect in which it is called good or bad), unless perhaps to a small extent some of the movements actually penetrate to the soul, and in this respect the dreams of good men are better than those of ordinary people. Enough of this subject, however; let us leave the nutritive faculty alone, since it has by its nature no share in human excellence.

There seems to be also another irrational element in the soul-one which in a sense, however, shares in a rational principle. For we praise the rational principle of the continent man and of the incontinent, and the part of their soul that has such a principle, since it urges them aright and towards the best objects; but there is found in them also another element naturally opposed to the rational principle, which fights against and resists that principle. For exactly as paralysed limbs when we intend to move them to the right turn on the contrary to the left, so is it with the soul; the impulses of incontinent people move in contrary directions. But while in the body we see that which moves astray, in the soul we do not. No doubt, however, we must none the less suppose that in the soul too there is something contrary to the rational principle, resisting and opposing it. In what sense it is distinct from the other elements does not concern us. Now even this seems to have a share in a rational principle, as we said; at any rate in the continent man it obeys the rational principle and presumably in the temperate and brave man it is still more obedient; for in him it speaks, on all matters, with the same voice as the rational principle.

Therefore the irrational element also appears to be two-fold. For the vegetative element in no way shares in a rational principle, but the appetitive and in general the desiring element in a sense shares in it, in so far as it listens to and obeys it; this is the sense in which we speak of 'taking account' of one's father or one's friends, not that in which we speak of 'accounting for a mathematical property. That the irrational element is in some sense persuaded by a rational principle is indicated also by the giving of advice and by all reproof and exhortation. And if this element also must be said to have a rational principle, that which has a rational principle (as well as that which has not) will be twofold, one subdivision having it in the strict sense and in itself, and the other having a tendency to obey as one does one's father.

Virtue too is distinguished into kinds in accordance with this difference; for we say that some of the virtues are intellectual and others moral, philosophic wisdom and understanding and practical wisdom being intellectual, liberality and temperance moral. For in speaking about a man's character we do not say that he is wise or has understanding but that he is good-tempered or temperate; yet we praise the wise man also with respect to his state of mind; and of states of mind we call those which merit praise virtues.

Book II

Virtue, then, being of two kinds, intellectual and moral, intellectual virtue in the main owes both its birth and its growth to teaching (for which reason it requires experience and time), while moral virtue comes about as a result of habit, whence also its name (ethike) is one that is formed by a slight variation from the word ethos (habit). From this it is also plain that none of the moral virtues arises in us by nature; for nothing that exists by nature can form a habit contrary to its nature. For instance the stone which by nature moves downwards cannot be habituated to move upwards, not even if one tries to train it by throwing it up ten thousand times; nor can fire be habituated to move downwards, nor can anything else that by nature behaves in one way be trained to behave in another. Neither by nature, then, nor contrary to nature do the virtues arise in us; rather we are adapted by nature to receive them, and are made perfect by habit.

Again, of all the things that come to us by nature we first acquire the potentiality and later exhibit the activity (this is plain in the case of the senses; for it was not by often seeing or often hearing that we got these senses, but on the contrary we had them before we used them, and did not come to have them by using them); but the virtues we get by first exercising them, as also happens in the case of the arts as well. For the things we have to learn before we can do them, we learn by doing them, e.g. men become builders by building and lyreplayers by playing the lyre; so too we become just by doing just acts, temperate by doing temperate acts, brave by doing brave acts.

This is confirmed by what happens in states; for legislators make the citizens good by forming habits in them, and this is the wish of every legislator, and those who do not effect it miss their mark, and it is in this that a good constitution differs from a bad one.

Again, it is from the same causes and by the same means that every virtue is both produced and destroyed, and similarly every art; for it is from playing the lyre that both good and bad lyre-players are produced. And the corresponding statement is true of builders and of all the rest; men will be good or bad builders as a result of building well or badly. For if this were not so, there would have been no need of a teacher, but all men would have been born good or bad at their craft. This, then, is the case with the virtues also; by doing the acts that we do in our transactions with other men we become just or unjust, and by doing the acts that we do in the presence of danger, and being habituated to feel fear or confidence, we become brave or cowardly. The same is true of appetites and feelings of anger; some men become temperate and good-tempered, others self-indulgent and irascible, by behaving in one way or the other in the appropriate circumstances. Thus, in one word, states of character arise out of like activities. This is why the activities we exhibit must be of a certain kind; it is because the states of character correspond to the differences between these. It makes no small difference, then, whether we form habits of one kind or of another from our very youth; it makes a very great difference, or rather all the difference.

2. Since, then, the present inquiry does not aim at theoretical knowledge like the others (for we are inquiring not in order to know what virtue is, but in order to become good, since otherwise our inquiry would have been of no use), we must examine the nature of actions, namely how we ought to do them; for these determine also the nature of the states of character that are produced, as we have said. Now, that we must act according to the right rule is a common principle and must be assumed-it will be discussed later, i.e. both what the right rule is, and how it is related to the other virtues. But this must be agreed upon beforehand, that the whole account of matters of conduct must be given in outline and not precisely, as we said at the very beginning that the accounts we demand must be in accordance with the subject-matter; matters concerned with conduct and questions of what is good for us have no fixity, any more than matters of health. The general account being of this nature, the account of particular cases is yet more lacking in exactness; for they do not fall under any art or precept but the agents themselves must in each case consider what is appropriate to the occasion, as happens also in the art of medicine or of navigation.

But though our present account is of this nature we must give what help we can. First, then, let us consider this, that it is the nature of such things to be destroyed by defect and excess, as we see in the case of strength and of health (for to gain light on things imperceptible we must use the evidence of sensible things); both excessive and defective exercise destroys the strength, and similarly drink or food which is above or below a certain amount destroys the health, while that which is proportionate both produces and increases and preserves it. So too is it, then, in the case of temperance and courage and the other virtues. For the man who flies from and fears everything and does not stand his ground against anything becomes a coward, and the man who fears nothing at all but goes to meet every danger becomes rash; and similarly the man who indulges in every pleasure and abstains from none becomes self-indulgent, while the man who shuns every pleasure, as boors do, becomes in a way insensible; temperance and courage, then, are destroyed by excess and defect, and preserved by the mean.

But not only are the sources and causes of their origination and growth the same as those of their destruction, but also the sphere of their actualization will be the same; for this is also true of the things which are more evident to sense, e.g. of strength; it is produced by taking much food and undergoing much exertion, and it is the strong man that will be most able to do these things. So too is it with the virtues; by abstaining from pleasures we become temperate, and it is when we have become so that we are most able to abstain from them; and similarly too in the case of courage; for by being habituated to despise things that are terrible and to stand our ground against them we become brave, and it is when we have become so that we shall be most able to stand our ground against them.

3. We must take as a sign of states of character the pleasure or pain that ensues on acts; for the man who abstains from bodily pleasures and delights in this very fact is temperate, while the man who is annoyed at it is self-indulgent, and he who stands his ground against things that are terrible and delights in this or at least is not pained is brave, while the man who is pained is a coward. For moral excellence is concerned with pleasures and pains; it is on account of the pleasure that we do bad things, and on account of the pain that we abstain from noble ones. Hence we ought to have been brought up in a particular way from our very youth, as Plato says, so as both to delight in and to be pained by the things that we ought; for this is the right education.

Again, if the virtues are concerned with actions and passions, and every passion and every action is accompanied by pleasure and pain, for this reason also virtue will be concerned with pleasures and pains. This is indicated also by the fact that punishment is inflicted by these means; for it is a kind of cure, and it is the nature of cures to be effected by contraries.

Again, as we said but lately, every state of soul has a nature relative to and concerned with the kind of things by which it tends to be made worse or better; but it is by reason of pleasures and pains that men become bad, by pursuing and avoiding these- either the pleasures and pains they ought not or when they ought not or as they ought not, or by going wrong in one of the other similar ways that may be distinguished. Hence men even define the virtues as certain states of impassivity and rest; not well, however, because they speak absolutely, and do not say 'as one ought' and 'as one ought not' and 'when one ought or ought not', and the other things that may be added. We assume, then, that this kind of excellence tends to do what is best with regard to pleasures and pains, and vice does the contrary.

The following facts also may show us that virtue and vice are concerned with these same things. There being three objects of choice and three of avoidance, the noble, the advantageous, the pleasant, and their contraries, the base, the injurious, the painful, about all of these the good man tends to go right and the bad man to go wrong, and especially about pleasure; for this is common to the animals, and also it accompanies all objects of choice; for even the noble and the advantageous appear pleasant.

Again, it has grown up with us all from our infancy; this is why it is difficult to rub off this passion, engrained as it is in our life. And we measure even our actions, some of us more and others less, by the rule of pleasure and pain. For this reason, then, our whole inquiry must be about these; for to feel delight and pain rightly or wrongly has no small effect on our actions.

Again, it is harder to fight with pleasure than with anger, to use Heraclitus' phrase', but both art and virtue are always concerned with what is harder; for even the good is better when it is harder. Therefore for this reason also the whole concern both of virtue and of political science is with pleasures and pains; for the man who uses these well will be good, he who uses them badly bad.

That virtue, then, is concerned with pleasures and pains, and that by the acts from which it arises it is both increased and, if they are done differently, destroyed, and that the acts from which it arose are those in which it actualizes itself- let this be taken as said.

4. The question might be asked,; what we mean by saying that we must become just by doing just acts, and temperate by doing temperate acts; for if men do just and temperate acts, they are already just and temperate, exactly as, if they do what is in accordance with the laws of grammar and of music, they are grammarians and musicians.

Or is this not true even of the arts? It is possible to do something that is in accordance with the laws of grammar, either by chance or at the suggestion of another. A man will be a grammarian, then, only when he has both done something grammatical and done it grammatically; and this means doing it in accordance with the grammatical knowledge in himself.

Again, the case of the arts and that of the virtues are not similar; for the products of the arts have their goodness in themselves, so that it is enough that they should have a certain character, but if the acts that are in accordance with the virtues have themselves a certain character it does not follow that they are done justly or temperately. The agent also must be in a certain condition when he does them; in the first place he must have knowledge, secondly he must choose the acts, and choose them for their own sakes, and thirdly his action must proceed from a firm and unchangeable character. These are not reckoned in as conditions of the possession of the arts, except the bare knowledge; but as a condition of the possession of the virtues knowledge has little or no weight, while the other conditions count not for a little but for everything, i.e. the very conditions which result from often doing just and temperate acts.

Actions, then, are called just and temperate when they are such as the just or the temperate man would do; but it is not the man who does these that is just and temperate, but the man who also does them as just and temperate men do them. It is well said, then, that it is by doing just acts that the just man is produced, and by doing temperate acts the temperate man; without doing these no one would have even a prospect of becoming good.

But most people do not do these, but take refuge in theory and think they are being philosophers and will become good in this way, behaving somewhat like patients who listen attentively to their doctors, but do none of the things they are ordered to do. As the latter will not be made well in body by such a course of treatment, the former will not be made well in soul by such a course of philosophy.

5. Next we must consider what virtue is. Since things that are found in the soul are of three kinds- passions, faculties, states of character, virtue must be one of these. By passions I mean appetite, anger, fear, confidence, envy, joy, friendly feeling, hatred, longing, emulation, pity, and in general the feelings that are accompanied by pleasure or pain; by faculties the things in virtue of which we are said to be capable of feeling these, e.g. of becoming angry or being pained or feeling pity; by states of character the

things in virtue of which we stand well or badly with reference to the passions, e.g. with reference to anger we stand badly if we feel it violently or too weakly, and well if we feel it moderately; and similarly with reference to the other passions.

Now neither the virtues nor the vices are passions, because we are not called good or bad on the ground of our passions, but are so called on the ground of our virtues and our vices, and because we are neither praised nor blamed for our passions (for the man who feels fear or anger is not praised, nor is the man who simply feels anger blamed, but the man who feels it in a certain way), but for our virtues and our vices we are praised or blamed.

Again, we feel anger and fear without choice, but the virtues are modes of choice or involve choice. Further, in respect of the passions we are said to be moved, but in respect of the virtues and the vices we are said not to be moved but to be disposed in a particular way.

For these reasons also they are not faculties; for we are neither called good nor bad, nor praised nor blamed, for the simple capacity of feeling the passions; again, we have the faculties by nature, but we are not made good or bad by nature; we have spoken of this before. If, then, the virtues are neither passions nor faculties, all that remains is that they should be states of character.

Thus we have stated what virtue is in respect of its genus.

6. We must, however, not only describe virtue as a state of character, but also say what sort of state it is. We may remark, then, that every virtue or excellence both brings into good condition the thing of which it is the excellence and makes the work of that thing be done well; e.g. the excellence of the eye makes both the eye and its work good; for it is by the excellence of the eye that we see well. Similarly the excellence of the horse makes a horse both good in itself and good at running and at carrying its rider and at awaiting the attack of the enemy. Therefore, if this is true in every case, the virtue of man also will be the state of character which makes a man good and which makes him do his own work well.

How this is to happen we have stated already, but it will be made plain also by the following consideration of the specific nature of virtue. In everything that is continuous and divisible it is possible to take more, less, or an equal amount, and that either in terms of the thing itself or relatively to us; and the equal is an intermediate between excess and defect. By the intermediate in the object I mean that which is equidistant from each of the extremes, which is one and the same for all men; by the intermediate relatively to us that which is neither too much nor too little- and this is not one, nor the same for all. For instance, if ten is many and two is few, six is the intermediate, taken in terms of the object; for it exceeds and is exceeded by an equal amount; this is intermediate according to arithmetical proportion. But the intermediate relatively to us is not to be taken so; if ten pounds are too much for a particular person to eat and two too little, it does not follow that the trainer will order six pounds; for this also is perhaps too much for the person who is to take it, or too little- too little for Milo, too much for the beginner in athletic exercises. The same is true of running and wrestling. Thus a master of any art avoids excess and defect, but seeks the intermediate and chooses this- the intermediate not in the object but relatively to us.

If it is thus, then, that every art does its work well- by looking to the intermediate and judgling its works by this standard (so that we often say of good works of art that it is not possible either to take away or to add anything, implying that excess and defect destroy the goodness of works of art, while the mean preserves it; and good artists, as we say, look to this in their work), and if, further, virtue is more exact and better than any art, as nature also is, then virtue must have the quality of aiming at the intermediate. I mean moral virtue; for it is this that is concerned with passions and actions, and in these there is excess, defect, and the intermediate. For instance, both fear and confidence and appetite and anger and pity and in general pleasure and pain may be felt both too much and too little, and in both cases not well; but to feel them at the right times, with reference to the right objects, towards the right people, with the right motive, and in the right way, is what is both intermediate and best, and this is characteristic of virtue. Similarly with regard to actions also there is excess, defect, and the intermediate. Now virtue is concerned with passions and actions, in which excess is a form of failure, and so is defect, while the intermediate is praised and is a form of success; and being praised and being successful are both characteristics of virtue. Therefore virtue is a kind of mean, since, as we have seen, it aims at what is intermediate.

Again, it is possible to fail in many ways (for evil belongs to the class of the unlimited, as the Pythagoreans conjectured, and good to that of the limited), while to succeed is possible only in one way (for which reason also one is easy and the other difficult- to miss the mark easy, to hit it difficult); for these reasons also, then, excess and defect are characteristic of vice, and the mean of virtue;

For men are good in but one way, but bad in many.

Virtue, then, is a state of character concerned with choice, lying in a mean, i.e. the mean relative to us, this being determined by a rational principle, and by that principle by which the man of practical wisdom would determine it. Now it is a mean between two vices, that which depends on excess and that which depends on defect; and again it is a mean because the vices respectively fall short of or exceed what is right in both passions and actions, while virtue both finds and chooses that which is intermediate. Hence in respect of its substance and the definition which states its essence virtue is a mean, with regard to what is best and right an extreme.

But not every action nor every passion admits of a mean; for some have names that already imply badness, e.g. spite, shamelessness, envy, and in the case of actions adultery, theft, murder; for all of these and suchlike things imply by their names that they are themselves bad, and not the excesses or deficiencies of them. It is not possible, then, ever to be right with regard to them; one must always be wrong. Nor does goodness or badness with regard to such things depend on committing adultery with the right woman, at the right time, and in the right way, but simply to do any of them is to go wrong. It would be equally absurd, then, to expect that in unjust, cowardly, and voluptuous action there should be a mean, an excess, and a deficiency; for at that rate there would be a mean of excess and of deficiency, an excess of excess, and a deficiency of deficiency. But as there is no excess and deficiency of temperance and courage because what is intermediate is in a sense an extreme, so too of the actions we have mentioned there is no mean nor any excess and deficiency, but however they are done they are wrong; for in general there is neither a mean of excess and deficiency, nor excess and deficiency of a mean.

7. We must, however, not only make this general statement, but also apply it to the individual facts. For among statements about conduct those which are general

apply more widely, but those which are particular are more genuine, since conduct has to do with individual cases, and our statements must harmonize with the facts in these cases. We may take these cases from our table. With regard to feelings of fear and confidence courage is the mean; of the people who exceed, he who exceeds in fearlessness has no name (many of the states have no name), while the man who exceeds in confidence is rash, and he who exceeds in fear and falls short in confidence is a coward. With regard to pleasures and pains- not all of them, and not so much with regard to the pains- the mean is temperance, the excess self-indulgence. Persons deficient with regard to the pleasures are not often found; hence such persons also have received no name. But let us call them 'insensible'.

With regard to giving and taking of money the mean is liberality, the excess and the defect prodigality and meanness. In these actions people exceed and fall short in contrary ways; the prodigal exceeds in spending and falls short in taking, while the mean man exceeds in taking and falls short in spending. (At present we are giving a mere outline or summary, and are satisfied with this; later these states will be more exactly determined.) With regard to money there are also other dispositions- a mean, magnificence (for the magnificent man differs from the liberal man; the former deals with large sums, the latter with small ones), an excess, tastelessness and vulgarity, and a deficiency, niggardliness; these differ from the states opposed to liberality, and the mode of their difference will be stated later. With regard to honour and dishonour the mean is proper pride, the excess is known as a sort of 'empty vanity', and the deficiency is undue humility; and as we said liberality was related to magnificence, differing from it by dealing with small sums, so there is a state similarly related to proper pride, being concerned with small honours while that is concerned with great. For it is possible to desire honour as one ought, and more than one ought, and less, and the man who exceeds in his desires is called ambitious, the man who falls short unambitious, while the intermediate person has no name. The dispositions also are nameless, except that that of the ambitious man is called ambition. Hence the people who are at the extremes lay claim to the middle place; and we ourselves sometimes call the intermediate person ambitious and sometimes unambitious, and sometimes praise the ambitious man and sometimes the unambitious. The reason of our doing this will be stated in what follows; but now let us speak of the remaining states according to the method which has been indicated.

With regard to anger also there is an excess, a deficiency, and a mean. Although they can scarcely be said to have names, yet since we call the intermediate person good-tempered let us call the mean good temper; of the persons at the extremes let the one who exceeds be called irascible, and his vice irascibility, and the man who falls short an inirascible sort of person, and the deficiency inirascibility.

There are also three other means, which have a certain likeness to one another, but differ from one another: for they are all concerned with intercourse in words and actions, but differ in that one is concerned with truth in this sphere, the other two with pleasantness; and of this one kind is exhibited in giving amusement, the other in all the circumstances of life. We must therefore speak of these too, that we may the better see that in all things the mean is praise-worthy, and the extremes neither praiseworthy nor right, but worthy of blame. Now most of these states also have no names, but we must try, as in the other cases, to invent names ourselves so that we may be clear and easy to follow. With regard to truth, then, the intermediate is a truthful sort of person and the mean may be called truthfulness, while the pretence which exaggerates is boastfulness and the person characterized by it a boaster, and that which understates is mock modesty and the person characterized by it mock-modest. With regard to pleasantness in the giving of amusement the intermediate person is ready-witted and the disposition ready wit, the excess is buffoonery and the person characterized by it a buffoon, while the man who falls short is a sort of boor and his state is boorishness. With regard to the remaining kind of pleasantness, that which is exhibited in life in general, the man who is pleasant in the right way is friendly and the mean is friendliness, while the man who exceeds is an obsequious person if he has no end in view, a flatterer if he is aiming at his own advantage, and the man who falls short and is unpleasant in all circumstances is a quarrelsome and surly sort of person.

There are also means in the passions and concerned with the passions; since shame is not a virtue, and yet praise is extended to the modest man. For even in these matters one man is said to be intermediate, and another to exceed, as for instance the bashful man who is ashamed of everything; while he who falls short or is not ashamed of anything at all is shameless, and the intermediate person is modest. Righteous indignation is a mean between envy and spite, and these states are concerned with the pain and pleasure that are felt at the fortunes of our neighbours; the man who is characterized by righteous indignation is pained at undeserved good fortune, the envious man, going beyond him, is pained at all good fortune, and the spiteful man falls so far short of being pained that he even rejoices. But these states there will be an opportunity of describing elsewhere; with regard to justice, since it has not one simple meaning, we shall, after describing the other states, distinguish its two kinds and say how each of them is a mean; and similarly we shall treat also of the rational virtues.

8. There are three kinds of disposition, then, two of them vices, involving excess and deficiency respectively, and one a virtue, viz. the mean, and all are in a sense opposed to all; for the extreme states are contrary both to the intermediate state and to each other, and the intermediate to the extremes; as the equal is greater relatively to the less, less relatively to the greater, so the middle states are excessive relatively to the deficiencies, deficient relatively to the excesses, both in passions and in actions. For the brave man appears rash relatively to the coward, and cowardly relatively to the rash man; and similarly the temperate man appears self-indulgent relatively to the insensible man, insensible relatively to the self-indulgent, and the liberal man prodigal relatively to the mean man, mean relatively to the prodigal. Hence also the people at the extremes push the intermediate man each over to the other, and the brave man is called rash by the coward, cowardly by the rash man, and correspondingly in the other cases.

These states being thus opposed to one another, the greatest contrariety is that of the extremes to each other, rather than to the intermediate; for these are further from each other than from the intermediate, as the great is further from the small and the small from the great than both are from the equal. Again, to the intermediate some extremes show a certain likeness, as that of rashness to courage and that of prodigality to liberality; but the extremes show the greatest unlikeness to each other; now contraries are defined as the things that are furthest from each other, so that things that are further apart are more contrary.

To the mean in some cases the deficiency, in some the excess is more opposed; e.g. it is not rashness, which is an excess, but cowardice, which is a deficiency, that is more opposed to courage, and not insensibility, which is a deficiency, but self-indulgence, which is an excess, that is more opposed to temperance. This happens from two reasons, one being drawn from the thing itself; for because one extreme is nearer and liker to the intermediate, we oppose not this but rather its contrary to the intermediate. E.g. since rashness is thought liker and nearer to courage, and cowardice more unlike, we oppose rather the latter to courage; for things that are further from the intermediate are thought more contrary to it. This, then, is one cause, drawn from the thing itself; another is drawn from ourselves; for the things to which we ourselves more naturally tend seem more contrary to the intermediate. For instance, we ourselves tend more naturally to pleasures, and hence are more easily carried away towards self-indulgence than towards propriety. We describe as contrary to the mean, then, rather the directions in which we more often go to great lengths; and therefore self-indulgence, which is an excess, is the more contrary to temperance.

9. That moral virtue is a mean, then, and in what sense it is so, and that it is a mean between two vices, the one involving excess, the other deficiency, and that it is such because its character is to aim at what is intermediate in passions and in actions, has been sufficiently stated. Hence also it is no easy task to be good. For in everything it is no easy task to find the middle, e.g. to find the middle of a circle is not for every one but for him who knows; so, too, any one can get angry- that is easy- or give or spend money; but to do this to the right person, to the right extent, at the right time, with the right motive, and in the right way, that is not for every one, nor is it easy; wherefore goodness is both rare and laudable and noble.

Hence he who aims at the intermediate must first depart from what is the more contrary to it, as Calypso advises-
Hold the ship out beyond that surf and spray.

For of the extremes one is more erroneous, one less so; therefore, since to hit the mean is hard in the extreme, we must as a second best, as people say, take the least of the evils; and this will be done best in the way we describe. But we must consider the things towards which we ourselves also are easily carried away; for some of us tend to one thing, some to another; and this will be recognizable from the pleasure and the pain we feel. We must drag ourselves away to the contrary extreme; for we shall get into the intermediate state by drawing well away from error, as people do in straightening sticks that are bent.

Now in everything the pleasant or pleasure is most to be guarded against; for we do not judge it impartially. We ought, then, to feel towards pleasure as the elders of the people felt towards Helen, and in all circumstances repeat their saying; for if we dismiss pleasure thus we are less likely to go astray. It is by doing this, then, (to sum the matter up) that we shall best be able to hit the mean.

But this is no doubt difficult, and especially in individual cases; for or is not easy to determine both how and with whom and on what provocation and how long one should be angry; for we too sometimes praise those who fall short and call them good-tempered, but sometimes we praise those who get angry and call them manly. The man, however, who deviates little from goodness is not blamed, whether he do so in the direction of the more or of the less, but only the man who deviates more widely;

for he does not fail to be noticed. But up to what point and to what extent a man must deviate before he becomes blameworthy it is not easy to determine by reasoning, any more than anything else that is perceived by the senses; such things depend on particular facts, and the decision rests with perception. So much, then, is plain, that the intermediate state is in all things to be praised, but that we must incline sometimes towards the excess, sometimes towards the deficiency; for so shall we most easily hit the mean and what is right....

If happiness is activity in accordance with virtue, it is reasonable that it should be in accordance with the highest virtue; and this will be that of the best thing in us. Whether it be reason or something else that is this element which is thought to be our natural ruler and guide and to take thought of things noble and divine, whether it be itself also divine or only the most divine element in us, the activity of this in accordance with its proper virtue will be perfect happiness. That this activity is contemplative we have already said.

Now this would seem to be in agreement both with what we said before and with the truth. For, firstly, this activity is the best (since not only is reason the best thing in us, but the objects of reason are the best of knowable objects); and secondly, it is the most continuous, since we can contemplate truth more continuously than we can do anything. And we think happiness has pleasure mingled with it, but the activity of philosophic wisdom is admittedly the pleasantest of virtuous activities; at all events the pursuit of it is thought to offer pleasures marvellous for their purity and their enduringness, and it is to be expected that those who know will pass their time more pleasantly than those who inquire. And the self-sufficiency that is spoken of must belong most to the contemplative activity. For while a philosopher, as well as a just man or one possessing any other virtue, needs the necessaries of life, when they are sufficiently equipped with things of that sort the just man needs people towards whom and with whom he shall act justly, and the temperate man, the brave man, and each of the others is in the same case, but the philosopher, even when by himself, can contemplate truth, and the better the wiser he is; he can perhaps do so better if he has fellow-workers, but still he is the most self-sufficient. And this activity alone would seem to be loved for its own sake; for nothing arises from it apart from the contemplating, while from practical activities we gain more or less apart from the action. And happiness is thought to depend on leisure; for we are busy that we may have leisure, and make war that we may live in peace. Now the activity of the practical virtues is exhibited in political or military affairs, but the actions concerned with these seem to be unleisurely. Warlike actions are completely so (for no one chooses to be at war, or provokes war, for the sake of being at war; any one would seem absolutely murderous if he were to make enemies of his friends in order to bring about battle and slaughter); but the action of the statesman is also unleisurely, and-apart from the political action itself-aims at despotic power and honours, or at all events happiness, for him and his fellow citizens-a happiness different from political action, and evidently sought as being different. So if among virtuous actions political and military actions are distinguished by nobility and greatness, and these are unleisurely and aim at an end and are not desirable for their own sake, but the activity of reason, which is contemplative, seems both to be superior in serious worth and to aim at no end beyond itself, and to have its pleasure proper to itself (and this augments the activity), and the self-sufficiency, leisureliness, unweariedness (so far as this is possible for man), and all the other attributes ascribed to the supremely happy man are evidently those connected with this activity, it follows that this will be the complete happiness of man, if it be allowed a complete term of life (for none of the attributes of happiness is incomplete).

But such a life would be too high for man; for it is not in so far as he is man that he will live so, but in so far as something divine is present in him; and by so much as this is superior to our composite nature is its activity superior to that which is the exercise of the other kind of virtue. If reason is divine, then, in comparison with man, the life according to it is divine in comparison with human life. But we must not follow those who advise us, being men, to think of human things, and, being mortal, of mortal things, but must, so far as we can, make ourselves immortal, and strain every nerve to live in accordance with the best thing in us; for even if it be small in bulk, much more does it in power and worth surpass everything. This would seem, too, to be each man himself, since it is the authoritative and better part of him. It would be strange, then, if he were to choose not the life of his self but that of something else. And what we said before' will apply now; that which is proper to each thing is by nature best and most pleasant for each thing; for man, therefore, the life according to reason is best and pleasantest, since reason more than anything else is man. This life therefore is also the happiest....

Chapter 14: Putting it all Together

If you're anything like me, you probably liked Kantianism when you were reading that section, and utilitarianism seemed correct when reading that section, and then virtue ethics seemed pretty good as well. And, if you believe in God, you're probably wondering how that blends (if at all) with any of them.

At this point, I'm going to try to synthesize what was best about the above theories, and offer my own view. You are by no means required to agree with me, of course—nor should you think that this is a "finished product." I learn something new all the time, and consider this view very much a work in progress.

Let's begin by refreshing our memories with regard to the features of each major theory (utilitarianism, Kantianism, and virtue ethics) that I (at least) find compelling.

What Utilitarians Seem to be Getting Right	What Kant Seems to be Getting Right	What Virtue Ethics Seems to be Getting Right
Morality *does* seem to be about reducing or preventing pain, and the promotion of happiness. Perhaps this is not the exclusive or even primary focus of morality, but the utilitarians certainly seem right to recognize the importance of pleasure and pain in our evaluation of moral claims.	It *does* seem to matter what reasons someone has for his or her actions. Someone who tells the truth from fear, or who saves a life for the sake of a reward just doesn't seem to merit the kind of moral praise that would be normally forthcoming.	One's "attitude" and general disposition with regard to morally right actions *does* seem to matter. Truly honest people don't struggle with honesty. Indeed, they probably rarely, if ever, even contemplate lying. This seems more morally impressive than the person who grits his teeth, digs in his heels, and barely manages to tell the truth despite his worst of intentions.
Non-humans *do* seem to have some measure of moral value. Perhaps non-human animals are not equal to humans in many respects, and perhaps they are not even morally equal (subject to debate, of course), but any theory that simply ignores or denies the moral status of non-human animals seems insufficient, at best, and misguided, at worst.	Respect *does* seem to be a central theme for our moral understanding. However we care to articulate it, the notion that all people deserve at least a baseline level of respect and dignity, that all people possess at least a baseline level of moral worth seems consistent with our moral intuitions.	The "virtue" approach *does* seem to help with that pesky "altruism v. egoism" debate within the field of ethics. It overcomes the self-interest concern by acknowledging that there need be no divide between one's own happiness and the demands of morality—indeed, it claims that our own happiness depends on our being morally good. In this way, virtue ethics renders the *good* life the good *life*—a life worth having, and therefore worth pursuing.

What Utilitarians Seem to be Getting Right	What Kant Seems to be Getting Right	What Virtue Ethics Seems to be Getting Right
Consequences *do* matter to us, morally speaking. Perhaps consequences are not the only things that matter, or are even the most important things, morally speaking, but results count. Someone can have all the best intentions, but if that person continually inflicts harm through ignorance, neglect, or just plain bad luck, we're unlikely to long uphold that person as a moral exemplar; nor are we likely to praise the person who "wants" to help others but just never gets around to actually doing so.	"Universalizability" *does* seem to be a handy tool for evaluating our actions. Whether we understand this in terms of the CI, or the Golden Rule, or any of the variations of the Golden Rule found in virtually every major religious tradition in the world, this idea that something is acceptable for one only if it would be acceptable for all is a powerful and potentially universal moral insight. Reason and self-consciousness *do* seem to be important qualities with regard to moral standing. We don't have to commit ourselves to the position that anything lacking in these qualities is completely lacking in moral standing, but the possession of these qualities does seem to qualify a creature for some sort of "special" moral standing—even if in no other respect than being a bearer of greater moral responsibility! Some have expressed this distinction in terms of moral "agents" (those possessing reason and self-consciousness) and moral "patients" (those lacking the qualities of agency, but still entitled to some degree of moral consideration).	Who one *is* (as opposed to what one does) *does* seem significant. Moral goodness seems to be about who one is, one's basic character, and in ways that can't be captured by a checklist concerning whether one has been naughty or nice. The vocabulary of admiration or disgust *does* seem important for our daily moral evaluations. We are more likely to speak of how someone is a "great man," or how "you disgust me," than to speak in terms of rules violated, or utility squandered.

I prefer to think of morality in terms of "health." In this sense, I suppose I am most closely aligned with virtue ethics.

Like ancient Greek and Roman philosophers, I think that one's "soul" can be healthy or ill, just as can one's body. For our purposes, we do not have to do the metaphysical heavy lifting and decide what exactly the "soul" is, or if it exists as something distinct from the body. Just think of the "soul" as a short and simple term used to express, if nothing else, one's mental and emotional life, and in particular with regard to one's character and overall experience of life. Obviously, for those who believe in God, there will be an important spiritual component to that understanding as well.

When our "soul" is healthy, we thrive. Much like when our bodies are healthy, we feel good. We enjoy life. Health is its own reward. It makes no sense to me to wonder why I should want a healthy body. As opposed to what? One riddled with injury or disease? *Of course* I prefer a healthy body, all else being equal. Who doesn't? So, too, with regard to a healthy soul. If I feel good when my soul is healthy, and bad when it is not, then my preference should be obvious.

Following Aristotle, I understand a healthy soul as one that is well equipped for the contingencies of life, and therefore less vulnerable to all the ways in which a soul can be "injured" or "infected." The virtues are the character traits that promote the health of the soul. I allow for some flexibility (and even outright uncertainty) as to which traits (and how many) count as virtues in this sense, but I think a handful, at least, stand out: courage, temperance, justice, truthfulness, generosity, compassion, and respectfulness. Wisdom, I think, is a comprehensive virtue that encompasses all the others. To say that one is wise is to say that one *is* courageous, temperate, just, truthful, etc.

I believe that the vicious do not prosper. I acknowledge that morally wretched people can acquire great wealth and power, lots of shiny and expensive toys, and might well be surrounded by great multitudes of "adoring" (perhaps sycophantic) admirers and associates. Nevertheless, in my experience and based on my observations, such people are not *happy* (though they might experience much pleasure). They seem to be plagued by emotional problems, and their relationships tend to be shallow, volatile, and fleeting. To the extent that these observations are correct, they reinforce my claim that the virtues promote a healthy soul, and that a healthy soul promotes happiness and life satisfaction.

We are social animals, by our very nature. We invariably find ourselves in community with others, and it matters to us how we are regarded by others. Taken to the extreme, this is a vice. There is nothing virtuous or healthy about being a slave to the opinions of others—especially when those "others" have no opinion of value! However, whenever I hear someone tell me that he "doesn't care what others think" I come to one of two conclusions: he's either a liar, or a sociopath.

We *should* care what others think of us. As social animals, our own happiness is dependent (to an extent) upon our ability to get along well with others. Moreover, our happiness and life-satisfaction is based (in part) on our self-respect, and our self-respect is based on our social standing and how we are regarded by others. It is difficult to flourish when I know that my peers are (rightfully) ashamed of me, or (rightfully) disgusted by my conduct. The virtues facilitate my being (rightfully) well-regarded, and therefore facilitate my self-respect, and therefore facilitate my happiness.

The "Kantian" element in my synthesis is present in the virtue of justice. Justice involves giving to each what they are due, treating like cases alike, and unlike cases differently. In essence, this is what it means to be *fair*. I think Kant's great contribution to our understanding of what it means to be morally good is how he has shined a spotlight on what I interpret to be the virtue of justice. Moreover, he has given us a particular tool (the CI) with which to test whether or not we are acting and deciding justly. Since determining what each is due is possible only by creatures capable of reasoning, those of us who can reason bear a greater moral burden than creatures that can't. This is reflected in Kant's emphasis on Reason. His PI is captured by the virtue of respectfulness. A respectful person honors the value and dignity of herself and others. The PI helps us to understand what it means to be respectful, and how to be conscientious in our treatment of others.

The "utilitarian" element on my synthesis is present implicitly in several of the virtues (e.g., generosity, compassion—even justice), as well as within the overall health metaphor. Utilitarians are right to recognize the importance of happiness and pleasure. There is something about suffering that should (and usually does) immediately trouble us, whether the suffering be our own or another's. Virtuous people are compassionate in the face of other's suffering, and are moved to diminish it, when possible. Note that we are moved by the suffering of non-human animals as well as that of humans. This honors the utilitarian insistence that non-human animals "count."

Our efforts, inspired by compassion, will often involve the virtue of generosity. It's important to note the role of both virtues. It's not enough merely to throw some money at someone who is suffering. A cold-hearted jerk can do that! Nor is it enough simply to "feel bad" for someone. How does that help?

A virtuous person is one who has an appropriate emotional response, as well as an appropriate intervention. While we need not necessarily employ an actual utility calculation when considering and responding to suffering, or the appeal of pleasure, utilitarians have given us a useful, concrete tool by which to take seriously the importance of happiness in our decision making. The centrality of happiness to morality is also present in the recognition that a healthy soul is its own reward, if for no other reason than because it makes us *happy* in that broadest, most holistic sense, over the span of our lives.

By now, many of you have no doubt noticed the neglect of divine command theory. There are reasons for that. The most obvious is that the divine command approach requires belief in a particular sort of deity. Not everyone (including not every one of you readers) believes in that sort of deity. Moreover, the particular requirements of any divine command approach will vary based upon the particular religious tradition, and even the particular denomination within that religious tradition. As such, it's hard to offer and incorporate the divine command approach without making some rather specific (and potentially alienating) commitments. That being said, I don't think that anything about my approach needs to conflict with, let alone contradict, the divine command approach. I would even go so far as to say that they are harmonious.

The 2nd century Christian bishop St. Irenaeus said that "the glory of God is a human being fully alive." Certainly, from a Christian perspective this is not meant to suggest that the moral life is somehow self-centered, or even human-centered. Not surprisingly, the Christian perspective is *God*-centered. Accordingly, anyone adapting my theory in this way would need to add at least one more virtue to the list: faith. What that quotation, and Christian theology in general, *does* suggest and support is that God does not expect, or desire, that our lives be bland, miserable, or servile. God wants us to live well. Our pursuit of happiness must be tempered by piety and virtue, of course, but that is for our own sake, not God's—and not merely in the stereotypical sense of avoiding Hell. Rather, a virtuous life, from a Christian perspective, is the best sort of life right here and now.

Christians believe that what God most wants is for us to be in right relationship with God. Beyond that, I think God wants us to flourish. This does not mean a life without suffering or setback, but neither does a purely secular account of flourishing presume an absence of suffering or challenge. Indeed, it seems that some of the virtues can only develop and be displayed in the context of challenge (e.g., courage), or suffering (e.g., compassion).

Remember what I offered from William Lane Craig many pages ago: "Kindness is good because that's the way God is; cruelty is evil because it is inconsistent with God's nature. Therefore He issues commands that forbid behavior which is cruel and prescribes behavior which is kind. Rape is cruel, not kind, and therefore it is forbidden by God and therefore wrong."

In God, we find the virtues in their perfect form. Kindness is a virtue because God is kind. Justice is a virtue because God is just. Generosity is a virtue because God is generous. Some virtues require rethinking, to be sure. After all, God has nothing to fear, so courage must be something different for God. Perhaps human courage is an approximation of God's perfect and unwavering dedication to God's own will? This interpretation is reinforced by the fact that "courage" is often translated as "fortitude" instead. In most cases, though, the analogy is pretty simple. God has provided us a blueprint, in God's own character, of what our own best character should be. From that character, we can reason our way to what sorts of actions are fitting, and guide our behavior accordingly.

I don't pretend that this is a "pure" divine command ethic, but nor do I pretend to any purity with respect to any of the other approaches. What I have maintained all along is that each approach captures something important and legitimate about morality, but that none, by themselves, exhausts the subject. If God exists, certainly God would have something to contribute to this discussion as well. Hence, my attempt to incorporate the divine command aspect as well. For any atheist (or agnostic) readers, understand that the purely "secular" version I have offered might have merits of its own.

Exercises for Wisdom and Growth

1. Do you think morality can have a strong and compelling foundation outside of a religious framework? Why, or why not? If moral principles are not built upon a religious foundation, then upon what would our moral principles be based?

2. Think of an example from your own life when the happiness or interests of one person (or a small group of people) was sacrificed for the happiness or interests of a larger group. Do you believe that was the morally right course of action? Why, or why not?

3. Do you believe pleasure and pain are relevant to moral decision-making? Why, or why not?

4. How important are motivations when it comes to our moral evaluation of people? If someone saves another person's life, but it was solely for the sake of a reward, does that detract from the moral worth of her action? Why, or why not?

5. Think of a time when you believed you were being unfairly treated differently from someone else. How did that make you feel? Do you believe the different treatment was morally wrong? To what extent does "fairness" enter into your understanding of morality?

6. How important is it for you to be respected? How can you tell when someone is treating you with respect? What about disrespect?

7. How would you describe someone with a (morally) good character? What is she like? What about someone with a bad character? What is she like instead?

8. Do you believe that someone with a "bad" character can be counted upon to act morally rightly, in spite of his character? Do you believe that someone with a "good" character will consistently act rightly? Based upon your answers, how important do you think character is to moral decision-making?

9. Which of the theories seems most appealing to you? Why? Did you combine ideas from different theories? If so, in what way? How would you describe your own understanding of ethical theory, at this point?

Chapter 15: Application (Animals)

> *Comprehension questions you should be able to answer after reading this chapter:*
>
> 1. What is "applied ethics?"
>
> 2. What major ethical theory is the foundation for Peter Singer's view on the treatment of animals?
>
> 3. Why does Singer think animals deserve equal moral consideration as humans?
>
> 4. What is "speciesism?"
>
> 5. What two conditions does Singer think must be met in order to justify inflicting suffering on animals (e.g., experimenting on them, or eating them)?
>
> 6. Does Singer believe animals should be given exactly equal rights and treatment as humans? Explain why or why not?
>
> 7. What are the four morally relevant differences between humans and animals, according to Bonnie Steinbock? Provide a brief explanation of each.
>
> 8. Why does Steinbock think that we are justified in granting privileged moral status even to humans who (like animals) do not possess those four morally relevant qualities you should have described in #7 above?
>
> 9. Although not specifically addressed in this chapter by either Singer or Steinbock, how do you think the status and treatment of animals would be considered and determined by each of the ethical theories: Ethical egoism, Emotivism, Simple Subjectivism, Ethical Relativism, Sentimentalism, Divine Command, Kantianism, and Virtue Ethics?

At this point, we have reviewed numerous interpretations of ethics. Among the candidates for how best to understand moral decision-making were ethical egoism (EE), subjectivism, Ethical Relativism (ER), divine command theory, utilitarianism, Kantianism, and virtue ethics. Within each chapter, we considered some possible applications to "real life" in order to see how these theories actually *work*. Our remaining chapters focus exclusively on what is known as applied ethics. Applied ethics is just what it sounds like: the application of ethical theories to actual situations, decisions, behaviors, etc. For each application, try to figure out how each of the theories we have considered would interpret the issues, and determine the morally right courses of action.

Our first application concerns the status and treatment of non-human animals.[168]

---

[168] Some of you might find the term "non-human animal" to be unusual. It just refers

Animals present all sorts of interesting moral questions.

- Do animals have any rights?
- Is it morally acceptable for humans to eat animals?
- Is it morally acceptable to experiment on animals?
- Is it morally acceptable to keep animals as pets?
- Is it morally acceptable to use animals for their furs of hides?
- Is it morally acceptable to use animals for entertainment (e.g., circus animals, zoos)?

It's pretty obvious that we (individually, and collectively) do things to animals that most of us would consider immoral if done to another human, no matter which ethical theory we adopt. I suspect that most of us would think it would be morally wrong to eat another human (except, possibly, under very specific and extreme circumstances—and possibly not even then!). I suspect most of us would think it would be morally wrong to experiment on other humans against their will, or without their knowledge. Indeed, tales of Nazi doctors who experimented on Jews in concentration camps, or of the Tuskegee Syphilis Experiment (in which doctors knowingly withheld treatment for syphilis on African-American test subjects in order to research the disease, thereby allowing the men to die needlessly, and to infect their wives or partners with the deadly disease as well), are presented as horror stories of unethical medical practices. I suspect most of us would think it would be morally wrong to force a fellow human to carry us around on his back, or perform tricks for our entertainment, and most of us would be horrified at the thought of skinning someone and then wearing his skin as clothing.

And yet we do those things to animals every day—or are at least complicit in those things by virtue of our buying furs and leather, buying tickets to rodeo or circus events, buying products tested on animals, etc.

If it would be immoral to do those things to a human, why would it not also be immoral to do those things to an animal? Unless we're just brazenly employing a double-standard, there would need to be some morally relevant differences between humans and animals to justify the different treatment and moral status. I say "morally relevant" because there are all kinds of obvious differences between humans and various animals, but those differences might not (or should not) make any *moral* difference. For example, cats are smaller than me—but so are children. If "being smaller" is a morally relevant difference, then if it's ok to experiment on cats, it should also be ok to experiment on children. If it's *not* ok to experiment on children, just because they're smaller, then it shouldn't be ok to experiment on cats just because they're smaller either. If there is a legitimate moral difference between humans and cats (or any other animal), then we'll need to establish why it's a *morally relevant*

---

to any creature that isn't a human. I use the term non-human animal to acknowledge that, technically, humans are animals too—albeit endowed with capacities other animals seemingly lack, to some degree, at least. For the remainder of the chapter, I will just use the simpler and more common term "animal" to refer to any animal that isn't a human.

difference.

Peter Singer

Peter Singer is a world-famous philosopher and animal-rights activist who believes that there is *no* morally relevant difference between humans and (many) animals, and that, therefore, much of our treatment of animals is not morally justifiable. The fundamental basis for Singer's view should be refreshingly familiar to you if you read the previous chapters: Singer is a utilitarian.

As a utilitarian, Singer believes that it is (generally) wrong to inflict pain, and (generally) right to relieve it, and that inflicting pain can only be morally justified if doing so causes a "greater good." Since utilitarians believe that what is relevant to moral goodness and badness is pleasure and pain, what makes a being "count," morally speaking, is whether or not it is capable of experiencing pleasure and pain. Singer relies explicitly on the utilitarian Jeremy Bentham to reinforce his point.

> *The day may come when the rest of the animal creation may acquire those rights which never could have been withholden from them but by the hand of tyranny. The French have already discovered that the blackness of the skin is no reason why a human being should be abandoned without redress to the caprice of a tormentor. It may one day come to be recognized that the number of the legs, the villosity of the skin, or the termination of the os sacrum are reasons equally insufficient for abandoning a sensitive being to the same fate. What else is it that should trace the insuperable line? Is it the faculty of reason, or perhaps the faculty of discourse? But a full-grown horse or dog is beyond comparison a more rational, as well a more conversable animal, than an infant of a day or it week or even a month, old. But suppose they were otherwise, what would it avail? The question is not, Can they reason? nor Call they talk? but, Can they suffer?*[169]

Most of us, I think, would readily acknowledge that many animals, and certainly the ones with which we have most contact (e.g., dogs, cats, cows, pigs, chickens, fish, horses, etc.), are capable of experiencing pleasure and pain. It seems obvious when animals cry out when wounded that they have experienced pain, just as it seems obvious that a cat purring when petted is experiencing pleasure (of some kind).[170]

If animals can (and do) experience pleasure and pain, then, from a utilitarian perspective like Singer's their pleasure and pain must be considered in addition to our own whenever we make decisions that affect them (e.g., eating them!). To be morally justified in inflicting pain on an animal, it must be the case that the pleasure/happiness generated (overall) outweighs their pain—but when we think in those terms, a great many of the activities most of us take for granted suddenly

---

[169] Jeremy Bentham, *The Principles of Morals and Legislation*, 1789, Chapter XVII, Section 1

[170] I say "most of us." For an interesting perspective suggesting that non-human animals do *not* feel pain (at least not in the same sort of way that humans do, I recommend the following article: http://www.reasonablefaith.org/animal-suffering#_edn1

become morally suspect. We'll first consider the most obvious (and daily) activity: eating meat.

Is it plausible to think that the pleasure you or I might experience in eating a steak (or chicken breast, or some slices of bacon) is great enough to outweigh not only the pain that the animal experiences at the moment of slaughter (and the traumas leading up to it), but also outweighs all of the future pleasures the animal might have had if it had lived out its "natural" life? However delicious bacon might be, the pleasure of eating it is limited, and fleeting. The pig's suffering is intense, and its own loss of potential happiness is permanent.

What mitigating factors might there be that could tip the cost-benefit analysis in favor of eating meat? One might point out that several people will eat the meat of a single animal, and therefore dozens of humans experience pleasure while only one pig suffers. This is a fair observation—though this would require that the collective pleasure of everyone who ate from the pig outweigh the pain (and loss of pleasure) of that pig. This is possible, of course, but is it plausible? Do we really think eating bacon is *that* pleasurable—so much so that it overwhelms the suffering experienced by the pig throughout all its life in the "factory farm" conditions that it experienced prior to being brought to the slaughterhouse, and then the brutally "efficient" and mechanized process of slaughter itself? From a utilitarian perspective, it is *possible* that eating pork can be justified in this way, but at the very least it would seemingly require much more humane methods of raising animals, and much more humane ways of killing them—not to mention more vigilance so that the meat is not wasted, left to go bad in overstocked supermarket refrigerators, etc. Beyond this, there are utilitarian arguments suggesting that a "greater good" could be served globally by *reducing* meat production given that vegetarian diets can feed more people than meat-based diets can, that meat production requires one hundred times the water (per acre) than does farming (on average), etc.

The same issues arise should someone claim that humans *need* meat in their diet. To be clear, the consumption of meat is not *required* for survival. There are over seven million vegetarians in the United States alone, and many tens of millions more in the rest of the world. It is unquestionably true that humans can survive (and live long lives) without eating meat. More debatable is the degree of "health" that humans can enjoy without the consumption of animal proteins. Much is said about the need for lots of animal protein if one is to be strong and athletic, and yet there are several professional athletes who are either vegetarian or vegan.[171] Indeed, the health *benefits* of a vegetarian diet are touted by many individuals and organizations, and include lower risks for heart disease and certain kinds of cancers. Even if one could establish that meat consumption *is* necessary for optimal human health, one would also have to establish that "optimal human health" produces so much more happiness than "less-than-optimal human health" that it outweighs the animal suffering—and we would certainly face the same issues considered above: we would be morally required to raise and slaughter animals more humanely, etc.

In practice, very few people (in my experience at least) actually try to argue that the happiness of eating meat actually outweighs the suffering of animals. Instead,

---

[171] Examples include legendary quarterback Joe Namath, tennis legend Martina Navratilova, Olympic medalist Carl Lewis, and pro-wrestler Daniel Bryan.

most people either don't think about it, don't care about it, or dismiss the animal suffering as unimportant (or at least less important than their desire for a bacon cheeseburger). If you don't subscribe to utilitarian thinking, and think that pleasure and pain are not what determines the moral rightness or wrongness of an action, then there is nothing inconsistent about such behavior. But, if you do think that pleasure and pain "matter," morally speaking, but nevertheless discount the pain of animals when it's your own pleasure at stake, then Singer would claim that you just might be a "speciesist."

The term "speciesism" was coined in 1970 by a British psychologist Richard Ryder, but made popular by Singer himself in his 1975 book, *Animal Liberation*.

Speciesism—the word is not an attractive one, but I can think of no better term—is prejudice or attitude of bias in favor of the interests of members of one's own species and against those of members of other species.

Racists violate the principle of equality by giving greater weight to the interests of members of their own race when there is a clash between their interests and the interests of those of another race. Sexists violate the principle of equality by favoring the interests of their own sex. Similarly, speciesists allow the interests of their own species to override the greater interests of members of other species. The pattern is identical in each case.

Think of all of the various "isms" in use (and usually decried) today: racism, sexism, heterosexism, ableism, classism, ageism, etc. What each "ism" has in common is an attitude and/or practice of marginalizing, discriminating against, or holding to be inferior (etc.), a subset of the population *for non-morally relevant reasons.* That last portion is an important disclaimer. Simply treating a portion of the population differently is not always morally suspect. Is it "criminalism" to "discriminate" against convicted criminals in the sense that they are not allowed to leave prison until their sentence is complete? Is it "patientism" to hold "inferior" the medical opinion of a patient as compared to the medical opinion of his or her doctor? Is it "childism" for a parent to "discriminate" against her child with respect to house rules, discipline, etc.? Presumably not. What makes an "ism" something morally objectionable is that there is no morally legitimate basis for the differential treatment or status.

Racism is generally condemned because there are no legitimate, morally relevant differences between persons solely on the basis of ethnicity.[172] Sexism is condemned on the assumption that there are no morally relevant differences between males and females solely on the basis of their gender. Classism is morally problematic on the assumption that income and wealth are not morally relevant to the determination of one's moral status or moral worth—and so on, for the rest.

Part of Singer's agenda is to show that the lack of consideration given to animals and the preference we give to ourselves as humans is similar to what takes place in racism or sexism, that "speciesism" should be added to our list of "isms," and is just as morally indefensible as the others in that list.

---

[172] Indeed, the very notion of "race" or "ethnicity" as a biological concept or in essentialist terms is dubious *at best.*

When we consider the usual (non-theological) reasons offered for why humans have greater moral status, or why humans deserve greater moral consideration than animals, one of the foremost differences offered between humans and animals is that humans possess and display "reason." Associated with reason are other notable traits: self-awareness, capacity for reciprocity, creativity, language use, etc.

For Singer, though, the appeal to reason is insufficient to demonstrate relevant moral difference, and to justify differential moral treatment. First and foremost, as a utilitarian, it is not reason that matters to Singer, but the capacity for pleasure and pain.[173] Certainly the ability to reason will affect how one interprets and even experiences pleasure and pain, and Singer will cede this point later, but greater reasoning capacity might, at best, *enhance* a creature's capacity for pleasure and pain. Reason does not establish it. Presumably, the "dumbest" of animals can still feel pain—just as can the "dumbest" of humans!

That last point is not merely meant in jest. Some humans are smarter than others (i.e., possess greater "reason" than others), but most of us don't deduce that the smartest among us are also the most morally valuable, and therefore "count" more when it comes to moral decision-making. Some humans are more sophisticated in their language use than others. Some humans speak multiple languages, with extensive vocabularies, and others can barely string together a coherent sentence in their native language. Despite those differences, most of us don't think that the most "linguistic" among us are more morally valuable, and should "count" more when it comes to moral decision-making. Nor do we think the more creative among us are (morally) worth more. Some people are more "in tune with themselves," and perhaps therefore more self-aware. Does this make those persons morally more valuable?

Equality is a moral idea not an assertion of fact. There is no logically compelling reason for assuming that a factual difference in ability between two people justifies any difference in the amount of consideration we give to their needs and interests. The principle of the equality of human beings s not a description of an alleged actual equality among humans: it is a prescription of how we should treat human beings.

For one trait after another, Singer would point out that we simply do not actually employ those traits as moral standards to justify differential treatment when it comes to humans, but only appeal to those differences to justify our treatment of animals. When it comes to humans, differences in reasoning ability don't matter (morally), but when it comes to animals, they do. This is just plain speciesism, according to Singer.

Singer argues (and he thinks most of us would agree with this) that everyone should be granted equal moral consideration. The only item of contention is who counts as "everyone." For most of us, "everyone" means all humans, and we no longer consider it morally justifiable to exclude *some* humans (e.g., African-Americans,

---

[173] For our purposes, the basic utilitarian foundation is the most important reply to the "reason" appeal, and it is beyond the scope of this chapter to address other concerns, but it should be noted that other animals display reasoning abilities as well, especially other primates, such as Chimpanzees. Other animals also appear to have at least crude abilities to communicate, some animals seem to be creative, etc.

women, homosexuals, people with disabilities, Jews, etc.) from that community of "everyone." If we persist anyway, we are labeled with one of those "isms," and suffer all the ensuing moral condemnation.

The fact that some people really are smarter than others, or more creative than others, or physically stronger than others, isn't thought to matter. Equal moral consideration is not based on actually equal ability. If we're determining who to hire for a job, then one person being smarter than another might be entirely relevant. If we're determining whether or not it's acceptable to rape someone, however, it doesn't seem like IQ should be part of that calculation. This holds true with respect to groups as well. It is a fact that, on average, males have more upper body strength than females. If we are trying to determine who is best suited for a job requiring lifting heavy things overhead, then it might not be unreasonable to *generally* prefer males over females—but upper body strength is not a measure of moral worth, and females are not somehow morally less important because (on average) they can do fewer pull-ups!

Similarly, it is undoubtedly true that humans have more powerful reasoning abilities than any other animals of which we are aware, but as a utilitarian that doesn't mean that we are more *morally* valuable. It might even be the case that humans are more sensitive to pleasure and pain by virtue of our reasoning abilities, but if this is true it might just mean that our pleasures and pains are weighted more heavily in the cost-benefit analysis, not that animals are excluded from the calculation entirely.

There are obviously important differences between humans and other animals, and these differences must give rise to some differences in the rights that each have. Recognizing this evident fact, however, is no barrier to the case for extending the basic principle of equality to nonhuman animals.

Because of their capacity for pleasure and pain, animals *count* in the same way and for the same reason that we "count." This does not entail that it is never justifiable to inflict harm on an animal, just like humans "counting" doesn't entail that it is never justifiable to inflict harm on a human. Singer's point is that we need to be consistent in each case: if the good outweighs the harm, then the infliction of suffering is morally justifiable. If it does not, then it isn't, and it doesn't matter whether the harm is inflicted on an animal, or a human. Pain is pain.

Is it ever justifiable to eat an animal, according to Singer? Certainly. So long as the happiness achieved truly does outweigh the pain. Is it ever justifiable to experiment on an animal? Certainly, under those same conditions. But, (and here is where Singer gets provocative), would you also be willing to eat an orphaned human infant, or a mentally-disabled person, under those same circumstances? Would you also think it morally acceptable to experiment on an orphan, or mentally-disabled person, under those same circumstances? If the answer is "no," aren't you just being speciesist?

If you are outraged at the comparison, think of it this way: if we acknowledge that animal pain "counts" just as does human pain, but think it morally acceptable to eat a chicken anyway, then (from the utilitarian point of view) we must have already established that the "good" is outweighing the "harm." But, in that case, why are we eating a chicken rather than a human?

If you just arbitrarily favor humans, you're being speciesist. If you think there is a relevant difference between humans and chickens, what is that difference? Presumably, intelligence. Humans are much smarter than chickens, much more self-aware and sophisticated. In a certain sense, pain "hurts more" for us, than for chickens. But, by that logic, what about humans that are as intelligent as chickens? Very young infants are no smarter than most of the animals we eat—indeed infants are clearly *less* smart than pigs, and yet we make bacon from pigs and not babies. If you're concerned about the harm inflicted on the families of these babies, that's why the hypothetical scenario proposed orphans.

You might reply that infants have the *potential* to become smarter than chickens or pigs. Assuming, for the sake of argument, that "potential" matters in this context, why don't we eat (or experiment upon) seriously mentally-disabled people, then? In those humans, there is no potential to become "smarter," and their intelligence is often *less* than that of the pigs we eat, and the chimps on whom we experiment.

Does this mean that Singer thinks we should eat babies and experiment on mentally-disabled people? *No*—though this is a sadly common misunderstanding of him.[174] He's *not* advocating that we eat babies, but he also thinks we shouldn't eat animals (most of the time) either—and for the same reason. He's *not* advocating that we should experiment on mentally-disabled people, but he also thinks we shouldn't experiment on chimps or dogs either—and for the same reason.

In order to justify the harm inflicted by meat consumption, experimentation, etc., Singer thinks that two standards have to be met:

1. The outcome satisfies the Greatest Happiness Principle (i.e., it maximizes happiness or minimizes unhappiness for all involved capable of pleasure and pain).
2. The good achieved is so worthwhile that we would, in principle, be willing to inflict the same harm on an infant orphan or mentally-disabled person in order to achieve the same end.

The first of these standards is just the general utilitarian justification of any act. Whatever it is we're proposing to do (e.g., eat meat, experiment on a chimp, etc.) must achieve a "greater good" in order to be justifiable at all. If it truly does serve that greater good, then the infliction of harm is morally justifiable, but a good way to test whether the outcome really is *that* valuable is to ask ourselves if we would do the same thing to a fellow human (with mental capacities equivalent to the animal in question).

If you were starving to death on an island, you just might think it morally acceptable to kill and eat the flesh of a severely brain-damaged human—or, you might think so on utilitarian grounds, at least. But, you probably would *not* think it morally acceptable to kill and eat that human if you just thought he would be delicious.

How often do you eat animal meat because you're starving to death, or even severely malnourished, as opposed to for the sake of taste, or mere convenience? If taste and convenience wouldn't justify slaughtering and eating a human just as smart

---

[174] Singer is familiar with being misunderstood: "It is always frustrating to be misunderstood. But I've had to put up with that frustration for a long time."

as that chicken, then why, other than speciesism, would it justify doing so to the chicken?

> *Since, as I have said, none of these practices cater for anything more than our pleasures of taste, our practice of rearing and killing other animals in order to eat them is a clear instance of the sacrifice of the most important interests of other beings in order to satisfy trivial interests of our own. To avoid speciesism we must stop this practice, and each of us has a moral obligation to cease supporting the practice. Our custom is all the support that the meat-industry needs. The decision to cease giving it that support may be difficult, but it is no more difficult than it would have been for a white Southerner to go against the traditions of his society and free his slaves: if we do not change our dietary habits, how can we censure those slaveholders who would not change their own way of living?*

Having considered the eating of animals, let us now turn to animal experimentation, using the same guidelines from Singer. If you thought a medical experiment would probably cure cancer, then you just might conclude (on utilitarian grounds) that experimenting on a severely brain-damaged human would be morally justifiable. But, what if the experiment was to see what happens when you spray oven cleaner in his eye? What if the experiment had already been done, the results were known, and the experiment was just being repeated to keep eligibility for federal grant money? Does the experiment on that brain-damaged man now seem frivolous and unjustifiable? Why is it "worth it," then, when the same experiment is done on a dog?

> *If the experimenters would not be prepared to use a human infant then their readiness to use nonhuman animals reveals an unjustifiable form of discrimination on the basis of species, since adult apes, monkeys, dogs, cats, rats, and other animals are more aware of what is happening to them, more self-directing, and, so far as we can tell, at least as sensitive to pain as a human infant. (I have specified that the human infant be an orphan, to avoid the complications of the feelings of parents. Specifying the case in this way is, if anything, overgenerous to those defending the use of nonhuman animals in experiments, since mammals intended for experimental use are usually separated from their mothers at an early age, when the separation causes distress for both mother and young.)*

In each case, Singer's basic position is the same: if the experiment is likely to "cure cancer," if it really will produce *so much good* that it would be morally acceptable to do the experiment on a human of limited mental capacity, then it would be acceptable to do the experiment on animals, and, given a rule-utilitarian concern about allowing human experimentation, we could (and may) proceed with the experiment on animals.

> *This is not an absolutist principle. I do not believe that it could never be justifiable to experiment on a brain-damaged human. If it really were possible*

to save several lives by an experiment that would take just one life, and there were no other way those lives could be saved, it would be right to do the experiment. But this would be an extremely rare case.

Similarly, if eating the flesh of an animal would produce so much good (e.g., prevent starvation and death) that it would be justifiable to eat the flesh of a human of diminished mental capacity, then it's justifiable to eat the animal. In the vast majority of cases, though, neither our dietary habits, nor our experiments, nor our treatment of animals in general, satisfies both of the standards described above. In practice, much of our treatment of animals is morally unjustifiable, and speciesist.

If we take Singer seriously, does this mean that animals must be extended all the same rights as humans? Wouldn't this produce absurd results? Would we have to give dogs the right to vote, for example? Certainly not—not even on the most ambitious reading of Singer.

Many feminists hold that women have the right to an abortion on request. It does not follow that since these same feminists are campaigning for equality between men and women they must support the right of men to have abortions too. Since a man cannot have an abortion, it is meaningless to talk of his right to have one. Since dogs can't vote, it is meaningless to talk of their right to vote. There is no reason why either Women's Liberation or Animal Liberation should get involved in such nonsense. The extension of the basic principle of equality from one group to another does not imply that we must treat both groups in exactly the same way, or grant, exactly the same rights to both groups. Whether we should do so will depend on the nature of the members of the two groups. The basic principle of equality does not require equal or identical treatment; it requires equal consideration. Equal consideration for different beings may lead to different treatment and different rights.

The idea here is simple: "rights" are based, in part, on the sorts of interests a being has (or can have). Males can't (currently) get pregnant, so it makes no sense to ask whether they should have the right to procure an abortion. Women *can* get pregnant, however, and it is arguably in a woman's interest to have reproductive control over her body, so it does make sense to at least debate whether women have a right to abortion services. Humans are rational, capable of rational choice, and have interests in self-determination within their communities. Accordingly, it makes sense to think that humans might have the right to vote. Animals, on the other hand, don't seem to have those same interests, and couldn't vote even if we legally extended them that right. So, it's just plain *silly* to ask whether equal moral consideration means that my cat gets to vote for the next President. On the other hand, although my cat doesn't have the right sorts of interests that would require us to let her vote, she *does* have interests in avoiding pain and fearful situations, so we would need to consider her interests if we were contemplating any actions that would cause her pain or distress.

Bonnie Steinbock

Not everyone agrees with Singer, of course, and the most obvious basis for disagreement is to argue that the capacity for pleasure and pain, while shared between humans and most animals, is not the sole relevant factor with respect to moral status, and that (consequently) there are more morally relevant differences between humans and animals than Singer admits.

While Singer's utilitarian foundation is explicit and obvious, Bonnie Steinbock's philosophical inheritance is less clear, though she seems to employ generally Kantian methods, given her emphasis on reason, as we shall see.

To begin, Steinbock acknowledges that we *do* have moral obligations to animals, and that we *should* attempt to reduce the amount of suffering we cause them, but she disagrees with Singer's claim that it is morally wrong to give preferential consideration to our own species, to be "speciesist." While the capacity for pleasure and pain is a prerequisite for moral consideration, she thinks that such capacity, by itself, does not demand equal moral consideration. If it did, counter-intuitive results would follow. As an example, she claims that if capacity for pleasure and pain were the only morally relevant features, then if both your dog and your young child were starving to death, we would have no (morally legitimate) reason to feed your child before feeding your dog—after all, both are roughly equal in their capacity for pain. However, she thinks most of us would find it absurd that we are not morally entitled to favor our child over our dog—so there must be something more to moral consideration and preferences than mere capacity for pleasure and pain.

In fairness, a utilitarian might respond that you have more emotional attachment to your child than your dog, so *you* will suffer more if your child starves than if your dog does. Therefore, there is a utilitarian basis to prefer the child. On the other hand, to preserve Steinbock's point we need only manipulate the example a bit. Make it *your* dog, but a child who is a complete stranger to you. In that case, would it still be wrong to prefer the child anyway? "You might be very attached to your dog, but have no attachment to the random child. I might feel much more love for my dog than for a strange child—and yet I might feel morally obliged to feed the child before I fed my dog. If I gave in to the feelings of love and fed my dog and let the child go hungry, I would probably feel guilty." Steinbock thinks that our moral intuitions still favor the child, probably *any* child over *any* dog. If this is "speciesism," she thinks there is nothing morally objectionable about speciesism.

Steinbock argues that there are several morally relevant differences between humans and animals that justify differential moral status.

There is, however, an important difference between racism or sexism and "speciesism." We do not subject animals to different moral treatment simply because they have fur and feathers, but because they are in fact different from human beings in ways that could be morally relevant.

I will refer to these morally relevant differences as the "four R's."

1. Reason
2. Responsibility
3. Reciprocity
4. Respect

We will begin with **reason**, because reason is what makes possible the other three "R's." Rather obviously, humans are capable of reasoning, and degrees of reasoning, that exceeds that of animals. While it is true that not all humans possess reason equally (i.e., however we wish to measure it, some humans are just plain "smarter" than others—especially when we consider very young children or adults with development delays or disabilities), all humans (barring some possible extreme exceptions) possess reasoning capabilities to *some* degree, whereas most animals do not possess reason to any significant degree.

The possession of reason is not some arbitrarily selected trait, chosen (in a conveniently speciesist manner) just because humans seem to have the advantage, but because reason is legitimately morally important given its relationship to the other three differences from our list.

Responsibility—specifically, ***moral* responsibility** refers to the fact that humans can (and are) held responsible for their actions in ways that animals are not. Most humans, most of the time, are held responsible for their actions. There are notable exceptions, of course. We don't hold very young children responsible for their behavior in the same way we do for adults, and we recognize that even with adults there might be mitigating circumstances such as mental illness. Nevertheless, we are confident that not only can the typical adult human be held responsible for his or her actions, but that he or she *should* be held responsible for those actions. That we are responsible for what we do is presupposed by, and seems foundational to, the very project of morality itself. What sense does it make to say that someone *should* do something, or refrain from doing something, if that person is not, ultimately, responsible for her actions? When we hold people responsible in this way, we are at least implicitly assuming that the person had the genuine ability to choose from amongst options, understood those options, and made a deliberate *choice* of one of those options. If the choice was a morally bad one, we hold the person responsible for it, and will condemn it, punish her, etc.

Can any of those things be said of animals? However clever our dogs or cats might be, or whatever tricks and feats of sign language a chimpanzee might learn, do we really think that animals are *morally responsible* for their actions? Do we really think animals are capable of rational, deliberate *choice* for which they can be held morally responsible?

If we call a dog a "bad" dog, we're not suggesting that the dog is morally evil, but that the dog doesn't behave in ways we like. Most of us understand that in terms of conditioning. The dog simply hasn't received proper training. In more serious cases, where the "bad" dog is also vicious and dangerous, we might take extreme actions such as euthanizing it—but even in those cases no one seriously suggests that the dog is morally bad, but rather just too dangerous to try to retrain. This interpretation seems to apply even to chimpanzees, who are extraordinarily genetically similar to humans (close to 99% genetically identical).

One such chimpanzee, the "animal-actor" chimpanzee named Travis, was quite intelligent, and capable of impressive feats of reason. According to accounts of his life, he could dress himself, open doors using keys, drink wine from wine glasses, eat at the table with his human family, log on to computers to look at pictures, use a remote control to watch TV, and even brush his teeth using a "water pik."

In 2009, Travis attacked a friend of his owner and handler. He literally ripped her face off. Her injuries included being blinded in both eyes, a severed nose and ears, numerous face lacerations, and the severing of both hands. When police arrived on the scene, Travis approached the patrol car, tried to open one door, smashed the side view mirror, and then actually opened the driver's door, at which time the police officer shot him several times.

There is a certain sense in which Travis was a "bad chimp." He did rip a woman's face off without provocation, after all. However, I don't imagine that any of us thinks that the "badness" of Travis' violence is the same kind of "badness" that would manifest if a fellow human were to have done the very same thing. It's important to acknowledge that the action, outwardly, could have been exactly the same (i.e., violent, unprovoked mutilation). But, if the actions are outwardly identical, but our judgments are nevertheless different, what could justify the different judgment? Among other things, the difference is that we think that humans are just more *responsible* for their actions than are animals (under normal circumstances). Because of our superior capacity for reason and deliberate, intentional *choice*, we hold humans (nearly any human) more responsible for his or her actions than we do those of *any* animal. For Steinbock, this is not a trivial difference, but one that is very much morally relevant.

Similar to our capacity for moral responsibility, Steinbock argues that humans are capable of **reciprocity** in a way that animals are not.

I was a vegetarian for over 15 years. During that lengthy span of my life, I never once ate any animals, though I had plenty of opportunities to do so. I don't think my vegetarianism would have meant a thing were I to have wandered into a pride of hungry lions, and had I attracted the attention of a hungry great white shark. It is obvious and irrefutable that, were I being mauled by a crocodile, my appeal to the fact that *I* didn't eat animals would fall on deaf ears. Magpies are notorious for taking "shiny things" (including jewelry left unattended). It simply doesn't matter that I have never taken anything from a magpie's nest, myself.

> If rats invade our houses, carrying disease and biting our children, we cannot reason with them, hoping to persuade them of the injustice they do us. We can only attempt to get rid of them. And it is this that makes it reasonable for us to accord them a separate and not equal moral status, even though their capacity to suffer provides us with some reason to kill them painlessly, if this can be done without too much sacrifice of human interests.

Reciprocity matters quite a bit, amongst humans. Indeed, for some it is a key capacity for membership in the "moral community," and it forms the foundation for social contract approaches to political philosophy. Humans are capable of making, and honoring promises. I won't steal your things, so long as you don't steal mine. The fact that I have been kind to you might well oblige you to be kind to me. Conversely, a retributive theory of justice would claim that the fact that someone harms you obliges you (or, more likely, the State on your behalf) to harm them (proportionally) in return.

None of these things apply to animals. The mere fact that I am kind to my cat and provide her food doesn't entail that she is morally obligated to be kind and provide food in return. Once again, for Steinbock this is not a trivial difference between me and my cat, but a morally relevant one.

Finally, the last of our "four R's" is the capacity for **Self-Respect**.[175] Respect—specifically, *self*-respect, refers to the fact that humans are self-aware in ways that animals are not, and both comprehend concepts like respect, dignity, esteem, justice, etc., as well as demand that these concepts be honored in their own person.

When I put my cat in her carrier whenever I take her to the veterinarian, she is terrified. No doubt the confinement causes her fear, as does the travel (via car) to an unfamiliar place filled with smells and sounds that are equally unfamiliar. I feel terrible whenever I have to take her to the vet because I know how scared she is, and I have no way of comforting her by explaining that nothing bad will happen, and that it's for her own good.

If someone were to force me into a cage against my will, and transport me to an unfamiliar location (despite my protests), I would certainly feel all the same fears and anxiety as does my cat. The confinement and uncertainty would cause me to suffer in at least a similar manner (if not identical) to that of my cat. But, Steinbock would argue that the experience would actually be *worse* for me, because I, unlike my cat, understand what is happening to me. I have an intellectual grasp of concepts like freedom and confinement. I know that I am being *kidnapped*, and held against my will. While my cat probably suffers from a vague anxiety, I might vividly imagine any number of possible tortures that might await me. I have a sense of self and am keenly aware that *I* am being held against my will, that *I* am helpless and vulnerable. My cat might actually be helpless and vulnerable, but I don't think she has any sort of cognitive grasp of "helplessness" or "vulnerability." What's more, while both my cat and I can feel fear from our imprisonment, I suspect that only I can feel outrage and indignation, because only I can grasp the presumed moral wrongness of what is happening to me. Similarly, while any animal being experimented upon would likely suffer from the fear and pain of it, a human (in addition) will be aware that she is being experimented upon! For that reason, when we suffer, our suffering is more intense than an animal's, even if the conditions are (externally) the same.

> But the desire for self-respect per se requires the intellectual capacities of human beings, and this desire provides us with special reasons not to treat human beings in certain ways. It is an affront to the dignity of a human being to be a slave (even if a well-treated one); this cannot be true for a horse or a cow. To point this out is of course only to say that the justification for the treatment of an entity will depend on the sort of entity in question. In our treatment of other entities, we must consider the desire for autonomy, dignity and respect, but only where such a desire exists.

For all of these reasons, because humans have "certain capacities, which seem to be unique to human beings, [and] entitle their possessors to a privileged position in the moral community" (i.e., reason, responsibility, reciprocity, self-respect), it is morally legitimate to prefer human interests over non-humans, and to relieve human suffering even if it means inflicting suffering on non-humans.

---

[175] Self-respect starts with an S, of course—but respect starts with an R, and it's very convenient to have four R's.

What about those extreme cases Singer offers, where a severely disabled human exhibits the same capacities of a non-human? Such humans seemingly possess none of those morally relevant capacities that seem so important for Steinbock. Does this mean that severely mentally disabled humans (or even fetuses and newborn infants) have lesser moral status than typical adult humans, and that we are being speciesist if we nevertheless prefer them over animals?

Steinbock thinks that even in those cases, there is still a reason to privilege humans over animals—though she admits the reasoning gets a bit murky.

> When we consider the severely retarded, we think, 'That could be me.' It makes sense to think that one might have been born retarded, but not to think that one might have been born a monkey. And so, although one can imagine oneself in the monkey's place, one feels a closer identification with the severely retarded human being. Here we are getting away from such things as 'morally relevant differences' and are talking about something much more difficult to articulate, namely, the role of feelings and sentiment in moral thinking.

In other words, we can *empathize* with a disabled human in a way that we can't with a non-human. We can imagine ourselves, severely disabled, and being experimented upon, but we can't imagine ourselves as a chimp in the same circumstances. From these feelings of sympathy, empathy, and protectiveness, we can still privilege *any* human to any non-human. She grants that this might be speciesism, but if so, speciesism is "stripped of its tone of moral condemnation."

For Steinbock, there are clear and morally relevant differences between humans and animals that justify our different moral status. That being said, even Steinbock acknowledges that many of our practices towards animals are morally unjustifiable.

> I have been arguing that we are morally obliged to consider the interests of all sentient creatures, but not to consider those interests equally with human interests. Nevertheless, even this recognition will mean some radical changes in our attitude toward and treatment of other species.

Even though humans are "worth more" than animals, according to Steinbock, that doesn't mean that animals are worth *nothing*, nor that we are justified in dismissing their interests altogether.

Conclusion

Like many moral issues, the status and treatment of animals is complicated. Clearly, the moral framework one adopts will have a significant impact on the conclusions reached. Not surprisingly, most animal rights activists (like Singer) are at least implicitly utilitarian, and focus on the capacity of animals to experience pleasure and pain to make their case. Those who resist the idea that animals are deserving of equal moral status or consideration usually highlight differences that eclipse our shared capacity for pleasure and pain. Steinbock is a good example from this camp.

What makes the moral status of animals so complicated and subject to debate is that animals (in general) exhibit some of the features that we consider morally relevant (e.g., capacity for pleasure and pain), but not others (e.g., reason, reciprocity, etc.)—or at least not to the same extent as humans. This is why animals are sometimes referred to as "marginal cases" of ethics. They are on the "margins" of moral consideration.

Our next chapter will focus on another marginal case (and marginal for the same reason): the moral status of fetuses, and of abortion.

Chapter 16: Application (Abortion)

Comprehension questions you should be able to answer after reading this chapter:

1. What is a "marginal case," and why is a fetus considered to be one?

2. What is the definition of murder (as employed in this chapter), and how might it (or might it not) apply to abortion?

3. Explain how "being alive" and "being a person" are different concepts, and why this might matter in the context of abortion?

4. What are some of the possibly morally relevant traits needed for personhood?

5. Explain the "deprivationist" account of the "badness" of death. How might it apply to abortion?

6. On the deprivationist account, why would contraception not necessarily be morally problematic?

7. Explain how Thomson uses the following thought experiments to argue for the moral permissibility of abortion: Violinist, "Seed people", Chocolate sharing.

8. In general, what sorts of things would matter (morally speaking) for each of the ethical theories, when considering the moral permissibility of abortion: Ethical egoism, Emotivism, Simple Subjectivism, Ethical Relativism, Sentimentalism, Divine Command, Kantianism, Virtue Ethics

---

The moral status of abortion involves questions and concerns similar to the moral status of animals. Both involve what are considered "marginal cases." Like animals, fetuses present a complicated ethical challenge because they exhibit or possess some features that we generally take to be relevant for moral status (e.g., being alive and, at a certain point, capable of sensations including pleasure and pain), but not others (e.g., rationality, the capacity for moral responsibility and reciprocity, etc.).

The treatment of abortion in this chapter presupposes an evaluation of the moral status of the fetus, and of abortion, that does not require any particular *theistic* worldview. It does not, for example, either assert (or deny) that a fetus has a soul, or that only God should determine when someone dies, etc. Certainly, if you believe such things to be true, this could strongly influence your views on abortion! However, this chapter will follow the model proposed by John Rawls:

Reasonable comprehensive doctrines, religious or non-religious, may be introduced in public political discourse at any time, provided that in due course proper political reasons—and not reasons given solely by comprehensive doctrines—are presented that are sufficient to support whatever the

comprehensive doctrines introduced are said to support.[176]

This approach was encouraged recently, specifically in the context of abortion, by President Obama.

> *Democracy demands that the religiously motivated translate their concerns into universal, rather than religion-specific, values. It requires that their proposals be subject to argument, and amenable to reason. I may be opposed to abortion for religious reasons, but if I seek to pass a law banning the practice, I cannot simply point to the teachings of my church or evoke God's will. I have to explain why abortion violates some principle that is accessible to people of all faiths, including those with no faith at all.[177]*

I have not just made any sort of political statement, and you shouldn't read too much into the approach I'm proposing. My reason for adopting it is simple: some of you believe in God (and that God forbids abortion). Others of you do *not* believe in God—and still others believe in God, but not that God forbids abortion. Yet others of you subscribe to a worldview that is not purely naturalistic, but that doesn't include the God of the Western theistic traditions (e.g., Hinduism). Any argument against abortion that rests primarily on a specific God's existence and condemnation of abortion is an automatic "non-starter" for any reader who doesn't believe in that God. Similarly, any argument for the moral permissibility of abortion that is based (even implicitly) on a purely naturalistic worldview will automatically be a "non-starter" for people of (any) faith. By appealing to shared values instead, we may avoid both horns of that dilemma.

One value shared by most of us is that murder is morally wrong. You might think that this would make the moral status of abortion a "no-brainer," but we're not as lucky as that. What *is* murder? Usually, murder is defined as the unjustified killing of an innocent person. There are several important terms in that definition.

"Killing" is easy enough. We can understand killing to be the active termination of a creature's life. Killing is not usually thought to be the same as "letting die." One is active (killing), the other is passive (letting die). If I swat a fly, I have killed it. If I do nothing to save a fly from a spider's web, I have let it die. While this distinction between killing and letting die is sometimes thought to be relevant in the discussion of the moral status of euthanasia or physician-assisted suicide, it's not particularly relevant in the context of abortion, as there aren't any methods of abortion that could be described as "letting die" as opposed to killing.

"Innocent" is a potentially interesting concept to explore. Innocent might refer to legal status, in which case "innocent" would be the state of not having been found guilty of a crime. A fetus would certainly be innocent, in that sense. Innocent might also refer to moral status. Someone might not have been found guilty of any crime via

---

[176] Rawls, "The Idea of Public Reason Revisited," in: Freeman, Samuel (ed.) *John Rawls: Collected Papers*, Cambridge: Harvard University Press, p. 591.
[177] http://www.nytimes.com/2006/06/28/us/politics/2006obamaspeech.html?_r= 0

any legal proceeding, but might nevertheless be "guilty" of having done something morally wrong (e.g., a murderer who never gets caught or convicted). Oddly enough, only from a certain religious perspective would a fetus be considered "guilty," in this sense (e.g., if you believe in the doctrine of Original Sin, and therefore that all persons are sinful and guilty before God from the moment of conception). From a secular perspective, however, a fetus is presumably morally innocent as well, if for no other reason than the fact that it has had no opportunity to do anything morally wrong yet!

"Unjustified" is a contender (along with "person") for the most morally relevant term in that definition. Very few people believe that killing—even killing *people*—is *always* wrong, without exception. Dedicated pacifists notwithstanding, most of us believe that there are at least *some* circumstances that justify killing. If, for example, you believe that there is a morally relevant difference between humans and animals, you probably think that killing animals is *justified* by virtue of the value of doing so for humans (e.g., for food, medical knowledge, etc.).

Many people believe that killing is justified in self-defense. If, for example, someone is trying to murder you, it would not surprise me at all to discover that you thought you would be justified in defending yourself, even if this meant using lethal force, and even though there would be no doubt that your attacker is a person.

Some people believe that killing is justifiable as a form of punishment (i.e., the death penalty), and some people believe that killing even *innocent* people is justifiable if a greater good can be achieved (e.g., "collateral damage" in war).

With regard to abortion, what will remain to be seen is whether there are any considerations that would justify the killing of the fetus. The usual candidates for such considerations are appeals to the health or life of the mother, the preference of the mother, the health status (e.g., disability) of the fetus, the financial status of the mother, or the suggestion that a fetus is not a person (and therefore does not have equal moral standing).

Finally, the concept of a "person" is often thought to be (arguably) the most morally relevant term in that definition of murder—though we will see that some philosophers try to establish the moral status of abortion without resolving the personhood of the fetus.

Earlier in this section, I used the example of killing animals. I'm confident that many of you think that killing animals is at least sometimes justifiable, and, if so, it's probably because you don't think that animals are "persons." In our previous chapter, we saw how Bonnie Steinbock tried to argue that very point. If a fetus is *not* a person, then its moral status is likely going to be more similar to that of an animal than to that of you, or me, or its mother. If you think that animals have moral standing, then what will likely matter to you is whether the interests of the mother trump those of the fetus in the context of abortion. If you think a fetus *is* a person, then what will matter is whether (and under what conditions) it is ever *justifiable* for one person to bring about the death of another.

In what follows, I will lay out what I take to be the central issues on abortion, offering what I take to be the most compelling (secular) reason why abortion would be considered morally wrong, and the most compelling reason why abortion might be considered morally acceptable.[178]

---

[178] Note that we will only be considering the *moral* status of abortion. Its *legal* and

To begin with, I want to dismiss the useless slogan that "life begins at conception." Of course it does! But, unless you think that every living creature is equally morally valuable and ought never to be killed (and I don't know anyone who seriously believes that!), the fact that a fetus is alive, and that the life of that fetus began when a sperm fertilized an egg is not morally relevant. What *is* morally relevant is what kind of moral standing the fetus has, and when it acquires that moral standing. Certainly, being alive is a prerequisite for even being considered for moral status (i.e., I don't think non-living things, such as my coffee cup, have any moral standing at all), but most of us think that more is necessary for moral standing than *mere* life.

What, beyond merely being alive, is relevant for moral status? Presumably, the possession of any number of "morally relevant" traits. For utilitarians, sentience (the capacity for sensation, especially pleasure and pain) is *the* trait needed for moral status. If that is what we take to be important for determining the moral status of the fetus, then certain biological details are relevant. For example, for approximately the first 8-9 weeks of the pregnancy, the "neural tube" (what will *become* the brain and nervous system) has not even developed yet, and the brain and nervous system don't become responsive until the second trimester (i.e., about 12 weeks into the pregnancy). Presumably, the fetus is not sentient prior to second trimester. If sentience is a prerequisite for moral standing, a first-trimester fetus should have no moral standing. As of the second trimester, it would—though it remains to be seen (from a utilitarian perspective) whether the fetus would "win" in the cost-benefit analysis.

Perhaps you don't think that sentience (or *mere* sentience) is what's most relevant for moral status, but instead appeal to our capacity for reason, or self-awareness, or personal responsibility. In that case, the status of the fetus is even more questionable, especially in the early stages of the pregnancy. Rather obviously, if the fetus literally does not yet have a brain, it couldn't possibly be "rational," or self-aware, or capable of any cognitive activities at all. A potentially disturbing implication of this line of reasoning is that it is by no means obvious that newborn infants have those sorts of capacities either! Indeed, for some, this kind of "slippery slope" reasoning ("if it's ok to kill a fetus because the fetus is not rational, then it's ok to kill infants too!") forms the basis for their conclusion that abortion is morally wrong.

I think there is a surprisingly simple way to avoid the intellectual quicksand of determining the personhood of the fetus, and the potential slippery slope arguments about when personhood is attained. I follow Judith Jarvis Thomson's strategy of just stipulating, for the sake of argument (if for no other reason), that the fetus *is* a person—and then seeing what might follow from that.

> I am inclined to agree, however, that the prospects for "drawing a line" in the development of the fetus look dim. I am inclined to think also that we shall probably have to agree that the fetus has already become a human person well before birth.... On the other hand, I think that ... the fetus is not a person from the moment of conception. A newly fertilized ovum, a newly implanted clump of cells, is no more a person than an acorn is an oak tree. But I shall not discuss

political status is another topic entirely.

any of this. For it seems to me to be of great interest to ask what happens if, for the sake of argument, we allow the premise. How, precisely, are we supposed to get from there to the conclusion that abortion is morally impermissible? Opponents of abortion commonly spend most of their time establishing that the fetus is a person, and hardly any time explaining the step from there to the impermissibility of abortion.

Let us suppose, for the sake of argument, that a fetus *is* a "person" (or at the very least is sufficiently "person-like" to have some sort of meaningful moral status). Does it follow from this that abortion is not morally permissible? Not necessarily, and we will return to Thomson later in this chapter to consider why not. For now, though, let's build a case for why abortion might be morally problematic.

To understand why it could be considered morally wrong to kill a fetus, we should begin by considering why we probably think it's morally wrong for someone to kill you or me. Then, if there are morally-relevant similarities between "us" and a fetus, then it might be wrong (by extension) to kill a fetus as well.

I think that, under most circumstances, it would be wrong for you to kill me. At the very least, I think it would be morally wrong because it would unjustifiably deprive me of something of great value: my life experience itself. This "deprivationist" account of the "badness" of death (and, by implication, killing) has had many spokespersons in the "philosophy of death" literature, and we will consider a few of them.[179]

Fred Feldman, for example, offers an example to illustrate how an event (or state of affairs) can be "bad" for someone. He imagines a girl born in a country in which girls are not allowed to learn to read and write, but are taught to do laundry and raise children instead. Having grown up in this country, the girl is reasonably satisfied, and thinks she has lived as she ought to have. To her dying day, she never realizes what might have been. Feldman imagines further that she has some natural gift for poetry, and would have excelled at it had she been allowed to learn to read and write, and would likely have grown to become a successful and happy poet, if given a chance. "I would want to say that it is a great pity that this woman had not been born in another country. I would say that something very bad happened to her, even though she never suffered any pains as a result."

As a result of such reflections, Feldman proposes that something "is extrinsically bad for a person if and only if he or she would have been intrinsically better off if it had not taken place." Death might well be extrinsically bad in just that way, since for most of us, most of the time, we would be intrinsically better off if it (death) had not taken place.

We can consider death to be a "negative evil": an evil of deprivation. Once we're dead, we can no longer experience pleasurable activities of any kind, nor even enjoy the mere possibility of enjoying such activities ever again.

---

[179] This deprivationist Intuition has pop cultural references as well: "It's a hell of a thing, killing a man. You take away all he's got and all he's ever gonna have." (Clint Eastwood's character, William Munny, from the 1992 film "Unforgiven.")

Death might be very bad for the one who is dead. If death deprives him of a lot of pleasure—the pleasure he would have enjoyed if he had not died—the death might be a huge misfortune for someone. More explicitly, death might be extrinsically bad for the one who is dead even though nothing intrinsically bad happens to him as a result. In my view, death would be extrinsically bad for him if his life would have contained more intrinsic value if he had not died then.[180]

This is a tricky issue. On the one hand, someone might claim that even a negative evil has to happen to *someone*, and the dead person who no longer exists (or at least no longer exists as a person on Earth) is no longer a "somebody" to experience the evil, so there shouldn't be any subjective harm. On the other hand, it is a powerful intuition that death deprives the *dead* of something, somehow. Thomas Nagel tries to resolve this problem by claiming that the person who *used* to exist can be benefited or harmed by death, and tries to show that our intuitions are in harmony with this idea. For instance, he claims we could and would say of someone trapped in a burning building who died instantly from being hit on the head rather than burning to death, that the person was lucky, or better off, for having died quickly. Of course, after dying from the head trauma, there was no one in existence who was spared the pain of burning to death, but Nagel claims that the "him" we refer to in such an example refers to the person who *was* alive and who *would have* suffered. Similarly, if someone dies before seeing the birth of a grandchild, and there is no life after death, there is no person in existence who is presently being deprived of anything at all, including, of course, births of grandchildren. But the person who *was* alive and who *would have* seen it, if not for death, has counterfactually and subjectively missed out on something.

The same kind of thing could be said about death as a negative evil. When you die, all the good things in your life come to a stop: no more meals, movies, travel, conversation, love, work, books, music, or anything else. If those things would be good, their absence is bad. Of course, you won't miss them: death is not like being locked up in solitary confinement. But the ending of everything good in life, because of the stopping of life itself, seems clearly to be a negative evil for the person who was alive and is now dead. When someone we know dies, we feel sorry not only for ourselves but for him, because he cannot see the sun shine today, or smell the bread in the toaster.[181]

To add one more philosopher to this deprivationist account, Martha Nussbaum argues that death is bad for the one who dies because it renders "empty and vain the plans, hopes, and desires that this person had during life." As an example, consider someone dying of a terminal disease. Subjectively, the terminally ill person is unaware of this fact, though some friends and family do know. This person plans for

---

[180] Feldman, Fred (1992). *Confrontations with the Reaper. A Philosophical Study on the Nature and Value of Death.* (Oxford: Oxford University Press.), 140.
[181] Nagel, Thomas (1987). *What Does it all Mean?* (Oxford: Oxford University Press.), 93.

a future that, unbeknownst to him, will be denied him, and, to the friends and relatives who objectively know of his impending death, "his hopes and projects for the future seem, right now, particularly vain, futile, and pathetic, since they are doomed to incompleteness." Moreover, the futility is not removed by removing the knowing spectators. "Any death that frustrates hopes and plans is bad for the life it terminates, because it reflects retrospectively on that life, showing its hopes and projects to have been, at the very time the agent was forming them, empty and meaningless."

This argument also helps to explain our intuition that death is especially tragic when it comes prematurely. While we might grieve the death of someone at any age, it seems especially bad when it is a child, or a young adult, that died. We sometimes explicitly state this in terms of the deceased having "so much left to do," or having their "whole lives ahead of them." It is not that death is unimportant when it is the elderly who die, but that, in many cases, the elderly have already had a chance to accomplish the goals they have set for themselves. Indeed, many times those who face impending death with tranquility are those who can say, of themselves, that they have already lived a long, full life—while those who most lament death are those who regret what they have failed to do in the time they had.

Note that this is a statement about when death is *most* terrible. The elderly also have lives of value, and can leave projects unfulfilled. Indeed, if we understand the badness of death in terms of rendering our current projects futile, it explains how death can be a bad thing for *anyone*. "Even if there should be a person for whom death arrives just as all current projects are, for the moment, complete and at a standstill— if such a thing ever happens for a person who loves living—still, the bare project to form new projects is itself interrupted; and it seems that this project is itself a valuable one in a human life." It is important to note that the sorts of projects referred to are not necessarily isolated, but can also be complex projects involving plans to do something, or certain sorts of things, repeatedly over the course of a complete life. Projects such as having a good marriage, or being a good philosopher, or a wine enthusiast, are subject to frustration by death not because some particular activity is interrupted, but because of the interruption of "a pattern of daily acting and interacting, extended over time, in which the temporal extension, including the formation of patterns and habits, is a major source of its value and depth." In short, death interrupts the most basic project of living a complete human life.

To summarize the point thus far, one of the reasons we might offer for why we would think it would be bad to be killed (and, in most cases at least, therefore morally problematic for someone else to kill us!) is because being killed would *deprive* us of all our future pleasures, joys, completion of life projects, and even the bare experience of life itself. To put it bluntly, death takes our futures away. On the assumption that our future is one of value, death has deprived us of something very valuable indeed.

What does any of this have to do with abortion? The connection should be (or should soon become) fairly obvious. Killing me (under normal circumstances) is morally wrong because it deprives me of a presumably valuable future. On the reasonably safe assumption that your future is also valuable, it stands to reason that killing you (under normal circumstances) would be morally wrong as well. The general pattern here is that if killing me is wrong because of the loss of my future, then if other creatures have futures like mine, killing them is also wrong.

Do other adults have "futures of value?" Presumably so. Therefore (under normal circumstances) killing other adults is morally wrong. Do teenagers have "futures of value?" Presumably so. Therefore (under normal circumstances) killing teenagers is morally wrong. Do young children have "futures of value?" Presumably so. Therefore (under normal circumstances) killing young children is morally wrong. What about new born infants? Presumably, the same argument applies. Now, what about fetuses? On the reasonably safe assumption that a fetus has a "future of value," it too would be "deprived" were it to be killed. We have a reason, then, to think that killing a fetus is (at least at first glance) morally wrong.

Before moving further, I want to address a quick point of clarification. Note that the preceding argument has relied upon a "future of value." There might be cases where the future of the person is *not* so valuable. Someone afflicted with a painful, terminal disease, for example, might not have a future that is so valuable. This might be the basis for an argument favoring euthanasia, or physician-assisted suicide, in some cases. Similarly, it might be arguable that some fetuses don't have "futures of value" (e.g., if they will be born with profound physical or mental disabilities, or into a life of poverty and abuse). In such cases, it might not be *obvious* that abortion would deprive such fetuses of a valuable future. These will be controversial cases, of course, but the point is that not *every* future need be assumed to be a "future of value."

We now have a basis for the claim that abortion is morally wrong (viz., because it deprives the fetus of a future of value). Does this mean that contraception is wrong as well? After all, couldn't someone argue that an egg, or sperm also have potential futures of value? Probably not. Neither a sperm, nor an egg, by themselves, have any meaningful possible future (as a person) at all! An egg, by itself, will get flushed out of a woman's reproductive tract if not fertilized and implanted. Millions of sperm are released with each ejaculation, the overwhelming majority of which simply die. Those that never escape the testes die and are reabsorbed by the male body. Only if the egg and sperm combine *and* successfully implant in the uterus is there a realistically viable subject with a possible future of value. So, even if you accept this deprivationist argument against abortion, it wouldn't entail being morally opposed to birth control as well.[182]

We have just seen how a philosophical case can be made for the *prima facie* ("at first appearance") claim that abortion is morally problematic, not by appealing to any potentially controversial theological claims, but by means of a deprivationist account of the "badness" of death (and killing). Does this mean that abortion is always morally wrong? Not necessarily.

Although it seems that there is something morally problematic "at first appearance," this doesn't necessarily mean that after further consideration, a case might not be made for the moral permissibility of abortion. We will see how this argument can be made from within the same "deprivationist" framework we have already employed.

One of the most famous philosophical arguments concerning abortion was made

---

[182] At the very least, it would form no basis for moral opposition to barrier methods of contraception, such as condoms. In fairness, one *could* make a case against certain other methods that work by preventing the implantation of the fertilized egg in the uterus.

by Judith Jarvis Thomson back in 1971.[183] Using a variety of thought experiments, she argues that woman are not morally required to provide "life support" for a fetus—at least under certain conditions.

Thomson assumes, for the sake of argument, that a fetus is a person (though she claims that this is clearly *not* true of a fetus in the first trimester, at least). Nevertheless, operating off of the assumption that a fetus *is* a person, she considers whether this entails that it is always wrong to terminate the life of a fetus. Her answer is, ultimately, "no"—that the "right to life" assumed to be possessed by persons is not a blanket "right not to be killed" but rather a "right not to be killed unjustly," and that various thought experiments can demonstrate that even in the case of non-ambiguous personhood and right to life, it is still sometimes morally acceptable to terminate that life.

Her most famous thought experiment is the "violinist" example. The details of this admittedly strange thought experiment are as follows: imagine that you are kidnapped and knocked unconscious. When you awake, you discover that you are in a hospital, and that a world-famous violinist has been surgically grafted to your body. Doctors explain that the "Society of Music Lovers" kidnapped you and grafted the violinist to your body, because the violinist had a fatal medical condition and would otherwise have died, unless he had been grafted to someone else and allowed to use that person's body as a life-support system. You were then dropped off at the hospital so that both you, and the violinist, could receive medical care. The doctors explain that if the violinist were to be disconnected from you, he would die, but that you need only sustain him in this way for nine months, at which point he can safely be detached and live on his own.

In this scenario, there is no question that the violinist is a "person." He is a fully functioning adult like you or me. To use our vocabulary from earlier in this chapter, there is also no question that he has a "future of value," and that to kill him (or allow him to die) would be to deprive him of that future. There is also no question that, if anyone has a right to life, this violinist also has it. Thomson then invites us to consider whether all of that means that we are morally obligated to submit to serving as a life-support system for this violinist for nine months, whether it would be morally wrong to remove him (thereby killing him), even though he has a "right to life."

In the event that anyone is thinking that the fact that you must only submit to the condition for nine months is relevant, imagine the term was longer? What if it were a year? Or nine years? Or the rest of your life? The amount of time is, in some sense, irrelevant. Thomson grants that although it might be "very nice" of you to serve as life support, a "great kindness," no doubt, you are not morally obligated to do so, and you have not done anything morally wrong if you refuse to act as life support, and demand to be disconnected. Although the violinist has a right to life, he does not therefore have a right to anything necessary to maintain that life, let alone any particular contribution from *you* to maintain it.

Even if you agree, you might think that this thought experiment offers only limited insight into the abortion debate. After all, given that you were kidnapped, and grafted to the surgeon against your will, the clear analogy here with abortion is in the

---

[183] *Philosophy & Public Affairs*, Vol. 1, no. 1 (Fall 1971).

case of pregnancies resulting from rape. Not surprisingly, even people are who generally "pro-life" will sometimes acknowledge exceptions in the cases of rape or incest. However, termination of pregnancies resulting from rape represent approximately 1% (or less) of the abortions performed each year.

A variation of this thought experiment involves the additional detail that providing life-support for the violinist will seriously impact the health of the host. This is clearly meant to be analogous to abortions done for the sake of health concerns for the mother. But, these cases are also relatively rare (roughly 10-12% of abortion cases cite "health reasons").

This is merely to say that if one's case for the moral permissibility of abortion was based solely on rape-related intuitions, or appeals to the health of the mother, the case would be very limited in application. Thomson does not limit herself in that fashion, however.

While terminating a pregnancy resulting from rape accounts for only 1% of abortions, and for health concerns for only 10-12%, terminating a pregnancy for reasons of "personal preference" account for the vast majority of abortions. According to the Guttmacher Institute[184], three-fourths of women surveyed about their abortions cited "concern for or responsibility to other individuals," three-fourths cited that that they "cannot afford a child," three-fourths say that having a baby would "interfere with work, school or the ability to care for dependents," and one-half say that they don't want to be a single parent or are having problems with their partner. In addition, 51% of women who have abortions were *using contraception* when the pregnancy occurred. In summary, slightly over half of all abortions involve women who were taking precautions to avoid getting pregnant, and when they become pregnant anyway, cite a variety of reasons of "personal preference" to explain their decision to terminate the pregnancy. To address these (more typical) sorts of cases, Thomson proposes a different thought experiment.

> *If the room is stuffy, and I therefore open a window to air it, and a burglar climbs in, it would be absurd to say, 'Ah, now he can stay, she's given him a right to the use of her house--for she is partially responsible for his presence there, having voluntarily done what enabled him to get in, in full knowledge that there are such things as burglars, and that burglars burgle." It would be still more absurd to say this if I had had bars installed outside my windows, precisely to prevent burglars from getting in, and a burglar got in only because of a defect in the bars. It remains equally absurd if we imagine it is not a burglar who climbs in, but an innocent person who blunders or falls in. Again, suppose it were like this: people-seeds drift about in the air like pollen, and if you open your windows, one may drift in and take root in your carpets or upholstery. You don't want children, so you fix up your windows with fine mesh screens, the very best you can buy. As can happen, however, and on very, very rare occasions does happen, one of the screens is defective, and a seed drifts in and takes root. Does the*

---

[184] http://www.guttmacher.org/pubs/fb_induced_abortion.html (Note: it should be obvious that multiple reasons have been given by the women surveyed, in some cases).

person-plant who now develops have a right to the use of your house? Surely not--despite the fact that you voluntarily opened your windows, you knowingly kept carpets and upholstered furniture, and you knew that screens were sometimes defective. Someone may argue that you are responsible for its rooting, that it does have a right to your house, because after all you could have lived out your life with bare floors and furniture, or with sealed windows and doors. But this won't do--for by the same token anyone can avoid a pregnancy due to rape by having a hysterectomy, or anyway by never leaving home without a (reliable!) army.

Clearly, this thought experiment is meant to be analogous to the typical cases of abortion, in which the pregnant women voluntarily engaged in activity that she knew *could* result in pregnancy, but in which she took (reasonable) precautions to prevent it. Even in these cases, Thomson argues that although the fetus ("seed people") might well be persons, and might well have a right to life, the fetus does not necessarily have a right to be maintained in that life by the pregnant woman if she does not wish to do so. Would it be *nice* to provide the life support all the same? Quite probably—but "nice" and "obligatory" are not the same, and Thomson uses yet another thought experiment to illustrate this point.

Imagine that a young boy is given a box of chocolate candy for his birthday. His younger brother would very much like to have some of it. If the older brother were to eat the entire box, all by himself, without sharing with his younger brother, we might think that he was being a bit stingy, or at least not being generous and kind, but it also seems like he would be within his rights. After all, the candy is *his*. Sharing it might well be a virtuous thing to do, but that does not imply that he is therefore morally obligated to do so.

To biologically-host the violinist when you were kidnapped and surgically attached against your will would certainly be going "above and beyond" your obligations. As such, it is a very, *very* nice thing to do, even though it is *not* morally obligatory (according to Thomson). This might correspond to pregnant women who carry their pregnancies to term, in spite of the rape, or in spite of a risk to their own health, or in spite of great personal cost in other ways (e.g., financial, emotional, employment, etc.). At the other end of the spectrum, Thomson imagines a woman who gets a late-term abortion simply to avoid having to postpone a vacation. In that case, although the woman might be within her rights, it is nevertheless "indecent" to have an abortion under those circumstances.

Conclusion

We started with a *"prima facie"* case for the moral wrongness of abortion based on a deprivationist account of the badness of death. In general, killing a person is morally wrong if for no other reason than because it deprives that person of his or her "future of value." By extension, if a fetus has a "future of value," then it would be wrong to kill a fetus as well.

What complicates the abortion debate, however, is that it's a mistake to think of a fetus in isolation, as if a fetus were some sort of free-floating person "out there" in the world somewhere, just hoping not be killed. A fetus is always (at least initially) literally *inseparable* from the woman who carries it, and her "future of value" must be considered as well.

It's not difficult to imagine how a case can be made (and, in real life, *is* made) that to carry the pregnancy to term would *diminish* the "future of value" of the mother, either by forcing her to endure additional trauma stemming from sexual assault (admittedly only 1% of cases, or so), or by risking her own life or health (10-12%), or by simply causing financial strain, relationship strain, or just plain disrupting the goals and vision of life for the woman in question (vast majority of cases).

The overwhelming majority of abortions (approximately 90%) take place during the first trimester of pregnancy, when the fetus has no developed brain or nervous system, and therefore nothing resembling self-awareness or conscious thought, values, goals, desires, etc. During the first trimester, to say that a fetus has a "future of value" is an abstraction and projection to be sure—in contrast to the clearly recognized "future of value" of the pregnant woman. In the vast majority of cases, then, (i.e., first trimester abortions), it seems reasonable that the woman's "future of value" trumps that of the fetus, and abortion is morally permissible. In most cases, then, while it might be "very nice" for a women to carry a pregnancy to term (against her preferences) and offer adoption, this is not morally obligatory. This becomes far less obvious the longer the pregnancy is carried, and the less speculative that fetus' "future of value" becomes.

Chapter 17: Application (Helping the "Less Fortunate")

Comprehension questions you should be able to answer after reading this chapter:

1. From within which major ethical theory is Peter Singer working?

2. Explain the general principle that Singer recommends when it comes to helping others.

3. What do you think Singer means by "comparable moral worth?"

4. Does Singer think that our moral obligations are diminished by how far away the needy person is, or by whether or not we know that person? Explain why or why not.

5. Does Singer think that our moral obligation is diminished by the fact that other people might be available to help as well? Explain why or why not.

6. What does Hardin mean by "lifeboat ethics?" What does he mean by the "tragedy of the commons?"

7. Why does Hardin think that helping the needy (at least in certain cases) actually does more harm than good?

8. What is Singer's response to Hardin's argument?

9. Explain the difference (according to Narveson) between starvation as an active verb, and starvation as a noun. Why does this distinction matter, morally speaking?

10. Explain the difference (according to Narveson) between killing and letting die. Why does this distinction matter, morally speaking?

11. Describe the "liberty" approach used by Jan Narveson.

12. What is the "ethics of the hair shirt," and why does Narveson reject it?

13. In general, what sorts of things would matter (morally speaking) for each of the ethical theories, when considering the moral status of helping others in need? Ethical egoism, Emotivism, Subjectivism, Ethical Relativism, Sentimentalism, Divine Command, Kantianism, and Virtue Ethics

In this chapter we continue the process of applying ethical theories and moral decision-making to particular issues. The focus of this chapter will be the moral status of helping others in need.

It goes without saying that people are more or less advantaged/privileged relative to others. We live in a world in which some people have multiple billions of dollars to their name, and can afford to spend what most of us would consider extraordinary sums of money on what many of us would consider luxury items. For example, a "private collector" purchased a single bottle of the 1947 vintage of Château cheval Blanc for $304,375. That amounts to $7609 per glass of wine.[185] At the same time, it is estimated that one person in the world dies *per second* from malnutrition.[186]

Is there anything morally problematic about individuals spending money on "luxuries," while other people literally *die* from lack of food, potable water, medicine, shelter, or some combination of all of these?

It's important, before attempting to answer this question, that we acknowledge that it does not apply only to the so-called 1% crowd or those with lavishly expensive taste in wine. I suspect that every person reading this chapter spends some amount of money each week, if not each day, on things that less fortunate people would label a "luxury" – even if that so-called luxury item is a cup of Starbucks coffee, a ticket to a movie, or some new clothes (when your "old" clothes still shelter you from the elements).

Think about it:
   You see a homeless person on the street, with a sign saying: "Hungry. Anything will help."

1. Are you morally obligated to help that person? Why or why not?
2. Are any *other* people morally obligated to help that person? Why or why not?
3. If anyone is morally obligated to help, what should that help look like? What form should it take?

There are entire communities of people around the world in desperate need of food, safe drinking water, and medicine.

4. Are you morally obligated to help those people? Why or why not?
5. Are any *other* people morally obligated to help them? Why or why not?
6. If anyone is morally obligated to help, what should that help look like? What form should it take?
7. Should the U.S. government provide foreign aid to help those people? Why or why not? What conditions, if any, should be attached to the offer of help? Is it morally justifiable for the government to tax people who would prefer not to help in order to fund that foreign aid? Why or why not?

Having studied numerous ethical theories in previous chapters, you should be

---

[185] https://vinepair.com/articles/five-most-expensive-wines-sold/
[186] http://www.theworldcounts.com/counters/global_hunger_statistics/how_many_people_die_from_hunger_each_year

able to develop general positions on the moral obligation (if any) to help others in need from within the framework of those theories – and this is a worthy and recommended exercise for you. What we will consider in this chapter, however, is what three particular philosophers have said on the issue. In some cases, their approach should feel quite familiar, and we will make the relevant connections when appropriate. In fact, the first philosopher we will consider should be very familiar indeed if you have read the earlier chapter on the treatment of animals.

Peter Singer

As you might recall from that previous chapter, Singer self identifies as a utilitarian. Accordingly, he believes that actions are morally right or wrong based upon their consequences: morally right if they maximize happiness for every creature involved and morally wrong if they do not.

Singer takes as a generally uncontroversial starting point the recognition that suffering and death from lack of food, water, shelter, or medicine is therefore "bad." If the suffering resulting from lack of resources is a bad thing, then relieving or preventing that suffering, generally speaking will be a good thing – which is to say the morally right thing. As a general principle, he proposes:

> *if it is in our power to prevent something bad from happening, without thereby sacrificing anything of comparable moral importance, we ought, morally, to do it. By "without sacrificing anything of comparable moral importance" I mean without causing anything else comparably bad to happen, or doing something that is wrong in itself, or failing to promote some moral good, comparable in significance to the bad thing that we can prevent. This principle seems almost as uncontroversial as the last one. It requires us only to prevent what is bad, and to promote what is good, and it requires this of us only when we can do it without sacrificing anything that is, from the moral point of view, comparably important.[187]*

On the surface, this might seem simple. Causing harm is morally wrong according to utilitarianism for the simple reason that it inflicts pain. The only way that causing harm could be morally justifiable is if we could demonstrate that doing so will somehow result in less pain than would otherwise have occurred. By extension, preventing harm is morally obligatory and failing to prevent harm (when we are in a position to prevent it) is only morally justifiable if we could demonstrate that permitting the harm to occur will somehow result in less pain than would otherwise occur if we prevented it. Consistent with the utilitarian cost-benefit analysis, preventing harm is not morally required of us if it would require the sacrifice of "anything of comparable moral importance." This is where the simplicity ends.

"Comparable moral importance" is admittedly a vague term. We might think that

---

[187] All quotations attributed to Singer in this chapter are from his essay: "Famine, Affluence, and Morality" by Peter Singer. *Philosophy and Public Affairs*, vol. 1, no. 1 (Spring 1972), pp. 229-243 [revised edition]. The entire text (along with many other writings by Singer) is available here: https://www.utilitarian.net/singer/by/1972-- --.htm

some examples are easy. For example if a child is drowning just a few feet from shore, and will clearly suffer from the panic of drowning, the physical pain of drowning, and (debatably) from the loss of all future pleasures, and the only "cost" to you in saving that child's life is the discomfort and inconvenience of wet pant legs, the choice seems clear from a utilitarian perspective: save the child! Dry pant legs are not of "comparable moral importance" to that child's very life.

That being said, examples can become increasingly "complicated." Using the example of spending money to provide necessities (such as food) to those in need, just what other expenditures would be considered of "comparable moral importance?" Using similar reasoning, is a Venti cup of coffee from Starbucks of "comparable moral importance" as the life of children? One organization claims that it can provide lifesaving nutrients to a child for $.20 per day.[188] The three dollars spent on that one Venti cup of coffee (without anything fancy or special, and without a tip) could instead provide food to keep one child alive for 15 days, or 15 children alive for one day. It's hard to argue that that cup of coffee is of greater moral value than the lives of 15 children!

But where does this reasoning end? As you might recall from the virtue ethics chapter, Susan Wolf argues that the life of a "moral saint" is not a desirable life, and that many of the things we do, though not fulfilling some grand moral imperative, are nevertheless perfectly justifiable for us to do based upon "reasons of love." There are certain things that we do, and pursue, because they make our lives worth living.

This is not to say that a cup of coffee, specifically, is one of those worthy objects of love, but we can certainly anticipate where Singer's notion of comparable moral importance would clash with Wolf's reasons of love. A passionate musician might find her life profoundly diminished in quality if she could no longer play her instrument, but Singer might claim that her valuable instrument is not of comparable moral importance to the lives of those in need, and should be sold with the proceeds donated to charity.

As another example, a "fashionista" might derive tremendous personal satisfaction from being sharply dressed, and giving up a versatile wardrobe could conceivably diminish that person's quality of life in a significant way. Singer, however, specifically rejects the moral legitimacy of preferring to be "well-dressed" as opposed to the practical value of merely keeping warm with respect to clothing. It seems likely that he would grant that spending resources to keep yourself warm in the winter is perfectly justifiable, but spending money on a stylish outfit solely for aesthetic reasons is not comparably morally important compared to the life of someone who might otherwise starve.

To make his principle even more stringent, Singer does not allow that proximity in space (location) or proximity of relationship makes any meaningful difference in terms of moral obligation. This principle according to which we are morally obligated to help others in need isn't diminished simply because the person is a stranger, nor because the person is "far away." Indeed, advances in technology have made it profoundly easier to help others even on the other side of the world compared to when Singer first published his essay (1972). One can donate money to disaster relief, for example, in less than a minute on a standard smart phone:

---

[188] http://www.kahbayarea.org/

http://www.redcross.org/
Considering that all creatures capable of pleasure and pain count equally (all else being equal) in the utilitarian cost-benefit analysis, the fact that the needy person is a "stranger" doesn't somehow diminish the obligation to help. The fact that I know someone doesn't somehow increase their value in the calculation of the greater good, and "relational proximity" ultimately matters no more than does geographic proximity. Nor is our moral obligation diminished by the number of other people who could conceivably help, whether they in fact help, or not.

There is a social psychological phenomenon sometimes referred to as "diffusion of responsibility." This is a phenomenon whereby a person is less likely to take personal responsibility for acting when others (who might themselves act) are present. In 1964, a New York woman by the name of Kitty Genovese was raped and murdered outside her apartment. Thirty-eight of her neighbors witnessed these crimes and not one of them called the police. Their inaction was explained in terms of diffusion of responsibility. Each had assumed that someone else was probably calling the police, and therefore felt no compelling responsibility to do so.

While it is perfectly fine to acknowledge the existence of the psychological phenomenon, Singer thinks that while it might *explain* inaction it does not *justify* it. According to him, the fact that other people also have a moral obligation to help those in need in no way diminishes one's own moral obligation, and the fact that other people fail to do what is morally right does not somehow excuse one's own failure. He acknowledges that many people don't see things the same way, but he replies that "the way people do in fact judge has nothing to do with the validity of my correlation." In other words, our intuitions, perceptions, and actual practices can be mistaken and morally unjustifiable.

If his general moral principle that we are obligated to help others in need when doing so doesn't require the sacrifice of something of comparable moral importance is correct, the fact that some people disagree, and the fact that lots of people don't comply, does nothing to negate the correctness of that principle.

In response to the objection that helping others is better done by government organizations than through private acts of charity, he states, in effect, that the combination of *both* is probably what is morally required of us.

> *I do not, of course, want to dispute the contention that governments of affluent nations should be giving many times the amount of genuine, no-strings-attached aid that they are giving now. I agree, too, that giving privately is not enough, and that we ought to be campaigning actively for entirely new standards for both public and private contributions to famine relief. Indeed, I would sympathize with someone who thought that campaigning was more important than giving oneself, although I doubt whether preaching what one does not practice would be very effective. Unfortunately, for many people the idea that "it's the government's responsibility" is a reason for not giving which does not appear to entail any political action either.*

One objection that he *does* take seriously in the revised version of his essay is an objection basically rooted in his own utilitarian framework: that helping the needy, specifically in the case of famine relief, fails to satisfy a utilitarian cost-benefit analysis because it merely postpones starvation and will ultimately *increase* suffering. Before addressing Singer's response to this concern, we will consider what is arguably its most infamous source: the "lifeboat ethics" argument of Garrett Hardin.

Garrett Hardin

In 1974, scientist and activist Garrett Hardin published what would become an infamous essay against providing food relief to starving people, specifically in Ethiopia (which was experiencing a devastating famine at the time). A basic premise with which he defended his position involved a "lifeboat" analogy with respect to natural resources. In terms of households, nations, and even the planet, we can imagine ourselves as passengers in a lifeboat, with limited resources, trying to survive while other people remain in the water, wanting to get on the boat. Without question, if we do nothing, the people in the water will die. However, since the lifeboat is already at capacity, letting any more people in will harm those already on board.

Harsh though it might sound, he claims that we are entirely justified in refusing to allow anyone else onto the boat. For anyone currently in the boat who feels guilty about their privileged position, he recommends that they volunteer to leap into the water and give up their spot to someone who (apparently) doesn't feel that same guilt! The fact of the matter is that there are not enough resources to save everyone, that some people will die, and that those in the fortunate position of survivor are not morally obligated to undermine that position for the sake of those in need.

He continues his metaphor by making it clear that, globally and economically speaking, the people in the boat represent persons from "privileged" nations while those in the water represent people from "underprivileged" nations. To make a bad situation worse, he points to the differences in population growth rates between "first world" and "developing" nations – a difference that ensures that disparities in resources and life expectancy will only increase over time.

As a contemporary example, in 2017 Niger had a growth rate of 3.2%. South Sudan had a growth rate of 3.8%. In fact, all 20 of the top 20 growth rate countries were in Africa or the Middle East.[189] The United States, in contrast, grew at a rate of .69%--almost 4.5 times *slower* than the growth rate of Niger. The difference in growth rates is accounted for by many factors, including a decline in infant mortality rates, and high fertility rates in high growth rate countries. For example, Niger had a fertility rate of 7.29 in 2015, averaging 7.29 children per woman.[190] The USA, in contrast, had a fertility rate of 1.84 in 2015--roughly ¼ the rate of Niger.[191]

A country with far fewer resources than the United States has substantially higher population growth rates. Not surprisingly, some of those people experience food insecurity.

Are wealthier countries such as United States morally obligated to provide from their own resources to feed the hungry people in other countries? Hardin says no, and that to do so, would ultimately only make the situation worse. Using his own data from 1974:

---

[189] https://www.statista.com/statistics/264687/countries-with-the-highest-population-growth-rate/
[190] https://www.statista.com/statistics/448648/fertility-rate-in-niger/
[191] https://www.statista.com/statistics/269941/fertility-rate-in-the-us/

Now suppose the U.S. agreed to pool its resources with those seven countries, with everyone receiving an equal share. Initially the ratio of Americans to non-Americans in this model would be one-to-one. But consider what the ratio would be after 87 years, by which time the Americans would have doubled to a population of 420 million. By then, doubling every 21 years, the other group would have swollen to 3.54 billion. Each American would have to share the available resources with more than eight people.

But, one could argue, this discussion assumes that current population trends will continue, and they may not. Quite so. Most likely the rate of population increase will decline much faster in the U.S. than it will in the other countries, and there does not seem to be much we can do about it. In sharing with "each according to his needs," we must recognize that needs are determined by population size, which is determined by the rate of reproduction, which at present is regarded as a sovereign right of every nation, poor or not. This being so, the philanthropic load created by the sharing ethic of the spaceship can only increase.[192]

That is, whatever burden is being placed on the resources of the "lifeboat" at present will only be magnified if the number of people "in the water" continues to increase and outpace the number of people with sufficient resources for themselves (i.e., those already in a "lifeboat"). He ties his notion of "lifeboat ethics" to an older idea of the "tragedy of the commons" (a term originally used by William Forster Lloyd in 1833).

The fundamental error of spaceship ethics, and the sharing it requires, is that it leads to what I call "the tragedy of the commons." Under a system of private property, the men who own property recognize their responsibility to care for it, for if they don't they will eventually suffer... If everyone would restrain himself, all would be well; but it takes only one less than everyone to ruin a system of voluntary restraint. In a crowded world of less than perfect human beings, mutual ruin is inevitable if there are no controls. This is the tragedy of the commons.

The idea here is somewhat simple and possibly intuitive: when something is "yours," you are motivated to take care of it much more so than if it belongs to "no one" or "everyone." A simple example of this is a public restroom. I am routinely horrified by the conditions of public restrooms, where it seems obvious that some people are making no effort to avoid making a mess – or possibly even making it a point to do so on purpose. Without going into too much detail, I've lost count of the number of times I've seen toilets where someone has urinated all over the seat and on the floor, and even times when someone has defecated on the seat or on the floor!

---

[192] All quotations attributed to Hardin are from the following essay: http://www.garretthardinsociety.org/articles/art_lifeboat_ethics_case_against_help ing_poor.html

Although I cannot say this with certainty, I'm very confident that those people treat their own bathrooms at home with much more care. It would truly surprise me if very many of those individuals would pee all over their own bathroom floor and then simply walk away. And yet, such actions are not all that uncommon in public restrooms.

To apply this intuition behind the tragedy of the commons to economic decisions and food resources, the assumption is that when people are responsible for their own resources they are much more motivated to take proper care of them. If, instead, resources are held "in common," and anyone may make a claim on these resources even if they have not taken care of them themselves, then people will exploit these resources, take advantage of the system, and the entire system will suffer as a result. In this scenario, Hardin thinks that "helping" with aid merely postpones (and increases) the suffering and death.

> *We must ask if such a program would actually do more good than harm, not only momentarily but also in the long run. Those who propose the food bank usually refer to a current "emergency" or "crisis" in terms of world food supply. But what is an emergency? Although they may be infrequent and sudden, everyone knows that emergencies will occur from time to time. A well-run family, company, organization or country prepares for the likelihood of accidents and emergencies. It expects them, it budgets for them, it saves for them. . . .*

> *What happens if some organizations or countries budget for accidents and others do not? If each country is solely responsible for its own well-being, poorly managed ones will suffer. But they can learn from experience. They may mend their ways, and learn to budget for infrequent but certain emergencies. For example, the weather varies from year to year, and periodic crop failures are certain. A wise and competent government saves out of the production of the good years in anticipation of bad years to come. Joseph taught this policy to Pharaoh in Egypt more than 2,000 years ago. Yet the great majority of the governments in the world today do not follow such a policy. They lack either the wisdom or the competence, or both. Should those nations that do manage to put something aside be forced to come to the rescue each time an emergency occurs among the poor nations?*

In other words, harsh though it might sound, at the international level if other countries "bail out" communities that have too large of a population for their current level of resources, then they will never "learn" and make the appropriate adjustments to their family planning and/or their economy. The outside aid will simply enable the poor resource management and prolong the suffering.

> *'But it isn't their fault!' Some kind-hearted liberals argue. 'How can we blame the poor people who are caught in an emergency? Why must they suffer for the sins of their governments?' The concept of blame is simply not relevant here. . . . As a result of such solutions to food shortage emergencies, the poor countries will not learn to mend their ways, and will suffer progressively greater*

emergencies as their populations grow. . . .

If poor countries received no food from the outside, the rate of their population growth would be periodically checked by crop failures and famines. But if they can always draw on a world food bank in time of need, their population can continue to grow unchecked, and so will their "need" for aid. In the short run, a world food bank may diminish that need, but in the long run it actually increases the need without limit.

Without some system of worldwide food sharing, the proportion of people in the rich and poor nations might eventually stabilize. The overpopulated poor countries would decrease in numbers, while the rich countries that had room for more people would increase.

Again, harsh as it might sound, Hardin is actually appealing to an implicitly utilitarian justification for not helping the needy – at least in the context he is describing. By providing aid, the "more fortunate" are simply propping up the circumstances and poor lifestyle choices of individuals or governments (or both). Because there is no need for them to change anything, they are unlikely to do so. The very same conditions that produced the "need" will continue to produce that same need in the future, requiring the more fortunate to continue to provide aid, which will continue to perpetuate the need, etc.

To break this cycle of dependency, the needy must do something different. At a personal level, people might need to make more responsible choices. At a national level, governments might need to change economic policies, or root out corruption, or abandon expensive military spending, etc. At a cultural level, communities might be forced to reconsider their beliefs and values concerning family planning. A culture with too many mouths to feed but that also rejects birth control and abortion might need to rethink that strategy.

In case it's not obvious, the utilitarian justification for this "tough love" is the assumption that the greater good is served not by providing help, but by those in need making the changes necessary so that the same conditions producing their suffering now will not continue to produce them in the future.

Singer was aware of this criticism of his general principle and replied to it in at least two fashions. The first is that even if those observations are true, it merely changes the *type* of help one should provide.

The conclusion that should be drawn is that the best means of preventing famine, in the long run, is population control. It would then follow from the position reached earlier that one ought to be doing all one can to promote population control (unless one held that all forms of population control were wrong in themselves, or would have significantly bad consequences). Since there are organizations working specifically for population control, one would then support them rather than more orthodox methods of preventing famine.

If the concern is that at the international level the cause of starvation is overpopulation, then in the short run some food aid might be appropriate, but in the long run providing resources for population control would be the "aid" that we are morally obligated to provide.

At a personal level, if the cause of someone being homeless and in need is drug addiction, then in the short run food and shelter might be appropriate, but in the long run our moral obligation might be to provide resources to combat drug addiction. The obligation remains, but the form it takes might have to be adjusted.

The second way in which Singer acknowledges this criticism is arguably more substantial. As mentioned earlier in this chapter, in the revised version of this essay, Singer acknowledges the credibility of this objection, up to a point, and makes a concession (of sorts).

> . . . for I now think that there is a serious case for saying that if a country refuses to take any steps to slow the rate of its population growth, we should not give it aid. This is, of course, a very drastic step to take, and the choice it represents is a horrible choice to have to make; but if, after a dispassionate analysis of all the available information, we come to the conclusion that without population control we will not, in the long run, be able to prevent famine or other catastrophes, then it may be more humane in the long run to aid those countries that are prepared to take strong measures to reduce population growth, and to use our aid policy as a means of pressuring other countries to take similar steps.

This is actually a significant concession. Acknowledging a bit of political pragmatism, Singer is recognizing that there might be certain nations where political corruption is so entrenched, or governments with such misguided priorities, that providing aid to those nations will not actually help the problem, but will only prolong it. In those cases, the right thing to do might well be to not provide aid, but perhaps direct resources to political and social change instead.

Thus far, we have heard from two people, both working from within some general utilitarian assumptions. Peter Singer claims that we have a moral obligation to provide for the less fortunate unless and up until the point something of "comparable moral value" is sacrificed. Garrett Hardin similarly appeals to the "greater good," but comes to a very different conclusion: the greater good is served by not providing aid, not prolonging the suffering, but forcing the needy to recalibrate their choices, or, at the level of entire nations, forcing governments to do the same. In sharp contrast to Peter Singer, and working outside the utilitarian approach, we have the libertarian approach advocated by Jan Narveson.

Jan Narveson

As is typical of good philosophers, Narveson begins by carefully defining his terms and distinguishing different meanings of the same term. For example, "starvation" can be understood either as an "active" or as a "passive" word.

The active form of "starvation" is the verb "to starve." That is something that is inflicted on someone else, and might be the moral equivalent of murder since it is the intentional killing of another person. However, "starvation" in the passive sense is a noun, a state of being. In this sense it is something that happens rather than something that is "inflicted," and is much closer to "letting die" than to murder. This distinction is important according to Narveson. With respect to our moral intuitions, we don't treat killing and letting die as a morally equivalent. Even if we think letting someone die is morally problematic, we wouldn't (presumably) recommend life in prison for letting someone on the other side of the world starve – otherwise, wouldn't this entail that nearly all of us are worthy of life sentences in prison?

> *As to the first, the argument for nonidentity of the two is straightforward. When you kill someone, you do an act, x, which brings it about that the person is dead when he would otherwise still be alive. You induce a change (for the worse) in his condition. But when you let someone die, this is not so, for she would have died even if you had, say, been in Australia at the time. How can you be said to be the "cause" of something which would have happened if you didn't exist?*[193]

This is a clever argument. Narveson is claiming that we can demonstrate that killing and letting die are not the same thing by recognizing the different causal relationship someone might have to each.

When you kill someone, you produce a change (i.e. death) that otherwise would not have occurred. When you let someone die, on the other hand, the change occurs completely independently of you. Theoretically, the death would have occurred if you were in a completely different location (e.g. Australia) or even if you never existed in the first place.

He is proposing that there is something conceptually dubious about claiming that you can somehow be the "cause" of something which would have happened even if you had never been born. If you are not meaningfully the cause of the death, then it seems questionable to say that you are morally responsible for it – or at the least it's a very different sort of responsibility than in the case of murder.

In addition to distinguishing different notions of starvation, he also distinguishes "justice" from "charity." Justice is something that is enforceable, that involves behavior subject to constraint, and is rooted in moral obligation. Justice refers to what is required of us. If we fail to do what justice requires, we have done something morally wrong, and we are justifiably subject to moral condemnation. Charity, on the other hand, he regards as something voluntary, and rooted in "feeling" rather than obligation.

For Narveson, the basic issues are as follows:

1. Is there a basic duty of justice to feed the starving?
2. If not, is there a basic requirement of charity to do so (and how strong is that requirement)?

In short, Narveson's answer to both of those questions appears to be "no." His

---

[193] All quotations attributed to Narveson are from the following source: Jan Narveson. *Moral Matters*, Broadview Press; 2nd edition (1999). Chapter 7. A copy of the entire chapter is available here:
http://www.csus.edu/indiv/g/gaskilld/ethics/feeding%20the%20hungry%20mm%2099.htm

justification for this is rooted in what he calls the "liberty" approach to these issues –
an approach known as Libertarianism in the political realm.

> *The most plausible answer, I think, is the point of view that allows different
> people to live their various lives, by forbidding interference with the lives of
> others. Rather than insisting, with threats to back it up, that I help someone for
> whose projects and purposes I have no sympathy whatever, let us all agree to
> respect each other's pursuits. We'll agree to let each person live as that person
> sees fit, with only our bumpings into each other being subject to public control.
> To do this, we need to draw a sort of line around each person, and insist that
> others not cross that line without the permission of the occupant. The rule will
> be not to forcibly intervene in the lives of others, thus requiring that our
> relations be mutually agreeable. Enforced feeding of the starving, however, does
> cross the line, invading the farmer or the merchant, forcing him to part with
> some of his hard-earned produce and give it without compensation to others.
> That, says the advocate of liberty, is theft, not charity.*

Generally speaking, this libertarian approach recommends that people be
allowed to conduct their lives as they see fit so long as they are not harming anyone
else. People will be allowed to live their life, and to spend their money, as they choose
without interference from others.

Requiring someone to provide food for the hungry against their will is a violation
of this liberty approach, an unjustified encroachment into the private life of someone
else. Obviously, people should be free to voluntarily donate their money as they see
fit, including famine relief. But, since we do not have a moral obligation to keep others
alive by paying for their food, we are not violating any moral requirements if we
choose not to do so, and we are therefore not subject to forced compliance (e.g.
through taxation) if we do not. To put it bluntly, if I never had an obligation to do
something, you are not justified in forcing me to do it.

From Narveson's perspective, this approach avoids concerns about utility
calculations entirely, since it does not consider utility in the first place. The debate
between Singer and Hardin concerning whether feeding the starving maximizes
utility or merely postpones (and increases) suffering is neatly sidestepped. In
addition, this approach avoids what Narveson derisively calls the "ethics of the hair
shirt."

For the sake of context, a "hair shirt" refers to a shirt of hair cloth, formerly worn
by penitents and esthetic monks in religious communities. The shirt was intentionally
uncomfortable so as to provide "mortification of the flesh." Today, the term also is
used as an adjective to refer to austere and self-sacrificing personalities or lifestyles.
The way Narveson is using the term, the "ethics of the hair shirt" seems to refer to an
understanding of moral obligation that places us in the service of others at the cost of
our own enjoyment and personal interests.

> *In stark contrast to the liberty-respecting view stands the idea that we are to
> count the satisfactions of others as equal in value to our own. If I can create a
> little more pleasure for some stranger by spending my dollar on him than if I
> would create for myself by spending it on an ice cream cone, I then have a*

putative obligation to spend it on him. Thus I am to continually defer to others in the organization of my activities, and shall be assailed by guilt whenever I am not bending my energies to the relief of those allegedly less fortunate than I. "Benefit others, at the expense of yourself -- and keep doing it until you are as poor and miserable as those whose poverty and misery you are supposed to be relieving!" That is the ethics of the hair shirt. How should we react to this idea? Negatively, I suggest. Doesn't that view really make us the slaves of the (supposedly) less well off?

If you recall the earlier chapter on ethical egoism and Ayn Rand, this sort of language should sound familiar. Rand argued that "altruistic" ethical theories (including, specifically, utilitarianism) were misguided and harmful because they obligate us to the service of others, and require us to sacrifice our own lives and own interests for the sake of anyone else who might have some sort of "need."[194] Like Rand, Narveson is proposing that it is perfectly legitimate to favor your own life and your own interests over those of others, and that you are not morally obligated to sacrifice those interests, even if they are "trivial" or of no "comparable moral importance."

Narveson appeals to what he thinks are common intuitions, in a fashion that might be reminiscent of Susan Wolf (again, see an earlier chapter), to reject Singer's claim that his moral principle does not recognize the legitimacy of "proximity."

Normal people care more about some people than others, and build their very lives around those carings. It is both absurd and arrogant for theorists, talking airily about the equality of all people, to insist on cramming it down our throats - which is how ordinary people do see it.

For example, a parent might honestly care considerably more about celebrating a daughter's *fiesta de quince años* than in saving the life of a hungry child on the other side of the world. Undoubtedly, the money that will be spent celebrating that daughter's birthday could be donated to a charitable organization and possibly literally save the life of another child, at least for a time. Singer and Narveson would draw profoundly different conclusions concerning this example.

From Singer's perspective, the fiesta is not of comparable moral significance to the life of that hungry child, and for that reason it is morally unjustifiable to dedicate resources for a coming-of-age party when it could be spent to save a person's life instead.

Narveson, on the other hand, doesn't recognize the moral obligation to save that hypothetical child in the first place, and while it might be very nice to donate the money instead, it is both reasonable and justifiable to celebrate the birthday instead.[195] That being said, Narveson does acknowledge that in some circumstances some amount of aid is probably morally appropriate.

---

[194] I encourage you to review that chapter for a fuller explanation of her perspective.
[195] This distinction between what would be "nice" and what is "morally required" is reminiscent of Thomson's argument for the moral permissibility of abortion from a previous chapter.

But the anti-welfarist idea can be taken too far as well. Should people be disposed to assist each other in time of need? Certainly they should. But the appropriate rule for this is not that each person is duty-bound to minister to the poor until he himself is a pauper or near-pauper as well. Rather, the appropriate rule is what the characterization, "in time of need" more nearly suggests. There are indeed emergencies in life when a modest effort by someone will do a great deal for someone else. People who aren't ready to help others when it is comparatively easy to do so are people who deserve to be avoided when they themselves turn to others in time of need.

By way of analogy, in my capacity as a professor I am sometimes asked to do things that technically fall outside my job description. Sometimes this is as simple as a student asking for directions to find a particular office on campus. I think providing whatever assistance I'm capable of in such circumstances is the decent thing to do, and I don't mind doing it, to be honest. Some sort of extreme stance according to which I refuse to even point a student in the right direction because to do so is making an unjustifiable demand of me seems to be a bit "extra." At the same time, if an endless stream of students came to me asking for directions, and I made a point to help every single one of them, every day, find where they need to go, at a certain point I wouldn't even be able to do my actual job, moral obligations notwithstanding.

Similarly, Narveson suggests that it might be a decent and appropriate thing to occasionally help someone in need when the need is urgent, and it is an "emergency." He rejects, however, the idea that we are obligated to make ourselves *equally needy* by virtue of continuing to help others out of our own resources.

One final issue that Narveson considers is more practical than philosophical – though it does have a connection to determining whether or not helping others in need is appropriate. Narveson points out that starvation is often the result of politics (e.g. corruption, war, etc.) rather than a lack of resources.

For example, from 1994 to 1998, at least a half million people (and possibly as many as a million) died from starvation in North Korea. This was the result of a combination of factors including draught, economic mismanagement, and an autocratic government that focused on military spending rather than food production and famine relief.

More than two billion dollars in international food aid was sent to mitigate the severity of the famine. Decades later, little has changed, with the North Korean government spending roughly 25% of its GDP on the military, while 41% of the population is undernourished.[196] As of 2017, many North Korean bellies remained hungry while the government conducted numerous tests of ICBMs. Meanwhile, Russia provided 5,200 tons of flour in food aid.[197] We can easily imagine Hardin calculating that providing food aid to North Korea merely enables the North Korean government to continue to neglect its own people for the sake of military spending, and will ultimately increase suffering over time. Similarly, from Narveson's

---

[196] http://www.bbc.com/news/world-asia-39349726
[197] http://english.yonhapnews.co.kr/search1/2603000000.html?cid=AEN20170718011600315

perspective, "helping" is not identical to "giving free food" in such cases, and food-relief to North Korea would probably not qualify as a suitable "emergency in life."

In contrast, more legitimate inspiration for charity would be natural disasters which cause short-term (and solvable) problems. For example, consider the 2017 flooding of Houston Texas neighborhoods. "Relief" in that case amounts to *temporary* distributions of food, water, and other necessities; *temporary* lodging in shelters, and (in some cases) Federal aid to help businesses and home owners repair flood damage. For those who choose to help, the need is urgent, and there is an "end in sight" with regard to that need, as opposed to an endless need that will always have to be filled.

Narveson neatly and conveniently summarizes himself as follows:

> *The basic question . . . is whether the hungry have a positive right to be fed. Of course we have a right to feed them if we wish, and they have a negative right to be fed. But may we forcibly impose a duty on others to feed them? We may not. If the fact that others are starving is not our fault, then we do not need to provide for them as a duty of justice. To think otherwise is to suppose that we are, in effect, slaves to the badly off. And so we can in good conscience spend our money on the opera instead of on the poor. Even so, feeding the hungry and taking care of the miserable is a nice thing to do, and is morally recommended. Charity is a virtue. Moreover, starvation turns out to be almost entirely a function of bad governments, rather than nature's inability to accommodate the burgeoning masses. Our charitable instincts can handle easily the problems that are due to natural disaster. We can feed the starving and go to the opera!*

Conclusion

The moral status of helping others in need is an issue that is urgent, timely, ever-present, and comprehensive. It reaches into massive political and economic issues such as health care and "entitlement" programs, tax policies, international aid, population control, reproductive choice, and foreign intervention. It touches us at the ballot box when we are voting our conscience, and on street corners when we see someone asking for money. Whether we find ourselves in the "privileged" position of being asked, or as the person in need of help, the issue is effectively impossible to escape (though many find ways to ignore it).

There are a variety of ways we might interpret the issue of helping the needy, and more possible answers as to whether we are morally obligated to do so than could possibly be addressed in this one, modest chapter. For our purposes, we considered Singer's utilitarian answer, Hardin's complication of that answer, and Narveson's libertarian rebuttal.

What do *you* think?

Notes

Notes

Notes

Notes

Notes